Broadcasting, Cable,
the Internet, and Beyond

The McGraw-Hill Series in Mass Communication and Journalism

Consulting Editor
Barry L. Sherman

Broadcasting, Cable, the Internet, and Beyond

An Introduction to Modern Electronic Media

Fourth Edition

Joseph R. Dominick
University of Georgia, Athens

Barry L. Sherman
University of Georgia, Athens

Fritz Messere
SUNY, Oswego

Boston   Burr Ridge, IL   Dubuque, IA   Madison, WI
New York   San Francisco   St. Louis
Bangkok   Bogotá   Caracas   Lisbon   London   Madrid   Mexico City
Milan   New Delhi   Seoul   Singapore   Sydney   Taipei   Toronto

McGraw-Hill Higher Education

A Division of The **McGraw-Hill** *Companies*

BROADCASTING, CABLE, THE INTERNET, AND BEYOND

 This book is printed on acid-free paper.

1 2 3 4 5 6 7 8 9 0 DOW/DOW 9 0 9 8 7 6 5 4 3 2 1 0 9

ISBN 0–07–290441–0

Editorial director: *Phillip A. Butcher*
Associate sponsoring editor: *Valerie Raymond*
Marketing manager: *Kelly M. May*
Project manager: *Christina Thornton Villagomez*
Senior production supervisor: *Lori Koetters*
Freelance design coordinator: *Laurie J. Entringer*
Cover illustrator: *Jose Ortega* © SIS
Senior photo research coordinator: *Keri Johnson*
Photo research: *Connie Gardner*
Supplement coordinator: *Susan Lombardi*
Compositor: *GTS Graphics, Inc.*
Typeface: *10/12 Palatino*
Printer: *R. R. Donnelley & Sons, Inc.*

Library of Congress Cataloging-in-Publication Data

Dominick, Joseph R.
 Broadcasting, cable, the Internet, and beyond: an introduction to modern electronic media / Joseph R. Dominick, Barry L. Sherman, Fritz Messere. — 4th ed.
  p. cm.
 Rev. ed. of: Broadcasting/cable and beyond. 3rd ed. ©1996.
 Includes bibliographical references and index.
 ISBN 0–07–290441–0 (softcover)
 1. Broadcasting—United States. 2. Cable television—United States. 3. Internet (Computer network)—United States.
4. Telecommunication—United States. I. Sherman, Barry L.
II. Messere, Fritz. III. Dominick, Joseph R. Broadcasting/cable and beyond. IV. Title.
HE8689.8.D66 2000
384'.0973—dc21   99–30379

http://www.mhhe.com

About the Authors

Joseph R. Dominick received his undergraduate degree from the University of Illinois and his Ph.D. from Michigan State University in 1970. He taught for four years at Queens College, City University of New York, before coming to the College of Journalism and Mass Communication at the University of Georgia where from 1980 to 1985, he served as head of the Radio-TV-Film Sequence. Dr. Dominick is the author of three books in addition to *Broadcasting, Cable, the Internet, and Beyond* and has published more than thirty articles in scholarly journals. From 1976 to 1980, Dr. Dominick served as editor of the *Journal of Broadcasting*. He has received research grants from the National Association of Broadcasters and from the American Broadcasting Company and has served as media consultant for such organizations as the Robert Wood Johnson Foundation and the American Chemical Society.

Barry L. Sherman is director of the George Foster Peabody Awards program and professor of telecommunications at the College of Journalism and Mass Communication, University of Georgia. Chairman of the department and associate director of the Peabody Awards from 1986 to 1991, he is also consulting editor for the McGraw-Hill series in mass communication. Dr. Sherman is a graduate of the City University of New York (B.A. 1974; M.A. 1975), and Penn State (Ph.D. 1979). In addition to *Broadcasting, Cable, the Internet, and Beyond*, he is the author of *Telecommunications Management: The Broadcast and Cable Industries*. His writings have appeared in a variety of professional and trade publications, including *Journal of Communication, Journal of Broadcasting and Electronic Media, Communication Education, Journalism Quarterly*, and *Channels*.

Frank (Fritz) Messere is chairman of communication studies at Oswego State University. In addition to his broad experience in radio and television production, he was external assistant to FCC Commissioner Mimi Wayforth Dawson and faculty fellow of the Annenberg Washington Program. Messere is coauthor of *Introduction to the Internet for Electronic Media*, and served on the National Experts Panel of Telecommunications for the Rural Policy Research Institute.

Preface to the Fourth Edition

New century. New look. In order to keep pace with the never-ending changes in electronic media, this fourth edition of *Broadcasting, Cable, the Internet, and Beyond* contains many new features.

New Title

The Internet has permanently changed the landscape of electronic media. Web sites offer alternatives to the traditional sources of news. Networks use the Web to promote their programs. Radio stations broadcast online. Companies such as broadcast.com aggregate links to radio and television content from across the globe. Consequently, it seemed only fitting to include the word "Internet" in the book's title and to regard it as an electronic medium along with broadcasting and cable.

New Content

The Internet appears in more than just the title of the fourth edition. A new chapter has been added that details the development of this new medium; explains its new vocabulary of ISPs, portals, and browsers; discusses its unique features; and examines its impact on the more-traditional broadcasting and cable media. Additionally, Internet content has been added to other appropriate chapters. For example, Chapter 2 ("History of Cable, Home Video, and the Internet") now includes a section on Internet history; Chapter 10 ("Rules and Regulations") discusses regulating the net; and Chapter 12 ("Ratings and Audience Feedback") contains a description of how the Internet audience is measured.

New Organization

The fourth edition also sports a new, streamlined organization that should fit better with the traditional semester system. The total number of chapters has been reduced from 19 to 14. The opening history chapters have been reorganized, and the third edition's two chapters on technology have been reduced to one.

Other changes include the addition of the new Internet chapter in Part Two of the book and a new chapter (Chapter 7, "The Business of Broadcasting and Cable") about the business aspects of the electronic media. This chapter integrates new material with information that previously was contained in several chapters in the third edition. It is hoped that this new arrangement will make it easier for instructors to cover this important aspect of the media.

Part Four ("How It's Controlled") has been shortened from three chapters to two. Similarly, the two ratings chapters in the third edition have been combined, and the chapter on international electronic media has been moved to the end of the book.

All in all, the authors hope this new structure will be more convenient and user-friendly.

New Themes

The fourth edition continues the use of thematically organized boxed inserts in every chapter that present extended examples or interesting snapshots of media leaders. The themes for this edition have been streamlined into four categories: Profiles, Ethics, Events, and Issues. Dozens of new boxed inserts have been added throughout.

New Writing Team

Previous adopters will note that a new author has joined the team. Frank "Fritz" Messere is an associate professor of communication studies at State University of New York at Oswego. Fritz is the author of a book about the Internet, and his expertise in the new media will be evident throughout this new edition.

New Supporting Materials

The fourth edition makes use of the World Wide Web to provide instructors and students with materials that enhance and complement the material found in the text. Each chapter of the book is supported by an interactive Web study guide that students can use to reinforce concepts in the text, communicate with others taking the course, study enrichment material, and practice for tests. For more information, see the McGraw-Hill Web site at www.mhhe.com/media.

Familiar Elements

Loyal users of the book will find many things that are familiar. The basic plan of the book has not been changed.

- Part One, "Foundations" (comprising Chapters 1, 2, and 3), reviews the history of electronic media and provides a simplified discussion of the technology of audio and video.
- Part Two, "How It Is" (Chapters 4, 5, and 6), is an overview of the current electronic media: radio, television, cable, and the Internet. Each chapter surveys the basic structure of the medium, examines the economic and societal forces that influence its operation, addresses relevant current issues, and concludes with a look at career prospects.
- Part Three, "How It's Done" (Chapters 7, 8, and 9), concentrates on the business aspects of the various media. Chapter 7 introduces the student to the role of advertising and the typical revenue streams and expenses of the various media. The next two chapters concentrate on programming. They highlight how broadcasting and cable operators select and schedule their content to appeal to an audience that is attractive to advertisers.
- Part Four, "How It's Controlled" (Chapters 10 and 11), examines the regulatory process. Chapter 10 discusses the basic rationale behind regulation and surveys the structure and function of the Federal Communications Commission and other organizations influential in media operation. The chapter also examines the Telecommunications Act of 1996 and its impact on contemporary media. Chapter 11 looks at media self-regulation and the response of industry and community groups to ethical and regulatory issues.

- The final part of the book, Part Five, "What It Does" (Chapters 12, 13, and 14), looks at audiences. Chapter 12 explains the important business of ratings research, while Chapter 13 examines the social impact of the electronic media. Audiences in other countries are the focus of Chapter 14, a survey of the world of international electronic media.

Every chapter has been updated and revised to reflect changes in this dynamic field. Charts and tables contain the most recent data available.

Additionally, the fourth edition carries through our attempt to create a book that would be both interesting for students to read and easy for teachers to use. The new edition emphasizes conciseness. We have tried to cut down on the details without sacrificing depth of coverage. We have maintained a conversational writing style and have included easy-to-understand figures and tables where appropriate. Like the third edition, each chapter opens with a list of "Quick Facts," which we hope will introduce the reader to the material in a bright and accessible way. Each chapter ends with a summary of key points, a list of the chapter's key terms, and suggestions for further readings and Web browsing.

Finally, we hope the fourth edition fulfills the goal we set when this book was first published: To produce a textbook that is informative and that captures some of the excitement, exhilaration, and immediacy that go with this industry.

Acknowledgments

First and foremost, the authors would like to acknowledge the contributions of Gary Copeland to our past editions. We particularly appreciate the high standards of scholarship and professionalism that he brought to this project.

We also would like to acknowledge the efforts of others that helped bring this edition to reality. On the industry side, especially helpful were James Duncan, Duncan's American Radio; Mark Fratrick and Rick Ducey of the National Association of Broadcasters; Val Carolin, CBS Radio Sales; Jeff Wise at WWHT-FM; Dee Collins of Cox Interactive; Jeff Carr, WTBS; Melanie Trulby at Interep; and Joseph Fazio at WHEC-TV.

In addition, a number of our colleagues offered helpful comments. Alison Alexander, Louise Benjamin,

Bill Lee, and David Hazinski are deserving of special thanks. We are also grateful for the help provided by all of our students, particularly Larisa Bosma, Vince Benigni, and Christina Saunders.

We would also like to thank those reviewers and focus group participants who offered helpful suggestions for improving the fourth and all previous editions: Steve Adams, Cameron University; Virginia Bacheler, State University of New York at Brockport; James Brown, University of Alabama, Tuscaloosa; Donna Dolphin, Monmouth College; Linda Fuller, Worcester State College; Ronald Garay, Louisiana State University; Mark Goodman, Mississippi State University; Douglas A. Ferguson, Bowling Green State University; Geoffrey Hammill, Eastern Michigan University; Mary Hart, Creighton University; Rick Houlberg, San Francisco State University; Suzanne Huffman, SMU, Dallas; Rebecca Ann Lind, University of Illinois at Chicago; John L. MacKerron, Towson State University; David Martin, California State University, Sacramento; David Reese, John Carroll University; Eric W. Rothenbuhler, University of Iowa; Pete Seel, Colorado State University; Noel Smith, Central Texas College; Geoffrey Valentine, Oklahoma Baptist University; Tom Volek, University of Kansas; Bob Vogel, Miami University of Ohio. Special thanks to John Gray Cooper, Eastern Michigan University.

Finally, as always, we say a big thank you to the team at McGraw-Hill who helped put this edition together. Valerie Raymond deserves an extra special salute for her efforts to keep this project on track and for providing professional expertise and guidance along the way. The authors wish we had half her energy. We also thank Phil Butcher for his continuing support of this book and the McGraw-Hill Series in Mass Communication. Other team members we would like to thank include Kelly May, our new marketing manager, who has done so much to support the text; Christina Thornton-Villagomez, our tireless and resourceful Project Manager; Keri Johnson and Connie Gardner, who pulled the photo program together; Laurie Entringer, who provided the beautiful text design; Lori Koetters, our Production Supervisor; and Susan Lombardi, our Supplements Coordinator.

In closing, we once again acknowledge the help and support of our families for standing by us and encouraging us as we went through yet another revision. It is to Candy, Eric, Jessica; Carole and Meaghan; and Nola and Katy that we dedicate this volume.

Joseph R. Dominick
Barry L. Sherman
Fritz Messere

Brief Contents

Detailed Contents

6
The Internet and New Media Today   120

Part Three
How It's Done

7
The Business of Broadcasting and Cable   143

List of Boxes

Broadcasting, Cable, the Internet, and Beyond

Part One   Foundations

Introduction

As we start a new millennium, it is obvious that the pace of change within the electronic media shows no signs of slowing down. Consider what has happened in just the few years since the previous edition of this book went to press (late 1995).

Thanks to the Telecommunications Act of 1996:

- Newly manufactured TV sets will be equipped with a V-chip that gives viewers the ability to block out unwanted programs.

- The ownership cap on radio stations has been removed, resulting in a wave of consolidation that has totally transformed the industry. Some companies now own more than 400 radio stations.

- The telephone and cable industries have started to move closer together as telephone companies offer cable TV and cable TV companies offer phone service.

In 1995, about 20 million Americans had access to the Internet. Latest figures suggest that more than 60 million will have access by the year 2000. The ultimate social effects of this new mass medium are difficult to predict, but its impact on traditional forms of news gathering and reporting has already been demonstrated:

- The story that prompted the Clinton-Lewinsky scandal first appeared on the Internet as part of the "The Drudge Report," a gossip-oriented Web site authored by lone-wolf, cyberjournalist Matt Drudge. Drudge single-handedly proved that one person, with the right Web connections, could shape the national news agenda.

- Speaking of the Clinton-Lewinsky scandal, the 119,000-word report about the affair prepared by independent counsel Kenneth Starr was published on the Internet at the same time it was released to reporters. About 25 million people saw the report in the first two days it was online. That's more than the combined total viewership of the three networks' evening newscasts.

- Although the majority of Americans (about 75 percent) still turn to television to learn about breaking news stories, the Internet is now the second most popular place to follow breaking stories.

The Internet has reshaped the electronic media in other ways as well:

- More than 100 Internet-only radio stations were on the Web at the beginning of 1999. Audio services such as **Spinner.com** target listeners who

spend most of their day in offices working with computers.

- Sites such as **Broadcast.com** offer live programming from television and radio stations, audiobooks, a CD jukebox, and special services not available from traditional radio and TV stations. The July 1998 initial public offering of stock in **Broadcast.com** set a Wall Street record.

- Broadcasters and cable programmers use their Web sites (such as **abc.com**, **espn.com**, and **mtv.com**) to cross-promote programming on their television networks and vice versa.

- In 1998, all the major record companies in America embraced a new technology called MP3 for delivering high-quality, CD-like music via the Internet.

On April 4, 1997, the FCC ushered in the new age of digital television. Stations in the top 10 markets began broadcasting at least some programs in the new format in 1998 and 1999. The plan calls for all stations to go digital by 2006, provided 85 percent of their markets have TV sets that can receive digital signals. Once they switch, their old analog channels then revert back to the federal government. What are some of the implications of this shift?

- Stations can use their signals to broadcast high-definition television (HDTV), with pictures much sharper and clearer than present-day analog pictures.

- Instead of HDTV, stations can also use their new digital space in the spectrum for additional channels. Thus, one station might provide news on one of its new digital channels and a talk show on the other. This opens up many new programming and revenue-generating possibilities.

- One possible digital format also allows for TV signals to be viewed on computer screens. Consumers would not have to buy a new TV set to get the new format and could watch TV and surf the net from one machine.

In 1995, direct broadcast satellites (DBS) and digital satellite systems (DSS) were just appearing on the market. By the beginning of 1999, more than 8 million of the small, 18-inch dishes had been sold and the market appeared to be growing. Some potential results of this trend:

- DSS may be on the way to becoming a serious competitor to cable systems.

- The large number of pay-per-view movie channels (more than 50 on some systems) may cut into the videocassette rental business.

Finally, if current trends continue, cable television will have a larger prime-time audience than the four major broadcast networks by the end of the year 2000. As of early 1999, cable audiences grew to record levels and network audiences continued to dwindle. As cable audiences grow, so do Internet audiences. As access speed to the Internet increases, will web-based portals compete with broadcasting and cable for viewers?

All of the development mentioned above suggest that the world of the electronic media will continue to change and will continue to have a great impact on society. This, in turn, suggests that it is important for students to appreciate these changes and what they mean for their future.

SUGGESTIONS FOR READING FURTHER

All of the chapters in this book end with a section called "Suggestions for Further Reading," which lists books you can read for additional information. This *introductory* chapter ends differently: It suggests why you should keep reading this book.

To be specific:

- Many of you will go on to careers in the electronic media. This book presents a foundation of information for you to build on as you pursue your professional goals.

- For those of you who do not intend to become media professionals, a knowledge of the electronic media will help you become intelligent consumers and informed critics of radio, TV, and online media. The electronic media are so pervasive in modern life that everyone should know how they are structured and what they do.

- Finally, all of you will spend the rest of your lives in the Information Age, an age in which the creation, distribution, and application of information will be the most important industry. At the core of the Information Age will be the electronic media. Everybody benefits from the scholarly study of an industry that will be a crucial part of business, education, art, politics, and culture.

In sum, the authors hope that what you learn in this book will be liberating in the traditional sense of a liberal education: We hope that the knowledge you acquire will free and empower you within this new millennium and this new era.

1 History of Broadcast Media

Quick Facts

 First radio broadcast: Reginald Fessenden, Christmas Eve, 1906

 First radio network company: NBC, 1926

 First "Top 40" radio broadcasts: 1952

 First public demonstration of TV: 1939 World's Fair

 Cost of first TV commercial: $4 (1941)

 Cost of commercial minute in 1999 Super Bowl: $3.2 million

"What hath God wrought?"

That was the message sent by wire from Washington, D.C., to Baltimore one spring day in 1844. Using a code made up of dots and dashes, Samuel Morse had demonstrated the potential of his new communication device—the telegraph. For the first time in history, it was possible to send a message across long distances almost instantaneously.

"Come here Watson. I need you."

Thirty-four years after Morse's invention, Alexander Graham Bell uttered those words into a telephone, a device that could send the human voice through a wire, making it even easier to communicate at a distance. Both the telegraph and the telephone are radio's ancestors, and their evolution anticipated many of the factors that would shape radio. Specifically:

- Both the telegraph and the telephone businesses supported themselves through commercial means.
- Big corporations came to dominate both industries.
- Both the telephone and the telegraph were point-to-point communication media. They sent a message from one source to one receiver.

Radio started off as a point-to-point medium until people discovered the advantages of broadcasting—sending the same message to a larger number of people simultaneously. But we're getting ahead of the story.

THE INVENTORS

In the late nineteenth century, efforts were underway to liberate electronic communication from the wire. Physicists such as James Maxwell and Heinrich Hertz demonstrated the existence of electromagnetic radiation, energy waves that traveled through space. Other researchers investigated the nature of these mysterious waves. None of them, however, was able to perfect a system of wireless communication. The creation of such a system—radio—was due to the efforts of many inventors. There are three, however, whose contributions bear special mention: Marconi, Fessenden, and De Forest.

Marconi and Wireless

Guglielmo Marconi, who came from a wealthy and cultured Anglo-Italian family, had seen a demonstration of the mysterious radio waves while a college student. Enthralled with the new discovery, a young Marconi started experimenting with radio transmitters and receivers. Eventually he was able to send a radio signal more than a mile.

Marconi was aware of the commercial possibilities of his experiments. He realized that the biggest potential use for his wireless communication system would be in situations where it was impossible to use traditional wire telegraphy: ship-to-ship and ship-to-shore communication. Accordingly, he traveled to Great Britain, the leading maritime country of the period, and applied for a patent. The British granted him a patent for his wireless telegraphy system in 1896, and Marconi formed his own company to manufacture and sell his new device.

As his company became successful, Marconi turned his efforts toward increasing the range of his signals. In December 1901, he successfully transmitted a wireless signal—three short beeps, the letter S in Morse code—across the Atlantic, a distance of more than 2,000 nautical miles. The age of radio was dawning.

Fessenden and the Continuous Wave

Keep in mind that Marconi was sending wireless telegraphy—dots and dashes. No one was yet able to send the human voice via radio waves. In order for this to occur, someone had to develop a new way of generating radio signals. Marconi used a technique that generated radio waves by making a spark jump across a gap between two electrodes. This was fine for Morse code, but the human voice was another matter. To transmit voice, or music or other sounds, what was needed was the generation of a continuous radio wave that could be transformed to carry speech.

Reginald Fessenden, a Canadian-born electrical engineer, came up with the solution. Working with the General Electric Company, he built a high-speed alternator, a piece of rotating machinery much like those used to generate alternating current for household use.

Fessenden tested his alternator on Christmas Eve, 1906. Wireless operators on ships up and down the eastern coast of the United States were amazed when through their headphones they heard a human voice speaking to them. It was Fessenden explaining what was going on. After some violin music and readings from the Bible, the inventor wished his audience a merry Christmas and signed off.

Guglielmo Marconi was able to build a lucrative communications empire on his wireless invention. Here a successful Marconi listens to radio signals in the wireless room of his personal yacht, Electra.

This first "broadcast" caused a mild sensation and marked a major technological breakthrough. As dramatic as the change from typewriter to word processor, the shift from the spark gap to the continuous-wave transmitter ushered in a new age for radio. Radio waves could now carry more than just dots and dashes.

De Forest and the Invisible Empire

Around 1910, the most popular way of receiving radio signals was to use something called a **crystal set.** Scientists had discovered that some minerals, such as galena, possessed the ability to detect radio waves. Moving a tiny wire, called a cat's whisker, over a lump of galena allowed the listener to hear the faint sounds of wireless telephony, as radio broadcasts were called back then. Crystal sets were cheap and easy to assemble, but they had one big drawback: They couldn't amplify weak incoming signals. If radio was to become a mass medium, something better was needed: a receiver that would boost the level of weak signals and make radio listening easier.

Lee De Forest found the answer during his experiments with something called a Fleming valve. This device looked like an ordinary light bulb. It consisted of a plate and a thin wire and was used to detect radio waves. De Forest discovered that the insertion of a small wire grid between the plate and the wire acted as an amplifier that boosted weak radio signals until they were easily detected. Hooking together two or three such devices could amplify signals millions of times. De Forest, realizing the potential of his invention—which he named the **audion**—for radio, wrote in his diary that he had "discovered an Invisible Empire of the Air." De Forest's invention made galena obsolete. The audion moved radio into the electronic age.

The inventor tried to create a market for his audion by using publicity stunts such as broadcasting phonograph records from the Eiffel Tower in Paris and a performance from the New York Metropolitan Opera. These early demonstrations had few listeners, but they did show that broadcasting was possible. It would take a few more years, however, before that idea gained wide acceptance.

Role of the Navy

De Forest's invention also got him into legal trouble. The Marconi company sued him, claiming that his audion infringed on their patents to the Fleming valve. Another patent battle over the audion dragged on for more than 20 years before reaching the Supreme Court. De Forest eventually sold rights to the audion, for a modest $50,000, to AT&T, who wanted to use it to amplify the signal of long-distance phone calls, and he turned his attention to other areas.

The audion contributed to improvements in transmission as well as reception. It subsequently was refined into the vacuum tube and formed the basis for all radio transmission until the 1950s, when it was replaced by the transistor and solid-state electronics.

BOARDROOMS AND COURTROOMS

Now that radio had been successfully demonstrated, the next step was to refine it and make it commercially rewarding. Accordingly, the next phase of broadcasting's evolution is marked by the activities of corporations more than of individuals. It's a tangled story, complicated by legal feuds, conflicting claims, politics, and war. It's also an important phase: Decisions made during this period permanently shaped radio's future.

Legal Tangles

To begin, let's review the situation as of 1910. Radio was still thought of as a point-to-point communication device—much like the telegraph and the telephone. Despite De Forest's demonstrations, broadcasting, as we know it today, did not exist. Radio's main use was still ship-to-ship and ship-to-shore communication.

Although Marconi's company (British Marconi) and its American subsidiary (American Marconi) dominated the business, there were other companies interested in radio: General Electric, AT&T, and Westinghouse. Each of these companies held patents on certain elements necessary to manufacture radio transmitters and receiving sets but no one company had patents that covered the entire process. Predictably, each company produced its own version of the inventions patented by the others so that it could enter the business. The result was a long and costly legal battle over patent infringements. Had something drastic not happened, radio's evolution might have been severely hindered.

Radio Goes to War

Something drastic—World War I—was not long in coming. The military benefits of radio were apparent from the start of the conflict. The U.S. Navy had equipped all of its warships with radio and operated three-dozen coastal radio stations. When the United States entered the war in 1917, the government, in the interests of national security, gave the Navy complete control over all radio operations, including all commercial stations.

This move had two important consequences for radio. First, the Navy assumed responsibility for patent infringement. This meant the various companies involved could pool their discoveries to improve radio communication. This is exactly what happened, and by the war's end in 1918, the technology was vastly improved. Second, during the war the Navy had taken control of 45 coastal radio stations and eight high-power transmitters owned by American Marconi. When the war ended, the Navy was reluctant to give them back because it was convinced that such an important function as international radio communication should not be controlled by a company (American Marconi) that was in turn controlled by a foreign power (Britain). In fact, bills were introduced in Congress to give the Navy exclusive control over radio's future. Obviously, some important decisions had to be made.

Birth of RCA

The first decision was what to do about the Navy. Commercial interests in the United States were opposed to any governmental intrusion into the free enterprise system and did not want the Navy controlling a potentially lucrative business. Consequently, the bills giving the Navy control over radio were never brought to a vote. Unlike some other countries, the United States chose not to put radio under direct governmental control.

The second problem was what to do about American Marconi and a possible British monopoly. To make matters even worse, with the Navy out of the picture, all of the prewar patent problems immediately resurfaced. The ultimate solution to the problem was suggested by the Navy: Buy out American Marconi and start a new company. Representatives from the U.S. government went to General Electric, the company with the most resources and financial clout, to handle the deal. After much tough negotiating, the management at Marconi agreed to the plan. Marconi would sell its American subsidiary to a new company—the Radio Corporation of America (RCA). Note that RCA would still be in the business of point-to-point communication and planned to make its money by sending wireless telegraphy and telephony to U.S. and international customers.

The next step was to solve the patents problem. Ultimately, RCA entered into a cross-licensing agreement with GE, AT&T, and Westinghouse that enabled each company to use the others' discoveries. The companies also agreed to divide the market: GE and Westinghouse would manufacture radio equipment, and RCA would sell it. AT&T would build the transmitters.

Ironically, just as these new agreements were falling into place, it became clear that the real future of radio would not be in point-to-point communication but in broadcasting—providing news and entertainment to the general public. Because of this, all of the agreements that were negotiated among these companies would soon fall apart as radio headed in a new direction.

BROADCASTING'S BEGINNINGS

Radio burst on the scene in the 1920s and soon became a national craze. There were several cogent reasons for the incredible growth of this new medium:

1. An audience of enthusiastic hobbyists, thousands of them trained in radio communication during the war, was available and eager to start tinkering with their crystal sets.

2. Improvements during the war gave radio better reception and greater range.

3. Business realized that broadcasting might make money.

Its beginnings were modest. In 1920, Frank Conrad, an engineer for Westinghouse, began experimental broadcasts from his Pittsburgh garage. Conrad's programs, consisting of phonograph recordings and readings from the newspaper, became popular with listeners who were picking up the broadcast on crystal sets. Westinghouse noticed the popularity of Conrad's program and began manufacturing radio sets that were sold by a local department store. As sales of radio sets increased, Westinghouse moved Conrad from his garage to a studio on the roof of the company's tallest building in Pittsburgh. This new station was licensed

by the Department of Commerce and given the call letters of KDKA (it's still on the air today, making it the oldest operating station). Conrad had established that there was a market for radio broadcasting.

Westinghouse quickly started other stations in Chicago, Newark, and other cities. RCA, GE, and AT&T also started radio stations. As the year 1922 began, there were 28 stations actively broadcasting; six months later there were 378; and by the end of the year, 570. Receiving sets were selling quickly; by the end of the decade almost one-half of the homes in America had a working radio.

The tremendous growth brought problems. For the listener, the biggest annoyance was interference. There were only a few frequencies available that gave good reception, and many stations were operating on them, which caused great difficulty for the listener as the competing signals interfered with one another.

At the corporate level, the problem was money. The cross-licensing agreement did not anticipate broadcasting. In 1923 RCA made $11 million from selling radio sets and only $3 million from its wireless telegraphy operation. AT&T, prohibited from manufacturing radio sets by the agreement, was obviously displeased. Friction soon developed between the members of the cross-licensing agreement over who had the right to do what. After a four-year imbroglio, the parties finally agreed to a plan that ultimately solved the problem. AT&T left the broadcasting business and sold its assets to the other companies involved in the agreement. In return, AT&T would be granted a monopoly over the wire interconnections that were used to link stations together into a network (see "Radio Networks" section). RCA won the right to manufacture radio sets and acquired WEAF, the powerful New York City station formerly owned by AT&T.

RADIO'S FAST TIMES: THE 1920s

Things happened quickly for radio in the 1920s. In eight years, from 1920 to 1927, radio went from a fad to a major industry and a major social force. We have already noted how big business got involved with early radio. The three other major developments of this period that helped to shape modern radio were the development of radio advertising, the beginning of radio networks, and the evolution of radio regulation.

The control room and studio of KDKA, Pittsburgh, generally considered to be the oldest broadcasting station in the nation. Note that early broadcasters had to be careful about loose wires.

Advertising

When broadcasting first started, nobody thought too much about how it was supposed to make money. Most of the early broadcasters were radio and electronics manufacturers. For these companies, radio was simply a device to help sell their products. Other businesses that owned large numbers of early radio stations were newspaper publishers and department stores. For these companies, radio was a promotional device; it helped sell more newspapers or attracted people to the store. Nobody envisioned that it might be possible for a radio station to make money.

In time, however, costs started building up. To compete successfully, stations required reliable equipment, special studios, and technicians and professional talent who had to be paid for their labor. Rising costs forced many stations off the air. Those that were left scurried to find some way to produce revenue.

It was the phone company that came up with the answer. Considering broadcasting an extension of the telephone, AT&T developed a system whereby anyone who had a message to deliver would come to

their station, pay money, give the message, and leave (just as people did when they came to a phone booth and made a call to a single person). AT&T called the arrangement "toll broadcasting." It wasn't long before advertisers began to appreciate the potential of this new arrangement. The Queensboro Corporation, a New York real estate company, was the first to buy time on WEAF. Others quickly followed.

Although it may seem odd today, this early experiment in commercial broadcasting was resented by many listeners. There was even talk of·a bill in Congress to prohibit it. By 1924, however, enough stations had followed WEAF that it was obvious the public did not object to radio ads. If anything, the audience liked the improved programming that came with advertising. By 1929, advertisers were spending more than $20 million on radio advertising and the new medium was on solid financial ground.

Radio Networks

There were three main reasons for the development of chain or network broadcasting in the mid-1920s.

The first stemmed from the broadcasters themselves and was primarily economic. It was less expensive for one station to produce a program and to have it broadcast simultaneously on three or four stations than it was for each station to produce its own program. The second reason came from the audience. The listeners of local stations in rural areas, far from the talent of New York, Chicago, or Hollywood, wanted better programs. Networking allowed big-name talent to be heard over small-town stations. A third reason was the desire of advertisers to increase the range of their programs beyond the receivers of local stations and thus multiply potential customers. Given the pressure from these three sources, the development of networks was inevitable.

After AT&T pioneered the interconnection of stations using their long distance phone lines, RCA, headed by David Sarnoff, set up a new company in 1926 to separate the parent company from the broadcasting operation. The National Broadcasting Company (NBC) was to oversee two broadcasting networks. The "Red" network consisted of the stations acquired from AT&T when the phone company left the broadcasting business, and the "Blue" network comprised of stations originally owned by RCA, Westinghouse, and GE. By 1933, NBC had 88 stations in its network.

A competitor came on the scene when the Columbia Broadcasting System (CBS) was formed in 1927. Under the direction of William S. Paley, CBS started with 16 stations, but by the end of 1933 the younger network had 91 members. Another network, the Mutual Broadcasting System, began operation in 1934. The radio networks would be the controlling force in broadcasting for the next 20 years.

Radio networks forever changed American society. First they stimulated national advertising. With one phone call, advertisers could procure nationwide exposure for their products. Second, radio networks brought to rural areas entertainment pre-viously provided to urban areas. Now everybody could hear the same comedians, big bands, Hollywood movie stars, and political commentators. Network radio stimulated the beginnings of a truly national popular culture. Finally, the networks changed American politics, as campaigns became truly national in scope. Politicians who mastered the new medium, such as Franklin Roosevelt did in his fireside chats, had a distinct advantage over their competitors.

Rules

Attempts to regulate the new medium can be traced back to 1903 when a series of international conferences were called to discuss the problem of how to deal with wireless communication. The result of these efforts for the United States was the Wireless Ship Act of 1910, requiring certain passenger vessels to carry wireless sets. Two years later, the pressure for more regulation increased when amateur wireless operators were interfering with official Navy communications. In the midst of this, the *Titanic* struck an iceberg and sank. Hundreds were saved because of wireless distress signals, but the interference caused by the many operators who went on the air after knowledge of the disaster spread hampered rescue operations. As a result, the public recognized the need to develop legal guidelines for this new medium. The Radio Act of 1912 required sending stations to be licensed by the Secretary of Commerce, who could assign wavelengths and time limits. Ship, amateur, and government transmissions were to be assigned separate places in the spectrum.

The problem with this law was that it envisioned radio as point-to-point communication and did not anticipate broadcasting. Consequently, as more stations went on the air, broadcasting for long periods at a time, interference became a severe problem.

By 1926 the interference problem had become so bad that it was obvious to all that some form of federal control was needed if radio was to avoid being suffocated in its own growth. In response to requests from the radio industry for legislation, Congress passed the **Radio Act of 1927.** Its key assumptions were the following:

- The radio spectrum was a national resource. Individuals could not own frequencies, but they could be licensed to use them.

- Licensees would have to operate in the public interest.

- Government censorship was forbidden.

In addition, a five-member **Federal Radio Commission (FRC)** was established to enforce the new law. Within five years the FRC had solved the interference problem and laid the groundwork for an orderly system of frequency sharing that would obtain maximum benefit for the public. In 1934, in an attempt by President Franklin Roosevelt to streamline government administration, Congress passed the **Communications Act of 1934,** which replaced

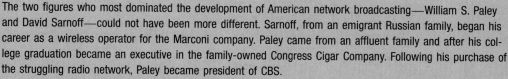

Profile: Sarnoff and Paley

The two figures who most dominated the development of American network broadcasting—William S. Paley and David Sarnoff—could not have been more different. Sarnoff, from an emigrant Russian family, began his career as a wireless operator for the Marconi company. Paley came from an affluent family and after his college graduation became an executive in the family-owned Congress Cigar Company. Following his purchase of the struggling radio network, Paley became president of CBS.

Sarnoff gained national attention when he was one of several telegraph operators who relayed messages about the sinking of the *Titanic*. Marconi took note of the young man who was quickly promoted into the managerial ranks of American Marconi and later RCA. Popular history suggests that in 1916 Sarnoff wrote a prophetic memo to his superiors at Marconi, predicting that radio would become a mass medium. Recent research suggests that the memo might have been written some years later, making it less prophetic. In any case, Sarnoff eventually became chief executive officer at RCA and managed the company until 1969. It was Sarnoff who made NBC a force in radio broadcasting and who was a firm believer in the potential of television. Sarnoff also championed color TV.

Paley was more interested in the programming side of the business. He signed Bing Crosby and Kate Smith to contracts at CBS. In 1948, he scored a programming coup when he lured a number of big stars—Jack Benny, Edgar Bergen, and others—from NBC to CBS. Paley's achievements extended into news broadcasting as well. Under his leadership, CBS assembled a crew of reporters that began a tradition of outstanding journalism at CBS. It was Paley who persuaded Edward R. Murrow, the famous war correspondent, to take an executive position at CBS.

Rivals most of their careers, Paley and Sarnoff left their own personal marks on American broadcasting.

---

the FRC with a seven-member **Federal Communications Commission.** The basic philosophy of the 1927 law, however, was not changed.

RADIO DAYS, RADIO NIGHTS: 1930–1948

The years from 1930 to 1948 can be termed the radio years. The new medium grew at a phenomenal rate, became an integral part of American life, developed new forms of entertainment and news programs, and ran into a few problems along the way.

Growth

Table 1–1 documents the skyrocketing growth of radio. Other statistics are equally impressive: from $40 million spent on radio advertising in 1930 to $506 million in 1948; from 131 network affiliates in 1930 to 1,104 in 1948. Keep in mind that this growth occurred despite a worldwide depression and another world war.

With growth came new problems. One had to do with questionable radio content. The FRC, with backing from the courts, was able to shut down radio broadcasts by quacks and swindlers, such as John R.

Brinkley, who used his station to promote bogus patent medicines, and Norman Baker, who touted his homemade cancer cure over KTNT in Iowa.

Another problem concerned FM (frequency modulation) broadcasting. Perfected by Edwin Armstrong (see boxed material), FM transmission was first publicly demonstrated in 1933. FM had two big advantages over AM (amplitude modulation): FM was less prone to static and had better sound reproduction quality. Armstrong took his invention to his friend David Sarnoff, now chief executive at RCA, who had supported the inventor's work in the past. Unfortunately for Armstrong, the time was not right for FM. Conventional AM radio was doing fine; it didn't need

Table 1-1	The Growth of Radio		
Year	Number of Stations	Percentage of Homes with Radio	Number of Employees
1930	618	46%	6,000
1950	2,867	95	52,000
1970	6,889	99	71,000
1999	12,276	99	150,000

Profile: Edwin Armstrong

In his early years, Edwin Howard Armstrong was fascinated by two things: radio and heights. In 1910, when he was 20, Armstrong built his own antenna to aid his experiments with radio. Armstrong liked to hoist himself to the top of his 125-foot tower to enjoy the view.

A few years later, while climbing a mountain, Armstrong worked out a method by which De Forest's audion could be modified to amplify incoming radio signals as well as detect them. Armstrong's invention, the regenerative circuit, would become part of almost every piece of radio equipment.

Armstrong's inventions were not overlooked by the radio industry. In 1913, David Sarnoff, chief inspector for the Marconi company, visited Armstrong's labs for a demonstration of his equipment. The two quickly became friends.

Armstrong's success in the laboratory, however, was not matched by success in the courtroom. Beginning in 1914, Armstrong became embroiled in a complicated legal struggle with Lee De Forest over who had actually first discovered the principle of regeneration, a battle Armstrong eventually lost.

Armstrong served in the Army during World War I and spent some time flying over France in rickety biplanes. While in the Army, Armstrong continued to invent devices that improved the quality of radio transmission and reception.

Armstrong's inventions brought him money and fame. In 1922, David Sarnoff, then head of RCA, signed a deal with Armstrong that brought the inventor more than a quarter million dollars in cash and stocks. A few months later, Armstrong, perhaps symbolizing his new on-top-of-the-world status, scaled the radio antenna atop the 21-story building owned by RCA. Armstrong even sent photographs of his feat to his friend Sarnoff. Sarnoff was not amused.

In the next few years, however, several events brought Armstrong back to earth. After some initial victories in his court fight with De Forest, Armstrong had a setback. The Supreme Court, operating more from technical legal rules than from scientific evidence, ruled against him in 1928.

For most of the next five years, Armstrong devoted his time to perfecting FM, an invention he hoped would bring him to new heights of fame and prosperity. When Sarnoff refused to back the new technology, their friendship began to evaporate.

Undaunted, Armstrong set up his own FM transmitter for demonstrations. By 1940, Armstrong was on top again. Other radio set manufacturers were impressed and paid Armstrong for the rights to manufacture FM sets. The FCC set aside part of the electromagnetic spectrum for commercial FM broadcasting. Even Sarnoff had changed his mind about FM and offered Armstrong $1 million for a license to his invention. Armstrong, probably remembering the earlier incident with Sarnoff, refused.

Word War II interrupted the development of FM. After the war ended, optimism for the new medium flourished again. This confidence, however, was short-lived. The FCC moved FM out of its former spectrum slot, and Sarnoff announced that RCA had developed its own FM system, one that did not rely on Armstrong's inventions.

The break between the two old friends was now total. Armstrong sued RCA for patent infringement and RCA martialed its massive financial and legal resources against him. The lawsuit lasted four years and drained Armstrong physically, financially, and emotionally. By 1954, Armstrong was near bankruptcy, depressed, and convinced that his creation of FM was destined to be a failure.

More than forty years in the future, looking back, we, of course, know that Armstrong was wrong. Despite the initial hardships, FM flourished. By the late 1990s, FM commanded more than two-thirds of the listening time of Americans. The inventor, however, would never see his invention succeed. In 1954, Edwin Armstrong, the man who was fascinated by heights, commited suicide by jumping out of the window of his thirteenth-floor apartment.

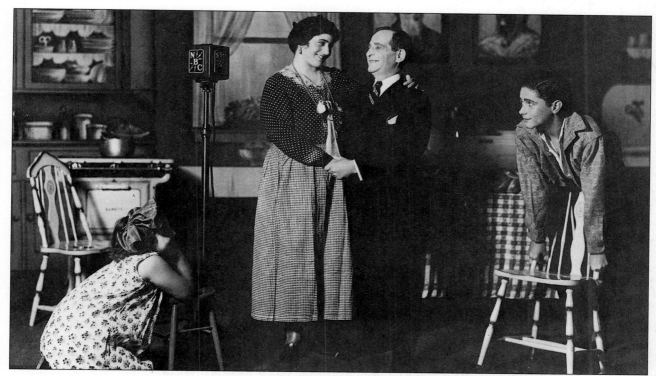

The Goldbergs: Rosalie, Molly, Jake, and Sammy. Gertrude Berg (Molly) was the creative force behind "The Goldbergs," a radio situation comedy that premiered in the early 1930s and moved to TV in 1949.

additional competition. In addition, RCA had made a major investment in AM and was more interested in getting a return on this money than in developing a new radio service. Finally, Sarnoff was committed to another developing technology, television, which he saw as more important. Consequently, RCA would not back the new radio technology. Dismayed, Armstrong built his own FM station but World War II intervened and halted its development. Nonetheless, at the end of the war there were about 50 FM stations in operation. The FCC dealt it another blow, however, by moving FM to a different spot in the radio spectrum, thus rendering obsolete about 400,000 FM receiving sets. Although its ultimate future would prove to be bright, FM struggled along for the next 20 years.

The last problem concerned NBC's two networks and the FCC. After a lengthy study of monopolistic tendencies in network broadcasting, the FCC ruled that NBC had to divest itself of one of its two networks. NBC sold its Blue network to Edwin Noble, who had become rich by selling Life Savers candy. Noble renamed the network the American Broadcasting Company (ABC).

Impact

By now, radio had become part of the country's social fabric. It was the number-one source of home entertainment, and the stars of early radio were familiar to the members of virtually every household in America. Radio news reports had a sense of immediacy that set them off from items in the newspaper. People trusted and depended on radio.

The social power of radio was demonstrated several times during this period. Franklin Roosevelt used his informal "fireside chats" to help push his legislation through Congress. In 1938, Orson Welles used a quasi-newscast style in a radio adaptation of *War of the Worlds* that featured Martians invading the United States. Many people thought the program was real and panicked. Finally, singer Kate Smith stayed on the air for 18 straight hours during a pledge drive for war bonds. She eventually raised more than $39 million.

Moreover, radio took advertising revenue away from the newspaper and magazine industries and radio newscasts effectively killed the "extra" editions of the newspaper. Radio also had an impact on the sound recording industry. The early radio networks refused to play recorded music, and the recording industry was reluctant to permit their records to be played on radio. As more and more people turned to radio for music, the recording industry nearly died during the economic downturn of the 1930s; it survived thanks to better marketing efforts and the popularity of the juke box, a coin-operated phonograph found in most drug stores, restaurants, and bars. Interestingly, the idea that playing records on the radio would be helpful to both industries had yet to catch on.

Programs

Radio programs during this time period were primarily music/variety programs, comedy, drama, and news. On the music front, big bands such as Tommy Dorsey and Benny Goodman became popular during the 1930s and 1940s. Variety shows featuring Bob Hope, Jack Benny, and Jimmy Durante were also crowd pleasers. Mystery shows, such as "The Shadow" (at one time starring Orson Welles), were popular, along with dramatic series such as "Grand Central Station." The biggest comedy hit of the

period was "Amos 'n' Andy," which went on the air in 1929. Although the show would be considered racist today, almost the entire nation stopped to listen to it during its 7 to 7:15 P.M. time slot.

Radio news got off to a slow start, but by 1930 the networks were carrying regular newscasts. The events of the 1930s gave radio news a boost as reporters and commentators described and analyzed events leading up to World War II. An impressive array of reporters, including Eric Sevareid, Edward R. Murrow, and William Shirer reported regularly from Europe. Millions of people in the United States would huddle around their radios to hear timely reports on the war's progress. The amount of network time spent on news more than doubled from 1940 to 1945. There were some notable individual achievements, including Murrow's dramatic accounts of the bombing of London. All in all, radio news reached its high point during the war.

After the war, the future for radio never looked brighter. It was America's number-one source of news and entertainment. Advertising revenue was increasing, and more and more people were listening. Radio's future, however, was about to be drastically changed.

David Sarnoff standing in front of a TV camera as he opens the RCA pavilion at the 1939 New York World's Fair. This was the first time a major news event was covered by television.

TELEVISION

Nine miles from Manhattan, in Flushing Meadows, Queens, a mosquito-infested swamp underwent a magical transformation. At a cost of $156 million, the New York World's Fair opened on that site in April of 1939. RCA, NBC's parent company, had chosen this event to make a public demonstration of its latest technological marvel—television. David Sarnoff, the head of RCA, called the invention "a new art so important in its implications that it is bound to affect all society." He was right.

The idea of TV goes back to the 1880s. Early TV pioneers such as Paul Nipkow and Boris Rosing correctly reasoned that if the elements of a visual scene could be scanned and broken down into a series of tiny electrical signals able to be transmitted and reassembled in a receiver, a viewable television picture would result. It took a while, however, to put this principle into practice.

After a series of false starts with mechanical scanning systems, two inventors, Vladimir Zworykin and Philo Farnsworth, were able to perfect a method of electronic scanning that would eventually become the basis for modern television. Working at RCA's research labs, Zworykin developed the "iconoscope," the eye of an electronic TV camera. Farnsworth grew up in Idaho and, working mainly by himself, developed an "image dissector," which, with a different design, accomplished much the same thing as Zworykin's iconoscope. The Depression of the 1930s forced Farnsworth to turn for financial support to the Philco Corporation, a radio set manufacturer and rival of RCA. Even at this early date, it was clear that corporate America would be behind future TV growth. It was also clear that the existing radio industry would be a major force in shaping the new medium. Consequently, TV came into being with an organized pattern (networks and local stations) and a support system (commercials) already in place.

Improvements in TV continued during the 1930s. Experimental TV stations went on the air. RCA and Farnsworth settled a patent suit, and RCA was permitted to use Farnsworth's invention to further enhance their TV system. By 1939, the new invention had improved enough to be ready for its public debut at the World's Fair.

The development of a commercial TV system was interrupted by the war. Station construction was halted, and all but a handful of stations went off the air. On another front, however, World War II accelerated the technology behind TV. Scientists involved in perfecting TV went into the military and studied high-frequency electronics. Their work greatly improved the U.S. system of radar and also advanced the technical side of TV. As the war neared its end, it was apparent that TV would be back, stronger than ever.

When the war ended, the broadcasting industry made immediate preparations to shift its emphasis from radio to TV. Assembly lines that had been used to turn out war materials were retooled to produce tubes and TV sets. Returning soldiers, skilled in radar operation, were hired by many stations that were eager to use their electronics knowledge. Set manufacturers made plans to advertise their new, improved products.

By 1948, television was clearly on its way; network programming was introduced; popular radio shows made the transition to TV; and the new medium created its own stars. When Milton Berle's program came on Tuesday night at 8 P.M., it seemed the whole country stopped to watch. Ed Sullivan, a newspaper columnist with no discernible TV talent, hosted a variety show that quickly followed Berle's show to the top of the ratings charts.

Lucille Ball and Desi Arnaz starred in "I Love Lucy." From 1951 to 1957, the show was always among the top three most popular TV programs.

Freeze

The growth of TV during 1948 was phenomenal. Set manufacturers couldn't keep up with the demand. More stations were going on the air and many more were seeking to start. It seemed as if every town wanted a TV station. Things got so hectic that the FCC declared a freeze on new TV station applications while it studied the future of TV.

The TV industry, however, was not in a state of suspended animation during the freeze. Stations whose applications were approved before the freeze were allowed to go on the air. By 1950, 105 TV stations were broadcasting. Further, the networks, using AT&T land lines, were able to complete a coast-to-coast hookup, which enabled live network broadcasts to reach 95 percent of the homes then equipped with TV. Despite the freeze, TV had grown to nationwide proportions.

The freeze thawed in 1952 when the FCC produced a document called the **Sixth Report and Order,** which addressed several issues:

- A table of channel assignments was constructed, structuring the provision of TV service to all parts of the United States.

Profile: Frieda Hennock

Frieda Hennock always valued education. Born in Poland, she moved to the United States when she was six. After graduating early from high school, she took law classes at night and finished her degree at the age of 19. She was admitted to the bar two years later and, not surprisingly, became the youngest woman lawyer in New York City. During the late 1920s she distinguished herself as a criminal lawyer but eventually her interest turned to corporate law. Her expertise and ability earned her a position at one of New York's leading law firms.

During the 1940s, Hennock became active in politics and raised money to support several prominent Democrats, including Harry Truman. In 1948, when all political experts were predicting a Truman loss in the upcoming election, Truman repaid Hennock for her past support by nominating her to the Federal Communications Commission. This gesture, however, may have been more symbolic than substantive since, at the time, Republicans in Congress were blocking all new presidential appointments until after the election, when, presumably, a Republican would hold the office. Hennock, nevertheless, displayed impressive political skills and gained support from both Democrats and Republicans. To almost everyone's surprise, her nomination was approved by Congress, making her the first woman on the commission and the only one out of 800 Truman appointees to be confirmed. (Truman, of course, also surprised everybody and won the 1948 election.)

Hennock joined the FCC at the start of "The Freeze," the period when the commission refused to consider new applications for TV stations while it worked out technical rules and regulations for the new medium. Her interest in education came to the surface. In the early days of radio, many educational institutions acquired broadcasting licenses only to give them up later after coming under pressure from commercial broadcasters who saw an opportunity for profit. When FM came on the scene, the FCC reserved 15 percent of the frequencies for use by educational institutions. The commercial broadcasters didn't object to this, since they didn't think FM would amount to much.

Hennock believed that a similar reservation should be made for educational TV stations, a position that immediately put her at odds with commercial broadcasters who wanted the frequencies for themselves. As they had done during the early days of radio, the broadcasters argued that they were the ones who could best provide educational programming through sustaining, or commercial-free, programs. Hennock's colleagues at the commission favored the broadcasters' position.

Despite the odds against her, Hennock mobilized support from educators, private foundations, and the media. In 1951 she was rewarded with a partial victory when the FCC proposed reserving about 10 percent of available TV channels for noncommercial educational broadcasting. Hennock, however, campaigned for 25 percent. Despite her efforts, when the freeze was lifted in 1952, only 12 percent of the channels available were set aside for noncommercial broadcasting. Hennock voiced her dissatisfaction with the ruling and continued to campaign for greater educational access to television.

Hennock's remaining years on the commission often found her at odds with her colleagues and the establishment. She opposed the proposed merger of ABC with Paramount Theaters. She argued against rate increases for AT&T. Since many of the new educational stations were in the UHF band, she spent her last days on the commission campaigning to make UHF stations more competitive with VHF stations.

Hennock completed her term in 1955, and Republican President Dwight Eisenhower did not reappoint her. She resumed her successful law practice until her death in 1960. Today's noncommercial broadcasters can be thankful that Frieda Hennock's determined efforts gave education a permanent place in the television spectrum.

- To accommodate the hundreds of applicants seeking a TV license, the FCC opened up new channels (14–69) in the ultra-high frequency (UHF) part of the electromagnetic spectrum to join the channels (2–13) already in use. (Most TV sets couldn't get the UHF channels without a special antenna, so the new channels started off with a technical disadvantage that would slow their development for years to come.)
- Anticipating the future, the commission set standards regarding color TV.
- Finally, thanks to the efforts of Frieda Hennock, the first woman FCC commissioner, 242 channels were set aside for noncommercial TV stations.

Television programming developed and flowered during the freeze period. This was the golden era of TV as high-quality plays authored by such notables as Rod Serling and Paddy Chayefsky were key parts of the prime-time schedule. The "Today" show, still going strong at this writing, premiered in 1952. The most significant situation comedy of the era was "I Love Lucy," starring Lucille Ball, a comedienne who would appear on TV in one form or another in four different decades. "I Love Lucy" was significant not only for its popularity but also because it was filmed in Hollywood, marking the beginning of the Hollywood involvement in TV, a trend that would grow over the next three decades.

RADIO'S PERIOD OF ADJUSTMENT

Faster than most people imagined, TV became the dominant news and entertainment medium. Although some people thought that radio might go the way of the blacksmith and the ice box, it managed to adjust and prosper.

At the risk of oversimplification, the coming of TV had four main effects on radio. First, it completely changed network broadcasting. After the freeze was lifted, mass market advertising moved to TV. By 1955, network radio was taking a financial beating, with revenues dropping by about 58 percent from 1952. As major radio stars like Jack Benny and Bob Hope shifted to TV, network radio programs lost audiences to the new medium. Pretty soon the once-powerful radio networks were reduced to providing 10-minute newscasts on the hour and some daytime programs. It would take network radio nearly 30 years to recover.

Second, television made radio turn to specialized audiences through the development of particular formats. Local stations, faced with more hours to fill since the networks cut back on their programs, looked for an inexpensive way to fill the time. They found it with the disc jockey (DJ) and recorded music. Abandoning the long-standing antagonism against playing records on the air, stations chose music that would appeal to a specialized audience. Some rural stations concentrated on country-and-western music, while some stations in urban markets developed a rhythm-and-blues format. Many FM stations played classical music. The most influential format developed in this period, however, was called Top 40. Capitalizing on the growing popularity of rock-and-roll and the growth of the "youth" culture,

Top 40 appealed to teens by playing a relatively small number of popular songs over and over. By 1960, hundreds of stations had adopted the format.

Third, the advent of TV brought the radio and record industry closer together. Contrary to past thinking, radio airplay helped sell records. The record companies kept radio's programming costs to a minimum by providing the latest hits free to the station. In return, the radio stations gave the record industry what amounted to free advertising. Record sales nearly tripled from 1954 to 1959.

Finally, television forced radio to become more dependent on local advertising revenue. Since they were no longer conduits for material produced by the networks, local stations became more responsive to their markets. They could play regional hits; DJs could make special appearances at local events; stations could provide more local news. All of this increased radio's appeal to local advertisers. In short, radio redefined its advertising base. In 1945, less than one-third of radio advertising came from local ads. Ten years later that proportion had nearly doubled.

To sum up, over the course of about a dozen traumatic years, radio made the necessary adjustments that enabled it to prosper in an era that was to be dominated by TV.

TV'S GROWTH CURVE: 1953–1962

The next 10 years saw an incredible surge in the fortunes of TV (see Table 1–2). In 1952, some 34 percent of households had TV. Ten years later 90 percent were equipped. There were 108 stations broadcasting in 1952. Ten years later there were 541. In the same period, the amount of money spent on TV advertising quadrupled. By any yardstick, TV was booming.

Table 1-2	The Growth of Television		
Year	Number of Stations	Percentage of Homes with Television	Number of Employees
1950	98	9	9,000
1970	862	95	58,400
1999	1,576	99	175,000

New Wrinkles

On the technology side, the Ampex Corporation in-troduced videotape recording in 1956. This inven-tion made it possible to store TV programs in a high-quality format that could be used again and again. Tape also made program production cheaper and would ultimately replace film in the production of many situation comedies. Finally, tape helped kill off live drama on TV. Before long, only news and sports were broadcast live; most other shows were either taped or on film.

RCA introduced color TV sets in 1954 and, after a slow start, color TV eventually caught on. By 1962, about a half-million color sets were sold and RCA announced it was finally making a profit from their sales.

As mentioned earlier, UHF TV stations got off to a slow start because their signals did not go as far as **VHF (very high frequency)** signals and TV sets were not equipped with the special antenna needed to pick up UHF broadcasts. In 1961, the FCC persuaded Congress to pass the All-Channel Receiver Bill, which required all television sets to be able to receive all TV channels, not just VHF. Even so, UHF grew slowly.

Two other technological milestones occurred dur-ing this period that were to prove highly significant for the future of TV. The significance of the first was immediately apparent. A rocket roared off Cape Canaveral in July of 1962 carrying *Telstar,* the first active communication satellite capable of relaying signals across the Atlantic Ocean. Only 25 years after Marconi's death, wireless signals were crossing the Atlantic in a way he had never imagined.

The ultimate significance of the second event was overlooked by virtually everybody. A new idea, in-troduced in the early 1950s, was gaining ground. People who lived in mountainous areas could not get good over-the-air TV reception. Residents of these areas hit upon a novel solution. They would put an antenna on top of one of the tall peaks and run wires down to the homes in the valley. The resi-dents would pay a fee to receive their programs over a cable. This system was called **community an-tenna TV,** or **CATV.** Later CATV would come to stand for cable TV. Conventional broadcasters thought that transmitting signals by cable was a clever idea but that it would have little general ap-plication. As the next chapter illustrates, they were mistaken.

Hollywood

Not all was going well for networks during TV's growth curve. The struggling DuMont Network, lacking stations in many of the major cities, went out of business in 1958. ABC was also having financial problems, but its merger in 1953 with Hollywood-based United Paramount Theaters brought fresh cash to the network and enabled it to become more competitive.

The merger also marked the beginning of a trend toward closer cooperation between TV and Holly-wood. The major film studios had initially been hos-tile to TV but they eventually realized that they could make money by producing series for the new medium. ABC led the way by signing a contract with Walt Disney studios for a one-hour weekly se-ries called "Disneyland." The show was a big hit and soon the other networks followed suit. By 1957 Hollywood had taken over much of the production work for prime time. (Interestingly, the Disney–ABC connection resurfaced in 1995 when Disney ac-quired ABC.)

Programming

Big money quiz shows, such as "The $64,000 Ques-tion" and "21" were popular at the end of the 1950s but quickly died out after a major scandal revealed that some of the shows were rigged. Adult westerns, such as "Wyatt Earp" and "Gunsmoke" also became popular; by 1959, there were more than 20 western series on the air. Television news grew slowly during these years, as nightly network newscasts were only 15 minutes long.

STABILITY FOR TV: 1963–1975

The next dozen years or so marked a fairly stable pe-riod in the history of broadcast TV. The networks were the dominant force of entertainment and news and enjoyed more or less steady financial growth. In any given minute of prime time, around 90 percent of the sets in use were tuned to network shows. Pro-gramming, while sometimes innovative, basically followed the formats from the 1950s. True, there were some events within the industry that ruined the placid mood, but compared with what was to come, these years seem almost tranquil.

Technology

On the technological side, the slow but steady growth of cable TV began to capture the attention of the broadcasting industry. The early developments of this new medium are detailed in the next chapter. For now, the main thing to note is that cable grew slowly during this time period, reaching only 10 percent of all TV homes in 1974.

Interestingly, UHF stations got a boost from cable. Cable systems had to carry all of the local stations in a market, including UHF. Once on the cable, the signal strength disadvantage of UHF no longer mattered, putting UHF and VHF stations on an equal footing and helping UHF increase its audience reach.

Finally, communication satellites become more important to TV. Those that followed Telstar were placed in a geosynchronous orbit, which meant that the satellites maintained their position relative to a point on earth and could serve as relays for ground stations. Satellites would eventually replace wires as the preferred medium for sending much of the content of broadcast TV.

Public TV

Noncommercial TV progressed slowly during the early 1960s, growing to 100 stations in 1965. A major development occurred in 1967 when a study sponsored by the Carnegie Foundation recommended a plan for what it called "public" TV. The term **public broadcasting** came to include a wide range of station owners: universities, school boards, state governments, school systems, and community organizations. Indeed, some of the problems that were to plague public broadcasting were in part caused by its heterogeneous nature. In any case, one of the important things about this report was a shift in philosophy: Noncommercial TV would no longer be limited to programs stressing formal instruction and education. Instead, it would provide an alternative to commercial programming. With amazing rapidity (just eight months later), Congress passed the **Public Broadcasting Act of 1967**, which created the Corporation for Public Broadcasting (CPB). The main function of CPB was to channel money into programming and station development. Two years later, CPB created the Public Broadcasting Service (PBS) to manage the network interconnection between the public stations.

Unfortunately, Congress never provided enough funds for public TV, making it difficult for public TV to establish any long-range plans. Nonetheless, the service presented some award-winning programs: "Masterpiece Theater," "Upstairs, Downstairs," "Black Journal," "Sesame Street," and "The Electric Company." By the late 1970s, however, its future was somewhat cloudy.

New Regulations

In 1971, after much debate about the harmful effects of cigarette smoking, Congress passed a law prohibiting the advertising of cigarettes on TV. Despite initial complaints from broadcasters that the new law would cost them more than $200 million in revenue, other advertisers quickly replaced the tobacco companies and TV ad revenues continued to increase.

Around this same time, the FCC was concerned that the networks were dominating TV. Accordingly, the commission announced the **Prime Time Access Rule (PTAR)** in 1970. In effect, this rule gave the

The cast of "All in the Family," a show that brought a harsh edge of realism to the situation comedy format.

Profile: Joan Ganz Cooney

Joan Ganz Cooney is the founder of "Sesame Street" and created the Children's Television Workshop.

Cooney graduated from the University of Arizona in 1951 with a degree in education. She worked as a reporter for two years before moving to New York to become a publicity writer for NBC. From 1962 to 1967 she produced public affairs documentaries for New York's public broadcasting station, WNET.

In 1966 Cooney was asked by the Carnegie Corporation to do a study of the possible uses of public TV in preschool education. The Children's Television Workshop (CTW) was founded in 1968 on the strength of her report, which found that in homes with children the TV set was on as many as 60 hours a week. The idea behind the CTW was to use TV to give poor children the same preparation for school that most middle-class children were getting. CTW's first effort, "Sesame Street," became a huge success, winning Peabody awards in 1970 and again in 1989.

Inducted into the Academy of Television Arts and Sciences' Hall of Fame in 1990, Cooney continues to search for innovative ways to use TV in education.

7:30–8:00 P.M. (E.S.T.) time period back to the local stations to program. The rule encouraged the growth of syndicated programs, such as "Wheel of Fortune," and made the syndication market an important one in TV programming.

Programming

There were several overlapping trends in TV programming during these years. In the early 1960s, programs containing violent content, such as "The Untouchables," were becoming popular and began a controversy—that continued into the 1990s—over the effects of TV violence. At the same time, CBS was successful with a number of rural comedies, such as "The Beverly Hillbillies" and "Green Acres." Escapist programs were also popular; "I Dream of Jeannie" and "Star Trek" both premiered during this period. Another notable trend in programming was the maturation of the situation comedy. "All in the Family" and "MASH" injected a new style of realism into the situation comedy. Finally, this period also marked the coming of age of TV news. The networks expanded their nightly newscasts from 15 to 30 minutes in 1963. In addition, audiences for local news shows were also increasing. At some stations, revenues from news programming was the station's most important source of income.

CHANGES FOR TV: 1975–1990

The period from 1975 to 1990 heralded great changes in the TV industry. New technologies emerged to compete with traditional TV, increased competition

lessened network domination of audience viewing, and the industry itself was reshaped by changes in the economic and business climate.

Competition

The growing popularity of cable TV, discussed in the next chapter, siphoned viewers away from broadcast TV networks. Premium channels, such as HBO, specialized cable channels, such as ESPN and MTV, and superstations, such as WTBS, became increasingly popular. Broadcast audience shares declined as more people opted for other viewing choices. In addition, videocassette recorders (VCRs) became increasingly common in American households. From only a handful in operation in 1978, VCRs were in more than 50 percent of homes by the end of 1987. Some people used VCRs to tape network shows and play them back at more convenient times, but many others used them to watch rented theatrical movies on tape, which also ate into the broadcast networks' audiences. In addition, a fourth network—the Fox Broadcasting Company, premiered in 1987, dividing the audience into even smaller segments. By the late 1980s, the three major networks' share of the audience had declined from 90 to less than 70 percent.

Mergers

There were important business developments as well. In 1985, Capital Cities Broadcasting acquired ABC. In an example of history coming full circle, GE, one of RCA's original owners back in 1919, reacquired RCA (and NBC) in 1986. A few years later,

Westinghouse, another early broadcasting pioneer, would acquire CBS.

Not surprisingly, one of the first tasks faced by these new owners was to improve the networks' financial status. All of the networks experienced budget cuts as the new owners concentrated their attention on the bottom line.

Public TV: Searching for a Mission

Public TV's recent history has been marked by two main themes: a general lack of money and a search for a purpose. A second Carnegie Commission Report, dubbed Carnegie II, was released in 1979. The report reviewed the problems that had plagued PBS from its inception: a lack of long-range funding from Congress, the lack of insulation of public TV from political squabbles, a clumsy managerial structure, and a need to define its mission.

Regarding the debate of public broadcasting's basic mission the following questions arose: Should public TV return to its original purpose during its inception in the 1950s and become an educational service? Or, should it provide more general-appeal programming as an alternative to commercial broadcasting? But, what exactly was an alternative? "High-brow" programming for the culturally elite or programs such as "Austin City Limits"? Should it compete with the major networks or become a service for minority interests? Which minorities? Such questions are still being asked today.

To make matters more complicated, cable networks were providing some of the material that had previously been the province of public TV and public TV was beginning to look more like a commercial network; The Discovery Channel, the Arts and Entertainment Network, and the Learning Channel presented educational and prestige programming that siphoned away some PBS viewers. And public TV stations, in an attempt to raise more money, adopted a policy of "enhanced underwriting," announcements from companies that helped underwrite the costs for programming and that sounded suspiciously like commercials.

Despite its problems, PBS still produced programming that garnered critical praise and loyal fans. "Sesame Street" celebrated its 20th year on the air in 1989 with its second Peabody Award. "Viet Nam: A TV History," "Nova," and "Cosmos" also won numerous awards. And regularly scheduled news and public affairs programs, such as "Washington Week in Review," and "Wall Street Week," score steady if not spectacular numbers in the ratings.

Programming

One of the biggest programming trends of the late 1970s was the emergence of the prime-time continuing episode series, also called prime-time soaps, such as "Dynasty" and "Dallas." Another significant trend was the shift back to warm and wholesome family situation comedy as exemplified by "The Cosby Show" and "The Wonder Years." News programming continued to expand both on cable and on broadcast TV. The Cable News Network (CNN) began in 1980 and prompted the broadcast networks to expand their own news programming by adding late-night and early-morning programs. By the mid-1980s, the networks were providing about 40 hours of news every week.

Technology

In the 1970s TV production equipment became smaller and easy to carry. One of the results of this was the development of **electronic news gathering (ENG)**, which revolutionized TV coverage. Using portable cameras and tape recorders, reporters no longer had to wait for film to be developed. In addition, ENG equipment was frequently linked to microwave transmission, which allowed live coverage of breaking news.

The 1980s saw the development of **satellite news gathering (SNG)**. Vans equipped with satellite uplinks made it possible for reporters to travel virtually anywhere on Earth and to send back a report. Local stations sent their own correspondents to breaking news events in Europe and Asia for live reports. Stations also formed satellite interconnection services that swapped news footage and feeds.

Another promising development, the **direct broadcast satellite (DBS)** got off to a slow start during this time period. DBS uses high-power communication satellites to send original programming direct to umbrella-sized dishes mounted on rooftops. Another satellite technology, the backyard satellite dish or **TVRO (for TV Reception Only)** also became common in the 1970s and 1980s. The TVRO business, however, ran into hard times after many programmers scrambled their signals and consumers had to pay monthly fees to receive the channels. More details on the development of satellite broadcasting can be found in the next chapter.

RADIO IN THE VIDEO AGE

Since 1960 the TV set has pushed radio from center stage. Television now dominates news and entertainment, and radio has carved out a new niche for itself. This section will examine the more-significant trends that have shaped modern radio.

High Tech

Radio became portable during the early 1960s because of the transistor, a tiny device that took the place of the vacuum tube. This made it possible to produce small, lightweight, and inexpensive radios. The invention of printed and integrated circuits shrank radio sets even further. Taking advantage of these and other developments, the Sony Corporation marketed the Walkman, a miniature radio–cassette player that produced high-quality sounds through lightweight earphones. Radio had become a truly personal medium.

FM

Perhaps the most significant event in the radio industry since 1960 has been the evolution of FM to being the preferred service among radio listeners. After a slow start, the number of FM stations nearly tripled from 1960 to 1980. The number of FM radios increased from 6.5 million in 1960 to 350 million in 1980. Listening patterns had totally changed: In 1972, FM held only 28 percent of the audience's total listening time and AM held 72 percent, but by 1995 the figures were reversed—72 percent FM and only 28 percent AM. Why the change?

First, FM was able to broadcast in stereo. This enhanced sound gave it a distinct advantage over AM among the many consumers who valued improved audio quality. Second, AM stations were hard to come by. Those wishing to go into broadcasting during this time period were almost forced to start FM stations because all of the AM frequencies were taken. Third, the new FM stations developed new formats, such as progressive rock and easy listening, that drew listeners. Faced with declining audiences, AM stations searched for a format that would be successful. Many went to an all-talk format, while others switched to golden oldies.

Radio Networks

The 1960s were dark days for network radio. Advertising revenues dropped, and fewer stations were network affiliates. Looking for some way to rebound, ABC split its original network into four spe-

AM radio rebounded in the 1980s and 1990s thanks to popular talk shows hosted by controversial figures such as Gordon Liddy.

cialized services that complemented the new specialized formats on local stations: Entertainment, Information, Contemporary, and FM. The idea worked, and ABC had doubled the number of its affiliates by 1970. NBC, CBS, and Mutual soon followed suit. Network radio bounced back, and by 1980 there were more than a dozen nets in operation.

This growth was accompanied by changes in network ownership. In 1987, Westwood One took over the NBC network. Consolidation in the radio network business would continue into the 1990s as Infinity Broadcasting took over Westwood One and eventually merged with CBS.

Coupled with this trend was the growth of radio **syndication** companies. Syndication companies, much like networks, send programming to local stations. The growing popularity of syndicated talk shows, such as those of Rush Limbaugh and Howard Stern, helped build the audiences of many AM stations.

Fine-Tuning Formats

The increased number of radio stations has made radio a highly competitive business. In an effort to attract an audience segment that is of value to advertisers, many radio stations have turned to audience research to make sure that the station's programming reaches its target audience. This research has produced a set of highly refined **formats** that have sliced the radio audience into smaller and smaller segments. For example, there are several subvarieties of the country format; album-oriented rock attracts 18- to 24-year-old males; and news-talk is geared for the over-45 male audience. In 1990, *Broadcasting Yearbook* listed 70 different formats, ranging from "alternative" to "Vietnamese." In the larger markets, a radio station that attracts only 10 percent of the listening audience will usually rank at or near the top of the ratings.

BROADCASTING IN THE 1990s AND BEYOND

The current state of the radio and television industries is contained in Chapters 4 and 5. This section lists the major highlights of the last few years that have shaped the present situation.

- *New networks.* The 1990s saw the emergence of the Fox Network as a major network player. Helped by its purchase of the rights to broadcast the National Football League and major league baseball and by some innovative programming such as "The X-Files" and "The Simpsons," the new network was moving toward parity with NBC, CBS, and ABC. In addition, two new networks, UPN (owned by Paramount) and the WB network (owned by Warner Brothers), also entered the scene. Network share of the audience continued to decline as cable, VCRs, video games, and home computers siphoned off more potential viewers.

- *Newsmagazines.* In programming, the biggest trend was toward prime-time newsmagazine programs. By 1995, the networks had scheduled eight hours per week of these programs and the trend showed no signs of letting up. Part of their popularity was economic. Newsmagazines cost less to produce than situation comedies and dramas.

- *Competition.* The **Telecommunications Act of 1996** made the video business more competitive by allowing telephone companies to offer television services. The ultimate impact of this change on broadcast TV has yet to be determined. The

The WB network positioned itself as the network that reaches young viewers with such shows as "Buffy the Vampire Slayer."

1996 act also relaxed the limits on television station ownership and made it easier for TV networks to own cable systems.

- *Consolidation.* As far as radio is concerned, the Telecommunications Act lifted the ownership limits on radio stations, prompting an unprecedented wave of consolidation in the industry. By the end of the decade, a few large companies, including Chancellor Media and CBS-Infinity, owned most of the larger-market radio stations.

In closing, as radio and television broadcasting enter a new century, it may be worthwhile to look back 100 years to see how far broadcasting has traveled. Back in 1900, Marconi was trying to send dots and dashes via wire telephony across the Atlantic. Experiments in television were still embryonic. It is doubtful that anybody alive in 1900 could have imagined how radio and TV would evolve in the next 100 years. By the same token, it is doubtful that anyone reading this book will be able to imagine what radio and television will be like in the year 2100.

SUMMARY

- Marconi, Fessenden and De Forest were early inventors who helped radio develop. General Electric, Westinghouse, and AT&T were companies that were interested in early radio. Each company held patents needed by the others, and, as a result, many legal battles hampered radio's early development.

- During World War I, the Navy took responsibility for patent infringement, which allowed for significant technical improvements in the medium. When the war was over, a new company, RCA, was formed and quickly became the leading company in American radio.

- The 1920s were a significant period for radio. Early stations were experimental, and the notion of broadcasting was discovered more or less by accident. The new fad grew quickly, and soon there were hundreds of stations on the air. Radio networks and radio advertising were developed, and the federal government took charge of radio regulation.

- The period from 1930 to 1948 was the "golden age of radio," as the medium was the prime source of news and entertainment for the nation. This situation changed as television came on the scene in the 1950s.

- Developed by Zworykin and Farnsworth, TV was first unveiled in 1939. After its development was interrupted by World War II, television quickly became popular, and by the mid-1950s it had taken radio's place as the number-one medium in the country.

- The FCC froze applications for TV stations from 1948 to 1952 while it determined standards for the new medium. After the freeze was lifted, TV growth skyrocketed. Networks dominated TV until the 1970s when cable emerged as a formidable competitor.

- Radio reacted to TV by becoming a localized medium that depended on formats to attract specific segments of the listening audience.

- Television's Fox network premiered in the 1980s, which caused ABC, CBS, and NBC further audience erosion. The ownership of all three major networks changed hands during the 1980s and 1990s. The Telecommunications Act of 1996 had an impact on both the TV and radio industries.

KEY TERMS

crystal set 8
audion 8
Radio Act of 1927 12
Federal Radio Commission (FRC) 12
Communications Act of 1934 12
Federal Communications Commission (FCC) 13
Sixth Report and Order 17

ultra-high frequency (UHF) 18
very high frequency (VHF) 20
community antenna TV (CATV) 20
Telstar 20
public broadcasting 21
Public Broadcasting Act of 1967 21
Prime Time Access Rule (PTAR) 21
superstations 22
electronic news gathering (ENG) 23

satellite news gathering (SNG) 23
direct broadcast satellite (DBS) 23
TVRO (for TV Reception Only) 23
transistor 24
syndication 24
format 25
Telecommunications Act of 1996 25

SUGGESTIONS FOR FURTHER READING

Archer, G. (1938). *History of radio to 1926*. New York: American Historical Society.

Barnouw, E. (1966). *A tower in Babel*. New York: Oxford University Press.

———— (1968). *The golden web*. New York: Oxford University Press.

———— (1975). *Tube of plenty*. New York: Oxford University Press.

Czitrom, D. (1982). *Media and the American mind*. Chapel Hill, NC: University of North Carolina Press.

Douglas, S. (1987). *Inventing American broadcasting*. Baltimore, MD: Johns Hopkins University Press.

Eberly, P. (1982). *Music in the air*. New York: Hastings House.

Fornatale, P., & Mills, J. (1980). *Radio in the television age*. Woodstock, NY: Overlook Press.

Hilliard, R., & Keith, M. (1992). *The broadcast century*. Stoneham, MA: Focal Press.

Lewis, T. (1991). *Empire of the air*. New York: HarperCollins.

Sterling, C., & Kittross, J. (1990). *Stay tuned: A concise history of American broadcasting*. Belmont, CA: Wadsworth.

Udelson, J. (1982). *The great television race*. University, AL: University of Alabama Press.

White, L. (1947). *The American radio*. Chicago: University of Chicago Press.

INTERNET EXERCISES

1. Visit our Web site at http://www.mhhe.com/beyond for study-guide exercises to help you learn and apply material in each chapter. You will find ideas for future research as well as useful Web links to provide you with an opportunity to journey through the new electronic media.

History of Cable, Home Video, and the Internet 2

Quick Facts

 Cost of monthly cable service 1950: $3.00

 Cost of monthly cable service 2000: $30 (est.)

 First satellite TV broadcast: NBC, 1962

 Cost of first home satellite dish: $36,000 (1979)

 First practical e-mail system: 1972

 First consumer VCR: 1975

 Development of the Internet: 1986

 Development of the World Wide Web: 1991

As we discussed in the last chapter, a sea change occurred in the radio business in 1978, when the majority of radio listening in America shifted from the AM band to FM. In 1998, a similar moment of significance took place, when ratings revealed that more Americans were watching cable programming in the evening than were watching one of the over-the-air broadcast networks. In scarcely a generation, cable has moved from a small-time adjunct to broadcast TV, to a huge and influential media business. This chapter traces the growth of cable and other alternatives to broadcast television, including satellites, VCRs, and the "new kid on the block"—the Internet and its network, the World Wide Web (WWW). Like many mass media today, cable's beginnings were modest and its early steps were halting. What follows is a small part of the cable success story.

DEMANDING WIVES AND POWERFUL ALLIES: THE STORY OF CABLE TELEVISION

On Thanksgiving Day 1949, KRSC in Seattle became the first operating TV station in the Pacific Northwest. Up in Astoria (near Portland), Oregon, there was at least one family with a television set. Back in 1947, Ed Parsons and his wife, Grace, were at a convention in Chicago, where they first saw TV. Grace wanted one in her home. So, Ed bought one by mail order. He tried to tell his wife they were too far from any TV stations to get any channels. "She figured I was an engineer; so there was no reason why she shouldn't have television," he later said. For months, the set sat idle. Ed thought it would end up as an interesting-looking table.

But the new station in Seattle kindled Ed's interest and inventiveness. He put together a system of antennas, amplifiers, and converters and tried to pull in a signal from Seattle. He took the rig all around town and even flew it in his own airplane. Ultimately, he found he got the best test signal from Seattle (where KRSC was testing its tower) from the top of the Astoria Hotel, just across the street from Ed and Grace's apartment.

Working out of his small radio repair shop, he built the antenna array and amplifiers needed to pull in KRSC, and he stretched antenna wire over to his apartment. As the new station signed on, the Parsons—and more than a dozen friends and relatives who crammed into their apartment—were the only people in Astoria who could watch it. Soon, however, Parsons was stringing antenna wire all over town for $125 per household. Grace was happily watching "Uncle Miltie," as were millions of other new TV viewers.

Back east, a big union boss was planning a brief trip. John L. Lewis was a man who usually got what he wanted. As president of the United Mine Workers, one of the nation's most powerful unions, he wielded enormous power. It was difficult to say no to Mr. Lewis, or to his legion of large, loud, and loyal "friends." One day in 1950, one of those friends—an executive secretary in the union—was expecting a weekend visit from Mr. Lewis. There was one major problem, though. The secretary lived out in Lansford, Pennsylvania, about 70 miles from Philadelphia, too far to receive a decent TV signal. And Mr. Lewis liked to watch TV, especially the Friday night boxing matches.

On the edge of town, near Summit Hill (the next town over), Bob Tarlton, a young veteran of World War II, was working at the radio and appliance store he and his father owned. Summit Hill was about 500 feet higher than Lansford. Fuzzy pictures from Philadelphia could be seen on the new TV sets the Tarltons had just started to sell. But they wanted to improve the picture (and sell some TV sets as a result). So they strung antenna wire from their store to a radio antenna in Summit Hill. The picture was greatly improved.

One day, a well-dressed, but rather swarthy and brusque man appeared in the Tarlton's shop. It was the union secretary from Lansford. He wanted that crisp, clear picture in his home for Mr. Lewis. It was an offer the Tarltons couldn't refuse. They ran a cable from a hilltop in Lansford, down to the union secretary's home. Mr. Lewis and his friend were pleased.

Soon, the Tarltons' other customers wanted to get on the antenna to improve their reception, especially those who had just bought a TV set from them. The Tarltons borrowed money from a local bank, improved their antenna system, and replaced common antenna wire with the newfangled coaxial cable the telephone company was using to promote long-distance service. They began charging customers $100 for installation, and a monthly fee of $3.

Through the early 1950s, in Astoria, Oregon, Lansford, Pennsylvania, and dozens of other small communities on the fringes of good TV reception, community antenna TV (CATV, or more commonly, **cable TV**) was catching on. By the end of the famous

TV freeze in 1952, 70 cable systems were serving about 15,000 homes in the United States. Five years later, 500 systems brought improved TV signals to about 350,000 homes. As President Kennedy took office in early 1961, about 650 systems served just under 700,000 subscribers.

Broadcasters weren't sure how to regard the new industry. At first they welcomed the fact that their signals were reaching homes that otherwise couldn't receive them. On the other hand, broadcasters planning on starting up new UHF stations might find that they could not make a profit unless they were carried on the cable. Their prosperity would be under the control of the cable operator, a situation broadcasters did not find appealing.

The FCC was reluctant to get involved. In 1958, the commission decided that it did not have the authority to regulate cable because cable was not broadcasting and used no spectrum space.

Meanwhile the cable industry continued slow but steady growth. By 1964 a thousand cable systems were in operation, mainly serving small- to medium-sized communities. Two years later the number grew to more than 1,500. At about this same time, the concept behind cable was changing. In addition to carrying local stations, cable systems began to import the signals of distant stations that were previously not available to the community. This development alarmed the broadcasting community. If several new stations were all of a sudden available in a market, the audience shares and the advertising revenues of the existing stations would decline, perhaps forcing some local broadcasters off the air. Particularly disturbed were the owners of UHF stations, whose operations were not very profitable to begin with. The broadcasting lobby asked the FCC for some protection.

A few years earlier, the FCC had committed itself to the development of UHF broadcasting to encourage the expansion of broadcast television. The growth of cable posed a threat to its policy. Accordingly, from 1965 to 1966, the FCC reversed itself by claiming jurisdiction over cable and issued a set of restrictive rules that protected over-the-air broadcasting. (The prevailing philosophy at the FCC at this time envisioned cable as merely an extension of traditional TV signals. Thus it is not surprising that any challenge to broadcasting by cable's development would be curtailed by regulation.) Cable systems had to carry all TV stations within 60 miles and couldn't carry shows from distant stations that duplicated those offered by local stations. In 1968 the

commission ruled that CATV systems in the top 100 markets had to get specific approval before they could import the signals of distant stations. Taken together, these rules effectively inhibited the growth of CATV and made sure that any growth would be limited to smaller communities. While all of these rules were being made, CATV systems were quietly improving their technology so that by the late 1960s many systems could carry as many as 20 different channels.

In 1972 the FCC, pressured by both traditional broadcasters and the cable industry, issued yet another set of rules. Among other things, these rules specified the following:

1. Local communities, states, and the FCC were to regulate cable.
2. There would be 20-channel minimums for new systems.
3. There would be carriage of all local stations.
4. More regulations on the importation of distant signals, including the nonduplication provision mentioned earlier, would be implemented.
5. Pay cable services would be approved.

Once again, the major impact of these rules was to discourage the growth of cable in urban areas. Cable was insignificant to city residents, who already received good reception from a number of local stations. Cable system operators were not encouraged to bring service to urban areas, since the stringing and installation of cable was expensive in densely populated areas, and once cable was installed the operators would have a big job making sure that no imported signal duplicated local programs. To top things off, a major cable company nearly went bankrupt. Cable did, however, grow in midsized markets, and by 1974 it had penetrated a little more than 10 percent of all TV homes. On balance, its future did not look promising. As we shall see in the next section, however, things changed.

Pay TV: An Idea ahead of Its Time

Early on, a number of entrepreneurs had the notion that cable could be used to control what programs went into any individual household. Specifically, they thought that one or more channels on a TV set could be used to send movies and sports, for a one-time or extra monthly fee. As early as 1953, Paramount Pictures built a cable system in Palm Springs,

California, and offered movies like "Forever Female" with Ginger Rogers, for $1.35. They also offered the Notre Dame–USC football game for $1.00. Only about 75 homes signed up for "pay as you look" service, and it ended—amid strenuous objections from TV broadcasters and fearful theater owners—less than a year later. Though similar pay TV ventures were tried in Oklahoma, Los Angeles, and elsewhere, the idea was tabled for nearly 20 years.

Cable Growth

There were two basic reasons for the explosive growth of cable in the late 1970s, one technological, the other regulatory. In 1975, a then little-known company in the pay-TV business, Home Box Office (HBO), rented a transponder on the communications satellite *Satcom I* and announced plans for a satellite-interconnected cable programming network. Cable systems could set up their own receiving dish and HBO would transmit to them first-run movies, which the operators could then sell to their subscribers for an additional fee. Although pay TV was not a new idea, HBO's new arrangement meant wider coverage of cable systems at a lower cost. Further, the new programming service provided a reason for people in urban and suburban areas to subscribe to cable. Now the big attraction was no longer better reception of conventional channels but content that was not available to regular TV viewers, including movies, sports events and musical specials. In a few years other cable-only channels were also distributed by satellite—Showtime, The Movie Channel, Christian Broadcasting Network—as well as independent local stations, dubbed "superstations," such as WTBS in Atlanta and WGN in Chicago. Other specialized cable networks—ESPN (sports), CNN (news), and MTV (music videos)—soon followed. Cable now had a lot more features to attract customers.

The second reason for growth came from the FCC. By the mid-1970s the commission realized, with some help from the courts, that its 1972 rules were stifling cable's growth. Consequently, the FCC postponed or canceled the implementation of many of its earlier pronouncements and changed its philosophy: It would henceforth encourage competition between cable and traditional TV. Eventually, as the Reagan administration advanced its deregulation policies, the FCC dropped most of its rules concerning cable. In 1984 Congress passed the **Cable Communications**

Ted Turner (shown here in his yachting days) used cable TV to take a struggling Atlanta UHF station and turn it into superstation WTBS.

Policy Act. The law, which was incorporated into the 1934 Communications Act, endorsed localism and set up a system of community regulation tempered by federal oversight. The FCC was given definite but limited authority over cable. The local community was the major force in cable regulation, which it exercised through the franchising process. The act gave cable operators, among other things, greater freedom in setting their rates and released them from most rules covering their program services.

Taken together, these two factors caused a spurt of cable growth, which attracted the interest of large media companies such as Tele-Communications, Inc. (TCI), which in turn invested in cable. This in turn caused cable to grow even faster. In fact, the growth was so great that many cable companies in a rush to get exclusive franchises in particular communities promised too much and had to cut back on the size and sophistication of their systems. Nonetheless, although the growth rate tapered off a bit in the mid-1980s, the statistics are still impressive. From 1975 to 1987, the number of operating cable systems more than tripled. The percentage of homes with cable went from about 14 percent in 1975 to 50 percent in 1987. Even the urban areas shared this growth and at least parts of many big cities were finally wired for cable.

By 1988 the cable industry had become dominated by large multiple-system operators (MSOs). The era of a locally owned "mom-and-pop" cable

Table 2-1	The Growth of Cable TV		
Year	Operating Systems	Subscribers (millions)	TV Homes (%)
1960	640	0.7	1.4%
1965	1,325	1.3	2.4
1970	2,490	4.5	7.6
1975	3,366	9.8	14.3
1980	4,048	15.5	20.5
1985	6,600	37.3	43.7
1990	10,200	54.0	58.0
1995	13,000	60.0	63.0
1998	10,850	65.9	67.2

Source: Compiled by the authors from various industry publications.

holds with TV in the United States were cable subscribers (about 45 million homes).

The spectacular growth of cable (detailed in Table 2–1) continued through the 1990s, though the pace slowed once the majority of American homes could receive cable, and more than half chose to do so. By 1990, more than 10,000 cable systems served nearly 6 in 10 TV homes. At mid-decade, cable was in more than 60 million homes. Today, cable is available to more than 97 percent of American homes. About 66 million homes subscribe, representing just about two in three homes with TV in the United States. Annual revenue to the cable industry from these subscribers is nearly $30 billion.

ALTERNATIVES TO CABLE

system was over. The top-10 MSOs controlled more than 54 percent of the nation's subscribers, and the largest MSO, TCI, alone had more than 10 million subscribers. In this same year, cable passed the "magic number": More than one-half of all house-

It should come as no surprise that the rise of cable led other innovators and entrepreneurs to get on the multichannel bandwagon. Leading the way were satellite; multichannel, multipoint distribution service (MMDS); and a huge consumer favorite: the VCR.

Profile: From Cottonseed Salesman to Cable King: Bob Magness and TCI

The media world was shaken in 1998 with the announced merger of two of its largest companies: telephone giant AT&T and cable power Tele-Communications, Inc., also known as TCI. The combined company, valued at nearly $50 billion, is a world leader in local and long distance telephone, cable television operations, and entertainment and information programming. It may be hard to believe, but global powerhouse TCI wasn't even founded until 1965. And it probably wouldn't have even existed if a young cottonseed salesman hadn't stopped to pick up a couple of hitchhikers whose truck had broken down one day in Paducah, Texas.

A native of Oklahoma, Bob Magness had served in a rifle platoon under General George Patton in World War II. After the war, he got a business degree from Southwestern State College in Texas, and went to work selling seed to farmers and ranchers. One day, after visiting a cattle rancher near Paducah, Magness stopped to help two workmen whose truck was stalled at the side of the road. He was amply rewarded for his Good Samaritan gesture.

It turns out the hitchhikers had been constructing a cable system in Paducah. Over lunch at a hamburger stand, they boasted how good a business cable television was getting to be. Magness was bitten by the cable bug. In 1956, with money he got by mortgaging his ranch, Magness built his first cable system in Memphis, Texas. Two years later, he moved to Bozeman, Montana, to build a system there. In 1965, he brought his cable operations to Denver, and he renamed his company TCI in 1968. A short time later, he brought in John Malone to help run his operations. For the next two decades, Magness and Malone grew the company into a cable and media superpower. At the time of his death in 1996, Bob Magness was Colorado's second-richest resident, with a net worth greater than $1 billion.

It makes one rethink the old notion that picking up hitchhikers is a bad idea.

The Satellite Sky

In 1945, science fiction writer Arthur C. Clarke wrote an article in *Popular Science* describing the elements of a satellite communications system. He theorized that global communications could be possible by reflecting signals off three satellites parked in orbit at equal distance from one another. It took a little over 20 years for this pipe dream to become a reality, spurred by the "space race" between the former Soviet Union and the United States.

In 1962, the first satellite TV transmission was made using *Telstar I*. Commentator David Brinkley reported from France to eager audiences in the United States that "there was no big news." He was mistaken. Satellite TV was on its way. By the early 1970s, Western Union had successfully launched the *Westar I* and *Westar II* satellites. The industry took its first major step into the entertainment field in 1976, when Home Box Office used satellite TV for the "Thrilla in Manila" heavyweight championship fight between Muhammad Ali and Joe Frazier. That same year, Ted Turner put his Atlanta station WTBS on satellite, and the Christian Broadcasting Network (later to become The Family Channel) became the first satellite-delivered basic cable network.

Proof that satellite TV had arrived came in 1979, when Nieman Marcus featured a home satellite dish on the cover of its famous Christmas catalogue. Price: $36,000. Throughout the 1980s, the price began to drop and dishes began to proliferate,
aided by crucial decisions in Congress and at the FCC. In 1984, the Cable Communications Policy Act (cited earlier) legalized the private reception of satellite TV programming. Hardware prices dropped below $5,000, and more than half a million home dishes could be seen dotting the American landscape, especially in rural areas unlikely to be served by cable TV due to low population density. The act also permitted program services, like HBO and Showtime, to scramble their signals and to require dish owners to subscribe (like cable customers) to these services.

TVRO: The Big Dish   By the late 1980s, direct-to-home satellite (*DTH*, in industry parlance) became a growth industry. Dubbed the **TVRO** (short for **"satellite television receive-only earth station"**), sales of the three-meter dish eclipsed first two million (1988) and then three million (1990) consumer households. But these dishes were too big and cumbersome to supplant cable TV in suburban homes. Some neighborhoods considered them unsightly and developed local codes restricting their use. The anti-piracy provisions of the cable act allowed for prosecution of those receiving program services illegally. Sales peaked, then plummeted. By the late 1990s, only about two million TVROs could still be seen strewn across the American landscape. To take off, satellite TV would have to become physically smaller, and cheaper; that development didn't take long.

The event that brought HBO into national prominence was the "Thrilla in Manila," a heavyweight championship match between Muhammad Ali and Joe Frazier that was distributed by satellite and cable.

Direct Broadcast Satellite

A new alternative to cable TV took the nation by storm in the mid-1990s. High-powered **direct broadcast satellite (DBS)** service provided for nationwide distribution of TV programming from a new generation of orbiting satellites to compact (18-inch) home dish receivers. The dishes were aimed at one of three satellites launched by Hughes Communications. With use of digital compression (see Chapter 3), these satellites could beam over 200 channels to subscribing households; the channels were offered in different packages by four competing organizations: DirecTV, United States Satellite Broadcasting (USSB), Echo Star and the Dish Network. In the 1990s, the new dish, mounted on a window ledge or near the chimney, became a new TV status symbol, not unlike the rooftop antennas of the 1950s.

By 1995, three million DBS dishes (also known as *DSS* service, for Digital Satellite System) had been sold. At the end of 1998, more than eight million—just under 1 in 10 TV homes in the United States—had DBS service. Clearly, cable had a new competitor. Further growth of DBS is expected as dish systems have become available for under $100, and monthly subscription services have dropped to rates comparable to cable (in the $30–$75 range). Moreover, as this book goes to press, the satellite industry is expecting regulatory relief from Congress that would allow DBS to include local TV channels among their channel offerings.

SMATV: Private Cable

Perhaps you have noticed a large satellite dish on the grounds of an apartment complex or atop a high-rise residential building in your community. This technology is known as **satellite master-antenna television,** or **SMATV.** SMATV is also known as "private cable." Like TVRO, SMATV rose rapidly in the 1980s when residents of apartment complexes (known as multiple-dwelling units, or MDUs) wanted cable service but were impatient in waiting for the wire to reach them. Instead, they turned to SMATV operators. SMATV companies provided the dish, downlinked the additional TV services off the satellite, and delivered service to homes in the complex by their own set of cables. In communities where cable was already available, SMATV operators were able to "skim" potential subscribers from the local cable systems by charging lower monthly rates. The lower rates reflected their much lower expenses (smaller facilities, no studios, simpler wiring, and so on). This

took place particularly in many of the new "upscale" condo communities proliferating in the mid-1980s near many large cities.

However, by the end of the 1980s SMATV growth had slowed. One reason was a slew of lawsuits filed by the cable industry arguing that private cable violated its rights to provide TV service in their franchise areas. Like TVRO, SMATV suffered from scrambling. Moreover, cable was becoming increasingly available to many communities that had originally relied on the satellite dish. Cable systems offered incentives to attract SMATV subscribers, including more channels and even lower rates. As a result, by the close of the 1990s, fewer than 1.5 million homes—less than 2 percent of TV homes—were linked to SMATV services. Many of these homes were looking to DBS as a less costly alternative.

Wireless Cable

As we have seen, because of construction costs, utility problems, and franchise disagreements, cable service lagged in the inner cities. In major urban areas satellite dishes, even the smaller ones now available, remain impractical. There is simply too little space. Yet people in major urban areas also want cable services, especially movies.

One solution is wireless cable, also known as **multichannel, multipoint distribution system,** or **MMDS.** MMDS makes use of short-range microwave transmissions to beam channels of video programming from a central transmitter location, such as the top of a tall office building. Receiving households use a small microwave antenna to pick up the signals and a special decoder called a **downconverter** to turn them into TV channels.

The same compression technologies that make DBS a reality hold promise for MMDS. Depending on the frequencies employed and the digital compression mode used, MMDS may eventually offer between 150 and 300 channels, which could make it competitive with traditional cable and the new DBS service.

However, MMDS service has been slow to catch on. One reason, of course, is competition from existing services. Another is that MMDS has attracted a number of entrepreneurs of questionable ethics. Many people have been persuaded to invest in wireless cable through high-pressure radio ads and TV infomercials. Temporary restraining orders have been issued on various unscrupulous MMDS companies.

By 1999, there were about 1.5 million wireless cable households. Though this figure represented fewer than 2 in 100 TV homes, this segment of the industry was optimistic about future growth, particularly as an alternative to computer modems and telephone hookups for the delivery of high-speed data and Internet services.

HOME VIDEO

For nearly half a century, Peter Goldmark was one of the true visionaries in telecommunications. From his laboratory at CBS had come high-fidelity sound recording, the long-playing phonograph record, and some of the basic research that resulted in color TV. Regarding home video, Goldmark made this prediction in 1976 (cited in *Videography,* July 1986, p. 61):

> I doubt that packaged video programs for home entertainment would be economically justifiable. It's speculative in so many ways, and basically a question of cost. Will people pay . . . for a first-rate entertainment program they know they may view only once or twice?

In fairness, Goldmark was talking about buying movies for home viewing. Nobody had yet conceived the idea of video rentals. However, the statement does reveal the speedy germination of a new industry that would have immediate and long-term impact on American TV. In less than 20 years the home video market exploded onto the media scene. Today broadcast and cable TV are just part of a total "home video environment." The TV set is now a video monitor, or video display terminal (VDT). Wedded to many home screens today is a range of attachments and accessories (which computer people call *peripherals*) that have helped transform the way we watch TV. This revolution began with the introduction of the **videotape recorder (VTR).**

The history of videotape recording is intertwined with the history of television provided in Chapter 1. Before the videotape recorder became a mainstay in the American home, it first had to be perfected in production studios, networks, and TV stations. Few inventions in media history have been as significant. After all, for more than six decades—from early inventors tinkering in the 1880s to the battle between CBS and NBC over color in the early 1950s—TV was *live.* What you saw was what was actually going on—in the studio or in the "great outdoors"—in front of the camera.

The Kinescope Recorder

Many older Americans look back fondly on the days when TV was "live." The experience was immediate, radiating a sense of danger and excitement. More often than not, something unexpected would happen: A "dead" character would come back to life when the actor thought the camera was off him, or an easy-opening refrigerator door would refuse to budge, despite pulling, yanking, and tugging by an undaunted young model.

There was good reason for TV to be live: No means had yet been developed to preserve a TV program in sufficient quality for postproduction or later broadcast. Until the mid-1950s there was only one means to record TV programs, and its performance was less than satisfactory. The **kinescope recorder** was a film camera especially equipped to shoot an image off the face of a TV screen.

The quality of a kinescope recording (or "kinny," as it became known) was not very high. For one thing, the scanning rate of the TV tube is $\frac{1}{30}$ of a second. Yet the frame rate of a motion picture camera is $\frac{1}{24}$ of a second. With the kinescope out of sync with the picture tube, a visible bar (the scanning beam) often appeared on the recording. In addition, the frame size of the film was different from the shape of the picture tube, leading to recordings with heads, feet, and assorted other body and picture parts cut off. There was also the delay involved from recording to replay, owing to the need for processing and drying time for the film. Finally, editing was virtually impossible: Who would want to assemble a bunch of fuzzy images together? Because of these limitations, kinescope recording was never an adequate means of preserving TV signals. Its primary use was to make up for the three-hour time difference between the east and west coasts. After one play, the kinny was usually discarded, which explains why so few of TV's great early programs can be seen today.

The Videotape Recorder (VTR)

On November 30, 1956, the videotape recorder (VTR) made its debut on "The CBS Evening News with Douglas Edwards." The color VTR was introduced by the Ampex Corporation a short time later. In fact, an impromptu debate between Vice President Richard Nixon and Soviet Premier Nikita Kruschev,

Events: Life in the Kinescope Days

Before the videotape recorder, video recording meant kinescope. There were so many problems with this process, however, it was no wonder that the networks eagerly welcomed a substitute. In addition to their poor quality, kinnies used expensive film stock. In 1954, American TV operations used more raw film for kinnies than did all the Hollywood film studios combined. NBC alone used more than one million feet of film a month to feed programs to stations in the different time zones.

Kinescope recording was also troublesome and a little nerve-racking. At CBS Television City in Hollywood, recording started at 4:30 P.M. to pick up the shows broadcast live at 7:30 in the East. Engineers recorded a 35-millimeter kinescope along with a 16-millimeter backup copy. When the first 34-minute kinny reel was done, a switch was made to a second kinescope machine. Then a courier grabbed the exposed reel and rushed it to a nearby film lab. Meanwhile, another courier took the 16-millimeter copy and, using a different route to minimize the chances that both reels would get caught in a traffic jam, rushed it to the same lab.

As the film came out of the dryers, it was spooled onto reels and packed into cans. The waiting couriers then rushed it back to the CBS projection room. These films were called "hot kinnies" because at airtime they were still warm from the dryer. At the same time, another set of couriers was heading back to the lab with the second kinny reels to be developed. If traffic was bad or if the film lab had problems, things could get tense. Veteran engineers recall several times when they were threading up a reel only a minute or so before airtime, and there were other occasions when they had to use the 16-millimeter backup copy. Despite these hardships, CBS never lost a show because of a kinescope processing problem. Nonetheless, everyone was relieved when magnetic recording was perfected.

was captured on videotape at an exhibition in Moscow in 1959. One highlight of this encounter (dubbed the "Kitchen Debate," since the exhibit also included a demonstration of a modern U.S. kitchen), had the future U.S. president sheepishly admitting that the Russians were ahead of America on certain things, such as space travel, but that "we are way ahead on other things, like color TV."

We will review the evolution of videotape recording, especially the various standards and formats used in the industry in the next chapter. Suffice it to say that for 20 years, from its debut in 1956 to the eve of the nation's Bicentennial birthday celebration in 1976, the video recorder was for TV stations, networks, and production facilities, not for home viewers. They were too cumbersome, large, and above all, expensive.

TV Recording Comes Home: The VCR

The VCR (videocassette recorder) revolution began with the introduction of the Betamax VCR by Sony in 1975. Crude by today's standards, the table model machine could record up to one hour of video. However, the machine touched off a fiery court battle between Sony and Universal Pictures.

Shockingly (at least to the movie studios and their major clients, the broadcast networks, for whom they produced the majority of programs seen on prime-time TV), Sony was promoting the machine's ability to tape broadcasts off the air! "Piracy!" claimed the studios. After a much-publicized legal battle, which came to be known as the "Betamax case," in 1984 the U.S. Supreme Court ruled that home taping did not violate copyright law. Not that they needed further encouragement, but this ruling essentially gave Americans a green light to tape TV shows.

In 1978 there were 175,000 VCRs in use in the United States. By 1982 nearly five million units were in use, representing about 9 percent of TV homes; in 1985, some 26 million homes had VCRs—about one-third of all households; and by 1988 the figure had doubled: 52 million VCRs were in use, representing just under 60 percent of homes. Today 85 million households own a VCR, representing about 9 in 10 homes in the United States.

At first, all home VCRs were table models, designed mainly to record TV shows off the air for later playback (a phenomenon known as **time-shifting,** the term reportedly coined by Sony executive Akio Morita). However, in a few short years technological

Akio Morita, chief of the Sony Corporation, the company that pioneered the development of the VCR.

development had reduced the size of the VCR and had made home color TV cameras practical realities. A second growth industry was created: home video moviemaking. Weddings, confirmations, bar mitzvahs, and other cultural rites are captured by camcorders (portable combination camera and VCR units), which have replaced 8-millimeter film as the medium of record. The proliferation of home camera equipment has been almost as spectacular as the rise of the VCR itself. In 1985 about half a million homes had portable video equipment. Today there are over 20 million camcorder units in use, about one in every five homes!

All of this home taping, off the air and in the back yard, has created still another growth industry: the sale of blank videotape. In 1985 the sale of blank tapes accounted for $233 million in consumer expenditures. Today blank tape sales produce over $500 million in annual revenues. Of course, much of this revenue does not benefit the U.S. economy, as the leading tape producers are companies located in Japan, Germany, and Mexico.

The Video Store

A major reason people buy VCRs is to screen movies. In scarcely 10 years, a new commercial establishment—the video store—has become an indispensable feature of our shopping districts and malls.

The pioneer of this portion of the home video business was Andres Blay. In 1977 Blay convinced 20th Century Fox to lease to him videotape versions of a few films, including *Patton*, *M*A*S*H*, and *The*

French Connection. His assumption that a few consumers would be interested in watching films at home was a gross miscalculation. Thousands of people were interested! Within months he was cranking out more than 20,000 copies per month (at a retail cost of $50). Home movie viewing had taken off.

Other entrepreneurs soon entered the picture. Some reasoned that it would be better to offer movies for home viewing on a rental basis than to require consumers to buy copies of the films. A leading entrepreneur in this phase of the business was Arthur Morowitz. The owner of a chain of movie theaters in New York (in Times Square and elsewhere), Morowitz reasoned that adults might want to rent X-rated (and other) films to watch in the privacy of their own homes. In the late 1970s he opened a chain of Video Shacks in the New York area, the prototypes for today's video retail establishments.

By 1984 about 20,000 specialty video shops were operating. Today more than 30,000 retail video establishments dot the landscape. Including department, convenience, and grocery stores, more than 90,000 commercial establishments offer videos for sale or rent. The video industry generates more than $16 billion in annual revenues; about $9 billion in rentals, and $7 billion in the sales of prerecorded movies.

As the president of the Video Software Dealers Association recently stated, "the simple truth is, consumers like to rent videos." Seven in 10 adult Americans will rent a movie at least once in a given year; 6 in 10 homes visit a video store at least twice monthly. More than half of all homes maintain a collection or library of videos. That's all good news to the home video business. But there are storm clouds on the horizon.

For one thing, industry concentration has tended to vest power in the hands of a very few chain "superstores," like Blockbuster Video, forcing many smaller operators, and even a few large chains like Wherehouse, out of the business. Also, fewer successful movies have emerged from Hollywood in the late 1990s meaning worse business for video store owners. For example, in 1996, only 8 films that had grossed more than $30 million at the box office came into the video market (compared to 16 in the previous years), leading to a first-ever drop in video rentals in 1997. In fairness, the success of *Titanic* in 1997 and 1998 forestalled the sinking of the video industry, at least for a time. But video stores face long-term problems, including competition from pay cable and DBS, which offer 50 channels or more of movie options, often for a lower price than the tape rental. Then there is the ongoing problem of inconvenience: Many consumers lack the time or interest in shopping, selecting, renting, and then rewinding and returning videos.

Finally, one core audience for entertainment, including movies and music, is spending less time with their television sets (and radios) and more and more time with their computers. A new media competitor has burst upon the scene: the home computer. And it has its own "network," the Internet and the World Wide Web (WWW). We close our brief history of electronic media with the story of the Web.

THE INTERNET AND THE WORLD WIDE WEB

True or False: The Internet and the World Wide Web are the same thing. False (sorry). The term **Internet** refers to the global interconnection of computer networks made possible by using common communication protocols. The **World Wide Web** is just one service available on this global network. Other Internet services we use, including Gopher, FTP, and e-mail, may function within a Web browser, but they are really separate network technologies. There are others, too, and more are in development. But our book is about sending sounds and pictures, mainly. So our discussion will focus on the development of the Internet and its primary audiovisual component: the World Wide Web.

Cold War and Hot Science: The Birth of the Internet

The Internet, like television and radio before it, is taking the world by storm. In fact, it's one of those new communications technologies that seem to have been invented and perfected overnight. In reality nothing could be further from the truth. The Internet, like television, was in development for decades. Like radio, the Internet was developed out of concern for military preparedness and assurance that the military could communicate in times of emergency.

The main impetus behind the Internet's development was the Cold War struggle between the United States and the former Soviet Union, which marked the period from the end of World War II in 1945, until the fall of the Berlin Wall in 1989.

In the early morning hours of October 4, 1957, the former Soviet Union astounded the world by launching Sputnik, the earth's first man-made satellite. This event would have a huge impact on U.S. technology, planting the seeds for the Internet. The race for space had begun, and the Soviets had clearly beaten the United States. Many people began to question how it was possible for the Soviet Union to completely surprise the United States with a new, possibly threatening technology. President Dwight D. Eisenhower called the nation's top military advisors and scientists to form a new agency called the **Defense Advanced Research Projects Agency (DARPA).** On January 7, 1958, DARPA was created to ensure that America would never again be taken by surprise by new technologies.

Sputnik demonstrated that the Soviets had intercontinental missile capability. In response, **SAGE (Semi-Automatic Ground Environment)** was formed to provide the United States with advanced warning against a possible Soviet attack. Many computing devices we take for granted came out of the top-priority SAGE project. For example, SAGE operators communicated with their computers by using interactive displays and light guns, the forerunners of today's mouse and laser pen systems. New information flowed into the computer constantly, which the operators could access in real time through standard telephone lines. Engineers developed **modems** (modulator/demodulators) to connect sensors to the SAGE computers. Another advanced feature of the project was the use of large-screen visual displays. Project designers were concerned that, in emergency situations, a great deal of data would have to be digested by SAGE workers very quickly, thus video displays were used to show the positions of incoming aircraft. While most 1960s computers were connected to teletypelike terminals that printed a line of information on paper every time the carriage return was pressed, SAGE operated using **video display terminals (VDTs).** Compared with the computers in private industry, the SAGE system was definitely on the cutting edge.

Post–Nuclear War: Would There Still Be a Dial Tone?

In the wake of the Cuban missile crisis in October 1962, when the United States and the Soviet Union stood on the brink of nuclear war, military commanders became convinced that it was going to be necessary to develop a communication system that could survive a missile attack. A lot was already known about building sophisticated voice and video networks. AT&T had interconnected the country with telephones by 1914, and the first coast-to-coast hookup for television was completed in 1951. But computer networks were relatively new and consisted mostly of using modems on a standard phone circuit to make an interconnection. Telephone switching centers were located near major cities, and they were sure to become targets of Soviet missiles. In order to make the nation's emergency communication system less vulnerable, a new approach to networking was necessary.

The Air Force hired the Rand Corporation to figure out a way to bolster American communication systems in case of war. Paul Baran of Rand had been pondering some hypothetical questions about the capabilities of different types of computer networks. He reasoned that, in order to make a communication system less vulnerable to attack, that system would need to take many paths to send messages. This concept was similar to the way neural networks work inside the human brain. If one brain cell is damaged, an alternate neural route around the damaged area can be found because of the millions of neural connections that exist. Baran was convinced that a computer network could mimic a neural network, but his ideas were so revolutionary few people in the telecommunications industry believed they were possible. It took Baran nearly five years to convince people that such a network could work. Meanwhile a British physicist named Donald Davies, working independently, had come to the same conclusion: A distributed network of information could provide redundancy of information. Davies thought that data should be broken up into small strings of bits that could be enclosed in "electronic packets," which would be able to move quickly within a communications network having many different connections. The notion of **packet switching** was born.

Packet switching provided the ideal solution to the problem of data loss during emergencies. Data packets were small, and, if a packet was lost, it could be sent and re-sent over the networks easily. With many interconnected computers, packets had several possible paths they could travel in order to reach their final destination. This distributed system could provide survivability in case of a missile attack, because, if one part of the network was destroyed, there would be other paths available. These concepts were at the frontier of computer science during the 1960s. Many computer scientists and telecommunications engineers wondered about the viability of such a system. There

was a great deal of speculation about whether data packets would get lost or flood the system if part of the network failed. It was time to put the theory to the test.

ARPANET: Forerunner of the Internet

Bob Taylor at DARPA decided to build the network that could survive nuclear war. In 1968, the ARPANET project was born.

Twelve different companies bid on the project. Bolt, Beranek, and Newman (BBN), a small engineering firm in Cambridge, Massachusetts, got the contract to begin development work on the basic network computer called the Interface Message Processor (IMP) machine. Not many people outside the firm understood precisely what the firm had been hired to accomplish, nor what the outcomes would be. For example, shortly after BBN received the contract for the IMPs, a note came from Senator Edward M. Kennedy's office congratulating the company on receiving a federal contract to work on the Inter*faith* Message Project!

Early work in computer interactivity was going on at several separate geographical locations simultaneously. Virtual reality experiments were already underway at the University of Utah, while Marvin Minsky and Seymour Papert were developing the field of artificial intelligence at MIT. How could all of the various universities and research labs working on DARPA projects communicate with one another? The solution was to build an interactive computer network that could share data quickly. Engineers at BBN realized that to make this happen they would have to devise a way of controlling network message traffic. The **Network Control Program (NCP)** was a scheme devised to provide this control. NCP became the forerunner of today's **TCP** or **Transport Control Protocol,** the switching system that controls modern communication networks.

In the fall of 1969, UCLA and Stanford became the first of many links in this distributed network. Success of the network was not immediate. Researchers at UCLA wanted to connect their new machine with another computer at Stanford. Sitting at a computer terminal at UCLA's computer lab, undergraduate Charlie Klein typed an "L." Stanford called back on a standard telephone and confirmed the computer had received an "L." Then Klein typed an "O," and again the researchers at Stanford confirmed an "O." Feeling more confident, Klein typed a "G," hoping to gain remote access to the Stanford computer. He hit

Profile: "Lick"—The Brain behind the Internet and the WWW

When Joseph C.R. Licklider wrote *Man–Computer Symbiosis* in 1960, his work inspired many to seriously consider the relationship between computer science and psychology. In 1962, ARPA's attention turned toward computers and "Lick," as he was known, was chosen to head up ARPA's behavioral science office. **Cybernetics,** the study of the interrelationship between man and machines was a new field of study, and Licklider was keenly interested in it. His ideas that a computer could serve as a problem-solving partner to humans, in real time, sounded like science fiction to many. Licklider even talked about creating an "Intergalactic Network" of interconnected computers and of a new concept called **time-sharing.** The notion of connecting computers together to function in some kind of an interconnected network was a radical idea. Though many computers had been interconnected into networks, the process was cumbersome and expensive; usually one communicated with computers using punch cards and "dumb" terminals.

Cold War tensions between the United States and the former Soviet Union prompted America to embark on research into many different technologies simultaneously. Computers and communication systems became a priority, and the military's SAGE project inspired Licklider to see computing in a new light. He reasoned that it didn't make sense to have many different computers using different operating systems, all of them unable to communicate with one another. The Intergalactic Computer Network should have a standardized connection, he thought. Soon after, Licklider began pulling together some of the nation's brightest young researchers to work on the project, among them Bob Taylor of Dallas, who by 1963 headed up DARPA's Office of Information Processing Techniques. Taylor had three terminals in his office at the Pentagon. One was connected to the University of California at Berkeley, another to the main computer at the Strategic Air Command in Santa Barbara, and the third to Lincoln Labs at MIT. Unfortunately, none of the computers could communicate with the others and they all required different log-in procedures. Taylor found the lack of interconnection frustrating.

Computers weren't small and they certainly weren't cheap, Taylor thought. Why not fund a networking project that would try to link them together? With networking, researchers at MIT could use resources at UCLA and vice versa. Taylor called on Larry Roberts, a brilliant 29-year-old scientist at MIT to help make this happen. The rest, as they say, is history. But Licklider's influence on DARPA and network computing in indisputable. "Lick was among the first to perceive the spirit of community created among the users of the first time-sharing systems," said Taylor. "In pointing out the community phenomena created, in part, by the sharing of resources in one time-sharing system, Lick made it easy to think about interconnecting the communities, the interconnection of interactive, online communities of people."

the carriage return, and both computers crashed, perhaps the first (but definitely not the last) time an attempted log-in failed!

Later that day, the bugs were ironed out of the log-in process and the first computers designed for networking were connected. Soon more nodes (sites) were added to the network. In 1970, the University of California at Santa Barbara and the University of Utah were connected; then MIT, Harvard, Carnegie-Mellon, and other major research universities were added. **ARPANET** became the first fully interconnected nationwide computer network.

Where It's @: The Rise of Electronic Mail

While designers of the ARPANET system had originally envisioned its primary use for the exchange of missile telemetry information and had planned for large database transfers using file transfer protocol (FTP), most users were actually using the network to send personal communications to their colleagues. In 1972, Ray Tomlinson of BBN, the company that designed the network, had invented the first practical network e-mail program. Tomlinson and all ARPANET users had their own specific computer accounts, but each user needed a way to separate his own name from the name of the computer system he was using. Looking at his teletype terminal, Tomlinson saw mostly letters and numbers. However, when he saw the @ sign, Tomlinson thought it could be used to combine one's personal user name with the name of his host computer system. Today, the @ has become one of the lasting symbols of our interconnected world!

The 1970s were pivotal for the development of ARPANET. Several public demonstrations of the network's capabilities convinced DARPA to extend packet-switching capability through the use of communications satellites and ground mobile radio transmitters. These efforts, known as **interneting**, began a research initiative designed to solve the problems associated with linking different kinds of networks together. Also, nodes connecting England and Norway broadened the international scope of the network. By 1976, Web pioneers Vinton Cerf and Robert Kahn had developed Transport Control Protocol (TCP/IP) to replace Network Control Program. With TCP/IP, the delivery of a message was the same, regardless of what information was contained inside the packet. A file sent over the network could just as easily be a document, a picture, or a set of numbers. This change in protocol now made it easier to send photographs, sounds, and other material over the network. With new nodes being added every month, ARPANET grew from its original two connections to more than 200 by 1981. Eventually it encompassed more than 1.5 million miles of interconnected telephone lines. While ARPANET's success was well known to many, its usage was still limited to people with high-level military clearance. It was still not a medium available to the masses.

USENET: Bringing Computer Networking to the Masses

Telenet, Tymeshare, and other commercial versions of ARPANET were introduced in the early 1970s, and interconnections with businesses became possible. By the late 1970s, many large corporations and most universities had the ability to connect to a computer network. Electronic mail continued to be the dominant application. In fact, in 1976 Queen Elizabeth sent her first e-mail message. Also that year Steve Bellovin, a graduate student at the University of North Carolina, created **USENET,** a system that enabled groups of computer users to send messages between the UNC campus at Chapel Hill and nearby Duke University in Durham. USENET operated like a bulletin board. A topic area was created, and computer users on the network could post their opinions on the topic. At first, most bulletin boards featured postings on computer-related topics. It wasn't long until politics (mostly liberal), music (mostly contemporary), and sex (mostly recreational) became popular topics on the system.

In the late 1970s, Matt Glickman, a high school student, and Mark Horton, a graduate student at the University of California at Berkeley, rewrote the USENET program to extend its capacity. Through USENET, faculty and students at dozens of universities, who were not previously authorized for ARPANET accounts, now had access to the network. USENET grew rapidly. Starting from just three sites in 1979, USENET grew into thousands of different newsgroups. As might have been expected, the ARPANET administrators objected to USENET's carrying discussions about drugs, sex and rock-and-roll over the network's computers (this was a military project, after all). As a result, an alternative routing system was created to route USENET newsgroup messages around the main ARPANET network. The bulletin boards would carry the prefix "alt," to distinguish these messages from the more traditional research, military, and computer science traffic.

Network users all over the country protested this new policy, which was seen by some as a form of censorship. Yet, as soon as the "alt" distribution system was devised, the number of newsgroups multiplied rapidly. Mythology has it that "alt.rockand-roll" was the first of the alternate newsgroups. Within five months, the ARPANET system administrators gave in to carrying the newsgroups without censorship. The concept of free access to all information is one that net users continue to prize greatly. Today, USENET newsgroup topics range from hip-hop music to collecting Barbie dolls to soap operas to weird sexual behaviors. Alt, indeed.

The various interconnected computer networks grew as users realized TCP/IP would provide greater flexibility than the many different proprietary systems that existed. There was no single initiative to create a vast worldwide interconnected network, yet that's exactly what seemed to be happening. One innovation, called **TELNET,** gave users the ability to connect to and control various computers from remote locations. Another innovation, Bob Metcalfe's Ethernet, allowed an array of computers to be connected into a single **local area network (LAN).** Now, it was possible for all kinds of computers to be linked together, both in the same office and literally around the world. These network innovations gave rise to widespread usage of e-mail and electronic bulletin boards, and they provided remote access to unique scientific databases. Government funding allowed more and more universities to join the network. By the early 1980s, a flourishing research community was interconnected.

Personal Computing: The New Mass Medium

The contribution of the personal computer to the growth of networking cannot be underestimated. Personal computers made it affordable for businesses to provide workers with individual computers instead of teletypes or "dumb" terminals, and, when Apple Computer introduced the Macintosh computer in 1984, the desktop publishing revolution began. Using concepts pioneered at Xerox Corporation's Palo Alto Research Center, the Macintosh offered users a streamlined operating system, a graphical user interface, and highly developed graphics. This revolution in desktop computers and the growth in networking capability allowed individuals to access networked materials, use e-mail, and develop materials for publication. Many people were

An early Macintosh computer.

beginning to predict a closer relationship between computers, communications, and a social usage for the network with Compuserve, America Online, Genie, and other services providing individual accounts. Also, in 1984 William Gibson's influential novel, *Neuromancer*, coined the term cyberspace, a place on a computer network that carves out a virtual world somewhere between reality and the imaginary.

To meet the growing demand for interconnection, domain name servers such as ".gov" for government, ".edu" for educational institution, and ".mil" for military unit were developed. It was no longer necessary to memorize numerical IP addresses. Now it was possible to send a message to a person's name at a particular institution (**<your-name>@hostinstitution.edu.country**). Networking was taking hold in many industrialized countries. EUnet (European UNIX network) provided users in the Netherlands, Denmark, Sweden, and the United Kingdom with e-mail and USENET services. BITNET and CSNET connected university and business users, while bulletin board systems (BBS) provided dial-up access to information in major urban areas.

With the success of interconnection came a realization that problems associated with speed and bandwidth would eventually grind the network to a halt. By 1985, the amount of networked traffic was gaining attention from NASA, the Department of Energy, and government agencies using the net. The National Science Foundation (NSF) proposed building a new high-speed network to ease data traffic. During this period of development, two different standards had emerged. ARPANET's TCP/IP coexisted with x.25, a different transmission protocol that was widely used in Europe and had many commercial applications in the United States. Now NSF pushed for one standard so that all systems could be interconnected into one "network of networks." A highly influential report, "Towards a National Research Network," issued by the National Research Council spurred then-Senator Al Gore to sponsor legislation to fund a super high-speed network using fiber optic technology. This set the stage for the development of the **information superhighway** concept. **NSFNET** would be a high-speed backbone that linked supercomputer centers at Cornell, San Diego, Illinois, and Pittsburgh. Instead of carrying messages at 56kps (kilobits per second), the new network could transmit messages at 1.5Mbps (megabits per second).

The Internet at Last!

The Internet was officially born in 1986, when NSFNET replaced the aging ARPANET with a faster network providing 30 times more bandwidth. Using TCP/IP technology, NSFNET allowed universities to link together in a "daisy chain" arrangement ultimately connecting to one of the supercomputer centers. For the first time, faculty at smaller institutions had the ability to run experiments on the nation's largest and fastest research computers. At the same time, commercial vendors recognized the importance of the developing trends and started work on commercial products that could take advantage of the unique networking characteristics of TCP/IP. As the 1990s arrived, private **Internet Service Providers (ISPs),** such as America Online (AOL), gave consumers access to the Internet, while large telecommunications corporations, such as MCI and AT&T, provided new backbone capability. Public access to the Internet was occurring at libraries and universities around the country, too. Cleveland Free-Net, generally regarded as one of the first community computer networks, had over 40,000 registered users by 1992. The WELL, San Francisco's community-based network, boasted becoming America's first "virtual community," with membership swelling from a few hundred in 1986 to nearly 10,000 by the early 1990s. During just a five-year period, between 1987 and 1992, the speed of the Internet backbone increased a remarkable 400 percent, while traffic on the net increased exponentially.

In Search of Search Engines: Sorting Out the Internet

By now, a tremendous amount of information was available on the Internet and most of it was free. But how could Internet users organize and sort out all this data? The answer to the question came from university researchers and computer companies who started to develop numerous tools for utilizing information available on the Internet. One of the first Internet crawlers was Archie, a robot-like program that checked FTP (file transfer protocol) sites to catalog which databases were publicly available. Gopher programs, available on most publicly accessible networked computers, provided a menu system that allowed the user to access resources on the Internet. And WAIS (wide-area information servers) systems were distributed by Apple Computer and others to provide users the ability to search many Internet servers simultaneously. With the capability of very-high-speed data access, affordable computers, and free databases available for searching, the stage was set for the introduction of the World Wide Web.

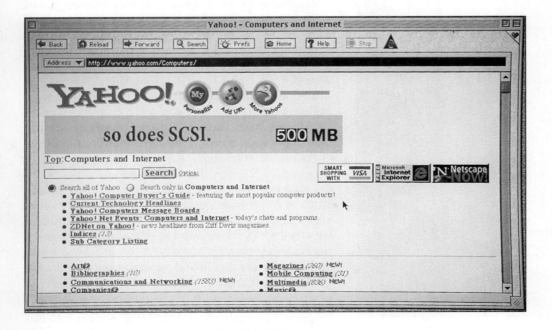

Yet Another Hierarchical Online Organizer. Yahoo's search engine is one of the most visited sites on the Web.

The Birth of the World Wide Web (WWW)

In March 1989, Tim Berners-Lee, while working at CERN, Europe's high-energy particle physics laboratory, circulated a paper that called for the creation of a program that used a graphical interface (pictures, as opposed to text) for requesting information available on networked databases. After the paper kicked around for more than a year, CERN gave Berners-Lee the job to write the program. He dubbed his concept the "World Wide Web." Here's how his revolutionary concept worked:

The vast majority of information on the Internet consisted of text: words in documents, and lines of letters and numbers. Berners-Lee's idea was to insert a system of **hyperlinks,** packets of computer commands, within the texts. By clicking a link, the program makes a request to the server. The server determines the location of the link through the use of a **URL (universal resource locator)** address, gets that information, and sends it back to the computer that requested it. Since the data inside the requested packets could be anything (text, video, audio, etc.), the Internet was now capable of displaying text, video, audio, or any combination, and the user did not need to know elaborate computer code to find it. The WWW was WWWonderful.

By the fall of 1991, the World Wide Web began running experimentally on several different computer systems in Europe and the United States. During the next year, various versions of the CERN browser were installed on some 26 different computers around the world for testing. In January 1993, Marc Andreesen, working at the National Center for Supercomputer Applications (NCSA), released the first version of Mosaic, the forerunner of Netscape Navigator. This revolutionary program made it even easier for computer users to find text, sound, and pictures on the Internet. At this point, World Wide Web traffic was still miniscule, roughly .1 percent of all the traffic on the Internet. That would soon change.

Mosaic and the World Wide Web together formed the "killer application" that was needed to make the Internet really take off among all sorts of people. The World Wide Web became an overnight sensation. Within six months the number of Web-based servers jumped from a few to over 200, and traffic increased tenfold as well. People outside of the research community began to take a real interest in the WWW. Everywhere newspapers, television, and magazines were talking about the new phenomenon. In 1994 Andreesen left NCSA to form Netscape Communications and the World Wide Web saw its first commercial applications.

The usage statistics for the Web are staggering; between 1993 and 1995 the number of Internet users more than tripled, from about 12 million to 40 million users. While only 22 countries had access to the Web in 1995, today more than 100 countries have regular service. And, the number of Internet-linked computers seems to be tripling every 18 months! Where there were just 100 Web sites in 1992, today there are more than a million sites housing 12 million pages of data, graphics, sound, and video and the number of pages of information is increasing by 250,000 every seven days. Data traffic is tripling every three years and will overtake voice as the dominant type of traffic on telephone lines by 2005. Cable TV is touting its high-speed modems as an alternative to land lines, just as satellite and microwave companies scramble to enter the Internet fray. At this moment, there is no way to predict where the growth of the Internet will taper off, or which companies consumers will turn to for their radio stations, TV shows, telephone calls, chat rooms, and Web sites. We do indeed live in interesting times.

SUMMARY

- Cable television began in the late 1940s and early 1950s, as viewers in mountainous and rural areas strove to be a part of the "TV craze." On the West Coast, Ed Parsons in Oregon rigged up a cable TV system to receive signals from Seattle. Back east, Bob Tarlton provided cable service in Pennsylvania and began to charge a monthly fee. At first, the FCC was reluctant to regulate the cable business, but under pressure from broadcast TV, a set of restrictive regula-

tions was put in place that stymied the growth of cable for over 20 years.

- Cable's period of explosive growth began in the 1970s, spurred by the adoption of new FCC rules, the spread of satellites for program distribution, and the rise of innovative programming services. Two important program concepts, pay TV (led by Home Box Office) and the "superstation" (developed by Ted Turner), were developed at this time. By the 1980s, more new program services appeared, like CNN and MTV, making cable increasingly attractive to TV households. Cable boomed, as more than half of all TV homes decided to subscribe to the service. Today, cable TV reaches more than 6 in 10 TV households and delivers a range of services to consumers, including video, data, and even telephone service.

- Cable's growth created competition, including direct broadcast satellite and the consumer favorite: the videocassette recorder (VCR). The first wave of home satellite dishes were large, cumbersome, and expensive. Nevertheless, TVROs dotted the landscape in the 1980s, with over three million units sold. A new generation of smaller and more-affordable satellite dishes appeared in the 1990s and have taken the video industry by storm. More than 10 million homes have some form of DBS service, and that figure will grow as satellite services add more channels, including local broadcast stations. Other alternatives to cable, including MMDS, or "wireless cable," have been less successful.

- The rise of the VCR has been spectacular. The home video business exploded on the scene in the 1980s, fueled by a landmark Supreme Court case legalizing home video recording, the arrival of affordable video recorders, and the rise of video rental shops. VCRs are in nearly 9 in 10 TV homes, and the video sales and rental business tops $16 billion in annual revenues.

- The newest of the so-called new media is the Internet and its video/audio segment known as the World Wide Web (WWW). The Internet is a byproduct of the Cold War between the former Soviet Union and the United States, arising from an initiative to link major universities and civil defense sites to avert (or survive) nuclear war. It arose from the creation of the Defense Advanced Research Projects Agency (DARPA) in 1957, following the successful launch by Russia of its Sputnik satellite. Innovations from DARPA included SAGE, a computer system designed to detect incoming Soviet missiles, and ARPANET, a network of connected computers designed to spread data among various defense installations so that a single Soviet bomb couldn't destroy all of our vital missile data. The innovative SAGE computers used video screens, modems, and early versions of the computer mouse. With its ability for computers in different

places to exchange data, ARPANET can be seen as the direct forerunner of the Internet.

- By the 1970s, most users of ARPANET were not using the system to exchange missile guidance information. Instead, researchers and college professors were using the system to exchange electronic messages. The concept of e-mail was taking shape. Also during this period, computer scientists began to design programs to enable different kinds of computers to exchange data and to standardize the exchange, whether the message consisted of text, sounds, or pictures. By the end of the decade, USENET, a simplified bulletin board system, and TELNET, a means of dialing into large computers from remote locations, were growing in popularity.

- Like VCRs, sales of personal computers skyrocketed in the 1980s. The Apple and IBM PC brought a new class of entrepreneurs, experimenters, and enthusiasts to the field of computing. Individual computer users in universities and businesses could now connect to one another to exchange data (and e-mail). In response to the growing demand, the National Science Foundation replaced the aging ARPANET infrastructure with a faster network that had much higher bandwidth. Hundreds, then thousands, of universities and schools soon logged on to the network. They were followed in the early 1990s by millions of home computer enthusiasts, using commercial gateways like Prodigy and America Online (AOL). An additional innovation introduced at this time was the easy-to-use search program, which made finding data on the net both fast and easy.

- The last piece of the puzzle was provided by Tim Berners-Lee, who coined the term *World Wide Web*. His innovative idea was to connect data on the Web via *hyperlinks,* packages of computer commands that computer users could execute with a simple click of the mouse. As a result, text, sounds, and pictures could be transmitted and received on the Internet virtually anywhere in the world, without the need for sophisticated or technical commands.

- Today, the Internet is taking its place alongside radio, broadcast TV, and cable television as a means of sending and receiving media content. Time will tell if the new Web replaces such "ancient" networks as CBS, NBC, and ABC.

KEY TERMS

cable TV   29
Cable Communications Policy
   Act   30
TVRO (Satellite television receive-
   only earth station)   32
direct broadcast satellite (DBS)   33
satellite master-antenna television
   (SMATV)   33
multichannel, multipoint
   distribution system
   (MMDS)   33
downconverter   33
videotape recorder (VTR)   34
kinescope recorder   34
VCR (videocassettes recorder)   35

time-shifting   35
Internet   37
World Wide Web   37
Defense Advanced Research
   Projects Agency (DARPA)   37
SAGE (Semi-Automatic Ground
   Environment)   37
modems   37
video display terminals (VDTs)   37
cybernetics   39
time-sharing   39
packet switching   38
Network Control Program
   (NCP)   38
TCP; Transport Control Protocol   38

ARPANET   39
interneting   40
USENET   40
TELNET   40
local area network (LAN)   40
cyberspace   41
information superhighway   41
NSFNET   41
Internet Service Provider (ISP)   42
hyperlinks   43
URL (universal resource locator)   43

SUGGESTIONS FOR FURTHER READING

Baldwin, T. E., & McVoy, D. S. (1983) *Cable communication.* Englewood Cliffs, NJ: Prentice-Hall.

Eddings, J. (1994). *How the Internet works.* Emeryville, CA: Ziff-Davis.

Hafner, K., & Lyon, M. (1996). *Where wizards stay up late: The origins of the Internet.* New York: Simon & Schuster.

Luber, S. (1993). *Infoculture: The Smithsonian book of Information Age inventions.* Boston, MA: Houghton Mifflin.

Parsons, P. R., & Frieden, R. M. (1998). *The cable and satellite television industries.* Boston, MA: Allyn and Bacon.

Randall, N. (1997). *The soul of the Internet: Net gods, netizens, and the wiring of the world.* Boston: International Thomson.

Reid, R. H. (1997). *Architects of the Web: 1,000 days that built the future of the Web.* New York: John Wiley.

Salus, P. H. (1995). *Casting the net: From ARPANET to the Internet and beyond.* Reading, MA: Addison-Wesley.

Southwick, T. (1999). *Distant signals: How cable TV changed the world of telecommunications.* Denver: The Cable Center.

Sterling, C. J., & Kittross, J. (1990). *Stay tuned: A concise history of American broadcasting.* Belmont, CA: Wadsworth.

Winston, B. (1998). *Media technology and society: A history.* New York: Routledge.

INTERNET EXERCISES

1.   Visit our Web site at http://www.mhhe.com/beyond for study-guide exercises to help you learn and apply material in each chapter. You will find ideas for future research as well as useful Web links to provide you with an opportunity to journey through the new electronic media.

3 Audio and Video Technology

Quick Facts

 Frequency response of voices and music: 15 kilohertz

 Frequency response of compact disc: 20 kilohertz

 Scanning lines, conventional television: 525

 Scanning lines, high-definition television: 1080

 First high-definition TV broadcasts: 1998

 Deadline for transition to digital HDTV: 2006

 Cost of digital HDTV set (1999): $5,000

Watching TV and listening to radio are the easiest things in the world to do. Just twist that dial, flip that switch, or punch that button and poof: Vivid sounds and picturesque images are yours (unless, of course, you're watching a test pattern). The ease with which we command TV and radio reception hides the incredibly difficult problems and complex technical processes involved in moving sound and pictures from their source to you. This chapter attempts to demystify the magic of radio and TV technology. We describe how the process works and, more important, why it matters. In many ways understanding the technical bases of electronic media helps you to understand its history, legal status, social and political power, and future.

BASIC PRINCIPLES OF MEDIA TECHNOLOGY

It's helpful to begin a discussion of technical aspects of radio and TV with some basic principles.

Facsimile Technology

All modes of mass communication are based on the process of facsimile technology. That is, sounds from a speaker and pictures on a TV screen are merely representations, or **facsimiles,** of their original form. We all learn and practice facsimile technology at an early age. Did you ever use a pencil or crayon to trace the outline of your hand on a sheet of blank paper? That's facsimile technology. Having one's face covered by plaster of Paris for a mask or sculpture is facsimile technology; so are having your picture taken and photocopying a friend's lecture notes.

In general, the more faithful the reproduction or facsimile is to the original, the greater is its **fidelity.** High-fidelity audio, or **hi-fi,** is a close approximation of the original speech or music it represents. And a videocassette recorder marketed as high fidelity boasts better picture quality than a VCR without hi-fi (known as H-Q, to distinguish video high fidelity from its audio counterpart). Indeed, much of the technical development of radio and TV has been a search for high fidelity: finding better and better ways to make facsimiles of the original sounds or images.

The second point about facsimile technology is that in creating their facsimiles, radio and TV are not limited to plaster of Paris, crayon, oils, or even pho-

tographic chemicals and film. Instead, unseen elements such as radio waves, beams of light, and digital bits and bytes are utilized in the process. Although you cannot put your hands on a radio wave as you can a photo in your wallet, it is every bit as much *there*. The history of radio and TV is directly linked to the discovery and use of these invisible "materials," from Marconi's radio experiments in the 1890s to the microcomputer technology of today.

In the technical discussion that follows, bear in mind that the engineer's goal in radio, TV, and cable is to create the best possible facsimile of our original sound or image, to transport that image without losing too much fidelity (known as signal loss), and to recreate that sound or image as closely as possible to its original form.

Transduction

Another basic concept is **transduction,** the process of changing one form of energy into another. When the telephone operator says "the number is 555–2796" and you write it down on a sheet of notepaper, you have transduced the message. Similarly, when you slip a CD in your boom box and stroll through the mall, you are transducing—although not all those around you will appreciate it.

Why does this matter? Well, getting a sound or picture from a TV studio or concert hall to your home usually involves at least three or four transductions. At each phase loss of fidelity is possible and must be controlled. And at each phase the whole process may break down into **noise**—unwanted interference— rendering the communication impossible. Although breakdowns due to transduction rarely occur, they do happen. Technicians were embarrassed when the sound went out during the 1976 presidential debate between Gerald Ford and Jimmy Carter. Closer to home, a cassette recorder with dirty heads can make Tchaikovsky sound like Marilyn Manson.

Television and radio signals begin as physical energy, commonly referred to as light waves or sound waves. When you hear a bird chirping in a tree, your brain directly perceives the event by processing the sound waves that enter your ears and vibrate your eardrums. You see the bird as your brain processes the reflections of light that have entered the eye and fallen on the retina. This is direct experience: no transduction, no signal loss; true high fidelity. To experience this event on radio, however, the following translations or transductions occur.

As we stand there with a microphone attached to a tape recorder, the bird's song is first changed into mechanical energy. Inside a dynamic microphone, the various sound wave pressures cause a small coil to vibrate back and forth in a magnetic field. This sets up in the coil a weak electrical current that re-produces the pattern of the original sound waves. Next, this current is amplified and varies the magnetic field in the *recording head* of the tape recorder—the device that stores a new signal on tape by rear-ranging the metallic particles on the tape. Thus the bird's song is translated into patterns of magnetic blips on a piece of audiotape. How well the trans-duction occurs is based on the quality of our facsimile. A big tape recorder with tape that is 2 inches wide, like those used to record orchestra perfor-mances, will produce bigger and better blips than those produced by a $20 cassette recorder that uses tape ⅜ of an inch across.

Now we have a mechanical facsimile of the chirp-ing, a pile of blips on a piece of tape. Next, we need to transduce that signal into electrical energy. In playing back the tape, the *playback head* of our recorder converts the signal stored on the tape into a small electrical charge. The amplifier detects the electricity, boosts it, and cleans it up. And, as stereo buffs know, the quality of our facsimile is now based on the quality or power of our amplifier. We are now halfway to hearing the chirp on our radio.

Next, we transduce the electrical energy into elec-tromagnetic energy. At the radio station we feed the amplified sound from the tape recording to the transmitter. Here the signal is superimposed, or "piggybacked," onto the radio wave (channel) as-signed to that station (a process called *modulation,* examined in detail later). The fidelity of the signal is based on the station's power, its location, its channel, and all sorts of other factors.

At home we turn on the radio and tune to the ap-propriate channel. Our antenna detects the signal and begins to reverse the transduction process. The energy is transduced first to electrical impulses as it enters our radio's amplifier. Next, it is transduced to electromagnetic energy, to vibrate the diaphragm of the radio's loudspeaker. At long last it is transduced back into its original form, physical energy, as we hear the chirp in the form of vibrations on our tym-panic membrane (eardrum). Note the many trans-ductions in this process.

What's the point of all this? Why does the trans-duction process matter?

Signal and Noise

First, the signal, or message, goes through many translations, with the possibility (even the necessity) of losing some information or adding some unneces-sary data at each phase. It's rather like playing the game "telephone," where several people whisper a simple message in turn. By the time the message gets to the last person, a lot of the original information has dropped out and some irrelevant information has crept in. In electronic terminology, losing infor-mation in the transduction process is known as **sig-nal loss.** As was explained earlier, the unwanted interference is known as noise. Now you can under-stand a term found in many advertisements for stereos and VCRs: the **signal-to-noise ratio.** In com-mon terms, this is a numerical representation of the amount of "pure" picture or sound information that remains after subtracting unwanted noise acquired during the transduction process. The higher the sig-nal-to-noise ratio, the higher the fidelity; the lower the ratio, the "noisier" the sound or picture.

Analog and Digital Signals

How information is converted from one form of en-ergy to another is an important aspect of transduc-tion. Until the 1980s, broadcast transmissions uti-lized **analog signals.** This means that to change the energy from physical to electrical impulses, an "anal-ogy" to the original sound or image replaced the matter itself. It sounds tricky, but the concept is sim-ple. Think of the grooves in a phonograph record. As the needle travels through the grooves, it vibrates in a pattern similar to the vibrations made by the guitar string or vocal cords it represents. This is not the original vibration, but an *analog* to it. Similarly, when the chemicals in a piece of photographic film change in response to the patterns of light reflected on it, the film is an analog recording of the events in front of the camera. By their nature, analog transmissions and recordings are subject to a great deal of signal loss and noise. They merely represent the original signal, itself a major limitation since the transmis-sions can never include all of the information present in the original sound or picture. And analog signals tend to decay over time and space. After all, records collect dust, get scratched, and warp in hot cars and on window sills. Photographs blur, tear, and fade.

Most of the excitement in broadcasting, home au-dio, and video today concerns **digital recording and**

transmission: Rather than creating an analog to the original sound or picture, the signal itself is utilized in the transduction process. Each element of the audio or video signal is translated into its digital equivalent—that is, a number—by means of a binary code. A binary code is one with only two values, such as "on–off," "yes–no," "open–shut," or 0 and 1. Computers use binary codes to process information. In digital recording, each sound is a unique sequence of binary numbers: 010, 011, 101, and so on. The picture or music is transduced by being "read," or *sampled*, by a beam of laser light, the same way the bar codes on your groceries are at the supermarket checkout. There are no needles, no friction, no wear, no scratches. More important, there is virtually no opportunity to introduce noise. When the signal is transmitted and played back, what we hear through the speakers and watch on the screen is a virtual duplicate of the original signal with the highest fidelity and excellent signal-to-noise ratio, meaning it is virtually noise-free.

A frequent topic of this text is the transition from analog to digital. Radio, TV, cable, and recording are all moving to digital means of production. As a result, they are merging with the computer: the technology that introduced and perfected digital communication. This phenomenon has received its own industry buzzword: **convergence.**

Oscillation and the Waveform

Another basic principle to both audio and video signal processing is the concept of oscillation. Recall that we hear sounds and see images as variations, fluctuations, or vibrations detected by our ears and eyes and interpreted by our brain. Remember too that every vibration has a unique signature or "footprint"; every sound and image has its own characteristics. How well we see, how acutely we hear, and how well we can recreate these signals as sounds and pictures depend on our ability to identify, store, and recreate those vibrations. In electronic terms, the vibration of air produced by our mouths, the instruments we play, and objects in our natural environment, as well as the vibration of light that accounts for every color and image our eyes can see, is known as **oscillation.** The footprint or image of an oscillation we use to visualize the presence of the invisible is known as its **waveform.** Figure 3–1 demonstrates the phenomenon of oscillation and the common waveform.

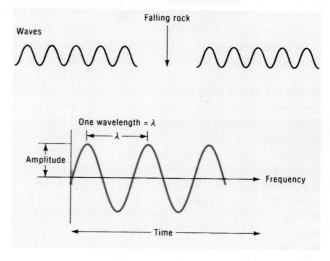

Figure 3–1

Principle of Oscillation and the Common Waveform

The most common way you and I can visualize oscillation is by dropping a rock into a pail of water. You know that the result will be a series of circles or waves, radiating outward from the spot where the rock fell, until dissipating some distance from the center (depending on the size of the bucket and the height from which we drop the rock). All audio and video signals produce a pattern like this, except that they are invisible to the naked eye. However, while we can't see the patterns with the naked eye, using the appropriate electronic equipment (such as an oscilloscope and a waveform monitor), we can detect them, use them, even create them ourselves.

Frequency and Amplitude

A major way in which we describe a wave is by its **frequency,** the number of waves that pass a given point in a given time. Originally measured in cycles per second (cps), frequency is more commonly measured now in **hertz (Hz),** in homage to early radio pioneer Heinrich Hertz.

In our example with the rock, depicted in Figure 3–1, the frequency is simply the number of waves that pass a given point in a single second. Note also from the bottom of Figure 3–1 that the distance between two corresponding points on a wave is called the **wavelength.** Also note that frequency and wavelength are inversely related. High frequency means a short wavelength; low frequency means a long wavelength. In the early days of radio, U.S. stations were classified by their wavelengths. Today we identify them by their frequencies.

A wave may also be described by its height or depth, from its normal position before the rock is dropped to the crest created by the splash. This is known as its **amplitude.** When choosing a section of beach to swim in, families with small children are likely to select those with slow, low, undulating waves—waves of low amplitude or, to use a radio term, long waves. Surfers will select a wild stretch of shoreline with frequent, mammoth-sized (high-amplitude) waves capable of picking the swimmer up and depositing her anywhere on the beach. In radio terms, these are the high-frequency short waves.

What's the significance of all this? For one thing, this is precisely how radio and TV work. As we examine in detail later, local radio stations wish to blanket their area with a strong local or regional signal. That's why AM signals use long waves. International broadcasters like the BBC and Radio Moscow seek to spread the word about their countries around the globe. Hence they use short waves to hopscotch around the world. The services of these and other shortwave broadcasters are traced in detail in Chapter 14.

Frequency Response

Consider a final point about oscillation and the waveform. How well we can record and play back music or pictures depends on the range of frequencies that our radio or recorder is capable of receiving or reproducing. This is known as the unit's **frequency response.** A radio set that can be tuned only to frequencies below 10,000 cycles and above 1,000 cycles will simply exclude very low and very high sounds. At the same time, a receiver with the best speakers, with a frequency response from 40 to 40,000 hertz, will be able to reproduce virtually all the sounds the human ear can hear. It's the difference between hearing a symphony orchestra on a CD player or through the tiny speaker in a telephone receiver. This is critical since the history of the popular arts is directly linked to the frequency response of the prevailing methods of signal processing.

In the recording industry the early success of banjo-playing minstrel-type performers, who frequently whistled in their acts, was in large part due to their audibility on 78-rpm records of limited, mainly high-frequency capability. Such stars as Al Jolson, Rudy Vallee, and Eddie Cantor fall into this class. Similarly, in retrospect, Elvis Presley's limited tonal range seems to have directly fit the limitations of the cheaply produced 45-rpm record popular in the 1950s, which was meant to be heard on a teenager's much abused "personal" record player (certainly not on Dad's hi-fi in the den). More recently, is it any surprise that the orchestrations, sound collages, and other experimentations ushered in by the Beatles' *Sergeant Pepper's Lonely Hearts Club Band* and by other groups in the late 1960s were aided by the developments of high-fidelity studio recording and FM stereo broadcasting? Today the complexities and acoustic calisthenics of rap and hip-hop performers (such as Busta Rhymes and Snoop Dogg) are made possible by the extended range of frequencies available with new audio components, such as digital consoles and CD players.

STEPS IN SIGNAL PROCESSING

Having mastered the basics of media technology, let's turn to how it's actually done. All electronic signals—radio, TV, cable, satellite, and computer—follow the identical path from their inception to our consumption. These steps are depicted in Figure 3–2.

STEP 1: SIGNAL GENERATION

This step involves the creation of the necessary oscillations, or detectable vibrations of electrical energy, which correspond to the frequencies of their original counterparts in nature. In plain language, signal generation involves getting the grooves onto a record, the vibrations into a microphone, the blips onto a strip of audiotape, or the bits and bytes onto a CD or floppy disk.

Figure 3–2

Steps in signal processing

(1) Signal generation

(2) Amplification and processing

(3) Transmission

(4) Reception

(5) Storage and retrieval

Audio Signal Generation

Sound signals are generated by two main transduction processes: mechanical and electronic. Mechanical methods, like microphones, phonograph records, and tape recorders, have been in use for many years. They are being replaced by digital electronics, such as CDs, DATs, and minidiscs. First, let's briefly review how mechanical methods work.

Mechanical Methods   Mechanical generation uses facsimile technology to create an analog of the original signals (by now you should be able to understand that technical-sounding sentence). That is, mechanical means are used to translate sound waves into a physical form, one you can hold in your hand, like a phonograph record or audiocassette.

Inside the microphone   One place where speech or music is mechanically recreated to produce electrical signals is inside a microphone. There are three basic types of microphones: dynamic, velocity, and condenser. Each produces the waveforms required for transmission in a different manner.

In a dynamic microphone a diaphragm is suspended between two electromagnets. In the center of the microphone is a coil of electrical wire, called a voice coil. Sound pressure vibrates the diaphragm, which moves the voice coil up and down between the magnetic poles. The result is an electrical pattern in the mike wire analogous to the frequency of the entering sound. Thanks to durable and rugged design similar to a sturdy kettle drum and good frequency response with voices and most music, dynamic mikes are frequently utilized in radio and TV productions.

Velocity microphones, also known as ribbon microphones, replace the voice coil with a thin metal ribbon. There is no diaphragm; the oscillations of the ribbon suspended between the electromagnetic poles produce the necessary electric signals. Velocity mikes produce a lush sound, particularly with the human voice, but they are very fragile and highly susceptible to wind damage. Very common in the "golden age" of radio, they are still widely used in recording studios. (You can see one on Jay Leno's desk on "The Tonight Show.")

In place of a diaphragm, condenser microphones use an electrical device known as a capacitor to produce electronic equivalents of sound pressure waves. The capacitor is an electrically charged plate.

The pattern of electricity in the plate (its amplitude and frequency) varies in relation to its distance from its stationary backplate. That distance is affected by the pressure of the incoming sound waves. While this might seem complex, the process is quite similar to the workings of your own ear. Without touching the volume knob on a portable stereo, you can vary its loudness simply by moving the headphones closer to or farther from your eardrums.

Condenser mikes feature excellent dynamic range but require external power sources to charge the capacitor and amplify the resulting electrical signal before it enters the standard amplifier. Thus most early condenser mikes were cumbersome and large, limiting their use in broadcast sound applications. Recent developments in microelectronics have led to a special class of condenser mikes in common use in telecommunications today. Electret condenser mikes feature an internal power supply unit, typically indicated by the presence of a small battery compartment inside the body of the mike or attached to its cable connector. Electret condenser mikes can be made extremely small (tie-tack, and clip-on styles) and still produce a crisp sound, especially with speech. Thus they are now the preferred mike for news personnel.

The tiny electret condenser is the preferred microphone in TV news due to its small size and rugged design.

Inside the phonograph record   Phonograph records are another means of mechanical transduction of audio signals. They've been around for more than a century, so the method must have its advantages. In recorded music, the sounds produced by musicians and singers are transduced into cuts made on each side of the central groove on the record (this is probably why songs are known as "cuts" in the popular music business). This process is known as **lateral cut recording.** As the turntable rotates, the stylus (needle) vibrates laterally as it follows the groove, creating the vibrations corresponding to the original words and music.

Over the years continuing improvements have been made in the production of records, turntables, needles, and other recording equipment. For example, the frequency response of the gramophone records of the early 1900s ranged from 200 hertz (G below middle C, for you musicians) to around 1,500 hertz (second G above middle C). Today a typical high-fidelity LP record ranges over eight octaves, from 40 to 12,000 hertz, which pretty much includes most of the sounds that are produced by voice and musical instruments.

Inside the tape recorder   The third way we begin sound signal processing is by converting sounds into electromagnetic "blips" on a piece of audiotape. Under a microscope, a piece of audiotape can be seen as a concentration of millions of metallic particles suspended in a plastic base. As the tape moves from supply reel to takeup reel on a tape recorder, the metal filings pass by a charged electromagnet known as the *tape head.*

Here's how the process works. Imagine that the microphones described earlier have generated the electromagnetic energy corresponding to the original sound pressure waves (that is, they worked). It is a simple matter to send that electromagnetic charge through a wire to the tape head. The head is now emitting a signal that is a facsimile of the original sound, only now it is in the form of a magnetic field. A small signal is being emitted throughout the head. As the tape passes, its microscopic metal filings are charged—they are shaped into an exact replica of the electrical patterns moving through the head. We have now created an analog signal, just like the grooves on a record or the oscillations in a microphone.

Why is it useful to know how tape recording works? A basic understanding of audio technology adds much to our study of the radio industry. First, an audiotape is never really erased or noise-free. The presence of the iron oxide particles on the tape at all times creates an audible hiss, even on the best tapes and best machines. Thus home and studio tape recorders frequently have noise-reduction circuits (such as Dolby) designed to suppress the sound of the hiss. Also special tapes have been manufactured that include metal and chromium oxide (CrO_2). In addition, since the tape heads are in constant contact with the tapes, there is plenty of opportunity for stray filings, dust, dirt, and so on to come in contact with the gap and cause poor recordings and playbacks. This is why it is critical to clean the heads frequently, both in the radio station and the home hi-fi. Isopropyl alcohol is usually used since, in addition to its cleaning properties, it is electrically neutral.

Second, by varying the width of the audiotape and the location of the head gap, we can create a variety of tape styles and formats. Professional audio facilities use tape that is two inches wide, capable of recording 8, 12, 16, even 24 or 32 separate sets of signals on one piece of tape. Consequently, such machines are known as **multitrack recorders.**

A common form of audiotape recorder in radio studios is the open-reel machine. The open-reel recorder employs two reels (the one full of tape is the supply reel; the empty one is the takeup reel). The tape is ¼ inch wide and usually can record two tracks in each direction, for a total of four tracks. Thus these are sometimes known as four-track stereo machines.

Radio stations also use audiotape cartridge players, or "carts," for their music, commercials, and station identifications. These machines use a special tape cartridge with only one reel. The tape winds past the heads and back onto itself. This allows for the musical selections to arrive quickly at their original starting point (in radio jargon, they are fast-cued). Cart machines record in one direction only, with a left-channel signal and a right-channel signal for stereo. Thus they are two-track machines.

Cassette tape recorders use a miniaturized reel-to-reel configuration enclosed in a small plastic housing. The tape is only ⅜ inch wide, and, as we all know from our home and car stereos, the tape can be recorded and played back on both sides. Thus there are four tracks of information crunched onto the small tape area. This is why cassette stereo units produce a lot of noise and hiss, and why the better ones allow for two or three types of tape (oxide, metal, standard) and noise reduction options (such as Dolby B and Dolby C).

Digital Electronics   As a trip to the nearest record store confirms, there has been a revolution in audio in recent years. Recordings and magnetic tapes have given way to compact discs (CDs) and digital audiotape (DAT), the digital compact cassette (DCC), and the minidisk (MD).

Digital audio was made possible by the development of a new means of signal generation, known as pulse code modulation (PCM). This and other modulation methods are seen in Figure 3–3. At the top of the figure is the original waveform: the shape of the original sound we seek to record and reproduce. Let's say it's the sound of a guitar solo. Below the waveform is its shape, transduced into an AM signal. Like a surfer on a wave, its new shape is a series of peaks and valleys, or changes in amplitude. Below that is the same waveform transduced into an FM signal. Now the message is in the form of a series of changes in the number of times it occurs in one second—that is, its frequency. At the bottom is the waveform translated into a digital signal. By sampling the amplitude of the wave at varying intervals (turning a laser beam on and off and measuring the length of the light beam at each interval), a digital version of the wave has been produced. This process is called **pulse code modulation,** since the oscillating beam "pulses" and turns the amplitude of the wave into a "code" that can be read by the laser tracking beam.

Foremost, unlike an analog signal, a digital wave is virtually constant—it is the identical shape on recording, on transmission, in the amplifier, and out of the speakers. Second, unlike tapes and standard phonograph records, CDs preserve the original sounds in a sterile, noise-free environment.

CDs   The information on a **compact disc (CD)** is carried beneath the protective acrylic coating in a polycarbonate base. In the base is a series of pits and flats. The pits vary in length in precise correspondence to the amplitude of the waveforms they represent. The flats represent no waveforms: utter silence. As the disc rotates, a laser beam is focused on the disc. Like a mirror, when the beam "sees" a pit, it reflects back a light wave that is a perfect replica of the original sound wave. Now it is a simple matter to transduce that wave into an electrical signal through amplifiers, to antennas, and into speakers. The result is a clean, nearly perfect sound (or picture). In technical terms, the frequency response ranges from 20 to 20,000 hertz (remember, the best

LP record ranges from 40 to 12,000 hertz), with a signal-to-noise ratio of 90 decibels, the common measure of the intensity of sound, which is pretty close to acoustic perfection.

Unlike with records and tapes, there is no friction or wear. Discs are comparatively immune from damage in routine handling and storage. With proper care, they should never warp or scratch, unwind, or jam in the player or get accidentally erased.

Writable compact discs, developed for the computer industry, add the ability to record audio (and video) signals. Thus far, they have not penetrated the home audio market to a significant degree, but another technology is becoming increasingly prevalent in radio stations, recording studios, and home hi-fi systems:

Digital audio tape (DAT)   Digital audio tape (DAT) machines are now the standard professional digital audio format for studio music recording. In addition, DAT recorders are a common feature in most radio stations. Thus far, home DAT sales have lagged. However, with prices dropping, DAT players are expected to take their place in the "audio stack" of many home audio systems.

One reason for the delay in consumer acceptance of DAT concerns copyright. Because digital audio tape recordings are as good as the original records or CDs, every DAT machine and blank DAT tape sold in America includes an excise fee collected by the U.S. Copyright Office. These fees, paid to music publishers and record companies, compensate performers for lost royalties due to digital taping. For this reason, prices for DAT machines and blank tape have remained high.

Digital compact cassette (DCC) and minidisc (MD)   Two other digital audio formats have recently appeared on the scene. **Digital compact cassette (DCC)** recorders, introduced by Philips Corporation, use tape that is the identical size of existing audiocassettes. In addition, DCC machines can play both standard audiocassettes and the new DCC cassettes.

This ability to play both standard and digital cassettes is known as "backward compatibility." Philips counted on this feature to speed consumer adoption of the DCC format. But things did not work out as planned, at least for Philips. In May 1997 it announced it was discontinuing the manufacture of DCC machines.

In 1993, Sony introduced a compact version of the

Figure 3-3

Modulation Methods

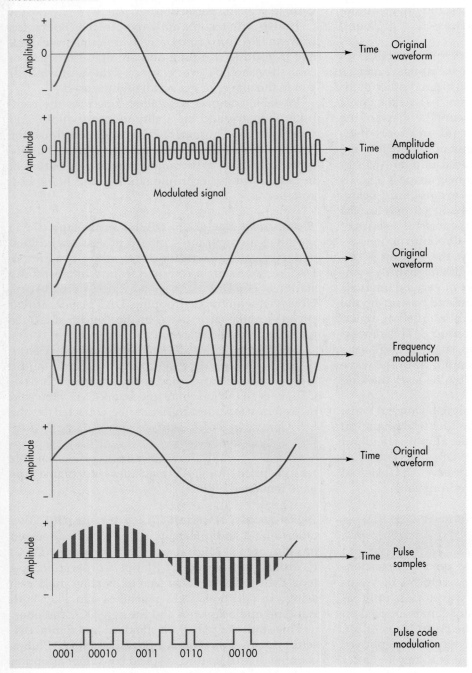

CD called the **minidisc (MD).** The minidisc is about 2½ inches in diameter, just about one-quarter the size of a standard CD. Designed mainly for walkabout stereos, the MD eliminates the problem many portable CD players have had: skipping as a result of laser mistracking. MDs can record up to 74 minutes of music. They can also read out text (liner notes, song titles, and so on).

Thus far, minidisc sales have been disappointing, but Sony remains committed to the format, probably since it also owns one of the largest recording companies in the world: Sony Music.

Video Signal Generation

Television's ability to transmit images is based on the technology of scanning. The TV camera scans each element of a scene line by line; the picture tube in your TV set retraces the scene. Earlier in the chapter we said tracing the outline of your hand is a way to create a facsimile representation of the hand on the sheet of paper, like the illustration in Figure 3–4(a). Let's change the game a little bit. Instead of drawing one continuous line, suppose we trace the hand by using a series of five parallel lines, as depicted in Figure 3–4(b). We move the crayon straight across. We lift it when it encounters the hand and return it to the paper when it passes by a "hand" area. The result is the rough facsimile of the hand in

Figure 3–4(b). Now, let's use 10 lines instead of 5. This tracing will provide a fairly good representation of the hand, as in Figure 3–4(c). Just for fun, let's alternate the tracing by doing every odd-numbered line first, then each even-numbered line. After two passes, top-to-bottom, the result is Figure 3–4(d). In this exercise we have actually demonstrated the workings of TV technology.

When done invisibly by the TV camera, the tracing process is called **scanning.** The process of alternating lines is known as the **interlace method.** And the process of replicating the scan on the picture tube to produce the image at home is known as **retracing.** The process originates in the TV camera and is recreated at home on the picture tube.

The Importance of Scanning   At this point you may feel saturated by needless technical information. Actually there are excellent reasons why this information is critical to understanding modern telecommunications.

Figure 3–4

Examples of Scanning

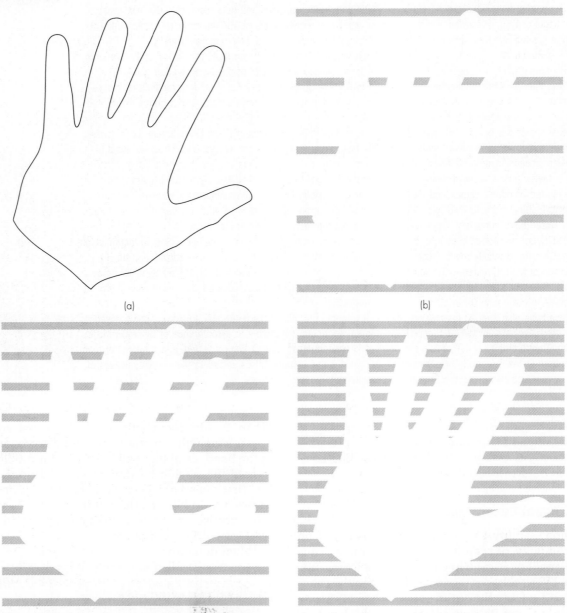

(a)

(b)

Standardization   First is the issue of standards. The number of lines utilized in the scanning process varies throughout the world. The United States uses a 525-line system adopted in 1941 by a group known as **NTSC (National Television Standards Committee).** A complete picture consists of two separate scans or **fields,** each consisting of 262½ horizontal scanning lines. The two fields combine to form a sin-

gle picture, called the **frame.** In the United States, the AC power system we use oscillates at 60 hertz. Thus, our TV system uses a 60-hertz scanning rate. Since two fields are needed to produce one frame, 30 complete pictures are produced every second.

     Much of European TV uses a system known as *PAL*, adopted several years after the U.S. system. Based on the DC power available there, European

Ethics: Negativland: Digital Artists or Rip-off Artists?

Digital sampling techniques allow virtually any sound or image to be reproduced and re-recorded, thereby raising a critical ethical dilemma. Is it ethical to borrow musical phrases from one song and then combine them with pieces of other songs? Most performers and musicians argue that their work should be protected from such digital manipulation. Others argue that the new technology has created a new art form. Composers should be free to use sounds and images from other works to create new ones, especially those that use the expropriated images for comedic or satirical purposes.

Negativland is one of those groups. The "band," if you can call it that, exists by purloining the work of other artists and turning compilations of those bits of work into their own songs. Their albums make use of hundreds of digital samples—from familiar rock guitar riffs, to snippets of conversations from TV talk shows, to slogans and jingles from radio and TV advertisements. The results are mixed (pun intended), but when it works, the effect can be insightful and interesting.

A few years ago, the Irish group U2 sued Negativland when it released an album titled U2, which included a vicious parody of the supergroup's "I Still Haven't Found What I'm Looking For." More recently, their *Dispepsi* CD made use of samples of dozens of soft drink ads to satirize the leading cola companies. Apparently too busy with their "Cola Wars," thus far Coke and Pepsi have failed to file suit.

Negativland caused quite a stir in late 1998 with the release of its new CD with the not-so-clever title of "Over the Edge Volume 3—The Weatherman's Dumb Stupid Come-Out Line." According to the band's co-leader Mark Hosler, five CD-pressing plants refused to manufacture the disc, apparently under pressure from the Recording Industry Association of America. Disctronics, a plant in Texas, said it was refusing to make the CD since it might contain unauthorized sound clips. Negativland immediately went on the offensive.

They wrote a protest letter to the RIAA, posted the letter on the Internet, and called for free speech advocates everywhere to rally to the group's side. For its part, RIAA's president and CEO, Hilary Rosen, called the group's concerns "misplaced" and said RIAA has had "absolutely no involvement with Negativland or its new release."

How will it all turn out? So far, to quote R.E.M., it's been mostly "Ignoreland."

TV uses a shorter scanning rate (50 hertz), with more scanning lines (625). Many Americans are startled to see how clear European TV is; that's due to the fact that it has 100 more lines of resolution.

Beyond better picture quality, the issue of standardization involves a lot of other important matters. Televisions and VCRs produced for one system will not work on the other. The same is true for videotape. (As an administrator for the Peabody Awards, one of the authors racks up hours in international telephone calls each year making sure programs are submitted in the proper format.)

High-definition television (HDTV) The scanning process is also directly involved in many of the current technical innovations in the TV medium. **High-definition television (HDTV)** utilizes up to 1,080 scanning lines, producing an image rivaling 35-millimeter film in quality. It also changes the aspect ratio (the ratio of screen width to screen height) of conventional TV. In standard TV the screen is four units wide and three units high. In HDTV, the ratio is 16:9 (sixteen units wide and nine units high), much like the frames of a motion picture.

As we trace in the "Television Today" chapter (Chapter 5), TV stations, networks, cable, and satellite systems are in the process of converting from the 60-year-old 525-line system to the new digital, high-definition system. Most TV stations in the nation's top markets began the transition to HDTV (also known as DTV—for Digital TV) in 1999. NFL games, the "Tonight Show," and many prime-time TV shows are already being transmitted in digital high definition, and the FCC has called for a complete transition to DTV by 2006.

While we're on the subject of scanning, the switch to DVT actually involves three sets of lines and two scanning methods. The new DTV sets are able to tune in TV signals using 480, 720, and 1,080 lines, all of which have much higher fidelity than traditional analog 525 NTSC. And, the new TV signals can be sent every other line (the traditional interlace method) or line by line—an alternative scanning method known as **progressive scan.**

Events: Handycam or "Panty-cam"?—The Camera with X-ray Vision

One of Sony's new, miniature home video cameras apparently boasts one feature not touted in the company's advertising. *Takarajima,* a Japanese men's magazine, reported that a certain model of Sony's popular Handicam camcorders could look beneath swimsuits and see through to the underwear of lightly dressed people when switched to its low-light "night shot" setting and when equipped with a cheap lens filter. The article included a number of photos of female models, some in wet swimsuits, others dry and fully dressed. The pictures showed something, all right, even to the naked eye.

Soon, the cameras and filters were flying out of stores all over the world. One camera shop in Boston sold 30 by noon the day after the publication of the report in a local newspaper. In Arlington, Virginia, one customer bought two of the cameras, which cost about $600 each. Sony hurriedly announced that it was discontinuing Handicams with the special infrared feature. However, by the time of the announcement, more than a million such units had been sold, almost half in North America.

That's a lot of electronic voyeurs.

So, what difference does this make? Plenty. Using 480 lines allows TV stations and networks to send more than one version of their channel (like NBC1 or CBS2). Broadcast TV is touting this feature so it can compete more successfully with its cable competitors, which have made multiple versions of their channels available for some years now (like ESPN, ESPN2, and ESPNews). And, using the progressive scan method brings TV much closer to the computer business, which has used progressive scan on its monitors for years now.

Closed captioning Closed captioning uses the blanking period between scans (the **vertical blanking interval**) to send additional information with the TV signal. Appropriate decoders provide captions for deaf viewers or specialty text services, such as news capsules or stock market reports, to specially equipped TV sets.

High Definition TV (HDTV). Experts disagree about whether consumers will be willing to pay thousands of dollars for a new TV set that provides a picture that rivals 35 millimeter film.

Figure 3–5

Inside the TV Camera

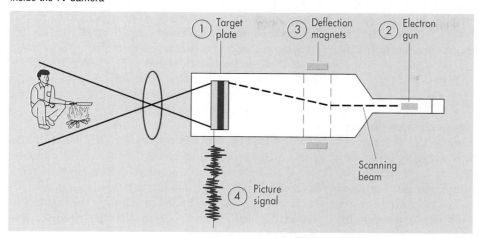

Inside the Camera: Pickup Tube   The purpose of scanning is to transduce physical light into electronic signals. The process occurs inside the TV camera, as depicted in Figure 3–5.

The first step in creating TV is the collection of an image by a lens. Inside the TV camera the image is captured onto a mirrorlike device called the **target plate** (1). At the base of the camera tube is an **electron gun** (2), which sends a stream of electrons toward the picture on the plate. Force fields created by **deflection magnets** (3) pull the beam up and down across the image, much as our crayon did in Figure 3–4. As the beam scans the picture, an electronic signal (4) is created, with each line in the original picture now taking the form of an electronic signal—the common waveform as illustrated in Figure 3–1. A black line is added after each horizontal line and after each complete scan to allow the image to burn into our retina. This is known as the **blanking pulse.** The signal that exits the camera thus contains two sets of information: picture plus blanking. At the camera control unit (CCU) or in the switcher, a third signal is added. The **synchronization pulse** enables the output of two or more cameras and other video sources to be mixed together and allows all the scanning processes to take place at the same time, from camera to receiver. The complete TV picture, picture plus blanking plus sync, is known as the **composite video signal.**

Tubeless Cameras: The Camera as Computer   Much of the excitement in TV imaging in recent years revolves around the introduction of tubeless, or solid-state, cameras. These cameras replace the pickup tube with a **charge-coupled device (CCD).**

The CCD image sensor consists of three semiconductor chips, which replace the conventional tubes in a standard vacuum tube camera. Each of the red, green, and blue chips can sample over 250,000 picture elements in a manner not unlike the way a printing press uses dots to produce a color newspaper photo. CCD cameras have a number of advantages over traditional vacuum tube designs. First, the chips are much smaller than the tubes they replace, allowing for smaller, lighter cameras. Second, since the CCD is flat, picture distortion is reduced. In addition, CCD cameras are rugged and durable. Today, these so-called "chip cameras" have become the preferred acquisition medium for much TV news. Inexpensive, small, lightweight, and durable, they have proved their worth under fire: first, in the Persian Gulf War, and later in such global hot spots as the Middle East, Bosnia, and Somalia. It is not uncommon today for news organizations (such as CNN) to send dozens of chip cameras into areas of crisis in hopes a few will be smuggled out with usable pictures. Unlike high-paid correspondents, the relatively inexpensive CCD cameras are considered expendable.

STEP 2: SIGNAL AMPLIFICATION AND PROCESSING

Now, we've successfully transduced sounds and pictures into electronic analog or digital signals. The next step is to boost those signals so that they can be transported from one place to another, and to mix them with other sounds and images so we can hear more than one musical instrument or see a great football catch from many different angles. In engineering terms, we're talking about signal amplification, mixing, and processing.

Audio Amplification and Processing

An **amplifier** is a device that boosts an electrical signal. Typically, in electrical circuitry the voltage or current of an input is increased by drawing on an external power source (such as a battery or an AC or DC transformer) to produce a more powerful output signal. Devices to perform this function range from the original vacuum tubes (whose development made radio and sound movies practical in the 1920s), to transistors (which emerged in the 1950s to enable manufacturers to reduce the size of radios and TVs), and finally to integrated circuits in the 1970s (which permitted "microelectronics").

Modern amplifiers perform functions beyond increasing the power of the sound (or video) source. An **equalizer** is a special kind of amplifier that is frequency-dependent. This means that it can work within a specified range of frequencies to adjust the amplification. Equalization, referred to as "EQ" by sound engineers and music trendies, enables a sound signal to be fine-tuned for its best tonal quality. For example, equalizers can be used to make bass sections (between 60 and 250 hertz) sound more fat, thin, or "boomy." An equalizer can also be used to boost vocal sections out of the "soup" of an orchestrated passage, and even to isolate, diminish, or remove poor-sounding sections or mistakes in vocals or music. Once limited to expensive studios, EQ is now available in home and car stereo systems. In fact, a tiny Walkman may have five EQ faders on it (and cost less than $50, on sale of course).

In addition, amplification circuitry allows for electronic special effects to be added. These include reverberation, which is simply the echo effect. Special amplifiers can create all sorts of effects, from echoes to "sing-along" doubling or tripling. They can even create artificial choruses and deep echo chambers. Other devices are available to play tricks on audio signals. Phasers (not the kind used by Kirk and Spock) manipulate frequencies to create the illusion of stereo from mono signals, pitch changers can turn an out-of-tune musician into an accomplished soloist, and tape

recorder motors can be manipulated to record sounds backward and to speed up or slow down recordings. In the 1950s and 1960s it was common practice for radio stations to use speeded-up recorders to re-record popular songs so that they played more quickly, allowing for more commercial and promotion time. And there is speculation that the practice continues today. Does it seem to you that some Top-40 music is faster on the radio than when you play those same recordings on your own machine?

Mixing Consoles and Control Boards   The next link in the audio production chain is the audio console, which combines sound sources into a single signal. In radio and TV stations the console is generally referred to as an **audio board** or simply "the board." In recording studios and motion picture sound studios the board is commonly known as the **mixing console.** Regardless of its name, the console is the central nervous system of the audio facility. It is the place where the various sound signals are input, selected, controlled, mixed, combined, and routed for recording or broadcast transmission. Let's examine each of these phases individually.

The first function of the board is to input sound sources. A major-market radio station may have five or six tape recorders, three or four turntables, an equal number of CD players, and perhaps seven or eight microphones spread among several studios but capable of being interconnected. A recording studio is even more complex. In any event, the central location where each enters the chain of sound processing is the board.

The board usually consists of an even number of dials or sliding bars called **inputs.** Eight, 10, 12, 24, and 32 input boards are common. Some inputs correspond to one and only one sound device. Others use select switches and patch bays to allow for a single input to control as many as four or five different sound signals. In this way it is possible for a 32-channel board to handle 50 or 60 separate sounds in one recording session.

Each input is controlled by a rotating dial called a *pot* (short for **potentiometer**) or, more common today, a sliding bar called a **fader.** By rotating the pot or sliding the fader, the board operator can control the sound level of each studio input. More elaborate boards allow for equalization and special effects at this stage as well. Boards also allow for each source to be measured or metered and for the outputs of various signals to be amplified similarly.

So, sitting at one location, the audio person can combine and compose the overall sound of a performance, which is called the **mix.** The mix distills all the audio sources. This is sometimes a single (monaural) or, most commonly, a two-channel (stereo) signal. On occasion it's a four-channel (quad) version. The result is preserved on record, audiotape, compact disc, videotape, DVD, or film, or it is broadcast live to viewers and listeners at home.

Desktop Audio   As you might expect, the rush to digital media has spread to the amplifier and control board. Today's high-memory, fast desktop computers can perform the same audio tricks as can the largest, most sophisticated mixing consoles. With a microphone, sound card, and a modem, many home computers can be turned into fully functional sound studios.

The result is a revolution in audio-signal processing. Radio executives today speak of the "tapeless" or "recordless" radio station, where all the announcing, music, amplification, and mixing is done on a desktop computer.

One company, Radio Computing Services (RCS) of Scarsdale, New York, calls its desktop system "Master Control" and touts it as the "paperless, cartless, all-digital studio." In its system, all audio signals—jingles, ads, musical selections, even telephone calls from listeners—are stored on computer hard drives. There are no tape machines, turntables, or microphones. In essence, an entire radio station is converted into a network of desktop computers.

Video Amplification and Processing

As the TV signal travels from the camera to the transmitter, several things happen. First, the electrical signal is amplified—increased in electrical intensity—and carried along a wire to a closed-circuit TV set, called a monitor, where it is viewed by the director and other production personnel. In most TV programs the inputs from several cameras and other video sources (tape machines, the graphics generator, and so on) are mixed together before they are transmitted. The **switcher,** the device used for mixing TV signals, is probably the first thing a visitor to a TV control room notices. The advanced models are impressive-looking devices consisting of several rows of buttons and numerous levers. The switcher is used to put the desired picture on the air. If camera 3 shows what the director wants to see, then pushing

the appropriate button on the switcher puts camera 3 on the air. If videotape machine 4 has the desired picture, then pushing another button puts it on the air.

The switcher also lets the director choose the appropriate transition from one video source to another. Simply punching another button generates what's known as a **cut**—an instantaneous switch from one picture to another. By using a fader bar the director can dissolve from one picture to another or fade an image to or from black.

If a special-effects generator is added, a host of other transitions are possible. One picture can wipe out another horizontally, vertically, in a diamond shape, or in many other patterns. In addition, a split screen with two or more persons sharing the screen at the same time is possible, as is **keying,** an effect in which one video signal is electronically cut out or keyed into another. The most common use of this process is **chromakey.** A specific color (usually blue) drops out of one picture and another picture is seen every place where that color appeared in the original picture. Weathercasters, for example, usually perform in front of a blue background, which is replaced by keyed-in weather maps or other graphics. (Performers must be careful not to wear clothing that is the same color as the chromakey blue, or they will appear transparent on screen.)

Digital Video Effects   As might be expected, digital technology has had an impact on video processing. Each TV signal can be converted into a series of binary code numbers that can be manipulated and then reconverted back into a TV signal. There are numerous types of digital video effects, or *DVE,* in industry parlance. They include freeze-framing, shrinking images in size and positioning them anywhere on the screen (as happens when an anchor talks to a field reporter and both pictures are kept on screen), stretching or rotating a video picture, producing a mirror image, and wrapping the picture into a cylindrical shape.

Desktop Video   One of the quiet revolutions in contemporary TV is based in video signal processing. Until the late 1980s, generating video special effects required large, expensive processing equipment. Only a few big-city TV stations and production centers had the capability to produce digital video effects (DVE).

In the early 1990s the Commodore and Apple computer companies merged the video signal with the personal computer. Windows and other operating systems for IBM and compatible computers soon made video manipulation possible on the typical desktop PC.

Today, DVE can be produced on a personal computer array costing less than $1,000. Advances in high-speed CD-ROM and DVD drives allow for storage and retrieval of photographic and television images. As a result, the kind of spectacular visuals once reserved for music videos with huge budgets, or for the promotional messages of the major networks, can now be produced by anyone with a camcorder linked to a PC. This revolution is known as "desktop video." As if to underscore the low cost and simplicity of the new DVE machines, one common setup is known in the industry as the "video toaster."

STEP 3: SIGNAL TRANSMISSION

We've now succeeded in selecting sounds and pictures, changed them from physical energy into electronic signals, and amplified and mixed them. The next step is to take them from point "A" to point "B," the process of signal transmission. As we read in the history chapter, the modern age of broadcasting began when scientists and inventors became able to do this over the air, without wires. Ironically, as the new century dawns, we are now trying to do it all over

again by wire—over the Internet. But let's not get ahead of the story.

Audio Transmission

As Chapter 1 described in detail, the radio pioneers found that electrical signals created by human beings could be transported across space so that buttons pushed here could cause a buzz over there. They soon replaced signals and buzzes with a voice at both ends.

The Electromagnetic Spectrum This magical process was made possible by the discovery and use of the **electromagnetic spectrum,** the electromagnetic radiation present throughout the universe. Figure 3–6 is a chart of the spectrum. A fundamental component of our physical environment, electromagnetic radiation is traveling around and through us at all times. We can see some of it (the narrow band of frequencies corresponding to visible light and color, or the "heat waves" that radiate off a parking lot in the summertime). But most of the spectrum is invisible to the naked eye and must be detected by human-made devices (like radio and TV tuners).

In the past century we have learned how to superimpose, or "piggyback," our own electronic signals on the natural waves in the environment, a process known as **modulation.** This is done by generating a

Figure 3–6

The Electromagnetic Spectrum

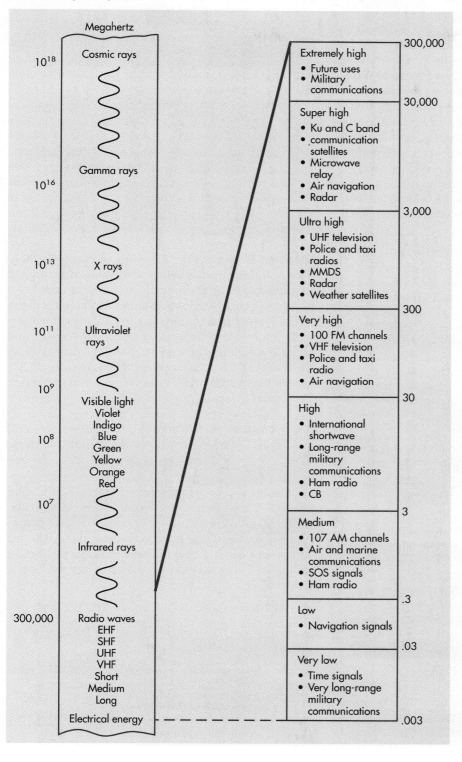

signal that is a replica of the natural wave. This signal, produced by a radio station on its assigned frequency, is called a **carrier wave.** It is "heard" on our radios as the silence that comes just before the station signs on in the morning, or after the national anthem at sign-off. The radio signal is created by varying the carrier wave slightly, in correspondence with the frequencies of the signals we mean to transmit. Our tuner, tuned to the precise middle of the carrier, interprets these oscillations and reproduces them as sounds in the speaker system. While this process may seem hopelessly complex, consider this metaphor. Suppose there is a natural rock formation in the shape of a bridge. Adding a bed of concrete atop the formation, we have propagated a carrier wave. When we ride a car across the bridge, we have superimposed a signal, or modulated the carrier wave.

Radio Frequencies   Only a small part of the electromagnetic spectrum is utilized for broadcasting and related transmissions. This range spans from long waves of very low frequency to extremely short waves of relatively high frequency. In general, the higher one goes in the spectrum, the more power and sophisticated electronics are needed in the modulation process.

Each new development in electronic media has taken us higher in the spectrum. Radio broadcasting began toward the low end of the spectrum, in the area ranging from 0.3 to 3 megahertz (mega = million), a region known as the medium waves. Included in this region is the range of 550–1,600 kilohertz (kilo = thousand), which is the range of the AM radio dial. In fact, in many countries AM is still referred to as the medium-wave (MW) band.

The high frequencies (which, with satellite and infrared communications, actually aren't so high anymore) range from 3 to 30 megahertz. These waves are utilized for long-range military communications, CB, and ham radio. Since high-frequency waves can be used to transmit signals over greater distances than can medium waves, this part of the spectrum has been used for over 50 years by international shortwave stations such as the BBC and the Voice of America. The shortwave band on a radio is sometimes labeled HF, for high frequencies.

The next group of radio waves used for telecommunications applications are the very high frequencies, or the VHF band. VHF ranges from 30 to 300 megahertz. Television stations 2 to 13, FM radio stations, police radios, and airline navigation systems are located in this band.

Above the VHF channels are the ultra high frequencies, or the UHF band, spanning the region from 300 to 3,000 megahertz. This part of the spectrum is used for TV stations 14 to 83, police and taxi mobile radios, radar, and weather satellites. In addition, it is UHF radiation that is modulated to cook our food in microwave ovens.

Much of recent telecommunications development has occurred in the next two radio bands: super high frequencies (SHF) and extremely high frequencies (EHF). SHF spans from 3,000 to 30,000 megahertz and EHF from 30,000 to 300,000 megahertz. Commercial satellites, which deliver pay cable channels, superstations, and satellite news, emanate from these bands, as do new developments in digital audio broadcasting, military radar, and air navigation.

Spectrum Management   Keeping track of all these uses of the electromagnetic spectrum is difficult, and requires substantial domestic and international regulation, a process known as **spectrum management.** In the United States, decisions regarding which services operate in which regions of the spectrum, and at what operating power, are handled primarily by the Federal Communications Commission (FCC). Here's how radio and TV service is administered in the United States.

Radio channel classifications   At the latest count more than 12,000 radio stations were on the air in the United States. Yet there are only 107 AM channels and 100 FM channels. How is this possible? The answer is spectrum management. By controlling operating hours, power, antenna height and design, and other factors, the FCC squeezes the 12,000 stations into the 207 channels. If you can imagine 12,000 cars competing for 200 parking spaces (kind of like the first day of classes), you have a sense for the task at hand.

● *AM channels and classifications.* The 107 AM channels are divided into three main types: 60 are clear channels, 41 are regional channels, and the remaining 6 are local channels. Here's how the system works: The **clear channels** are frequencies that have been designated by international agreements for primary use by high-powered stations. Such stations use ground waves in daytime and sky waves at night to reach a wide geographic area, often thousands of miles. The United States has priority on 45 clear channels. Stations on these frequencies include some of our oldest and strongest. Class A stations, like WABC in New York at 770 kilohertz, WJR in Detroit at 610 kilohertz, and KMOX (1120 kilohertz) in St. Louis, have the exclusive right to the clear channel after sunset. They operate at high power, from 10,000 to 50,000 watts. Class B AM stations use the clear channels but must operate at reduced power at night to avoid interference. Their wattages range from 50 to 250 kilowatts. Class C stations are designated as **regional stations.** Ranging in power from 500 to 5000 watts, Class C's must share channels with numerous other stations. To do this they generally use directional antennas and strategic placement to blanket their main population areas. Over 2,000 Class C stations share the 41 regional channels. Other Class C stations operate on **local channels.** These stations are mostly at the right or top end of the dial (above 1230 kilohertz). They are limited in power to 1,000 watts by day and 250 at night.

- *FM channels and classifications.* In 1945 the FCC set aside the region from 88 to 108 megahertz for FM. This allowed room for 100 channels, each 200 kilohertz wide. This means that when your FM radio is tuned to 97.3 the station is actually radiating a signal oscillating from 97.2 to 97.4 megahertz. Of the 100 channels, 80 were set aside for commercial use. The remaining 20 channels, located from 88 to 92 megahertz, were reserved for educational and noncommercial stations.

To facilitate the development of commercial FM, the FCC divided the United States into three regions. Zone I includes the most densely populated areas of the United States: the Northeast. Zone I-A covers the southern California region. The rest of the country composes Zone II. FM stations also use A, B, and C designations. Class A FM stations operate in all zones, Class B's in Zone I, and Class C's only in Zone II.

Each class is defined by its **effective radiated power (ERP)**, the amount of power it is permitted to use. Class C FMs are the medium's most powerful. They can transmit up to 100,000 watts (ERP). They may erect transmitters with a maximum **height above average terrain (HAAT)** of 2,000 feet. Class B's can generate up to 50,000 watts ERP at 500 feet HAAT, and class A's are authorized to a maximum of 3,000 watts ERP at 300 feet HAAT. At maxi-

mum power and antenna height, Class C's can cover about 60 miles, Class B's about 30, and Class A's up to 15.

Sidebands and subcarriers   The bandwidth of FM (200 kilohertz) allows these stations to transmit more than one signal on their channel. Such signals use the area above and below the station's carrier frequency, known as the **sideband.** The most common use of the sideband is to disseminate separate signals for the left and right channel to broadcast stereo. This is called **multiplexing.** If you have an old FM stereo receiver, it may be labeled an FM multiplexer.

FM station operators may use additional spectrum space to send multiplex signals, which can be tuned only by specially designed receivers. To do this, stations apply to the FCC for a **subsidiary communications authorization (SCA).** Such services include the "background" music one hears in malls and elevators, a Talking Book service for the blind, telephone paging, data transmission, and special radio services for doctors, lawyers, and some others.

Although technically the process is not the same, AM stations can use their carrier waves for other purposes as well. Many AM stations transmit a subaudible tone used in utility load management. A subscriber, such as a business, rents a special receiver. During peak electric use hours the station transmits a tone that turns off the subscriber's appliances. When the peak load period is over, another subaudible tone turns them back on.

Video Transmission

As might be expected, the TV signal, with its complex set of information (including picture, sound, color, blanking, and synchronization signals), requires enormous amounts of space in the electromagnetic spectrum. More than any other reason, this explains why there are over 12,000 radio stations but only about 1,500 TV stations on air in the United States.

The Television Channel   Each TV station requires a bandwidth of 6 megahertz. This is equivalent to enough space for 30 FM radio stations and 600 AM stations!

Our TV system was perfected in the 1930s and 1940s when amplitude modulation (AM) techniques were considered state-of-the-art. For this reason it was decided to transmit the TV picture information via AM. Two-thirds, or 4 megahertz, of the TV bandwidth is used for picture information. The sound signal is essentially a full-range FM, or frequency-modulated, signal, oscillating at 25 kilohertz above and below its center (carrier) frequency. The remainder of the video channel is occupied by protective guard bands that keep the various encoded signals from interfering with one another.

TV Allocations   The complexity of the TV signal and its vast need for space caused the FCC in the 1940s and 1950s to assign it a place higher in the electromagnetic spectrum than any that had been utilized in prior years.

Channels 2 to 13 are located in the **very high frequency (VHF)** portion of the spectrum, the area ranging from 54 to 216 megahertz. Interestingly, a sizable portion of the VHF band is not used for TV purposes. The area between channels 6 and 7 includes the space for all FM radio stations as well as aircraft-control tower communication, amateur or "ham" radio, and business and government applications.

Channels 14 to 83 lie in the **ultra-high frequency (UHF)** portion of the band, the region between 470 and 890 megahertz. There is another gap, this time between channels 13 and 14, which is reserved for government communications.

VHF stations 2 through 6 can achieve excellent coverage transmitting at a maximum of 100 kilowatts. Channels 7 to 13 require power up to a ceiling of 316 kilowatts. However, channels 14 and above need power up to 5,000 kilowatts to generate an acceptable signal (the UHF maximum is 10,000 kilowatts). In addition, more sophisticated antenna arrays are required. So viewers often have difficulty locating UHF stations on their dial, and, once stations are located, tuning and maintaining a clear signal are also problematic. The FCC's freeze on new stations from 1948 to 1952 (discussed in Chapter 1) also hurt UHF's development. The existing stations were all VHFs and had established loyal audiences before UHF even got started.

For these technical and historical reasons VHF stations have tended to travel "first class" in the TV business, while UHF properties have typically been relegated to the "coach" section.

From NTSC to ATSC: Digital TV Channels   In 1997, the FCC finalized its plans for the transition from analog to digital television broadcasting. Each existing TV station was given a second channel, 6 megahertz wide, to use for its new digital broadcasts. A set of transmissions standards set by an industry group—the **Advanced Television Standards Committee (ATSC)**—was adopted. (For engineering and computer fans, the standard uses the MPEG-2 video compression format and the 8-VSB modulation format). In addition, a timetable was set for TV stations to move from analog to digital. By May 1, 2003, stations are supposed to have half of their programming simulcast in digital high definition. By the following May 1, the percentage is set at 75 percent; by May 1, 2005, 100 percent. The complete transition from analog to digital TV should be completed across America by year's end 2006, when stations are supposed to return their old NTSC channel to the FCC to auction for other uses.

Satellite Transmission

A common sight on lawns, homes, and businesses is the satellite dish, which has become an important means of radio and television transmission. These dishes are all pointed up to the sky to one or more of the dozens of communications satellites in orbit about 22,000 miles above the earth. These satellites are powered to move at the same rate as the earth rotates, a technique known as **geosynchronous orbit.** For all intents and purposes, the satellites are "parked" in their unique orbital slots.

Satellite terminology   Satellite technology has introduced a new vocabulary into telecommunications. Because of the complexity of their operations, the amount of information they carry, and the power needed to send a signal through the Earth's atmosphere and back, satellites operate in the **super-high frequency (SHF)** portion of the electromagnetic spectrum. Just as new developments led radio and TV to move up the spectrum, the same has happened in satellite communications. The first geosynchronous satellites were assigned to the area ranging roughly from 4 to 6 gigahertz (gHz, or billions of cycles) in an area known as the **C band.** Newer, more-powerful satellites operate from 12 to 14 gigahertz, a region known as the **Ku band.**

Direct Broadcast Satellite   The late 1990s have seen a new form of satellite communications, known as **direct broadcast satellite,** or **DBS.** DBS makes use of newer, higher-powered satellites with a much larger footprint than traditional C- and Ku-band "birds" (as satellites are sometimes called). In addition, rather than require a three-meter dish (the size you see in some back yards), DBS receivers are only 18 inches wide. They can be made to work successfully on a rooftop or window ledge, much like the TV aerials of yesteryear.

Marketed by such firms as DirecTV, The Dish Network, and USSB, DBS has enjoyed widespread consumer acceptance. By the year 2000, its advocates predict direct broadcast satellite may reach as many as one in four TV households.

Digital Audio Broadcasting   If we can get direct satellite-to-home TV, why can't we also get direct satellite-to-car radio? Well, we just might. **Digital audio broadcasting (DAB)** combines the technique of pulse code modulation (PCM), which made CD audio practical and popular, with super high frequency transmission (such as that used for satellites and microwaves). The result is CD-quality sound from a home or car radio without the need for records, tapes, discs, or your local radio station.

In 1997, the FCC auctioned off part of the spectrum to two companies—CD Radio and American Mobile Satellite—who promised to deliver CD-quality radio to cars and homes. In particular, CD Radio promises 50 channels—30 music and 20 news/talk/information—available nationwide as soon as early 2000. Instead of an antenna, cars will be equipped with a small receiving dish, embedded on the roof or in the hood of the car. It remains to be seen whether Americans will embrace or resist this new service.

Back to the Future: The Return to Wired Communications

As we traced in Chapter 1, the modern era of broadcasting began with the liberation of the telegraph by Marconi's wireless. Ironically, a century later, much of the change in contemporary telecommunications is due to the return to prominence of *wired* communications. This trend is led by the phenomenal growth of cable television and the rise of the Internet.

Cable Transmission   Shortly after World War II a new type of cable, called **coaxial cable,** was developed to support the burgeoning telephone industry. In addition to handling thousands of simultaneous telephone conversations, this cable was soon found to be an excellent conduit for disseminating TV signals. Since then, cable TV has become an increasingly widespread and important means of TV signal propagation.

Coaxial cable, or "coax" for short, consists of two electronic conductors. At the center is a copper wire shielded by a protective insulator called the **dielectric.** Outside the dielectric is a wire mesh, typically made of copper or aluminum. This conductor is shielded by a durable plastic coating, the outer body of the cable. This design gives the cable some special properties. The shielding keeps the signals within a confined space, reducing the electrical interference common in normal wiring (like that in household appliances). Coaxial cable can also carry its own power source, which allows signals to travel comparatively long distances with little signal loss or noise. In addition, good shielding allows the coax to last many years without contamination by water or other invasive materials.

Over the years, as the materials used to make coaxial cable and the types of transmission and amplification equipment used by cable systems were refined, the number of TV signals transmittable by cable increased. In the 1950s cable TV systems could carry only three to five TV signals. In the 1960s transistorized components and new cable materials raised cable channel capacity to 12 channels. The cable explosion in the 1970s came about as further technical refinements allowed cable systems to carry as many as 60 TV channels, as well as a range of other services, from FM radio to data, text, and other services.

As you can see, local cable operators can exert a kind of media power that broadcasters cannot. Within certain limits (see Chapter 5), they—not the FCC—can control where a given TV station is placed on the cable. In addition, cable systems can reuse their own frequencies simply by installing two cables side by side. Thus systems of 100 or more channels are possible. Moreover, a cable company can construct a system that allows communication from the receiver to the headend, enabling two-way, or interactive, communication.

Another advantage of cable is **addressability,** the ability of a cable system to send a program to some houses that request it and to not send it to those that don't. Addressability is important in the development of pay-per-view TV, where only a portion of subscribers are willing to pay extra to watch a recent movie or sports event.

This flexibility accounts for cable's great expansion in recent years, detailed in Chapter 2. Originally a source of improved reception of only three or four nearby TV stations, the cable has become a broadband source of local and regional broadcast stations, distant superstations, sports, movies, and other special-interest channels to more than two-thirds of the nation.

For nearly half a century, two different wires connected most homes, for communications purposes. The common "twisted pair" brought telephone calls into and out of the home. The "coax" connected subscribing households to a cable television company. However, both telephone companies and cable systems are now installing a new kind of cable, which allows the telephone companies to provide video service and the cable companies to handle telephone calls. Battle lines are forming due to this new means of video signal distribution.

Fiber Optics Fiber optic cable is a kind of "wireless wire." Instead of the copper and aluminum elements found in coaxial cable, fiber optic cable contains strands of flexible glass.

Fiber optic technology makes use of digital communications. That is, the electrical signals normally transmitted through conventional wire are replaced by light pulses transmitted by a laser light source. These on–off (binary) pulses are decoded at the receiving source by a photodiode, a small, light-sensitive device. The process is similar to the way CDs produce high-quality sound.

Fiber optic cable has excellent potential in its applications to telecommunications. Glass is less expensive than aluminum and copper. Electrical interference is nonexistent since there is no real electricity in the wire. Optical fiber is thinner and more flexible than coax. Perhaps most important, the bandwidth is virtually limitless, unlike the relatively narrow band that fits into traditional coaxial cable. On the downside, amplifying fiber optic signals is hard to do, as is connecting and switching fiber optic transmissions.

Fiber optic technology is at the center of the struggle now emerging between the telephone and cable industries. Many regional telephone companies are replacing their copper wires with fiber optics. As regulatory barriers fall and the telephone companies are allowed to offer video services to the home, it's likely that the conversion to fiber will occur much

A fiber optic bundle. Eventually fiber optics will replace the copper wires that now carry TV and telephone signals.

more quickly. Cable companies are also experimenting with fiber. By 1995 all of the top cable companies were installing fiber optics in at least part of their systems. The benefits of fiber over the traditional copper cable are significant: clearer video and audio, low maintenance costs, and a virtually unlimited capacity for video services. The huge amounts of signal capacity needed for HDTV, for example, are not a problem with fiber optics.

Today, the fiber optic market is a bright spot in the telecommunications economy. Telephone companies and cable systems are racing to replace their trunk lines with fiber optic cable.

The pure, noise-free digital signal passing through the fiber connection into the home can be a telephone call, a radio show, a modem connection to the Internet, or a TV program. It should not be a surprise to the reader, then, that radio, TV, cable, and telephone companies are in the process of entering each other's businesses to one degree or another.

STEP 4: SIGNAL RECEPTION

We've now modulated, amplified, mixed, and transmitted an audio or video signal. The next step is reception: capturing that signal on a receiving device, such as a radio or TV set. As you might expect, the once-simple task of tuning a radio or dialing in a TV station has become quite complex. Just think of how many different remote control devices you own, or how many different boxes are connected to your TV set. Let's trace trends in some common audiovisual reception devices.

Radio Receivers

AM (MW) Band Receivers   The location of AM radio in the medium-wave part of the spectrum has several advantages. Long telescopic antennas are normally not needed and a good signal may be received even when the radio is in motion. This makes AM ideal for car radios. AM radios can take almost any form, from microscopic transistor versions to large table-top models. Normally, good reception is only a matter of moving the receiver slightly for best tuning.

However, consider the disadvantage: a check of the spectrum chart shows that the MW band is precariously close to the bandwidth of electrical energy. Thus AM radios are prone to interference and noise, heard mostly as static. In cars, energy produced by engines and electrical systems can often be heard on AM. At home, one can "hear" vacuum cleaners, lights turned on and off, and so forth.

Another limitation of AM reception has to do with its limited frequency response. As you know, AM stations generate signals in a bandwidth only 10,000 hertz wide. Recall that the human ear can hear a bandwidth about twice that. As a result, you may have noticed that AM sounds somewhat thinner or tinnier than FM (with full 20,000-hertz response). AM is best with speech and music of limited orchestration. Hence news/talk and sports tend to be popular AM formats.

AM Stereo   In the 1980s new developments in transmission and reception devices held promise in improving the AM signal. However, a debate over technical standards and the atmosphere of deregulation at the FCC left first three, then two, noncompatible competing systems.

Despite millions of dollars in investment in new transmission equipment, AM stereo has largely been a disappointment to broadcasters. It is available mainly as an option in luxury cars. It is virtually unknown in home or walkabout radio receivers. As some in the industry lament, it simply brings a static-filled signal to two channels instead of one!

FM Receivers   The evolution of the FM receiver has followed an interesting path. From the beginning, the noise-free dynamic range of FM made it a natural element for the hi-fi enthusiast's home audio system. Thus many FM receivers did not have amplifiers or speakers attached to them; they were separate tuners that had to be plugged into the hi-fi system. However, when FM boomed in the late 1960s, consumers demanded FM in forms they had become familiar with in AM: in cars, transistor radios, table models, and so on. Thus most radios manufactured after 1970 were capable of both AM and FM reception. As a result, FM moved from an "add-on accessory" to the most important part of the radio receiver.

Since the FM signal requires a line of sight from transmitter to receiver, there are some potential pitfalls in signal reception. First, FM normally requires a long antenna, in the shape of a telescoping rod or a wire. Reception can also be improved by attaching the radio antenna to a TV antenna and in some areas by hooking the receiver to the cable TV system.

Moreover, FM signals tend to be blocked by buildings or moving objects. This situation is commonly experienced in cars. Unlike the AM signal, this type of signal loss is seldom heard as static. Instead, the signal simply disappears and returns, as if it were being turned on and off repeatedly. To solve this problem, many FM receivers have features that lock in the carrier frequency of the transmitting station. Such techniques may be seen on your radio sets as automatic frequency control (AFC) or quartz lock. A car radio typically has a separate switch for local and distance (DX) reception on FM.

Multiband Receivers   Today virtually all radios offer both AM and FM bands. New radios recently previewed by the National Association of Broadcasters have a continuous-tuning feature that allows a listener to go from an FM station to an AM station without pressing a switch to change bands. In addition, many receivers offer access to a range of other bandwidths that provide various radio services. A radio with the HF, or shortwave, frequencies provides access to the services of international broadcasters. Some receivers can monitor channels used by police and fire services. Other radios feature a weather band, capable of tuning the nearest government weather station for use in general aviation. Becoming more popular are radios with "TV sound": These allow listeners to keep up with "soaps" and sports while at the beach or at work.

Digital Tuners   A useful feature of many radios is the digital tuner. Using the same techniques as a digital watch or clock, digital tuners display a station's frequency in real numbers, instead of a line on a dial. The numbers may be presented on a liquid crystal display (LCD) or on a light-emitting diode (LED).

Digital tuners perform some impressive functions.

When equipped with a numeric keypad, they enable the listener to program specific frequencies. This can be critical for international shortwave listening, where different stations often occupy the same channels at different times. They enable clock radios and radio–tape recorder combinations to operate with up-to-the-minute accuracy. And they can be programmed to tune themselves, either to sample the bandwidth for strong signals (scan) or to find and stop at the nearest strong station (seek).

"Smart Radios"—Radio Broadcast Data System   Digital tuners make possible a new generation of "smart" radio receivers. Using their subcarrier frequencies, in addition to sending voices and music, radio stations can send other signals to their receivers. On such radio sets, a small display terminal can provide a readout of the station's dial location, call letters, format, and even the title and artist of the song being played. Weather forecasts can display a map; news and sports reports can show stock tickers, scoreboards, and so on.

These new smart radios are known as **Radio Broadcast Data Systems,** or **RBDS.** Advertisers are excited by one new feature called "coupon radio," which allows the listener to record information from the RBDS screen (such as a secret password) and use that information when making a purchase.

TV Receivers

Improvements in our media devices usually are confined to making the items either grossly large or incredibly minute. For example, consider the contrast in radios between nearly piano-size boom boxes and personal stereos custom-fit to the human ear canal. These same developments in the TV medium head the list of new developments in TV reception.

Large-Screen TV   In the early 1970s wall-size TV screens began appearing in bars, nightclubs, and conference facilities. Today they are slowly creeping into the home video environment.

Large-screen TVs come in two main types. Projection TV systems beam the red, green, and blue elements that compose the color signal through special tubes to a reflecting screen suspended at a distance from the video unit. This is the type of system most commonly seen in sports bars.

Solid-state, large-screen systems do not have sep-arate beam and screen components. These receivers make use of new developments in computer imaging, such as the charge-coupled device (CCD) discussed earlier. The picture tube is made up of a matrix of over 200,000 red, blue, and green light-emitting elements. Excellent color, crispness, and detail are achieved. In addition, the screen is flat, free from the type of distortion common in standard curved vacuum tube systems. Although expensive, these solid-state, large-screen systems are beginning to move from sports stadiums to the home video market.

Small-Screen TV   For some TV enthusiasts smaller is better. These folks like to take the TV with them to the ball game, the beach, the office, or elsewhere. To satisfy this demand, manufacturers have introduced the visual equivalent of Sony's revolutionary Walkman radio design. Sony and its competitors, Casio and other Japanese manufacturers, have merged microprocessor technology and display expertise with years of experience in the production of transistor radios to produce smaller and smaller TV sets.

To date, a couple of major problems have hindered the diffusion of this technology. For one thing, the screens are so small, they tend to produce very low light levels. Hence they can get drowned out by bright sunlight (a big limitation if you're at a day baseball game or the beach). Another fault is inherent in the medium: unlike radio, a TV must be watched (at least some of the time) to be enjoyed. For obvious reasons the Watchman thus has limited suitability to such proven portable radio activities as driving a car and jogging.

Digital TV Sets   How many times have you tried to watch two or three TV programs simultaneously? Using a remote control or nimble fingers, you flip continuously from one to the other—playing a sort of TV musical chairs—and end up missing the important parts of all programs. Well, if you're an inveterate flipper (like the authors), the digital receiver is for you. The integrated microchips that make tubeless cameras and micro-TVs practical have made it possible for the TV screen to display more than one channel at a time. The technique is known as **picture-in-picture,** or **PIP.**

Digital TVs also perform other electronic tricks. Suppose, when watching a baseball game, you decide to try to steal the catcher's signs to the pitcher. **Zoom** allows you to fill the entire picture with just one small detail you would like to see, in this case the catcher's hands. To really get the sign, you can stop the picture momentarily, a technique known as **freeze frame.**

By 1999, the major TV set manufacturers, led by Sony and Panasonic, had introduced large-screen, digital television sets capable of receiving standard 525-line NTSC and the new 480-, 720- and 1,080-line digital high-definition signals. They are still a bit pricey—in the range of $5,000 to $8,000.

TV/Computer Convergence

As we have seen, the move to digital TV is expected to bring two different TV screens together: the computer monitor and the TV set. Such combinations are reaching the marketplace (Gateway's computer/TV combination, dubbed the "Destination," comes complete with a 35-inch screen and costs $3,000), but early consumer reaction is lukewarm. It seems that people either want to watch TV, or surf the net, and they still want to do these things on different devices. Interestingly, recent surveys show that as many as 4 in 10 computer users have a TV set nearby so that they can keep an eye on the TV while they e-mail or play computer games.

STEP 5: STORAGE AND RETRIEVAL

The final step in audio and video technology is the storage and retrieval of sounds and moving images. As we all know, old programs never die: They live on forever in reruns. Some of the great growth industries in mass media in recent years are based on improved means of storing and accessing images, including the video store, nostalgic TV networks like "Nick at Night," "TV Land," and, yes, the Nostalgia Network. In fact, one of the benefits of the World Wide Web is that the content of all the memory of all the computers connected to the Internet in all the world is accessible to any single user. Increasingly, that content includes sounds and pictures, not merely text. Yet, not too long ago (in the 1940s and 1950s), radio and TV were still "live," as recording methods were noisy and inefficient. Even today, the complex signals involved in speech, music, motion pictures, and TV tax the storage and processing capacity of even the fastest microcomputers, so we're still a bit away from dialing up on our PC any movie ever made. Let's see where things stand with respect to radio and TV storage and retrieval.

Audio Storage

Phonograph Recording   The old standby, the phonograph record, has been around since the turn of the century. From that time, the sizes and speeds have been changed, but the basic design has remained consistent. Today, the most common record format is the 33⅓ revolutions per minute (rpm), 12-inch, high-fidelity recording.

Magnetic Tape Recording   The development of magnetic tape recording was revolutionary for both radio and TV. Unlike earlier recording methods, such as disc and wire recordings, magnetic tape was of very high fidelity. For all intents and purposes, radio and TV programs recorded on magnetic tape sounded just like they were "live." Tape recorders became the heart and soul of radio and TV stations.

The three most common forms of tape in use in radio today are open reel (reel-to-reel), cassette, and cartridge. Radio stations tend to rely on cartridge and open reel; the cassette recorder is the most common home recording device. High-quality cassette recorders are often used by radio reporters to record meetings and to do interviews in the field.

Most manufacturers have not abandoned production of analog tape recorders. Many musicians and audio engineers prefer their rich, full sound when compared with the crisp, clean sound of digital recordings. Tape manufacturers, including Sony, BASF, 3M, Ampex, and others, continue to make better and better products of these types. Thus, reel-to-reel and cassette audio recorders promise to remain in use for some time to come. Digital recording (CD, DAT, and MD) has already been discussed (see pages 54–56).

Video Storage

Magnetic Video Recording   As we stated in Chapter 2, the **videotape recorder (VTR)** made its network debut with "The CBS Evening News with Douglas Edwards" on November 30, 1956. But it hardly resembled today's tabletop VCR. For nearly 20 years, TV's tape machines were the size of a refrigerator-freezer and required two people to operate them. The reels of tape, as big as 35 mm film cannisters, were two inches across (thus, these were called two-inch recordings). But they produced excellent, long-lasting copies of TV programs.

The next revolution in videotape recording was started by the Japanese. At the forefront of the emerging field of microelectronics, Sony technicians, in the late 1960s, perfected a means of storing the complex video signal on narrower tape, moving at slower speeds.

The idea was to stretch the magnetic tape around the revolving recording head so that there was virtually continuous contact between the tape and the recording head. For an analogy, imagine that instead of taking a single piece of chalk to one blackboard at the head of the class, your instructor had a piece of chalk in each hand and foot and was surrounded by a huge cylindrical blackboard.

This technique became known as **helical-scan tape recording,** since the heads are positioned obliquely to the tape and the lines of picture information produced on the tape form the shape of a helix.

The birth of a standard: three-quarter-inch VTR   The helical-scan recorder had many advantages. Tape width shrank from 2 inches to ¾ inch, which had financial as well as technical advantages. The tape could be packaged in a protective case; thus the videocassette became popular. Most important, the size of the tape recorder shrank. In the early 1970s it became practical to send cameras and recorders into the field for coverage of breaking news and live sporting events. Although a number of helical-scan recorders had been introduced, by 1975 the industry had standardized. The 2-inch machine gave way to the ¾-inch VTR.

The VTR was soon a fixture in TV production. After its introduction, recorders became small, portable, and usually dependable. Editing from one machine to another became easy, especially with the development of computer-assisted editing equipment. And the entire field of broadcast news changed: The era of electronic news gathering, or ENG, was launched.

Home video   In 1976 Sony introduced its first Betamax **videocassette recorder** (priced at $1,200); today the home **VCR** has become the centerpiece of a revolution in the way we view TV.

The key was the development of high-density recording. Basically, the difference between broadcast-quality ¾-inch VTR and the ½-inch system introduced in the late 1970s is that the new system eliminated guard bands on the videotape, providing more room to store the picture signal on a reel of magnetic tape. Essentially, the ½-inch machines sacrificed some picture quality for smaller, lighter, and cheaper recorders with longer recording times. Clearly, the compromise was worth it: In 20 years, more than 80 percent of the households in the United States acquired VCRs.

Initially there were two competing varieties of ½-inch helical-scan VCRs. Machines produced by Sony and its licensees used the Beta format; machines produced by other manufacturers used VHS tape and electrical components. For 10 years, a debate raged about which systems produced the better signal, with most technicians and industrial video users concluding that the Beta system had slightly superior performance. However, in the interim the TV consumer had decided on the standard. Since more machines and prerecorded tapes were available in the VHS format, by the mid-1980s the home market had more or less standardized in the VHS format. Even Sony began producing VHS machines.

Beta videotape didn't die off, however. A hi-fidelity version, Beta-SP, became a vital part of professional TV production. At home, ½-inch tape was shrunk even further, into a compact version of VHS (VHS-C), and another popular Sony format, only 8 mm wide.

Digital Video Recording   It should come as no surprise that the digital revolution sweeping the audio industry soon spread to television recording. The first wave of digital video recording was the appearance in the early 1990s of **digital videotape.** Today, many TV studios boast camera and editing systems that utilize digital videotape. Sony's system is easy to spot: Its equipment uses the DV prefix to denote digital videotape. "DVC-Pro" is the line of machines in widest distribution.

In a way, digital videotape is a hybrid recording system, combining the analog system of putting images on magnetic tape with the new digital sampling techniques. With the increasing processing and storage capacity of today's computers, it's possible to go all-digital. Why have tape at all? Why not store all the TV sounds and images on a computer hard drive? More and more TV facilities, from CNN International to large-station newsrooms, have no VCRs in sight. Systems like "Media 100" and AVID are moving TV news and entertainment programming production from editing suites to desktop computer consoles.

Profile: Her Own Personal TV Network: JenniCamLive

By all measures, Jenni R. is an average, ordinary, regular person. Born in Harrisburg, Pennsylvania, in 1976 (the year of the nation's bicentennial), she grew up in a typical middle class home, went to college, got a degree in economics, and got a job as a Web designer for a company in Washington, DC. Jenni's got a small apartment, a boyfriend, two cats (Macadamia and Spree), and a tank full of tropical fish.

What's extraordinary about Jenni is that she has placed her life onto the Internet, streaming everything from her morning exercise routine, to bathing her cats, to doing her laundry, for all the world to see. She began JenniCam while a junior in college. First, the site was free. Jenni then instituted a $15 annual fee so web surfers could continue to watch her put on her makeup, chat with boyfriend, Jeff, or talk on the phone with her mom back in Pennsylvania. Today, more than 15,000 people subscribe to JenniCam. Many millions have visited her home page. She has been profiled in major magazines, on dozens of popular Web sites, and she has appeared on TV talk shows, including "Leeza," where "the crowd acted like I was some sort of exhibitionist freak, which I'm not," she said to an ABC reporter.

Jenni's fame has even attracted the attention of cable TV executives, including Leo Hindery of TCI. And why not? As we reveal in Chapter 2, cable built its business by appealing to narrow audience segments. As JenniCam illustrates, that narrowing can potentially be reduced to a single person.

Is there anything Jenni won't let her loyal audience see? Most of the 700 e-mails she gets every day ask her to appear naked and show her sex life on the Web. While Jenni admits at least one encounter got on the Internet, she usually turns off JenniCam. Boyfriend Jeff isn't keen on broadcasting their intimate moments. "He makes me turn off the lights and pull up the covers," Jenni recently told ABC News. "The viewers aren't so happy about that, but oh well."

The Digital Video Disc player may ultimately replace the VCR.

WEBCASTING: AUDIO AND VIDEO STREAMING

We close this section on audio and video technology with a technique that's blurring the lines between computers, TV sets, and radio receivers. The technique, called **streaming,** allows sounds and moving pictures to be transmitted on the World Wide Web and other computer networks. And, it allows these complex, high-memory transmissions to travel on slower, comparatively low-capacity bandwidths, such as 28.8 or 56k modems or across traditional telephone lines.

Streaming audio and video makes use of two nifty shortcuts called **buffering,** and **compression.** To put a complex radio or TV signal on the Web, the signal is "shrunk" into a much simpler form, using techniques of digital compression. Essentially, the complex signal is sampled, and redundant, nonessential information is stripped away, to be added back later (in decompression). Even so, music and moving video images are still too complex to transmit in real time over narrow bandwidths, like telephone lines. The solution is to stop playback for a short time so the computer hard drive can store the necessary information. It then begins playback, all the time replenishing the drive with new, incoming signals. This is the buffering technique.

Playing sounds and moving images on the web requires special software. Featuring brand names like RealAudio, RealVideo, Shockwave, VDO, Vivo, and NetShow, these programs allow desktop computers to become more like radio and TV receivers. The software displays controls similar to a radio or TV set (with tuning buttons and volume controls). There are now literally hundreds of radio and TV stations that can be heard and seen on any computer hooked to the net (so long as it has a soundcard, speakers, and the appropriate media player software). Add a microphone, a camera, an MIDI keyboard, and a CD-ROM or DVD drive, and any computer can become the personal equivalent of a radio or TV station, "broadcasting" its messages to any similarly equipped computer anywhere in the world.

SUMMARY

- Broadcasting, cable, and new media make use of facsimile technology, reproducing sound and sight in other forms. The better the correspondence between the facsimile and the original, the higher the fidelity.

- Transduction involves changing energy from one form to another; it is at the heart of audio and video technology. Transduction can be analog—the transformed energy resembles the original—or digital—the original is transformed into a series of numbers.

- Audio and video signal processing follows five main steps: signal generation, amplification and processing, transmission, reception, and storage/retrieval.

- *Signal generation.* Audio signals are generated mechanically, by using microphones and turntables; electromagnetically, by using tape recorders; and digitally, by using laser optics. Television signal generation involves the electronic line-by-line scanning of an image. An electron beam scans each element of a picture, and the image is then retraced in the TV receiver.

- *Amplification and processing.* Audio and video signals are amplified and mixed by using audio consoles and video switchers. Today's digital technology enables sophisticated signal processing and a variety of special effects.

- *Transmission.* Radio waves occupy a portion of the electromagnetic spectrum. AM radio channels are classified into clear, regional, and local channels. FM stations are classified according to power and antenna height. The wide bandwidth of an FM channel allows for stereo broadcasting and other nonbroadcast services. On the horizon is Digital Audio Broadcasting, or DAB. The traditional systems of transmitting a TV signal are (1) over-the-air broadcasting utilizing electromagnetic radiation on channels located in the VHF and UHF portions of the spectrum and (2) by wire through a cable system using coaxial cable that can carry more than 100 channels of programming. New distribution technologies include fiber optics, satellite transmissions, and new forms of digital distribution. Television and radio are moving to new forms of digital distribution. On the TV side, the FCC has mandated a switch to digital high-definition television by 2006. That process is currently underway at the nation's TV stations and networks. In radio, two companies have promised national digital radio distribution via satellite, which is committed to providing CD-quality radio to homes and cars.

- *Signal reception.* Radio receivers pull in AM, FM, and other signals, in monaural or stereo. New digital multiband receivers are becoming more prevalent. In TV, large and small-screen receivers have attained record sales in recent years, abetted by new digital capabilities and "smart" remote control devices.

- *Storage and retrieval.* New technology is reshaping audio and video storage and retrieval. Phonograph records, compact discs, and videotapes are being supplemented and may ultimately be replaced by digital storage media, such as recordable CDs, digital video disks (DVDs), and high-capacity disk drives on computers. A comparatively new phenomenon, audio and video streaming, permits radio and TV stations to send their complex signals onto the Internet. Today, any home computer with a soundcard, a CD-ROM drive, and a microphone can produce and distribute its own radio and TV programs. The impact of this development on traditional radio, TV, and cable is unclear.

KEY TERMS

SUGGESTIONS FOR FURTHER READING

Alvear, J. (1998). *Web developer.com guide to streaming multi-media*. New York: John Wiley and Sons.

Angel, J. (1998). *Realmedia complete: Streaming audio & video over the web*. New York: McGraw-Hill.

Baldwin, T. F., & McVoy, D. S. (1987). *Cable communication*. Englewood Cliffs, NJ: Prentice-Hall.

Benford, T. (1995). *Introducing desktop video*. Indianapolis: I.D.G. Books.

Benson, K. B. (1991). *HDTV: Advanced television for the 1990s*. New York: Intertext/McGraw-Hill.

Bertram, H. N. (1994). *Theory of magnetic recording*. New York: Cambridge University Press.

Casabianca, L. (1992). *The new TV: A comprehensive survey of high definition television*. Westport, CT: Meckler.

DeSonne, M., ed. (1996). *International DTH/DBS*. Washington, DC: National Association of Broadcasters.

Horn, D. T. (1991). *DAT: The complete guide to digital audio tape*. Blue Ridge Summit, PA: Tab Books.

Luther, A. (1997). *Principles of digital audio & video*. Norwood, NJ: Artech House.

Marlow, E. (1991). *Shifting time and space: The story of videotape*. New York: Praeger.

Mott, R. L. (1990). *Sound effects: Radio, TV and film*. Boston: Focal Press.

O'Donnell, L. B., Benoit, P., & Hausman, C. (1993). *Modern radio production* (3rd ed.). Belmont, CA: Wadsworth.

Paulsen, K. (1998). *Video & media servers: Technology and applications*. Woburn, United Kingdom: Butterworth-Heinemann.

Pohlmann, K. C. (1992). *The compact disc: Handbook of theory and use* (2nd ed.). Madison, WI: A-R Editions.

Rhoads, E., ed. (1995). *The radio book.* West Palm Beach, FL: Streamline Press.

Robin, M., & Poulin, M. (1997). *Digital television fundamentals.* New York: McGraw-Hill.

Soderberg, A. (1995). *Desktop video studio.* New York: Random House.

Whitaker, J. (1997). *HDTV: The revolution in electronic imaging.* New York: McGraw-Hill.

Zolzer, I. (1997) *Digital audio signal processing.* New York: John Wiley.

INTERNET EXERCISES

1. Visit our Web site at http://www.mhhe.com/
    beyond for study-guide exercises to help you learn
    and apply material in each chapter. You will find
    ideas for future research as well as useful Web links
    to provide you with an opportunity to journey
    through the new electronic media.

Part Two How It Is

4 Radio Today

Quick Facts

 AM stations on air: 4,800 (1999 est.)

 FM stations on air: 7,500 (1999 est.)

 Share of listening to FM radio: 80 percent

 Number of country radio stations: 2,500 (est.)

 Number of college radio stations: 800 (est.)

 Average radio salary: $20,000

 Howard Stern's annual salary: $20 million (est.)

My name is RADIO! My influence shall abide!
I, Magic Box, am something years ago
The wizards dreamed of in Arabian Nights.
Science has conceived and brought to birth
More wondrous far than legends' figments
*   wrought*
By the ingenious bards of long ago. . . .
I feel like a spirit medium that can bring
The listener what'er he wishes from the void.
Do you want multitudes of thoughts, all types?
Full measure comes with the revolving dial;
The masters wait to pour out symphonies
That rock the world and set your soul on fire. . . .

Robert West, "My Name Is Radio!" (1941)

We'll be looking for caller number 10 but first
you've got a lock on a 30-minute block of rock
direct from stereo compact disc on the hot new
Z-93 . . . Hot . . . hot . . . hot . . . hot.

DJ on large-market FM station (1999)

Satellites! The Web! High-definition TV! . . . Amid the furor of today's communications explosion it's easy to overlook persistent, enterprising, unassuming radio. If nothing else, radio is resilient. It has withstood frontal attacks from an array of new media services, each promising to sound the death knell of the radio business. But in every instance, from the introduction of sound pictures in the late 1920s to the arrival of TV in the 1940s, from the birth of music TV in the 1980s to the rise of the Internet in the 1990s, radio has rebounded, reformulated, and, most important, remained.

Radio today is as vital as ever. It is chameleonlike in form: from the supertiny Walkman to the suitcase-sized "boom box." It is omnipresent: Most households have five radios or more. It fills the air: There are more than 12,000 stations on the air in the United States alone. And it seems to meet our needs: Somewhere on that dial there can be found almost every form of music, all kinds of advice, hundreds of ball games, and special events. Perhaps most important of all, in the face of an unprecedented flow of competition from within and outside the industry, radio remains economically viable.

Why do we continue to tune in to radio? As we pointed out in Chapter 1, radio has been around longer than any other electronic medium. Like baseball, hot dogs, and apple pie (to borrow a commercial slogan), radio has become a part of our culture and tradition.

Radio is the most intimate of the mass media. It's portable—and personal. It is with us wherever we go, from the exercise room to the classroom (You! Put that Walkman away!); from the car to the transcontinental airplane.

And, as communications grow more global in nature (see Chapter 14), at its heart, radio is a local service medium. We rely on it to get the weather and the traffic report, and to hear a reassuring voice as we face our daily activities. We often define our friends and relationships by our radio habits. Don't agree? Look around any college campus. How many students are wearing T-shirts or sporting bumper stickers on their cars touting a local radio station?

Sometimes in our crush to credit TV for almost everything good or ill in our culture, there is a tendency to overlook radio. Let's not make that mistake. To borrow from some of its supporters, let's remember: Radio is red hot! In fact, "heat" is the appropriate metaphor. Everything about radio—from its competitive policies to its flamboyant personalities—tends to be intense. Let's don our insulated gloves and delve into the radio business.

THE "THREE C's" OF RADIO TODAY: COMPETITION, CONSOLIDATION, AND CONTROL

Radio today is marked by three major trends, which can be labeled the "three C's." These trends are **competition, consolidation,** and **control.** With many thousands of stations on the air, and consumers faced with many attractive alternatives to radio (like TV, CD and DVD players, VCRs, and computers), radio *competes* vigorously for listeners. With radio deregulation (discussed more fully in Chapter 10) has come radio *consolidation,* the ownership of more and more stations by fewer and fewer large corporations. The combination of competition and consolidation has led to enormous *control* in the radio business, including the development of narrower, intensively researched radio formats, and the rise of satellites and computers in radio operations, the meat of the material in Chapter 8. For now, let's see about the "three C's."

Competition in Today's Radio Business

Any discussion of the radio business must begin with one word: competition. Radio is arguably the most competitive of contemporary media. By almost every criterion there is more "radio" than anything else. There are more radios than there are TVs (about three times as many). There are five times as many radio stations as there are daily newspapers and nearly 10 times as many radio stations as TV stations. About the only thing there is less of in radio is advertising revenue. To understand commercial radio today, we must begin with its economics.

For some reason many people have difficulty with economic terminology but few fail to understand the intricacies of pizza. So imagine you and a group of friends have just been served two pizzas at your favorite restaurant. As usual, the pies have been sliced. Let's see where the cuts are.

Advertising Revenue   Pie 1 (Figure 4–1) is apportioned on the basis of 1997 advertising revenue. In 1997 advertisers spent nearly $190 billion trying to convince the American public to buy their products. The bulk of that spending, over $50 billion, went to the newspaper and magazine business. Television got the second biggest slice, about 24 percent, or $45 billion. A lot went to direct mail; nearly a quarter went to other media, like billboards, bumper stickers, and blimps. Look at the paltry radio slice: 7 percent of total advertising expenditures, representing about $13 billion. Lesson number one, then, for radio, is that if this pizza party were given in honor of America's leading advertising vehicles, you would leave comparatively hungry.

The Station Universe   Pie 2 (Figure 4–2) is divided on the basis of radio station type. There are about 12,300 radio stations on the air. Four in 10 stations (39 percent) are commercial AM stations. Although many of these are powerful stations emanating from large cities, the majority of AM stations are relatively low-powered, local operations serving the small and midsized communities that constitute the essence of "middle America."

A slightly larger proportion (45 percent) of radio stations are commercial FM operations. Because of their relatively late arrival on the scene and their technical requirements (described in detail in Chapter 3), the majority of the FMs are currently allocated to midsized and large-sized cities. Recently, however, the Federal Communications Commission (FCC) allocated around 700 new FM stations to small communities.

The remainder of radio stations, about 2,000, or 16 percent, are designated noncommercial stations. Most noncommercial stations are FMs.

The point of this pie is that radio today is largely a

Figure 4–1

Advertising Revenue by Medium

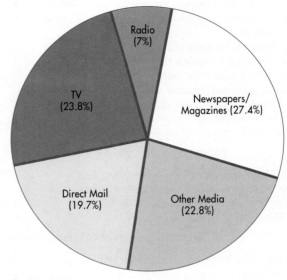

Source: McCann-Erickson.

locally based medium. Many stations are commercial AMs, trying to operate on the advertising revenue available from local advertisers in the smaller markets. Large cities are increasingly being dominated by FM commercial stations, where major advertisers call the shots. Within the noncommercial

Figure 4–2

Types of Radio Stations, 1999

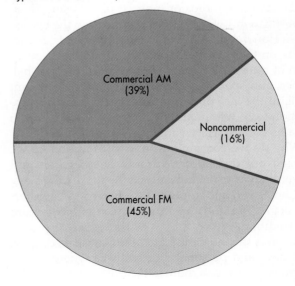

Ethics: Outrageous Radio

Howard Stern is perhaps the most infamous and controversial of a number of radio personalities who are earning a reputation for "outrageous radio." Increasing competition for advertising, especially in the nation's largest markets, has led to an unprecedented series of incidents, which have stretched the bounds, some observers say, of good taste and fair play. Outrageous radio is also known as "raunch radio," and its air personalities are often called "shock jocks."

In St. Louis, a radio station aired phone messages from a well-known TV weatherman talking about a love affair and played an interview with a woman who claimed the weatherman was harassing her. The next day, the weathercaster died in a fiery plane crash that appeared to be a suicide.

In Chicago, a DJ suggested to listeners that a TV anchorwoman—recently widowed—was pregnant by a Chicago Bulls player. She soon sued for defamation.

Ostensibly to "encourage reading," a station in Fort Worth told its listeners that cash was hidden somewhere in the main city library. Eight hundred people stormed the building, damaging and destroying thousands of books in the process.

Two disc jockeys in Denver kicked off their new show with a half-page newspaper advertisement that resembled the popular "fold-in" section in *Mad* magazine. When properly folded, the ad produced an attack on a competing station, complete with a four-letter expletive not normally seen in a family newspaper. The competitive station had had its own problems recently, when its morning team made jokes about a man who suffered a seizure and drowned in a lake as his two children watched.

A Memphis radio station caused a run on the banks when a morning team took a call on the air from someone claiming that all old $20 bills would be no good and would have to be exchanged for the newer (and uglier, if more colorful) ones. The call was fake, but the panic was real. Hundreds of people stormed local banks, and the station's General Manager apologized for his morning team's practical joke. Lesson learned? Hardly. After an industry tip sheet reported the episode, the prank was repeated by other morning teams in Richmond, Seattle, Greensboro, and other cities.

And the redoubtable Mr. Stern himself made international headlines when the Canadian Broadcast Standards Council ruled that stations in Montreal and Toronto breached the industry's Code of Ethics by carrying his morning program. It didn't help that the controversy provoked Howard to go on the offensive against Canadians in general, and French-speaking Canadians in particular. As the CBSC delicately put it, Mr. Stern used "abusive and discriminatory comments directed at French Canadians and other identifiable groups."

In response to these and other excesses, the FCC has increased enforcement of its rules regarding pranks and hoaxes. It has levied considerable fines for indecent language (including $1.2 million for a variety of transgressions by Mr. Stern). But the bottom line is that outrageous radio seems to attract audiences. Like "tabloid TV," raunch radio has become a part of the modern media scene.

environment the pressure is on to find funding: from the federal government, from religious organizations, from foundations, from university administrations or student fees, or from individual listeners.

Share of Audience   The point of both pies becomes clearer with one more statistic in view: share of audience. Today, almost 80 percent of all radio listening is to FM stations. In some cities, like Terre Haute, Indiana; Tallahassee, Florida; and Johnstown, Pennsylvania; FM share of audience is above 90 percent. In fact, many radio listeners, especially younger ones, rarely, if ever, tune to the AM band.

So, to sum up the competitive battleground, commercial radio is a business where more than 12,000 stations compete for a comparatively small percentage of national advertising expenditures. In commercial radio, approximately equal numbers of AM and FM stations compete for audiences, though most radio listeners prefer the FM band. It should not be surprising, then, that the most profitable radio stations are the big FM music stations in the major cities and the powerhouse AM news/talk stations that deliver older listeners, and that many stations, both AM and FM, report modest profit at best or are in a constant struggle to survive.

Consolidation: The Big Radio Groups

The increasingly competitive nature of the radio business is reflected in the kinds of companies now involved in the medium. For nearly one-half a century, radio was generally a small business. Owners were also operators and lifelong residents of the community in which the station operated. Many owned other businesses in the area, such as automobile dealerships, restaurants, and even local newspapers. Reflecting this ownership pattern and the "homespun" environment in which they operated, such stations were commonly referred to as "mom-and-pop" stations.

Today, mom-and-pop radio has largely disappeared. Why? The competitive situation traced in the previous section was not lost on the radio business. Led by the National Association of Broadcasters—the industry's largest lobby group and trade association (see Chapter 11)—throughout the 1990s the radio business successfully lobbied Congress for regulatory relief. Their argument was that radio had become so competitive, with so many stations competing for such a small advertising segment and with so many stations losing money, that radio group owners should be able to own more stations. In addition, the argument went, a single owner should be able to operate more than the two stations (an AM and an FM) they were permitted to own.

For many years, radio *group owners* were restricted to owning only 14 stations total (seven AM and seven FM). In addition, they could not own more than two stations in a single market (one AM, one FM); within one market they could not own more than one station in the same bandwidth, such as two AMs and two FMs). After some modification in the early 1990s, the passage of the **Telecommunications Act of 1996** literally changed the rules of the radio business, and in less than two years the entire radio landscape shifted.

The new rules allow a single radio group owner to own as many stations as it wants. There are no national ownership caps. Even within markets, groups can amass more stations. For example, in cities with more than 44 stations, one company can own up to eight stations (no more than five AM or FM). In cities with 30 to 44 stations, a single company can own seven stations (up to four AM or FM). In midsized communities (15 to 30 stations) a single company can control six stations. Even in smaller towns (with up to 15 commercial stations), a single group can control 5 stations (up to 3 AM or FM).

As a direct result of these new rules, the radio business changed radically, at least in ownership, in the late 1990s. Local ownership gave way to the rise of the radio **supergroup.** By this, we do not mean rock-and-roll bands, like Hootie and the Blowfish, the Dave Matthews Band, or Aerosmith. The supergroups we refer to are radio's largest companies, which control most of the listening—and therefore most of the revenue—in radio today.

Table 4–1 lists the largest radio groups by overall revenue. Leading the pack is Chancellor Media, with nearly 500 stations and revenue of more than $1.7 billion. Like the big fish gobbling a school of smaller ones, Chancellor emerged in the 1990s from a combination of Chancellor Broadcasting and Evergreen Media. The new company then acquired stations from Viacom, Gannett, and Bonneville. Most recently, Chancellor Media absorbed Capstar in late 1998, forming the nation's largest radio group.

Chancellor, based in Dallas, owns at least one station in each of the nation's top 12 radio markets, and 17 of the top 20. It controls five stations in New York and Los Angeles; six in Chicago; seven in San Francisco, Detroit, and Cleveland; and eight in Phoenix. Chancellor's radio power is not concentrated in major cities, however. The company also owns stations in Jackson, Mississippi; Texarkana, Texas; Dover, Delaware; and Ogallala, Nebraska.

Another powerhouse group, in terms of total stations, is Clear Channel Communications. Clear Channel, with its home base in San Antonio, Texas, controls about 450 stations, including the assets of Jacor, a large radio group it acquired in 1999. Clear Channel owns seven stations in Los Angeles, and eight in Miami, San Diego, Cleveland, and Cincinnati.

Together, Chancellor and Clear Channel control nearly 1 in 10 commercial stations in the United States. From a revenue standpoint, the two groups account for roughly $3 billion of the estimated $13 billion in advertising revenue in radio, or almost one in four radio advertising dollars.

Thus, the power of radio groups is not measured solely by the number of stations owned by the group; how much advertising the group amasses is also significant. For example, Infinity Broadcasting, which is 80 percent owned and operated by CBS, owns fewer than 200 radio stations. Yet, it is ranked second in overall revenue, with more than $1.6 billion. Simple arithmetic reveals that the typical Infinity station earns more than $10 million in annual advertising revenue. In fact, Infinity owns many of the

Rank	Group	Revenue*	Stations
Table 4–1	**America's Leading Radio Groups**		
1	Chancellor Media Corp.	$1,765,421,000	488
2	Infinity (CBS)	1,687,457,000	164
3	Clear Channel Communications	1,240,644,000	453
4	ABC, Inc.	339,822,000	35
5	Cox Broadcasting, Inc.	279,279,000	59
6	Entercom Communications Corp.	193,564,000	41
7	Heftel Broadcasting Corp.	184,748,000	39
8	Emmis Communications Corp.	171,538,000	16
9	Cumulus Media, Inc.	167,209,000	207
10	Susquehanna Radio Corp.	152,475,000	22
11	Sinclair Broadcast Group, Inc.	141,603,000	53
12	Citadel Communications Corp.	140,941,000	102
13	Bonneville International Corp.	120,912,000	15
14	Greater Media, Inc.	116,420,000	16
15	Jefferson Pilot Communications Co.	101,664,000	17
16	Beasley Broadcast Group	85,715,000	30
17	Spanish Broadcasting System	82,785,000	11
18	Saga Communications, Inc.	77,132,000	41
19	Journal Broadcast	67,378,000	36
20	Tribune Co.	57,071,000	4

*Estimated 1998 revenue.

Source: *Broadcasting & Cable*, October 12, 1998, pp. 33–45.

nation's highest-billing radio stations, including all-news powerhouses WCBS and WINS in New York, KNX and KFWB in Los Angeles, and WBBM and WMAQ in Chicago. As morning man Don Imus is fond of pointing out, Infinity's WFAN in New York, an all-sports station, is the nation's most profitable radio station, with annual advertising revenue above $50 million.

The list of radio group owners is filled out with a number of other influential and respected names. Fourth on the revenue ranking is Disney's ABC Inc., a fleet of 35 stations reporting revenue above $300 million. ABC has been a leader in radio since the 1950s, and its list of radio assets includes talk radio leaders WABC in New York, KABC in Los Angeles, WLS and WMVP in Chicago, and WJR in Detroit. In Atlanta, ABC owns the two largest country radio outlets, WKHX-FM and WYAY-FM.

Other groups known for effective management, innovative programming, and profitable radio operations include Cox, Emmis, Heftel, Susquehanna, Bonneville, and Sinclair.

A New Kind of "Doo-wop": Duopoly and LMAs   It is kind of ironic (or at least coincidental) that the medium of radio, built in part on early rock-and-roll music known as "doo-wop," has given new meaning to that shop-worn bit of slang. Where once doo-wop referred to the sound produced by harmonizing street-corner singers (Frankie Lymon and the Teenagers, The Coasters, and The Drifters, for example), today its homonym "duop" refers to the in-market control of radio listening and revenue by a few large group owners.

As we have seen, the FCC now permits a single company to own as many as eight stations in a single radio market. In addition, the FCC permits one company to manage the assets of another in the same market without being in violation of ownership rules. Known as a **lease management agreement** or **local market agreement (LMA),** the arrangement permits one station or group to control the programming, operations, and sales of additional radio stations in the same marketplace.

Radio Business Report, a leading trade magazine,

Mel Karmazin, one of the most influential people in radio, became president and chief operating officer of CBS in 1997. He reorganized CBS by spinning off its radio stations and outdoor advertising holdings into a new company, Infinity Broadcasting.

has estimated that nearly 75 percent of all radio stations are in the hands of "superduops," groups owning or controlling at least three stations in the same service in a market (three AMs, three FMs, or both). By 1999, only 7 markets in the top 100 were "unconsolidated," down from 9 in 1998, and 16 in 1997. For an illustration, consider New York City, where Infinity, Chancellor, and Emmis account for more than half of all radio listening, and nearly 75 percent of all revenue; or Chicago, where just under half of all radio listening goes to Chancellor, Infinity, or Cox stations, and the three groups earn two in three radio ad dollars; or Philadelphia, where Infinity, Chancellor, and Greater Media attract more than 7 in 10 radio listeners and 8 in 10 dollars in radio advertising.

Is ownership consolidation in radio a good thing? Advocates of this trend maintain that group ownership allows for economies of scale (more efficient programming, better news gathering) to keep big-city radio exciting and interesting. Critics charge that group owners lack the sensitivity to community concerns that "mom-and-pops" have. If you're planning

a radio career and favor local independent ownership, you may wish to consider small-market radio. If you're heading for New York, Chicago, Los Angeles, or other large markets, the "corporate culture" is no doubt in your future.

Control: Radio Programming and Promotion

The last "C" of radio today is *control*. With increasing competition and consolidation has come a desire on the part of radio managers to gain more and more control of the programming, promotions, and marketing of their stations. Radio today is marked by the kind of rigorous product and consumer research used to sell all kinds of consumer products, such as soap, cigarettes, and cheese. Like all consumer items, the process begins with a full understanding of the attributes of the product. In the case of radio, the product is its *programming*. Let's examine the major trends in radio programming today.

RADIO PROGRAMMING TODAY

At the risk of sounding stereotypical, a snapshot of radio listeners today might include a teenager "zoning in" to a personal stereo on a school bus, a middle-aged executive listening in a luxury automobile, a city youth listening to an oversized "boom box," a trucker listening while traveling the highway in an 18-wheel rig, and a secretary listening to a desktop radio while at a computer workstation. It is highly unlikely that each is listening to the same type of station.

With more than 12,000 stations on the air and more than 25 local stations typically available for most listeners, and while competing for audiences against tape and CD players, TV, the Internet, movies, and even live entertainment like concerts and theater, radio has become a focused and highly targeted medium. That is, rather than programming to meet the broadest tastes of the largest numbers of people in their listening areas, most stations today cater to a narrow market segment, the core of listeners who prefer a certain type of programming. The two key components of this trend are target audience and format.

The concept of **target audience** emerges from advertising research, which shows that the majority of purchases of a given product are made by a minority of the public: the target market for that product. For example, the overwhelming majority of beer is purchased by men between the ages of 21 and 49, teenagers account for most movies attended, and adults over 45 take the most European trips. In developing their campaigns, advertisers try to identify the target market for a product and then to develop appeals that meet the needs of this group.

Commercial radio today, particularly in the largest cities, is programmed in precisely the same fashion. Reflecting this trend, in fact, cities themselves are known in the business as "markets." Management identifies a target audience by its age, gender, music preferences, lifestyle, and other information, and it develops a program strategy to satisfy that group. The program strategy is known as the radio station's **format.** A successful radio station consistently delivers its intended target audience, in both aggregate size (quantity) and lifestyle preferences (quality). Its listeners are an identifiable subgroup, largely similar in age, gender, income, habits, leisure pursuits, and other characteristics. This makes the station attractive to advertisers: the name of the game in commercial radio.

Table 4–2 lists the top 10 commercial radio formats, in terms of number of stations and share of audience. Chapter 8 details how a format evolves from conception to execution. Until then, let's identify the major formats and their typical target audiences.

Country

Today, country radio is king. There are almost 2,500 radio stations playing country music, representing about one in four commercial stations. As a radio format, country music has decided advantages. Its appeal is broad. People of all ages listen to country; unlike album rock, for example, it's a cradle-to-grave experience. Like most of the preferred formats, it delivers more women than men. Even so, large audiences of both sexes respond to the music. Country fans are loyal: They tend to listen to a single favorite station for long periods of time, making these stations a prime target for advertisers.

The growth in popularity of country music in the 1970s and 1980s led to the development of various derivatives. "Traditional" or "classic" country stations consider themselves the purest players of the format. The emphasis in music is on the country-and-western standards of 20 or 30 years ago.

"Contemporary" or "modern" country stations concentrate on current hits on the country charts, particularly the most up-tempo or upbeat tunes.

Table 4–2	Commercial Radio Formats		
Rank	**Format**	**Number of Stations***	**Audience Share****
1	Country	2,941	11
2	Adult contemporary: oldies; soft	2,003	14
3	News/Talk and Sports	1,331,	15
4	CHR/Hot AC	618	10
5	Adult standards/Easy listening/Beautiful	600	4
6	Hispanic	474	6
7	Black/Urban contemporary	452	11
8	Religion	404	2
9	Rock/Album rock	240	7
10	Modern rock/Alternative	231	7

Sources: *M Street Report (December 1997); **Duncan's American Radio (Spring 1998).

Strong airplay is usually given to the "superstars" of country, like Garth Brooks, the Dixie Chicks, and Brooks and Dunn.

Regardless of the music orientation, most country stations are "full-service" operations. Announcers tend to be friendly and helpful, directly involved in community events. Unlike some of the other contemporary formats, most country stations provide news, weather, and other information to their listeners. Remote broadcasts are common, from concerts and fairs to shopping malls and drive-ins.

Part of the continuing appeal of country music is its success on both AM and FM. Country is heard nearly evenly on the two bands. This means that the format has participated in the FM boom but also remains viable in AM. Like rock-and-roll, country radio is here to stay.

By the late 1990s, however, there were some chinks in country radio's armor. After a decade of growth, the country radio boom leveled off. The number of country stations peaked at nearly 2,600 stations in 1996; by 1999, the number had slipped below 2,500. Too, while country radio represents 25 percent of stations, it accounts for only 11 percent of radio listening (down from 15 percent just a few years ago). This is because country's strength is concentrated in medium and smaller markets. Though popular, country stations do not lead listening in the nation's most populous markets, like New York, Los Angeles, Chicago, Boston, and Philadelphia, to name a few.

Adult Contemporary

Just behind country in total number of stations is adult contemporary (AC). Adult contemporary runs along a continuum from "soft hits" to "oldies." AC/soft stations emphasize current music with a soft, lyrical, and melodic beat. Celine Dion, Shania Twain, LeAnn Rhimes, Whitney Houston, and Mariah Carey are typical female artists played often on modern AC stations; their male counterparts include Phil Collins, Elton John, Lionel Richie, Harry Connick, Jr., John Tesh, and Michael Bolton.

AC stations that take the "oldie" route play soft, nonmetallic, rock-and-roll hits from the 1960s to the early 1990s. The songs played were usually big hits in their day by the best-known bands of their time. The Beach Boys, The Beatles, The Supremes, and other mainstays of the rock-and-roll charts are featured prominently on AC/oldies stations.

In AC, announcers are generally pleasant, friendly, innocuous, and noncontroversial. In fact, many listeners would be hard put to name the announcers at their favorite AC station (aside from a funny morning team), since the main reason they listen is for the music.

AC stations are popular because they tend to attract the audience most in demand by advertisers and marketers: women between the ages of 25 and 54. The appeal of AC is wide: from urban areas to rural, from college-educated to grade school, from upper income to the poverty line. But AC is particularly strong "where it counts" to many advertisers: among middle- and upper-income housewives and working women in urban and suburban areas.

AC's strength in the bigger markets and attractive suburbs accounts for its large listenership. Today, about 14 percent of all radio listening is to some kind of AC station. As with country, however, the news is not all good for AC. The number of AC stations has been declining lately due to a rebound among both news/talk and contemporary hit radio (CHR). The target audience of women, particularly younger women, is attracted to other formats, especially CHR and black urban contemporary (discussed in a later section). Older women often migrate to adult standards (also discussed later). Still, AC remains a well-known and highly profitable radio format.

News/Talk and Sports

News and talk is a broad radio format. At one end of the scale are *all-news* operations, usually AM stations in major metropolitan areas that program 24 hours a day of news, sports, weather, and traffic information. Examples are WINS and WCBS in New York, WBBM in Chicago, and KNX and KFWB in Los Angeles. At the other end of the scale are *all-talk* stations, which rotate hosts and invite listeners to call in on a range of topics—current affairs, auto mechanics, and counseling in every area, even sex. Examples are New York's WOR, WIOD in Miami, and KSTP-AM in Minneapolis. Between these extremes there are many *news and talk* stations, some of which mix play-by-play sports and occasional musical segments into the format. However, even the "hybrids" center their programming on information services.

More than 200 stations are *all-sports* operations. Most are in large cities, particularly the cities that boast teams in the four major professional sports leagues: Major League Baseball, the National Football League, the National Hockey League, and the National Basketball Association. All-sports stations

Some country artists, such as Shania Twain, have recordings that are played on both country and contemporary hit radio stations.

The radio and the recording industries have a mutually beneficial relationship. The recording companies supply stations with free music. Radio stations play the music on the air which, in turn, helps sell recordings.

typically frame play-by-play action of these professional teams and major college games with nonstop discussion, analysis, and debate about sport teams, athletes, and coaches.

Whatever its unique interpretation, talk radio is a popular format, particularly on the AM band. In fact, more than half of all AM listening today is to news/talk and sports stations. Part of the appeal of news/talk and sports is its audience composition. The news format attracts "big numbers," particularly during important drive time in the morning and afternoon. It follows that people who listen for news, traffic, and weather information are on their way to jobs. This makes them an ideal target for advertisers.

By the dawn of the new century, news/talk and sports was among commercial radio's fastest-growing formats, accounting for more than 1,300 stations and about 15 percent of all radio listening. Nationally syndicated personalities like Rush Limbaugh, Don Imus, G. Gordon Liddy, Dr. Joy Browne, and Dr. Laura Schlessinger, among others, were reaching millions of listeners each day. At the local level, news, talk, sports, and information stations were rife with acerbic commentators, smart-talking "jocks," computer gurus, cigar aficionados, and gabbers of all political stripes.

Contemporary Hit Radio

Targeting a younger audience than AC is the contemporary hit radio format, or CHR. Contemporary hit radio may also be referred to as Top-40 or current-hit radio. This radio format is like an audio jukebox. The emphasis is placed on the most current music, the songs leading the charts in record sales. The music played is almost always bright or up-tempo. Slow songs, long songs, and oldies (even those only a few months old) are avoided. Songs play again quickly (a program strategy known as **fast rotation**) and are removed from the playlist as soon as there is evidence that their popularity is declining. Top 40 is a misnomer: Today's CHR stations may play as few as 20 or 30 songs.

"Screamers" are common on CHR stations. Disc jockeys (DJs) tend to be assertive, high-energy personalities who sprinkle their shifts with humor, sound effects, and gimmickry. Contemporary hit radio stations sound "busy" compared with ACs: The air is filled with contests, jingles, jokes, buzzers, whistles, and, above all, hits. Currently about 10 percent of all listening is to this format; the majority of stations using the format are FM stations in large markets. Contemporary hit radio is most popular with the age group that buys single records and hot albums: preteen, teen, and young adult women. This is the group in recent years that has made mammoth stars of Jewel, Goo Goo Dolls, Sheryl Crow, and Matchbox 20.

Once thought to be a format in decline, CHR has rebounded remarkably in recent years. There are numerous reasons for this turnaround. First, a spate of new artists appeared on the scene. Many were solo female performers, whose songs of independence, emotional turmoil, and love found and lost, resonated with the core audience of teen and young adult women. Such artists include the aforementioned Jewel and Sheryl Crow, as well as Alanis Morissette, Sarah McLachlan, Natalie Imbruglia, and long-time torchbearers Natalie Merchant and Stevie Nicks. In addition, a new kind of CHR called "hot adult contemporary" (Hot AC) found success with older women (ages 25–49), moving these women away from their allegiance to oldies and soft rock standards. Groups such as Hootie and the Blowfish, Fastball, Semisonic, Third Eye Blind, and The Backstreet Boys appealed to this group with melodic tunes that sounded very much like the mellow rock of the 1970s and early 1980s. Contemporary radio also began to merge with the sounds of America's inner cities, giving rise to two important formats: Hispanic and black/urban contemporary.

Ethnic Formats: Hispanic and Black/Urban Contemporary

Next in share of listening are the so-called "ethnic" formats, those radio stations that target minorities in major cities. The leading ethnic formats are Hispanic and black/urban contemporary. Together these formats can be heard on almost 1,000 stations and they account for more than 17 percent of all radio listening. In fact, "ethnic" may be a misnomer: their growing popularity indicates that people of many cultures enjoy these stations, mostly because of the attractive beat and rhythms of their music.

Hispanic Radio   Hispanic radio was the growth format in the 1990s, with the number of stations more than doubling in the decade. Today, nearly 500 stations consider themselves Hispanic and garner about 6 percent of radio listening.

The rise of Hispanic radio is due to two factors. The first is the growing population and economic clout of the Hispanic community. Today, the His-

panic population in the United States is approaching the total population of Canada. Advertisers spend more than $1 billion each year to reach this important group, more than $300 million in radio advertising.

The format also benefits from the rising popularity of its music. Subgenres like Banda, Ranchera, and Salsa have attracted large and loyal followings and made stars of such artists as Shakira, Enrique Iglesias, Chayanne, Frankie Negron, Pepe Aguilar, and La Mafia.

Black/Urban Contemporary   The black or urban contemporary (UC) format refers to the percussive, up-tempo sounds of the stations in America's major cities. Black is actually a misnomer for the format: people of all racial and ethnic backgrounds enjoy the music. Urban contemporary arose out of the "disco craze" of the mid-1970s, when a gyrating John Travolta captivated the culture and sent a new generation to the dance floors. By the 1990s, rap music had emerged to create a new force in UC. Today variations of the format range from rap, hip-hop, and "house" music to more traditional rhythm-and-blues and soul music stylings. Hot urban contemporary artists in recent years include Divine, Dru Hill, Keith Sweat, Mary J. Blige, Usher, Monifa, and R. Kelly. Like Hispanic radio, the urban format is played on about 500 stations, most in major cities with large African-American populations.

Adult Standards/Easy Listening/Beautiful Music

If Hispanic and urban radio is growing, the format known variously as "adult standards," "beautiful music," and/or "easy listening" may be losing audience. Beautiful music, or "easy listening," refers to the stations that program "wall-to-wall," "background," or "elevator" music. One of the stalwarts of FM (which stood for "fine music" in its early days), easy listening is an evolving format. Where once the "rules" called for only instrumental music (Mantovani, 101 Strings, Tony Matola, and so on), today it is common to hear Rod Stewart, Barbra Streisand, Jewel, Billy Joel, and Phil Collins in the format.

The primary reason for this change is the aging audience for the format. Beautiful music appeals mainly to older listeners, those above 45 years of age. Today's mature audiences grew up after the dawning of the age of rock-and-roll. They are as likely to relax and unwind to pop tunes as they are to lush orchestrations.

Beautiful music stations tend to have unique program elements. Music is generally played continuously; breaks for commercial announcements and news segments, if used, are kept to a minimum. Announcers have pleasant, low-key styles. They will never shout at you. Contests and other aggressive promotions are eschewed in favor of "image-enhancing" station events (sponsorship of appropriate music performances, for example).

The success of the format is not based on audience size, although in many markets beautiful stations boast big audiences. Rather, these stations attract a high-quality audience of professionals and managers. In addition to being high earners, this audience tends to listen to the radio for long periods of time and to be loyal to a single station or to very few stations.

Album Rock: Modern and Classic

Album rock is a long-lasting legacy of the progressive rock movement of the late 1960s and early 1970s. At this time, rock artists began to experiment with the form, producing theme albums (such as the Beatles' *Sergeant Pepper,* The Who's *Tommy,* and *The Wall* by Pink Floyd). The length of songs played on the radio began to increase, from two minutes to five minutes or more. Like classical and jazz before it, album rock developed a core of informed, dedicated, loyal listeners: most of them young adult males. In fact, of all the major formats, album rock is most heavily targeted, or *skewed,* to male listeners. Over 60 percent of the album rock audience is male.

There are two main types of album rock stations. Those attracting younger males (teenagers and young adults in the 12- to 34-year-old age group) are known as *alternative* or *modern rock* stations. This is the group that has made superstars in recent years of such artists as Goo Goo Dolls, Cake, Eve 6, Candlebox, Semisonic, Fuel, and Fastball.

Those stations seeking aging male baby boomers (like the authors of this text), are known as *classic rock* stations. Their core audience of 25- to 54-year-old listeners is loyal to the music of the supergroups of the 1960s, 1970s, and early 1980s, including the Rolling Stones, The Doors, The Police, U2, the Allman Brothers, and others. Proof of the enduring appeal of older rock artists to both older and younger males is the fact that the most successful tours in recent years have been mounted by such aging rockers as the Stones, Pink Floyd, Aerosmith, Kiss, Mötley Crüe, and Black Sabbath, giving new meaning to the phrase "long live rock."

Together, classic and modern rock stations number nearly 500 and represent about 15 percent of all radio listening.

Other Formats

Together, the formats just described account for almost 90 percent of radio listening in the United States. The additional 10 percent is filled out by a number of other formats.

Religious stations appeal to a variety of faiths, but Christian stations are most plentiful. In addition to delivering inspirational talks, many religious stations include music in their format. Those targeting the black audience are generally known as gospel stations. Religious stations tend to be most popular among older women (above the age of 50). The majority of religious stations (60 percent) can be found on the AM dial, usually at the high end of the dial where local stations are most plentiful.

By mid-decade, there were more than 400 stations playing some form of religious format. Despite its proliferation, religious stations lag in listenership. At any given point in time, fewer than one in 50 radio listeners is tuned to religion.

While classical music and jazz are the backbone of public radio stations (see the discussion that follows), some 50 or so commercial operations play each of these formats. Classical stations attract a very upscale listener: between 35 and 54 years of age, typically college-educated and professional. The jazz enthusiast shares a similar profile. Although the number of classical and jazz aficionados is small (compared, say, with the audience for adult contemporary), the "high quality" of their listeners makes these stations potentially attractive advertising vehicles.

It sometimes appears that there are almost as many other formats as there are radio stations. Filling out the dial there are Portuguese, Greek, Polish, German, and other foreign-language stations. Over 20 stations program exclusively to Native Americans and Eskimos. Russian-language WMNB in New Jersey and KMNB in Los Angeles have become popular among the many immigrants from the former Soviet Union. Clearly, commercial radio is in an era of expanding format diversity.

Noncommercial Radio

The bulk of America's radio stations seek profits through advertising sales, but about one in six stations does not. Into this class fall approximately 2,000 noncommercial radio stations. There are three main types of noncommercial stations: community, college, and public.

Community stations are those that are licensed to civic groups, nonprofit foundations, local school boards, or religious organizations. There are about

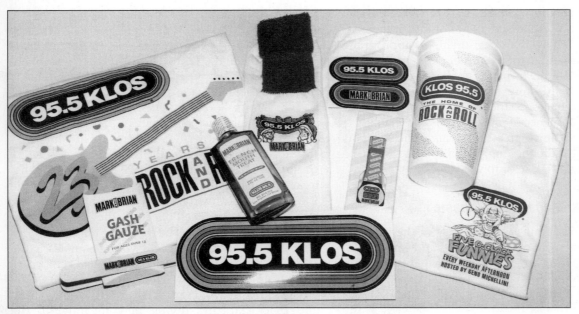

Promotional items, ranging from T-shirts to mugs, are essential elements of radio today.

Events: Catch a .WAV—Radio and the Personal Computer

There is much discussion today about "the new information superhighway," which will bring over 500 channels of TV plus the contents of newspapers, photographs, and other data to our home screens, possibly through our personal computers. While much of this discussion is so much "pie in the sky," radio has led the way in the online revolution.

Today, many desktop computers are equipped with a soundcard and a pair of stereo speakers. Words and music can be created and stored in computer files, usually identified with the suffix .WAV on the file name to indicate sound waves as the file's content. Add a modem, and presto! Radio programs can be transmitted and received anywhere in the world. Today, a range of radio programs are wending their way around the world on the Internet, the global computer network.

The technique of streaming described in Chapter 3, allows radio stations to move their signal onto the World Wide Web. More than 500 stations now simulcast their signals on the Internet; more than 6,000 maintain Web sites to promote their air personalities, special events, and sports programming.

Long-distance, computer-assisted radio listening has led to the rise of services known as "Webcasters." AudioNet is the leader in this fast-growing new media segment. A quick trip to Audionet.com provides an instant link to hundreds of radio stations. Located in a trendy section of Dallas, AudioNet streams the signals through an array of dozens of computer servers there and in more than 50 other American cities. In return, the stations permit the company to run its own Internet advertising, often in the form of a brief sound bite (or is it "byte"?), which plays just before the distant radio station begins to play on the user's computer.

It is unclear whether online delivery of radio will take the medium to new levels of influence. One recent check of the America Online service found much of the .WAV files full of miscellaneous bits from the Howard Stern program, including at least five versions of Stern saying "bababooey."

500 of these stations, which operate in the FM band (between 88 and 92 megahertz), providing a range of services including coverage of local issues, study-at-home classes in conjunction with local schools, religious services, and other "home-based" activities.

College radio is a broad category comprising about 800 stations licensed to universities and some secondary schools. About 650 of these stations are members of the Intercollegiate Broadcasting Society (IBS).

College stations are a diverse group. However, most of them share a similar programming pattern. The musical mix is eclectic and "progressive," featuring program blocks of new wave, new age, reggae, folk, jazz, and other alternatives to standard formats. Many college stations operate as training sites for students planning broadcast careers. Thus, in addition to announcing, staffers gain experience in news, play-by-play sports, public affairs, and promotions.

Public radio stations are also known as *CPB-qualified stations*. These stations meet criteria established by the Corporation for Public Broadcasting (CPB), enabling them to qualify for federal funds, and to receive programs from National Public Radio (NPR).

In 1998, standards for CPB-qualified stations were tightened. Today's public radio stations must have professional staffs of at least five full-time members; must operate at least 18 hours per day, seven days a week; must operate at full power (250 watts AM and 100 watts FM); and must demonstrate sufficient local financial and listening support to justify federal grant monies. As a result, eight stations have lost their NPR affiliation; up to 80 more have been considered endangered. On the positive side, research studies on public radio audiences suggest that NPR listening is growing and that federal appropriations seem secure for the foreseeable future.

As one might expect, the audiences for public radio tend to be comparatively smaller than those for commercial stations. Nationwide, public radio averages about a 2 percent share of audience at any given time. This compares with shares of 6 to 15 percent for highly ranked commercial radio outlets. However, in some cities public radio attracts sizable audiences.

The public radio audience is somewhat highbrow. Studies have shown that the majority of listeners to public radio stations have college degrees and many listeners have advanced and professional degrees. You may recall that this profile overlaps the target audience of some commercial radio formats, such as advertiser-supported classical and jazz stations and beautiful-music operations.

Figure 4–3

A Radio Station Table of Organization

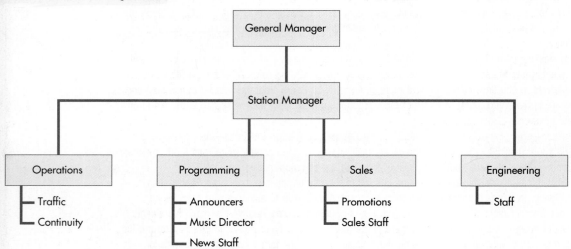

Among the most-listened programs in public radio are NPR's leading news programs, "Morning Edition" and "All Things Considered;" "Performance Today", "Talk of the Nation"; and "Fresh Air with Terry Gross." Such shows as "A Prairie Home Companion," hosted by Garrison Keillor, and "Car Talk" attract a large and loyal following.

RADIO STATION ORGANIZATION

Regardless of their size, radio stations tend to share an organizational pattern. Figure 4–3 illustrates the flow of managerial control common to radio stations. The illustration is typical of a radio station in a midsized market, such as those described earlier in the section on radio economics.

There are typically four "core departments" at each station: operations, programming, sales, and engineering. **Operations,** also known as the *traffic department,* has the responsibility of placing advertising on the station in accordance with the contracts signed with advertisers. This is a difficult task: At any given time dozens of different contracts are in force, each with varying schedules for airtime, length, position, and so on. For this reason most radio stations have automated their traffic departments with computer systems. The operations director or traffic manager heads this important department.

The **program department,** headed by the program director, has overall responsibility for the sound of the station, including music, news, and public affairs. Stations with a music format may also employ a music director to oversee the development and implementation of the format; news/talk stations may appoint a news director to handle the logistics of news and public affairs coverage.

The **sales department** is very important. Sales personnel are fond of pointing out that theirs is the only department that makes money; all of the others spend it. Led by the sales manager, this department is responsible for the sale of commercial time to local, regional, and national advertisers. Depending on the size of the station (and the size of its commercial client list), stations may employ both a local sales manager to oversee local sales and a national sales manager to handle spot advertising accounts. Today's commitment to research and promotion makes these important functions of this department, prompting many stations to value highly a promotions director and research manager.

In public radio, the sales department is replaced with a fundraising unit, typically led by the **director of development.** This staff plans, organizes, and executes the station's fundraising efforts, including pledge drives, grant applications, program underwriting, and related activities.

The **engineering department,** headed by the chief engineer, basically has one function: to keep the station on the air with the best signal possible. Many radio stations once had large engineering staffs, with as many as 5 to 10 full-time employees, but relaxed federal regulations, improved electronic equipment, and competition from other businesses for engineering talent led to the streamlining of engineering

Issues: College Radio: Vital Alternative or Electronic Sandbox?

As commercial radio becomes more and more consolidated, researched, formatted, and otherwise controlled, college radio has taken on immense importance to musicians and record labels. "Alternative" artists and "independent" labels, in particular, turn to college radio to stimulate interest in music that is unlikely to be played, at least initially, on commercial radio. As a result, many mainstays of college radio have become big-time bands, including Marilyn Manson, Hootie and the Blowfish, Eve 6, and others.

At the same time, college radio faces the kind of competitive pressures faced by NPR and other enterprises dependent on public monies for their support. As higher education tightens its belt, university administrations are questioning their investment in student-run radio—especially when these administrations are an object of scorn or ridicule by DJs or commentators on the stations.

College radio has often hurt its own cause. For example, the student station at the University of Missouri lost a significant sum after reuniting the group Big Star for a concert on campus. The university shut the station for a month while it got its books and management in order. A station at a branch campus of the State University of New York was fined over $20,000 for broadcasting a rap song deemed "indecent" under FCC guidelines.

The debate centers on the proper role of college radio. Should the goal of college stations be to provide training for students in radio operations and programming, thereby eschewing a more "professional" sound? Should the format appeal mainly to college students on campus? Or, should college stations program to the broader "college community," including faculty, staff, and listeners throughout the station's coverage area? On countless campuses the debate rages, including recent controversies in Las Vegas (KUNV), Pasadena (KPCC), Santa Monica (KCRW), and elsewhere.

Sometimes, college radio runs into problems even when it has the support of the university and the campus community. WUOG-FM at the University of Georgia is widely known and respected for its support of new music, from Athens' own R.E.M. and the B-52s to the more recent sounds of Widespread Panic, Five-Eight, and the Woggles (who took their name from the station's call letters). Recently, the university authorized a power increase. Alas, the stronger signal was blamed for interfering with the university's computer network, muffling local telephone calls, and overriding the sound system at a fine arts performance in the university theater.

departments. Some stations retain the services of a consulting engineer, who works part-time, as needed, to keep the station in prime operating condition.

Top-level management of, and responsibility for, a radio station is in the hands of the general manager (GM) or station manager. The GM is responsible for business and financial matters, including station revenues and expenses, short- and long-term planning, budgeting, forecasting, and profitability. The GM must run the station in accord with local, state, and federal regulations. The GM is responsible for maintaining and representing the station's image in the community. General managers also hire the major department heads, establish their goals, and monitor their performance.

Some large stations, particularly those in large markets and those owned by station groups, have both a GM and a station manager. In this case, the station manager has responsibility for the day-to-day operations of the radio station, such as hiring and firing, making sure the bills are paid, and keeping up employee morale; the GM reports to the "home office," representing the station to its corporate ownership, to the community, and to federal, state, and local regulatory bodies.

Traditionally, the route up the corporate ladder into the management of radio stations starts in sales; most radio GMs have a background as account executives, promotion directors, or research managers. However, it is not unheard of for GMs—even station group owners—to come from the music or announcing ranks. At a radio management meeting one will hear many well-modulated announcer voices; a very high percentage of owners and operators are former DJs.

Radio consolidation is leading to new management structures. In most markets, groups operating multiple stations have consolidated sales by using one sales staff to sell commercials on as many as eight stations. The engineering and traffic departments have been similarly streamlined. However, most duopolies prefer to keep programming and general station management decentralized. As radio is still primarily a local service medium, it makes sense to maintain local control of what the station sounds like, as well as what it's like to work there.

GETTING A JOB: RADIO EMPLOYMENT TODAY

The consolidation of radio, due to rising competition, increasing group ownership, duopolies, and LMAs, has had a measurable effect on radio employment. Total radio employment has dropped by about 10 percent since duopoly rules went into effect.

With consolidation continuing, one industry analyst predicted that by the year 2000, 25 percent of those working in radio in 1992 would be out of the business.

The news is not all bad, however. Opportunities for women and members of ethnic minority groups have been increasing in radio in recent years. For example, in 1977 the percentage of women in radio jobs was 28, and ethnic minorities accounted for only 10 percent of employees. By 1990 almost 40 percent of the radio workforce was female, and the percentage of ethnic minorities had risen to 15. Today, the radio workforce is about 17 percent ethnic minority, and about 42 percent female.

Most of the new opportunities for ethnic minorities and women have occurred in sales and announcing positions. Today the majority of salespeople at many large stations are women. Whereas in 1985 black and Hispanic announcers were virtually unheard of (and unheard) outside of "ethnic" stations, radio today has an increasingly multiethnic and multicultural sound.

The FCC estimates that about 70,000 people work in the radio business. The majority work at commercial radio stations. Noncommercial radio employs about 4,000 people. The remainder of radio jobs are at corporate headquarters and networks.

Radio Salaries

Salaries in the radio business are largely a function of the size of the market. Overall, the average radio salary is low—only about $20,000 per year. In smaller markets most people, especially announcers, earn at or slightly above minimum wage. A salary of about $15,000 is typical for most small-market air personalities. However, in larger markets, top personalities—particularly the popular DJs in the lucrative early-morning time period—can earn seven-figure salaries. Table 4–3 compares radio salaries by occupation and size of the market.

In radio, the better-paying jobs are in sales. Account executives in large markets exceed $100,000 in annual income. The nationwide average is over $140,000 per year for radio sales managers in major markets. This trend is also apparent in smaller markets. For example, a small-market sales manager averages about $60,000 per year in earnings, nearly twice as much as the average salary for the program director. In fact, in some markets a successful sales manager might even make more than the GM.

Talent is still sought after and rewarded in radio. The morning personality in a large market will command more than $140,000 per year; a highly rated morning team can earn as much as a half-million.

Table 4–3	Radio Salaries					
	Market Size*					
	Large		**Medium**		**Small**	
Job Title	**1–5**	**6–25**	**26–50**	**51–75**	**76–90**	**91+**
General manager	$230,000	$130,000	$147,300	$88,400	$76,600	$87,260
Sales manager	150,750	110,500	86,800	65,400	62,300	58,600
Program director	141,800	79,000	70,100	47,300	42,500	N/A
Morning person	145,000	50,200	N/A	N/A	N/A	N/A
News director	54,400	39,000	35,400	29,000	34,400	24,100
Promotions director	57,200	40,700	37,200	24,500	25,900	29,250
Traffic director	41,300	30,260	28,000	25,800	24,400	23,600

*Based on population, as ranked by Arbitron.

Salaries are averages, based on questionnaire responses. N/A indicates too few responses to produce meaningful data.

Source: *Radio Ink*, October 12, 1998, p. 70.

SUMMARY

- Judging by the number of radio stations on the air and by the number of radios in homes, there is no doubt that the medium has survived the threat of TV. However, radio receives less than 7 percent of total advertising expenditures. This means that radio is arguably the most competitive of the electronic media businesses.

- Radio stations, once family-owned operations, now are merged into groups of stations owned by corporations. Fueled by relaxed ownership regulations, these corporations are leading the consolidation of the radio business. Duopolies allow a single owner to operate as many as eight stations in a single community.

- Because of intense competition, most stations have turned to format radio, targeting their programming toward specific factions of society. Some fear these trends are resulting in the franchising and depersonalization of the medium.

- Three kinds of noncommercial radio stations—community, college, and CPB-qualified—compete for audiences with their commercial counterparts. Affiliates of National Public Radio (NPR) are the most influential in this group, though they are subject to the uncertainty of federal funding, and face increasing technical, employment, and programming requirements.

- Most radio stations have four major departments: operations, programming, sales, and engineering. The GM is responsible for all of the executive decisions at a station.

- Radio consolidation has caused considerable shrinkage of the workforce. However, opportunities continue for women and minorities, and positions in sales, promotion, and programming can lead to lucrative careers in senior management.

KEY TERMS

competition   79
consolidation   79
control   79
Telecommunications Act of 1996   82
supergroup   82
lease management agreement   83

local market agreement (LMA)   83
target audience   84
format   85
fast rotation   87
community stations   90
college radio   91

public radio stations   91
operations   92
program department   92
sales department   92
director of development   92
engineering department   92

SUGGESTIONS FOR FURTHER READING

Adams, M., & Massey, K. (1995). *Introduction to radio: Production and programming.* Madison, WI: Brown & Benchmark.

DiTingo, V. (1995). *The remaking of radio.* Boston: Focal Press.

Engleman, R. (1996). *Public radio and television in America: A political history.* Thousand Oaks, CA: Sage.

Hausman, C., Benoit, P., & O'Donnell, L. (1996). *Modern radio production (4th ed.).* Belmont, CA: Wadsworth.

Keith, M. (1997). *The radio station (4th ed.).* Boston: Focal Press.

Laufer, P. (1995). *Inside talk radio.* Secaucus, NJ: Carol Publishing Group.

Looker, T. (1995). *The sound and the story: NPR and the art of radio.* Boston: Houghton Mifflin.

Lynch, J. (1998). *Process and practice of radio programming.* Lanham, MA: University Press of America.

MacFarland, D. (1997). *Future radio programming strategies (2nd ed.).* Mahwah, NJ: L. Erlbaum.

Norberg, E. (1996). *Radio programming: Tactics and strategy.* Boston: Focal Press.

INTERNET EXERCISES

1. Visit our Web site at http://www.mhhe.com/beyond for study-guide exercises to help you learn and apply material in each chapter. You will find ideas for future research as well as useful Web links to provide you with an opportunity to journey through the new electronic media.

5 Broadcast and Cable TV Today

Quick Facts

 Network share of audience (prime time) 1975: 90 percent

 Network share of audience (prime time) 1997: 47 percent

 Number of TV networks 1975: 3

 Number of TV networks, 1999: 7

 Percent of TV homes with cable: 67 (1999)

 Percent of TV homes with HBO: 30 (1999)

One word sums up the television industry today: transition. Traditional broadcast television is in transition, as TV stations spend millions of dollars to upgrade to digital high definition. Those stations once had three networks from which to choose their entertainment, news, and sports programming. Today, the original three (ABC, CBS, and NBC) are joined by Fox, the WB Network, UPN, and the newest network Pax TV. As if stations and networks did not have sufficient competition already, the viewing audience has discovered intriguing new options for their home leisure, including cable, home video, video games, and the newest of the "new media," the Internet. This chapter takes a brief look at the dynamics of television today, particularly the broadcast and cable businesses. The next chapter presents a snapshot of the new media, especially the World Wide Web.

TELEVISION NOW

Watching TV is one of America's favorite pastimes. More than 98 percent of the homes in America—nearly 100 million homes—have at least one TV. Of the homes with TV sets, 98 percent have a color set. Nearly three-fourths of the homes in the United States have more than one set. More than a decade ago the census reported that more American homes had TVs than indoor toilets; that disparity continues to grow.

According to the A. C. Nielsen ratings company, the average American home has the TV set on more than seven hours each day. Those viewers have a lot of choices. The typical TV household today receives 45 different channels of programming.

TYPES OF TELEVISION STATIONS

There are over 1,500 TV stations in operation today. The various types of stations are depicted in Figure 5–1.

Commercial and Noncommercial Stations

The stations depicted in Figure 5–1 can be divided into two categories: commercial and noncommercial. The primary distinction between the two is the way in which each type of station acquires the funds to stay on the air. Commercial stations—77 percent of the total number of TV stations—make their money by selling time on their stations to advertisers. Noncommercial stations are not allowed to sell advertis-

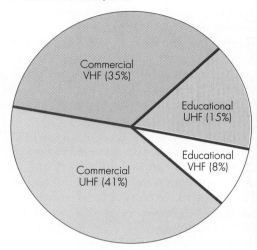

Figure 5–1

TV Stations on the Air, 1999

- Commercial VHF (35%)
- Educational UHF (15%)
- Educational VHF (8%)
- Commercial UHF (41%)

ing. These stations, which were set aside by the FCC for educational, civic, and religious groups, must adhere to the FCC mandate not to sell advertising time. They survive strictly through donations from individuals, businesses, and the government.

VHF and UHF Stations

Another way to categorize stations is by the channels on which they broadcast. Stations that broadcast on channels 2 to 13 are called **VHF,** or **very high frequency,** stations. Those stations that broadcast on channel 14 and above are called **UHF,** or **ultra-high frequency,** stations.

VHF frequencies have historically been the preferred channels for broadcasters. During the 1950s and most of the 1960s, TV sets often did not have the capability to receive UHF signals. The quality of the UHF signal was also judged to be inferior to that of a VHF signal.

Cable technology has erased many of the distinctions between VHF and UHF broadcasting. Cable TV provides the subscriber pictures of equal quality whether the station is VHF or UHF. Cable has also made selecting a UHF station as easy as selecting a VHF. On some cable systems UHF stations are reassigned to a VHF channel.

Figure 5–1 reveals that the most common type of TV station today (more than 650 stations, or 41 percent) is a commercial UHF facility. About 550 stations (35 percent) are commercial stations operating in the VHF band. There are nearly 250 noncommercial UHF facilities (15 percent) and about one-half that number of noncommercial VHF stations.

Of course, like the situation in radio today, the commercial stations do not share equally in TV revenues. And noncommercial TV faces the same problems of funding that public radio faces.

The broadcast TV business is actually two businesses in one. There is **network television,** a system in which ABC, CBS, NBC, and some newer networks develop program schedules for their affiliate stations. The networks sell most of the advertising in those programs (a process traced in detail in Chapter 7), which is how they make most of their money.

Then there is **local television** business, which revolves around scheduling programs and selling advertising in the many cities and towns in which TV stations can be found. Managers of these stations earn their revenue primarily through the sale of advertising in their community and their region.

Let's first take a look at the network TV business.

NETWORK TELEVISION

For many years the TV business (like the U.S. automobile business) was dominated by three giant companies. At the peak of their power in the 1960s and 1970s ABC, CBS, and NBC dominated the viewing habits of the nation. That dominance was especially acute in prime time: the evening hours during which the overwhelming majority of American households were watching TV. On the East Coast and in the far West, prime time ran from 7:00 P.M. to 11:00 P.M.; in the Midwest and certain parts of the Rocky Mountain region, prime time spanned 6:00 P.M. to 10:00 P.M.

At the height of their prime-time power the three major networks commanded more than 9 in 10 of all TV homes with the TV set on. With competition from new sources—most notably Fox, cable, and home video (see Chapter 2), the 1980s saw the beginning of a significant decline in the networks' audience share. For example, the three networks drew 91 percent of U.S. TV households in prime time in 1978. By 1986, their share had slipped to 75 percent. By 1992, the network share for ABC, CBS, and NBC had slipped to 60 percent. The 1997–98 TV season saw the lowest-ever ratings for the networks. Combined, ABC, CBS, and NBC attracted only 47 percent of TV households.

Fox Broadcasting Company

The Fox Broadcasting Company (FBC) was launched in 1986 by Australian media magnate Rupert Murdoch. Murdoch had purchased the former Metromedia stations and was interested in using his newly acquired TV studio (20th Century Fox) to produce programs for these stations. The decision was made to introduce programming slowly—first, one day of the week (Sunday), then gradually extending it throughout the week.

Today Fox network programming is available seven nights per week. Many successful shows now attract audiences and advertisers to Fox, including "Ally McBeal," "The Simpsons," and "King of the Hill."

New Networks

Motivated by the success of Fox and the revenue potential of the network TV business, two new players recently entered the game.

The United Paramount Network debuted in January of 1995, anchored by "Star Trek: Voyager," the latest installment of its science fiction franchise. Like Fox, UPN began with two evenings of programming, with plans to expand beyond prime time to other days and other day parts.

By 1999, UPN was broadcasting five nights per week. However, its ratings were low, compared with Fox and the "Big Three" networks. And, aside from an animated version of the comic strip "Dilbert," the network boasted few successful shows.

Another new network is WB, backed by multimedia conglomerate Time Warner. WB Network launched in 1995 with comedies at its core, including "Father Knows Nothing," and "Unhappily Ever After." If these programs seem suggestive of Fox series, perhaps this is because the WB Network was led at launch by two of Fox's founders: Jamie Kellner and Garth Ancier.

By the close of the 1990s, WB seemed to be outpacing UPN, propelled primarily by the success of two shows with huge followings (especially among teenagers)—"Buffy the Vampire Slayer," and "Dawson's Creek." However, neither network attracted more than 5 percent of the prime-time TV audience overall, and both reported to their shareholders that they were losing money. But that wasn't enough to keep another competitor from entering the fray.

Pax TV, founded by long-time TV station owner Lowell "Bud" Paxson, launched in the Fall of

A scene from the Peabody Award winning series, "Ally McBeal." "Ally" was often the top rated show on the Fox Network during the 1999–2000 season.

1998. Unlike the WB and UPN, which aggressively courted the teenage, inner-city crowd, Pax TV targeted older, more-conservative audiences (perhaps because Mr. Paxson was an evangelical Christian and proponent of "family values"). The anchor programs for Pax TV were reruns of the popular CBS shows "Dr. Quinn, Medicine Woman" and "Touched by an Angel." Early ratings for the new network were meeting its projections. That's the good news; the bad is that these projections called for only one in one hundred TV households (a rating of 1).

Issues: Portal Power: TV Networks and the Internet

One way that TV networks are planning for the future is by joining forces with Internet services. A key focus of these ventures is the portal—the gateway to the Internet provided by an especially popular Internet service or search engine. A number of "portal partnerships" have occurred in recent years, and more are expected.

In 1998, NBC joined forces with CNet's Snap service. That $38 million deal was followed by a $200 million strategic alliance between Disney/ABC and Infoseek. In 1999, CBS News aligned with America Online (AOL), TCI's @home cable Internet connection allied with the popular Excite service, Fox paired with search engine Yahoo!, and the USA Networks partnered with Lycos (including USA's Ticketmaster division), a merger with a combined asset value of more than $18 billion.

Is all this a precursor to the day when we'll watch the evening news or "ER" on the Internet? It's too early to tell. As those of us who surf the web know all too well, the Internet is still evolving. And early indications are that TV and the Web seem to differ in some important respects. A report in *Broadcasting & Cable* (February 15, 1999, pp. 73–74) found some interesting opinions on portal partnerships. Analyst Bill Bass of Forrester Research said, "Traditional media companies haven't done well on the Internet. In traditional media, what wins is content. What wins on the Internet is commerce." Another industry observer, Harold Vogel, put it another way. "Nobody knows how it will evolve. It's like bumper cars hitting each other and seeing where they can take this."

The End of Network Television?

With seven networks now competing for audiences (especially in prime time), and with growing attention paid by viewers to cable, home video, and the Internet, some observers have speculated that network television is a "dinosaur" business. Through the 1990s, audiences shrank, program costs rose, and advertising revenues were flat, at best. The result is that a TV network is no longer the steady source of corporate profits it used to be. For example, the combined revenue of ABC, CBS, NBC, and Fox was about $11 billion in 1997, with earnings of just under $400 million. The profit margin was a miserly 3.4 percent.

Will network TV go away? Unlikely. Even at their worst, network programs still attract larger audiences than do cable, the VCR, and the Internet. Think of the size of the audience for the Super Bowl—or for an episode of "Ally McBeal," or "Buffy," or "Friends." It's many times larger (usually by a factor of 10 or more) than the number of people watching wrestling on cable or reading their e-mail on AOL. But reducing costs as a way of maximizing revenue has become a way of life at the TV networks. Look for this trend to continue apace in the new millennium.

LOCAL TELEVISION

The major networks seem to get all the attention in the TV business, even though they account for only about a third of all the advertising revenue spent on the medium. This section looks at where the rest of the dollars go—to about 1,200 commercial TV stations.

Figure 5–2 rates the various types of TV stations in economic terms. The rankings range from "five-star" stations, which traditionally have been the most profitable, to "one-star" stations, which have faced considerable financial hardship and apathy among America's TV households.

Television's Cash Cows: Network Owned-and-Operated Stations

At the top of the rankings of commercial TV stations there are those that are owned outright by the corporate parents of the three established TV networks—ABC, CBS, and NBC. In industry parlance, these are owned-and-operated stations, or "O&Os," for short. These are the five-star stations in Figure 5–2.

Network O&Os have traditionally been the most profitable of all TV stations. Located primarily in the VHF band, O&Os are considered the flagship sta-

Figure 5–2

Rating the TV Stations

	VHF	UHF
Network O&Os	★★★★★	★★★★
"Big Four" network affiliates	★★★★	★★★
WB/UPN/Pax affiliates	★★★	★★
Independents	★	★
Low-power TV	½★	½★

tions of their networks. Situated in the largest TV markets, they often boast the call letters of their networks. In addition to owning NBC, General Electric is the parent of WNBC in New York and KNBC in Los Angeles, plus stations in Chicago, Denver, Miami, and Washington, D.C. Westinghouse/CBS owns WCBS in New York and KCBS in Los Angeles, as well as other stations in Minneapolis, Chicago, and Miami. Disney/ABC O&Os include WABC (New York), KABC (Los Angeles), plus additional TV stations in Chicago, San Francisco, Philadelphia, and Houston. Purchasing its own stations has been a cornerstone of the Fox strategy to achieve parity with the other major networks. It has invested hundreds of millions of dollars to purchase such stations as WNYW in New York, KTTV in Los Angeles, WTTG in Washington, and WFLD in Chicago.

Ownership by a major network guarantees a steady supply of programming to these stations and a high profile for potential advertisers. Owned-and-operated stations are typically local news leaders in their marketplace. The fact that they emanate from the corporate or regional headquarters of their networks permits economies of scale and access to programming and personalities that other stations can't match.

For these reasons network O&Os have traditionally been the most profitable of all TV stations. Annual profit margins above 50 percent have been commonplace. Even as the ratings of their parent networks decline, O&Os remain "cash cows" for their companies, returning, on average, more than 30 cents in profit for each dollar of sales.

Cash Calves? Major Network Affiliates

The second-most-profitable class of TV facilities are those affiliated with a major network. In industry parlance, such stations are network-affiliated stations, or **affiliates** for short. Traditionally, the best affiliation to have was with one of the three "old guard" networks, ABC, CBS, and NBC. Like O&Os, most of these affiliates have been leaders in local news and public service in their communities. Many have been in operation since the dawn of TV (the early 1950s), and over the years they have cultivated enormous goodwill among their viewers.

But the world of TV affiliation has changed dramatically in recent years. In 1994, for example, Fox invested $500 million in New World Communications, a group of 12 stations, 8 of which were long-time CBS affiliates. The terms of the deal included switching the affiliations, naturally, from CBS, NBC, and ABC to Fox, in such cities as Dallas, Detroit, Atlanta, Cleveland, Tampa, and St. Louis.

In the wake of this bombshell, viewers across the country were unsure where to find CBS shows, as they moved to new channels (including some highband UHF's). In response, CBS and the other traditional networks tried to shore up relationships with long-time allies to prevent further Fox defections. For example, CBS signed an unprecedented 10-year joint-venture agreement with Westinghouse to keep its programs on KPIX-TV in San Francisco and KDKA in Pittsburgh. As part of the deal, NBC affiliates WBZ (Boston) and KYW (Philadelphia) switched to CBS. The 10-year deal lasted only one: In 1995 Westinghouse acquired CBS.

Today, about 200 stations each are aligned with CBS, NBC, ABC, and Fox.

WB, UPN, and Pax Affiliates

Affiliates of these newer networks are next in our hierarchy of TV station profitability. Each new network launched in 1995 with about 100 affiliated stations. By the end of the decade, WB outpaced UPN in distribution, but each network boasted sufficient affiliates to reach more than 90 percent of America's TV homes. Pax TV launched in late 1998 with about 90 affiliates, covering about 75 percent of U.S. TV households. Its distribution was supplemented by deals with cable companies to carry Pax TV programs in areas without a broadcast affiliate.

In Figure 5–2, we grant three stars for operating revenue and ratings potential to VHF affiliates of these new networks; two to those that broadcast on the UHF band. Indeed, the overwhelming majority of WB, UPN, and Pax affiliates are located on the

higher band. But viewers will find their shows regardless of where they are, especially if they attract the kind of following that "Buffy," "Dawson's Creek," and other popular shows do.

Independents: A Vanishing Breed

An **independent TV station** is one that does not align itself with a major network. With seven networks from which to choose, independent TV stations appear to be a vanishing breed. When the last edition of this book went to press, some 100 stations were independent, relying on their libraries of movies, syndicated programs, and local professional sports to fill their program schedules. Today, fewer than 50 stations do not affiliate with either ABC, CBS, NBC, Fox, or one of the newer networks.

For this reason, we assign one star to independents. In major markets, an independent station (especially one on a lowband VHF frequency) can still be viable, particularly if it is the home of the broadcasts of local baseball, basketball, and/or hockey teams (provided the teams are playing and not out on strike, of course). However, in smaller markets, where the stations are likely to be located on highband UHF channels, remaining independents struggle for viewers and advertising support.

Low Power to the People: LPTV

A newer, relatively unknown force in TV are **low-power television (LPTV)** stations. The FCC authorized this new service in 1982 to create openings for minority ownership of TV stations and to increase the number of broadcast offerings in a community. To promote minority investing in these stations, the FCC promulgated rules that would show preference for minority applicants. In theory, lower-power TV would increase broadcast offerings to communities by increasing the number of TV stations that served those communities.

To restrict coverage to the community to which an LPTV station is licensed, the FCC placed limits on the power of LPTV stations. An LPTV station can transmit at 100 watts VHF and 1,000 watts UHF. Regular TV stations can be assigned transmitter powers 1,000 times more powerful than these. This low power (hence the name) limits the signal to a very small area. Some owners of LPTV stations are hoping that the FCC will change its rules from limiting the coverage by capping the broadcast power to limiting the coverage by barring interference: The station may operate as powerfully as it wishes so long as its signal does not interfere with that of another station on the same channel.

Today, about 500 LPTV stations are in operation. Located mainly in rural areas (Alaska has the most LPTV stations), LPTV has faced financial hardship to date. In most cases LPTV operations have been unable to compete with affiliates and full-power independents for attractive programming. Their limited broadcast range has made it difficult for LPTV to interest advertisers in the medium. This is why we place LPTV at the bottom of our rankings of TV stations, with only ½ star.

However, LPTV still holds promise as a venue for special-interest and minority programs. Spanish-language services like Univision and GEM align with LPTV stations. LPTV was given an additional boost by Congress in 1998, which exempted these stations from the mandated switch to HDTV imposed on full-power stations.

TV STATION OWNERSHIP

Generally, one wouldn't ask "who" owns a TV station, but rather would ask "what." Television stations are so expensive that few individuals can afford to own them. Instead, most TV stations are owned by companies that own other stations and networks, or by investment groups.

For many years, TV station ownership was strictly regulated, with the number of stations a group could own limited to 12, to prevent concentration. Recent years have seen significant streamlining of TV station ownership. Today, a single TV group can own as many TV stations as it likes, so long as the total number of U.S. TV homes reached by those stations does not exceed 35 percent. However, even that restriction may be relaxed to 50 percent or more in coming years.

The leading TV group owners are listed in Table 5–1.

Today, Fox is the largest station owner, with 23 stations reaching the cap of 35 percent of TV households. The leading Fox-owned stations include New York's WYNY, Los Angeles's KTTV, and Chicago's WFLD. Fox also owns stations in Philadelphia, Boston, Dallas, Atlanta, Houston, and even Greensboro, North Carolina, and Austin, Texas.

CBS is the second-biggest TV group, boasting 14 stations and roughly 31 percent coverage of U.S. TV

homes. With the exception of its station in Detroit, CBS's stations are all VHF. Most hold the coveted low dial position (Channel 2, 3, 4, or 5). Cash cows, indeed.

In contrast, Paxson Communications' fleet of 50 stations, the backbone of the Pax network, combined reach about 29 percent of TV households, making it the third-largest TV group. However, none of these stations has a dial position lower than 14 (WPXA in Atlanta). Most Pax-owned stations are in smaller cities, like Albany, New York; Fresno, California; Shreveport, Louisiana; and Cedar Rapids, Iowa.

Other leading TV group owners include Tribune, NBC, ABC, Gannett, A.H. Belo, Sinclair, and Cox. Each of these companies, and the others in Table 5–1, also hold other diversified media interests, including networks, newspapers, and cable systems.

PUBLIC TELEVISION

Not all TV stations are in it for the money (at least, not overtly). Some 400 TV stations are considered noncommercial operations. These stations, owned primarily by governmental organizations, universities and school boards, and religious organizations, form the backbone of an often-struggling but ongoing alternative to commercial TV, the public television service.

In 1999, the Public Broadcasting Service (PBS) celebrated its 30th anniversary. There was much to celebrate. At its launch, PBS provided programming to 128 stations and boasted a budget of $7 million. Today, PBS provides programming to more than 350 noncommercial stations serving the United States, Puerto Rico, the Virgin Islands, Guam, and Samoa. Nearly 98 million homes in the United States watch PBS in a typical week, including about 35 million children. The fiscal year 2000 budget for PBS was $300 million.

In some ways, PBS operates as commercial networks do. It provides a means of national distribution of programs (its satellite distribution network was operational in 1978, before those of NBC, CBS, and ABC). Its national programs attract large and loyal followings, from "Sesame Street" to "Nova" and "Masterpiece Theater." But PBS differs from the commercial networks in some important ways.

Public TV programs rarely match the ratings of those on commercial TV. In fact, the PBS audience is typically 2 percent of the homes in the United States. The highest-rated PBS series of all time, Ken Burns'

Table 5–1	TV's Top 25 Station Group Owners		
Rank	**Group Owner**	**Stations**	**Percent of TV Households**
1	Fox Television Stations, Inc.	23	35.3%
2	CBS Stations, Inc.	14	30.8
3	Paxson Communications Corp.	50	29.2
4	Tribune Broadcasting	20	27.6
5	NBC	13	26.6
6	ABC, Inc.	10	24.0
7	Chris Craft Television, Inc./United Television, Inc.	10	18.3
8	Gannett Broadcasting	21	16.3
9	Hearst-Argyle Television, Inc.	32	16.0
10	USA Broadcasting	13	15.4
11	A. H. Belo Corp.	20	14.2
12	Sinclair Broadcast Group, Inc.	56	13.8
13	Paramount Stations Group	19	13.6
14	Univision Communications, Inc.	12	13.4
15	Telemundo Group, Inc.	8	10.7
16	Cox Broadcasting	11	9.7
17	Young Broadcasting	13	9.0
18	E.W. Scripps Co.	10	8.1
19	Hicks Muse Tate & Furst	27	7.9
20	Post-Newsweek Stations, Inc.	6	7.2
21	Meredith Broadcasting Group	11	7.0
22	Raycom Media, Inc.	13	6.7
23	Media General	14	5.1
24	Clear Channel Communications	19	4.4
25	Granite Broadcasting	10	4.1

Source: *Broadcasting & Cable*, January 25, 1999, pp. 44–64.

"The Civil War," attracted an average of just under 9 percent of U.S. homes, a figure that would probably have led to its quick cancellation were it a series on ABC, CBS, or NBC.

However, while small in aggregate size, the audience for public TV is high in income, education, and influence. PBS viewers tend to be important opinion leaders in their communities. A high proportion have college and advanced degrees and hold key leadership positions in government, business, education, and the arts in their communities.

Surveys find that the viewing audience has come to rely on public television for some of its programs, particularly its news reports (especially the highly regarded nightly "NewsHour") and children's programs ("Sesame Street," "Reading Rainbow," and the like). That the public supports public television is borne out by the fact that viewers pledge nearly $500 million each year to local public TV stations.

Public television has been an early advocate of digital television. Indeed, in some large cities, the PBS stations were broadcasting in high definition before local commercial stations. In 1999, PBS promised a full schedule of children's programs in DTV for its member stations, including high-definition versions of "Barney," "Wishbone," and "Teletubbies." Thus, PBS, considered somewhat imperiled in the belt-tightening period of the late 1980s and early 1990s, seems secure, at least for the foreseeable future.

Ethics: Public TV for Sale? The Commercialization of PBS

Finding funding for public television has always been a struggle. In recent years, a more fiscally conservative Congress has questioned its investment in a TV service whose programs and personalities can occasionally be perceived as politically aligned with the opposition. In fact, former Speaker of the House, Newt Gingrich even went so far as to call for the elimination of federal support of public broadcasting. The hue and cry died down at just about the same time Newt resigned his speakership amidst the recent White House scandal.

Corporate underwriting for public television programs has similarly faced a decline. For one thing, large companies like General Motors, Texaco, Mobil, IBM, and others, have faced rounds of belt-tightening, mergers, and acquisitions. Support for the arts is often a frequent casualty of such events, under the banner of "downsizing." Like Congress, large corporations are not fond of funding programs they sometimes find are at cross-purposes with their lobbying activities or their corporate agendas. So, buying ads on commercial TV seems a safer alternative than funding public TV shows.

What is PBS to do? One answer has been to relax its underwriting guidelines, which have generally limited what (and how much) could be said to identify a program's sponsorship. For example, old rules allowed only a 30-second announcement of a show's underwriters, with a maximum of 15 seconds for a single corporation. Corporate spokespersons could not be used, and the announcements typically could not show corporate mascots or promote the attributes of the firm's products.

FCC underwriting rules have been relaxed in recent years. Today, public TV underwriting announcements are sounding more and more like regular commercial advertisements. Naturally, many commercial broadcasters are not amused. They point to the increasingly commercial nature of public TV, including the sale of videos, "Barney" dolls, and the successful merchandising of hundreds of "Sesame Street" items.

Even so, don't look for public TV underwriting to match the advertising revenue of commercial TV. As PBS President Ervin Duggan mentioned in a recent speech, "Corporations do not understand the waywardness and anarchy . . . that are at work in the (public television) system."

Apparently, some public TV managers have recognized one benefit of expanded underwriting. In Minneapolis and Dallas, a huge outcry was caused by revelations that the managers of the local public TV stations were making more money than their counterparts at commercial stations: as much as $350,000, including bonuses. Who said you can't get rich in noncommercial television?

CABLE TELEVISION

As we all know, there is a lot more TV that meets the eye than the amount that can be tuned in with a pair of rabbit-ear antennas atop the TV set. In fact, for most television viewers, the set-top or rooftop antenna has become a relic of the past. With its impressive roster of program services; its multiplicity of channels; and its promise of better pictures, better sound, and even Internet access and other services, cable TV today has become a strong competitor to the traditional TV networks and their affiliated stations.

Over the years, cable has grown in gross revenues, from a small adjunct to over-the-air broadcasting to a huge business in its own right. In 1980, for example, cable was a $3 billion business—about a fourth the size of the TV business. Today, cable revenues exceed $30 billion annually, placing the cable business revenues on a par with the total revenues of over-the-air TV.

Just a few years ago virtually all cable systems were 12-channel operations. Attaching the TV set to the cable generally filled most of the channels from 2 to 13. In the mid-1970s new cable systems offered 35 channels, requiring most TV homes to have a converter box. By the 1980s many older systems were upgraded and new franchises were awarded to companies providing 54 or more channels. New technologies like fiber optics and digital compression, enable some cable systems in the 1990s to boast well over 100 channels.

Nationwide, more than two-thirds of the nation's cable systems, representing three-fourths of all cable viewers, provide over 30 different channels of programming. Nearly one in two cable subscribers can view 54 or more cable channels.

Clearly cable provides more viewing alternatives. Whether more TV is *better* TV is an important question that we address in some detail in a later chapter.

Cable Programming

The cable business today is something like a shopping mall. There may be room for 100 retail stores in a new mall, but how many will actually sign a lease? Which stores will be most popular with shoppers, and thereby take the lion's share of the profits? While some stores will be "mass merchandisers," attempting to bring in lots of customers with discounting practices and volume sales, others will be specialty stores or boutiques, aiming at a narrowly selected clientele (like teens and young adults for Benetton and urban professional males for Brookstone). The same situation applies in the quest for cable audiences.

There are now well over 200 program services available to cable, with an additional 30 or more in the planning stages. Some are "mass marketers," like Sears or Macy's; others are boutiques, like Banana Republic or The Sharper Image, Ltd.

For convenience, cable programming today can be divided into three broad classifications: basic cable services, pay cable services, and specialty services. Let's examine each in detail.

Basic Cable Services   The backbone of cable is its lineup of basic services. These are the program services available for the lowest subscription charge. There are two main types of basic services: local and regional broadcast signals and advertiser-supported cable services.

From "must carry" to "retransmission consent": Local/regional broadcast signals   For years cable systems were obligated to provide space on their systems to retransmit local TV stations within their communities. Such rules, known as "must carry," were declared unconstitutional in 1985.

As a result, cable operators were able to retransmit the TV signals of stations in and near their communities without compensating those stations. Local broadcasters fought diligently in the ensuing years to receive some form of compensation for cable carriage of their services. In 1993, new regulations were implemented by the FCC to resolve this dispute. Broadcasters were instructed to choose either "must carry" or "retransmission consent." With a selection of must carry, the cable company was required to air the local TV station, but the station was not entitled to any form of compensation. Broadcasters choosing retransmission consent were required to negotiate

some form of compensation from the cable system in return for their signals' being carried on the cable.

In the wake of the new rules, the major networks and leading station groups generally made their stations available free to local cable operators. In return, as compensation, they were provided channel space on cable systems for new services, such as regional news channels (see Chapter 9).

The net effect of the rules is that most cable systems continue to carry the programming of most TV stations in their service area. Local and regional broadcast channels remain the backbone of basic cable programming.

Advertiser-supported basic cable services   The second classification of basic cable services is advertiser(ad)-supported cable networks, program services specifically designed to reach cable audiences. Like the broadcast networks (ABC, CBS, NBC, and Fox), they carry national advertising. They also provide opportunities for local cable systems to place their own advertising spots.

The leading ad-supported cable networks include three channels offered by Turner Broadcasting Systems: CNN, Headline News, and Turner Network Television (TNT); the Black Entertainment Network (BET); the Arts and Entertainment Network (A&E); the Nashville Network (TNN); Nickelodeon; the Weather Channel; and MTV. Some basic services are dedicated to women (Lifetime, Oxygen), and some to education (The Learning Channel). The Cable News and Business Channel (CNBC) caters to consumer and business news; the Courtroom Television Network provides extended coverage of crime and legal issues.

Pay Services   Pay services became popular in cable in the 1970s as a source of home viewing of theatrical motion pictures, major sports events, and entertainment specials. They are called pay services, since subscribers must pay an additional fee to receive the service. Their selling feature is original programming that is not available on broadcast TV, most typically commercial-free movies and home-team sports.

The giant of pay cable is Time Warner's Home Box Office. HBO boasts nearly 30 million households, just under one in three TV homes in the United States. Time Warner also owns Cinemax, present in about 15 million homes. Viacom's two services, Showtime and The Movie Channel, are chief competitors to HBO and Cinemax. Showtime serves

The crude but funny Kenny, Stan, and Kyle from Comedy Central's "South Park." Although the top-rated show on Comedy Central, "South Park" was typically seen in less than two percent of all U.S. homes.

about 15 million homes; The Movie Channel about 8 million. Other pay services with a movie emphasis include Encore and Starz, Movieplex, The Sundance Channel, Flix, and BET Movies.

Regional sports services represent a strong and growing segment of pay cable programming. Fox scion Rupert Murdoch has made a specialty in recent years of acquiring regional sports channels around the country (as well as owning teams, like the L.A. Dodgers and the Manchester United soccer club). Viewers can pay an extra fee each month to watch the exploits of their favorite teams on Fox Sports Arizona, Fox Sports Chicago, Fox Sports New York, Fox Sports Bay Area, Fox Sports Rocky Mountain, and more than a half dozen others. However, Fox hasn't bought them all (at least not yet). New York sports fans can subscribe to Cablevision's Madison Square Garden (MSG) network, and those in the Boston area can see their beloved Red Sox, Celtics, and Bruins on New England Sports Network (NESN).

Specialty Services   Some additional services available from cable include regional news channels, electronic program guides (EPGs), local governmental channels, juke-box-style music channels (like "The Box"), shopping channels, even a channel devoted to state lotteries (The Lottery Channel). And cable is scrambling to provide non-TV services in the new millennium, including Internet access and local telephone service. Still, as this book goes to press, most

people pick cable because of its television implications: more channels. Let's look at how the cable industry prices and packages its program offerings.

Packaging Cable Services: The Trail of "Tiers"

Cable is marketed to attract different types of customer households. The monthly charge for basic service has been regulated by the FCC, to keep cable affordable to most homes in the United States and to guarantee carriage of most popular services (including local broadcast services and some of the ad-supported basic services discussed above). These regulations were eliminated in 1999, amidst a loud outcry from consumer groups concerned about escalating cable rates.

While the majority of revenue to cable companies is provided by basic subscribers, profitability in the cable business is often based on the number of homes that upgrade to higher levels of service. To create different service levels, cable operators package their offerings in groups, with each succeeding level costing more per month. This process is known as **tiering.** Let's trace the trail of "tiers," from initial wiring of a home for cable to attracting the most lucrative cable households.

Types of Cable Households   In the cable business not all homes are created equal. Cable companies make clear distinctions between the types of households in

Figure 5–3

The Cable Subscriber Pyramid

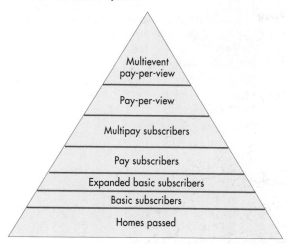

Total U.S. TV households

their service areas, on the basis of which program options they elect. The various types of TV homes in the United States can be viewed as a pyramid, as illustrated in Figure 5–3.

Homes passed   The base of the pyramid consists of those households in the United States that are in an area served by cable TV. This statistic is known as **homes passed (HP).** Homes passed are all households that could subscribe to a cable system if they wanted to. The cable literally passes by these households.

In real numbers, there are about 100 million homes with TV in the United States. About 97 million homes are located in an area served by cable, for an HP figure of about 97 percent.

Cable households   The next level of the pyramid are those HPs that decide to subscribe to cable TV. This figure can be calculated as the ratio of subscriber households to HPs. The resulting percentage is sometimes called the cable system's **basic penetration.** For example, if a cable system passes 100 homes and 85 take the cable, the basic penetration rate is 85 percent. Obviously, a cable operator would like all HPs to take cable service—that is, a penetration rate of 100 percent. This ideal world does not exist. The percentage of households that elect to subscribe varies widely in cable areas. Some suburban systems have enough "upscale" consumer house-

holds to boast over 90 percent basic penetration. Other systems, including many in poor inner-city and rural areas, report penetration rates below 50 percent. Industrywide, about two-thirds of HPs are cable subscribers, about 67 million homes.

Pay households   Those cable homes that pay an additional fee for the pay services listed earlier (such as HBO or Showtime) are known as **pay households.** Through the period of cable's massive growth—from the mid-1970s to the mid-1980s—as many as 90 percent of all cable subscribers also took a pay service. Faced with competition from new media outlets (mainly video stores), the percentage of pay units began to drop in the late 1990s. Today about 33 million homes have pay cable, representing about half of cable homes and one in three TV households in the United States.

Multipay households   There are two types of pay cable households: those that elect just one pay service and those that subscribe to more than one. The homes that take more than one service are known as **multipay households.**

Multipay subscribers pay the biggest cable bills—$75 per month or more—much of which is additional profit for the cable company, since it can negotiate reduced rates from pay services to "bundle" its program offerings and since pay tiers are not regulated by the FCC.

Pay-per-view   Near the top of the subscriber pyramid are those households that can choose their pay programming selectively by ordering it as desired from the cable company. This is known as **pay-per-view,** or **PPV.**

PPV requires special cable technology. Pay-per-view homes require cable boxes that can be isolated by the cable company and separately programmed (so that only the home that orders the event will receive it). Such devices are known as **addressable converters.** Addressable converters are available in about two-thirds of cable homes.

At the top of the cable pyramid is **multievent PPV,** also known as **impulse PPV.** As channel capacity increases and addressability spreads, cable executives expect consumers to buy on impulse, to purchase many different events each month on a PPV basis. This optimism is based on the great success of boxing matches, wrestling events, concerts, and other events offered on a PPV basis in recent years.

Cable Ownership

Cable TV is different from broadcasting in one important respect. Whereas there is a history of federal caps on the number of broadcast stations that can be owned by a single entity, no such limits have been imposed on cable ownership. In other words, a cable entrepreneur can own as many systems and boast as many subscribers as can be amassed, subject to antitrust law and a rarely enforced cap of 30 percent of national households. Consequently, the cable business is marked by a concentration of ownership by a large number of **multiple-system operators (MSOs).** Owners of only one system are known as **single-system operators (SSOs),** or simply **cable system operators (CSOs).** The MSOs dominate the business, as depicted in Table 5–2.

The largest cable MSO is Tele-Communications, Inc. (TCI) with nearly 12 million subscriber households. TCI announced its intention to merge with telephone giant AT&T in 1998, a union that is being completed as this book goes to press. The second-largest MSO is Time Warner Cable, a subsidiary of the entertainment giant, which also owns HBO and Cinemax. Time Warner's cable systems amount to nearly seven million homes. Together (including Time Warner subsidiary TWE-Advance/Newhouse, the fourth-largest MSO), TCI and Time Warner account for roughly 25 million subscriber households. This means that roughly one in three cable bills in the country is paid to one of these two huge companies. Other major MSOs include MediaOne, Comcast, Cox, Cablevision Systems (the owner of the MSG Network, as well as the New York Knicks and the New York Rangers), Adelphia, Jones Intercable, and Century.

The largest individual cable systems are located in major suburban areas, and range from about 250,000 to about a million subscriber households. The largest single system is Time Warner's operations in New York, which boasts more than a million homes. Other large single systems include Cablevision's on Long Island, New York; Time Warner's in Orlando; the Cox cable system in San Diego; and AT&T's (formerly TCI's) operations in Puget Sound, Pittsburgh, and Denver.

Cable Economics

Unfortunately, it is difficult to evaluate cable systems using a "five-star" rating system like we did for the various types of television stations. But some industry rules of thumb can apply.

Table 5–2	Top 25 Cable MSOs	
Rank	**Multiple-System Operator (MSO)**	**Subscription Households**
1	*AT&T Broadband Communications (Formerly TCI)	11,455,400
2	Time Warner Cable	6,577,500
3	MediaOne	5,102,948
4	Time Warner Entertainment-Advance/Newhouse	4,500,000
5	Comcast	3,894,572
6	Cox Communications	3,697,749
7	Cablevision Systems	3,347,975
8	Adelphia Communications	2,150,586
9	Jones Intercable	1,493,087
10	Century Communications	1,471,397
11	Falcon Communications	1,462,850
12	Charter Communications	1,329,224
13	InterMedia Partners	1,291,764
14	Lenfest Group	1,202,652
15	Marcus Cable	1,085,652
16	TCI/Time Warner	1,080,000
17	TCA Group	872,232
18	Cable One	727,620
19	FrontierVision Partners	635,712
20	Multimedia Cablevision	513,295
21	TW Fanch	456,900
22	Prime Cable	440,015
23	CalPERS/Comcast	435,028
24	CableVision Communications	387,091
25	Mediacom	367,075

*TCI was renamed AT&T Broadband Communications in mid-1999.

Source: *Cablevision,* January 25, 1999, p. 46.

With high up-front capitalization and operations costs, it might appear that making money in cable is difficult, if not impossible. But the truth is that cable can be an enormously profitable enterprise. After all, few businesses find subscribers writing a check to them every month, year after year, "just for TV." Add to this phenomenon the increase in revenues from advertising, the rise of PPV, and additional income from Internet and telephone services, and the result is a rosy outlook for cable economics.

Despite enormous construction costs, cable systems can come quickly to profitability. Once systems pass the construction phase, expenses tend to become controllable, if not constant. For example, adding a new household might bring in $25 per month in subscriber fees but might cost only $5 to wire and program. Simple arithmetic indicates a 500 percent profit margin!

For these reasons cable operations have received particularly glowing reports from financial analysts. The increasing value of cable systems is driven home by a key industry indicator: cost per subscriber. When a cable system is sold, cable investors and industry observers divide the sales price by the number of subscriber households to arrive at this figure. It is a good measure of how much a cable system is truly worth.

In 1977 the typical cable system sold for under $400 per subscriber. By 1980 the figure had risen to about $650. By 1985 cable systems were selling for over $1,000 per subscriber household. Today cable systems trade in the $2,000–$2,500 range! Few industries can match the pace of this economic growth.

WORKING IN TELEVISION

We close this chapter with a look at television stations and cable operations as places to work and build careers. First, we look at how television facilities are organized and staffed. Then, we take a look at salaries. In short, where are the jobs and how much do they pay?

TV Station Organization

The organizational structure of a TV station varies according to the size of the organization. There is no specific way in which all stations are organized, but there are some general areas common to most TV stations. Figure 5–4 presents a typical organizational structure for a station in a large community.

At the top of the organizational ladder is the general manager (GM), or station manager—two different names for the same job. This person is ultimately responsible for the operation of the station. If the station is part of a group of stations, the GM usually is a vice president in the parent organization.

TV stations are generally divided into five divisions, each division having its own head who reports directly to the station manager. The five areas are sales, engineering, business, programming, and news. Each of these areas is vital for the efficient operation of a TV station.

Sales   Sales is the most important part of the TV station—at least according to anyone in the sales department. This division of the TV station is headed by a general sales manager. It is her or his job to oversee the sales staff—both local and national. The salespeople for the station are called account executives or sales representatives.

The sales department is also in charge of **traffic** and **continuity.** Traffic is not the helicopter reports but that

A small satellite receiving dish. Many experts predict that direct satellite for home delivery of video signals will become a serious rival to cable.

Profile: Clash of the Titans: Ted Turner and Rupert Murdoch

As we've seen, the two most important executives of the radio era, William S. Paley and David Sarnoff, were fierce competitors who didn't like each other very much. Flash forward a generation. Two of the titans of television today are Ted Turner and Rupert Murdoch. Apparently they don't like each other either.

Both Turner and Murdoch began their careers by inheriting a modest media company. In 1952, Murdoch took the helm of the *Adelaide News,* a struggling daily in his native Australia. Through business acumen and aggressive acquisition strategies, by the late 1990s Murdoch had built a media empire worth more than $25 billion.

One key to Murdoch's success has been his unmatched ability to create media products with appeal to popular tastes. His tabloid newspapers, famous in Britain for photos of seminude women and the latest gossip about the peccadillos of government and public figures, have been very successful and much imitated. Perhaps the most famous headline in newspaper history appeared on page one of Murdoch's *New York Post:* "Headless Body in Topless Bar."

On the television side, Murdoch's Fox Network successfully challenged ABC, NBC, and CBS with a similar formula. "Beverly Hills 90210," "In Living Color," "Married with Children," and the Fox-produced "Inside Edition" all appealed, some say, to our baser instincts. And they attracted audiences the way Murdoch's newspapers gained readers.

Ted Turner took over his father's billboard advertising company in 1963. To diversify the company, he invested in the new business of independent television, acquiring the bankrupt Channel 17 in Atlanta and Channel 36 in Charlotte, North Carolina.

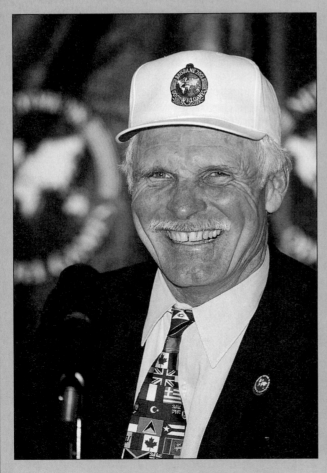

Ted filled the airtime on these new stations with sports, wrestling (almost a sport), and cheap reruns of old TV shows. In the mid-1970s, he partnered with another fledgling business—cable TV—to make Atlanta's channel 17 available to thousands of cable viewers throughout North America. By 1980, his idea for an all-news TV channel, Cable News Network, had become a reality. By the 1990s, Turner Broadcasting had grown into one of the most profitable, diversified entertainment conglomerates in the world. Turner merged his operations with Time Warner in 1996. Ted became vice chairman, and he was rich enough to announce a personal donation of $1 billion to the United Nations.

The conflict between Murdoch and Turner is greater than the corporate struggle for viewers between the various Fox and Turner networks (or parent News Corporation and Time Warner ventures). It seems personal. The clash came to a head recently in New York City. As might be expected, Time Warner was initially reluctant to make space on its cable system in New York for Fox News Channel, a competitor to its own CNN. New York mayor Rudy Giuliani intervened and threatened to put Fox News on its own municipal channel on the city's system. Some pointed out that the mayor's motives could be called into question since his wife was a reporter for WYNY, the TV station owned by Murdoch in New York. It didn't hurt that the mayor's conservative politics were more in line with Rupert Murdoch's than Ted Turner's (whose wife, Jane Fonda, was something of a legend among liberals for her stand during the Vietnam war).

During the imbroglio, Turner compared Murdoch to Adolf Hitler; Murdoch's *New York Post* questioned Turner's sanity in huge headline stories. The situation was resolved late in 1997, when Time Warner agreed to add Fox News to its channel lineup in New York and both organizations pledged to drop the numerous pending lawsuits. Still, don't expect to see Mr. Turner sitting in Mr. Murdoch's box at Dodger Stadium (now that the team is owned by News Corporation). Likewise, don't bother looking for Rupert in Ted's box at Turner Field, home of his (and Time Warner's) Atlanta Braves.

part of the station that schedules commercials and verifies that scheduled commercials are aired properly. Traffic departments are responsible for the program logs that tell the people in the control room when each video event is to occur. The continuity department makes sure the station's schedules have no interruptions between commercials and programs.

The verification that an advertisement was played is just as important as scheduling it. If the scheduled commercial doesn't air or only partially airs (say, because of an equipment malfunction) then the sponsor is entitled to a **make-good**—a free commercial in the same time category—to replace the commercial that didn't air. Make-goods are given in lieu of returning the advertiser's money.

Engineering   The second major division in a TV station is engineering. Engineering is the most important part of the TV station—just ask any engineer.

The engineering department is responsible for the maintenance of the equipment, including the transmitter. If there is an equipment failure, it is up to a member of the engineering department to find the problem and correct it.

In sufficiently large or unionized stations engineers run the audio/video equipment. People who load the video machines, edit, run the audio board, and push the buttons on the switchers are from the engineering department. Camera operators are also usually from this department. In smaller stations or nonunion shops there may be no hard-and-fast rules about who uses what equipment.

Business   The third area of the TV station is the business division. The business division is usually headed by the business manager. Most business managers feel that they run the most important division of the station. Accounts payable (money owed *by* the station) and accounts receivable (money owed *to* the station) are handled in this division. Everyone who is owed money *by* the station and everyone who owes money *to* the station has his or her paperwork go through this division. Receptionists and secretaries are also a part of the business division.

Programming   The fourth and, according to the people who work there, the most important area of a TV station is programming. The program director, often

Figure 5–4

The Organizational Structure for a TV Station

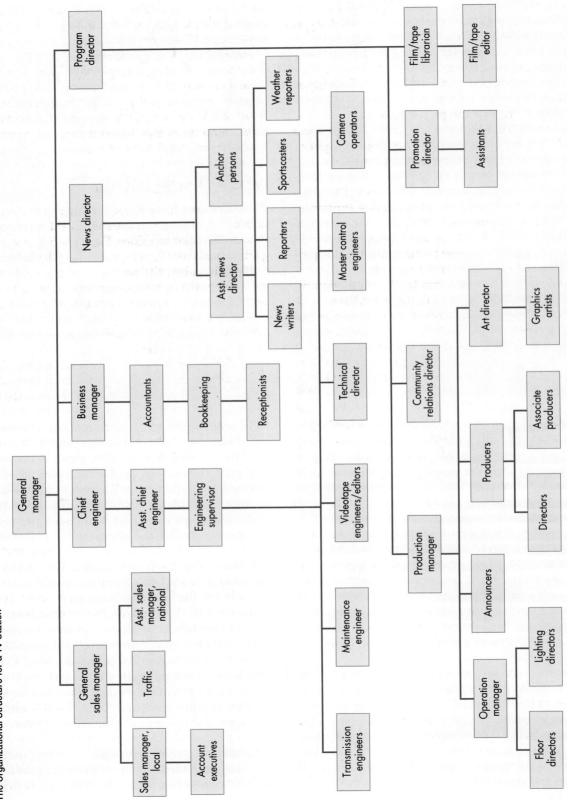

abbreviated PD, oversees a number of subdivisions and, in consultation with the station manager, is responsible for the purchase of all new programming for the station and the scheduling of the programming during the broadcast day.

Under the program director, three subdivisions can be identified at most stations. Usually the largest subdivision is run by the production manager, who oversees studio workers such as floor managers and lighting directors, art directors and videographers, producers, directors, and production assistants.

The second subdivision is headed by the community relations director and her or his staff. This division is usually in charge of public service announcements. The community relations director may also be in charge of TV programs examining minority interests at the station or may be the official spokesperson for the station at community events.

The third subdivision is run by the promotion director, who typically has three duties. First, the promotion director oversees the creation and placement of messages that promote programs, movies, specials, and the station's image. Second, she or he plans and runs activities designed to gain publicity—such as sponsoring a local charity road race. Third, the promotion director is responsible for the purchase of advertising in other media. This person is in charge of the commercial aspects of promoting the station, whereas the community relations director is usually seen as being in charge of the altruistic side of the station.

News   The fifth division is news, which, as any newsperson will tell you, is the most important part of the station. The news division is headed by the news director, who is in charge of the reporters, news writers, anchors, sportscasters, and weather forecasters. The news division of a station is supposed to operate independently of influences from the other divisions and so is separate from all other divisions. The smaller the station is, the harder it is to maintain this independence. As with the other division heads, the news director reports directly to the station manager.

News has a special place in broadcasting. Stations with active news departments become more important to—and are viewed more favorably by—the communities they serve. The overall quality of a station is often judged by how good its news department is. The value of a station during a sale can be affected by the reputation of the news department; a good news department is considered an asset to a station.

Departmental Evaluation   As indicated, each department thinks it is the most important department at the station. Which department is really the most important? Are the sales executives right that the station would close its doors if they were not finding sponsors? Are the programming and production people right when they argue that without them there would be nothing to sponsor? Or, do the engineers, who insist that without them there wouldn't be any signal, have the better claim?

Cable System Organization

Cable systems have a similar organizational structure to TV stations, but use slightly different names to denote the major functions. Figure 5–5 provides an organizational chart for a typical cable television system.

First, in cable, the manager of the cable system may be known as the general manager, as in broadcast TV, or as the system manager. At one time, these executives were called "sysops" (short for "system operator"). Today, that designation is more common to computer networks.

The technical side of the cable business is handled by the chief technician (**chief tech,** in cable parlance). Roughly equivalent to the chief engineer on the broadcast side, the chief tech supervises cable installation and maintenance and has the additional burden of coordinating and dispatching field crews to maintain and improve cable service throughout the system.

The sales function in cable includes advertising sales, but it also involves the important task of recruiting and retaining subscribers. Thus, the promotion function in cable is a bit broader than on the broadcast side. For this reason, cable promotion executives tend to be called **marketing managers** (rather than promotion directors). Similarly, office management requires more people than is common in broadcast TV. Cable systems often have more than one retail location, at which numerous **customer service representatives (CSRs)** process bills, hand out converters, and take complaints from subscribers.

Finally, the programming department in cable is slightly different from its counterpart in broadcast TV. In cable, the program director is the liaison between the various program services and the local system. Locally produced programs (such as home shopping and local call-in programs) typically fall under the aegis of the **local-origination** (or **LO) producer,** the rough equivalent of the community affairs director in broadcasting. Cable systems with full-fledged

Figure 5–5

Cable System Organizational Chart

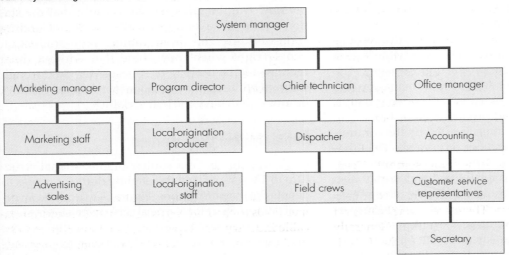

local news operations (see Chapter 9), may also boast a separate news director and production staff.

All told, however, cable systems and TV stations are staffed and managed in similar ways. Critical departments include general operations, programming, sales, and engineering.

THE JOB OUTLOOK

Before we look at the job picture for broadcast and cable television, some general observations can be made. The first line of this chapter stated that TV is an industry in transition. That means that the jobs (and salaries) described below are frequently changing—as are technology, ownership, programming, and distribution. So one kernel of good advice is to keep an open mind about your career choice. The job you seek today may not even exist when you graduate. If it does, it's apt to require a set of skills other than those you acquired in the classroom or on an internship.

A second thing is true about a career in television—whether broadcast or cable: Both are "cottage industries"—that is to say, despite the power and influence of their programming, the industries are in fact quite small. All told, the combined television workforce represents fewer than a quarter million people, including all employees of both commercial and nonprofit TV stations and networks, and of cable systems and headquarters. Like other small industries, a move up the career ladder

requires skill, dedication, and perseverance. Too, much like the popular game "six degrees of Kevin Bacon," you'll find it quite easy to find a link between your current employer or co-workers and other managers and employees from other stations, networks, or organizations. Thus, it is good advice to maintain positive relationships as you move along the career path and to not "burn bridges" by exhibiting the kind of workplace behaviors apt to catch up with you later on. As the old saying goes, it's not *what* you know, but *who* you know (and what they think of you as a co-worker or boss).

Finally, the trend toward industry concentration and automation traced throughout this text has had great impact on the media workforce. Generally speaking, there are fewer jobs in areas like production, and the power of trade associations, unions, and guilds has diminished. At the same time, the competition for audiences and from new media has led to job growth in other areas, like web site development, sales, marketing, and promotion. Workforce growth in the news area has also occurred, as more and more TV stations and cable systems look to TV news as a means of driving viewer interest and attention.

Broadcast TV Job Trends

About 80,000 people work in TV today—nearly 70,000 in commercial TV, with the remainder in public TV. The highest earnings tend to be in the north-eastern and northern states; the lowest are in the south. Salaries depend on a number of factors: the size of the community in which the station is located, whether the workers at the station are unionized, the dominance of a station in its market, and so on.

Sales executives are usually paid on a commission basis. To survive, they must sell time. If they are not good at selling time, they rarely make enough to live on and so move on to a different field. If they can sell, then TV can be very lucrative. There is always a strong demand for good salespeople in broadcasting, and TV is no exception.

Production crews and those who appear on the air are represented by unions at some stations. Organized, that is, unionized, stations almost without exception pay their employees better than nonunion stations in the same area. There are several different unions representing workers at a station. Generally performers are represented by AFTRA, the American Federation of Television and Radio Artists. Engineers and production people are usually represented by NABET, the National Association of Broadcast Engineers and Technicians; IATSE, the International Alliance of Theatre and Screen Employees; and/or IBEW, the International Brotherhood of Electrical Workers.

Unions usually represent the workers at contract renewal time, when management and union come to agreement on compensation and work responsibilities.

Reflecting national trends, unions have been in decline in TV. Whereas nationwide the number of employees belonging to a union was once as high as one in three, today fewer than one in six workers belong to a union. This trend has also been felt in TV, as the power of NABET, IATSE, and other organizations is much less today than it was in the 1960s and 1970s.

Pay in TV is largely determined by the size of the market one works in. Simply put, the larger the city, the more money you will earn. In addition, on average, VHF stations pay more than UHF stations, and network affiliates pay better than do independents. Commercial TV tends to pay better than public television, although public broadcasters tend to have higher job security than their counterparts at commercial stations.

As is true for most businesses, managers make the most money in TV. Nationwide, the typical GM earns over $50,000 per year, over $100,000 in the nation's top-50 TV markets. As in radio, sales managers make the most money. In fact, you would be hard-

pressed to find a sales executive in a top-10 TV market earning less than $150,000 per year.

Next to sales, salaries in the news department are the highest in TV. In the top-10 markets, anchors and reporters can earn six-figure salaries. The downside is that salaries slip significantly in smaller markets.

Engineering and programming positions, from the video editor to the camera operator, tend to provide steady employment at stable but lower salaries than high-profile sales and news jobs offer. There is less volatility from market to market in salaries and employee benefits.

Cable TV Job Trends

During the era of cable's great expansion, from the late 1970s to the mid-1980s, it was estimated that the cable industry was expanding by an average of 1,000 new jobs per month. This is an astonishingly high figure, particularly since this expansion coincided with an era of high national unemployment and a serious economic recession.

Cable employment slowed in the late 1980s and early 1990s, as most systems completed their construction, and many cable networks faced cost-cutting due to increasing competition. Today, the cable workforce is approaching 125,000. About 1 in 10 cable employees is found at network or MSO headquarters; the remainder at local cable systems around the country.

Whereas the size of the staff in a radio and TV station is usually based on the size of the station's home city, in cable, the number of employees is based on the number of subscriber households. That is, systems with more homes hire more people. This makes sense: large systems are more likely to sell advertising and to program their own channels. They also need more customer service representatives, installers, and technicians. A large system (more than 100,000 subscriber households) is about the size of a large TV station, with 75 or more full-time employees. Midsized systems (25,000 to 100,000 subscribers) are more like large radio stations, with 25 to 50 people on staff. Small cable systems (under 25,000 households) are run like small-market broadcast stations, both radio and TV, with fewer than 20 total employees.

Unlike broadcasting, cable is a decidedly blue-collar industry. Most jobs fall into the technical or office/clerical category. Technical jobs generally require training in fields like electronics and engineering.

Profile: A Breath of "Oxygen": Television Executive Geraldine Laybourne

By all accounts, Gerry Laybourne was headed along a traditional career path for women of her generation. After graduating from Vassar College and getting an M.S. degree in elementary education from the University of Pennsylvania, she began teaching school in the 1970s. Like millions of parents and teachers everywhere, she soon became dismayed at the prospect of competing with television for the attention of her students. And she began to wonder why so much TV programming for children was of such poor quality. How could more high-quality children's shows similar to PBS's "Sesame Street," and "Mr. Rogers" make it to TV? Would there be a market for such shows on a commercial network?

It wasn't long before Gerry Laybourne acted on her impulses. She joined the fledgling Nickelodeon network in 1980 and was named president of Nickelodeon and Nick at Nite in 1989. Under her leadership, Nickelodeon became the top-rated 24-hour cable network. It also won numerous Peabody, Emmy, and Parent's Choice Awards for its programming excellence. By 1995, Gerry Laybourne was vice chair of MTV networks, the parent of Nickelodeon. She left MTV Networks in 1996 for a brief stint as president of Disney/ABC Cable Networks, which included the Disney Channel.

In 1998, Gerry Laybourne linked up with two of the other "most powerful women in television," Oprah Winfrey and Marcie Carsey (of the Carsey-Werner-Mandabach TV production team responsible for such shows as "Cosby," "Roseanne," "Grace under Fire," and "Cybil"). Under the banner of Oxygen Media, the group announced a new 24-hour cable service, and a broad Internet presence, all targeted to the diverse needs and interests of America's women.

Oxygen was set to launch its cable service on December 31, 1999, with some 20 million cable homes. Its position on the Internet was bolstered by the purchase of three women-oriented sites on AOL, including Thrive, Moms Online, and Electra (and, of course, Oprah Online). With a commitment to original production, the library of Oprah Winfrey and Carsey-Werner-Mandabach programs, and a vital Web presence, Oxygen is expected to breathe new life into the world of women's media. Says Ms. Laybourne, "there's a lot of things we can do to help women. What this is all about is creating a brand that will help women manage their lives."

Cable recruits its technicians from trade schools, community college electronics programs, and vocational-technical (vo-tech) schools. Job applicants are also sought from related communications fields, including the telephone and data-processing industries.

Because of its history and tradition as a service business (and not "show business"), cable salaries have typically lagged behind those in broadcasting.

One reason for lower salaries and wages is the relative lack of union membership in the cable business. Whereas most telephone employees and many broadcast technicians belong to unions, less than 10 percent of the cable workforce is unionized. However, as cable operations become more profitable, they are also becoming more like broadcast stations.

As we have seen, many cable systems are actively seeking advertising dollars.

Nationwide, the typical general manager of a cable system earns about $60,000. Other high-paid positions in cable include treasurer or finance director ($65,000), human resources director ($55,000), program manager ($58,000), and marketing director ($52,000). Lower-paying positions include office manager ($32,000), vehicle and maintenance operator ($35,000), and technician ($28,000).

Women and Minorities in TV

Like many other industries in the United States, TV has been, historically, primarily a white, male-dominated

The job outlook in television has brightened, especially for women and minorities.

industry. Steps were taken in the late 1960s and early 1970s to begin to rectify the imbalance, but changes have been slow in coming.

Overall, women hold about 4 in 10 jobs in television today, and members of minority groups (including African Americans, Hispanic Americans, Asian Americans, and Native Americans) represent nearly 30 percent of TV employees. The good news is that those percentages have been on a slow and steady increase in recent years.

On the negative side, women still tend to find themselves in office positions. More than 87 percent of office and secretarial staffs remain female. Ethnic minorities tend to find themselves in technical and operations positions. However, gains for both women and members of minority groups have been seen in recent years in the more lucrative areas of sales and news. Today, more than half the broadcast sales workforce, and 45 percent of the cable sales force is female. On the news side, about one in two news anchors and reporters are women, reflecting the population. One in five TV newspersons is a member of a minority group. However, entry into management is another matter. Less than one in five TV news directors is a woman, and only 1 in 10 minorities heads a TV news department.

Like much of American industry, there remains a rather large gender gap. Men make more than women in both broadcast and cable TV. All told, women's salaries lag about 10 percent behind those for men in similar positions. Some good news for women is that they have tended to get larger pay increases than men in recent years. However, the gender gap remains real and persistent.

In 1998, the leading trade magazine, *Broadcasting & Cable,* noted that of the top 25 TV groups, none was headed by a woman or minority. No woman or minority sat atop any of the seven broadcast networks or a major cable programming company. Those trends were among the reasons that FCC Chairman William Kennard (himself an African American) was pushing hard to increase opportunities in television for female and nonwhite owners, operators, and employees.

SUMMARY

The popularity of television with American viewers has made it an important and highly profitable business. However, it is also a business in transition, facing new competition for viewers and from new technologies.

- More than 1,500 TV stations compete for audiences. Commercial stations earn their revenue primarily from advertising sales. Noncommercial stations rely on government funds, grants, and donations from viewers. Television stations are of two main types: VHF stations (channels 2–13), and UHF stations (channels 14 and above). VHF stations are generally more watched and more profitable.

- Network television is a segment of the TV business in which local TV stations agree to carry programs from a major network in return for monetary compensation and a share of their advertising slots. The network business was dominated for many years by ABC, CBS, and NBC. Newer networks are now on the scene, including Fox, UPN, WB, and Pax TV.

- The local television business relies on sales to local and regional advertisers. The most successful local TV stations are those owned and operated by a major network, or those owned and managed by a large-TV-station group owner. Weaker TV stations include independents and low-power operations. About 400 stations are public television operations. PBS provides programming to most of these stations, and its children's shows, news, and documentaries have attracted viewers and continuing government support.

- Cable television has grown in recent years to become an important component of the television landscape. Cable is in more than two-thirds of America's TV homes, and more than 200 different program services compete for space on the cable. The cable business makes its money by marketing and selling to different levels of customer homes. Revenues are enhanced by moving customers from basic service to pay, multipay, and new services, including Internet access and local telephone service. The cable business is dominated by large, multiple-system operators, most of whom also have ownership interest in cable programming services, telephone services, and broadcast TV services.

- Both broadcast and cable television facilities are organized into separate staffs, which typically include general management; programming; sales, marketing and promotion; and engineering. Job growth has been noted in the marketing and sales areas, as well as in local news, as cable systems and local TV stations aggressively court viewers faced with more and more options.

- In general, the best salaries are earned by employees of large TV stations and cable systems, and by employees in sales or general management. While opportunities for women and members of ethnic minority groups have risen in recent years, the television industry still lags behind other industries in employment and salary equity.

KEY TERMS

VHF; very high frequency   97
UHF; ultra-high frequency   97
network television   98
local television   98
affiliates   101
independent TV station   101
low-power television (LPTV)   101
tiering   106
homes passed (HP)   107
basic penetration   107

pay households   107
multipay households   107
pay-per-view (PPV)   107
addressable converters   107
multievent PPV   107
impulse PPV   107
multiple-system operators
    (MSOs)   108
single-system operators
    (SSOs)   108

cable system operators (CSOs)   108
traffic   111
continuity   111
make-good   111
chief tech   113
marketing managers   113
customer service
    representatives   113
local-origination (LO)
    producer   113

SUGGESTIONS FOR FURTHER READING

Auletta, K. (1991). *Three blind mice: How the TV networks lost their way.* New York: Random House.

Baldwin, T.F. and McVoy, D.S. (1988). *Cable Communications* (2nd ed.). Englewood Cliffs, NJ: Prentice-Hall.

Day, J. (1995). *The vanishing vision: The inside story of public television.* Berkeley, CA: University of California Press.

Ellis, E. (1998). *Opportunities in broadcasting careers.* Lincolnwood, IL: VGM Career Horizons.

Engleman, R. (1996). *Public radio & television in America: A political history.* Thousand Oaks, CA: Sage.

Johnson, L. (1994). *Toward competition in cable television.* Cambridge, MA: MIT Press.

Mogel, L. (1994). *Making it in broadcasting: An insider's guide to career opportunities.* New York: Collier.

Parsons, P., & Frieden, R. (1998) *The cable and satellite television industries.* Boston: Allyn and Bacon.

Sherman, B. (1995). *Telecommunications management* (2d ed.). New York: McGraw-Hill.

Sherman, B. (1999). *The television industry standard.* New York: Gerson-Lehrman.

Walker, J., & Ferguson, D. (1998). *The broadcast television industry.* Boston: Allyn & Bacon.

Waterman, D., & Weiss, A. (1997). *Vertical integration in cable television.* Cambridge, MA: MIT Press.

Weaver, D. (1998). *Breaking into television: Proven advice from veterans and interns.* Princeton, NJ: Peterson's.

INTERNET EXERCISES

1. Visit our Web site at http://www.mhhe.com/beyond for study-guide exercises to help you learn and apply material in each chapter. You will find ideas for future research as well as useful Web links to provide you with an opportunity to journey through the new electronic media.

6 The Internet and New Media Today

Quick Facts

 Projected number of Web users in the year 2002: 250 million

 Projected Internet e-commerce sales in the year 2001: $6 billion

 Time it takes to download a 5 MB file at 28.8Kbps: 23 minutes

 Number of Americans who had used the Internet in 1998: 70 million

 Percentage of Americans who say they've listened to radio on the Internet: 13 percent (1998)

 Percent of Web users who think online news sources are less credible than television or cable news sources: 20 percent

INTRODUCTION

It is clear from the content of the previous chapter that the television industry today can be summed up with one word: *transition.* The language of the Internet is quite different from that of traditional broadcasting—*Gateways, routers, ISPs, portals, push technology, Java,* and domain names—and the unfamiliarity of the language suggests that new media are really quite different from traditional electronic media. The history of information services reinforces this notion. The development of the Internet occurred among people with specific interests, such as computer hobbyists, businesspeople, and scientists. Discussions on early bulletin boards often centered on computers and software usage. These services weren't anything at all like the mass media. But now the Internet is evolving rapidly, and it seems to be changing into a mass medium. Broadcasting and cable networks all have Web sites. There are sites streaming video and radio stations broadcasting live. The media presence on the World Wide Web is important and growing. This chapter takes a look at the new media, who's on the "information superhighway," and how choices are made about which lane to travel. Not to worry, though, you won't need a degree in computer science to follow this road map.

In the Beginning Was the Word: Teletext

The Internet's growth has been nothing short of phenomenal. Some of the pioneering information-based services available to the general public started first in Europe with the use of television signals or the telephone system. In America, large American newspaper publishers, trying to come to grips with the new electronic communication systems, also experimented with various kinds of information services to determine whether there was a consumer market for purchasing information. These first systems were called **teletext.**

Britain pioneered an early teletext system called CEEFAX, a one-way system that sent data to your home TV by encoding information within the television signal. Although the system could display large amounts of data, it was slow and had limited graphics capability. It never caught on in the United States.

Toward the end of the 1970s, U.S. newspaper giants Knight-Ridder and Times-Mirror spent millions of dollars trying to develop **videotex,** an information service designed to serve as electronic newspapers. Some of these early services were based on essentially the same television technology as teletext, but they accessed the information via the telephone. Videotex also had limited graphics capabilities. These early experiments did not generate much interest among test-market users either, and the services lost millions of dollars for the companies. By 1982, most American newspapers had scrapped the idea of making money off of one-way, text-only newspapers displayed on television screens.

Minitel

The French telephone company introduced Minitel, a **videotext** system that connected special terminals to the telephone. Unlike CEEFAX and other one-way information systems, videotext systems are completely **interactive.** French Telecom gave terminals to customers in lieu of providing a printed telephone directory. There were few offerings other than the telephone directory, and service was slow. But then Minitel service offerings began to grow. People who had telephone service were potential users, so there was a ready-made

Ceefax

BBC Television Centre
Wood Lane,
London W12 7RJ
Telex: 265781

**News & general
enquiries:**
01-743 8000
Ext. 3701 or 3703

Sport & Finance:
01-580 4468
Ext. 2880

**Engineering
Information:**
01-580 4468
Ext. 2921

market for service providers and no real competition from private information networks. During the first years of operation, the government heavily subsidized the service.

As people began using the system, the number of services on Minitel grew rapidly. Escort services, interestingly, were soon available in large numbers, but, before long, other businesses began seeing opportunities. Today, Minitel offers a wide gamut of services—for example, banking, e-mail, and ordering take-out food for home delivery. Since Minitel is really an extension of the phone, its ubiquity makes it an enticing service for millions of French, but it was not the same technology as the Internet.

Hometown America Gets Wired—Slowly

CEEFAX and Minitel may seem unfamiliar to you, but AOL and Prodigy are probably not. Here's a point we need to make: Commercial development of information services has been somewhat different in America than throughout the rest of the world. While many foreign governments tried to promote growth of their information and computer industries—such as CEEFAX in Britain and Minitel in France, most communication innovations in America have tended to be the efforts of private entrepreneurs. Even though the U.S. government (in 1969) built ARPANET, the original communications network, this network generally limited access to government, educational, scientific, and military personnel. It was entrepreneurs who used that technology to start up and build the first information services to serve businesses and the home consumer in the United States.

In 1978, William Von Meister, a telecommunications entrepreneur, envisioned a "home information utility" linked by computers. He started a computer bulletin board service called The Source. Meister's brainchild became the first home computer network, but he quickly ran into financial trouble. Publishing giant Reader's Digest decided it couldn't ignore this potential area, and two years later it bailed out Meister in a $6 million takeover.

In 1980, Compuserve, another pioneering information service, came online, joining The Source in the role of nationwide private information providers. H&R Block, the tax preparation firm, started Compuserve with the intention of linking tax services with information services. While that aspect of the business never caught on, Compuserve maintained its business focus by providing in-depth discussion areas related to business, commerce, and technology.

When IBM entered the home computer market in 1981, the world's largest computer company legitimized the new personal computer for business. At that point Commodore, Apple, IBM, and other companies made personal computers in a wide range of prices for consumers to purchase. Unfortunately, customers weren't ready to embrace information providers without reservations.

New Markets: Prodigy and America Online

Prodigy soon joined The Source and Compuserve in 1985. Sears, Roebuck and IBM, Prodigy's owners, conceptualized their services differently from other **computer bulletin boards.** For one thing, Prodigy's monthly subscription price was fixed as opposed to charging the customer by the minute. However, the real difference was how the service was conceived; Prodigy was designed to serve as an online magazine. With flat-fee pricing, unlimited access, and e-mail all at one low price, the service looked like a real bargain to many customers. And Prodigy didn't just download information from wire services; it provided unique content specifically geared toward its users, much the same way a magazine would. When the service started, Prodigy began a multimillion-dollar promotional campaign for subscribers, and it quickly became a household name.

Prodigy distinguished itself from other services by offering users an exciting new graphical interface, albeit with rather crude graphics. As in magazines, advertisements would be tied to the specific content on the text page. Prodigy hoped that subscribers would be enticed by the prominent advertising to request additional screens of product information. Since Sears was a part owner of the venture, it also hoped to replace its aging catalog shopping service with a modern online shopping network. This idea of a separate revenue, in addition to the flat monthly access fee, transformed the notion of the online service provider from a bulletin board to a content provider/editor.

Also in 1985, a small startup company, Quantum Computer Services, began offering information services specifically geared to the tastes and interests of the average American consumer. Quantum provided a user-friendly log-on screen, with point-and-click menu options specifically geared toward Commodore computer gamers. Quantum officially became America Online in 1989, and to broaden its appeal it offered special areas within its service for Macintosh, Apple II, and IBM machine owners. AOL also saw discussion or chat rooms as an important way of distinguishing itself from Prodigy. Rather than making discussion forums ancillary to other services, AOL put them out in front.

Despite offering services with a broad appeal, America Online did not meet with immediate acceptance. Four years after beginning national operation, America Online was looking like an also-ran, with only 200,000 subscribers while both Prodigy and Compuserve had over a million.

Internet service providers (ISPs) did not become overnight sensations in the United States. They met with opposition from many home computer owners and with varying degrees of acceptance from others for a number of reasons. Access numbers were limited mostly to large urban areas. Thus, if you lived outside that calling area, you needed to make a long-distance call to get a connection. With the per-minute telephone charge and modem speeds of only 300 and 1,200 baud per second, these services were much too slow to download any significant computer databases or visual images. These factors tended to keep the majority of people from using information services frequently.

Several events, however, changed the telecommunications marketplace as the 1980s came to a close, and the fortunes of AOL, Compuserve, and Prodigy were about to change dramatically. First, the growth of competition in the long-distance telephone business increased dramatically after the breakup of AT&T. As a result, by 1990 the cost of long-distance calling began to decline by nearly 50 percent compared with 1985 long-distance rates. Users who lived in suburban areas saw the price of their usage drop, and that meant that the costs associated with dialing into a network declined as well.

At the same time a new generation of computers emerged. Black-and-white or amber screens were replaced with color displays. Users became more interested in using graphics and images with their computers. Finally, slower modems were replaced by new ones that made networking much faster. These factors, coupled with the introduction of Microsoft's graphical interface (Windows) made online services much more attractive to the average user.

America Online and Prodigy took advantage of innovations in the hardware. They embarked on high visibility advertising campaigns to encourage people to try their services. Compuserve consolidated with The Source and introduced a graphical interface in an attempt to compete for the new generation of users. AOL sent out millions of trial software packages in the mail and included them in magazines, hoping to entice people to connect for a trial period. Millions of Americans signed up. But while America Online's customer base exploded, technological change was going to force all of these companies to alter their business plans dramatically.

ISPs Grow, Business Plans Fail

Recall that ARPANET had demonstrated in 1969 that networked computers could be made to share complex information; by 1988, more than 100,000 host computers were interconnected into a huge network called the Internet.

The growth in the number of users connected to the Internet spurred tremendous innovation in computer networking services. In 1989, both Compuserve and MCI provided gateways making it possible to e-mail to locations around the globe. E-mail could now move between different commercial providers through the Internet. Other important network search tools were introduced in quick succession between 1989 and 1992. But it was Tim Berners-Lee's development of the **World Wide Web** and the introduction of the Mosaic browser in 1993 that spurred the growth of local Internet service providers. Suddenly, it seemed that overnight the general population began talking about the new communications revolution. Small Internet service providers (ISPs) sprang up in cities like neighborhood convenience stores. Frequently these ISPs offered easy, unlimited access to the Internet and e-mail, and the necessary software for accessing net services tools for a set monthly fee.

The sudden growth of the Internet challenged AOL, Prodigy, and Compuserve in two areas (1) retaining current customers and (2) the attraction of new users. In fact, while the different services were originally conceptualized on the idea of providing unique services to specific users, over time they had become much more like one another. Many customers who began comparing services and prices realized that they could get standard Internet services from a local ISP oftentimes for less money. **Churn,** customer turnover, became a problem for national services.

Newspapers and magazines were beginning to experiment by putting sections online. Since ISPs were frequently local or regional, there were no more long-distance charges and fewer repeated busy signals. In comparison, AOL, Prodigy, and Compuserve provided its customers with many useful and unique services but initially gave them very limited access to the World Wide Web. For example, AOL customers who wanted to use the World Wide Web found that America Online's system didn't work well with Netscape. Some people began predicting the demise of AOL and Compuserve, claiming that customers would leave these services once they became sophisticated Web users.

The Growth of the World Wide Web and What Came After

The phrase "Surfing the Net," coined by Jean Armour Polly, sums it all up. The relative ease of searching for information and the ability to link from one page to another halfway around the world put incredible power into the hands of the user. The World Wide Web became a "killer application"; something that convinced many people that they should buy personal computers.

In 1993, Mosaic became the first browser for personal computers, but there were only about 50 locations around the world with Web pages running. That changed quickly. During that year alone, the number of Web pages grew 340,000 percent, and while that sounds too incredible to be true, it really does make sense. There were only a few sites initially running Web pages in 1993, but there were nearly two million computer hosts already attached to the Internet and each one of those sites had the capability of becoming a Web site immediately. The only thing a site administrator needed to do was to set up an index page in the **HyperText Markup Language (HTML).** Once content pages were linked to that index, a new Web site was born. Fairly soon after the release of Mosaic, many universities started experimentally displaying pages with this new form of hypertext media. The large publishing companies also started sites immediately. The Web spread quickly.

By the fall of 1994, there were more than three million Internet host sites connected worldwide. Network Solutions, the company charged with the task of registering Internet domain names (such as McDonalds.com and ESPN.com), was registering new names at a rate of 2,000 per month. (The network was also now 400 times faster than the original system.) Within two years the number of Internet hosts tripled again to nearly nine million. (See Figure 6–1.)

The introduction of the World Wide Web and the tripling of the size of the Internet within a 24-month

Figure 6–1

Internet Growth 1993–1996

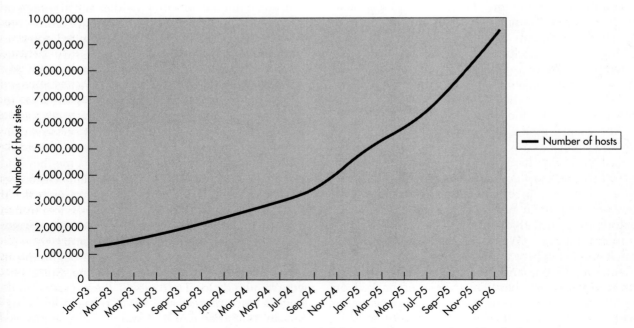

Source: Matthew Gray www.mit.edu/people/mkgray/net/intrnet-growth-raw-data.html

period encouraged a frenetic rush to get into the information business. Innovations both at the user and corporate levels changed the Web very quickly. Online publications blossomed, personal web pages started popping up everywhere, college professors put their syllabi on the Internet for students to access, cooks posted their favorite recipes, and Web soap operas started up—as did thousands of different small enterprises directly related to a new concept called "e-commerce." Few people made any money except those sites that charged a fee for the titillating views of sex that they offered.

As with any great new invention, new industries are created to support previously unrealized needs. Now that information was being added to the World Wide Web quickly, usable **search engines** became very important. Large search engines such as HotBot, AltaVista, and Excite send "Web crawlers" around the net during off-peak hours of the night cataloging pages. These search companies then index the pages based on a scan of the keywords contained within. In turn, these companies make money by placing advertising banners at the top and bottom of the search pages and by forming partnering relationships with online e-commerce sites.

Founder and chief executive officer of America Online, Steve Case got into the computer business by delivering Atari games to personal computer owners.

The growth of the Internet has elicited all kinds of speculation about what the net will look like in the next millennium. The current growth of the Internet shows no sign of slowing down. Perhaps more important to note, however, is that fact that the fastest growth taking place is now outside the United States. The Global Internet Project predicts that there will be 120 million computers connected to the Web, with over 250 million users, by 2002. Forecasts for Internet commerce are equally impressive. Jupiter Communications, a research company that specializes in Internet research, predicts that e-commerce sales will reach $6 billion by 2001. In order to put that figure into perspective we need to remember that Internet revenues were only $550 million in 1997.

There are several aspects of network usage and development that are likely to continue to grow for the next few years. In the next section, we'll examine some of the current and projected uses of the Internet.

INTERNET BASICS

The Internet is cyberspace; there's no one place where it resides. It would be difficult to imagine one person having to manage a piece of real estate as big as the Internet. But, that's the point. The Internet is not REAL estate. It's not owned or managed by any one person, or government, or company. A number of different groups have the responsibility for coordinating the Internet and setting specifications to make it work. Among the different groups charged with managing cyberspace is the Internet Society, a not-for-profit organization that helps to promote global connectivity. Membership to the Internet Society is open to anyone. The Internet Society sponsors a number of important working groups such as the Internet Engineering Task Force. This group focuses on setting technical standards to ensure that as new technology and software are developed they will be compatible with the network.

Several other organizations play important roles in making the Internet work efficiently. Internet Operators' Providers Services (IOPS) group was formed by the large network service providers such as AT&T, Sprint, and MCI to handle network congestion while Network Solutions was given the task of registering Internet names for organizations that want to have a unique address on the Internet. Tim Berners-Lee, the inventor of the Web, heads up the **World Wide Web Consortium (W3C)**, which is run jointly by the MIT Laboratory for Computer Science, the National

Profile: Steve Case, Bob Pittman, and AOL: Branding the Internet

Stephen McConnell Case, the man behind AOL, admits that he didn't even like his computer course in college. But those who know Case are not surprised that his determination fueled America Online's long climb into the enviable position as the world's largest Internet service provider. What was surprising is that it happened at all.

Alvin Toffler's book *The Third Wave* talked about the potential for an electronically linked community; it made a lasting impression on Case. So, after college and a series of middle-level jobs, when Case found himself (at 25) frustrated by the bureaucracy in corporate America, he left his day job to work with William Von Meister, the founder of The Source. Meister's new venture, Control Video Corporation, allowed people to download games into home computers. The service Playnet was launched in 1983, almost exactly when the game market crashed in the mid-eighties. Things didn't go well.

Soon, CVC was restructured into Quantum Computer Services. Investors ousted Meister and chose Case to start Q-link, an online game/chat service. Tight money, tiny offices in suburban Washington, D.C., and long hours characterized the time. On the first night of service, Q-Link logged on 24 users until the system crashed. By 1985, Quantum had 10,000 users, but profits were tiny.

Quantum Computers and Case wandered through a series of business deals over the next few years. None of them made the company a fortune. Deals with Apple, Commodore, and Tandy didn't provide the hoped-for profits. With fewer than 75,000 customers nationwide, and no strong national brand name, Case decided it was time to give Quantum a name that would provide instant recognition. He adopted the name America Online in 1989 because of the potential for brand recognition that the three letters AOL provided.

Perhaps one of the characteristics needed for success is the determination to follow a strong vision. For the next three years, AOL just struggled along. There was no World Wide Web and online was not an exciting place to be, but Case still clung to the idea of an online community that had formed years earlier. To fulfill that vision, the company needed to go public and raise cash; however, Case found that investors thought he was too young to execute his vision. Jim Kimsey, another Quantum holdover, replaced him as chief executive officer. Despite losing his title to grey-haired Kimsey, Steve Case chose to remain and became a millionaire overnight when AOL first traded publicly in 1992.

Though tiny compared with Prodigy and Compuserve, America Online pioneered a lively, easy-to-use service that was completely different from other online companies. AOL's point-and-click startup was truly easy to install, and it didn't have the annoying banner advertisements. It looked like AOL was really on to something, but rags-to-riches stories are always filled with plot twists and turns of events that prove the fortitude of the hero. The story of AOL and Steve Case's success is no different. Paul Allen and Bill Gates, Microsoft founders, both became interested in buying the company. AOL was at a crossroads. Many of the original investors wanted to sell out, but Case and many of the employees were opposed to that idea. They had come this far, why not push the envelope? Fending off a hostile takeover, Case emerged as AOL's chief, and his vision was to grow AOL very big, very fast.

Institute for Research in Computer Science and Automation in France, and Keio University in Japan. Together these organizations provide the guidance necessary for the network to grow and expand.

Standards and Protocols

While Internet standards and protocols are decided upon by the various organizations we discussed, no single organization has control or say as to how the network can be used or what can be sent over the network. A commercial user providing online shopping has as much right to use the Web as a public library or a government agency. Individuals have the same rights, too. The question of knowing where and to whom to send a message or where to locate specific information on the Web is resolved by giving a unique address to each site. If your computer is connected to an Internet Service Provider (ISP) or network, you are part of the Internet. When you type

Stephen McConnell Case is a bit of a paradox. He's described by employees and associates as introverted, observant, and self-contained. Yet, at the same time, Case preaches the online gospel like no other. Both of these characteristics served him well. His no-nonsense, quiet style allowed him to make quick business decisions, while his showmanship in selling the virtues of online services is unmatched.

AOL went through a period of incredible growth. Between 1994 and 1996, subscribers increased from 900,000 to 6.2 million, but as the system grew more and more complex, its frailty began to show. The problems came to a head in 1996 when AOL suffered a 19-hour blackout. The system failure brought many problems to light, but it also pointed out that millions of Americans now relied on electronic communication. Showing a picture of Steve Case, a *New York Post* headline screamed: CHAOS@AOL.COM! When AOL started offering unlimited service at the end of 1996 to counter this negative image, the online service encountered a huge increase in traffic. With AOL's phone lines jammed in early 1997, however, New York's Attorney General sued AOL for oversubscribing the service. At one point, tens of thousands of frustrated AOL customers e-mailed Case personally to complain. His e-mail account crashed. Though Steve Case had become the poster boy of the new millennium, the picture was not flattering. Something needed to change.

Bob Pittman had been in the cable network business. Pittman was always impeccably dressed and had an easy, confident style. At Warner Brothers he oversaw the launch of MTV and five other networks. They became cable powerhouses. When Pittman came to AOL at the height of the crisis in 1996, some people wondered why. Robert Warren Pittman gave up a $1 million salary to take half that amount at AOL. The company seemed besieged by troubled service and troubling financial problems. Though Pittman was charismatic and charming, he was also a tough-minded, strong leader. Many within the company began to worry that Case would be out; perhaps their own jobs were in jeopardy too. This concern proved unnecessary.

Pittman knew how to analyze the market, and in early 1997 he realized that, despite the problems it faced, AOL was the *only* brand name in Internet service. He also noticed that AOL users watched less television than the average American. Pittman knew what to do. AOL had developed a number of strong "program" channels, attractive sites where people shared common interests. Pittman started to use these channels like television, he sold advertising on them. He brought in new content. Amazon.com, Barnes and Noble, and 1-800 Flowers began to advertise, while companies like CBS agreed to become paying tenants of the various channels. AOL quickly outpaced the competition as subscriptions jumped above nine million. Soon after, AOL bought long-time rival Compuserve. In 1998, AOL scooped up Netscape Communications in a $3.8 billion takeover. Netscape helps AOL position itself for the fast growing e-commerce segment of the Internet market.

So, why did Pittman take a huge pay cut to take on AOL problems? Perhaps it was the challenge. In the face of speculation that Microsoft would bury AOL—or that the Web would make AOL an unnecessary service, Case and Pittman provided the leadership to make AOL succeed, and America Online survived to emerge as the Web's first portal. Today AOL's familiar "You've got mail" has become synonymous with logging on to the Internet for nearly three out of every five Web users. And, Pittman got a cool $40 million in stock valuation for convincing Wall Street and the world that Steve Case was right, an electronic community *could* change the world.

an address or link to a Web page, a request for information is made through the ISP gateway to the specific server housing the requested information. A router computer keeps tabs and sends the information packets to the correct destinations.

A **Universal Resource Locator (URL)** provides the key to retrieving the correct information and then getting it delivered to the requester's address. Each URL is hierarchical, designating a specific protocol (such as *www* for World Wide Web or *FTP* for file transfer protocol). Next is a secondary **domain name** and then a primary domain name. Secondary domains are usually the company or institutional name (such as McDonald's or IBM). Top-level domains such as .com (pronounced "dot com") in the United States help to provide a unique address or destination. Outside of the United States, the top-level domain names also reflect a geographical region of the world. Messages emanating out of Great Britain have a .uk domain while .ca indicates a domain in Canada.

Old and New Domains

In the United States the following top-level domains were established initially:

.com (originally for businesses, but now anyone can register dot com)

.edu (for educational institutions)

.net (for organizations directly related to networking)

.org (for organizations, including nonprofit organizations)

.mil (for the U.S. military)

.gov (for federal government sites)

These top-level domains also provide a context for the site that we access or send messages to. Dot com (.com) is usually a commercial establishment, while dot edu (.edu) is an educational institution. As more and more people begin to use the Internet, companies are putting their secondary and primary domains in their television or radio advertising. It's quite common now to see *www. honda.com*, for example, in the bottom portion of the television screen within a Honda commercial.

When Internet fever struck, most organizations set out to get their own domains. As a result, the list of available domain names is dwindling. In 1997, the organizations that oversee the Internet approved seven more top-level domain names:

.arts (for cultural and entertainment entities)

.firm (for businesses or firms)

.info (for information services)

.nom (for private individuals)

.rec (for recreation and entertainment)

.store (for businesses offering goods to purchase)

.web (for entities related to the World Wide Web)

E-mail and Browsers

The most popular services on the Internet are e-mail and the World Wide Web. There are many different e-mail packages that offer various levels of flexibility, but there are only two main browsers used for the World Wide Web. Netscape Navigator and Microsoft Explorer are the most popular commercial applications that run on today's personal computers. Currently Microsoft's Explorer seems to be winning the browser wars, with approximately 60 percent of all Web users having a version installed on their computer hard drives. Netscape Navigator claims almost all of the rest of the market.

Browsers allow us to communicate with various public Web sites anywhere in the world by interpreting and displaying the contents of an HTML (HyperText Markup Language) document. Both Netscape Navigator and Internet Explorer follow a set of standards about what can be displayed on screen. The protocols or standards are defined by the World Wide Web Consortium (W3C). These standards are constantly evolving too. As protocols for HTML become more refined, the capability of browsers to provide higher levels of functionality for the user will increase. However, as smart as browsers are, they are mostly just fancy text-reading programs.

Plug-ins

An HTML page may contain, in addition to text, many different types of files that can display unique

Microsoft's Internet Explorer and Netscape Communicator—The two leading web browsers.

graphics, photographs, or even animations. The trick is to get your browser to correctly identify the file type and start up the appropriate "plug-in" application to deal with the file. Plug-in software is downloaded from home-page sites for the browsers or from third-party software companies, usually for free.

Audio, video, and interactive applications can also be displayed on your browser page with the plug-in helper applications. For example, Quicktime, an application that allows the playback of video movies, starts up when the browser senses an .mpeg (motion picture expert group) suffix tag at the end of a file. Similarly, a program such as Real Audio begins to run when the browser encounters a .ram file suffix, assuming that your browser has the needed plug-in stored in the necessary folder on the hard drive.

Newer versions of multimedia plug-ins such as Quicktime allow your computer to display "streaming" audio or video. That means the file will start playing before the file has been fully downloaded. At times, there may be a delay in the downloading of a mediated file and you may see a "rebuffering" message. This happens when the network gets jammed with Internet traffic. At times it can seem to jam up easily.

Plug-ins extend the capabilities of browsers beyond video. Shockwave, from Macromedia, and Java, from Sun Microsystems, provide for interactive experiences by creating subprograms that run in the background of the browser environment. Both of these programs are being used at game sites to allow the computer to load and display interactive graphics and audio quickly and seamlessly.

Pulling an Elephant through a Straw— Downloading the New Media

Almost as soon as the World Wide Web came into existence, entertainment and information executives began looking for ways to use the new medium to deliver content and to charge the user for it (of course). In 1995, big newspapers put up sites, then television and cable networks started sites. Some Internet service providers such as Prodigy tried publishing "hip" **webzines** (online magazines) hoping to lure demographically attractive web surfers. These first innovative experiments were not commercially successful. Text-based sites such as Time Warner's SPY didn't do well. Online soap operas failed too.

Modem connection speeds in 1995 were much slower than they are today. As a result, the "wait period" or download time for mediate entertainment material was just too long for most people. The president of Prodigy, Ed Bennett, who had spent years involved in electronic media as head of VH-1, was quoted once as saying that "downloading music and video on the Web was like pulling an elephant through a straw."

Long download times still discourage many people from using the multimedia capabilities of the World Wide Web. This is changing, but it will take some time before most home users will have instantaneous downloading capability. The Web's backbone speed and capability continues to grow, and overall the speed of the Internet has dramatically increased over the last five years. In addition, home modems have increased in speed. Many new computers have 56k modems built in, and cable modems have improved the ability to download files even more dramatically. Some businesses and homes have faster **Integrated Services Digital Network (ISDN)** connections or Ethernet connections. Both of these services are faster than home modem connections. But, downloading a large file can still be a chore. Here's a comparison of times for downloading two minutes of MPEG video (about a 5 MB file):

Modem Speed	Approximate Time
14.4 kps modem	45 minutes
28.8 kps modem	23 minutes
56 kps modem	12.5 minutes
128 kps (ISDN line)	5 minutes
10 Mbs (cable modem)	12 seconds

Even though streaming video helps reduce the wait because the clip starts playing soon after some of the file loads, this clip will only be a small window within your browser's display area. Cable ISPs such as Roadrunner and @Home point out that it is possible to download video clips quickly using cable access technology. But, even with high-speed cable connections, it will be some time before we're able to get a large enough data stream into the home to display a 30-minute broadcast quality video over a home Internet connection.

Portals

When surfing the World Wide Web, a user needs to start someplace. As the browser opens, it goes to a designated "home" location. Frequently when software comes preloaded on a computer, it will be set to

Events: Students Took Control of the Web

In 1994, Jerry Yang and David Filo, two graduate students at Stanford were doing what students all over the world do when faced with a seemingly impossible amount of work to finish. They were goofing off! Both of these students were several months away from finishing their dissertations in engineering. Instead of studying, they were spending most of their time surfing the new World Wide Web. In 1993, Web sites began springing up all over. Yang and Filo took notice and began to keep track, listing them in a hierarchical order. Working out of their trailer, they spent days—then weeks—indexing. To speed the process along they wrote a software program to locate, identify, and index the various sites. As the Web began to grow bigger, their list began to grow quickly.

Those in the know say that if Yang and Filo had started two years earlier it would have been a silly exercise, but two years later major competitors were playing catch-up. So, Yahoo! started just at the right time. Along the way they were assisted by Marc Andreesen, founder of Netscape Communications, who as a graduate assistant created the Web browser. The rest, as they say, is history, but the history of student upstarts would be incomplete if we stopped here. Undergraduates contributed to the development of the Web, too.

Also in 1994, at the other end of the country in Ithaca, New York, Todd Krizelman and Stephan Paternot came up with a fairly simple idea while surfing the Web in their dorm room at Cornell University. Why not create a one-stop Web site that would intertwine personal interaction with information and news of the day? The two undergraduates ran with the idea. With $15,000 they managed to raise from friends and family, theglobe.com was launched. Krizelman and Paternot marched down to the student union and hired their first employees, paying them with pizza slices. Three years later when Michael Egan, the former owner of Alamo Rent-A-Car, invested $20 million in the company, it became the largest individual investment ever made in a new media company.

Today both Yahoo! and theglobe.com are worth hundreds of millions of dollars in this new media environment where it seems that a good idea and your portal's name on the World Wide Web may be your most important corporate assets.

go to the computer manufacturer's home page. Subscribers who join an ISP such as America Online, will find the company's home page loads into the computer automatically. After a bit of use, some people change their home pages because they find a preferred location, but research suggests that many people stay with the same browser and home site that came loaded with their computer. Search engine sites (e.g., altavista.com), news sites (e.g., cnn.com), and other sites that have a full range of search/ news/ chat/shopping options (e.g., theglobe.com) frequently are chosen by users as their default browser page. These all-in-one starting places are called portals.

Portal is defined as an entrance or doorway. It's one of the many new words that has entered the Internet lexicon. **Portals** are becoming increasingly important to the Web. Here's why: You could think of a portal as a starting place for people to begin their cyberjourney. When the Web was introduced to the general public in 1994, people surfed around in this experimental medium. However, even within its short history, the World Wide Web has become vast and very sophisticated. With tens of millions of pages on the Web, how does one know where to begin? Therefore the notion of beginning a cyberjourney at a comprehensive starting place that offers good suggestions for where to start is increasingly important as the size and breadth of the World Wide Web grows.

Yahoo!, one of the largest portals, is a very popular destination for news, entertainment, and shopping. Portals serve a number of functions at once. They provide a means of searching for information, but they also may provide e-mail, shopping, directory services, and reference materials as well. Another important function of the portal is to provide a way for users to get links and recommendations about other Web sites they could visit. This function allows portal managers to recommend other businesses with whom they have established business relationships. Finally, one vital aspect of having a successful site is that it is able to attract advertisers who want to reach a large number of eyeballs to view their Web announcements.

Rank	Top 10 Digital Media/Web Properties	Unique Visitors (000s)
1	AOL Network	37,956
2	Microsoft Sites	30,130
3	Yahoo! Sites	29,495
4	Lycos	28,513
5	Go Network	22,771
6	Geocities	19,257
7	The Excite Network	18,225
8	Netscape	18,001
9	Time-Warner Online	12,180
10	AltaVista Search Services	11,237

Source: MediaMetrics Web site **www.MediaMetrics.com,** January 1999.

Communities

Another popular model for the Web is the **virtual community.** A virtual community is a place where people can congregate, chat, and share ideas. In some ways, America Online is the ultimate community, giving millions of members access to specific channels of information and chat. These member services are separated from the free services available to all on their Web pages. In order to access them, you need to be an AOL subscriber. Delphi is another example of an online community. Delphi offers groups the opportunity to establish either public and private discussion forums without special software or browser plug-ins. Anyone can start a discussion group, and while the services are free, products and services advertisements are integrated into the services offered.

Geocities.com is a different virtual community, offering a range of services where individuals can build their own free Web sites and use e-mail. Three million people use Geocities as their virtual home. After defining an area of interest, such as art or music, pop culture or technology, a Web page is placed within a "neighborhood" housing people with similar interests. E-mail is free to Geocities homesteaders. Similarly, Tripod.com divides its community into 14 broad categories such as money and business, sports, travel, and the like. These sites give away a piece of virtual real estate (an oxymoron), and they offer advertisers the ability to place ads in the specific communities of interest. Theglobe.com is yet another portal community. Each of these sites has unique features available to its members.

The Bottom Line

At the moment there are a few ways to make money on the Web. A company can sell connections to the Web as an Internet service provider. It can sell space and sponsorships for ads on its Web site, or it can sell goods via a catalog or auction. Of course, a company could offer any combination of these services. While most analysts are convinced that the Web will become a lucrative form of media eventually, it is still in a formative stage.

Revenues from the Internet are growing. Internet advertising revenue reached $1.5 billion in 1998. It is expected to surpass $2 billion in 1999. While these figures are very small compared with television and cable's advertising revenues, they represent a substantial growth in Web advertising from only a few million dollars in 1995.

Sales and Growth Rates for Major Search Engines 1997

Company	Primary Source of Revenue	Sales (1997)	Growth over 1996 (%)
Yahoo!	Advertising based	203.3 million	201%
Lycos	Advertising based	55.1 million	152
Excite	Advertising based	50.2 million	239
Infoseek	Advertising based	34.6 million	129

Source: Hoover.com.

Despite this growth, at the beginning of 1999, few media sites on the Web have made money from their Web content. That's not unusual for startup businesses, especially in new technology areas. Traditional media companies have had some difficulty in duplicating their standard advertising business model, that is, charging advertisers who use their electronic channel to reach viewers. For example, ABC.com can't show a 30-second commercial on its web page. Banners are just not the same.

Several different kinds of companies viewed the Internet as a gold mine for generating revenue. Some have made money, others have not. Compuserve and The Source charged users on a per-hour basis. Prodigy thought that users would pay a monthly subscriber fee that could be supplemented by advertising and online sales. Overall, these plans have not worked out. America Online wanted to get a large number of monthly subscribers to access their content and use their chat rooms. Small Internet service providers (ISPs) wanted to charge a per-hour connect fee to generate revenue, but many switched over to a flat fee under increasing competitive pressures. The high cost of network expansion, development of the World Wide Web, and the growing competition from companies such as Microsoft Network and ATT Worldnet made it difficult for ISPs to make substantial profits. Many have consolidated or been driven out of business. Only AOL realized that it was going to have to become larger and diversify into new areas to increase revenue.

Search engine companies are looking for business models to follow. Yahoo!, Excite, Infoseek, and other Web crawlers began experimenting with banner advertisements at the top or bottom of the search results pages in 1995. Banner ads were tied to the search request. Based on the keyword from the user, a related banner is displayed. For example, a person searching for information on cars could pull up a banner linking you to a Ford site. Banners are potential revenue streams for these companies, but few companies have shown both substantial profits and the likelihood of long-term growth based solely on banner revenues. All the different search engines have an inventory of unsold space. The solution seems to be to branch out into new revenue areas. Today, companies have determined that a commerce-based model, perhaps in conjunction with advertising, holds promise for the future.

One of the real paradoxes of the new media and the information revolution is that now that all this information is available, people may be suffering from trying to interpret too much information on small computer screens. The information revolution has arrived and many people claim that they are inundated with too much information. No doubt the way people surf the Web and use the various services available to them needs to be focused clearly. This conundrum has not been lost on Internet companies.

OWNERSHIP AND ALLIANCES

The World Wide Web is becoming a household commodity. As with household commodities, brand names play a prominent role in choosing products and services. There are a number of companies that have already established themselves as brands customers recognize; portals such as AOL, Yahoo!, Microsoft, Netscape, and Excite have established themselves as recognizable Internet brands.

Portals are forging relationships with content providers to make their offerings more attractive to visitors. By providing strong online content with page sponsorship, portals are hoping to increase their revenues. These companies also realize that cross-promotion is essential to ensure that people will visit the Web site. For example, Yahoo! developed a partnership with Fox Broadcasting in 1999. This means that Fox now has the potential of benefiting from increased visibility to all the people who use Yahoo! as their entry to the World Wide Web. In return, the Yahoo! brand name gets advertised on Fox television and cable programming. Business interrelationships such as this one have the potential for developing **synergy** in many cross-promotional schemes.

Media companies are counting on Web users to continue to visit the larger portal sites. Research on Web usage illustrates a fairly high degree of repeat visitations to portal sites. As 1999 began, a spate of mergers between large media companies, Internet service providers, and portals occurred. For example, Netscape was purchased by AOL, suggesting that AOL wanted to bolster its web presence for non-AOL customers and gain access to Netscape browser and server technology at the same time. And, At Home, AT&T's high-speed Internet cable service, combined with search engine Excite. Similarly, a proposed merger between Lycos and USA Networks and the Home Shopping Channel would have created a linkage between a portal site and home shopping.

MEDIA: NEW AND OLD

A Neilsen Media Research study concluded that one out of every three Americans, some 70 million people, had used the Internet by the end of 1998. That figure represents a 25 percent increase in just nine months. Further, it is predicted that one out of three American homes will have Internet connections by the end of 1999. Some communications historians like to remind us that the pace of innovation for the World Wide Web is similar to that of other electronic media. For instance, it took about eight years for radio to find a place in 50 percent of all American homes. So if you think of 1994 as the first year an Internet browser was widely available, the World Wide Web went from zero to 33 percent penetration in just four years. At this rate, the Web will equal or beat radio's 50 percent penetration mark well before the year 2002, the eight-year mark.

Technological advancements have made it easy to transmit high-quality graphics and photographic images over the Internet. Applications such as Shockwave can provide interactive functionality within the browser environment. New, faster Internet backbone connections will greatly increase network speed. It seems that all the disparate elements of the Internet are coming together to make the World Wide Web a unified presentation system, called the new media.

The World Wide Web and Electronic Media

Consider how the Internet could change our expectations about what broadcasting and cable services should be. Program producers can coordinate programming both on television and on their Web sites. There is the potential to use the Web as a secondary platform to move viewers from one medium (TV/cable) to another (the Web) and vice versa.

Obviously cross-promotion is already taking place. Did you miss "ER" this week? If you're the producer of "ER" you'll want to encourage the audience to visit the Web site. Give visitors a quick plot summary, include one or two small streaming video segments that highlight the episode, and encourage viewers to come back to the show next time. Right? Yes, but there's much more than simple cross-promotion activities.

Producers of "Dawson's Creek" hope viewers will follow the show's plot line interactively. "Dawson's Creek" can run separate story threads that only appear online. The Web site is designed to look like Dawson Leery's computer desktop with icons that give viewers access to his e-mail, chat, text documents, and favorite Web sites. Text documents and chat are updated daily by one of the show's staff writers. After watching the show, viewers can log on to the Web site and find out what the characters think about the events in the TV story line. Product sponsorship takes on a new role, too. Rather than just using banners for advertising, product information and links are integrated directly into the desktop. Dep, one of the show's sponsors, has product demonstrations and hair-styling consultations available online.

The potential to link services on the World Wide Web to either television or radio is common now. If you want more information on a story you've seen on CNN, you can go to CNN.com. More information is immediately available. Cross-promotion appears to be effective. For example, SNAP.com site traffic increased a whopping 200 percent after NBC began on-air promos for the service. Similarly, Web users expect services that they can't get on traditional media. For example, radio listeners who miss a segment of NPR's "All Things Considered" can go to the NPR Web site to download the segment they missed. Some people believe that synergy between traditional electronic media and the Web will make it possible to transfer viewers or listeners from a broadcast medium to the Web and vice versa. In doing so, producers keep audiences looking or listening to their product longer.

The World Wide Web is much more than a means of interlocking promotions between broadcast media and the Internet. New concepts in coordinated marketing and programming will develop rapidly in the next few years. The Web is a very powerful secondary brand outlet, but it may also entice new advertisers who have not been using radio or television. More important, the Web's growth rate worldwide shows no sign of letting up. This blue-sky growth gives producers the opportunity to expand to new audiences beyond their current geographical boundaries. In this global market, the new European Union and the North American Free Trade Agreement have taken on greater importance and the Web is an international marketing tool. This section of the chapter focuses on the Web and its relationship to existing electronic media.

Radio: AM, FM, and the Web

Over the last 80 years radio has survived the introduction of numerous forms of competition by constantly evolving and changing. Radio lost network stars and its biggest shows to television in the 1950s, leaving it to find specific niches to fill; along came Top 40 radio. Elaborate car stereos, cassettes, and compact disc walkmans provided alternative ways for people to hear high-quality music on the go; talk radio grew. Radio consolidated and changed again. Will the growth of the Internet radio and other new technology media such as direct satellite broadcasting create another challenge for radio? Absolutely!

It's an old comedy routine: There's good news and bad news. First the bad news: Online users appear to be listening to over-the-air radio less. Studies of more than 1,300 online users completed at the end of 1998 suggest new trends in the way people use media. According to Arbitron, Internet users reportedly spend 13 percent less time listening to the radio. As more Americans go online, radio's listenership is likely to drop even more.

Does this signal the end of radio? We doubt it, but the research does show a fair bit of dissatisfaction among current listeners of over-the-air radio. For example, one out of six listeners polled say that radio doesn't play the music they want. And, the number of people who indicate they listened to Internet radio doubled in 1998, up from 6 percent to 13 percent. While this represents only a small percentage of Americans, that number will grow rapidly as Internet penetration grows and the technology improves. Net listenership appears to be doubling every year. There's substantial room for growth in the Internet radio segment.

Now for the good news: Listeners say they want more from radio's Web sites. Those polled say they want the Web to be another avenue for programming. Stations could program several different formats on the Web. Local Web sites could publish updated concert information, merge promotional activities with other local online sites, and provide a feedback line or dedication line. In fact, the Web gives radio many new capabilities the audio medium lacks by itself.

People who currently listen to Web radio are likely to listen to stations outside of their market area now. An oldies station in Washington, D.C., may now compete with a local oldies station in upstate New York or many different oldies stations all across America. The potential reach of an Internet station extends beyond the physical over-the-air coverage area in Washington, D.C.

Internet Radio doesn't need to rely upon an over-the-air signal to penetrate thick building walls. Webcasting just needs a computer hooked to the net; so, Internet radio could build listenership during key dayparts when office listenership is traditionally low. But, what radio programming will be like both on and off the Web in the year 2005 and beyond is anyone's guess.

Changing the Face of Broadcast News

Technological Changes   First, Americans turned to radio for breaking news. Then, with ENG equipment and satellite news gathering, television started broadcasting breaking news. Then CNN came along. Now news is changing again. Michael Silberman, the executive editor of MSNBC, says that online news services are as likely to be the first choice for breaking news. In fact, in 1999, MSNBC.com had a larger daily viewership than either MSNBC or CNN television. Silberman says he's bullish about the Web's future.

New standards for encoding Internet video such as MPEG-4 are being developed now. Coupled with high-speed access, these new technologies will enhance the distribution of quality pictures and sound over the Internet, which, in turn, will have a staggering impact on news coverage. The cost of collecting and distributing new stories will decline. Once producers have the opportunity to send high-quality pictures over the Web, breaking news coverage will be extended to any place in the world with access to a high-quality Internet connection. Distance will no longer be a barrier. No need to worry about a satellite uplink, and the costs associated with using satellites will evaporate. Local television news crews will become potential sources in the new global media environment. Producers and editors could choose from many more variations of stories. The immediacy of news and the increased choice of pictures could cloud our news judgment or alternatively increase our perspective in an increasingly shrinking world.

A Recent Example of the Change in News   As 1998 started, few Americans knew of Matt Drudge. Published from a small apartment just off Hollywood Boulevard in Los Angeles, *The Drudge Report*, (http://www.drudgereport.com/) broke the details of an investigation into allegations that President William Jefferson Clinton had an extramarital affair with a White House intern. The story catapulted Monica Lewinsky, Linda Tripp, and others into the limelight, making the Clinton–Lewinsky scandal the primary news story for more than a year. The funny thing is that *Newsweek* was conducting the actual investigation that Drudge reported. They had been "scooped" on their own story by an Internet upstart, Matt Drudge.

Many dismiss Drudge's publication as nothing more than a scandal sheet, yet *The Drudge Report* is frequented by hundreds of journalists every day because it has dozens of links to national and international newspapers, wire services, magazines, and writers and columnists such as George Will and Dave Barry. It has become a convenient portal from which to launch a search on the top stories of the day's events. So the irony is that, while many journalists dismiss *The Drudge Report*, they visit the site daily.

Public Reaction to Changes in News   How are Americans reacting to this new influx of news? Web users turn to news and weather sites frequently. Looking at the tallies for the most frequently requested terms (besides sex) on search engines illustrates that current events and weather information are frequently among the top requests. And evidently Web users put a good deal of faith in online sources. Studies completed at the end of 1998 found that more than 80 percent of Web users think online sources are as trustworthy as their newspaper, broadcast, and cable counterparts. Other good news surfaced for Web publishers, too. Consumers do not seem to distrust the information gleaned off Web sites that have active advertising. Of the 2,200 Internet users surveyed, only 3 out of 10 users said they were concerned about the objectivity of a site that reviewed a CD title and then provided a button linking the visitor to an e-commerce site selling the item. Some industry observers speculate that consumer acceptance of e-commerce and advertising will help Web publishers pay for the cost of maintaining the site.

Television on the Web, and WebTV

When snippets of video started to appear on the Web, some futurists speculated that broadcast television would die out as thousands of video channels of programming became available on the Internet. But rumors of television's demise seemed to have been overstated. While video is available on the Web right now, its small postage stamp size and fuzzy pictures don't encourage viewing over a long time period. One important question being debated is whether broadcast-quality television will ever be possible over the Internet for the home user; this is perhaps the most complex issue for the engineers and planners trying to predict the future of the new electronic media.

One reason that video quality is low is because broadcast television pictures are very complex, data-intensive files that are continuously being updated.

WebTV turns a TV set into a computer screen.

These complex files would quickly clog up the stream of material fed into a standard telephone modem, even a 56 kps modem. Further, there is a real debate about whether cable modems (at 10 mbs) would even be fast enough for full motion video if many people sharing the same server in a neighborhood were downloading signals at the same time. So, if the Internet can't deliver enough data to the home browser fast enough, then the question is moot, right? Maybe.

The new digital television system adopted by the United States uses very sophisticated **CODEC** (compressor/decompressor) technology to squeeze lots of data into the standard TV channel. Engineers predict that similar video compression technology will trickle down to the home user over time. In fact, the new MPEG-4 standards allow for the streaming of high-quality video over the net. The IP **multicast backbone** (Mbone) is another technology that media companies are experimenting with. So, while the current Internet won't allow for the deliver of broadcast video to the home today, future developments may make high-quality Web video a reality.

Video *is* being used on the Web, today, nonetheless, and its usage is growing. Sites such as Broadcast.com and ABCnews.com are using streaming video to broadcast up-to-the minute news, concerts, old television shows, video conferences, and distance learning courses over the Web. More than 40 television stations broadcast news and information regularly from the Broadcast.com portal. That number is increasing steadily. RealNetworks, movie studios, and game sites such as SONY.com, are among the most innovative users of interactive Web video. As cable Internet services grow, we'll see an increase of both commercial usage and personal transmission of video.

WebTV is another service that is expanding. When it was first introduced, some people dismissed it as an IOP (Internet for old people) service. That's because with the WebTV device, it is possible for a user to get access to the World Wide Web without buying a home computer. But then the struggling company was purchased by Microsoft and as you can imagine, things changed quickly. In 18 months, WebTV was transformed from an Internet also-ran to a sophisticated, enhanced television service. Subscription rates soared too. WebTV is now among the top 10 largest ISPs in the country.

BEYOND

The rapid growth of the Internet is unparalleled in the recent history of electronic media. Only radio and then television had similar adoption rates. But exactly what effect the accelerated growth of the World Wide Web will have on traditional electronic media is difficult to predict. The following are some likely scenarios.

Home electronics are becoming digital. Digital cameras, camcorders, and the introduction of DVD players demonstrate consumer acceptance of new technology. When this equipment is coupled with a powerful home computer and Internet connection, the individual family has the ability to become a Web-based publisher. This is an opportunity that the individual's analog counterpart never could have provided. We will embrace a personal electronic publishing trend in the same way that cable television

Although he didn't actually invent the Internet, Vice President Al Gore was helpful in bringing about the "information highway."

viewers are embracing new, more highly defined cable networks. Television networks will continue to suffer an erosion of large viewing audiences as more media choice is provided. New Web operations are not confined by geographical considerations. Networks and portals will serve narrowly tailored audiences.

Technology makes the Internet increasingly attractive to distribute and deliver audio and video directly to the consumer. Web delivery of CD-quality audio, books on tape, and spoken newscasts will change media merchandising. Audiotapes are likely to be replaced by completely solid-state walkman-type players that will provide CD-quality music and programming on interchangeable flashcard memories.

Hard-drive digital VCRs will provide consumers with the ability to record and play programs simultaneously. Web-based search wizards will allow consumers to predefine recording interests and automatically begin recording when an interest match is found. For example, if you were a fan of the WNBA's Phoenix Mercury, the digital VCR will automatically begin recording when it encounters a scheduled event.

Because Internet radio and television do not require federal licenses, new stations will develop based on specific interests. Web networks with the latest technologies will provide users with 360-degree panoramic views, three-dimensional viewing, and automatic language translation. High-powered computer graphics will create a new sense of realism in scenery and movement in action games.

Distribution of adult-oriented material and anti-social material is likely to expand on the Web, much to the dismay of many religious, governmental, and family groups. Fringe groups and radical groups have greater access to espouse their views on Web sites. Fraud and privacy issues are increasingly important in the future, as e-commerce grows into a multibillion-dollar industry. Adoption of worldwide policies for the instantaneous free flow of information and data between different countries will become more important.

CAREER PATHS: SOMEWHERE, OUT THERE . . .

Can you work in one of many new exciting career fields in cyberspace? No, sorry. You'll have to work here on earth. But as the World Wide Web continues to grow, both in the United States and around the world, job opportunities related to Web-based product creation, sales, and site management continue to increase; people trained in computer science, programming, and in the telecommunications field are thus currently in high demand.

You don't have to be a computer genius, however. Internet growth is creating many nontechnical jobs too. There are good jobs available for people who have the ability to use Web development products and desktop publishing software packages today. Demand is likely to continue. Industry leaders emphasize the need for good communication skills, the ability to follow a task through to completion, and an eagerness to learn as prerequisites to successful Internet employment. And, many people stress the importance of doing internships as a means of gaining experience and making those valuable first connections. Take heed.

At the moment, Internet communications is a lucrative field in which to pursue a job. Exactly how lucrative it is relates to the skills you bring to the job (not surprisingly). The Association of Internet Professionals (AIP) surveyed current professionals to gain some information about average salaries within several segments of the Internet industry. What they found was encouraging for individuals who want to enter some aspect of this work. According to the AIP, average salaries for Web designers and creative directors hovered around $46,000 while site managers averaged about $54,000 per year.

Web software system programmers were among those at the top of the survey making an average of $72,000. Technical positions edged out marketing specialists who reported making an average of $65,000 yearly. Directors of online services and company CEOs both reported earnings in the low to mid $70s. Bear in mind that these are average salaries. Starting salaries are always lower.

Meet Dee Collins. She's the City Site Manager for Cox Interactive Media's popular Web site Sybercuse *(http://www.sypercuse.com)*. After graduation from college Dee pursued a career in radio, and in 1988, she landed a job at WYYY-FM, an adult contemporary power-house in Syracuse. Collins started doing mid-days at Y-94, but she was eventually moved into promotion and marketing for WSYR, one of Cox's five radio stations in Syracuse.

In August 1995, Cox started community Web sites in cities where they had media properties. Though Sybercuse was not the first community portal in central New York, it had the advantage of cross-promotion. Cox began promoting it on their stations. Dee was asked to run the small operation and through most of 1997 she was the sole producer of the Web site, where she did all kinds of jobs including programming and selling the site. But as the number of visits grew, so too, did the operation. By the summer of 1998, Cox approved expansion of the site, adding a producer, graphic artist, and salesperson. Dee became Sybercuse's City Site Manager.

Today, Sybercuse.com is an important media outlet in central New York, programming current local chat and forums. The site also provides extensive information on Syracuse area community happenings, including a daily digest of events. The site has audio clips and Looksmart, giving users real flexibility in navigating the pages.

Collins' role is like an editor for a broadcast news operation or a newspaper. She decides on content, develops links, provides audio clips from WSYR, the AM news-talk outlet. Like other online communities, Sybercuse has streets and places of interest. It allows users to build Web sites, and holds forums and chats on issues of local interest.

How does Dee know what to program? "It's like any full service radio station. You focus on content and choose the areas your listeners are interested in," she says. "Everyday we need to decide what are the impor-tant events. We look for local angles to national stories. For example, the school shootings in Littleton, Colorado upset a great many people locally. So, we set up a forum where people could express their thoughts on the terrible tragedy."

When people log onto the site, they can choose from many different areas such as news, community events, sports, and entertainment. The effectiveness of banners and sponsored ads are measured by the click-through response. Cox sends information on the numbers of page views each page receives and this gives Collins an opportunity to evaluate what works and what doesn't. Banner and ad sales began taking off in 1998 and the site became a regular destination for local residents. "Big companies began advertising on Sybercuse first," says Collins. "Now when medium-size companies start Web advertising, things will really take off." And, while she has sales target figures to reach, Sybercuse, like most Web portals, hasn't turned a profit yet.

Dee Collins loves her job; she says it's the best job she's ever had. So, what are her goals for the future? She thinks the future is in interactive media. Ten years from now, she wants Sybercuse to be the #1 place to turn for local information. Is that really realistic? At the moment only about 25 percent of all families have Internet access in the Syracuse market. That leaves room for 75 percent growth. Dee Collins has good reason for optimism.

SUMMARY

- The first information services were one-way text ser-vices called teletext. Britain's CEEFAX was an early ver-sion that was transmitted over the air. In France Minitel, a large-scale interactive text service started. Although America pioneered computer networking, information services were not quick to start up. In the early 1980s, The Source and Compuserve became early informa-tion service providers. They were joined by Prodigy and America Online toward the end of the 1980s.

- By 1984, a new generation of computers made graph-ics display a greater priority. AOL and Prodigy adopted graphics interfaces that attracted many home computer users. However, high interconnect long-distance charges and hourly rates prevented many from using information service providers frequently. As long-distance rates came down, more and more users connected to the network.

- The Internet is owned by no single organization. Several organizations, such as the Internet Society and the World Wide Web Consortium, set guidelines for its standards and its operation. When a Universal Resource Locator address is typed into a browser, a request for information is made from the gateway to the server housing information. Domain names help to provide pathways for information.

- Microsoft Explorer and Netscape Navigator are the most popular browsers available for the World Wide Web. Web sites that provide many customer services are called portals. They may be search engine sites, virtual communities, or information/shopping sites. Portals frequently contain banners or other forms of advertising. While ad revenues have risen dramatically over the past few years, most companies providing content on the World Wide Web are still looking for the best way to package content and advertising for consumers to use.

- 1998 and 1999 saw the merger of several large Internet companies: AOL purchased Netscape Communications; Yahoo! merged with broadcast.com and geocities.com; Disney purchased Infoseek; and @Home merged with Excite. Further consolidation is likely to take place as content providers and Internet service providers look for ways to develop mass audiences.

- New media is the term applied to the convergence of audio/video technologies with the World Wide Web. Some media companies use the Web as an ancillary means of reaching target audiences. Broadcasters are experimenting with streaming video applications, such as MPEG-4, to see if it is possible to distribute quality video on the Internet. Technological obstacles to the transmission of quality video over the Web include problems of downloading large video files quickly. Cable modems may provide for much faster download times in the future.

- Web users report a reduction in over-the-air radio listening; Web radio listenership, on the other hand, is on the rise. Studies point to the fact that millions of Americans turn to the Web for breaking news stories. WebTV is a new service that allows users to display both TV programs and the World Wide Web on their television screens. In the past year, WebTV's customer base has increased dramatically.

- As the World Wide Web expands, so, too, do job possibilities. Jobs in desktop publishing and graphic arts are in demand as are positions in computer programming, site management, and marketing. Because the Internet continues to grow rapidly, job prospects continue to look bright.

KEY TERMS

teletext   121
Videotex   121
videotext   121
interactive   121
computer bulletin boards   122
Internet service providers
   (ISPs)   123
World Wide Web   123
churn   123

HyperText Markup Language
   (HTML)   124
search engines   125
World Wide Web Consortium
   (W3C)   125
Universal Resource Locator
   (URL)   127
domain name   127

webzines   129
Integrated Services Digital Network
   (ISDN)   129
portals   130
virtual community   131
synergy   132
CODEC   136
multicast backbone   136

SUGGESTIONS FOR FURTHER READING

Cairncross, F. (1997). *The death of distance*. Cambridge: Harvard Press.

Dodd, A. Z. (1998). *The essential guide to telecommunications*. Upper Saddle River, NJ: Prentice-Hall.

Eddings, J. (1994). *How the Internet works*. Emeryville, CA: Ziff-Davis Press.

Grant, A. E. (1996). *Communication technology update* (5th ed.). Boston: Focal Press.

Horak, R. with Miller, M. A. (1997). *Communication systems and networks*. New York: MIS Press and M&T Books.

Kerland, D., Messere, F., & Palombo, P. (1996). *Introduction to the Internet for electronic media*. Belmont, CA: Wadsworth Publishing.

Lubar, S. (1993). *Infoculture*. Boston: Houghton-Mifflin.

Negroponte, N. (1995). *Being digital*. New York: Vintage Books.

Sinclair, J. (1998). *Web pages with TV HTML*. Rockland, MA: Charles River Media.

Swisher, K. (1998). *aol.com*. New York: Random House.

United States Department of Commerce. (1991). *The NTIA infrastructure report: Telecommunications in the age of information*. Washington, DC: U.S. Government Printing Office.

Winston, B. (1998). *Media technology and society*. London: Routledge.

INTERNET EXERCISES

1. Visit our Web site at http://www.mhhe.com/ beyond for study-guide exercises to help you learn and apply material in each chapter. You will find ideas for future research as well as useful Web links to provide you with an opportunity to journey through the new electronic media.

Part Three | **How It's Done**

The Business of Broadcasting and Cable 7

Quick Facts

 Most expensive advertising time slots: 1999 Super Bowl

 Amount of money spent on local radio advertising: $11.9 billion (1998)

 Projected growth of radio sales for the year 2000: 10 percent

 Most profitable television station in the United States: WNBC-TV, New York

 Cost of a 30-second advertisement time slot during Ally McBeal: $177,000 (1999)

 Ratio of advertising dollars spent on TV versus billboards: 10:1

 Total Cable advertising revenue: $10 billion (1998)

INTRODUCTION

It's time for a short quiz. One question: What is the primary product that a radio or television station has to sell? Here are the choices:

a.   Entertainment.

b.   Advertising time.

c.   Eyeballs and ears.

d.   All of the above.

If you answered *c,* you're right.

Let's dwell on this for just a minute. Commercial mass media has a unique dual nature. The mass media technology is designed to link audiences with program suppliers and with sponsors. Broadcasting and cable operations need to provide listeners and viewers with programs that meet their tastes and needs. Stations transmit programs in order to attract an audience. A commercial radio station, for example, doesn't make any money unless it has an *audience* that some advertiser pays money to reach. Television stations that broadcast network programs make some money from the networks by broadcasting programs, but that's because an advertiser is paying a network to reach a certain audience.

So, while it's true that stations are attracting audiences because of their programming, it is the advertising revenue generated as a result of having a desirable audience that really pays for the programming. Mass media technology provides a means of reaching a large number of people simultaneously, and as a result it is an economical way of linking audiences with advertisers via television and radio programming. You are the product a broadcasting station is selling to an advertiser.

In all electronic media there is this kind of interplay between the technology, the consumer, and economics. For example, there is also an interplay for the cable industry, but it works just a little differently from broadcasting. Obviously cable has advertising, and thus cable, too, must be selling the audience's attention to advertisers (unless a consumer is willing to pay extra money to receive noncommercial channels such as HBO). But, there is a difference between over-the-air broadcasting and cablecasting. Cable companies also charge viewers a monthly subscription fee for the privilege of receiving cable programming. In fact, the majority of cable's revenue is generated by the monthly franchise fee that consumers pay to receive the service. Cable thus has a *dual* income; cable operators sell advertising *and* they collect revenues

from a monthly subscription service. Some cable companies are also offering high-speed Internet access as a service, which would act as a third source of income for these companies. (AT&T/ TCI wants to offer telephone service over cable, too.) Of course, cable operators also have a different cost structure because cable is a different technology than over-the-air broadcasting: Cable franchisers have a large video distribution network to maintain, while broadcasters just have a transmitter. The business model for radio and television is thus different than for cable; both cable and broadcasting must be technology-dependent.

This chapter will address the economics of broadcasting and cable, and, while economics is sometimes referred to as a dismal science, advertising revenues for broadcasting and cable are anything but dismal. They've grown steadily since broadcasting's beginnings. We need to understand how a station generates revenue and spends money. Broadcasting and cable are big businesses, after all. Without profits, there would be no money for program development; no programming. Exploring the relationships that exist between broadcasters and advertisers and within the industry will give us some insight into how the business works.

COMPETITION AND ELECTRONIC MEDIA

Radio, television, cable, and satellite broadcasters all face competition from other services. The amount of competition often helps the government determine how closely it will monitor and control the mass media facility. Chapter 10 goes into regulation in detail, but let's discuss a few basic principles here. Generally the amount of government oversight of the electronic media is tied to how competitive that media is. If there is more competition, there is less regulation.

Radio is less heavily regulated than television, for example. There are more than 10,000 commercial radio stations compared with a little more than 1,200 commercial television stations. Guess which medium has fewer regulations regarding ownership? With cable television there are different rules, too. There are very few places in the United States where there is more than one cable operator in a franchise area. As a result, the cable operator can be mandated to provide government and public access channels for the local municipality. The point we are trying to make is simply this: The different electronic media have different levels of competition and face different amounts of government oversight as a result.

If a medium faces no competition, there is a **monopoly.** It's hard to find a place in the United States today that only receives one radio station and no other distant radio or television signals. If there were such a town, the station in that town would have a monopoly on advertising. If there are a limited number of competitors—say, only three national commercial television networks, we would call that an **oligopoly.** Here the limited number of competitors means that each of the networks will probably gain a share of available advertising revenue. If a market faces complete competition—say, a large radio market with 25 or more radio signals available, it is possible to let the listeners decide which stations will become popular and thereby gain a large share of the advertising dollars. We call this a "marketplace" solution, or **pure competition,** because the competitive forces within the market make each station try hard to gain a share of the advertising revenue. Within this last category, it is possible for weak stations to go out of business or get purchased by larger group owners when they do not succeed in gaining a sufficient audience.

Competition among Different Media Types

This may seem obvious to you, but let's state it anyway. People use the various forms of media differently. To some extent competition is defined by how we use a specific medium and what competition it faces from all other competitors. For example, the competition for specific listeners among radio stations must be different from the competition for viewers on television. As we noted in Chapter 4, radio is the most intimate of the mass media. It is a highly portable and personal medium. It is more likely to compete against other portable devices such as cassettes and CDs for your attention than against cable or television. Radio programming centers around music, news, and talk. There is practically no drama. Comedy on radio is more like stand-up than situational. Radio is omnipresent. People can listen in places where watching television would be difficult. Someone jogging or driving a car is obviously the type of person who would be listening to radio, not watching television. Workers in an office are likely to listen to the radio in the background; in fact, some have started listening on their computers via the Internet.

Television is used differently than radio. Many people get home, kick off their shoes and sit down to watch a little TV. The term "couch potato" engenders thoughts of someone at rest, but the term is rarely applied to radio listeners! Television is more likely to compete with cable and movie rentals for its viewers. We can compare other media too. Obviously billboards must compete with radio, but newspapers have the potential to compete with both radio and television, depending on where and when people read their papers. You get the point.

Advertisers will frequently buy different media in order to reach as many customers as possible. They will also frequently spread their messages over different times in the broadcast day to ensure the broadest dissemination of their message. A look at Figure 7–1 shows that time spent listening to the radio and watching television is greater than any other media, thus advertisers are *particularly* concerned with these two media.

Determining a Medium to Buy and Figuring Out Its Cost

There is a triangular relationship in the media business between programmers, media sellers, and media buyers. How does the advertiser actually decide to buy time from one radio station over another, or why does an appliance store use television as opposed to the local newspaper for advertising? As we learned in Chapters 4 and 5, broadcasters need to develop successful programs that certain people will want to listen to or watch. To determine just how successful a TV program is, you need to evaluate how many viewers watch the program. Finding out about the age, gender, and income of viewers is important too. Stations can use that information to attract certain advertisers. You will learn about measuring an audience in Chapter 12. In this chapter we need to focus on how the advertiser decides to allocate dollars.

Marketers and advertisers generally put together a buying plan developed on three basic elements: (1) population or market size, (2) effective buying income, and (3) retail sales for each geographical area where they sell their products. If the product is a national or regional product, advertising agencies and marketing firms collect data relevant to that status and may develop a **buying power index (BPI)** for the specific markets they're interested in. If the media plan is sizable—that is, if there is a substantial amount of money allocated for advertising the product, the advertiser may use the services of a company that provides information regarding the amount of money that competing national advertisers spend on various media. Research companies break down advertising expenditures according to specific classifications of products, such as breakfast cereals. This

Figure 7–1

Consumer Media Usage

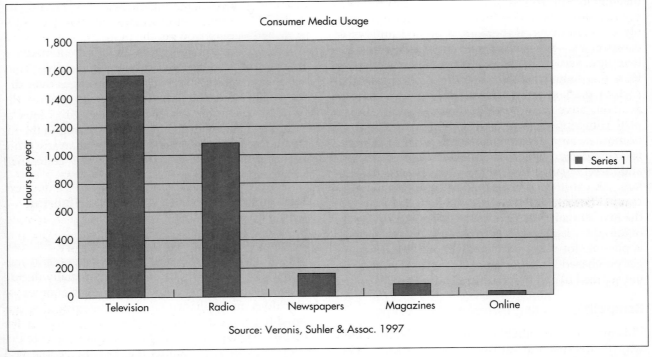

Consumer Media Usage

Source: Veronis, Suhler & Assoc. 1997

Source: Veronis, Suhler & Associates 1997

information provides the advertiser with a way of gauging what the competition is spending on media.

After data collection, the advertiser will develop media plans for the product. Frequently, sophisticated analysis will be used for allocating advertising funds to buy time on broadcasting stations. For example, a national restaurant chain may target the Durham, North Carolina, market for spending because the chain is expanding the number of restaurants in that area. A *brand manager* will want to purchase airtime on television stations for a two-week period prior to the opening of each new store. The time segments available for commercials in radio and TV are called *spots,* and this term is also used to refer to the commercials themselves.

Media buyers use various formulas for determining the effectiveness of ad placement. One such measure, called **gross rating points (GRPs)** gives the buyer a way to evaluate a run of x number of commercials over the specific time period that has a consistent rating for the target audience. **Gross impressions,** another measure, reflects the total of all persons reached by each commercial in the advertis-

ing campaign. Using this kind of information to determine audiences and effectiveness, advertisers will calculate how much money they want to spend to achieve their marketing goals.

Nationally advertised brands such as Coke or McDonald's may decide to purchase broadcasting time on national television and cable networks, or they could choose to buy time on network affiliates or independent stations on a market-by-market basis. Frequently, nationally advertised brands will also help out the local retailer through cooperative advertising. (We'll discuss these differences in greater detail a bit later in this chapter.) Occasionally an advertiser will select or not select specific media based solely on cost (e.g., a firm may decide it cannot afford to advertise during the Super Bowl).

Placing the Ad

Once advertisers determine what kind of media they want to buy (radio only, for instance) and when (morning drivetime), they can begin to evaluate the benefits of purchasing time on one or more specific media outlets. Generally, advertising time is sold for a specific number of spots and it covers a specific period of time. For example, a nursery wouldn't want its "Spring Gardening Sale" spots aired in the middle of July. So, the media buyer will specify beginning and ending dates for the advertisement to run. Time buyers want to be able to compare the cost of doing business at station A with another media facility (station B) down the road. For the sake of this example, we're going to use radio, but both radio and television stations publish *rate cards* (see Figure 7–2) to help time buyers evaluate the cost of advertising. The next step is to find out how many potential listeners you can reach for your money.

Frequently rate cards will reflect charges based on different numbers of spots. As an advertiser purchases more time, the cost per spot decreases.

CPM: Measuring the Cost of Advertising on Two Stations

Media buyers use a standard formula to figure out the actual cost of a commercial spot. The unit cost is expressed as the cost to reach 1,000 audience members. **Cost per thousand** is abbreviated **CPM,** where the *M* stands for the Roman numeral 1,000. To calculate the CPM of a radio station you need to know the cost of the spot and the size of the audience. For example, if the shoe store owner wanted to advertise on station WXXX, which charged $240 per spot and had a listening audience of 20,000 people, the CPM formula would look like this:

$$\text{WXXX CPM} = \frac{\text{Cost of spot}}{\text{Audience (000s)}} = \frac{\$240}{20} = \$12.00$$

Thus, the CPM, or cost of reaching 1,000 listeners, would be $12.00 on WXXX. Now, compare this CPM with that of station WZZZ, a station that has a similar listenership in terms of demographics. While the cost of advertising on WZZZ is slightly higher, it also has a slightly larger audience. The cost of advertising on WZZZ is $270 per spot for reaching 30,000 listeners.

$$\text{WZZZ CPM} = \frac{\text{Cost of spot}}{\text{Audience (000s)}} = \frac{\$240}{30} = \$9.00$$

If the media buyer were to compare the costs per thousand for the two stations, WZZZ would be a better buy. Even though WZZZ charges slightly more per spot, the CPM (cost per thousand) is lower because it has a larger listening audience.

CPM is a good way of expressing *efficiency*—that is, the cost of reaching a thousand potential buyers of the product. For advertisers, the goal is generally to reach the largest potential audience for the smallest dollar investment, but sometimes it is useful to spend more money to reach audiences with specific demographic characteristics.

Local Markets

Obviously the above scenario for developing a media buy doesn't apply to all situations. Many advertisers are just not large enough to hire an advertising agency or a media buyer. In many smaller markets, a station sales representative will work directly with a store owner to develop a commercial. Once the commercial is written and approved, it will be turned over to the station's production manager to execute. The sales representative will then schedule the spot in the station's commercial rotation for play.

The sales representative and the store owner might develop a long-term contract that reflects a discount for sponsoring a specific time slot—say, the 8 A.M. news. The sales rep will place a **standing order** for the shoe store's commercial to run over a specific period (maybe several weeks or months, for example). Now no other advertiser will be able to sponsor the morning newscast for the duration of the standing order. In this example, the station's sales rep is acting like an account executive by servicing the needs of the local shoe store. The sales representative will need to see the shoe store owner regularly to develop new ideas for the news sponsorship.

Small-market radio stations frequently don't subscribe to a ratings service. As a result it may not be possible to calculate the CPM on small-market stations. In rural America, where some towns only have a weekly newspaper and one or two local radio stations, a store owner may simply work out the best deal possible with some or all of the local media available in the area.

BROADCASTING SALES PRACTICES
Radio Sales

There are more than 12,000 radio stations in the United States. Five out of every six stations are commercial stations. They derive their revenues by selling listeners to potential advertisers who have products or services they want to promote. In Chapter 4, we stated that the goal of a radio station is to gain a

Figure 7–2

Radio Advertising Rate Card

RATE CARD

TIME	MONDAY-FRIDAY	SATURDAY	SUNDAY
AM DRIVE **5:30A-10A** *"MARTY &* *PAIGE IN THE* *MORNING"*	$255	$90	$75
MIDDAY **10A-3P** *"KEVIN"*	$255	$300	$180
PM DRIVE **3P-8P** *"JAVA JOEL"*	$315	$180	$180
EVENINGS **8P-12A** *"SHAWN MICHAELS"*	$180	$150	$90
OVERNIGHTS *"DANGER BOY"*	$30	$30	$30
THREE DAYPART TAP **6A-8P**	$270	$225	$150
FOUR DAY PART TAP **6A-12A**	$240	$180	$120
BTA **MON-SUN 6A-6A**	$180	$150	$105

"The supply of time is totally inelastic. No matter how high the demand, the supply will not go up. Yesterday's time is gone forever and will never come back. Time is, therefore, always in exceedingly short supply!" –
Peter Drucker

10/16/98

large number of a certain type of listener. Radio sales is closely tied with demographic analysis and program planning. An all-news format radio station does not *expect* to have a large number of adolescents in its listening audience. An analysis of listening habits for people ages 12 to 18 would show that adolescents and young adults tend to listen to radio stations that concentrate on playing music appropriate to their age group.

The all-news radio listeners, according to research, however, will tend to be older (35+) and more affluent than listeners of most other radio formats. So, while the all-news format station might actually have many fewer listeners than a station that caters to the young adults (say an urban contemporary format), it may actually charge the advertiser *more* for those listeners. A look at the type of sponsors might reveal that those interested in buying time on the all-news station are likely to be more upscale than the advertisers on a station trying to reach a much younger audience. Luxury cars, travel cruises, and commercials for brokerage houses or insurance are likely to be advertised on all-news radio.

The Search for Spots   As we mentioned earlier, there are three types of advertising purchases made in broadcasting. The term *local*, meaning local spot sales, refers to the sale of commercial advertising by stations to advertisers in their immediate service area. Auto dealers, appliance stores, and restaurants are frequent local advertisers. As we noted, salespeople will call on local businesses and attempt to sell them ad time.

Station ad rates are pegged to the *share of the audience* that is listening to the station at a given time. Shares are determined by Arbitron (see Chapter 12), which publishes radio ratings reports. The larger the share is, the more money a station can charge for its commercial spots. Most stations give discounts if an advertiser buys a large number of spots (called a *package*) and if the advertiser commits to buying spots that will run over an extended period of time.

Ads cost more or less depending on the time period in which they air. The rate card reflects the radio day as it is broken down into **dayparts.** The most expensive daypart during which to advertise is *morning drive time,* and *afternoon drive time* is the second-most expensive. The largest number of listeners are in the audience during morning and evening drive. Commuters are frequent targets of advertising; tire and battery sales, insurance, and convenience stores

are frequently advertised during these time periods. Special sections of a ratings book will usually highlight average commute times for each *radio market.* The time between morning and evening drive is called *daytime.* Daytime is also an important advertising time. *Evening* is the next daypart, followed by late night or overnight. When an advertiser buys a package that will run on a station throughout the broadcast day, the term *run of schedule (ROS)* is used to designate that the spots are played during all the dayparts.

Radio stations also make use of **cooperative advertising,** or simply *co-op.* Many local retail stores sell items made by national manufacturers. In a co-op arrangement, the national firm will share the cost of advertising with the local business. Thus the Maytag Company might pay part of the cost of local radio time purchased by Green's Appliance Store. Local retailers like co-ops because, in addition to helping them pay for the ads, the ads are often produced by national ad agencies and are high in production value. Co-ops allow local retailers to tie their businesses in with a national campaign. Stations need to provide affidavits showing how many times the co-ops run. In fact, at some stations one or more members of the sales staff are assigned exclusively to deal with co-op plans.

The term *national spot sales* refers to the sale of commercial radio time to major national and regional advertisers. For example, Ford and General Motors buy national spots so that their commercials are heard all over the country but at different times on different stations. The local Smith Ford dealership or the Jones GM dealer will buy local spot sales. Frequently, national brands have regional managers to handle the ad campaigns, which can vary greatly from one region of the country to the next. For example, Goodyear probably won't advertise with snow tire commercials in the South or the Southwest.

National spot sales are normally made on behalf of local stations by station *representation firms,* or *reps.* Reps maintain offices in the nation's biggest cities, like New York, Los Angeles, Dallas, and Atlanta, which are also home to the nation's leading advertisers and their agencies. Suppose Coke's media buyers want to buy spots on classic rock stations all over the United States. They will contact rep firms that may handle many different stations in markets around the country. The Coke media buyer places one order but buys air time for many different individual stations using this technique.

The third type of radio advertising is *network sales*, which is the sale of commercial advertising by regular networks, such as ABC, Mutual, and CBS, or special radio networks that carry specific programs such as a local college football game. National spots are aired within the programs and carried on each station in the ad hoc network. Although local stations receive no revenue for carrying the program, there may be some available time within the programs for local spot sales. Sporting events can usually be sold locally at a premium, making carriage of the game a lucrative event for the local station. Some specialized programs, such as "American Top 40," are distributed via satellite to local stations with national spots included within the program. Local spots can be inserted at the top or bottom of the hour for these weekly specials.

The Future of Radio Sales   Take a look at Table 7–1. It displays radio revenues reaped by advertising agencies since 1965; the revenues are broken down by type of expenditure. In 1970, about 30 percent of all radio buys were national spot sales. Local sales accounted for about two-thirds of all revenue. Network radio was in substantial decline at this time (before satellite distribution), with advertisers spending less than 4 percent of their radio budgets on network programs. Today, nearly 80 percent of all radio sales are local. National spot sales account for only one out of every six dollars of radio advertising. The majority of these sales go to the top-rated stations in the largest markets. But in the last few years, network radio has rebounded thanks to diverse personalities such as Howard Stern, Rush Limbaugh, Don Imus, and Dr. Joy Browne. We will trace this trend in more detail in Chapter 8.

How does advertising affect radio's future? Radio is poised to bloom over the next few years. During the previous two decades, radio garnered only about 7 percent of all advertising dollars. So even though more and more stations were licensed, the radio advertising pie wasn't really growing. However, in the next few years industry analysts predict a renewed interest in radio, with a growth rate close to 10 percent. In addition, radio group owners have started consolidating with billboard advertisers, making the radio/billboard combination a more attractive place for ad dollars. Finally, national spot advertising is expected to grow now that group owners have the ability to market broadly through the multiple station groups that were created during the consolidation after the Telecommunications Act of 1996.

Table 7–1	Radio Advertising Volume, 1965–2002			
Year	Network	National Spot	Local	Total

	Revenue (millions of dollars)			
Year	**Network**	**National Spot**	**Local**	**Total**
1965	$ 60	$ 275	$ 582	$ 917
1970	56	371	881	1,308
1975	83	436	1,461	1,980
1980	183	779	2,740	3,702
1985	365	1,335	4,790	6,490
1990	433	1,626	6,780	8,839
1995	512	1,741	7,987	10,240
1997	498	2,407	10,741	13,600
1998	557	2,743	11,900	15,200
2002	800	3,900	16,400	21,100*

*Projected by Veronis, Suhler & Associates.
Source: McCann-Erickson.

As in the TV business, national spot advertising is usually sold on the basis of station popularity, as measured by ratings. Almost without exception the highest-rated stations will get the majority of advertising expenditures. Media buyers usually go with these higher-ranking stations, leaving the other stations out of the huge advertising expenditure. Stations ranking considerably above their competition thus outbill and outearn their competition, usually by a wider margin than their ratings advantage. Consequently, a station's share of the audience is an extremely important sales tool for a media rep. The higher-ranking stations are much easier to sell to media buyers.

Public Radio Stations   Public, educational, and noncommercial radio stations are difficult to categorize. There are many noncommercial radio stations that operate on tiny budgets, frequently operating as part of a high school or college communications program. Some of these stations operate on a part-time basis, while others are full-service stations. It is possible that the FCC will require a part-time noncommercial station to share its frequency with other noncommercial entities in an urban area.

Public radio stations are affiliated with National Public Radio. These stations carry network and syndicated programs reflecting the entire range of programming from news to classical music, from "Prairie Home Companion" to "Talk of the Nation."

Many are well financed by local educational or community entities. Other stations rely heavily on listener support. Unlike PBS, which acts as a television program distributor and syndicate, National Public Radio is a program producer and supplier. Because educational and noncommercial radio stations run the gamut from extremely small to very large, it is difficult to generalize about personnel and budgets. Noncommercial stations can solicit corporate or advertiser support through underwriting. Unlike commercial advertising, underwriting cannot make a *call to action,* such as "to order your . . . call 555-XXXX now." The announcement should be completely factual. Many NPR stations ask for listener support as part of their way to raise the funds necessary to buy programming.

Television

America's 1,500 full-time television stations are much more complex structurally than radio stations. Television stations have a greater reliance on outside programming sources than radio. Radio stations rely either on a local talent for playing music for a local audience or satellite programming that is demographically specific to that audience. Television network programming is primarily based on shows of a fixed length that are meant to reach very large audiences. It makes sense, therefore, that television programming is acquired, aired, and sold rather differently than is most radio programming.

In small to medium-sized television markets, almost all of the stations are affiliated with one of the four big television networks, or with UPN, WB, or Pax TV. Affiliates downlink the network feed off a geostationary satellite. During those times when the network is supplying programs, the television station is responsible for retransmission of the network programs for that market and for station breaks at designated times. Station breaks between network programs allow the local stations to sell advertisers **adjacencies,** local spots that are aired next to prime-time, daytime, late-night, and weekend network programming. Those few minutes adjacent to network programs usually command a premium and are very lucrative for affiliated stations.

The amount of money that a particular station or network can charge sponsors is influenced by several factors, such as the number of people predicted to watch a given program or to watch during a given time period and the number of commercials the ad-

vertiser wishes to place with the station or network. In general, the amount that the broadcaster will charge is based on the estimated number of people viewing a program. The larger the ratings estimate, the more a station or network will charge for the spot.

Several economic factors affect the way the industry works, but competitive programming is the primary factor (see Chapter 9). Networks are important producers of programming. They develop different kinds of shows to cover many time slots throughout the broadcast day, including the crucial prime-time hours between the evening news and late news. But, when there is no network feed, television stations turn to the **syndication** market. Shows that were once successful on the network are frequently syndicated to local stations. These former prime-time reruns compete with other syndicated programming produced exclusively for local distribution, such as the popular game show "Jeopardy," reality-based programming like talk shows or magazines, and first-run syndication. Last, all of these shows compete with locally produced programming. Local news and information shows are also important programs for television stations. As you can see, television programming is quite different from that of radio.

Network Sales—Getting Things Upfront   Even though audiences for the television networks are slipping near or below the 50 percent mark, network television is still a cost-effective way to reach large numbers of Americans at one time. Advertisers buy time slots within individual programs on the networks to reach the large mass audience. Television viewing is most heavy during the fall and spring; it's lightest during the summer. Media buyers purchase network time to meet the specific needs of their client's products, frequently paying more for special times of the year such as the pre-Christmas selling season or special occasions such as the Olympics.

The television advertising year is broken down into a number of different sales periods, but most networks like to see their revenue **upfront.** This sales period begins in early summer and ends before the fall television season begins. National advertisers buy time on the new season before it starts because this assures advertisers that they control time slots within the popular program time periods or program nights. Upfront is an important time. Network sales produce the *revenue stream* that they use to pay

In the 1920s, at the very beginning of commercial broadcasting, William Paley created a partnership between CBS and radio stations around the country. The affiliates' success was due in large part to the success of the network. The network–affiliate relationship has become one of the cornerstones of American broadcasting. Today that relationship is changing.

Networks are looking for ways to make their programming more accessible to viewers. Television stations carry their programming, but public access to network programming is limited. Network viewing shares have been decreasing steadily for the last 10 years. Now networks are looking to change the relationship and use cable to increase viewership of their shows.

In 1999, both Fox and ABC said that they needed to redefine their long-term relationships with affiliates, and network executives now seem confident that they can change the business model. ABC, for example, wants to start replaying episodes of its programming on a new cable channel the same day they're showed over the air. Some ABC affiliates are worried that the network has declared war. One local TV executive who sits on the ABC affiliate board called the highly tense posturing a "deadly embrace."

NBC announced that it would rerun episodes of its prime-time programming on cable two weeks after the show airs on the network. Executives even question the value of relying on local stations to broadcast network shows. For example, Robert Wright, President of NBC, said that he would broadcast NBC shows on local cable channels if the network couldn't work out acceptable deals with local affiliates. Fox, which pays no station compensation, has acted even more aggressively. It told stations that it wanted to claim more advertising time for itself, thus reducing some of its affiliates' most lucrative spot sales.

At the heart of the problem is the large amount of money networks pay stations in the form of compensation. Over the years, television networks have seen profit margins decline or disappear while profits at local television stations have skyrocketed. But some affiliates are skeptical of network intentions. They point to the huge profits of the network owned-and-operated stations and say that this current push is simply an attempt to allow networks to own more local television stations or control the business more directly.

Since most affiliates are in long-term contracts with networks, television stations find that they have few weapons in their arsenal against the networks. Stations *could* refuse to air network shows they didn't like or that got low ratings; they would preempt the network with a local program. Preemption hurts a network because it loses a portion of the national audience every time an affiliate preempts a program.

The television network business is undergoing significant change. As digital television starts up and cable grows, business relationships between local stations and networks must change too. How will the relationship between affiliates and networks change? What should the network business model look like in 2005? Answer those questions and you'll find a good-paying job in television.

for the cost of programming, to pay affiliates for carrying their programs, and to pay the creative talent to develop new programs. In other words, when a network sells more **inventory** before the season starts, it is better able to gauge revenues for the upcoming season, something Wall Street seems to appreciate. Cable networks have also started to sell upfront inventory for their programs, too.

National advertisers also buy time in the **scatter market.** The four quarters in the scatter market correspond to the seasons of the year. Buying time this way can be very cost-effective for advertisers. If the actual audience share does not meet preseason estimates, the cost for buying that time slot will decrease in the scatter market. The reverse can be true too. For example,

if analysis of a new television show's audience reveals a greater, particularly strong viewership among females 25 to 45 (a very attractive demographic), advertising agencies may decide to buy time during that show in the scatter market even though the rates increase. Buying time in the scatter market allows an advertiser to use a *planning cycle* more effectively and some networks give ratings guarantees for these purchases since *hard* numbers can be ascertained from overnight ratings. But, broadcast networks also offer guaranteed audience targets in the upfront market to protect the incentive to buy time early. This strategy seems to be working; upfront sales for the 1999 television season netted some $6 billion.

Networks collect large sums of money from ad-

National advertisers, like Pepsi, spend about $25 billion annually on TV commercials.

vertisers because they offer buyers the promise of reaching large audiences, but they must rely on affiliates to carry their programming in order to make good on delivering the numbers. Networks pay affiliates **compensation** for carrying programs. The amount of compensation is based on the size of the "market" area the affiliate serves. Large metropolitan stations such as those in New York and Chicago get a much larger share of compensation than smaller-market stations, such as a TV station in State College, Pennsylvania. Remember that most five-star stations are actually owned and operated by the networks. In essence, networks pay compensation to themselves when they carry their own programs, along with all the other group owners who have affiliated stations. However, the network owners sometimes make very little money on their network operations; they make a tremendous amount of money on their owned-and-operated stations. WNBC in NYC is the most profitable station in the country.

The Economics of Networking   The finances of network television programming are very complex. In the 1970s, when the networks were at the peak of their power, the government barred them from owning financial interests in their programs (Financial-Syndication rules). These government regulations, which allowed independent producers to develop, were relaxed in recent years as more competitors have entered the television marketplace. Today tele-

vision networks can own some of their own programming, and they can develop new programming with the intention of profiting from the show when it is placed into the syndication marketplace.

Television programming, particularly dramas and high-profile situation comedies, are very expensive to produce. The per-episode cost can be well over a million dollars to produce. Much of the cost is personnel. Programs that survive the first few weeks of a television season sometimes go on to become hits and run for years. Programs such as "Seinfeld" and "Frasier" are prime examples. However, it is not unusual for networks to lose money the first season that a program airs. That's because the cost of production, promotion, and compensation exceeds the revenue the networks derive from the sale of time until a new show finds its audience and starts making money.

In order to make network television profitable, networks charge a large amount of money for a 30-second spot during the most popular programs. Table 7–2 shows the costs to advertise on some popular network programs. Even though costs are high, particularly for "ER" and "Frasier," the CPM for these shows is only about $12.00 because the shows garner high ratings. The CPM cost for advertising on a network is actually in line with many national brands' advertising budgets. Network television still provides a truly mass audience, even though audiences are getting smaller.

Issues: Networks' Profits and the Financial Syndication Rules

We recall from earlier chapters the stories of the growth of the networks and how this growth made both David Sarnoff and William Paley wealthy, famous, and powerful. Today, the economic situation is different from the heady days when networks commanded 90 percent of the viewing audience. In 1998, only two of the four major television networks reported profits for the year.

Fox Broadcasting posted a miniscule $10 million profit on television network sales of more than $1.6 billion. NBC boasted a $470 million profit on sales of nearly $3.8 billion, thanks in large part to some of its highly successful Thursday-night lineup.

Together ABC and CBS television networks lost more than a third of a billion dollars. CBS alone racked up a huge $235 million loss, mostly due to the 1998 Winter Olympics; CBS owned-and-operated stations, on the other hand, made more than half a billion dollars. ABC lost a cool $100 million on its television network even though it made $850 million on its cable and international distribution operations.

Don't worry, all four media companies are financially sound. But, what's going on? The way television networks make money is changing.

The television network business is sound, but the costs associated with buying shows and with mounting network operations are very high. At the same time, the television network business is mature. So media companies are looking for ways to get more out of their investments in programming. They want to branch out into cable and Internet ventures to reach new customers, and they want to reinvent their relationship with affiliates. For example, CBS has cultivated the situation comedy "Everybody Loves Raymond" since early 1996. TV critics panned the show early on, and it finished the first year ranked 83rd. Most other shows would have been canceled, but in its second season CBS moved the show into one of its coveted Monday-night time slots and gave it a ton of promotion. Within a season it moved into the top 40 shows. In 1998 "Raymond" finished 13th for the season, frequently hitting in the middle of the top 10. This isn't about programming, though, it's about economics. Read on:

Before 1995, FCC rules barred CBS and the other networks from owning a piece of the shows they broadcast. If a show didn't perform well, the network could cancel and try a new program. Many times the networks split the development cost with the show's producers, but these were costly failures. Since then, however, networks could invest in the opportunity to recoup their investments in syndication. TV experts claim that CBS could net nearly $100 million when "Everybody Loves Raymond" is offered into syndication in the year 2000. Currently CBS owns part of more than half of its prime-time lineup. The other networks are also invested in their own programming. Touchstone, whose parent company is ABC, owns parts of "Boy Meets World" and "Sports Night." NBC has a financial interest in "NewsRadio," among other shows. The financial considerations involved in show development may encourage networks to give extra needed time for shows like "Everybody Loves Raymond" to find an audience and become successful. This new strategy could be very lucrative for networks that have lost tens of millions of dollars over the last few years.

Table 7–2	Cost of 30-Second Time Slots for Prime-Time Programs, 1999 Season
ER	$551,000
Frasier	470,000
Monday Night Football	380,000
Touched by An Angel	277,000
The Simpsons	248,000
Ally McBeal	177,000
Law and Order	154,000
Dawson's Creek	96,000
The Jamie Foxx Show	43,000

Source: *Broadcasting and Cable*, September 28, 1998.

Networks usually negotiate to broadcast the program at least twice: once in either the fall or spring 13-week season and one rerun in the summer or near a holiday. Television producers share in the costs with the network. Producers, too, may actually lose money in the first showing of a hit series, but they tend to make money in the *back-end* market. This means that when a program goes into syndication, the show can make a tremendous amount of money for the producers because it is sold to television stations on a market-by-market basis.

Sports provide a real dilemma for television networks. Televised professional sporting events are

Events: Gillette, Rupert Murdoch, and the Super Event

In 1939, the Gillette razor company paid $200,000 for the rights to broadcast the World Series by radio. Paying this sum of money, large for 1939, established the facts that sponsoring sports was both costly and profitable. This event triggered the beginning of a relationship between sports teams, players, and the product sponsors who like to be associated with them. The target was to reach males in the audience.

Networks quickly realized there was money to be made by selling advertising within these mega-events. Today Rupert Murdoch wants to control sports broadcasting. In the last few years, Murdoch's News Corporation, the parent company of Fox, has purchased a financial stake in 19 of the 23 networks that broadcast regional sporting events. These deals do not include teams in the National Football League that already play games seen over the Fox television network.

Murdoch wants to offer advertisers the convenience of one-stop spot shopping. Buyers can go to one organization and make buys on most teams in the three primary professional sports. News Corp. is the first real competition to ABC/ESPN, which has long dominated professional sports. However, there is a difference. While advertisers buy network time on ESPN, spots shown on News Corp. are primarily national spot sales. There's more flexibility.

Today the NFL dominates. In the 1998–99 football season, ABC, CBS, ESPN, and Fox all carried NFL action and aired 2,200 spots promoting various NFL games. Of all sporting events, the Super Bowl is king. Each year a handful of advertisers ante up a royal sum for 30 seconds of time in the most coveted of advertising time periods.

Super Bowl XXXIII's nine minutes of advertising time raked in a cool $150 million for the Fox network, averaging $1.6 million for a 30-second spot. America's biggest corporate names, including IBM and Pepsi hurried to sign up, and Anheuser-Busch was willing to pay a premium on top of that to be the only beer advertiser during the mega-event.

Viewers wait eagerly to see commercials. High-profile advertising has become a tradition during the Super Bowl since Apple Computer ran a now-famous commercial introducing the Macintosh in 1984.

Meantime, Fox will need all the revenue it can get. The network signed a new deal with the NFL for future broadcasts for well over $4 billion. Payments at this level will make it difficult for Fox to turn a profit, but television networks continue to pay high figures to sports franchises to secure the elusive male viewer.

---

becoming increasingly expensive as the salaries for sports stars rise to astronomical levels. Most sports teams do not make sufficient revenues from gate sales to pay the athletes' salaries. Team owners rely on royalties from the broadcast of games and merchandising. Since sporting events have little potential as reruns, there are very few ways for networks to recoup the cost for the rights to air the event (especially with declining viewership). When costs exceed the ability to charge advertisers for the product, they lose money. In recent years, some networks have lost money broadcasting certain professional sports. If this trend continues, some sports may be forced to move off of television networks and into pay-per-view.

Syndications and Local Sales Stations will fill nonnetwork time with TV shows that have been purchased in the syndication market. Syndicated programming may be composed of network reruns such as "Seinfeld," "Home Improvement," and "The X-Files," or the shows could be developed specifically as *first-run* syndication. First-run syndications such as "Jeopardy," "Jerry Springer" and "Judge Judy" are shown directly on local television stations.

When a television station buys a syndicated show package, it buys the rights to show each episode a certain number of times in the local market. For example, suppose WEEE-TV decided to pay $10,000 per episode for the rights to show 150 episodes of "Mad About You" three times each. (Striped across the five-day week, 150 × 3 is 450 daily showings of "Mad About You"; this will provide approximately 1½ years of local programming for the station.) This deal, worth $1.5 million dollars for the program producer, would be based (1) on the size of the market and (2) on how much other TV stations in that market might be willing to bid for the rights to the show. (Reruns of "Seinfeld" and "Mad About You" tend to be among the most expensive shows in syndication.)

If the producers were able to strike similar deals in just 60 of the 240 television markets in the United States, they would be very happy and very rich. To carry this example to a conclusion, WEEE-TV sells the number of commercial minutes available within each "Mad About You" episode locally or in national spot sales. The station must make back the cost of syndication plus enough money to cover station overhead, station commissions, and meet a profit target. You can see that the amount of money needed to support showing network reruns, particularly big hits, on the local station can be very high.

Syndicated programming runs the gamut from sophisticated coproductions to quiz shows to fairly vulgar talk shows. Some programs don't cost any money at all; *barter* syndication programs are provided free to television stations, but they have national spots embedded in them. As we noted with radio, stations are obliged to carry the spots if they carry the programs. Frequently these shows will include a couple of 30-second holes where local spots can be inserted by the local station. On some quiz shows, viewers will see products being given away as prizes. These products are given by sponsors as consideration for the promotional value of having them seen on the show, making quiz shows relatively inexpensive to produce. Next time you watch "Wheel of Fortune," note how many automobiles are on the floor as grand prizes.

News and informational programs are extremely important local products for the station to sell. Many stations operate large and sophisticated news departments capable of programming several hours per day on the station. Time sold during and adjacent to highly rated local news programming often generates large profits for TV stations. Networks encourage affiliates to have strong local news since they often run directly before the network news. A good local newscast can provide a strong lead-in for the network newscast. With the higher ratings numbers, higher spot prices can be charged.

National Spot Advertising   National spot advertising consists of commercials that national advertisers place on selected stations across the nation. For example, makers of harvesting equipment might wish to purchase ads in a large number of rural markets. Buying time on the network would be inefficient for them since it would be unlikely that many people in New York City or Los Angeles would be shopping for harvesters. Local advertis-

ing consists of commercials that are shown on the broadcast station in your area and that feature products and services in the local community served by the TV station.

Most spot buying is handled by a local station's *national representative* (or simply *rep*) firm. The rep represents local stations to national and regional buyers. National reps make it easier for buyers to purchase time by being a central contact point for a given station. Usually a national rep will represent only one station in a given market. This prevents conflicts of interest.

Reps will also offer programming advice and market research to help the station increase its number of viewers. This advice is not altruistic, however; an increase in viewer numbers means better ratings. Reps have an easier time selling time at higher rates to national advertisers for stations that have the highest ratings in their areas. More time sold at a higher cost means more profit for the rep (whose fee is a percentage of sales) as well as for the station. Since the goal of the rep is to sell commercials on each of the many stations he or she represents in a given market or region, this kind of advertising is usually known as the *spot business.*

As Figure 7–3 indicates, the spot business today is a sizable advertising segment, averaging about $11 billion annually in billings. National or regional spot advertising is the lifeblood of many TV stations, especially those in major markets. Automotive retailers, national restaurant chains, entertainment enterprises, and computer/office equipment suppliers tend to use national spot sales heavily. Firms with a particularly impressive track record for their clients include Katz, Telerep, and Blair.

Local Spot Sales   Today an increasing amount of the advertising revenue of a local station comes from the sale of advertising time to local merchants. Local car dealerships, appliance stores, lawyers, and others seek to tell people about their services and products through advertising on the local station.

Stations employ salespeople, called *account executives,* to visit potential advertisers and to demonstrate how advertising on their TV station will increase business. As we noted earlier, a good account executive will help the client develop an advertising strategy based on the amount of money the advertiser has to spend. Like the radio example we used earlier, the account executive should help the client plan the time of the year in which to advertise and the time of the

Figure 7–3

TV Sales by Type (in $ billions)

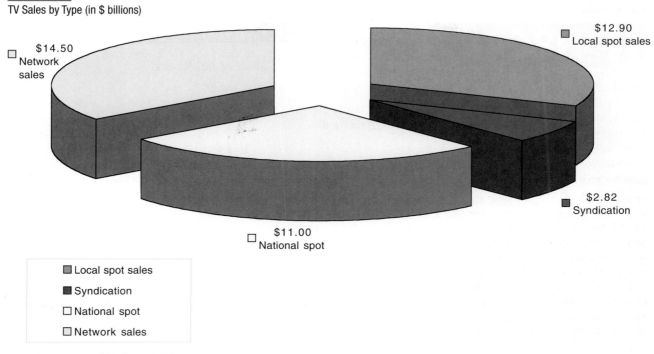

$14.50
Network
sales

$12.90
Local spot sales

$2.82
Syndication

$11.00
National spot

- ▨ Local spot sales
- ■ Syndication
- ☐ National spot
- ☐ Network sales

Source: *Broadcasting and Cable*, January 4, 1999.

broadcast day during which to advertise and may, particularly in smaller markets, help write commercials. Account executives are usually paid a *commission*, a percentage of the value of advertising they sell.

The primary tools of the account executive are the ratings and the list of prices for advertising, which are on the rate card. Figure 7–4 is a sample rate card. Note that the TV rate card is much more specific than the radio rate card (refer to Figure 7–2). The cost of advertising is based on the show the client chooses to advertise in.

In terms of advertising revenues, local businesses are increasingly important to local stations. In the last 30 years, local advertising from local merchants and service providers has increased from 35 to nearly 50 percent of total sales. By 2000, local advertising is expected to pull ahead of the national/regional spot market, with annual volume in the $12 to $14 billion range.

Cable Television Sales National cable television sales is similar to that of network television, and it is becoming an increasingly important venue for advertisers. National advertisers buy time both upfront

and in the scatter markets. The Television Advertising Bureau predicts that the growth of advertising for cable will remain at 13 percent, a very healthy figure. Basic cable national advertising was approximately $6.6 billion in 1998 and total cable ad revenue was close to $10 billion. Car manufacturers and general merchandise retailers tend to be the largest advertisers. In certain weeks of the year, some late-night and weekend cable network ratings exceed the lower-rated broadcast networks. In addition, cable has a very strong children's television audience. These factors point to the prospect of steady growth in national cable sales. Comparatively speaking, cable sales could grow more than those of over-the-air television.

Local cable television spots air across many different basic cable networks simultaneously. By coordinating the station break times on different cable networks, local franchisers are able to show commercial **pods** of local spot sales. In addition, many larger cable franchises now cover large urban and metropolitan areas of major U.S. cities. Local cable revenue is expected to become much more important in the next few years.

Figure 7–4

Television Rate Card

FOR INTERNAL USE ONLY

Effective 3/31/97-6/29/97

10NBC/WHEC
2nd Quarter 1997
Rate Card

DAY	TIME	PROGRAM	LEVEL I	LEVEL II	LEVEL III	LEVEL IV	LEVEL V	LEVEL VI
M-F	5A-530A	NBC News at Sunrise	$60	$50	$40	$30	*$20	$10
M-F	530A-6A	News 10NBC A.M. Live	75	60	*50	40	30	25
M-F	6A-7A	News 10NBC A.M. Live	140	120	*100	80	60	50
M-F	7A-9A	Today Show	190	*170	150	130	110	90
M-F	6A-9A	AM Rotation	120	100	90	*80	70	60
M-F	9A-10A	Live with Regis & Kathie Lee	200	160	*140	125	110	90
M-F	10A-11A	Jenny Jones	55	*45	40	35	30	25
M-F	11A-12N	Leeza	75	*65	55	50	40	30
M-F	12N-1230P	News 10NBC at Noon	90	*80	70	60	50	40
M-F	1230P-1P	American Journal	70	60	50	*40	35	30
M-F	1P-3P	Days of Our Lives/Another World	115	*105	95	75	60	50
M-F	3P-4P	Sunset Beach	80	70	60	*50	40	30
M-F	4P-5P	Dr. Quinn, Medicine Woman	100	*80	60	40	30	20
M-F	5P-530P	Live at Five	250	200	*175	150	125	100
M-F	530P-6P	Inside Edition	250	200	*175	150	125	100
M-F	6P-7P	News 10NBC at Six	575	525	*475	425	375	325
Sat	6P-7P	News 10NBC at Six	350	*300	250	200	175	150
Sun	6P-7P	News 10NBC at Six	450	*400	350	300	250	200
M-F	7P-730P	Real TV	250	*225	200	175	150	125
M-F	730P-8P	Extra	250	*225	200	175	150	125
Sa-Su	7P-8P	Inside Edition/Siskel & Ebert	225	200	175	150	*125	100
M-Su	11P-1135P	News 10NBC at Eleven	525	*475	425	375	325	275
Thu	11P-1135P	News 10NBC at Eleven	1000	900	800	*700	650	600
M-F	1135P-1235A	Tonight Show with Jay Leno	250	225	*200	175	150	125
M-F	1235A-135A	Late Night with Conan O'Brien	45	40	*35	30	25	20
M-Th	135A-205A	Later	40	35	30	*25	20	15
M-F	205A-405A	NBC Nightside	35	30	25	*20	15	10
Fri	135A-235A	Friday Night	40	35	30	*25	20	15
Sat	1130P-1A	Saturday Night Live	375	*350	300	250	200	175
Sat	1A-2A	Viper	45	40	35	*30	25	20
Sun	1135P-1235A	Extra Weekend	90	80	70	*60	50	40
Sun	1A-2A	Dr. Quinn, Medicine Woman	50	45	40	35	*30	25
Sat	7A-9A	Saturday Today	100	90	80	*70	60	50
Sat	8A-9A	Sunday Today	100	90	80	*70	60	50
Sun	9A-10A	Meet the Press	150	120	110	*100	90	80
Sa/Su	12N-6P	Weekend Rotation:Sports/Movies	150	125	*100	75	50	25

■191 East Avenue Rochester, NY 14604   (716) 546-5670   FAX: 454-7433   www.10NBC.com   WHEC-TV A DIVISION OF HUBBARD BROADCASTING INC.

Figure 7–4

Television Rate Card   *(continued)*

DAY	TIME	PROGRAM	LEVEL I	LEVEL II	LEVEL III	LEVEL IV	LEVEL V
Mon	8P-9P	Jeff Foxworthy Show/Mr. Rhodes	$550	$450	*$400	350	300
Mon	9P-11P	NBC Monday Night Movie	1100	*1000	900	800	700
Tue	8P-830P	Mad About You	1000	*900	800	700	600
Tue	9P-930P	Frasier	1700	*1500	1400	1300	1200
Tue	9P-10P	Frasier/Caroline in the City	*1200	1000	900	800	700
Tue	10P-11P	Dateline NBC	950	*850	750	650	550
Wed	8P-9P	NewsRadio/Chicago Sons	600	500	450	*400	350
Wed	9P-10P	Wings/Just Shoot Me	600	500	450	*400	350
Wed	10P-11P	Law & Order	950	850	*750	650	550
Thu	8P-830P	Friends	2600	*2400	2200	2000	1800
Thu	9P-930P	Seinfeld	4000	*3500	3000	2500	2000
Thu	9P-10P	Seinfeld/Fired Up	3100	2900	*2700	2500	2300
Thu	10P-11P	ER	4000	*3800	3500	3200	3000
Fri	8P-9P	Unsolved Mysteries	450	*400	350	300	275
Fri	9P-10P	Dateline NBC	750	700	*625	550	475
Fri	10P-11P	Homicide	450	*400	350	300	275
Sat	8P-9P	Dark Skies	500	450	*400	350	325
Sat	9P-10P	The Pretender	500	450	*400	350	325
Sat	10P-11P	Profiler	500	*450	400	350	325
Sun	7P-8P	Dateline NBC	800	700	*600	500	400
Sun	8P-9P	3rd Rock/Boston Common	700	*600	500	400	350
Sun	9P-11P	NBC Sunday Night Movie	1200	*1100	1000	900	800
M-Su	8P-11P	Prime ROS	*550	500	450	400	350

SPECIAL NOTES: All submissions on avails must be at asterisk (*) level. All sports and specials are on weekly sports and specials sheet.

Fixed: Level 1
Pre-emptible with notice: Levels 2, 3, 4
Immediately pre-emptible without notice: Levels 5 & 6

:10-Second Availabilities - 60% of the :30 rate
:15-Second Availabilities - 65% of the :30 rate
:60-Second Availabilities - Twice the :30 rate

All programming subject to change without notice.
Program rate available upon request.

Home shopping networks such as QVC do millions of dollars of business every year.

Public Television   Public television stations can be small or large, depending on the markets that they serve. Funding for a public station comes from a variety of sources. Fewer federal and state dollars are available for public stations, and as a result underwriting rules for television were relaxed in the mid-1990s. They cannot "sell" time as commercial stations do, so public stations generally rely upon underwritings and local revenue-raising promotions for a portion of their budget. Underwritings for public television are much more commercial-like than they were 10 years ago. Stations will now show the corporate logo of the underwriter, in addition to noting the specifics of its goods or service.

Public television stations also rely upon corporate and individual members to help pay for the costs of programming. Corporate underwriting usually means that a local company will help pay for the cost of the specific programming. Shows such as "The Computer Chronicles" will have a national and local underwriter. The show's production costs are underwritten by the national sponsor, while the station may use a local computer store to pay for the rights to air the program. Membership drives usually occur twice each year, the goal of which is to resubscribe current station members and add new ones to the roster. During these membership periods the station will run a heavy schedule of specials and promotions.

Promotions tend to center around art auctions, community fundraising events, and similar activities that raise revenue for the station. PBS also makes substantial use of its image as the place for quality programming in order to raise funds. During special membership drives, local stations will broadcast concerts and specials by noted performers as a way of generating new station members. Concert specials will often be followed by the star herself asking for your pledge of support. In the same vein, PBS stations use their children's television stars, such as Barney or Big Bird, to help raise funds for the station.

OTHER ASPECTS OF BROADCAST SALES
Station Identification and Promotion

Station identification is extremely important since the sale of time is directly related to the number of listeners the station has and, generally, the greater the listenership the greater the potential number of sponsors. So stations try to make themselves identifiable to their listeners and sponsors through the use of slogans and promotional contests.

Radio stations will use a combination of call letters and their *frequency* (location on the radio dial) as a means of promoting themselves. Number and letter combinations like "95X" often connote music preference in the same way that "Lite102" has meaning for the listener. These combinations are recorded in diaries at "sweeps" times and a rating for the station is determined. Frequently, a radio station will *trade out* commercial time for products or services that the station can give away. Contests can be used

Ethics: Radio Promotion: Chaos out of Control?

While promotion is increasingly important in the hotly competitive environment of radio today, there are indications that some stations are going overboard in their efforts to lure audiences. Some examples:

- A morning DJ for a Phoenix station pogo-sticked the entire 26-mile route of the Boston Marathon—it took him two and a half days—and wound up with severe knee damage.

- An Abilene, Texas, DJ tried to raise money for the United Way by spending 81 straight hours on a Ferris wheel. One night, while adjusting his sleeping bag, he fell off. Lucky for him, he was at the bottom of the wheel at the time. The Ferris wheel attendant who immediately rushed to his aid, however, was *not* so lucky; he was hit by the wheel and suffered a concussion.

- A radio station in Rhode Island bought a huge billboard to promote the repair of its high-powered transmitter. The sign, which said "More Power Than God," led to a deluge of complaints, led by the Greater Providence Council of Churches. "We never intended people to take us as literally as they did," said the sheepish general manager. The sign was removed shortly thereafter.

- An FM station in Sacramento, California, ran a Smash the Zoo promotion, in which all five members of the station's controversial morning "Zoo Crew" sat in an old car that had all the window glass removed. Listeners were given sledgehammers and allowed to pound on the car. The car was supposed to rest on a platform so that people swinging the sledgehammers wouldn't be able to reach the open windows. Unfortunately, the platform never arrived. With the DJs in easy reach, members of the crowd started flailing away with 10-pound sledgehammers. Luckily, the promotion was stopped before anybody got hurt.

Listeners are well aware of the treasures to be had in radio promotion. A teenager in suburban Chicago considers himself a radio contest connoisseur. Since 1990, he has won 250 movie passes, 150 compact discs, 75 sets of concert tickets, 20 "Walkman"-style radio receivers, 5 stereo sets, 4 sets of airline tickets, and a Jeep Wrangler. Not to be outdone, in Los Angeles, a group of computer hackers was arrested for taking control of radio station phone lines during station contests, blocking all but their own calls. Until shut down by police, the ring had received $22,000 in prize money, two Hawaiian vacations, and two Porsches.

as a means to build listenership and loyalty. Promotions vary greatly based on the size of the market and the station.

Good ratings are vital. Just one ratings point can translate into thousands of dollars in extra sales for a station. In the last few years, many stations have increased the value of the prizes given away during sweeps in an effort to raise the diary numbers and ultimately their ratings. Expensive sports cars and cash prizes in excess of $10,000 or $20,000 are not unusual prizes.

Radio stations also use another type of promotion to raise listenership: Commercial-free rides encourage extended listening. Commercials are then clustered together at the end of, say, "twenty minutes of nonstop music." When a station changes its overall format, it may change just prior to ratings period. After an advertising blitz, stations might begin a "commercial-free" month during that sweeps period. Station sales for the next quarter or half of the year will be set by the numbers garnered during the ratings

period. Frequently listeners are drawn to the station during the commercial-free month but often revert back to old listening habits when commercials resume. Usually most stations realize that they need good numbers all year long, so promotion tends to be an ongoing process.

Television has a great need for promoting programs and personalities. Television promotion tends to be somewhat different from that of radio. You'll see few contests, and even fewer opportunities to win the sports car of your dreams on TV. Instead, television promotion tends to be divided up into two specific categories: the promotion of specific shows or the copromotion of events in coordination with a sales event.

Promotional announcements, or *promos,* are short announcements that publicize a program on the station. These messages remind you of the content of a show—"Tomorrow on 'Geraldo': Satanic transvestite drug-abusing prostitutes who want to adopt"—or they may just remind the viewer of an upcoming

"Judge Judy" was one of the most successful shows in syndication in the late 1990s.

program—"News tonight at 11." The process of promoting a television show is important and costly for broadcasters. Remember that every 10- or 20-second promotion is time that a television station cannot sell. Obviously a station must make a commitment to advertising itself and its shows. Viewers won't immediately know when they can watch "Judge Judy" unless the station tells them (but some viewers do use the TV listings!).

Local television news is another area in which stations need to promote themselves. Does the station have a particular focus on local government? An investigative team? Or special family healthcasts? Does the station specialize in covering a particular local sports team? Viewers will need to know what distinguishes one station's news programming from that of the competition. Solid promotions are necessary to build audience and, as a result, revenue through high-priced advertising.

Other Announcements

The second type of announcement is the *public service announcement (PSA)*. These announcements, as the term implies, are unpaid. Every year broadcasters perform millions of dollars worth of public service by offering timely announcements to their audience without charge. At the national level, PSA campaigns are organized and managed by the National Association of Broadcasters and the Advertising Bureau.

Local radio and television stations frequently donate airtime and talent to produce or cosponsor local events that raise millions of dollars for local charities and people in need. For example, when an exceptionally ferocious storm hit the Syracuse area in late 1998, tens of thousands of people lost power, heat, and water for more than a week. Thousands of people lost their homes. The Cox group of radio stations set about collecting donations for the needy and raised $250,000 in donations in a matter of days. This is one of many examples of how local broadcasters can use PSAs to help the needy.

THE FUTURE OF BROADCASTING AND CABLE SALES

Super is an appropriate word. It describes the general outlook for electronic media as we enter the new millennium. Media research groups and analysts from Veronis, Suhler and Associates; McCann-Erikson; Katz Media; and others point to above-average growth for almost all media, with electronic media such as radio, television, and cable leading the pack. That's good news for those readers hoping to get a job in one of the electronic media fields after graduation.

Sales managers for television and radio stations usually like to point out that sales are among the top-paying jobs in the field. Further, they insist that as sales managers, they hold the most important jobs in broadcasting. If the salespeople didn't do their job well, there would be little money for programming. We think there's something to what they say.

SUMMARY

- Electronic media outlets such as radio, television, and cable sell audiences to advertisers. The audience gains entertainment or information, and media outlets sell the audience's attention to advertising agencies.

- Different media outlets compete for audience attention. For example, television competes against video outlets such as cable and video rentals. Radio competes against audio competitors and outdoor advertising. Cable gets revenue through advertising but makes the majority of its income charging subscribers access fees.

- The amount of competition in the marketplace frequently defines the kind of programming that is appropriate. In a monopoly there is no effective competition. When there is a great amount of competition, ratings define who the leading media outlets are. In comparing the various outlets to place an ad-

vertisement, media buyers look at the cost of advertising on the different media. Cost per thousand is a way to compare the cost of advertising on different media.

- Both radio and television have different ways of selling time to advertisers. Local, national spot, and network sales provide venues for advertisers to focus in on audiences or advertise broadly. Television networks are complicated media outlets. Networks pay compensation to affiliates for carrying their programs. Stations fill their broadcast times with syndication and local programming when networks do not provide programming.

- There are several types of announcements on radio and television. Promotions help to provide excitement for the station or its programming. Public service announcements (PSAs) provide free announcements and publicity to not-for-profit organizations.

KEY TERMS

monopoly   145
oligopoly   145
pure competition   145
buying power index (BPI)   145
gross rating points (GRP)   146
gross impressions   146

cost per thousand (CPM)   147
standing order   147
dayparts   149
cooperative advertising   149
adjacencies   151
syndication   151

upfront (sales)   151
inventory   152
scatter market   152
compensation   153
pods   157
station identification   160

SUGGESTIONS FOR FURTHER READING

"Advertising Outlook: How the pie will be sliced in '99." (1999, January 4). *Broadcasting and cable*. Washington, DC: Cahners.

Alexander, A., Owers, J., & Carveth, R., Eds. (1993). *Media economics: Theory and practice*. Hillsdale, NJ: Lawrence Erlbaum.

Broadcasting and Cable. (1999). *Broadcasting and cable yearbook*. Washington, DC.

Dizard, W. (1994). *Old media/New media*. White Plains, NY: Longman.

McLuhan, M. (1964). *Understanding media: The extensions of man*. New York: McGraw-Hill.

Owens, B., Beebe, J. H., & Manning, W., Jr. (1974). *Video economics*. Lexington, MA: Lexington Books.

Parsons, P., & Frieden, R. M. (1998). *The cable and satellite television industries*, Needham Heights, MA: Allyn & Bacon.

Sherman, B. L. (1995). *Telecommunications management* (2d ed.). New York: McGraw-Hill.

Sissors, J. Z., & Goodrich, W. B. (1992). *Media planning workbook*. (3d ed.). Lincolnwood, IL: NTC Business Books.

Tapscott, D. (1996). *The digital economy: Promise and peril in the age of networked intelligence*. New York: McGraw-Hill.

Walker, J. & Ferguson, D. (1998). *The broadcast television industry*. Needham Heights, MA: Allyn & Bacon.

Warner, C. & Buchman, J. (1993). *Broadcast and cable selling*. Belmont, CA: Wadsworth.

Wimmer, R. & Dominick, J. R. (1998). *Mass media research* (5th ed.). Belmont, CA: Wadsworth.

INTERNET EXERCISES

1. Visit our Web site at http://www.mhhe.com/beyond for study-guide exercises to help you learn and apply material in each chapter. You will find ideas for future research as well as useful Web links to provide you with an opportunity to journey through the new electronic media.

Radio Programming 8

Quick Facts

 Number of Americans who listen to radio each week: 250 million (1999 est.)

 Number of Americans who listen to Rush Limbaugh each week: 15 million (1999 est.)

 Percent of radio audience under age 35: 55

 Radio's most important time of day: 6 to 10 A.M. (Morning Drive)

 Most popular program on National Public Radio: "Car Talk"

 Favorite sport of talk radio listeners: Football

To unlock the secret of radio programming today, it's helpful to turn to the biological sciences. Biologists define *symbiosis* as "the living together in intimate association or close union of two organisms," especially if mutually beneficial—like silverfish and army ants or coral and sea creatures.

Symbiosis is also an especially good term to use to describe radio programming today. Radio enjoys a close and mutually beneficial relationship with a variety of other "organisms." The popularity of music from feature films (from *Saturday Night Fever* in 1975 to *Dirty Dancing* in 1987 to *Pulp Fiction* in 1994 to *Titanic* in 1998) illustrates how radio is intertwined today with the movie business. The rise of MTV and its host of imitators, (such as Country Music Television, VH-1, and the Box) point to radio's interrelationship with TV, especially cable. But radio's most symbiotic relationship is with the popular music business: the world of records, tapes, and discs. Since radio is more than an electronic jukebox, we will also examine the dynamics of information programming on radio: the nature of "news radio" and "talk radio."

RADIO REGULATION AND FORMAT DESIGN

For this symbiotic relationship to work, it's necessary for radio stations to have the freedom to choose the programming they want to provide to their communities. Section 326 of the Communications Act, the law that empowered the FCC to govern broadcast operations, states:

> Nothing in this Act shall be understood or construed to give the Commission the power of censorship over the radio communications or signals transmitted by any radio station, and no regulation or condition shall be promulgated or fixed by the Commission which shall interfere with the right of free speech by means of radio communication.

In short, the FCC has neither the right nor the power to control radio programming. Radio stations are free to program their airtime however they may. In certain specific areas, such as political advertising, obscenity, and indecency, the FCC has introduced legislation regarding programming. However, the bulk of radio programming—music, news, and information—is largely free of governmental intrusion. In fact, this characteristic is one of the fundamental distinctions between the sound of American radio and that of the rest of the world. Basically, American radio is programmed to satisfy listener tastes and not, as in government-owned systems, to serve political or bureaucratic interests.

We call this situation "format freedom." Faced with the task of filling 20 or more hours per day, 365 days a year, radio programmers are "on their own." Their task is simple: to provide attractive programming to meet the informational and/or entertainment needs of an audience. In commercial radio, the audience must be large or important enough to be of interest to advertisers. Public stations must entertain and inform their listeners to an extent that justifies financial support from government agencies, foundations, business underwriters, and the listeners themselves. If the task seems especially formidable, at least the programmers don't have to worry about direct governmental intrusion. (Maybe life is easier for the program director of Radio Iraq.)

A MATRIX OF RADIO PROGRAMMING

Types of radio programming today are mapped in Figure 8–1.

Across the top of the matrix of radio programming are the sources of radio programming. **Local programming** is original programming produced by the radio station in its station or from locations in its immediate service area. **Prerecorded** or **syndicated programming** is programming obtained by the station from a commercial supplier, advertiser, or program producer from outside the station. The most common sources of programming of this type are records, tapes, and compact discs. Prerecorded programs may also be received by stations through telephone lines, by microwave relay, or by satellite. Stations that belong to a network such as ABC, CBS, or National Public Radio are permanently interconnected, usually by telephone lines or satellite transponders. Unlike syndication, **network pro-**

Figure 8–1

Types of Radio Programming

		Source		
		Local	Prerecorded/ Syndicated	Network
Type	Music	1	2	3
	News/Talk	4	5	6

gramming is regularly scheduled; that is, with few exceptions, network programs run the same time each day at every station on the network.

Top to bottom in Figure 8–1 are the two main types of radio programming. Most plentiful in radio today is *music programming,* from opera to country, from "adult standards" to progressive jazz. *News/talk* covers the broad spectrum from news and traffic reports to sexual advice, from stand-up comedy to stock tips.

Music

Now, let's examine the kinds of radio programs that fall into each box. In box 1 is locally produced music programming. Once a staple of radio programming, when many stations employed their own orchestras, original music emanating from studios or area concert halls is heard today on only a few stations (mostly noncommercial). Some rock stations have had success promoting the music of local bands. For example, WNNX (99X) in Atlanta, a modern rock station, has broadcast numerous live performers from its studios and has successfully marketed these performances on disc and tape. Some programs heard nationally today began as local productions. American Public Radio's "Prairie Home Companion," hosted by affable Garrison Keillor, started in this fashion. However, locally produced music is becoming increasingly rare and is thus the smallest segment of the matrix.

The biggest element of radio programming today is box 2, prerecorded and syndicated music. Nearly 9 of 10 radio stations rely on some kind of music as the backbone of their schedule, and that music is most likely coming from a CD, a tape recorder, or a satellite transponder. This is the high-intensity world of format radio, described in detail later.

Pronounced dead and buried by industry observers just a few years ago, network music programming (box 3) has undergone a renaissance in recent years. Joining the long-running orchestral and opera broadcasts (such as the Texaco-sponsored Metropolitan Opera, and the New York Philharmonic, Philadelphia Orchestra, and Chicago Symphony broadcasts) have been the live broadcasts of Westwood One, the Los Angeles–based radio network. Rock-and-roll music has been the network's strong suit, featuring live national broadcasts of concerts by the Rolling Stones, Eric Clapton, U2, and the Red Hot Chili Peppers.

Howard Stern, one of the personalities behind the growth of radio syndication. Stern's sometimes controversial show is heard in numerous markets across the country.

More recently, Westwood One has moved into the urban area, with a series of live concerts hosted by comedian Sinbad, with performances by Earth, Wind & Fire; Deniece Williams; and The Emotions.

News/Talk

Locally produced news/talk programming (box 4) includes the many news, sports, weather, and traffic reporters at work in radio today, as well as a range of local hosts of political, civic, medical, and financial information shows. As we saw in Chapter 4, news and talk stations have the largest staffs in radio, including hosts, anchors, reporters, producers, and a host of technicians.

You will note from Figure 8–1 that there is a dashed line between boxes 5 and 6: syndicated and network radio. This is because the two forms are in the process of growing and combining.

Profile: Trust No One: The Strange Case of Art Bell

Art Bell is the unlikeliest of national radio celebrities. He did spend 20 years as a disc jockey, playing rock and roll around the Southwest, including a stint at 91-X in Tijuana, just south of San Diego. But he tired of the travel and the relentless meddling of program directors and left radio for a successful engineering career in cable TV, building systems in San Diego and Las Vegas for Times-Mirror. But Bell never lost the radio bug, and in the late 1980s he agreed to host an overnight show on KDWN (K-Dawn) in Las Vegas. After a short time talking the usual political talk, Bell began concentrating on what he calls "the unusual"—reports of aliens, UFOs, apparitions, and supernatural events. The program soon became a lifeline for legions of listeners preoccupied with the netherworld.

Broadcasting via satellite from his home in Pahrump, Nevada (not too far from the mysterious Area 51 where the U.S. government is said to have secretly discovered and studied UFOs), today Bell boasts over 400 affiliated stations and a weekly audience over 10 million strong. Bell treats those listeners to a steady stream of talk about extraterrestrial life, alien encounters, government conspiracies—indeed the whole "X-Files" mantra. One regular caller to his weekday program "Coast to Coast AM" (and "Dreamland," its weekend incarnation), is Mel from Washington, who claims there is a hole on his property into which cars, refrigerators, and cows can be thrown without touching bottom.

Bell gained attention in late 1996 when an amateur astronomer told a national audience that a mysterious object was trailing the Hale-Bopp comet. In March 1997, 37 members of the Heaven's Gate cult committed suicide, claiming the comet-following object was a spacecraft that would take them home to "a higher plane of existence." Bell said he had never heard of the cult and was not responsible for the deaths.

Most recently, the Internet and the radio underground were abuzz, certain that Art Bell himself had been abducted by aliens. Without warning, at 2:25 one morning Bell told his audience he was quitting broadcasting, due to a "threatening, terrible event . . . which I cannot tell you about." Jacor, the giant radio company that syndicates "Dreamland," was taken by surprise. Speculation ranged from a government plot to silence Art Bell to a publicity stunt designed to inflate his contract with Jacor.

A few weeks later, Bell was back in business, denying that his departure was a publicity stunt, a contract ploy, or a government plot, for that matter. The departure had something to do with family problems, centering around his son. Or did it? Trust no one. The truth is out there.

For example, many popular talk personalities who have been successful in one market are now being syndicated via satellite to many other markets. Howard Stern of WXRK in New York (whose talent is talk, despite the fact that he's featured mostly on rock stations) is on the air in about 20 markets, and his audiences are large and loyal. Another syndicated talker is WFAN (New York) personality Don Imus. Imus is heard on 30 stations around the nation, including affiliates in Boston, Washington, and Seattle.

Other leading syndicated radio talkers are Dr. Laura Schlessinger, Jim Bohannon, Bruce Williams, G. Gordon Liddy, Michael Reagan, Dr. Dean Edell, and Doug Stephan. Even if you are not familiar with these personalities, you've probably heard of the reigning king of talk radio: Rush Limbaugh.

Limbaugh, a conservative commentator, is heard on more than 600 stations, with a weekly cumulative audience of about 15 million Americans. While many listeners disagree with his politics, there is no denying his contribution to the radio business. When his program began to attract attention about 10 years ago, AM radio was in decline. Most AM stations were bankrupt or near-bankrupt. The AM listening audience was shrinking. Thanks to the popularity of Rush, his legion of imitators and his ideological opposites (like liberal Tom Leykis), the AM band rebounded. By 1998, talk radio was the leading format in the top 25 metropolitan areas, reaching a daily audience of more than 10.5 million adults each day, most on their way to or from high-paying jobs.

MODES OF RADIO PRODUCTION

Just as radio programmers have a full menu of types and sources of programming, they likewise have a range of ways to produce those programs for their audiences. This is just one example of the many

Dr. Laura Schlessinger's talk show has millions of loyal listeners.

decisions that have to be made by radio managers. We call these choices modes of radio production. The various modes are depicted in Figure 8–2.

At the left end of the continuum is **local, live production.** When radio stations employ their own announcers or newscasters locally and play CDs and tapes that they themselves own, they are using this mode of production.

Live-assist production occurs when radio managers use syndicated programming, such as reels of prerecorded music and satellite-delivered music services, but retain local announcers and DJs as the backbone of their program schedule. In this case the live air personality assists in the implementation of the syndicated schedule, hence live-assist.

Semiautomation refers to the reliance of the local radio station on the services of the syndicated program producer. The music is typically played on large tape machines or comes in via satellite. When a break

point for a commercial or program announcement is reached, smaller tape machines are triggered to play by a subaudible cue tone on the master tape or broadcast in the satellite transmission. In a semiautomated system the station occasionally inserts live personalities, perhaps in morning programs or for news and local weather breaks. But the backbone of the programming is the syndicated music schedule.

At the far end of the radio production continuum is **turnkey automation.** This refers to fully automated radio stations that take one of two main forms. Some automated stations consist largely of a satellite dish and a control board. The satellite dish downlinks a radio program service, such as country, rock, or beautiful music. In some cases the service has been so localized that time, weather, and news information is sent by satellite or computer to the program producer in time for the announcers thousands of miles away to prepare the inserts.

Other turnkey automation systems rely on CD players or tape machines interfaced with a computer console. The program director uses a computer program to prepare the logs, which plan all the music, information, and commercial elements, including their order, length, and frequency. Once the manager has approved the logs, the same or another computer at the station controls the program schedule, selecting the music, commercials, and cartridge

Figure 8–2

Modes of Radio Production

Local, live	Live–assist	Semiautomated	Turnkey automation

Developing the Music Format

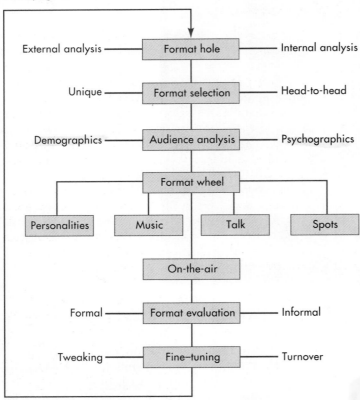

ment? In addition, the programmer must decide on how the programs will be produced for the audience. Will format freedom reign, giving local control to program directors and disc jockeys? Will outside consultants make many program decisions, with the goal of assisting local announcers and personalities? Will the station be programmed from afar via satellite, with only occasional local break-ins? Or, will the station be essentially a radio music box, completely automated and controlled by management personnel and their desktop computers?

CREATING THE RADIO FORMAT

The myriad of options facing radio management regarding programming can be answered by the process of creating and refining a format. In radio terminology, the format is the overall sound and image of the radio station: its comprehensive approach to its talk, music, advertisements, promotional strategies, community relations, personalities, and other factors. There are three keys to a successful format:

1. To identify and serve a predetermined set of listeners.

2. To serve those listeners better than the competition.

3. To reward those listeners both on and off the air, so they become consistent customers for the products and services advertised on the station.

In radio today, the format reigns supreme. It is both an art and a science, combining such artistic expressions as the musical talents of singers and groups and the diverse personalities of deejays and talk-show hosts with the social and behavioral sciences, including polls, surveys, and focus groups.

RADIO MUSIC FORMATTING

Today, more than 8 of 10 radio stations overall, and 9 of 10 on FM, choose some form of music as the backbone of their programming. The process of developing a radio music format is detailed in Figure 8–3.

tapes with news and weather from bins of prerecorded tapes, discs, and other recording media.

New developments in radio automation rely on the enhanced audio-processing capabilities of today's computers. It is now possible to have a music radio station without a single record, tape, or compact disc. All voice and music elements can be stored in digital computer format and played on demand from the desktop computer of the general manager or program director.

The task facing radio program managers is formidable. They must decide whether to emphasize talk or music or strive to operate a full-service station. Having made that decision, they must determine where the programming should come from. Will it all emanate locally? Should the station acquire a music library? If not, which program sources should be used? Should the station purchase a satellite dish? For what services? Should it affiliate with a network? If so, which one(s)? And to what degree of commit-

THE "FORMAT HOLE"

Whether placing a new station on the air, acquiring an established station, or reevaluating the programming of an existing station, radio broadcasters have two main choices about how to fill their airtime. They may try to outdo the competition in a given service by programming the same format—most of the nation's largest markets boast at least two of radio's major formats, from contemporary hit radio, to urban, country, and rock—or the station may decide instead to inventory and analyze radio programming in the market in search of an unfulfilled programming need. Managers may decide to try modern rock, progressive jazz, or other formats in areas where these services were previously not heard.

Whatever the choice, the secret to successful radio programming is to carve a unique niche, one that will deliver a large enough audience to attract advertising revenues to that station. In the radio business the phrase used is "find the format hole." The process is dependent on two sets of factors: internal and external.

Internal factors affecting the analysis include the ownership of the station, its dial location, power, technical facilities, and management philosophy. For example, it would not make much sense for a station at 99.5 on the dial to play contemporary music if a competitor is already playing this format at 101 FM. It would not be wise for a 5,000-watt AM station at 1570 on the dial, with a full-service country format, to compete against a 50,000-watt powerful station in that format at 720 on the dial.

The process of external analysis begins with a competitive market study, which examines the existing stations, including their technical properties, their ownership, their financial performance, their ratings, and, of course, their current formats. If there are competitors, are they strong? Or do they have program weaknesses (bad musical selection, poor announcers, weak promotions, and so on) that make them vulnerable to competitive attack?

Other external factors include geography and population characteristics (country/western in Wichita, laid-back "new age" in Los Angeles, nostalgia for the aging population of West Palm Beach, for instance).

The search for the format hole yields one of two outcomes: the station selects a new or different format that is unavailable in the market, or it decides to compete in the same format with one or more existing stations. The former choice makes the station unique; the latter we refer to as becoming a head-to-head competitor.

Audience Analysis

The goal of radio programming is to attract and maintain an audience. So it makes sense that one of the primary steps in creating a music format is audience identification. In format radio, every station must ascertain its **target audience,** the primary group of people sought by the station's programming. As we traced briefly in Chapter 4, the target audience is usually defined by its principal **demographics,** including age, gender, racial/ethnic background, income, and other descriptors.

The radio audience is also defined by listeners' attitudes, beliefs, values, hobbies, lifestyles, and motivations for listening. These kinds of audience attributes are known collectively as **psychographics.** Following are some industry rules of thumb regarding demographics and psychographics.

Listener Demographics   One reason radio has remained and even rebounded in the TV, cable and Internet eras, is its phenomenal reach. As we have seen, radio is an intensely personal medium that reaches almost all Americans on a daily basis. All told, radio reaches over 250 million people each week. Just under half of all Americans over the age of 12 listen to radio between 6 and 10 A.M. on weekdays. From 6 A.M. to 6 P.M., radio reaches more people than TV, cable, newspapers, magazines, and computers and online services. In short, radio has excellent demographics.

Radio managers divide the U.S. population into standard demographic categories. Gender is demographically defined in terms of men and women (naturally enough). Combined, men and women over age 12 are considered "persons." Those 18 and above are "adults" in a radio ratings book. The standard age cutoffs (known as "age breakouts," or simply "breaks," in the radio business) are tots (ages 2–11), teens (12–17), 18–24, 18–34, 18–49, 25–34, 35–54, and 55 and above (the growing audience of "senior adults"). Demographic research indicates that radio is primarily a "young" medium (even though radio is over 100 years old: Nearly 55 percent of the radio audience is under the age of 35; a third of the radio audience falls into the 25–44 age range, and the largest groups of female listeners (who make most consumer purchases) are in the 25–54 and 18–34 age ranges.

Ethics: Paid to Play: Payola

In the late 1950s, the DJ became "king" of the radio business. Big-name DJs in major markets, like Howard Miller in Chicago and Murray the K in New York, had become well known to thousands of loyal listeners, and they exerted considerable influence in the record business. Simply put, if they liked a song and played it over the air, the song had a good chance of success.

This fact did not go unnoticed by the record industry, which showered DJs and music directors with gifts and gratuities, known as **payola.** Lucky "jocks" received cars, golf clubs, vacation trips—you name it. But the gravy train apparently ground to a halt in 1960, when, following a series of highly publicized hearings, Congress enacted legislation making the acceptance of payola a criminal offense, punishable by a $10,000 fine. Since then, most stations have had their DJs and PDs (program directors) sign affidavits guaranteeing compliance with the payola statutes.

However, payola has never really vanished. In the ensuing 40 years, attempts to influence radio programming personnel by record companies and artists' management have taken on new, sometimes "subterranean" forms. Recently, two record promoters were indicted for making payments exceeding $250,000 to PDs at nine stations. It was also alleged that at least three of the PDs were provided free cocaine in return for their endorsements of the promoters' artists.

The Department of Justice has launched an investigation into a payola scheme in which it is alleged that a Spanish-language record label was funneling as much as $10,000 per month to radio stations for playing the company's artists. The payments were said to be getting to the program directors and disc jockeys through a personal courier: an independent promoter well-known for his interest in Spanish-language artists and performers. Such promoters are familiar to program and music directors in all formats. Most of the time, however, they bear small gifts, like T-shirts, mugs, golf balls, pastries, and, of course, lots and lots of free CDs. Cash gifts and free cocaine are unusual incentives to play records, and are highly illegal.

Thus, the ideal radio format appeals to women, especially those in their mid-30s—hence the popularity of country and adult contemporary (soft rock), the two leading radio formats. Radio stations attracting males would be wise to seek an older, professional audience (beautiful music/adult standards), aging "baby boomers" in their late 40s (news/talk or classic rock), or younger (25 to 34) music aficionados (modern rock).

Nationally, the black and Hispanic audience together represent about 15 percent of all listeners—a large and growing group. Thus, there has been the rapid rise of black/urban/contemporary, Hispanic, Hot AC, and other radio formats described back in Chapter 4.

Radio programming begins with an analysis of these demographics, but not on a national basis. The first step is to look at these and other descriptive characteristics as they occur in a station's local market. Younger demographics might send a program director toward a younger format; older, to an older sound. But at best, demographics provide only a partial picture of the radio audience.

Listener Psychographics With about 20 distinct formats competing for a share of the radio audience,

and with more than one station and as many as five or six programming the same format in many cities, stations have developed more detailed methods of identifying their audiences. The current rage in radio research is listener psychographics (see Chapter 12), also known as *lifestyle* or *qualitative research*. *Psychographic research* is an attempt to understand radio listeners according to their attitudes, values, beliefs, leisure pursuits, political interests, and other factors. For radio programmers today, the age and gender of the audience are insufficient data: They need to know how their listeners view the world (and how their selected radio stations fit into that world).

A number of interesting psychographic studies of the radio audience have been conducted in recent years. Perhaps the best known of these was the "Radio W.A.R.S." series. Conducted in the mid-1980s for the National Association of Broadcasters by the research firm of Reymer and Gersin, these studies are still pertinent today despite some format evolution. Radio W.A.R.S. examined the psychological dimensions of radio listening. In other words, what are the listeners to the major formats *really* like? Let's take a look at some of the results.

Contempory hit radio (CHR)   The research revealed that listeners to Top-40 stations tend to fall into two main psychographic groups. One group listens primarily to hear new music with an up-tempo beat and a lot of urban rhythms (the kind of music heard on boom boxes). Reymer and Gersin called these listeners "new music trendies" and "get-me-up-rockers." Another subset of the format seemed attracted to CHR because it returned them to the format's heyday in the late 1950s and early 1960s. For them, listening to CHR was motivated by the desire to be put into a romantic, nostalgic mood. Songs about young love, funny DJs, and lots of oldies are what they want. Images of "Wolfman Jack" playing "Teen Angel" on a late Saturday night in southern California come to mind.

As the 1990s end, this research seems quite predictive. Today, multiple forms of CHR are becoming increasingly popular. The "urbanized" approach has led to the rap, Latin, and dance-influenced CHR, known in the trade as "churban" (CHR + urban contemporary). The nostalgia-fed CHR that treasures older standards has led to the rise of the "arrow" format (arrow = all rock-and-roll oldies) developed by the influential CBS radio group.

Follow-up research by radio advertising firm Interep tells us even more about the CHR crowd. Their late 1998 report found that most CHR listeners (56 percent) were women and were active consumers of soft drinks and alcoholic beverages. Compared with other groups, they attended more movies, ate in more restaurants, and used computer online services more than did listeners to the other popular formats. In addition, CHR listeners were also more likely to listen to Spanish, alternative, urban, and modern rock stations than were listeners to other formats like country, adult standards, and news/talk.

Modern rock   Rock listeners were found to be radio's most "socially motivated" listeners, considering themselves music experts. Three main subgroups were discovered. About 22 percent of rock listeners were labeled "uninvolved disloyals," listening solely for music, with disdain for DJs, contests, and most of all commercials. One-fifth of listeners to the format were found to be "mindless loyalists," plugging into radio rock to tune out the world. Another 20 percent of rock fans were "plugged-in smarts," looking for sophisticated and unpredictable music.

Again, trends in radio programming today reveal the predictive nature of psychographic research. Mod-

Wyclef Jean of the Fugees. About 300 stations across the country have adopted a rhythm and blues/rap format.

ern rock stations tend to reflect the world view of the "plugged-in smarts." Many listeners to this format see themselves on the cutting edge, in fashion, style, and especially music. Most modern rock stations capitalize on this perception: Their disc jockeys affect a certain "insider" attitude; station promotions, slogans, and even buttons and bumper stickers usually have a decidedly modern and antiestablishment look. Other rock stations target the "uninvolved" or the "mindless loyalists." For them, playing familiar mainstream music is complemented by uninterrupted musical sweeps, inoffensive DJs, and a more traditional graphical identity (think Grateful Dead T-shirts).

Of course, the "Radio W.A.R.S." studies were just one set of psychographic evaluations. The sample was national in scope; thus it is entirely possible (and likely) that listener motivations are different in Keokuk, Iowa, and Honolulu, Hawaii. For this reason many stations conduct their own psychographic listener studies. We shall examine those modes of research in Chapter 12.

Figure 8-4

Hot Clock for a Country Station

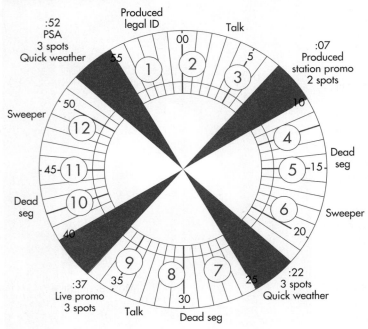

Figure 8-5

Hot Clock for a Rock Station

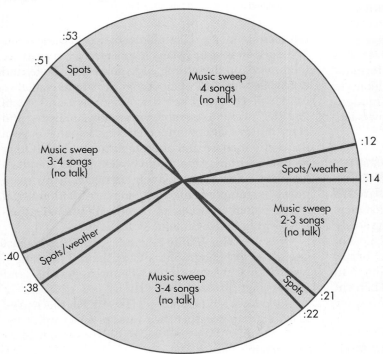

The Hot Clock

The next step in radio music programming involves the implementation of the schedule: the planning and execution of the station's sound. Most radio programmers today employ a version of a useful chart known as the **hot clock,** "format wheel," or "sound hour." Figures 8–4 and 8–5 are sample hot clocks.

Radio Dayparts   The format wheel looks like the face of a clock, with each element of the station's on-air sound—music, commercials, news, sports, promotions, and so on—scheduled at its precise interval in the programming hour. The hot clock performs two main functions. First, it enables programmers to get a visual image of an otherwise invisible concept, their "sound." Second, it enables programmers to compare their program proposals with the competition. In this way programmers make sure that at the time they air music, the other station plays its commercials; that the news does not air on both stations at the same time; that it is unlikely that the same song will air simultaneously on both stations; and so on.

Normally programmers use a different clock for each important scheduling period. Figure 8–6 illustrates how radio use varies throughout the day from Monday to Friday and on weekends. Find the peaks on each chart, and you have discovered the medium's key **dayparts** (important time periods).

Morning drive   Let's examine the Monday-to-Friday graph first. The highest point on the graph is radio's most important time period: Monday to Friday in the early morning. For convenience, programmers usually identify the boundaries of this time period as 6 A.M. to 10 A.M. Since most listeners are preparing to commute or are commuting to work and school, this is known as **morning drive time.** In most radio markets this is radio "prime time." This is where radio managers in the major markets commit their greatest program re-

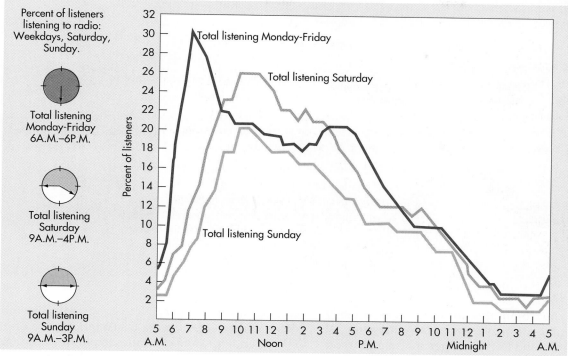

Figure 8–6

Radio Listening throughout the Day

Percent of listeners listening to radio: Weekdays, Saturday, Sunday.

Total listening Monday-Friday 6A.M.–6P.M.

Total listening Saturday 9A.M.–4P.M.

Total listening Sunday 9A.M.–3P.M.

Source: Courtesy Arbitron.

sources. The highest-paid radio personalities toil in this time period, frequently earning salaries in the mid- to high-six-figure range. Stations go to great expense and effort to have the top-rated morning show. Recently, the competitive battle has taken outrageous turns, leading to the rise of "shock jocks."

Another recent trend in morning drive is based on trends in the population. Americans are working longer and longer hours. As you've probably noticed, traffic is generally worse than ever before. Thus, morning drive has begun earlier. In many large cities, the top radio talents begin their shifts at 5 A.M. Some still work until 10 A.M. (often repeating elements from their earliest hours), others make way for the midday team at 8:30 or 9:00 A.M.

Evening drive The next "hump" in the Monday-to-Friday graph is seen in the late afternoon. This is radio's second-most-important time slot: 3 P.M. to 7 P.M., **evening drive time.**

The audience for evening drive radio is only about two-thirds the size of that for morning drive. This is because not

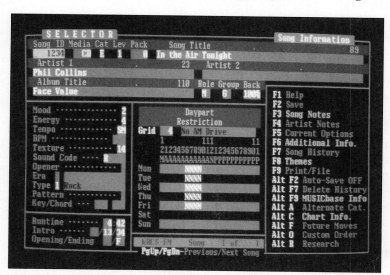

While hot clocks help programmers visualize the sound of their radio stations, most make use of computers to program their airtime.

everyone who commutes to work goes directly home. Also, the attractiveness of late-afternoon TV (Oprah Winfrey and Jerry Springer, for example) and early TV newscasts captures much of the audience at this time. People at home are more likely to watch these shows than listen to radio.

One programming element above all tends to dominate this daypart: traffic. Take a look skyward the next time you find yourself in afternoon city traffic. Chances are you'll spot multiple helicopters and a few light airplanes with radio station logos on them, each promising the best traffic reports for their stations.

Daytime There is a nice plateau in the weekday chart where radio listening holds steady at about one in five people. This is the fast-growing **daytime time period,** from 10:00 A.M. to 3:00 P.M. The popularity of portable radios in the home and workplace makes this one of radio's most important time periods.

The noon hour is especially critical to radio programmers in daytime. This is because of the popularity of listening to radio on lunch breaks. Many music stations air special programs designed for their target audiences at this time. AC stations may feature an "Oldies Cafe"; CHR stations may feature a "Danceteria"; and an album-rock station may run a "Metallic Lunchbox."

Evening and late night Note how radio listening slides in the early evening (as America turns on its TV sets and PCs) and continues to plummet through the night until dawn. Thus two less important Monday-to-Friday dayparts for programmers are **evening** (7:00 P.M. to midnight) and **overnight,** or **graveyard,** from midnight to 6:00 A.M.

Most stations revert to format in the evening and late-night hours. That is, they play long, extended versions of the preferred programming of their most dedicated listeners. Since it is harder to sell commercials in these dayparts (due to the comparatively small audience), the loyal listener is rewarded with longer musical programs, specials, and other extended programming.

Weekend radio Looking at the weekend plots on Figure 8–6 immediately reveals the most important time period to programmers and advertisers: Saturday in the late morning and early afternoon. This is when we are most likely to turn the radio on, as we clean the house, wash the car (or the dog), and head to the park or beach. There is a modest peak on Saturday evening, when radios are turned on at family or neighborhood gatherings and parties.

Note that at no time on Sunday does radio listening exceed levels achieved on Monday to Friday or on Saturday. The best time on Sunday seems to be in

Boom family @ NBC.com

the late morning, around 10:00 A.M. But with many listeners at church or sleeping late, this time slot is usually not a prime programming period.

At minimum, stations will use a hot clock for their Monday-through-Friday schedule in the morning drive time period, the midday time slot, the afternoon drive slot, and for the evening schedule. Stations may also employ a weekend clock for the daytime slots comprising late morning through the early afternoon.

Of course, these days radio hot clocks are rarely constructed with a compass or by outlining a paper pie plate, as was common "back in the day." Instead, program directors plot their show elements on their desktop PCs. Still, the process is the same, as is the terminology. Here's how the hot clock is put together:

Filling the Clock: Radio Programming Terminology

There are three main types of information depicted in the hot clock: commercial and promotional matter, music, and news/talk segments. The number and location of the commercial positions normally are set first by the general manager in consultation with the sales and program managers. Their job is to decide how many commercials will run and in which parts of the hour. While some beautiful music stations run as few as 8 or 9 commercial minutes per hour, some rock stations run as many as 15 or 16, and up to 20 or more in peak seasons such as the Christmas rush. The FCC has no strict limit on the number of commercial minutes per hour, but many stations hold the line at 18. The decision on number and placement of commercials is crucial. Although commercials pay for everything else on the station, too many spots—a situation called advertising **clutter**—may cause listeners to tune out or, worse, to tune elsewhere. In addition to scheduling commercial matter, stations will also use the format wheel to schedule their promotional announcements, including contests and giveaways. The commercial and promotional segments of the hot clock are normally known as **spot sets.** Somewhat confusingly, they may also be called *stop sets* since the music stops during these breaks.

The musical segments of the hot clocks are typically broken down into two or three subcategories, such as current hits (given the most airplay); recurrents, recent hits that are still popular; and gold, for golden oldies. Sometimes programmers use key words to denote the various song categories, such as

"power cuts" or "prime cuts" for the most popular current songs, "stash" or "closet classics" for obscure oldies, and "image cuts" for songs that seem to match the format perfectly, such as Beatles' love songs for adult contemporary. Some programmers use color-coding schemes. Red typically denotes power cuts, green may identify a new song in heavy rotation, and gold is used to signify an oldies set.

The area of overlap on the format wheel, where one program element ends and another begins, is known as a **segue,** pronounced "segway." The purest segue is one in which the musical segments blend from one song into another, without DJ interruption. But there are other options. The transition may be made by naming the artists and saying something about the previous song, a procedure known as a "liner." The station identification may be made ("ID"). The announcer might give the time and temperature ("T&T"). She might promote an upcoming feature ("teaser") or highlight a list of program and promotional activities ("billboard"). A promotional announcement ("promo") might be made. The air personality might promote the next artist or album ("front-sell"), or announce the performers of the last set of songs ("back-announce" or "back-sell"). Or the DJ might cover the time to the next musical set ("sweep") with comedy, ad libs, or listener call-ins ("fill"). With this glossary in mind, see if you can determine the program "sound" of the stations depicted in Figures 8–4 and 8–5.

Once the hot clock has been set, the format is in motion and the station is on the air! But the programming process is far from over.

Format Evaluation

Music programming is a particularly dynamic task. Audience tastes are constantly changing. A new pop star is always appearing on the charts. Listeners tire quickly of some songs. Others remain in our ears and minds seemingly forever. So, how does the music programmer select the songs for the wheel? When does a song get pulled? This is the difficult process of format evaluation, the next step in radio programming.

One good way to start is by keeping track of record sales at local and regional retail outlets. Many record stores provide this information to the radio stations in their area (next time you buy a CD, see if it is inventoried at the time of purchase).

Another way to keep track of musical tastes is by checking with trade publications, commonly known as **tip sheets.** Leading stations in the major formats provide these publications with a weekly report of the songs they are featuring, known as a **playlist.** In return they get "intelligence" about the popular songs and artists around the nation and in their geographical region. The major record labels use these report cards to make sure their artists are receiving airplay.

Influential charts include those in *Billboard* and *Radio and Records,* the two leading weekly trade publications. Other tip sheets appear in *Cashbox, Hits, Variety,* and *The Gavin Report.*

Most stations also keep track of what their listeners are telling them about their format. **Call-ins,** telephone calls to the station, are logged to determine how listeners feel about the songs, artists, and personalities on the station. Stations use lists of contest entrants and telephone directories to conduct **call-outs:** Short (5- to 10-second) selections of the music, known as **hooks,** are played over the phone and listeners are typically asked to rate the song as one they like a little, are unsure about, or like a lot.

Stations also assemble groups of their listeners in large rooms and conduct **auditorium tests.** In this forum up to 200 or 300 songs can be "hook-tested." Or stations may select a small group of listeners (from 3 to 15) and conduct in-depth interviews about their musical preferences; this is a **focus group study.**

If the task of evaluating the format sounds complex, that's because it is. For this reason many stations hire outside experts to help select their music, conduct their audience research, train their DJs, organize their promotions, and perform similar programming tasks. Such services are provided by program and research consultants.

There are essentially two main types of radio consultants. **Specialized consultants** provide expertise in one particular area, such as research, music selection, promotion, or financial management. **Full-service consultants** provide "soup-to-nuts" services, from how to decorate the radio station to how to deal with crank phone callers. A recent survey revealed almost 50 different radio consultants operating in the programming field. Some industry leaders are Paragon Research of Denver; The Research Group out of Bellevue, Washington; Shane Media of Houston, headed by program guru Ed Shane; and Roger Wimmer's The Eagle Group, also based in Denver.

Fine-Tuning the Format

The final phase of radio format evolution is fine-tuning. Using data based on listener reaction, as indicated by audience ratings, station research, phone calls, and other means, the program manager makes changes in the schedule. The changes can range from minor to drastic. Minor changes involve substitutions in the musical mix, reformatting the various time periods, moving personalities around throughout the day, and so on. Major adjustments include replacing air personalities (most typically in morning drive); developing new promotional campaigns, including occasional call-letter changes; and firing music directors (a relatively common occurrence). The most drastic change is to abandon the format altogether and to try a new type of music, targeted to a different audience demographic. In recent years "format turnover" has been increasing at a spectacular rate. In the late 1990s some estimates indicated that as many as 20 percent of radio stations change formats in a given year.

Despite the apparent complexity of the process of radio music formatting, it remains popular and rewarding work. Major-market program and music directors can look forward to high incomes, great visibility in the high-gloss world of popular music, and excellent "perks," like backstage passes to concerts and limo rides with the stars. Of course, some of these perks approach the limits of legality, which brings us to the problem of payola (see box on page 172).

NEWS/TALK AND SPORTS FORMATTING

On the surface it might appear that programming a radio station without music is a simpler task than formatting rock-and-roll or country. The format strategies of talk radio, however, are just as complex as those in the various music formats. How much news? How much telephone interview? What types of personalities? Sports? Which and how much? And, like the music formats, how many commercials? When?

The first consideration for a station planning a spoken-word service is to determine the type and amount of talk. There are two extremes in the format. At one is the all-news operation, providing summaries and spot news reports around the clock. Leading the way in this format are such classic all-news operations as WINS in New York, WBBM in Chicago, KFWB in Los Angeles, KYW in Philadelphia, and KIRO in Seattle. At the other extreme are all-talk stations, which lean

Figure 8–7

Hot Clock for an All-News Station

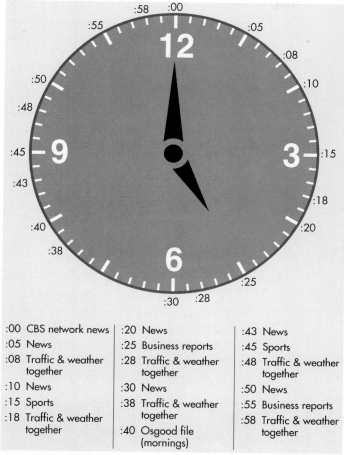

:00	CBS network news	:20	News	:43	News
:05	News	:25	Business reports	:45	Sports
:08	Traffic & weather together	:28	Traffic & weather together	:48	Traffic & weather together
:10	News	:30	News	:50	News
:15	Sports	:38	Traffic & weather together	:55	Business reports
:18	Traffic & weather together	:40	Osgood file (mornings)	:58	Traffic & weather together

Source: Courtesy CBS Radio.

heavily on the concept of the telephone call-in as the basis for their programming schedule. On this list are such stalwarts as New York's WOR and WABC, KOA in Denver, and WWWE in Cleveland.

Just like their musical counterparts, most news/talk radio stations use a format wheel to schedule their programming. Examine the clocks for an all-news station and an all-talk station in Figures 8–7 and 8–8.

All News

First, let's look at the all-news wheel. There are three basic elements in the sound hour: news segments, feature segments, and commercial matter. Typically news stations provide network news at or near the top of the hour. This provides the audience broad national and

international coverage, which the station can interpret or "localize" for its audience in other news segments. Some all-news stations break for network news reports at other times, typically at the 30-minute mark (the "bottom of the hour").

Credible announcers are a critical ingredient to the success of the all-news operation. Announcers must sound confident and authoritative. For this reason many all-news operations prohibit announcers from delivering commercial "pitches." This is to avoid hurting the newscaster's credibility, which might result from the announcer's reporting a natural disaster, for example, and then segueing to a used-car spot.

Feature programming at an all-news station runs the gamut from the expected (weather, sports, and traffic) to the more specialized (political, economic, and health reports). These reports usually are presented in a streamlined fashion—in units of three minutes or less.

By definition, all-news stations need to be bright, brisk, and dependable. News listeners tend to be "no-nonsense" information seekers. When they tune in to an all-news station, they expect to become well-informed quickly. For this reason the format wheel in all-news tends to spin rapidly; program elements are repeated regularly throughout the day. Phrases such as "give us 15 minutes, we'll give you the world" and "around the globe in 20 minutes" give evidence of this speedy rotation, especially in key dayparts like morning and evening drive. In this regard, the programming pace at an all-news station is similar to that at a Top-40 station.

News/Talk

Compared with all-news stations, those emphasizing talk tend to be "laid-back." News segments are common, particularly at the top and bottom of the hour, with the remainder of the program hour filled by features, interviews, and telephone call-in segments. As an example, inspect the hot clock for an all-talk station (Figure 8–8).

Note the more leisurely pace of the talk format. Talk segments of five to seven uninterrupted minutes are commonplace, like the "music sweeps" in adult contemporary and adult standards. These are presided over by talk-show hosts. Unlike the announcers on all-news stations, who tend to be interchangeable (credibility, rather than individuality,

Figure 8–8

Format Wheel for an All-Talk Station

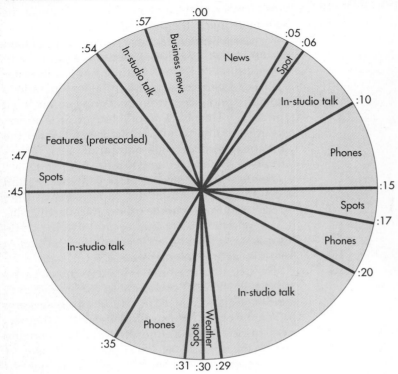

is the key for them), talk hosts are distinct personalities. Some boast political beliefs on the left of the political spectrum; others at the far right.

Feature elements are more commonplace in the talk format. Many stations have "resident experts" in such fields as medicine, psychiatry, finance, law, economics, and politics.

The prohibition of the reading of commercials by the announcer in the all-news format rarely extends to talk radio. In fact, talk-show hosts tend to be expert "pitchmen" (and women), who frequently give broad testimonials for their sponsors' products, sometimes longer than the 30 or 60 seconds the sponsor paid for.

Both news and talk tend to carry play-by-play sports on their schedule. In large markets there is considerable competition to land the broadcast rights to professional and major college sports in those cities. Smaller news and talk operations sign on to carry regional professional teams, as part of a network. Many also carry local college and high school games.

Talk radio is in a growth phase, fueled by sensational scandals and politically charged news events. Research on the audience, conducted by the trade magazine *Talkers,* is informative. The talk radio audience is mostly male (53 to 47 percent female); mostly mature (60 percent are aged 45 or older); mostly white (65 percent; 19 percent African American, and 7 percent Hispanic American); and mostly smart (75 percent with more than a high school education). Republicans outnumber Democrats (22 percent to 18 percent), but most talk radio listeners describe themselves as Independents (48 percent), Libertarians (8 percent), or "other" (4 percent). For what it's worth, the favorite food of talk radio fans is Italian (20 percent), football is their favorite sport, and their music formats of choice are country and adult contemporary (18 percent each).

NONCOMMERCIAL RADIO PROGRAMMING

As we traced briefly in Chapter 4, noncommercial radio programming is a "mixed bag," depending largely on the type of facility. Recall that there are three main classes of noncommercial facilities: public, university, and community.

One of the most popular programs on National Public Radio is "Car Talk," hosted by Tom and Ray Magliozzi.

Ethics: Love Is on the Air

One of the offshoots of the so-called sexual revolution of the late 1960s and early 1970s was the phenomenon known as "sex-talk" radio. As broadcast historians Pamela Johnson Sybert and F. Leslie Smith recounted in a recent report, sex-talk evolved from "Feminine Forum" on KGBS-AM (Los Angeles). On the show, which started in the spring of 1971, host Bill Ballance would announce a topic and invite women over 18 to call and make comments. Sample topics: "What place do you like to do it best?" "Tell us about your office affairs," and "How do you turn on your man?" The comments were recorded, edited, and aired the following day in the midday time period. The ratings went through the roof.

For the next two years, sex-talk radio took off. Similar shows were soon on the air in Cleveland, Detroit, Miami, New York, San Francisco, Dallas, and other cities. However, many listeners complained, the National Association of Broadcasters condemned the format, and the FCC opened an inquiry into the matter. The FCC chairman called the format "prurient trash." By late 1973, the format had all but disappeared.

Fast forward to today. Sex-talk is back, only in a different form. Nowadays, the host is more likely to be a woman than a man, the shows are mostly found in the late-night period, and they are more likely to be on FM rock stations than on AM.

One leading example of this format is the nationally syndicated "Love Phones" program, hosted by psychologist and sex therapist Dr. Judith Kuriansky (just "Dr. Judy" to her fans). At the local level, recent efforts include Erin Somers' "Passion Phones" on WKTS in Orlando, and "Loveline" hosted by "Dr. Drew" Pinski on KROQ in Los Angeles. With co-host Diane Farr and comedian Adam Carolla, "Loveline" recently moved to MTV, where it has become a popular late-night offering.

Sexual therapy on radio and in music television (especially with a comedian on the panel) raises some ethical questions. How real are the sexual problems under discussion; are the callers feigning their dysfunctions? How valid is the advice given to legitimate callers, given that there is little time to delve into background life experiences (not to mention the lack of a physical examination)? Since these shows exist mainly to entertain (or titillate, according to their critics), how appropriate are the topics under discussion? How often is sexual abstinence advocated? Are unusual sexual practices advertised or encouraged by these programs, in an era of widespread incidence of sexually transmitted diseases? What do you think?

Public Radio Stations

Public radio stations are those that meet guidelines for federal grant assistance through the Corporation for Public Broadcasting. CPB-qualified stations must employ at least five full-time employees, must broadcast at least 18 hours per day, and must demonstrate sufficient funding and listening support to justify the receipt of federal grant monies. These so-called CPB-qualified stations, numbering about 400 nationwide, are the backbone of the National Public Radio network, which boasts the well-known programs "All Things Considered," "Morning Edition," "Performance Today," and "Car Talk." CPB-qualified stations may also feature the programs offered by a smaller competing network, Public Radio International (PRI), of which Garrison Keillor's "A Prairie Home Companion" is perhaps the best known. As this book went to press, rumors were rampant of a possible merger between NPR and PRI.

Typically, CPB-qualified stations rely on NPR and PRI for about a quarter of their daily schedule. The remainder of the schedule is filled with locally originated music and public affairs programs. The overwhelming majority of CPB-qualified public stations play classical music as the backbone of their schedule. Other forms of music receiving airplay include jazz, opera, folk, and show tunes.

Public radio is following some of the same trends as commercial radio. For one, the industry has embarked on a major series of studies of its audience. Begun in 1998 by Audience Research Analysis, an independent firm located in Maryland, the studies provide important insight into the demographics and psychographics of the public radio audience. By the year 2000, the research had profiled minority listeners to public radio; "givers," those who pledge money to public radio; and public radio's important but small "Generation X" listeners.

In concert with expanded audience research, public radio has been diversifying its programs. Newer offerings include quiz/entertainment programs ("Wait . . . Don't Tell Me"), magazine shows (like Ira Glass's "This American Life"), and new music

Figure 8–9

WUOG Program Guide (Used with permission)

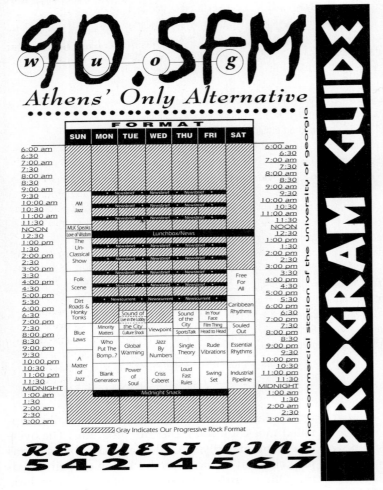

("Music from the Heart of Space"). And, like commercial radio, NPR has had some executive turnover. Taking over as president and CEO of NPR in December 1998 was Kevin Klose, a long-time journalist from the Washington Post, and the former head of the United States International Broadcast Bureau (IBB), the overseer of the Radio Free Europe and Radio Liberty services, among other positions (see Chapter 14).

College Radio

Although over 150 NPR-affiliated stations are operated by universities, we do not mean these when we speak of "college radio." Instead, we are referring to about 800 stations licensed to American colleges (and some high schools) that do not meet the CPB

criteria. Many are operated as student activities or training centers; most feature "alternative" programming schedules to both NPR and commercial radio. The musical mix at most college stations is eclectic and progressive. For example, examine the program schedule for WUOG, the student station at the University of Georgia (Figure 8–9).

As we have seen, commercial radio formatting is tightly structured and controlled. For this reason, college radio is where many new performers receive their initial exposure and airplay. This was the case for bands like R.E.M., Talking Heads, the Police, U2, INXS, and, more recently, Hole, Creed, Everlast, Eve 6, and the Dave Matthews Band.

Most college stations are active in news and public affairs programming. Again, the structure and approach of these services is an amalgam. Stations affiliated with journalism and mass communications programs may have news and public affairs schedules that emulate those at commercial operations. Others rely for news programming upon volunteer efforts by their staffers. In such cases schedules tend to be sporadic and content-varied, to say the least.

Community-Station Programming

If diversity is the word to describe college radio, the term is equally suited to the broad category of community radio stations. Community stations are operated by civic associations, school boards, charitable foundations, and, increasingly, religious organizations.

Most community stations use a **block programming** approach. Unlike commercial formats, where the music, talk, and commercial elements are generally consistent throughout the day, in the block scheme, programming is divided into two- or three-hour blocks appealing to different audiences at different times. Educational outlets, for example, may begin the day with a two-hour block appealing to elementary-age students. Midday might be used for in-home college-level instruction, and the afternoon dedicated to social studies programming for secondary schoolers.

The trend toward diversity in programming at noncommercial stations extends to the religious stations. While virtually all religious operations make live broadcasts of church sermons and activities a vital part of their programming day, beyond that there is great variation. Among Christian stations, for example, at various times one can hear old-time Gospel, solemn hymns, even rock, known as "contemporary Christian." And within the religious radio milieu, there are "networks." For example, the Protestant Radio and Television Center makes a range of programs available to over 700 stations. Its flagship service, "The Protestant Hour," has been on the air continuously since the 1930s.

A newer religious broadcaster making an impact today is Reverend James Dobson's "Focus on the Family," based in Colorado. By the late 1990s, the ministry's media division had produced and distributed numerous high-quality radio dramas and children's programs to hundreds of radio stations. Its drama on the life of theologian Dietrich Bonhoeffer received a prestigious Peabody Award in 1998.

SUMMARY

- There are strong ties between radio and the music business: it is evident that airplay means higher record sales. The advent of MTV and CDs has also reinforced the interdependence of these businesses.

- Radio programming can derive from local, prerecorded or syndicated, and network sources. Radio shows can be produced in four ways: local-live, live-assist, semiautomation, and turnkey automation.

- Stations strive to make their formats unique. One way of achieving this is to analyze the market of a particular city and to find a format hole.

- When a station attempts to choose a format, internal factors that are considered include ownership, dial location, power, technical facilities, and management philosophy. External factors such as strength of competitors, geography, and demographics also need to be analyzed. The new trend is toward psychographic research, which tells programmers the type of listener each musical category attracts.

- Station managers plan their programs on a hot clock. This helps them visualize the sound of a station. A program schedule is divided into dayparts, including morning drive, daytime, evening drive, evening, and overnight.

- Talk radio has seen spectacular growth in recent years, resuscitating the AM band, and providing its listeners a range of services, from all-news, to sports, financial advice, and psychological counseling.

- On the nonprofit side, public radio stations receive programming from two major network sources: National Public Radio (NPR) and Public Radio International (PRI). College stations tend to emphasize diversity and block programming; religious and community stations offer everything from chapel broadcasts to rock-and-roll.

KEY TERMS

local programming   166
prerecorded/syndicated
    programming   166
network programming   166
local, live production   169
live-assist production   169
semiautomation   169
turnkey automation   169
target audience   171
demographics   171
psychographics   171

payola   172
hot clock   174
dayparts   174
morning drive time   174
evening drive time   175
daytime time period   176
evening (daypart in radio)   176
overnight (daypart in
    radio)   176
clutter   177
spot sets   177

segue   177
tip sheet   178
playlist   178
call-ins   178
call-outs   178
hook   178
auditorium tests   178
focus group study   178
specialized consultant   178
full-service consultant   178
block programming   182

SUGGESTIONS FOR FURTHER READING

Adams, M. H. and Massey, K. (1995). *Introduction to radio: Production and programming.* Madison, WI: Brown & Benchmark.

Clark, L. (1996). *Shock radio.* New York: Forge.

Ditingo, V. (1995). *The remaking of radio.* Boston: Focal Press.

Hausman, D., Benoit, P., & O'Donnell, L. (1996). *Modern radio production* (4th ed.). Belmont, CA: Wadsworth.

Keith, M. (1997). *The radio station* (4th ed.). Boston: Focal Press.

Laufer, P. (1995). *Inside talk radio: America's voice or just hot air?* Secaucus, NJ: Carol Publishing Group.

Looker, T. (1995) *The sound and the story: NPR and the art of radio.* Boston: Houghton Mifflin.

Lynch, J. (1998). *Process and practice of radio programming.* Lanham, MD: University Press of America.

MacFarland, D. T. (1997). *Future radio programming strategies: Cultivating leadership in the digital age* (2d ed.). Mahwah, NJ: Erlbaum.

Norberg, E. (1996). *Radio programming: Tactics and strategy.* Boston: Focal Press.

INTERNET EXERCISES

1. Visit our Web site at http://www.mhhe.com/beyond for study-guide exercises to help you learn and apply material in each chapter. You will find ideas for future research as well as useful Web links to provide you with an opportunity to journey through the new electronic media.

TV Programming 9

Quick Facts

 Percent of Americans who cite TV as most credible news source: 53 (1997)

 Percent of Americans who cite the Internet as most credible news source: 1 (1997)

 Average cost per episode of TV newsmagazine: $900,000

 Cost per episode of NBC's "ER": 13 million

 Number of new program ideas pitched to TV networks each year: 10,000 (est.)

 Number of successful new TV series each year: 1–3 (average)

We study television for a lot of reasons: its social impact; its effect on politics; its influence on modes of conversation, fashion, and relationships; and on and on. Throughout this book, we've looked at its ownership, its financial structure, its employment patterns, and the like. But for the majority of the public, television is really only about one thing: programming. And that programming, whether it's found on the broadcast networks, local TV stations, cable, satellite, or the Internet, has only two main functions: information and entertainment. Simply put, people watch TV programs for either news or entertainment. In this chapter, we examine how television programming is made. First, we look at information programming—the often-controversial topic of television news. Next, we'll examine the field of entertainment television—how TV manufactures "stars and stories" for the entertainment of a large, loyal, and eager public. But first, we bring you the news.

THE RISE OF TELEVISION NEWS

The Roper Studies

Every few years the Roper Organization conducts surveys asking people to identify (1) their main source of news and (2) the news source that they perceive to be the most credible. The trends in popular opinion on these questions are summarized in Figures 9–1 and 9–2. From 1963 on, TV was named most frequently as the primary source of news. Its lead over second-place newspapers increased steadily. The proportion of people naming radio fell steadily from the 1960s, as did the magazine category (which was never named by more than 1 in 10 people to begin with). Few people over the years named "other people" as their primary news source.

Television news also has received high marks on credibility. Since 1961 TV has been cited as the most believable source of news. By 1992 TV was named as most credible more than two to one over newspapers.

While TV news credibility has taken some hits lately (we'll get to that later), today, TV is the primary source of news for more than two-thirds of the American public. Newspapers continue to slip, with less than 40 percent of the public using them for their primary news source (and about half that number subscribing to a daily newspaper). For the first time, the Internet made the list in 1997, as the primary source of news for 2 percent of the general public. But the net has credibility problems. Thus far, only about 1 percent of the general public finds the Internet as the source it would most trust among the major news media.

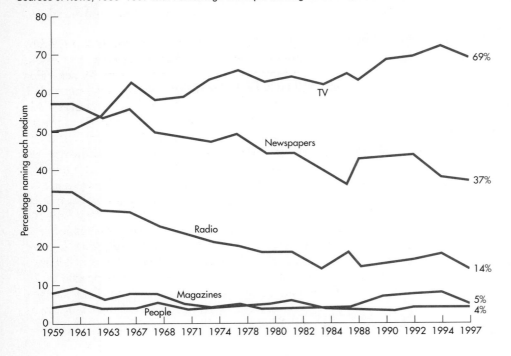

Figure 9–1

Sources of News, 1959–1997 with Percentage of People Naming Various Media as Their Source of Most News

Figure 9–2

Media Credibility, 1959–1997 with Percentage of People Naming Various Media as the One They Would Believe If They Got Conflicting Versions of a News Story.

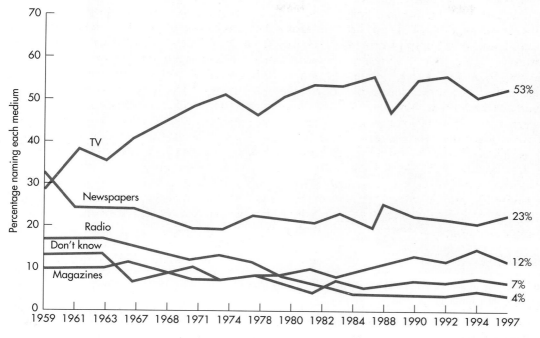

A BRIEF HISTORY OF TV NEWS

Although the wording of the questions has caused some debate about the validity of the Roper findings, they clearly indicate the rise of TV as a news source in our era. How did this happen? When did TV become our eyes on the world? The Roper studies suggest that it happened in the early 1960s—November 22, 1963, to be exact.

The Kennedy Assassination: The Death of Camelot and the Birth of Television News

President John F. Kennedy had been warned by his advisors not to go to Dallas. Like many places in the South, the city was torn by political and racial unrest. But he decided to go. The press hinted that there might be trouble when a president perceived as a liberal traveled to a staunchly conservative city. A large contingent of the media was on hand as the president's motorcade passed the Texas School Book Depository. Shots rang out. The president was mortally wounded.

Within five minutes, news of the shooting moved on the United Press wire service. Within 10 minutes

the three TV networks had interrupted their afternoon lineups of game shows and soap operas. Receiving the news from a young Dallas reporter named Dan Rather, an emotional Walter Cronkite told the nation on CBS that its president had been slain.

Assassinations in other nations might have led to governmental chaos and public violence, but in the United States it turned people to their TV sets. For four days all regular programming was suspended and people sat, seemingly transfixed by the story unfolding on TV. The full resources of the TV medium were turned to this one event. Television was there when President Kennedy's widow Jacqueline returned with the coffin to Washington and when the accused assassin, Lee Harvey Oswald, was himself gunned down by a Dallas nightclub owner, Jack Ruby. And TV permitted the nation to attend the funeral, as world leaders came to pay their respects.

More than 9 in 10 Americans were said to have watched the TV coverage that fateful weekend. Watching, too, were over 500 million people in 23 countries, as the coverage was fed to a new device that had recently been launched: the communications satellite.

On his third birthday, John F. Kennedy, Jr. salutes the casket bearing his father's body. More than 500 million people worldwide watched the events of that weekend in November of 1963.

Network news had just been expanded from 15 to 30 minutes. It consisted mostly of silent newsfilm and "talking heads." Local news was even more primitive: Many stations focused their efforts on sassy "weather girls"; their anchors would read a national story and a dog food commercial with the same officious presentation that they had employed in radio. But those days were over. In one weekend, TV news had seized the public consciousness. Things would never be the same.

No longer was TV news the stepchild of print or of its progenitor, radio. As 1963 drew to a close, both NBC, with the formidable team of Chet Huntley and David Brinkley, and CBS—with the "most trusted man in America," Walter Cronkite, were telecasting 30 minutes of nightly news. By 1965 the national news was in color. This became important as events both at home and abroad began to capture and command the TV news eye.

Television News Comes of Age

Today there is a certain nostalgia for the era of the 1960s and early 1970s, a period in history bounded by the Kennedy assassination in 1963 and the Water-

gate scandal, which ended in 1974 with the resignation of President Richard Nixon. Aging "baby boomers" (people born after World War II, who reached adolescence in the 1960s) tend to recall the time as a period of playful experimentation, blue jeans, rock-and-roll, and "flower power." There certainly were moments of fun, but the decade was marked by violent confrontations, social upheavals, and cultural change. And for the first time in history it all happened in front of the TV cameras. Three major events occurred in this period. Each event became forever intertwined with the growth of TV journalism.

Television and Civil Rights   In 1962, Dr. Martin Luther King, Jr., outlined a new strategy:

> We are here today to say to the white men that we will no longer let them use their clubs in dark corners. We are going to make them do it in the glaring light of television.[1]

And it worked—TV was there. It was in Little Rock in 1957 to capture the violence following the integra-

[1]In David J. Garrow, *Protest at Selma* (New Haven, CT: Yale University Press, 1978), p. 111.

tion of Central High School. It was in Montgomery, Birmingham, and other southern cities to witness sit-ins at lunch counters and bus stations. It was in Washington to cover the hundreds of thousands who rallied for civil rights in 1963. Television was in Detroit, Watts, and Newark to cover civil disorders, presenting searing images of white police chiefs turning dogs and fire hoses onto defenseless demonstrators. It revealed the hatred of white suprema-cists, including the Ku Klux Klan, as throngs of peaceful protesters filed through their towns. Later it demonstrated black anger and frustration, as it turned its cameras on arsonists and looters in the summer riots of 1965 and 1967, and following the as-sassination of Dr. King in 1968.

Television in Vietnam   A second major news event of the 1960s took place thousands of miles away. But it, too, harnessed the power of TV—particularly its ability to bring distant events into America's living rooms. The event was the war in Vietnam. Although Vietnam has been called "the first television war," TV had gone to Korea in the early 1950s. This early coverage, however, lacked the immediacy that would characterize Vietnam reporting. The years in which the war was actively fought by Americans (1961–1975) were indeed the "television years." During this period, TV news made virtually all its major advances: portable cameras, satellite relay systems, color, videotape replay, and on and on. This was the era when TV's first generation of reporters (Eric Sevareid, Chet Huntley, Charles Collingwood, and others), who had been trained in radio or print jour-nalism, gave way to a new wave of youthful re-porters who had grown up in the age of TV. In this group were Ed Bradley, Ted Koppel, Steve Bell, and John Laurence.

Like the civil rights movement, the war in Viet-nam provided a training ground for the new people and techniques coming to TV. As a result, the public was deluged with daily reports, with illustrations of American and enemy dead, with dramatic "point-of-view" shots from cameras mounted on helicopter gun ships and later in the bellies of evac-uation aircraft.

For many who lived through those years, the war is remembered as a series of indelible TV images: the whirr of engines as choppers evacuated wounded soldiers; GIs "torching" a village with their Zippo lighters (reported first by Morley Safer on CBS in 1965); antiwar demonstrators chanting

"the whole world is watching" as they clashed with police during the 1968 Democratic National Con-vention in Chicago; the execution of a prisoner by Saigon police chief Lo An (aired on NBC in 1968); panic-stricken South Vietnamese clutching the landing gear of evacuation aircraft in 1975; and flotillas of rafts and fishing boats crammed with refugees as the "boat people" fled their country in the late 1970s.

One Small Step   TV news grew concurrently with the U.S. space program. Beginning with Alan Shepard's space flight in 1961, "space shots" became a major focus on TV news, leading up to the lunar landing of *Apollo 11*.

In the summer of 1969 Neil Armstrong set foot on the moon, an event witnessed by the largest global TV audience up to that time, an estimated 600 mil-lion people on six of the seven continents. NASA had carefully orchestrated the event as a TV program, having mounted a small camera (provided by RCA) on the steps of the landing craft, in front of which as-tronauts Armstrong and Edwin "Buzz" Aldrin would cavort. The two unfurled and planted an American flag, stiffened by an aluminum rod to give the appearance that it was fluttering in some imagi-nary lunar breeze. Within minutes President Nixon was on a split screen to talk to the astronauts by tele-phone. Two hours later the world audience watched as the astronauts blasted off for the return trip to Earth. The astronauts had provided for this unique TV angle (the first point-of-view shot from outer space) by setting up another RCA camera in the lunar soil.

TV News Becomes Big Business

Civil rights; Vietnam; the space race; and subsequent events like the Watergate scandal (in 1974 and 1975), the hostage crisis in Iran (in 1980), and the explosion of space shuttle *Challenger* (1986) brought TV news to the forefront. The major networks expanded their news coverage (ABC's "Nightline," for example, be-gan as a nightly update of the hostage situation). An entire cable network—CNN—was launched in 1980, dedicated to news. Local television news also grew. And for good reason. It had become a profit center for television stations, accounting for as much as one-third to one-half of all advertising revenues. Following are some major trends in TV news in its growth period of the 1970s and 1980s.

"Happy Talk"   Throughout its history, TV news had been identified with its anchors and reporters. Newscasters, at both the national networks and local stations, tended to appear strong, serious, some would say staid, and conservative. At the networks there were Walter Cronkite, Eric Sevareid, John Chancellor, David Brinkley, Nancy Dickerson, and many others. In New York there were Bill Beutel and Jim Jensen; in Chicago, Fahey Flynn; in Los Angeles, Clete Roberts; in Miami, Ralph Renick. In every major city there were established figures in news, each with impeccable credentials and an aura of journalistic integrity and self-assurance.

In the late 1970s, a new breed of newscaster began to appear. Men were younger, more daring, and even "dashing," frequently dressed in the most modern clothing styles, many with facial hair (previously avoided—except for the stately mustache sported by Cronkite).

For the first time women began to appear in the anchor position. Like the new breed of male newscasters, they were young and attractive. On-camera looks, charisma, charm, and sex appeal became at least as important as journalistic training and ability.

Not only did this new breed look different, but they acted differently from their predecessors. They talked to each other on the air. Sometimes they talked about the news reports they had just seen; sometimes they just seemed to be engaging in the kind of gossip and repartee found in most offices. This new approach to TV news was lambasted by the more serious print media, which called it "happy talk." There was concern that TV news was moving away from issues toward personalities, away from information to entertainment, and away from serious news to "sleaze." Research seemed to support these claims. Studies found that stations with the happy-talk format featured more sensational and violent content than did traditional newscasts. They also had higher ratings.

ENG and SNG   Another new trend in TV news was its dependence on new communications technologies. The trend can be summed up in two three-letter abbreviations: ENG and SNG.

Electronic news gathering, known as **ENG,** emerged in the mid-1970s, when portable video cameras and recorders became commercially available. The basic elements of ENG included a lightweight TV camera and small videotape recorder, which could be handheld by the cameraperson.

Today's ENG equipment includes camera–recorder combinations, known as camcorders.

ENG revolutionized TV news. Prior to the introduction of ENG, TV news relied on cumbersome and costly film equipment. Film stock needed to be processed and physically assembled or edited. It could not be reused. Film cameras required unwieldy and obtrusive lights. With ENG, cameras and recorders could go anywhere. Events could be recorded in full, with natural sound, and the most important parts could be edited together electronically, in a speedy and cost-efficient manner.

At the same time, the dawn of **satellite news gathering (SNG)** had arrived. Satellite news gathering refers to the use of mobile trucks mounted with satellite communications equipment to report local, national, and international events. SNG trucks and vans could transmit up to communications satellites the pictures and sounds gathered by ENG. The satellites sent the signal back down to local stations and networks to use in their news programs. It was thus possible to obtain live news pictures from virtually anywhere in the world.

Today many stations own "flyaway uplink" vans, capable of transmitting events live to a satellite and back to earth, to the studio. CNN and the major networks have access to satellite up-link equipment small enough to cram into a suitcase.

The News as "Show Biz"   With increasing profitability inevitably came the "ratings war." News directors began to follow ratings with at least as much concern as their counterparts in the sales and programming departments. At local stations the competition for audiences was most intense during the periods when the Nielsen ratings company conducted surveys of local TV viewing (see Chapter 12). These periods are known as **sweeps.**

In TV the sweep periods occur four times a year—in February, May, July, and November. In a quest for "number 1" status, many local news operations took to programming series of short documentaries, known as **minidocs,** during these times. Many minidocs aired during the sweeps focused on sensational topics, including teenage prostitution, spousal and child abuse, and religious cults. They were accompanied by extensive advertising campaigns on the air and in print, on billboards and buses. In many ways the hoopla surrounding news was not unlike that which accompanied the premiere of a new motion picture. In fact, TV news became the stuff of movies and TV shows—*Broadcast News, Switching Channels,* "Max Headroom," "Murphy Brown"— suggesting that the TV newsperson had become a modern icon.

A number of **news consultants** emerged to provide the expertise required of news managers in this competitive environment. Leading news consultants included such firms as Frank Magid, Reymer and Gersin, and McHugh-Hoffman. Consultants provided advice to stations to use in selecting their talent, designing their sets, using graphics, devising sweeps-weeks promotions, and other areas. Their research techniques, ranging from focus-group tests to viewer surveys, are analyzed in Chapter 12.

TV NEWS TODAY

As television stations, networks, and cable systems face increasing competition—from each other, from the Internet, from radio, from magazines, and even from some "smart" mobile pagers—news has become increasingly important. Following are some key trends in television journalism.

Coventuring

One important trend has been the development of cooperative ventures by television news outlets with other stations in their market, with their "arch rival" cable systems, and even with their oldest competitors, the local newspapers. As the costs of the new "toys" of TV news mount, and as new means of delivering information become increasingly available to consumers (such as computer online services and interactive cable), news managers have recognized that **coventuring** makes good business sense.

Coventuring with other TV stations in the market usually occurs between a local news leader at a network affiliate and an independent station. The news leader buys time on the independent station to program an alternative version of its local news, which offers viewers a choice of different stories. In return, the affiliate garners a larger audience, which it can use to attract advertisers to buy commercials on either or both stations. For example, in 1995 CBS affiliate WCCO in Minneapolis began "News of Your Choice" with independent station KLGT. The arrangement allowed viewers the option of switching between channels 4 and 23 at 10 P.M., for different versions of WCCO's late news. Similar news coventures have begun in Tampa, Portland, and other markets.

Television news outlets are also coventuring with news/talk radio stations. For example, in Washington, D.C., NBC affiliate WRC-TV and all-news station WTOP-AM (a CBS affiliate) have entered into a news partnership. Under the arrangement, WRC has mounted a robotic camera in the heart of WTOP's newsroom. WTOP's reporters are encouraged to report live from the radio newsroom to WRC's newscasts; radio editors frequently ask WRC-TV reporters to go live on WTOP with breaking news events. The coventure bore fruit during a recent snowstorm when residents who had lost their power or were stranded in their cars were able to receive up-to-the-minute information on road conditions from WRC's mobile crews and weather-related cancellations from WTOP's computerized list.

If cooperation with competing independent TV stations and radio wasn't shocking enough, in the 1990s some local TV stations began to "sleep with the enemy"—local cable systems. The idea is to use the resources of local affiliates to feed specially customized newscasts to cable subscribers in a given community. Typically, special short newscasts, known as "inserts," are produced for the residents served by a local cable company. These air only in the cable area; over-the-air viewers stay with the affiliate newscast. The phenomenon is known as **local-local news,** since the cable subscriber receives an even more localized version of a local newscast. One particularly successful "local-local" venture is based in San Francisco. NBC affiliate KRON-TV provides local news segments to more than a dozen cable systems in the Bay Area. Segments are updated three or four times a day and are broadcast twice an hour. The newscasts are specially targeted for the region that each cable system operates, including the city of San Francisco, the east Bay, south Bay, and Marin County areas.

At the corporate level, coventuring has become commonplace. CNN, for example, has been aggressively partnering with other elements of the Time Warner empire. In sports, CNN and Sports Illustrated have created CNN/SI, an all-sports cable service. Programs on CNN include entertainment coventures with *Entertainment Weekly* and *People* and a financial program with input from *Fortune* magazine. This coventuring got off to an inauspicious start in 1998, when CNN and *Time* combined for an apparently fallacious report called "Operation Tailwind," which claimed that the U.S. military had pursued and released poison gas on American deserters during the Vietnam war.

Regional Cable News

Another significant trend in the 1990s has been the rise of *regional* cable-news channels. Unlike "local-local" news, which offers quick cut-ins or news summaries to cable viewers, **regional cable-news services** are 24-hour localized versions of CNN.

The pioneer in regional cable news is News12 Long Island, created by Cablevision to serve nearly one million subscribers in Nassau and Suffolk counties, suburbs of New York City. Inside the city limits, Time Warner's NY1 provides news around the clock to cable viewers in Brooklyn, Queens, the Bronx, Manhattan, and Staten Island. Suburban Los Angeles is served by Orange County Newschannel, a venture of Orange County *Register* and *Freedom* newspapers. Similarly, Chicagoland Television (CLTV) uses the resources of the *Chicago Tribune* to provide regional cable news to the second city and its suburbs.

By the year 2000, some two dozen regional cable-news services were operating in all parts of the United States.

News-on-Demand

Regional cable news is blazing the trail to the next generation of television news, known as **news-on-demand.** On-demand news services allow viewers to watch only those news services they may be interested in. For example, a sports enthusiast can select a steady diet of highlights from today's games, a "news junkie" can view all the day's significant events, while a third viewer can stay in constant contact with the current Doppler radar report.

TV news operations are scrambling to create partnerships with Internet service providers (ISPs) and search engines, for the purposes of providing news-on-demand. For example, there is the multi-million-dollar partnership between CBS and American Online. CNN, through its CNN Interactive division, has joined with the @Home service to link its news, sports, weather, and other offerings to subscribers. The "portal partnerships" described in detail in Chapter 5, are driven by news-on-demand, which is expected to be among the primary driving forces of Internet growth in the next decade.

Global News

Ironically, at the same time TV news delivery becomes more and more localized through regional cable and news-on-demand, it is also moving in an opposite direction. The success of Cable News Network has generated competition in serving the global news audience.

As we've seen in Chapter 5, Fox News now competes with CNN in the United States, as do other information-based channels, like MSNBC, CNBC, and Bloomberg News (primarily a financial news service).

News Corporation's Sky News offers an alternative to CNN in Europe, southeast Asia, and other regions of Rupert Murdoch's considerable reach. BBC World, a coventure of the venerable British Broadcasting Corporation and the Pearson publishing giant, competes worldwide with CNN. In fact, the service became available in the United States in February 1995, as BBC Americas.

International news channels are not limited to the English language. France's TF-1 and Canal Plus have teamed to create an all-news service for the French-speaking world. Not to be outdone, Telemundo and Reuters Television Ltd. have joined forces to create "Telenoticias," a 24-hour global service entirely in Spanish.

So, as a new century dawns, television news remains an important part of the media landscape. For local TV stations, it is a profit center, and a critical source of viewer attention, identification, and loyalty. For networks, like CNN, ABC, CBS, and Fox, news is more than a "necessary evil." It helps them earn and retain the credibility of the viewer, especially when those viewers tend to distrust what they often hear on talk radio, or read on the Internet. Speaking of the Internet, reliable and credible news helps web surfers separate the few grains of wheat from the tons of chaff available on the World Wide Web. News-based pages help the new medium earn the trust (and the business) of many consumers put off by the vitriolic—and often downright scurrilous—content of most web pages. The news for TV news is mostly good. Now let's see how TV news gets made.

THE TELEVISION NEWS TEAM: TELEVISION-NEWS COMMAND STRUCTURE

Television news is a collaborative craft. It is not unusual for a large-market station to boast more than 100 people in the news department. The major networks still maintain hundreds of news personnel. CNN alone employs over 1,000 people at its Atlanta headquarters. Coordinating the efforts of these small armies is no easy task, especially with the pressures of both the deadline and the bottom line. Thus TV news organizations tend to follow rigid command structures, outlined in Figure 9–3.

For convenience, Figure 9–3 separates TV news production into two phases. Phase I, the left side of the chart, refers to tasks and processes that take place primarily before the broadcast begins. This phase is called preproduction. The right side of the diagram covers the personnel involved on the air, or the production phase.

Phase I: Preproduction

The News Director   Overall responsibility for the news department falls to the news director. News directors tend to have a solid background in TV news, many as former reporters or anchors. The news director hires news personnel, establishes news and editorial policy, and evaluates the newscast in "post-mortem" screenings with the staff of the news department. Today's news directors are increasingly concerned with budgets, making sure the news is produced at a profit. The exciting, high-pressure nature of the job has led to a typical job tenure in the range of about three years (see box on page 174).

News Producer   If the news director is the "boss" of the news operation, the news producer is the czar of any given newscast, such as the "11 o'clock Report," or "The Noon News." The producers maintain editorial control over the stories that make up their individual TV newscasts. The producers prepare the story lineup, determine the stories' lengths, and decide how they will be handled. The producer of each newscast will proofread all copy, select the graphics, and be present in the control room to make last-minute changes during the newscast.

Most news operations have special segments or "beats," such as consumer affairs, health, arts and entertainment, and, of course, sports and weather. These beats are headed by unit producers, who assume overall responsibility for these segments.

Assignment Editor   The main job of the assignment editor is to dispatch reporters and photographers to cover news stories. The job requires great organizational skills. At a local station, as many as five different crews may be out in the field at one time. At a network, literally dozens of crews need to be dispatched and returned to the studio for editing and other production tasks. To assist in this complex task, assignment editors maintain a **future file.** This is an annotated listing of upcoming news stories, scheduled as many as 30 or 60 days in advance. Traditionally a

Figure 9–3

TV News Command Structure

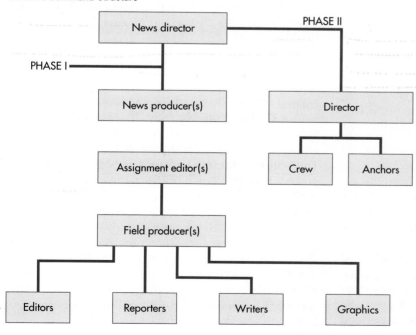

In a recent poll, 9 in 10 TV news directors reported they liked their jobs because they work best under pressure. They find deadline pressure "exhilarating." But there is a flip side to their exhilaration. More than half of the male news directors reported they had job-related personal problems. Although most were married at the time of the survey (80 percent), one-half of those polled admitted they were having marital problems. Nearly a third had been divorced at least once. Also, 42 percent admitted they had at least one drink daily; a third were smokers. Not surprisingly, the lifestyle of the news director was extracting a high price in health: One in four admitted to having serious job-related health problems, ranging from anxiety and depression to coronary artery disease.

The 44 women news directors polled matched their male counterparts in some lifestyle characteristics and not in others. Like male news managers, more than 9 in 10 relished the pressure of the business. About the same proportion of women as men smoked cigarettes. However, unlike the male news directors, most women managers were unmarried. Fewer found the need to drink alcohol on a daily basis. But women news manager's reported job-related stress more than their male counterparts (or they were more likely to admit their problems than are the men). In any case, the job of TV news director clearly takes a sizable toll on one's personal life.

series of file folders is each labeled with upcoming dates and filled with events for each day; many future files today are stored in computers. Of course, the future file is useless when breaking news occurs: A plane crash or tornado really taxes the skills of the assignment editor.

Field Producer   If there is sufficient lead time to prepare for a story, such as a space shuttle launch or a murder trial, it may be assigned to a field producer. The field producer will prepare research and background information, scout locations, and perform other valuable advance functions for the reporter and photographer, who will be busy working on other stories. On breaking stories of great magnitude (an assassination attempt or a skyjacking, for example), the news director may assign a field producer to coordinate the coverage.

Reporter   Reporters receive their orders from the assignment desk and begin their research, usually on the telephone. They set up interviews and determine shooting locations. Typically the reporter has been teamed with a photographer. At small stations, regional news channels, and some budget-conscious large stations, the reporter may be a "one-man band," responsible for shooting her own stories. The reporter proceeds to the scene, obtains interviews and other video, and returns to the studio to supervise the editing, write and announce the voice-over and lead-in copy, and, if part of the newscast, get dressed and made up for the newscast.

Writers   It is a sad fact that many of today's reporters may be selected for their on-camera appearance rather than their journalistic skills. For this reason most stations and networks employ newswriters to script the newscast. Writers may prepare the material for reporters and anchors. They frequently prepare the clever lines used to introduce the newscast (**teasers**) or to attract the audience to return after commercial breaks (**bumpers**).

Editors   Most newscasts consist of separate stories, called **packages,** linked by the anchors and reporters. Each package is a complete story, edited together with its own voice-over and graphic material. The editor is the person who puts the package together. Typically the reporter returns from the field with too much material, all of it shot out of sequence. He may have done the introduction to the story six or seven times; there may be dozens of separate pieces to an interview. The reporter (and sometimes the field producers, unit producer, producer, or news director as well) retreats with the editor to a small editing room to make sense of the mayhem of the typical field report. In many small news operations, reporters edit their own packages.

TV news has benefited greatly in recent years by the development of digital editing systems, such as AVID, Media 100, and Sony's ES-7 (see Chapter 3).

Phase II: On the Air

Director and Production Crew
As airtime approaches, pressure shifts from the news producer to the director. The director is the studio boss. The director is the person who "calls the shots" during the newscast, selecting the camera shots and calling for the packages to roll. The director is assisted by the full range of TV crew personnel. Pushing the buttons that correspond to the many cameras and videotape recorders is the technical director. Selecting the sounds, from microphones to music, is the audio director. In the studio are two or three camera operators. A floor director gives cues to the anchors and reporters, instructing them as to which camera is on and when the commercials are coming. The director is in communication with the people who put words and pictures on the screen, the graphics and videotape operators.

Anchors and reporters rarely read from the printed copy they appear to be holding. Reporting to the director are the people who operate a machine, the teleprompter, or "prompter," for short, that projects the script, using mirrors and reflectors, into a space just in front of the cameras. This is where the anchors look to read their copy.

Today the director has the added burden of coordinating live reports from the field, which may involve pressurized last-minute harangues with satellite companies, helicopter pilots, and panicky reporters. Helping the director with this range of diverse tasks will be one or more assistant directors, who may be assigned to help with time cues, supervise the insertion of video material, or monitor the preparation of graphic material.

As if the job wasn't difficult enough, during the broadcast the director is in constant communication with the news producer to keep the program on time and to allow for last-minute additions and deletions. Most of this activity takes place during commercial breaks, the only respite from the mania in the studio and control room during a broadcast.

Anchors
It is important to note how far down we have come in Figure 9–3 before mentioning the people who get most of the attention in TV news: the anchors. Like it or not, the anchors are the celebrities in TV news. Most have the bankrolls and wardrobes to prove it.

Simply put, the anchors represent the newscast to the viewer. The viewing public recognizes the anchors as the news spokespersons for the station. For good or ill, frequently the anchors *are* the station's newscast. For this reason anchor salaries often reflect their celebrity status. It is estimated that Dan Rather of CBS, Peter Jennings of ABC, and NBC's Tom Brokaw, each earn around $7 million annually. At the local level large-market anchors have been known to command upward of $500,000 per year, with the median in the $200,000 range.

What do anchors do to earn these salaries? Their primary responsibility is to read the news in a trustworthy and authoritative fashion. In some cases they actually write their news copy (their networks claim this is the case with Rather, Jennings, and Brokaw). In addition, anchors need to be good interviewers, especially when handling live reports from the field. The venerable Walter Cronkite and his heir, Mr. Rather, have carried the additional duties of executive producer, with editorial control of the "CBS Evening News."

Most analysts point out that the network anchors remain solid journalists with excellent credentials. However, this is not always the case at the local level. There is growing evidence that some anchors are selected primarily for their on-camera charm and good looks, independent of their writing and reporting abilities. Stories abound in the trade and popular press about anchormen and women who look great but are largely ignorant about the nature and practice of journalism.

The struggle between show business and journalism is among the current issues and controversies surrounding TV news.

CRUMBLING CREDIBILITY? ISSUES IN TV NEWS

We opened the chapter with the famous Roper polls, which suggests that TV is the most credible source of news for the American public. Take another look at Figure 9–2. Can you see the recent drop in TV news credibility? There is ample evidence that TV news is losing some respect as an information source.

One of the main reasons for this decline is the perceived preoccupation with scandal, known variously as the "tabloidization" of news, "pack journalism," or the TV news "freeding frenzy." The seemingly limitless and boundless coverage of violent, sexy (or both) stories began with the O.J. Simpson arrest and trials, which began in 1994, and has since led to coverage of the JonBenet Ramsey killing, the "nanny murder" trial of Louise Woodward, and, most recently, the misadventures of Bill Clinton and Monica Lewinsky. Critics claim the "legitimate" news organizations are spending too much time and effort on these stories, at the expense of other, more important topics. Faced with increasing competition and driven by profit, managers of major media outlets point to the increased ratings this coverage creates. They can also make a strong claim, at least in the case of Bill Clinton, that such scandals represent legitimate news.

For many years the National Opinion Research Center has conducted surveys tapping the degree of confidence the public has in various American institutions, including the press.

In the early 1970s (the height of the press's triumphant Watergate period) confidence in the press was high. One in four Americans expressed great confidence in the press; only 15 percent expressed little or no faith in it. Today the situation has reversed. A quarter of the population has little confidence in the American press; less than one in five place great faith in it.

The medium may not be helping its own cause. With an emphasis on ratings, with stories about satanism, cult worship, prostitution, and aliens replacing investigative reports and public service efforts, today's news has become just another form of TV entertainment, which brings us to our next topic.

TV ENTERTAINMENT PROGRAMMING

Most of us use the mass media for relaxation, escape, and diversion— in a word, entertainment. Entertainment does not come cheap in TV and cable. A major TV network might spend more than $25 million a week on nonnews programming. The entertainment programming business is an integral part of modern broadcasting and cable.

There are three basic ways in which a TV station or cable company can acquire programs: network, syndication, and local origination. First, we provide brief definitions of these terms. Then we examine each major program source in detail.

As you might expect, **network programming** refers to original programming funded by, produced

for, and distributed by the major TV networks. Television stations contract with networks to carry network shows. Recent popular network programs include "NYPD Blue" and "Drew Carey" on ABC, "Frasier" and "Friends" on NBC, "Walker, Texas Ranger" and "Touched by an Angel" on CBS, and "Ally McBeal" and "The Simpsons" on Fox.

Syndication refers to TV programming sold by distribution companies to local TV stations and cable services. Syndication companies sell two kinds of shows: off-network (series that have appeared on the networks and are being rerun by local stations or cable systems) and first-run (shows expressly produced for syndication). Some off-net successes in syndication include "The Cosby Show," "Seinfeld," and "Home Improvement."

First-run powerhouses are mostly talk and game shows, like "Oprah," "Wheel of Fortune," and "Jerry Springer." However, some dramatic programs in recent years have been successfully marketed through syndication, led by the beach boys and babes of "Baywatch."

Local origination refers to programs produced by local TV stations (or cable companies) for viewers in their own communities. The most common forms of local origination programs are the local news and talk shows that most TV stations and cable systems carry daily. In the 1950s and 1960s many stations featured cartoon programs for kids hosted by "talent" from the station (typically a cameraman or technician frustrated in an earlier career in vaudeville or theater). If you don't remember these local shows from your youth, your parents probably do.

NETWORK TELEVISION: THE BIG FOUR, PLUS THREE

From the beginnings of TV in the late 1940s, to the late 1970s, TV programming was dominated by three commercial networks: CBS, NBC, and ABC. For more than a generation these networks were America's great entertainers. Their programs, ranging from Ed Sullivan's "Toast of the Town" to the Super Bowl, attracted millions of viewers. In the 1980s, a new service emerged as a fourth network: Rupert Murdoch's Fox Broadcasting Corporation, or FBC. In the mid-1990s, two newer networks struggled for a share of television's huge audience: Paramount (UPN) and Warner Brothers (WB). They were joined in 1998 by broadcaster Lowell "Bud" Paxson's Pax TV network.

The network program process is designed to attract audiences for advertisers—not to create "art" or "culture." This is why the first 50 years of network TV have not generally been associated with such terms as "landmark" or "masterpiece."

Despite commercial pressures to produce revenue over quality, some programs do aspire to greatness. Some historians assert that the best of network TV will stand the test of time alongside the masterpieces of art, drama, and film. Recently, John Carman, the respected TV critic for the *San Francisco Chronicle*, compiled his list of TV masterworks. His list included "Your Show of Shows," the legendary NBC variety program starring Sid Caesar, Carl Reiner, and Imogene Coca and written by Woody Allen, Neil Simon, Larry Gelbart, and Carl Reiner, among others. Also on the list were ABC's landmark "Roots" miniseries (1977), CBS's "Lonesome Dove" (1989), and NBC's "An Evening with Fred Astaire," which aired in 1958.

Carman had less difficulty coming up with the list of all-time TV turkeys. Though there are many candidates for the label "worst television program of all time," few can argue with Carman's selections. On the list were ABC's "Turn On" (a 1969 clone of NBC's "Laugh In"), which barely made it through one episode; "Supertrain," an NBC series aboard a high-speed train that had about the same success record as Amtrak; Fox's late-night entry, "The Chevy Chase Show," which was put out of its (and our) misery after a short run in 1993; and "Pink Lady and Jeff" (1980, NBC), which featured the Japanese rock duo of Mie Nemeto and Kei Masuda and comedian Jeff Altman. It didn't help that neither Mie nor Kei spoke English.

Affiliation

The backbone of any network is the group of stations that carry its programs. Stations that receive network programming are known as **affiliates.** Traditionally, roughly 200 stations were affiliated with each of the "big three" of ABC, CBS, and NBC. Following its major expansion in 1994 (with the acquisition of New World and its investment in other properties), the Fox lineup approached parity with ABC, CBS, and NBC, at about 200 stations.

With roughly 200 stations each, the major networks cover nearly all of the U.S. homes with TV. This is critical, because national coverage enables them to sell the nation's leading advertisers commercials within their programs.

The newer networks are at a comparative disadvantage, each launching with about 100 affiliated stations. By the end of the 1990s, the WB network boasted the widest coverage, with about 90 percent of TV households in areas served by WB affiliates. UPN and Pax covered less than 9 in 10 U.S. households but were distributing their programs on local cable in some areas to boost their coverage.

To become an affiliate, the local TV station signs a contract, known as an **affiliation agreement,** with the network. Historically, the major networks have paid stations a fee for broadcasting network programs. This fee is known as **network compensation.** The fee has ranged from under $500 to more than $10,000 per hour, depending on the station's coverage area, market size, and popularity.

Due to the newly competitive marketplace, in recent years things have changed dramatically in network compensation. The high costs of original programming (like $13 million per episode for "ER"), and rights to sports events have caused the major networks to rethink their affiliation agreements. Negotiations are underway to reduce or eliminate network compensation, to make affiliates share the cost for more-expensive programs, or to get affiliates to agree to trade some of their airtime for more promotional spots by the major networks.

Affiliates may elect to carry the network shows, or they may refuse them. Programs that are carried by the station are said to have **cleared;** those that are refused are known as **preemptions.** In recent years many affiliates, especially those of the "big four," have exercised their right to refuse network programs, thereby producing some strained network–affiliate relationships and some widely publicized defections to other networks.

In return for their investment in programming and their affiliation payments, the networks gain access to the mass audience. Through their system of local affiliates, the networks have the potential to pull together a huge simultaneous audience, which they can sell to a national advertiser for a concomitantly large price. The name of the game is the audience.

Networks try to attract either a large, undifferentiated audience, as was the case with "Roseanne," or a relatively smaller audience that has the demographic profile that advertisers find attractive, as is the case with "Dawson's Creek," with its large 18- to 34-year-old audience. It's a high-stakes game. The network with the most successful programs will make the most money. The one with fewer viewers or the wrong kind of viewers will have bad news for its shareholders, and its suffering affiliates will respond appropriately.

The Network Programming Process

Network programming is cyclical: like baseball, it has its own seasons, pennant races, winners, and losers. First, let's examine the ground rules.

Financial Interest and Syndication Rules With the exception of news, sports, and a limited number of other programs, historically the networks did not own the shows that filled their nightly schedules. Fearing monopoly in entertainment production by the big three, in the early 1970s the FCC adopted a set of regulations known as the **financial interest and syndication rules.** In show-biz jargon the regulations were known as "fin-syn." In a nutshell, the rules limited network participation in the ownership of programs produced for them and in subsequent syndication. Rather than paying outright for their shows, the networks paid **license fees** to production companies. After the network run, programs were sold into syndication, but *not* by the networks. After nearly two decades of legal wrangling, the fin-syn rules were substantially modified by the FCC in 1993 and were abandoned entirely by the end of 1995.

The net effect was that networks were allowed to own their own shows and to sell them in syndication following the completion of their network runs.

By the late 1990s, the networks were actively involved in the production of their own programs. CBS was a partner in "King of Queens" and "Everybody Loves Raymond." NBC owned "Will and Grace" and was a partner in "NewsRadio" and "Homicide." As owners of studios (see the section on studios that appears a bit later in the chapter), ABC (Disney), UPN (Paramount) and WB (Warner Brothers) were likewise directly involved in program ownership.

Prime-Time Access Rule The FCC implemented the **prime-time access rule (PTAR)** in 1971. The rule restricted the amount of time an affiliate could accept from the network, in effect allowing networks to control no more than three hours of the four-hour prime-time nightly schedule (with some exceptions). Since TV viewing increases through the evening, naturally the networks maintained control of the three hours from 8:00 P.M. to 11:00 P.M. (7:00 P.M. to 10:00 P.M. in the Central Time Zone). This created a one-hour segment for local affiliated stations to fill by themselves. PTAR further prohibited network affiliates in the top 50 markets from filling this time (known today as "prime access" or simply "access") with off-network syndicated reruns.

Although the intent of the rule was to encourage production by non-Hollywood companies and maybe even stimulate local production, the reality is that most stations turned to syndication in this time period. Evening game shows became particularly popular, especially "Wheel of Fortune," and "Jeopardy."

PTAR had another lasting effect: It enabled independent stations to compete on more-equal terrain with network affiliates in the very important hour when people were sampling the TV schedule to make their nightly viewing choices. By programming their best shows here (ironically, a lot of popular old network shows that could not be shown on network stations), many new independent stations were able to siphon viewers from affiliates to themselves.

As with fin-syn, there was great pressure to modify or abandon PTAR. The FCC scrapped most of the PTAR requirements at the end of 1996. Still, "access" survives as an important lead-in to network prime-time programming.

Network Seasons Network programming is organized around two seasons. The fall premiere season begins in late September and runs through the end of October. This is when new programs are launched and returning programs begin showing new episodes. The so-called second season runs from mid-January through the end of February. This is when the networks replace low-rated programs with specials and new series.

At one time the two seasons were distinct. The three networks premiered their new shows in one week in late September; the second season almost always occurred in early February. Today, however, there seems to be one continuous season.

A daredevil tries to set the world record for walking on a beam between two balloons on an episode of Fox's popular "Guinness World Records Primetime." Fox helps its ratings by running some original episodes of this show during the summer.

Fox was especially instrumental in this trend. Fox staggered the introduction of its new programs, sprinkling premieres throughout the year. A particularly effective strategy included running new episodes of hit shows, like "The Simpsons" and "Beverly Hills 90210," in the summer, when ABC, NBC, and CBS were in reruns. The same strategy has been pursued by the newer networks, UPN, WB, and Pax.

In past years the network season lasted 39 weeks. As many as 32 episodes of a new show would be ordered, with the remaining 20 weeks occupied by specials and reruns. Today escalating production costs, competition, and a declining success rate have led the networks to order as few as 8 or 10 new episodes of a series, with an option to repeat at least two. This is one reason the season has shrunk (or expanded to year-round, depending on one's point of view).

Who gets the orders? Production of TV series is

dominated by a few large studios, increasingly owned by huge communications conglomerates. These are the major studios, or "the majors," for short. However, some hit shows come from outside these huge conglomerates. A small number of independent producers ("independents," for short) exert significant influence over the network programs we see. Let's start with the majors.

The major studios   The major studios in TV production are familiar names, although their ownership may be less familiar. Columbia/Tri-Star is one of these, producing such shows in recent years as "Mad About You" for NBC, "The Nanny" and "L.A. Doctors" for CBS, and "Dilbert" for UPN. In 1989 Columbia/Tri-Star was bought by Sony for $3.4 billion.

Another firm with major studio status in Hollywood is MCA-Universal, which was sold in 1995 by the Japanese firm Matsushita to Seagram's, the major Canadian maker of alcoholic beverages. Recent TV shows produced by MCA-Universal include "Northern Exposure," "Law and Order," and the short-lived "Hollyweird."

Another foreign-owned major is Twentieth Television, part of Rupert Murdoch's News Corporation empire. While Twentieth produces some programs for its own Fox network ("X-Files," "That 70s Show," and "The Simpsons"), it also provides programming to its competitors (such as "Chicago Hope" for CBS and "Snoops" for ABC).

Not all of the programming majors are foreign-owned. Warner Brothers, owned by Time Warner, is the home studio of such recent shows as "Full House," "Family Matters," "Murphy Brown," and "ER." Paramount, a part of the Paramount-Viacom communications conglomerate, is the source of such shows as "Frasier" and 1999 debut programs "Chaos Theory" and "Special Unit 2," plus its own enormously successful "Star Trek" series.

The TV programming arm of the Mickey Mouse media empire, Disney, is its Hollywood-based Walt Disney Studios and Buena Vista Television divisions. Such shows as "Blossom," "Boy Meets World," "Ellen," and "Home Improvement" have come from Disney sound stages. Disney is also a partner in other series, like the animated "PJs" on Fox and the WB youth drama "Felicity."

Independent producers   The networks also order programs from a small number of independent producers who have had a series of network successes. One of these is Stephen J. Cannell, whose success with "The Rockford Files," "Baretta," and "The A-Team" led to network orders for "Wiseguy," "21 Jump Street," "The Commish," and "Marker," one of the first shows on the UPN network.

Carsey-Werner was founded by former ABC programmers Tom Werner and Marcy Carsey. Their first show, "Oh! Madeline!" was forgettable. Their second was "Cosby." Carsey-Werner is now a powerhouse TV independent, responsible for such recent successes as "Roseanne," "Grace Under Fire," "Cybill," and "3rd Rock from the Sun."

Stephen Bochco is another influential independent, with a track record on network TV, including "Hill Street Blues" and the development of "L.A. Law." Bochco's recent mega-hit is "NYPD Blue." His most spectacular failure was "Cop Rock," a short-lived series featuring singing detectives on ABC.

Co-productions are common in network television. For example, "Felicity" is a coming-of-age drama from Imagine Television in association with Disney's Touchstone Television for the WB Television Network.

Aaron Spelling is another famous independent producer. His two monster hits "Dynasty" and "Hotel" were preceded by "Love Boat" and "Fantasy Island." His recent efforts include "Beverly Hills 90210," "Melrose Place," and "7th Heaven."

Dreamworks, the film studio created by Steven Spielberg, David Geffen, and Jeffrey Katzenberg, has been entering television in a big way. With former ABC programmer Ted Harbert at the helm, Dreamworks has produced the ABC comedy "Spin City," and the less successful "Arsenio" (a sit-com starring the former late-night talk host), "High Incident," and "Ink." Its fall 1999 projects included "Freaks and Geeks," a teen-oriented high school drama for NBC, and "Sick in the Head," a comedy (for Fox) about a psychiatrist's office.

Other well-known independents are Witt-Thomas-Harris ("Beauty and the Beast," "It's a Living," and "Everything's Relative") and Mozark Productions ("Designing Women," "Hearts Afire," and "Delta"), the company of Linda Bloodworth Thomason and Harry Thomason, famous friends of Bill Clinton.

"Pitching" a Program Programs get on the air through two primary means. Some are commissioned by the network, whose research and development discovers public interest in a particular program concept. It is said that the late NBC program executive Brandon Tartikoff ordered "Miami Vice" by telling producer Michael Mann to "give me MTV with cops!" Similarly, after meeting Mr. T at a Hollywood party, Tartikoff is reported to have handed Stephen J. Cannell a piece of paper reading: "'The A-Team,' 'Mission Impossible,' 'The Dirty Dozen,' and 'The Magnificent Seven,' all rolled into one, and Mr. T drives the car!"

More commonly, new program ideas are introduced, or "pitched," to the networks by their producers. The pitch can be based on an idea or **concept,** a short story narrative, known as a **treatment,** or a sample script. It is estimated that the networks are presented with as many as 10,000 new program ideas each year in one form or another. About 500 are chosen for further development.

At this point the lawyers, accountants, and agents get involved. Most commonly, the program (by now known as a "property") is developed under the terms of a **step deal**—an arrangement by which the program is put together in a series of distinct phases. The network will "front" the major portion of the development money for the program, in return for creative control over the show's content. The network gets **right of first refusal,** the contractual right to prohibit the production company from producing the program for another client. The step deal also enables the network to appoint additional writers to develop the concept or "punch up" the script.

About one-half of the optioned ideas will lead to the step deal or fully scripted stage. From this pool the networks will order about 30 or 35 **pilots,** or sample episodes, each costing in the range of $750,000 to $1.25 million to produce. By early spring about a dozen of these pilots will result in series orders; 10 of these twelve are likely to be canceled before the second season. Sometimes, in the late spring or summer, networks will run pilots that didn't make it, in an effort to recover some of their production costs.

Network program costs While the concept of a show, its location, and its stars are certainly important, for TV executives perhaps most important is its cost. Table 9–1 presents typical production costs for various program types.

The most expensive program type is the lavish, multipart network miniseries, which costs more than

Table 9–1	Typical Costs for Network Programs
Program Type	**Cost per Episode ($ millions)**
Major miniseries	$4–7
Movie of the week	3–5
Adventure/mystery/drama	2–4
Situation comedy	0.9–2.0
Reality/newsmagazine	.75–1.5

$5 million per hour to produce. With profits declining and competition increasing, you might think that these high production costs have made the networks avoid the production of miniseries. But the opposite has been the case. High-concept miniseries create "event" programming for the major networks, giving them programming to promote, and giving viewers a reason to watch them, instead of one of the "upstart" networks, or, heaven forbid, cable. In recent years, NBC has offered the $30 million "Merlin," which followed in the wake of the successful "Gulliver's Travels" and "The Odyssey." On the way for network runs are such classics as "Crime and Punishment" and a $150 million, six-hour network version of "The Bible."

The next-most-expensive program type are movies made for TV. In industry parlance, these are referred to as movies of the week (MOWs), "made-fors," or more cynically "disease of the week" shows. Typically these shows are contemporary dramas revolving around personal relationships, tragedy, domestic strife, or recent criminal cases. Some made-fors receiving attention recently were those based on the O.J. Simpson and Menendez brothers murder cases; Amy Fisher's adventures with Joey Buttafuoco; and Princess Diana's life and death.

Adventure, mystery, and drama series are next-most expensive, costing, on average, between $2 and $4 million on a weekly basis. As we have mentioned more than once, "ER" broke the bank on this form of television production in 1998, when NBC agreed to renew the show from Warner Brothers for $13 million per episode. This deal sent shock waves through the industry, with producers of other popular dramas pressing their networks for more money for big name stars, exotic locations, and expensive special effects. The cash-strapped networks have responded as you might think: by seeking less expensive shows to offset the high cost of miniseries, made-fors, and action hours.

Profile: Wrestling Mania: A Ratings Body Slam

Despite the multiple millions cable networks are spending on "high concept" original programming, the most popular program on cable week-to-week is wrestling. In fact, in one of the recent all-important sweeps periods (February 1999), wrestling occupied the top 3, and 8 of the top 10 places in the Nielsen cable ratings. USA Network's "WWF Wrestling" led the pack, with a rating of 4.4 (more than 4 million homes). Turner's "WCW Monday Night Nitro Live!" and its competitor's "Monday WWF Wrestling" were close behind, each with a rating of 4.2 (though Turner's grapplers had a few more households). More than 40 million Americans watch wrestling in a given week, and WWF and WCW are available in over 100 countries.

The appeal of wrestling is nothing new. When television was young in the 1950s, wrestling was a staple of the prime-time schedules of the major networks, making celebrities of Gorgeous George, Bobo Brazil, Handsome Johnny Baron, and Farmer Don Nelson, among others. After a time, NBC, CBS, and ABC moved away from wrestling, as their program schedules (and, it was presumed, their audiences) matured. By the 1990s, however, they soon rediscovered the apparently endless appeal of large men behaving badly in their undergarments. NBC has sometimes preempted its popular "Saturday Night Live" for a series of wrestling events under the banner of "Saturday Night Main Events." Fox TV has programmed similar specials. And wrestling has been the top money-earner for pay-per-view, with recent events like WCW's "Halloween Havoc," "Superbrawl VIII," and "Bash at the Beach" grossing millions, at a household cost of $29.95 and up.

The real heavyweights in TV wrestling are Ted Turner and Vince McMahon. Turner started World Championship Wrestling (WCW) to fill his new channels in the 1980s. It is now one of the more profitable arms of the Time Warner empire. Its arch rival is McMahon's Worldwide Wrestling Federation (WWF). Today, WCW and WWF slug it out night after night, week after week, each trying to outdo the other for excitement, spectacle, and sometimes it seems, outright repugnance. While "Billionaire Ted," (as Vince calls him) generally stays above the fray, McMahon is one of the ongoing characters in the WWF saga. Recently, McMahon stirred up a furor by hurling an on-camera epithet at crowd-favorite female wrestler Sable. His wrestlers generally are more "edgy" than those on WCW, having been seen to lip-synch profanities or to engage in gestures normally reserved for the boys' locker room. McMahon has been accused in the past of exhibiting homophobia, and of advocating the use of steroids among his wrestlers. He has survived these charges to build a TV property—Titan Sports—worth millions (if not billions, like ol' Ted). Diamond Dallas Page, The Undertaker, Hitman Hart, Hulk Hogan, and Goldberg are as famous in some TV households as are Calista Flockhart, Jennifer Aniston, and Jay Leno. Speaking of Leno, the Tonight Show host recently teamed up with Diamond Dallas Page against Hulk Hogan and Eric Bischoff in a pay-per-view event. Leno's team won. Hogan and Bischoff took it on the chin, so to speak.

Fortunately for the networks, the most popular program type is also one of the least costly. Situation comedies cost about $950,000 to $1.5 million per episode. Sitcoms can hold the line on cost since most are shot in a studio as opposed to an expensive location; they are recorded in "real time" before an audience, which keeps the need for editing and special effects to a minimum; and today most are shot on videotape, which is cheaper than using film. Most dramas, on the other hand, however, continue to use film.

As situation comedies become more popular, their costs increase, mainly in the area of star salaries. By the end of its run in 1998, "Seinfeld" was costing NBC about $3 million per program. Similarly, Paul Reiser and Helen Hunt were persuaded to continue on "Mad About You" for another season (1998–1999) with the promise of $1 million *each* per episode (bringing the show's total cost to $3.25 million per half-hour).

The "bargain basement" of network TV are so-called reality shows, including news documentaries and "infotainment" series. For example, CBS's highly rated "60 Minutes" costs about $900,000 per hour and ABC's "20/20" is budgeted in the $750,000 range. "Dateline NBC" is a bargain for NBC, budgeted at only $650,000 per hour. The low cost of reality shows is one reason for their proliferation in recent years.

Cable Network Programming

We covered the programming of cable and pay-cable networks in Chapter 5. However, it is useful to note here how these networks are programmed in comparison with the broadcast networks.

Theatrical Motion Pictures   As we have seen, the bulk of the program schedule (over 80 percent of airtime) on the major pay cable services, including HBO/ Cinemax and Showtime/The Movie Channel, consists of theatrical motion pictures. Most of these are licensed to the pay service by the "majors," Hollywood's largest studios.

The studios normally make their films (known as "titles" in the trade) available to pay cable a year after their first theatrical release. There is a narrower release "window" for pay per view (PPV) of six months or less. Sometimes studios will delay the pay release of major box office hits in order to continue to reap profits at the box office. Occasionally a theatrical release may be so disappointing that the studio will release the film to cable and home video within weeks of its theatrical debut.

Some distributors make their films available to multiple pay services simultaneously. However, to offset viewer dissatisfaction with pay services ("they all play the same movies"), there has been a trend toward studios' signing **exclusivity deals** with pay services. Such contracts guarantee first cable release to one pay service.

Theatrical motion pictures are also the backbone of a number of the advertiser-supported cable networks, including the USA Network, TBS Superstation, and Lifetime. These films are normally sold in **packages,** series of titles made available by a distribution company for sale to cable networks and local TV stations. In fact, it was Ted Turner's acquisition of virtually the entire MGM film library (including *Gone with the Wind*) that enabled his launch of Turner Network Television (TNT) and Turner Classic Movies (TCM). American Movie Classics (AMC) has also carved its niche by acquiring distribution rights to large packages of older film titles.

Cable-Original Movies   In their quest to keep pay cable attractive to consumers despite competition from video stores and other sources, cable programmers are producing their own movies. Some have been released for theatrical distribution first, to be followed by a pay-cable run. Others have been produced for a premiere on the cable network, to be followed by theatrical or home video release.

The typical made-for-cable movie today has a budget in the range of $4 million to $8 million. This is less than half the typical budget of a feature film but about a third higher than the cost of a "movie of the week" on one of the broadcast networks. For the extra cost, the cable "made-for" can typically attract a more well-known cast and take on more delicate or controversial subject matter than is the norm on broadcast TV.

HBO has been a leader in the production of cable original movies, producing between 10 and 15 each year. Among its recent offerings were the space epic "From the Earth to the Moon" (budgeted at $65 million), "The Rat Pack," "A Bright Shining Lie," and "Winchell." Showtime is also committed to original films, with the critically acclaimed "Baby Dance," "The Wall," and "Mandela and de Klerk," among its recent productions.

Cable Series   In their early days, cable and pay cable relied almost exclusively on movies, sports, and concerts for their programming. The few cable series that did run tended to be the low-budget, easy-to-film variety (Las Vegas acts, stand-up comedy, showbiz chatter, and so on). One sign of the maturity of the cable business is the emergence of regularly scheduled "high-profile" series from many cable networks. In fact, more TV programming is produced today for cable networks than for the traditional broadcast networks.

Some recent cable-original series of note were "The Larry Sanders Show" and "The Sopranos" on HBO; USA Network's "Pacific Blue"; VH-1's "Behind the Music" and "Legends"; MTV's "The Real World"; and dozens of others.

Generally, cable services produce their original programs at lower cost than do the commercial TV networks. This cost savings is achieved in various ways. First, smaller independent production companies are often used instead of the costly majors. To cut overhead expenses that pile up while shooting in a big studio lot, many series are shot on location or in major cities outside the United States, where the dollar is stronger than local currency. Canada and England have become very popular production sites, with Toronto and London "standing in" for Los Angeles and New York.

In addition, cable networks often engage in coproduction ventures with foreign networks and production companies, many of which have had trouble

Most cable networks aim for niche audiences, such as this program about Thomas Edison on the History Channel.

getting their programs into the lucrative American market.

Public Television Programming

Although the dominant networks (in terms of audience size and budget) are the major commercial broadcast and cable firms, public TV remains a vital source of national programming. Today some 350 full-power noncommercial TV stations have the same needs as their commercial counterparts: to fill their schedule with programming attractive to audiences. To do so, these stations rely on the Public Television Service (PBS).

PBS operates in reverse fashion from the commercial networks. Whereas NBC, CBS, ABC, and Fox funnel money to production companies and pay stations to carry their programs, PBS charges membership dues to its affiliates (over 90 percent of all public TV stations). In return, PBS provides programs funded by pooled station funds, the CPB, foundations, individual contributions, and other sources. PBS itself produces no programs. Instead, through its National Program Service (NPS), it serves as a conduit to program producers, usually avoiding the suppliers common to network scheduling.

A key difference between the commercial networks and PBS is that the stations (not the network) decide when to carry national programs. The most popular programs on PBS form the "core schedule," which is designated for same-night carriage. PBS recommends but cannot require stations to air these shows the same night that they are fed by satellite to member stations. Same-night carriage helps PBS promote its shows nationally. Although most PBS affiliates air the core schedule the same day, many PBS shows are taped and delayed for days or weeks. And within limits, which vary from show to show, stations frequently rerun PBS shows. Thus unlike CBS or NBC, a PBS show may or may not air nationally in a given day, and when it finally does run, it may be rerun long before the summer.

On average, PBS today distributes about 1,500 hours of programming per year to its member stations (about four hours per day). The bulk of PBS programming consists of news and public affairs (about 40 percent). This includes programs like "Frontline," "Wall Street Week," and "The News Hour." Next most common are cultural programs, such as "Mystery," "The American Experience," "Dance in America," and "Live from Lincoln Center." Children's programs make up just over 1 in 10 PBS shows, from "Sesame

Street" to "Teletubbies" to "Where in the World Is Carmen Sandiego?" "How-to" shows are nearly as common, from "The Frugal Gourmet" to "Julia Child" to "Antiques Roadshow." Filling out the PBS schedule are shows that are strictly educational (like "Newton's Apple" and "Reading Rainbow") and a very small sprinkling of sports (mostly tennis and soccer).

PBS strives to avoid the producers that are common to commercial TV. Nearly 40 percent of producers for public TV considers themselves "independent." Just over one in four programs on the network come from one of its member stations, and about 7 percent emanates from international producers. The remaining shows are developed and funded by unique consortiums of stations, philanthropic groups, corporations, foundations; you name it!

THE WORLD OF TV SYNDICATION

After the networks (broadcast, cable, and PBS), the largest purveyors of programming are the **syndicators:** the companies that sell programs directly to TV stations and cable services. The growth of independent TV stations, the arrival of cable and new broadcast networks, and the introduction of the VCR have created tremendous new demands. Where once syndication meant only two things—movies and network reruns—the syndication universe today ranges from films to talk shows, music videos, and adventure yarns, to "how-to" tapes on everything from exercise to hunting water buffalo. Today TV syndication is a $5 billion annual business.

The Syndication Market

There are two primary buyers or markets for syndicated programming. The traditional market for syndication is local TV. Today over 1,300 local TV stations obtain syndicated programming to fill their program schedules during time periods without network programs or local programs (mainly news).

The second market for syndicated programming is the cable networks. The chief cable buyers of syndication are the advertiser-supported services, like TBS Superstation, the USA network, Lifetime, and others.

The annual NATPE programming bazaar attracts thousands of TV executives and producers from around the globe.

The Syndication Bazaar

In 1963, a small group of TV programmers got together with an equally small group of syndicators to pool their resources and streamline their efforts. From those humble beginnings has come an annual show-biz extravaganza known as NATPE International.

By 1999, nearly 17,000 TV executives—including programmers, syndicators, and even some stars—attended NATPE International, the annual gathering of the National Association of Television Program Executives. Part Hollywood hype and part consumer trade show, the convention has become the place where new syndicated programs are unveiled and, most of all, plugged. Syndicators lure buyers to screening rooms. Liquor flows. Premiums—like cowboy hats from producers of westerns—abound. And sometimes deals are made.

Types of Syndicated Programming

What does one see at NATPE? Despite the vast array of programming available, it is possible to classify syndicated programming into three main types: motion pictures that have completed their theatrical run, whose home video and pay-cable releases are sold to stations in **movie packages;** programming originally produced for one of the major TV networks, sold to stations as **off-net syndication;** and original programming produced expressly for syndication, known as **first-run.** Each type of syndication is distributed in a unique way.

Movie Packages   Movies are a mainstay of the program schedule for the pay-cable networks (from HBO and Showtime to Encore and Starz), many TV stations, and many basic cable networks (including USA, Lifetime, American Movie Classics, and Turner Classic Movies). Even network affiliates need movies for parts of their daytime, late-night, and weekend programming. There are lots of movies out there: It is estimated that since the sound era began in 1927, over half a million films have been produced in the United States alone. Keep that figure in mind when you get the feeling in a video store that you have seen everything.

From the earliest days of TV, movies have been the backbone of syndication. The new TV stations needed something to show; facing declining attendance, the motion picture business needed a new revenue source. The venture was a match made in heaven (if not Hollywood). Early on, it became unwieldy to sell movies one at a time. Thus the distribution companies (originally subsidiaries of the major studios) began to package the movies as a collection of titles. Today, with the exception of a very few blockbusters (such as *Titanic*) movies sold in syndication are packaged.

Stations acquire the rights to movies under **license agreements.** The agreements generally run from three to six years and allow the station to show a movie up to six times or more during the period covered. Typically packages of recent box office successes (known as A movies) cost stations more than older and less-popular films (known as B movies). In a market like New York City, *As Good As It Gets* may license for as much as $500,000, whereas *I Was a Teenage Werewolf* can run for as little as $50.

Off-Net Syndication   Say what you will about the commercial broadcast networks—their imitative schedules, their lowest-common-denominator programs, and their so-called demise in recent years. The fact remains that network programs enjoy great popularity, which sustains over time. In the jargon of syndication, network shows have "staying power" and "legs." Old network programs never die: They are sold to stations and cable services as off-net syndication.

Off-net series are packaged for syndication in a manner similar to motion-picture packaging. The station or cable service pays for a certain number of episodes in the series and gets the right to show each title a number of times. Six runs over a period of six years is commonplace. The price per episode for off-net programs varies widely. It depends on the size of the TV market, the popularity of the show in its first run, the number of programs available, and so on.

Normally at least 100 episodes of a network show are needed to launch it in off-net syndication. The ideal number of episodes is 130. Why? Since there are 260 weekdays in a year, an off-net episode can run exactly twice annually when programmed in a time period each Monday to Friday. This process of scheduling a show to run in the same daypart each weekday is known as **stripping.**

Shows that have recently eclipsed the magic number and scored a hit in off-net syndication include "Seinfeld," "Friends," "Home Improvement," and "The Simpsons."

First-Run Syndication   Programs that make their debut in syndication, without a prior network life, are known as first-run syndication. Traditionally first-run syndication has been characterized by cheap, easy-to-produce programs designed to be strip-programmed.

Game shows and talk programs have fit the bill perfectly over the years and have been the bulk of first-run syndication. Today's dominating syndicated quiz programs are "Jeopardy" and "Wheel of Fortune." The queen of syndicated talk is Oprah Winfrey. She has been joined in first-run syndication by Rosie O'Donnell, Jerry Springer, Leeza Gibbons, Regis and Kathy Lee, and a host of others.

Not all syndicated originals are cheap quiz and talk programs. Buoyed by Paramount's success with "Star Trek: The Next Generation" and "Deep Space Nine," as well as the worldwide appeal of "Baywatch," first-run action/adventure series have been proliferating lately. Many of these shows are long on action, short on dialogue, and skimpy on costuming. In this category fall such first-run epics as "Xena" and "Hercules," and the newer "Relic Hunter," "Avalon," and "Beastmaster: The Legend."

Barter Syndication

At one time, TV stations would purchase syndicated programming on a "cash and carry" basis. However, for a number of reasons cash sales of syndicated programming have declined in recent years. For one thing, the "bottom line" consciousness of the TV industry has made station managers reluctant to take million-dollar gambles on syndicated programs. The record number of mergers and buyouts has left little cash to speculate in program investment. And syndicators have had difficulty extracting payments from stations on installment plans. Many stations have been late in paying their bills; some (especially UHF stations with huge inventories) have defaulted altogether.

Thus, high prices have combined with low cash flows to create a new form of syndication finance. Just as the term was used in the days of fur trappers and Indian agents, *barter* refers to the trading of one commodity for another of similar value. In TV, the valuable commodity offered by the syndicator is programming; the item of value at the station is its airtime. In **barter syndication** the syndicator provides the program to the station free or at a substantially reduced cost per episode. In return, the station sacrifices some of the advertising slots in the show. The syndicator can integrate its own ads into the show, or the syndicator can act like a TV network, calling on major advertisers to place ads in each of the markets in which the program plays.

In barter syndication, the key to the syndicator is market clearance. The more markets the program plays in, the larger is the national audience that can be offered to advertisers. Clearing 80 percent of the nation's TV markets is considered good; over 90 percent clearance is excellent.

Advertising revenues from barter syndication have increased dramatically in recent years. In 1988 barter revenues to syndicators represented about $800 million. Today barter syndication is a $2.5 billion business.

LOCAL TELEVISION PROGRAMMING

The last piece of the programming puzzle is provided by individual TV stations and cable systems through their original, locally produced programs.

Local programming has been a growth area in recent years as TV stations and cable systems seek a unique identity when faced with new competitors like satellite DBS and the Internet.

Local Television Stations

Faced with escalating syndication costs, lagging network performances, and the loss of local advertising dollars to barter, TV stations are placing increasing emphasis on their own local programming. As we saw in a previous section, the bulk of the local TV budget goes to local news.

Many local TV stations have expanded their local news "hole" from early fringe and late night to include morning and noon programs. In virtually all large cities, there are locally produced alternatives to "Today" and "Good Morning America." Some local

Barry Diller, head of the USA Networks and creative force behind WAMI in Miami.

stations are moving from news and talk to comedy, drama, and music programming.

At the forefront of local production is WAMI in Miami, the brainchild of Barry Diller, former Fox TV head, who is now at the helm of USA Networks. WAMI is a 4,000-square-foot storefront studio on Lincoln Road, in the heart of Miami Beach's historic and trendy Art Deco district. WAMI has a staff of more than 150 (mostly young) employees, who produce more than 14 hours of original programming per day. WAMI boasts the usual news and talk shows. It also features unique exercise programs (where octogenarians work out alongside 20-something supermodels), sports, and dance and music programs. WAMI also runs historic TV programs made in and around Miami, which are archived by the Louis Wolfson II Media History Center.

Diversity is the key word in local TV production. Survey after survey of general managers and program directors suggests that local production of everything from situation comedies to dramas will increase in the early 2000s.

Local Cable Programming

Just as the future of TV stations may lie in their ability to develop local programming, the cable industry is making similar forecasts.

As we documented earlier in this chapter, cable systems have been especially vigorous in developing news and sports programs as an alternative to local affiliates in their service areas. The rise of regional cable news has been a boon to local cable channels.

Other community channel services on the rise include on-screen TV program guides, electronic bulletin boards that feature classified and personal advertising, and electronic "tours of homes" offered by area realtors.

PROGRAMMING STRATEGIES

Now that we understand the various types and sources of TV programming today, we close this chapter by providing a taste of the techniques of TV programming. Space precludes a full discussion of how TV programmers determine their schedules. This process fills entire books and full-semester courses at many institutions. The books listed at the end of the chapter provide a good beginning point to an understanding of TV programming in practice. Now, on to the "taste test."

There is an old saying in television: "People don't watch stations, they watch programs." This means we select the station to watch based on programming rather than selecting the program because of the station that transmits it. It is also a reminder of the importance of programming to the success of TV.

The first step in programming is to define the potential audience. Cartoons shown while children are in school or a football broadcast when men are at work may attract small audiences, but not the numbers possible if the cartoons are run after school or the football game is shown on Sundays when most men aren't working.

Programmers must also have some idea about what groups prefer the shows that are available to be used. "Murder She Wrote" generally attracted women and older men as its main group of viewers. To have optimum viewership it was necessary to schedule "Murder She Wrote" at a time when these people would be in front of their TV sets. Sunday evenings following "60 Minutes" seemed like a good idea to CBS. The show was a mainstay in that time period for over a decade. The time period was inherited by a show with appeal to a similar demographic: "Touched By an Angel."

Obviously, programming must entail more than merely placing a program that appeals to a particular audience at a time when that audience may view it. There are a number of techniques that programmers use to maximize viewership. Once you have viewers, you want to hang on to them.

Audience Flow

Audiences will tend to stay with the TV station they are watching until something they dislike shows up on the screen. In some ways audiences take on inertia-like properties, viewing the same station until forced to change. The proliferation of remote controls has changed this tendency, since viewers no longer are required to get out of their chairs to change the channel, but inertia still influences viewing. The movement of audiences from one program to another is called **audience flow.**

The successful programmer will build and hold an audience from show to show. This means putting together programs that generally attract the same audience.

One reason for the continuing success of "Oprah" is that her issues-based talk program provides the perfect lead-in to local news. At the network level, programmers try to build their evenings around a core audience. NBC's powerful Thursday evening block was designed to keep and attract women 25–49, flowing nicely from "Friends," to "Caroline in the City," to "ER" in 1998. Similarly, Fox had arranged its schedule on Monday nights to hook younger women, with a block of "Melrose Place," and "Ally McBeal."

Counterprogramming

Counterprogramming is a technique wherein the programmer decides to go for a different audience than the competing station or network is trying to attract.

Independent TV stations have long counterprogrammed network affiliates in their market, programming children's programs when their competitors carried local news, or male-oriented local sports when affiliates were in the female-oriented prime-time blocks. Cable networks have also been master counterprogrammers. One example is the success of ESPN's "Sportscenter," which comes on at 11 P.M., when many local TV stations go to their news programming. CNN carries its most popular talk program, "Larry King Live," when the major networks go to their dramas and situation comedies. One more example: Remember that Fox block on Monday evenings, with "Melrose" and "Ally"? It should come as no surprise that this was a counterprogram strategy to ABC's "Monday Night Football."

Challenge Programming

Challenge programming is the opposite of counterprogramming. In challenge programming, the TV network or station goes "head-to-head" with the same type of programming as a major competitor, or goes after the same demographic with a different program with similar audience appeal. Local stations often go head-to-head with their afternoon talk shows, such as "Oprah" against "Jerry Springer." They do this in local news and may also compete with morning talk and noontime information shows.

One famous example of challenge programming concerned the decision by CBS and NBC in 1994 to go head-to-head with high-profile medical dramas. CBS sought to win Thursday evenings at 10 (9 Central) with "Chicago Hope." NBC set its sights on the same time period with "ER." ABC was happy to stay on the sidelines by counterprogramming with "Prime Time Live." When the smoke cleared, NBC had won the battle; by winter 1995, CBS had moved "Chicago Hope" to Monday nights. By 1999, "ER" was a staple of NBC's Thursday schedule. "Chicago Hope" was earning respectable ratings on Wednesday nights, though it was running behind ABC's "20/20" and NBC's "Law and Order."

A FINAL WORD

Programming is the "fun" part of TV. It is what attracts viewers so that the station or network can sell time to advertisers, to make money. A great deal of thought and effort is put into deciding which programs fit where. The reason for this concern in programming is not primarily that the station or network cares whether viewers are entertained or informed but that this is how they make their money.

SUMMARY

- TV programming takes two major forms: news and entertainment.
- Television news is the nation's primary source of news and is regarded as credible by a large portion of the public.
- Television news reached maturity when President Kennedy was assassinated. The 1960s events such as the civil rights movement, the Vietnam war, and Neil Armstrong's first step on the moon came to life in people's living rooms.

- The 1970s and 1980s were marked by money and machines. Television news became a significant profit center for local TV stations and cable. Anchor salaries rose. Electronic news gathering and satellite news came on the scene.
- The 1990s saw growth in TV news due to new networks, regional cable news, and more global competition.
- Many people are involved in the preproduction stage of the newscast. They are the news director, news producer, assignment editor, field producer, reporter,

writers, and editors. Those involved in the production stage include the director, the studio production team, and the anchors.

● Television stations can obtain entertainment programming through networks, syndication, and local origination. The commercial networks—ABC, CBS, NBC, and Fox—provide broad, mass-appeal programming. Three newer networks, Paramount's UPN, Time Warner's WB, and Pax TV, have aligned with independent stations to compete for the huge TV audience.

● Historically, networks have relied on outside sources for their programs—in particular, the major Hollywood studios and a cluster of well-known independent producers. Recently, the networks have expanded the scope of their own in-house productions. The networks receive a great number of suggested story lines. Because the number is so large, there is only a slight chance that any one idea will be accepted.

● Movies of the week and made-for-TV movies are the most expensive types of programming. Situation comedies and reality programs, on the other hand, are the cheapest to produce.

● As cable matures, it has directly affected the networks. Cable has been producing higher-quality shows and the effects can be seen in the ratings.

● Syndication has become a popular source of programming. To understand fully the syndication business, one must be aware of NATPE trade shows and types of syndication.

● Local TV stations achieve an identity by producing local shows; therefore, many community and cable stations are trying this technique. Because they will be saving money and providing original programming, these stations are likely to survive in the future.

● TV programming strategies include audience flow, counterprogramming, and challenge programming.

KEY TERMS

electronic news gathering
   (ENG)   190
satellite news gathering
   (SNG)   190
sweeps   190
minidocs   190
news consultants   191
coventuring   191
local-local news   191
regional cable-news services   192
news-on-demand   193
future file   193
teasers   194
bumpers   194
packages   194

network programming   196
syndication   196
local origination   196
affiliates   197
affiliation agreement   197
network compensation   197
cleared   197
preemption   197
financial interest and syndication
   rules   198
license fees   198
prime-time access rules (PTAR)   198
concept   201
treatment   201
step deal   201

right of first refusal   201
pilots   201
exclusivity deals   203
packages   203
syndicators   205
movie packages   206
off-net syndication   206
first-run   206
license agreements   206
stripping   206
barter syndication   207
audience flow   208
counterprogramming   209
challenge programming   209

SUGGESTIONS FOR FURTHER READING

Auletta, K. (1991). *Three blind mice: How the TV networks lost their way.* New York: Random House.

Block, A. B. (1990). *Outfoxed: Marvin Davis, Barry Diller, Rupert Murdoch and the inside story of America's fourth television network.* New York: St. Martin's.

Blum, R. A., & Lindheim, R. D. (1987). *Primetime: Network television programming.* Boston: Focal Press.

Boyd, A. (1997). *Broadcast journalism: Techniques of radio and TV news* (4th ed.). Oxford; Boston: Focal Press.

Carroll, R., & Davis, D. M. (1993). *Electronic media programming: Strategies and decision-making.* New York: McGraw-Hill.

Cremer, C. (1996). *ENG: Television news* (3d ed.). New York: McGraw-Hill.

Eastman, S. T. (1997). *Broadcast/cable programming: Strategies and practices* (5th ed.). Belmont, CA: Wadsworth Publishing.

Gross, L., & Vane, E. (1994). *Programming for TV, radio and cable.* Boston: Focal Press.

Howard, H., Kievman, M. & Moore, B. *Radio, TV and cable programming* (2nd ed.). Ames, IA: Iowa University Press.

Leshay, J. (1993). *How to launch your career in TV news.* Lincolnwood, IL: VGM Career Horizons.

Picard, R. (1993). *The cable networks handbook.* Riverside, CA: Carpelan.

Yorke, I. (1995). *Television news.* Oxford; Boston: Focal Press.

INTERNET EXERCISES

1. Visit our Web site at http://www.mhhe.com/ beyond for study-guide exercises to help you learn and apply material in each chapter. You will find ideas for future research as well as useful Web links to provide you with an opportunity to journey through the new electronic media.

Part Four How It's Controlled

Rules and Regulations 10

Quick Facts

 License terms for TV and radio stations: 8 years

 FCC has five commissioners, six bureaus, and about 2,200 employees

 Number of states that permit cameras in the courtroom: 47

 Date by which all newly manufactured TV sets must contain V-chip: January 1, 2000

 Amount spent by National Association of Broadcasters on lobbying in 1998: $3.1 million

The first significant legislative update to electronic communications law in 62 years was passed in February of 1996. The Telecommunications Act of 1996, among other things, changed ownership limits on broadcasting and cable properties, opened up potential competition between the cable and telephone industries, and mandated that newly manufactured TV sets contain a computer chip that can be used to keep unwanted programs from entering the home. The effects of this new law have already changed much about the broadcasting and cable industries (see Chapters 4 and 5) and will probably have even more of an impact in the future.

This chapter will first examine some of the established forces that shape the overall form, structure, and operation of broadcasting and cable regulations and then look at the rules and regulations themselves, with an emphasis on the new Telecommunications Act.

RATIONALE

Unlike many other industries, broadcasting has always had special requirements and special responsibilities placed on it by government. What makes it different? There have been two main rationales for treating broadcasting as a special case: (1) the scarcity theory and (2) the pervasive presence theory.

The **scarcity theory** notes that the electromagnetic spectrum is limited. Only a finite number of broadcast stations can exist in a certain place in a certain time; too many stations can interfere with one another. This means that only a limited number of aspiring broadcasters can be served and that the government must choose from among the potential applicants.

In addition, the scarcity theory holds that the spectrum is such a valuable resource that it should not be privately owned. Instead, it is treated like a public resource, owned by all, like a national park. The government treats those fortunate enough to broadcast as trustees of the public and imposes special obligations on them, such as requiring that they provide candidates for public office equal opportunities to use their stations.

Recent technological advances such as cable TV, which offers would-be broadcasters a large number of channels, have prompted a reevaluation of the scarcity theory. Many critics would argue that it is outmoded. Others, however, point out that, as long as the number of people wishing to broadcast exceeds the available facilities, scarcity still exists.

The **pervasive presence theory** is of more recent origin. It holds that broadcasting is available to virtually all of the population and, once the TV or radio set is turned on, offensive messages can enter the home without warning, reaching both adults and children. This situation is fundamentally different from encountering an offensive message in a public forum. If you're out in public, you're on your own. You might encounter things that offend your sensibilities. Should you meet someone wearing a T-shirt with an offensive word printed on it, your only recourse would be to turn away. The home, however, is not the same as a public place; you should not expect to encounter unwanted offensive messages there. Consequently, the pervasive presence theory holds that you're entitled to some protection. Thus the basic intrusiveness of broadcasting allows the government to regulate it.

HISTORY

How did the government get involved with broadcasting regulation in the first place? In 1910 Congress passed the Wireless Ship Act. Only four paragraphs long, it basically mandated that large oceangoing passenger ships must be equipped with wireless sets. It had little relevance to broadcasting, primarily because broadcasting as we know it did not yet exist. Two years later the Radio Act of 1912 was passed. Spurred by the sinking of the *Titanic* and the need to ratify international treaties, the 1912 act required those wishing to engage in broadcasting to obtain a license from the Secretary of Commerce. Further, to prevent interference among maritime stations, it provided for the use of call letters and established the assignment of frequencies and hours of operation. The law also strengthened the regulations concerning the use of wireless by ships. As was the case with the earlier law, the 1912 act still envisioned radio as point-to-point communication, like the telegraph, which uses the spectrum only sporadically, and did not anticipate broadcasting, which uses the spectrum continuously. Consequently, for the next eight years or so, when most wireless communication was of the point-to-point variety, the law worked reasonably well. As the 1920s dawned, however, and radio turned into broadcasting, the 1912 act quickly broke down.

As related in Chapter 1, the number of broadcast stations greatly increased and available spectrum space could not accommodate them. Interference quickly became a serious problem. By 1926 the interference problem had gotten so bad that many parts of the country could no longer get a consistently clear broadcast signal. Consequently, after prodding from President Calvin Coolidge, Congress finally passed a new law—the Radio Act of 1927.

The 1927 Radio Act

Although more than 70 years old, the **Radio Act of 1927** still demonstrates the basic principles that underlie broadcast regulation. Embracing the scarcity argument, the key provisions of the act were the following:

1. The recognition that the public owned the electromagnetic spectrum, thereby eliminating private ownership of radio frequencies.

2. The notion that radio stations had to operate in the "public interest, convenience or necessity."

3. A prohibition against censorship of broadcast programs by the government.

4. The creation of a five-member **Federal Radio Commission (FRC),** which would grant licenses, make rules to prevent interference, and establish coverage areas with its decisions subject to judicial review.

Over the next few years, the FRC enacted technical standards that eliminated the interference problem and further elaborated the concept of the public interest. In one case, the FRC denied the license of a station in Kansas because it broadcast prescriptions for bogus patent medicines (see boxed material). The federal court system affirmed this decision, thus demonstrating that the FRC was not restricted to an examination of solely technical matters and could indeed look at content.

The Communications Act of 1934

The 1927 act was superseded seven years later when President Franklin Roosevelt streamlined the government's regulatory operations concerning communication. In response to Roosevelt's recommendations, Congress passed a new communications act **(The Communications Act of 1934),** which expanded the membership of the FRC from five to seven members and gave the organization a new name—the **Federal Communications Commission.** The powers of the new commission were broadened to include all wireless and wire forms of communication (including the telephone), except for those used by the military and the government. The 1927 law was regarded so highly that much of it was rewritten into the new legislation and the key provisions previously outlined were left unchanged.

Like most laws, the 1934 Communications Act has been amended and reshaped, usually in response to a current problem or to changing technology. For example, in 1959, Congress amended the act to make it illegal for people to rig quiz shows. Three years later, Congress passed the **Communications Satellite Act,** which expanded the regulatory powers of the FCC. With all of its various revisions, the 1934 law remained the nation's most influential broadcasting law until the passage of the 1996 Telecommunications Act, which is discussed in detail in a later section.

Cable Regulation

The history of cable regulation has been marked by major changes of direction. When cable first came on the scenes in the 1950s, the FCC refused to regulate it since cable didn't use over-the-air frequencies. By the 1960s, however, cable became a viable competitor to broadcast stations and the FCC responded to pressure from broadcasters and enacted regulations that effectively hampered cable's growth in large markets. By the 1970s, cable operators were exerting their own pressure on the commission, which eventually issued a new set of rules that were somewhat more favorable to cable.

While all of this was going on at the federal level, cable systems were also bound by regulations at the state and local levels. Thus a company that owned cable systems in 20 communities might be faced with 20 different sets of local rules. The most important local rule established exclusivity. Local governments awarded an exclusive franchise to a single cable company to serve a community or neighborhood in exchange for the provision of specialized community channels, payment of a franchise fee, and maintenance of low rates. Many companies, in their zeal to obtain a franchise, overpromised and had to scale down their systems, creating some bad feelings between them and the local governments.

Profile: Dr. Brinkley and His Goats

One of the key cases decided by the new Federal Radio Commission concerned station KFKB ("Kansas Folks Know Best") in tiny Milford, Kansas. Licensed to Dr. John R. Brinkley, KFKB ("The Sunshine Station in the Heart of the Nation") became one of the most popular stations in America during the 1920s, primarily because of the notoriety surrounding its owner. John Romulus Brinkley was the son of a medical doctor. At an early age he decided to follow in his father's footsteps and entered medicine. Young Brinkley graduated, if that's the right word, from the Eclectic Medical University of Kansas City. (He apparently finished his course of study in a few weeks, paid $100, and received a diploma.) Forty states did not recognize degrees from his college, but that left "Dr." Brinkley eight others he could practice in. He eventually wound up in Milford and opened a modest hospital, which he immodestly named after himself. If that wasn't enough, he also set up the Brinkley Research Laboratories and the Brinkley Training School for Nurses.

Brinkley had studied a little bit about the workings of human glands. He also was a shrewd judge of human nature. Consequently, he began to advertise his rejuvenation operations over KFKB. Designed to restore sexual drive in middle-aged men, the actual operation consisted of grafting or injecting material from the sexual organs of male goats into his human patients. The operation was done under local anesthesia and took only 15 minutes. The cost was a rather significant sum in those days—$750. (The goats, of course, paid a much higher price.) One interesting touch introduced by the doctor: Patients could pick their own goat in advance from the doctor's private herd, sort of like picking out a lobster for your dinner from a tank at a seafood restaurant. As time passed, Brinkley was touting his operation as a cure-all for skin diseases, high blood pressure, insanity, and paralysis.

KFKB was the perfect medium for Brinkley's advertising. At the time, thanks to the doctor's investment, it was one of the most powerful stations in North America. Twice a day, people from Saskatchewan to Panama could hear the doctor's own radio talk show, in which he promoted his operation, gave precise instructions on how to get to Milford, and even advised prospective patients on how to transport the $750 safely.

People flocked to Milford and Brinkley became a rich man. In an era when legitimate doctors were making an annual salary of about $5,000 Brinkley was pulling in about $125,000 a year. He owned his own airplane, his own yacht, and a fleet of cars, and usually wore a couple of 12-carat diamond rings.

In addition to his gland operations, Brinkley also started selling his own prescription drugs. On a show called "The Medical Question Box" Brinkley would read letters people had written him about their ailments. He would then prescribe his medicines by number. Pharmacists all over the region were supplied with the Brinkley formulas, which usually consisted of ingredients such as alcohol and castor oil. For each bottle that was sold, the pharmacist would give a cut to Brinkley.

Not all was rosy, however. Kansas City newspapers attacked the doctor's methods, the American Medical Association exposed Brinkley's quackery, and the Federal Radio Commission eventually revoked his broadcast license and further defined the principle that programming must be in the public interest. Undaunted, Brinkley ran for governor of Kansas as a write-in candidate and nearly won. Since KFKB was no longer open to him, Brinkley bought a station in Mexico, XER, 500,000 watts strong, and kept his messages blanketing North America. Eventually the doctor moved to Del Rio, Texas, across the border from XER, and continued his medical practice there, this time specializing in cures for enlarged prostate glands. When a competing doctor opened up a similar practice in Del Rio, Brinkley moved to Little Rock, Arkansas.

Once in Arkansas, Brinkley's troubles began. Malpractice awards to discontented patients, back taxes, legal fees, the costs of running his Mexican station, and his extravagant lifestyle soon exhausted even Brinkley's sizable bank account. The doctor had to declare bankruptcy. As if that wasn't bad enough, the U.S. government finally persuaded Mexico to ease international radio interference problems by shutting down XER and similar stations. Less than a year later, at 56, J. R. Brinkley succumbed to a heart attack, thus ending the career of one of early radio's unsavory but colorful broadcasters.

Figure 10–1

The Federal Communications Commission

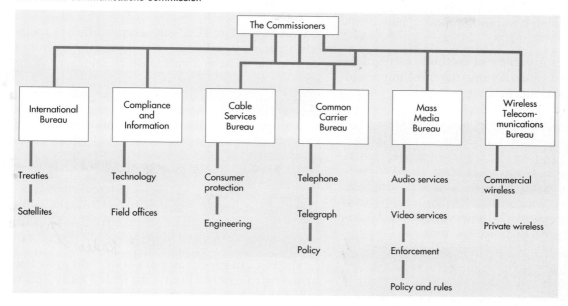

Reexamination

The 1980s saw a general trend toward deregulation. The FCC abolished many regulations that pertained to radio, simplified license renewal applications, and eased operating regulations for TV stations. Congress got into the spirit by extending the license terms for both radio and TV stations and by passing the **Cable Communications Policy Act of 1984,** which allowed cable systems the freedom to set their own rates.

By the 1990s, advances in technology and changes in the business arena prompted Congress to take another look at regulation. New communication technologies such as direct-to-home broadcasting via satellite and the Internet presented new opportunities and challenges. Telephone companies were interested in providing video programming, and some cable companies were actively exploring the possibility of offering phone services. In response to these and other forces, Congress passed the **Telecommunications Act of 1996** (discussed in the next section), which had a major impact on all areas of electronic media.

REGULATORY FORCES

Broadcast and cable policy results from the interaction of several factors. Legislative, administrative, judicial, political, and economic forces are all important deter-

miners of regulation. Drawing upon the model used by Krasnow, Longley, and Terry in *The Politics of Broadcast Regulation,* this section examines eight key components in the process: the FCC, Congress, the courts, the White House, industry lobbyists, the public, state and local governments, and the marketplace.

The Federal Communications Commission

The FCC currently consists of five commissioners, one of whom serves as chair, appointed by the president and confirmed by the Senate, for staggered five-year terms. Political balance is achieved by requiring that no more than three members can be from one political party.

Serving the commissioners are six bureaus: International, Wireless Telecommunications, Compliance and Information, Cable Services, Common Carrier, and Mass Media. Figure 10-1 shows this arrangement.

The **Mass Media Bureau** is most relevant to broadcasting and cable. Created in 1983, this bureau is charged with overseeing both over-the-air broadcasting and cable. The Mass Media Bureau has four divisions:

1. Audio Services, responsible for AM and FM radio.

2. Video Services, which handles UHF and VHF TV.

3. Enforcement, responsible for upholding FCC law.
4. Policy and Rules, which handles planning, revising existing laws, and proposing new regulations.

The FCC uses a variety of methods to regulate broadcasting and cable. Among the most important are licensing and policymaking.

Licensing   Licensing is the primary function of the FCC and the most important method of regulation. The FCC must approve applications for new station licenses, license renewals, and transfers of ownership to a new licensee. Note that the FCC grants licenses only to stations; it does not license networks. Each of the major networks, however, owns local stations that must have their licenses renewed.

Each radio and TV station must apply for a license renewal every eight years. When a license comes up for renewal, the FCC must determine if the station has operated in the public interest. In past years, the FCC required stations to submit sizable amounts of information along with their renewal applications. The current renewal application for most stations now fits on a postcard (some supporting documentation, however, is also required). Cable TV systems are not licensed by the FCC. Instead, this is the responsibility of the local governments that grant the franchise. The specific regulations and procedures surrounding the granting and renewal of broadcast licenses will be discussed later in the chapter.

Policymaking   Another regulatory tool is policymaking. Under the public interest guidelines, the FCC can enact rules governing some aspect of broadcasting and/or cable. To enact a rule, the commission must announce a proposal and allow for public comments. Moreover, the FCC can't put most new rules and regulations into effect until it publishes a summary, usually in a publication called the *Federal Register*.

Another component of the policy process involves planning for the future. The FCC maintains an Office of Plans and Policy, which analyzes trends and attempts to anticipate future policy problems. In 1991 this office issued a particularly bleak report on the future of conventional TV broadcasting, concluding that the audience and the revenues of that industry were in an "irreversible, long-term decline." In turn the FCC asked broadcasters to sub-

mit possible changes in FCC rules that would help the broadcasting business to be more competitive in the future.

Enforcement   The FCC has several different methods it can use to enforce its decisions, ranging from a slap on the wrist to a virtual death sentence. At the mildest level, the FCC can issue a letter of reprimand that scolds a station for some practice that is not in the public interest. Usually, unless the station persists in provoking the FCC, that ends the matter. Other legal remedies include a cease-and-desist order (which makes a station halt a certain practice) or a fine (called a forfeiture). A station can be fined up to $25,000 a day to a maximum of $250,000 for each separate violation. Infinity Broadcasting, for example, the company that syndicates the "Howard Stern" show, has been fined nearly $2 million by the FCC for broadcasting indecency.   *Radio*

The FCC, in effect, can put a station on probation by failing to renew a license for its full term. This is called short-term renewal and usually ranges from six months to two years. The idea behind short-term renewal is to give the commission a chance to take an early look at a station to determine if past deficiencies have been corrected. Infractions likely to bring short-term licenses involve deceptive promotions, lack of supervision of station facilities, and violation of equal employment practices.

The FCC can sound a death knell for stations by refusing to renew a license or revoking one currently in force. Although this action is used sparingly, it does occur. Since 1990 the FCC has denied the renewals of TV stations in Chicago and San Francisco and a radio station in Ohio for misrepresentation.

Congress

The FCC regulates broadcasting with Congress looking over its shoulder. The FCC is a creature of Congress. Congress created the FCC and, if it wished, Congress could abolish the FCC. (In fact, in 1982 Congress changed the status of the FCC from a permanent agency to one that had to be reauthorized every two years.) The U.S. Congress is an important part of broadcasting and cable regulation because of its power to enact and amend laws. It was Congress that passed the Communications Act of 1934 and the Telecommunications Act of 1996.

In addition to these two essential communication laws, Congress has enacted other legislation that has had an impact on broadcasting and cable. For example, in 1969, it prohibited cigarette advertising on TV and radio and in 1990 it passed a law that concerned children's television programming.

Moreover, although it sounds odd, Congress can affect regulatory policy by doing nothing. If it so chooses, Congress can terminate pending legislation or postpone it indefinitely by tabling it. It did this most recently in 1994 when it failed to act on a bill designed to set up the new "information superhighway" and forced its sponsors to resubmit it.

Congress can also exert pressure in nonlegislative ways. First, Congress controls the budget of the FCC. If the FCC has acted in a way that displeases the Congress, the commission may find its budget reduced. Further, all presidential appointments to the FCC must be approved by Congress. This gives Congress the opportunity to delay or block a particularly sensitive appointment. Finally, Congress can hold public hearings that highlight, at least in general terms, how Congress feels about a topic. The FCC, in turn, may get the message and shape its policies accordingly.

The Courts

If Congress looks over one shoulder of the FCC, the federal court system looks over the other. If a broadcaster, cable operator, or a citizen disagrees with an FCC decision, he or she appeals it to the federal courts. Most cases concerning broadcasting are decided by the U.S. Court of Appeals for the District of Columbia, whose decisions are subject to review by the Supreme Court only. Courts, however, do not act on their own. They wait for others to initiate actions. If a complaint is raised, courts do not normally reverse an agency's decision if the agency acted in a fair, nonarbitrary way and if the FCC actually has jurisdiction over the matter in question.

Although it does not get involved in many of the decisions of the FCC, when the judicial system does get a chance to speak, it has shown itself to be an important factor in determining broadcast policy. It was a court decision that articulated the pervasive presence rationale behind broadcasting regulation and affirmed the FCC's right to regulate indecent programming. Another court decision totally revamped the renewal hearing process. Before 1966, only those who would be affected by technical interference or economic hardship caused by the renewal or granting of a station's license could appear and offer evidence and testimony at a hearing. Then, in the WLBT case, the Court of Appeals ruled that private citizens had the right to participate in the process and citizen involvement grew rapidly in succeeding years. Deregulation has somewhat diminished citizen involvement, but the WLBT case established the right of citizens to intervene.

Of course, courts do not exist in a vacuum; they interact with many of the other forces active in regulating broadcasting. Federal judges are appointed by the president with the approval of the Senate. Congress writes and rewrites the laws that the courts interpret. Court decisions, as with WLBT, alter, for some groups, the ease of access into the regulatory process. Broadcasters and citizens can bring lawsuits to attract judicial attention. All in all, courts play a pivotal role in the regulatory process.

The White House

If it were possible for the FCC to have a third shoulder, the White House would be watching over it. The influence of the executive branch may not be as visible as that exerted by the Congress and the courts, but it is nonetheless potent.

In the first place, the president has the power of appointment over both FCC commissioners and judges. With regard to the FCC, since many members do not serve out their full terms, the president can fairly quickly establish a slate of congenial commissioners. Although the Communications Act limits the number of commissioners from one political party to no more than three, most presidents are able to find people who express the administration's prevailing political philosophy. Furthermore, the president can designate any of the sitting commissioners as chair at any time, without congressional intervention or approval. As a result, the president can set the regulatory tone of the FCC.

Second, the White House has its own agency that specializes in the broad field of telecommunications—the **National Telecommunications and Information Administration (NTIA)**. Housed in the Commerce Department, the NTIA allocates radio frequencies that are used by the federal government, makes grants to public telecommunications facilities, advises the administration on telecommunications matters, and represents the administration's interests before the FCC and the Congress. The NTIA is one of those organizations that will play as big a role in broadcasting and cable policymaking as the president desires.

Third, the various Cabinet offices can also influence

broadcasting and cable policy. The Department of Justice can prevent mergers that might result in antitrust problems, and the State Department represents the United States in international matters dealing with satellite orbital slots and mass communication–related businesses. The State Department's role will become more important in the future thanks to the growth of international communication systems.

Finally, the White House can influence policy by initiating communication legislation. Although the president cannot introduce bills in Congress, the White House can draft a bill and usually find a friendly member of Congress to propose it. In that same connection, the president also has the power to veto any unfavorable communication laws passed by Congress. Of course, Congress can also override a presidential veto.

Industry Lobbyists

A lobbyist is a person who represents a special interest and tries to influence legislators' voting behavior. Some people regard lobbyists as a negative force in policymaking, but it should be pointed out that they serve a necessary information function. Many lawmakers regard lobbyists as an asset; they help the lawmaker learn about the impact of pending bills on various segments of society. Lobbying has gone on in Washington for more than 200 years and is a deeply ingrained part of the political process. It comes as no surprise, then, that the broadcasting and cable industries maintain extensive lobbying organizations whose task is to make the industry's wishes known to the FCC, Congress, the courts, and the president.

Each of the major networks maintains its own lobbyists, as do a host of trade associations: the National Association of Broadcasters (traditionally the most influential for the broadcasting industry), the National Cable Television Association (the NCTA—the NAB's rival in the cable industry), the Association of Independent TV Stations, the National Association of Public TV Stations, the National Religious Broadcasters Association, and the National Association of Farm Broadcasters—to name just a few.

Lobbying tends to work best in a negative sense. It seems easier for lobbyists to stop something they consider bad from happening than it is for them to get something good to happen. Some of the biggest lobbying successes stem from the blockage of proposed legislation. For example, in 1994 the Clinton administration proposed charging royalty fees to

Eddie Fritts, president of the National Association of Broadcasters (NAB), the chief lobbying organization for radio and TV stations.

broadcasters and other users of the electromagnetic spectrum. Lobbyists responded quickly to the proposal and exerted pressure on lawmakers. A month later the administration dropped the idea.

Finally, the expense and energy that must be expended to support lobbying groups mean that one key player in the policy arena is underrepresented— the general public. Most citizens' groups lack the expertise, time, and money to maintain full-time lobbyists. As a result, policymaking tends to be influenced far more by the industry than by the average citizen. There are, however, a few ways in which citizens get involved in the process, and this is the focus of the next section.

The Public

Citizen involvement in broadcasting policy was at its high point in the 1970s. Citizen interest or media reform groups were active in more than 30 states in

1974 and had filed almost 300 petitions to deny the licenses of stations coming up for renewal. By the early 1980s, however, dwindling financial support, longer license terms, and a general emphasis on deregulation combined to weaken the power of these groups.

This decline does not mean that members of the public are shut out of the regulatory process. Some public interest groups still remain, most notably the National Coalition on Television Violence, the American Family Association, and Viewers for Quality Television. These groups generally try to put pressure on Congress and the broadcasters by generating favorable public opinion for their causes. Finally, the public influences policy in a more general manner through its election of both the president and members of Congress, who in turn help shape communications policy.

State and Local Governments

Federal laws supersede state and local regulations, but many states have legislation that covers areas not specifically touched on in federal communications law. For example, almost every state has a law dealing with defamation (injuring a person's reputation) and/or reporters' rights to keep sources confidential. Many states have their own laws covering lotteries (the conduct of contests and promotions) and statutes covering fraudulent or misleading ads. Public broadcasting, moreover, is regulated by many states through acts that spell out the ownership, operation, and funding of educational radio and TV stations. And, of course, broadcasters must comply with local law governing taxation and working conditions.

States and cities can also enact laws that protect the privacy of subscribers to local stations. Information about personal viewing habits cannot be released to unauthorized persons or organizations (this prevents, for example, a political candidate from obtaining from a cable company the information that his rival subscribes to an adult movie channel). Communities can also collect a franchise fee, subject to limitations, from a cable operator and determine the duration of the franchise agreement.

The Marketplace

In its move toward deregulation the FCC has often used the phrase "let the marketplace decide." It follows, then, that the marketplace has become an important factor in determining broadcasting policy. But what exactly is "the marketplace"? Broadly speaking, it's a place where buyers and sellers freely come together to exchange goods or services. Obviously, with regard to broadcasting and cable, there is no single place where buyer and seller are physically present. In this circumstance the marketplace notion refers to general economic forces, like supply, demand, competition, and price, that shape the broadcasting and cable industries. More and more, the FCC appears to be turning toward the marketplace as the ultimate determiner of the public interest. For example, the FCC refused to issue a single technical standard for AM stereo, propose rules for the TVRO (television reception only) industry, or get involved in the selection of radio program formats. In each case the FCC deferred to the marketplace.

This shift reinforces the basic change in recent broadcast regulatory philosophy. In the past broadcasters had been viewed as public trustees of the airwaves, obligated to offer public service to the community in which they are licensed. Under this rationale the best broadcasters are not the ones that compete best in an economic sense but the ones that provide the best service as determined by the FCC. There were times when the FCC attempted to coerce the industry into making greater public service commitments than economic incentives would dictate. The marketplace notion views the spectrum as an economic asset that will be utilized best if the government steps back and lets the law of economics take over. In short, the marketplace will encourage those services that the public wants.

The marketplace approach has its advantages: It can promote efficiency, encourage the creation of new services, and encourage diversity. On the downside, the marketplace is only responsive to economic forces and is not sensitive to social needs. Further, the real marketplace seldom approaches the ideal model posited by economic texts. Once they enter the market, for example, big companies exert far more clout than smaller companies.

As the century closed, both Congress and the FCC were taking a closer look at the marketplace concept. In some areas, such as children's programming, the notion was abandoned in favor of regulation. In others, as evidenced by the fact that the Telecommunications Act of 1996 encouraged marketplace competition between cable and phone companies, the impetus seems to be in the other direction. In any event, it seems likely that the marketplace will continue to be an important factor in broadcasting and cable for the foreseeable future.

Now that the general forces that influence broadcasting and cable regulation have been introduced, the remainder of this chapter concentrates on more specific regulatory issues—namely, the following: (1) the main federal laws pertaining to broadcasting, cable, and related technologies; (2) the FCC's regulatory responsibilities; (3) other federal laws that apply to the area; (4) laws pertaining to electronic journalism; (5) advertising regulations; and (6) international rules. A note of caution: This is a turbulent area; by the time you read this section, things may have changed. Like industry professionals, students, publishers, and textbook authors face the task of keeping up with this dynamic area. Check the book's Web site for recent developments.

FEDERAL LAW

The two pieces of federal legislation that have the most relevance for broadcasting and cable are the Communications Act of 1934 and the Telecommunications Act of 1996.

The Communications Act of 1934

The Communications Act of 1934 and related pieces of legislation are found in Title 47 of the U.S. Code. Title 47 is divided into chapters. The chapter most pertinent for our purposes is Chapter 5, "Wire and Radio Communication." Chapter 5 is further divided into subchapters which incorporate the 1934 act. For example, subchapter 1 presents the general purposes of the act and creates the Federal Communications Commission (FCC). Other sections in subchapter 1 define the terms and the organizations and functions of the FCC. Subchapter 2 deals entirely with telephone and telegraph regulations and is not a concern here. Subchapter 3 contains provisions relating to radio and TV, and it is this part of the act that has most relevance for broadcasters. Some of the key sections most often mentioned in the trade press are:

- *Section 301.* Users of the electromagnetic spectrum must be licensed by the FCC.
- *Section 312.* Candidates for federal office must be given reasonable access to broadcast facilities.
- *Section 315.* Use of broadcast facilities by candidates for public office is outlined. (This provision

is so important that an entire section is devoted to it later in this chapter.)

- *Section 326.* The FCC is forbidden to censor the content of radio and TV programming.

Subchapter 4 of the act, among other things, specifies how decisions of the FCC may be appealed. Subchapter 5 spells out the sanctions and penalties that the commission can use against offending stations. Subchapter 6 contains miscellaneous provisions.

The Telecommunications Act of 1996

Heralded by its supporters as a law designed to usher in the new Information Age, the final impact of the Telecommunications Act of 1996 has yet to be felt. The law covered a wide range of topics and some of the most important are described below.

The new law significantly eased ownership restrictions of broadcast properties. In television, one person or organization can now own as many stations as they want (the old law limited ownership to 12) as long as the combined reach of the stations does not exceed 35 percent of the nation's TV homes (the old law set a 25 percent cap). The law also allows common ownership of cable systems and broadcast networks, and it allows existing broadcast networks to start a new network (but bars an existing network from acquiring another existing network). The law has eliminated overall radio station ownership caps and liberalized the rules concerning local ownership. In large markets, one organization can own as many as eight radio stations.

The law has extended the license renewal terms to eight years for both radio (seven years under the old law) and television (five years under the old law). In addition, the new law has opened the door for more competition in the cable and telephone industries. It allows telephone companies to provide video programming and allows cable companies to offer local telephone service. Cable systems will have more leeway in setting their rates under the new law. Large cable systems' rates for basic and extended basic cable channels were deregulated in 1999.

The new law also requires new TV sets to be equipped with a **V-chip** that would enable parents to control access to programs they find objectionable. The V-chip works in tandem with a rating system that the television industry has instituted for its programs. More on the V-chip in the next chapter.

THE ROLE OF THE FCC

License Granting

An earlier section of this chapter contained a general introduction to the FCC's licensing function. This section concentrates on the specifics. Applying for a license to operate a new station is a fairly complicated process. (In fact, there are only a limited number of radio and TV frequencies available that would not cause major interference problems with existing stations. Most persons who want to get into broadcasting generally do so by purchasing an existing facility. Many rules discussed below would also apply in this situation.) After finding an available radio frequency or TV channel, all applicants must meet some minimum qualifications.

Personal Qualifications   First, the applicant must be a U.S. citizen or an organization that is free from significant foreign control. Next, the applicant must meet certain character qualifications, but the law is vague on what exactly constitutes a "good" or "bad" character. In practice, the FCC usually looks at things that are directly relevant to the potential future conduct of a potential broadcaster, although recent developments suggest that the commission has begun to look more closely at general character qualifications as well. In 1990 the FCC required broadcasters to report all convictions for felonies, all convictions for serious misdemeanors, any adverse civil judgments involving antitrust or anticompetitive activity,

and any cases of misrepresentation to government agencies. Such activity, said the commission, could jeopardize the broadcaster's ability to hold or acquire a license.

Financial and Technical Considerations   The new applicant must assert the financial capability to build and operate a new station. In addition, as might be expected, all applicants must demonstrate that they can meet all of the technical requirements set forth in commission rules concerning equipment operation. The applicant must also propose an affirmative action employment plan to assure the hiring of minority group members and women.

Diversity of Ownership

Throughout its history, the FCC has endorsed the philosophy that diversity of ownership was a desirable social goal. In recent years, however, the commission has relaxed many of its rules limiting ownership.

As mentioned above, the Telecommunications Act of 1996 permitted one organization to own an unlimited number of radio stations nationwide and as many as eight in a single market. The numerical cap on national TV station ownership was lifted so that one organization can own as many stations as it wants provided the total audience reach of the stations does not exceed 35 percent. Unlike radio, an organization can own only one TV station in a market.

President Clinton and Vice President Gore display the V-chip—a device that will allow parents to block objectionable content from their TV sets.

The Telecommunications Act also did away with the prohibition against cable TV and telephone system cross-ownership in the same market.

The FCC still has a prohibition against newspaper and broadcast station ownership in the same community. (Newspapers that owned broadcast properties before 1975, the year this regulation was passed, were permitted to keep their stations.) The FCC, however, can and has granted waivers to this rule if the newspaper can show that its ownership of a broadcast station will serve the public interest. Similarly, a TV station cannot own a cable system that serves the same area as the TV station. TV station owners, however, can own cable systems in other markets. As this book went to press, some members of Congress were urging the FCC to relax its ownership rules even more.

Competing Applications

What happens when there is more than one applicant for a license? This situation commonly occurs when a license for an existing station is contested by one or more competitors. On the one hand, giving preference to the current license holder might close out newcomers who could do a better job. On the other hand, ignoring past performance could be unfair to a station that had served the public well and ought not be replaced by an untested newcomer. After wrestling with this question for many years, the FCC settled on a method called **renewal expectancy.** If an incumbent station had provided substantially sound and favorable past service, it would be difficult for a challenger to be granted the license over the established station. The Telecommunications Act strengthened this philosophy so that currently a station can expect to have its license renewed unless it has committed some serious violation.

Renewal Forms   What does the FCC look for in a license renewal? The postcard form gives a pretty good idea. The form makes sure that the station's most recent Ownership Report, which lists owners and shareholders, is on file with the commission. The postcard form also makes sure the licensee is an American citizen, checks for the extent of foreign control, and asks if the station has maintained for public inspection a file that contains those documents required by commission rules.

License Denials   What must a station do to have its request for license renewal denied? One big reason for denial is lying to the FCC. If a licensee knowingly gives false information to the commission (such as concealing the actual owners of the station), the license is in jeopardy. Unauthorized transfer of control is another serious offense. Programming violations alone, such as violating the indecency rules, have rarely led to nonrenewal. Moreover, the FCC is unlikely to deny a license renewal on its own initiative. Cases that are not routinely passed (perhaps 2 to 3 percent of the total) are brought to the commission's attention by private citizens who file a petition to deny. Of these, only a tiny fraction of licenses (less than 1 percent of the total) are not approved at renewal time. Nonetheless, the threat of nonrenewal is perceived as real by many broadcasters and is a potent weapon in the FCC's enforcement arsenal.

The FCC and Cable

Cable TV systems are not licensed by the FCC. Instead, state and local governments grant franchises. The length of the franchise period is also set at the local level, usually at some period between 10 and 15 years. (Many franchises are not exclusive and some cities can authorize **overbuilds,** allowing two cable companies to serve the same area.) When a franchise comes up for renewal, and earlier, if the cable operator asks for early renewal, the cable operator's service record is examined. Unless the operator has failed to live up to the franchise terms or has provided inferior service, there is a strong presumption that the franchise will be renewed.

Although the FCC does not license cable systems, the 1984 Cable Communications Policy Act does give the commission some power to regulate cable. Eight years later, sparked by consumer complaints over rising rates and lack of service, the **Cable Television Consumer Protection and Competition Act of 1992** put more legal restrictions on cable. In short, the act stated that cable systems had to carry the signals of broadcast stations that served the cable system's market (called the **must-carry rules**). In turn, broadcast stations could either agree to be carried on the cable or waive their must-carry privilege in return for the right to negotiate a fee from the cable system for the use of their signal (called **retransmission consent**). Many stations opted for retransmission consent and worked out a deal with the local cable operators to be compensated by free promotions or advertising time on the cable system.

The 1992 act also gave the FCC the right to regulate the rates of most cable systems (the FCC promptly reduced rates) and to set minimum customer service requirements. The Telecommunications Act of 1996 changed directions in this area and, effective April 1, 1999, rate restrictions concerning upper-tier cable services were abolished. Further, smaller cable systems and those with competition from other sources (such as a telephone company that provides a video service) are exempt from regulation.

The FCC and Emerging Technologies

Several recent forms of communication technology don't fit nicely into traditional molds, and the FCC has made special rules for them. In general terms, the commission has taken a light touch toward regulation in order to encourage experimentation and development.

Multichannel, multipoint distribution service (MMDS), also known as "wireless cable," is free from most FCC content regulation. MMDS sends programming via microwave to receivers equipped with special antennas. Thus far MMDS has been used mostly in urban areas to transmit pay-TV services (HBO and Showtime) to apartment buildings and private homes. When they first started in the early 1980s, MMDS systems were limited to carrying only a few channels. Today, however, thanks to digital signals and compression technology, MMDS systems can carry a large number of programming sources. The FCC has tried to encourage MMDS as a competitor to cable. The 1992 cable act made it easier for MMDS systems to obtain programs from major cable suppliers and declared MMDS operators are not subject to the must-carry rules but do need consent from broadcast stations before carrying their signals. MMDS systems are classified as subscription services and not broadcasters. Consequently, they are exempt from the application of various broadcast rules, including section 315.

Direct broadcast satellite (DBS) systems provide programming to subscribers who purchase receiving dishes and decoders. Two DBS services, DirecTV and United States Satellite Broadcasting System, started operation in 1994. Although not classified as broadcasting, DBS is still subject to certain rules. The 1992 cable act decreed that DBS operators must provide reasonable access to federal political candidates and follow the provisions of section 315. The act also required them to obtain the permission of broadcasters before carrying their signals.

The Telecommunications Act provided that telephone companies could enter the video market in several configurations. They could become an MMDS operator, a common carrier, a cable TV operator, or a new form of video provider called an **open video system (OVS).** An OVS is a cross between a cable system and a common carrier. The telephone company programs some channels with content of its own choosing but must allow other program providers access to the system. As far as regulation goes, OVS systems are certified by the FCC and not franchised by local communities, but the local government can collect a share of the OVS revenues, similar to the franchise fee paid by cable systems. OVS systems are also exempt from most rate regulations.

Equal Opportunities: Section 315

From radio's earliest beginnings Congress recognized that broadcasting had tremendous potential as a political tool. A candidate for political office who was a skilled demagogue might use the medium to sway public opinion. By the time the 1927 Radio Act was written, Congress had already seen how some skilled communicators could use the medium for their own advantage. Consequently, what would eventually be known as **section 315** was incorporated into the 1927 act.

The crux of section 315 in the current act is the following:

> If any licensee shall permit any person who is a legally qualified candidate for any public office to use a broadcasting station, he shall afford equal opportunities to all other such candidates for that office in the use of such broadcasting station.

Sounds simple enough, but, in operation, section 315 can prove complicated. Note that section 315 talks about equal *opportunities* as opposed to equal *time.* If a station provides a candidate with 30 minutes of prime time, it cannot offer an opponent 30 minutes at 3:00 A.M., nor can it offer the second candidate 30 one-minute spots throughout the day. The station would have to provide 30 minutes in prime time. Note further that section 315 does not obligate a station to provide free time to a candidate unless free time was first offered to an opponent.

Also note that the section is not self-triggering. A station is under no obligation to tell opponents that a candidate has used its facilities. The station is

Issues: Fairness Doctrine: To Be or Not to Be

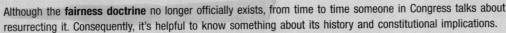

Although the **fairness doctrine** no longer officially exists, from time to time someone in Congress talks about resurrecting it. Consequently, it's helpful to know something about its history and constitutional implications.

In the late 1940s, the fairness doctrine was born when the FCC encouraged broadcasters to comment on controversial issues of public importance, provided they covered all sides of the issues. Broadcasters thought the doctrine was unconstitutional, and a case eventually reached the Supreme Court. In response, the Court relied on the scarcity principle to justify more regulation for broadcasting than for newspapers and ruled that the right of the public to receive information was paramount and took precedence over the rights of the broadcasters. Thus, the fairness doctrine was constitutional.

The controversy didn't end there, however, and broadcasters continued to pressure the FCC to clarify or modify the doctrine. For its part, the FCC was never an enthusiastic supporter of the doctrine, and in 1981 the commission asked Congress to repeal it. Many members of Congress, however, favored the doctrine and refused to act. In 1985, the FCC released a study which concluded that the fairness doctrine was not serving the public interest and once again asked Congress to abolish it. Once again, Congress refused.

Finally, after a federal court ruled that the fairness doctrine was not part of statutory law but was simply a regulation of the FCC, the commission went ahead and abolished the doctrine on its own. Several efforts by Congress during the 1980s and 1990s to write the doctrine into federal law were unsuccessful, and as of this writing the doctrine is still defunct; that is no guarantee, however, that things will stay that way in the future.

When it was in force, the doctrine imposed a duty on broadcasters to identify controversial public issues and present balanced programming to address those issues. Broadcasters were under special obligation to seek out opposing viewpoints. Note that, unlike section 315, the fairness doctrine never said that opposing views were entitled to equal time; the doctrine simply stated that some reasonable amount of time should be devoted to these views.

required to keep political files, however, and a candidate can easily examine these to see if any of the other candidates had made use of the station. The opponent must request equal time within a specified time interval. Also keep in mind that section 312 of the Communications Act requires broadcasters to provide reasonable access for candidates for federal office. They can, however, require candidates to pay for this time.

In addition, there are rules governing how much stations can charge candidates for purchased time. Broadcasters are prohibited from charging more for political time than they do for other kinds of commercials. The rules also make sure that a station doesn't charge candidate A $1,000 for a spot while charging candidate B $5,000 for an equivalent spot.

Other complications also arise. Who is a legally qualified candidate? According to the commission, there are three criteria:

1. The candidate must have announced publicly an intention to run for office.

2. The candidate must be legally qualified for the office (to run for president, you must be a U.S. citizen and at least 35 years old).

3. The candidate must have taken the steps spelled out by law to qualify for a place on the ballot or have publicly announced a write-in candidacy.

This means that if a highly popular president nearing the end of a first term in office, generally expected to seek reelection, appears on TV and harshly criticizes a likely opponent, section 315 will not be triggered because, technically speaking, the president has not announced publicly for the office. Similarly, suppose the 30-year-old leader of the Vegetarian party announced plans to run for the presidency. The law would not apply since a 30 year old is not legally qualified for the office.

Section 315 applies only among those candidates actually opposing each other at that moment. This means that it works differently during a primary than it works during a general election. During a primary, an appearance by a candidate for the Democratic nomination to an office would not create equal opportunity rights among those running for the Republican nomination. Once the primaries are over, however, an appearance by the Democratic nominee would mean the Republican nominee would probably be entitled to an equal opportunity to appear.

Section 315 raises a question regarding the definition of "use" of a broadcasting facility. Broadly speaking, a use occurs when the candidate's voice or picture is included in a program or commercial spot. A program or commercial about a candidate in which the candidate does not appear would not qualify. Most of the time, a use is fairly easy to recognize. Sometimes, however, it's trickier. What happens if the candidate appears in a role that is totally different from that of candidate? How about the candidate who makes a guest appearance in a skit on "Saturday Night Live"? Or, what about a candidate for the U.S. Senate who appears on a wildlife program and discusses his love for fishing? Could his opponents claim equal time under section 315? The commission has ruled that a candidate's appearance is a use even if the candidate is appearing for a completely unrelated purpose and never mentions his or her candidacy. Thus if the host of a children's show on a local station becomes a legally qualified candidate, each time he or she appears on the kiddie show the opposition is entitled to a comparable amount of time for free.

But what about the situation where an incumbent president who has already announced for reelection holds a press conference? Does this mean that all the other candidates are entitled to equal time? A similar situation occurred in 1959 when a minority party candidate for mayor of Chicago requested equal time because the current mayor who was running for reelection was shown in a series of film clips used on the evening news. Congress reacted by amending section 315 and providing these exceptions. Section 315 does *not* apply to the following:

1. Bona fide newscasts.

2. Bona fide news interviews.

3. Bona fide news documentaries in which the appearance of the candidate is incidental to the subject of the documentary.

4. On-the-spot coverage of bona fide news.

Questions can also be raised about exactly how much time an opponent is entitled to. Usually if the candidate appears or the audience hears the candidate's voice in a 30- or 60-second spot, opponents are entitled to 30 or 60 seconds, even if the candidate was on screen for a few seconds only. But, if the candidate was on screen or on mike for only a portion of an interview show, opponents are entitled to an amount of time equal only to that featuring the candidate. For example, if a candidate appears for 15 minutes on an hour-long "Late Show with David Letterman," opponents are entitled to 15 minutes, not a whole hour.

OTHER FEDERAL LAWS COVERING BROADCASTING AND CABLE

In addition to the provisions of the Communications Act of 1934 and the Telecommunications Act of 1996, broadcasters and cable operators must abide by other relevant statutes that relate to their operations. This section discusses five topics to which such laws apply: children's TV, copyright, obscenity, equal employment opportunities, and antitrust.

Children's Television

The **Children's Television Act of 1990** imposed an obligation on TV stations to serve the informational and educational needs of children through programming designed especially to serve those needs. The legislation also put a cap on the number of commercial minutes allowed in children's programs (10½ minutes per hour on weekends and 12 minutes per hour on weekdays) and established a multi-million-dollar endowment for the funding of children's educational programs. The FCC also ruled that, starting in 1997, TV stations had to present a minimum of three hours per week of educational programs. Failure to provide such programming would result in additional scrutiny by the FCC when the station's license came up for renewal. The commission has taken an active role in enforcing these provisions and many stations have received fines for exceeding the commercial-minute guidelines.

Copyright: Trying to Keep Up

Copyright law protects intellectual property; it allows creative people, such as writers, photographers, and painters, to control the commercial copying and use of intellectual property they create, such as books, films, phonograph records, audio- and videotapes, and sculptures.

In its simplest terms, the current copyright law protects works that are "fixed in any tangible means of expression." This includes phonograph records,

Bill Nye, the Science Guy. This is the type of program that would go toward fulfilling the FCC's quota of three hours per week of educational programs aimed at children.

dramatic works, motion pictures, TV programs, computer programs, and sculpture. Ideas and news events are not copyrightable (you could, however, copyright your particular written or recorded version of a news story). Copyright protection lasts for the life of the author plus 50 years (70 years if the work was created during or later than 1978). Frequently the creator of a work transfers the copyright so that in some cases the owner is not necessarily the creator. To be *fully* protected a work must contain notice of the copyright (usually consisting of the letter C in a circle, the copyright owner's name, and the date of origination) and must be registered and deposited with the Copyright Office in Washington, D.C. Nonetheless, any fixed form of an idea is now granted some protection from the moment that it is fixed in a tangible form.

Once a work is copyrighted, the owner has the right to authorize works derived from the original

(for example, a novelist could authorize a movie script based on the book), to distribute copies of the work, and to display and/or perform the work publicly. Even though a work has been copyrighted, others can borrow limited amounts from the material under the doctrine of *fair use*. Critics, for example, can quote from a work without needing permission.

Let's take a closer look at how copyright laws apply to broadcasting and cable, starting first with performance rights. An author is entitled to a royalty payment when his or her work is performed publicly. When a copyrighted work is broadcast over the air—that is, when a radio station plays a record, *that* constitutes public performance. The broadcasters pay royalties for such performances. The audience for the material pays nothing.

Music Licensing   There are more than 12,000 radio stations and 1,500 TV stations in the United States, and it would obviously be difficult for artists and performers to negotiate a royalty agreement each time their songs were played on the air. Accordingly, private music licensing organizations were established to grant the appropriate rights and to collect and distribute royalty payments. In this country, performing rights are handled by the **American Society of Composers, Authors and Publishers (ASCAP), Broadcast Music Incorporated (BMI),** and the **Society of European Stage Authors and Composers (SESAC,** which, despite its name, handles U.S. clients).

The major licensing firms grant what is known as **blanket rights,** whereby media firms pay a single fee to the licensing agency based on a percentage of their gross revenues. In return the stations get performance rights to the agency's entire music catalog. These rights do not come cheaply. Radio stations in large markets might pay around $75,000 annually for music rights. Stations in medium-sized markets might pay $15,000 to $30,000. The licensing agencies distribute this money to composers and publishers. The amount of the licensing fee has been a source of friction between broadcasters and music licensing organizations since the 1920s. New licensing rates are negotiated every several years, so the fee will probably continue to cause problems in the future as well.

Other Copyright Areas   Cable systems do not pay royalties to independent or network-affiliated stations that are carried on the system. Cable systems may carry the programming of superstations (such as WGN) for a fee that is then distributed to program

Events: Copyrights around the Campfire

You can probably imagine the scene: A group of Girl Scouts sitting around a glowing campfire, eating s'mores and singing . . . nothing.

That unlikely scenario may have been the case had the American Society of Composers, Authors and Publishers (ASCAP) had their way. In 1996, ASCAP announced that the Girl Scouts had to pay license fees if they sang or played any of the songs published by ASCAP's nearly 70,000 members. A spokesperson for ASCAP said, "They can buy paper, twine, and glue for their crafts. They can pay for the music too." ASCAP threatened to sue the Girl Scouts if they didn't pay the fees, which ranged from $300 to $1,500, depending on the size of the Girl Scout camp.

The threat, of course, caused a great deal of consternation around the campfire. Some old standards, such as "Puff, the Magic Dragon," and "This Land Is Your Land," were no longer heard because they were on ASCAP's list. Counselors went scrambling to find out if the girls could sing "Kumbaya," without being sued. (They could—it's not on the list.) Was "Ninety-Nine Bottles of Beer on the Wall" on the list? No one was willing to check out the list of the four million songs licensed by ASCAP and posted on the Internet, At some camps, Girl Scouts were reduced to dancing the Macarena in silence.

A *Wall Street Journal* article publicized the Girl Scouts' problems. In an example of the media enforcing social norms (see Chapter 13), ASCAP was soon hit with a wave of unfavorable publicity. There was something un-American about making youngsters pay for songs they sang while at camp. ASCAP was portrayed as a greedy, insensitive organization.

ASCAP quickly realized that the money they would make by collecting the license fees was not worth the cost of the bad press. The group relented and said it never really intended to make the girls pay after all. The Girl Scouts could sing again—for free.

---

suppliers. The rules concerning copyright and VCRs are straightforward. A person can tape a program off the air and watch it at some other time without fear of copyright violations. Movies and other prerecorded videocassettes can be rented and viewed without paying a copyright fee. Renting a cassette and copying it at home, however, is illegal since such copying may take away potential sales and rental income for the copyrighted material.

The Internet represents a new channel on which authors can publish their works. The Copyright Act of 1976 stated that its provisions would apply to any new medium so that any work posted on the Internet is entitled to copyright protection. Web sites are also protected. In practical terms, however, there are many gray areas concerning the notion of "fair use" as it relates to the Web and about the liability of Internet service providers whose subscribers illegally distribute copyrighted material. Further, when it comes to a global medium, such as the Internet, enforcement of copyright regulations is difficult.

Obscenity, Indecency, and Profanity

Section 1464 of the U.S. Criminal Code states that anybody who utters profane, indecent, or obscene language over radio or TV is liable to fine or imprisonment. Both the FCC and the Department of Justice can prosecute under this section. If found guilty, violators face a fine of up to $10,000, possible loss of license, or even jail. This seems clear enough. A couple of problems, however, quickly surface. First, remember that the FCC is prohibited from censoring broadcast content. Second, how exactly do you define obscenity, indecency, and profanity?

Let's take the easy one first. Profanity is defined as the irreverent or blasphemous use of the name of God. Practically speaking, however, the FCC has been unwilling to punish stations that air an occasional curse. Particularly in the era of deregulation, it is unlikely that profanity will become a major issue.

Obscenity and indecency are another matter. The struggle to come up with a workable definition of obscenity has been long and tortuous and will not be repeated here. The definition that currently applies to broadcasting is the definition spelled out by the Supreme Court in the *Miller* v. *California* (1973) case. To be obscene, a program, considered as a whole, must (1) contain material that depicts or describes in a patently offensive way certain sexual acts defined in state law; (2) appeal to the prurient interest of the average person applying contemporary local community standards ("prurient" is one of those legal words the courts are fond of using; it means tending to excite lust); and (3) lack serious artistic, literary, political, or scientific value. Obviously, most radio and TV stations would be wary of presenting programs that come anywhere near these criteria for fear of alienating much of their audience. Consequently, the FCC tends not to issue too many decisions based on the obscenity criterion alone.

But what about cable? Some of the movies commonly shown on certain cable channels go much further than what is shown on traditional TV. The 1984 cable act made it a crime to transmit obscenity over cable. Further, state and local franchise agreements can prohibit obscene programming. Even though cable content is far more daring than over-the-air TV, subscribers are unlikely to see the kind of movies that would be defined as legally obscene. In fact, most hard-core or XXX-rated films are released in two versions, one for theatrical or videocassette release and a less explicit version for cable. In practice, then, obscenity, as legally defined, is seldom at issue in broadcasting and cable.

This leaves the area of indecent programming—the area in which the FCC has chosen to exercise vigilance. Indecent content refers to content that is not obscene under the *Miller* standards but still contains potentially offensive elements. To be more specific, here's the common legal definition of broadcast indecency:

> Something broadcast is indecent if it depicts or describes sexual or excretory activities or organs in a fashion that's patently offensive according to contemporary community standards for the broadcast media at a time of day when there is a reasonable risk that children may be in the audience.

For example, a program that simply contains nudity is not obscene, although some people might be offended. Further, four-letter words that describe sexual or excretory acts are not, by themselves, obscene. They may, however, be classified as indecent.

The Seven Dirty Words Case   George Carlin is probably the only comedian ever to have his act reviewed by the Supreme Court. Here's how it happened. On the afternoon of October 30, 1973, WBAI-FM, New York City, a listener-sponsored station licensed to the Pacifica Foundation, announced that it was about to broadcast a program that would contain sensitive language that some might find offensive. The WBAI DJ then played all 12 minutes of a George Carlin rou-

tine entitled "Filthy Words." Recorded live before a theater audience, the routine analyzed the words that "you couldn't say on the public airwaves." Carlin then listed seven such words and used them repeatedly throughout the rest of his monologue.

A man and his teenage son heard the broadcast while driving in their car and complained to the FCC; it was the only complaint the commission received about the monologue. The FCC decreed that the station had violated the rules against airing indecent content and put the station on notice that subsequent complaints about its programming might lead to severe penalties. Pacifica appealed the ruling, and an appeals court sided with WBAI and chastised the FCC for violating section 326 of the Communications Act, which prohibits censorship. Several years later, however, the case made its way to the Supreme Court and the original FCC decision was reaffirmed. The Court said, among other things, that the commission's actions did not constitute censorship since they had not edited the monologue in advance. Further, the program could be regulated because the monologue was broadcast at a time when children were probably in the audience. Special treatment of broadcasting was justified because of its uniquely pervasive presence and because it is easily accessible to children. Thus the FCC could regulate indecent programming.

In the years following the *Pacifica* decision, many radio broadcasters pushed the limits by developing a new format called "raunch radio" or "shock radio." The FCC warned stations of possible fines for this content and suggested it might be more appropriate if presented after midnight when fewer children were in the audience. Congress got into the act in 1988 when it ordered the FCC to enforce a 24-hour ban on indecency, but this ban was overturned by a court decision. After several years of political and legal wrangling, the FCC and the courts have agreed to a "safe harbor" provision that protects indecent material if aired between 10 P.M. and 6 A.M.

Stations that run afoul of the FCC's rules on indecent content risk a substantial fine—about $10,000 for one offense, with some fines going much higher. Howard Stern, for example, was fined almost $2 million for his transgressions.

Indecent Content and Cable   Cable channels generally have a much wider latitude with programming that might be considered indecent. In fact, the 1984 cable act did not authorize the regulation of indecent material. The act differentiated between obscene and indecent material and permitted regulation of the former only. In addition, federal and state courts have found that the FCC's *Pacifica* ruling does not apply to cable. (George Carlin was able to perform his "Filthy Words" routine on HBO without incident.) The courts argue that cable is not as pervasive as broadcasting (you have to order it and pay additional fees for it) or as easily accessible to children (subscribers could buy and use lock boxes to limit viewing).

Indecency and the Internet   There are probably more than 10,000 sites on the Internet that contain sexually oriented material. The ubiquity of this material and the ease with which it could be accessed by minors prompted Congress to include the Communications Decency Act as part of the Telecommunications Act of 1996. Basically, the law made it a crime to transmit indecent and obscene material over the net to anybody under 18 years of age.

The constitutionality of this act was immediately called into question, and the case went to the Supreme Court. The Court ruled that the Internet was entitled to the highest degree of First Amendment protection, similar to that afforded books and magazines, and ruled the act unconstitutional. Note that legally obscene content on the Internet does not qualify for First Amendment protection so that the Court's ruling is most relevant to indecent material.

Equal Employment Opportunities

Broadcasters and cablecasters are bound by federal law prohibiting job discrimination based on race, color, sex, religion, or national origin. Further, they must adhere to regulations set down by the Equal Employment Opportunity Commission. Although not directly responsible for enforcing all equal employment opportunity (EEO) provisions, the FCC has made it clear that it will assert jurisdiction over this area in broadcasting and cable.

In the wake of a 1998 Court decision that found the FCC's EEO operating rules unconstitutional, the commission suspended many of its EEO reporting requirements and is considering a new set of regulations.

Antitrust

Broadcasting and cable are businesses and, as such, are subject to antitrust laws. These laws date back to the 1890s and protect business against unlawful

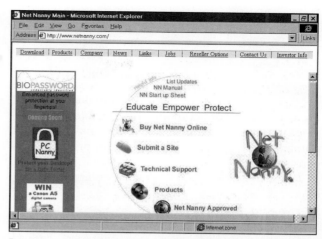

Preventing children from adult content on the Internet. NetNanny is a program that allows parents to block any words, phrases, Web sites, IRC chat rooms, and newsgroups from being accessed by their children.

restraints and monopolies. Although much of the antitrust litigation in recent years has concerned newspapers, the antitrust laws also have relevance for the electronic media. Over the years, as we have seen, the FCC has enacted rules that tried to maximize the diversity of ownership of broadcast facilities. At the same time, there has been a trend in the industry toward greater concentration in media ownership and growing conglomerate involvement. Since policymakers are relying more and more on the marketplace as a substitute for regulation, and antitrust laws govern the marketplace, look for more reliance on these laws in the decade to come.

THE LAW AND BROADCAST JOURNALISM

There are several areas of law that are most relevant to the news-gathering and reporting duties of stations and cable channels. Some of these laws cover topics that are common to both print and electronic journalists (such as libel and invasion of privacy). Other laws are more relevant to video reporters (such as the restrictions on cameras in the courtroom). Further, many of these laws vary from state to state, but some have raised constitutional issues that have been addressed by the Supreme Court.

This section covers four areas that are highly relevant to the broadcast press: (1) defamation, (2) privacy, (3) protection of confidential sources, and (4) use of cameras and microphones in the courtroom.

Defamation

The law regarding **defamation** is concerned with the protection of a person's reputation. A defamatory statement injures the good name of an individual (or organization) and lowers his or her standing in the community. The law of defamation makes sure that the press does not act in an irresponsible and malicious manner. As we shall see, erroneous stories that damage the reputations of others can bring serious consequences.

There are two kinds of defamation: libel and slander. **Slander** comes from spoken words; in other words, slander is oral defamation. **Libel** is defamation stated in a tangible medium, such as a printed story or a photograph, or in some other form that has a capacity to endure. Since libel exists in a medium that can be widely circulated, the courts treat it more seriously than slander, which evaporates after it is uttered. Broadcast defamation is usually regarded as libel rather than slander.

Broadcast journalists have become particularly wary of suits alleging libel because they can carry sizable cash awards to the victims if the media are found at fault.

Elements of Libel   If someone brings a libel suit against a station or cable channel, he or she must prove five different things to win. First, the statement(s) in question must have actually defamed the person and caused some harm. The material must have diminished the person's good name or reputation or held the person up to ridicule, hatred, or contempt. Harm can be such things as lost wages or physical discomfort or impairment in doing one's job. A prime example of a defamatory statement would be falsely reporting that a person has been convicted of a crime. The second element is publication. This usually presents no ambiguities; if a story was broadcast, then it fulfills the publication criterion. The third element is identification. A person must prove that he or she was identified in a story. Identification does not necessarily have to be by name. A nickname, a cartoon, a description, or anything else that pinpoints someone's identity would suffice.

The fourth element is fault or error. To win a libel suit, a party must show some degree of fault or carelessness on the part of the media organization. The degree of fault that must be established depends on who's suing, what they are suing about, and which state's laws are being applied. As we shall see, certain individuals have to prove greater degrees of fault than others. Finally, in most instances the individual has to prove the falsity of what was published or broadcast.

Defenses against Libel   When a libel suit is filed against a broadcast reporter and/or station, several defenses are available. The first of these is truth. If the reporter can prove that what was broadcast was true, then there is no libel. This sounds a lot easier than it is since the burden of proving truth, which can be an expensive and time-consuming process, falls on the reporter. Moreover, when the alleged libel is vague and doesn't deal with specific events, proving truth may be difficult. Finally, recent court decisions suggest that in many circumstances people who bring libel suits against the media must bear the burden of proving the defamatory statement false. All of these factors diminish the appeal of truth as a defense.

Note that libel suits concern defamatory statements of fact only. There is no such thing as libelous *opinion,* since no one can prove that an opinion is true or false. In 1990, however, the Supreme Court ruled that expressions of opinion can be held libelous if they imply an assertion of fact that can be proven false. Labeling a statement as an opinion does not necessarily make it immune from a libel suit.

A second defense is privilege. Used in its legal sense, privilege means immunity. There are certain situations in which the courts have held that the public's right to know is more important than a person's reputation. Courtroom proceedings, legislative debates, and public city council sessions are examples of areas that are generally conceded to be privileged. If a broadcast reporter gives a fair and accurate report of these events, the reporter will be immune to a libel suit even if what was reported contained a defamatory remark. Keep in mind, however, that accurately quoting someone else's libelous remarks outside an official public meeting or official public record is not a surefire defense against libel.

The third defense is fair comment and criticism. People who thrust themselves into the public arena are fair game for criticism. The performance of public officials, pro sports figures, artists, singers, columnists, and others who invite public scrutiny is open to the fair comment defense. This defense, however, applies to opinion and criticism; it does not entitle the press to report factual matters erroneously. A movie critic, for example, could probably say that a certain actor's performance was amateurish and wooden without fearing a libel suit. If, however, the critic went on and falsely reported that the bad acting was the result of drug addiction, that would be a different story.

In 1964, in the pivotal *New York Times* v. *Sullivan* case, the Supreme Court greatly expanded the opportunity for comment on the actions of public officials. The Court ruled that public officials must prove that false and defamatory statements were made with "actual malice" before a libel suit could be won. The Court went on to state that actual malice meant publishing or broadcasting something with the knowledge that it was false or with "reckless disregard" of whether or not it was false. In later years the Court ruled that public figures also must prove actual malice to win a libel suit.

In effect, two different degrees of fault are used as standards in libel cases. In many states a private citizen must simply prove that the media acted with negligence. For some states negligence means that accepted professional standards were not followed. Other states take negligence to mean that a reporter did not exercise reasonable care in determining whether a story was true or false. A few states define negligence in relation to whether the reporter had reason to believe that material that was published or broadcast was true. Public figures and public officials are held to a higher standard; they must also prove actual malice. (Note that the really big financial awards in libel cases come from what are called "punitive damages"—awards levied by juries to punish the offending media outlet. To win punitive damages, even a private citizen must prove actual malice.)

Invasion of Privacy

The right to privacy is a relatively new area of media law. Stated simply, it means that the individual has a right to be left alone—not to be subjected to intrusions or unwarranted publicity. The right to privacy is not specifically found in the Constitution, although many have argued that the right is implied in several amendments. Like defamation, laws concerning privacy differ from state to state.

Not surprisingly, invasion of privacy is a complicated topic. In fact, legal experts suggest that it actually covers four different areas. The right of privacy protects against (1) unwarranted publication of private facts, (2) intrusion upon a person's solitude or seclusion, (3) publicity that creates a false impression about a person (called "false light"), and (4) unauthorized commercial exploitation of a person's name or likeness.

Private Facts   Disclosure of private facts occurs when a broadcast station or cable channel reports personal information that the individual did not want to make public. Disclosure resembles libel in that the individual must be identifiable and the facts must cause the individual humiliation or shame. Unlike libel, however, the facts revealed are true and may not necessarily damage a person's reputation. For example, suppose that a TV station shot footage of you in a hospital bed after cosmetic surgery when your face was swollen, black and blue, and generally ugly-looking. The station then ran the tape without your consent on the six-o'clock news with your name prominently mentioned as part of a series it was doing on the hospital. It's possible you might have a case for invasion of privacy. To qualify as the basis for a suit, private facts must be highly offensive to a person of "reasonable sensibilities."

When faced with an invasion-of-privacy suit, the media have several defenses. The reporter might argue that consent was obtained before the information was released. Information obtained from a public record is generally immune to invasion-of-privacy actions. Last, the reporter could argue that the information was released in connection with a newsworthy event.

Intrusion and Trespass   **Intrusion** is an invasion of a person's solitude or seclusion without consent. The intrusion may or may not include **trespass,** which is defined as physical presence on private property without the consent or approval of the property's owner. Thus using a telephoto lens to secretly take pictures through a person's bedroom window could constitute intrusion. Secretly sneaking through the yard to take pictures through the bedroom window with a regular lens would probably constitute trespass and intrusion. Problems with intrusion and trespass generally crop up in the news-gathering stage. In fact, a reporter can be sued for trespass or intrusion even if he or she never broadcasts the information that was gathered.

Whether some news-gathering technique violates a person's right of privacy depends on how much privacy a person should normally expect in the particular situation involved. For example, people in their living rooms have a right to expect that they will not be secretly photographed or have their

(A)

Your TV station airs "On the Crime Beat," an investigative reporting show similar to the networks' "48 Hours," or "Street Stories." One of your reporters learns that the Department of Alcohol, Tobacco and Firearms (ATF) is going to raid a local house looking for illegal firearms. Your reporter knows the local ATF agent who will lead the raid. The ATF agent invites your reporter and camera crew to go along with the agents and tape the whole event.

The agents, armed with a legal search warrant, and your camera crew arrive at the house. The agents knock and identify themselves. An elderly woman opens the door a crack, and the agents push their way in with your crew, cameras rolling, right behind. The woman objects to the presence of the camera. She asks repeatedly that her picture not be taken. Nonetheless, your crew videotapes her and other scenes inside the house.

After the search, the woman sues your station for invasion of privacy. Your "On the Crime Beat" crew says you have nothing to be concerned about. They were invited into the house, the scene of a legitimate news event, by the ATF agent acting under a valid search warrant. Should you worry?

(Yes. You should probably worry a lot. A valid search warrant did not give the agent the right to invite whomever he wished into the house. In a similar case the court stated that such an invitation went beyond the scope of the warrant. A private home is not a soundstage, said the court, and should be safe from intrusions such as this. P.S. The agent should also worry. His actions may also get him into legal trouble.)

(B)

Your political reporter is putting together a package covering some unusual events concerning the city council. Council member Green finished last in a field of six in the primary election. A month before the general election, council member White, with two years remaining in her term, resigned for health reasons. Green, realizing he couldn't be reelected to the council, apparently arranged a deal with the other members. Green resigned his position and was then immediately reappointed by the other council members to fill the two-year term left vacant by White's resignation.

Your reporter sums up her report with a commentary that states that Green "slithered back into office." Green files for defamation, claiming that the phrase "slithered back into office" is tantamount to calling him a snake or some other derogatory term. Do you have a problem?

(Probably not. Remember that Green is a public official and the courts have always protected vigorous discussion of the actions of public officials. Your reporter's statement would probably qualify as fair comment.)

words recorded. People walking down a public street have less expectation of privacy.

Broadcast journalists can generally avoid charges of trespass by securing the consent of the owner of private property before entering it. In some limited instances during fires and natural disasters police or fire officials might control property and can grant consent to reporters to enter. Reporters, however, do not have the right to follow an unruly crowd onto private property without the consent of the owner or the police. In addition, TV reporters might be guilty of trespass if they enter, with cameras rolling, private property that is open to the public—like a place of business.

The concept of trespass assumed greater importance in a 1996 case involving the Food Lion grocery store chain and the ABC newsmagazine "Prime Time Live" over a report that Food Lion was violating health standards. Rather than sue for defamation, Food Lion charged that ABC had committed trespass when it gained access to nonpublic areas of a grocery store under false pretenses and taped employees with a concealed camera. The jury agreed with Food Lion and brought back a $5.5 million judgment against the network (on appeal the fine was later reduced to $300,000). The Food Lion case made investigative reporters reexamine some of their journalistic techniques.

False Light   A reporter can cast a person in a **false light** in several ways: omitting pertinent facts, distorting certain information, falsely implying that a person is other than what he or she is, or using a photograph out of context. A suit that alleges invasion of privacy through false light is similar to one brought for defamation (in fact, the two are often brought at the same time). A person can't be put in false light by the truth. Thus, like libel, there must be a false assertion of fact. In addition, the misinformation must be publicized. Finally, to win a false light suit, some people might have to prove actual malice on the part of the media. Unlike libel, in false light suits the false assertion is not defamatory. In fact, suits alleging false light have been brought over the publicizing of incorrect information that was flattering to the person. People who bring false light suits seek compensation not for harm to their reputation—how others feel about them—but for the shame, humiliation, and suffering *they* feel because of the false portrayal.

Commercial Exploitation   This area tends to be more of a problem area for advertisers, promoters, agents, and public relations practitioners. Basically, it prohibits the unauthorized use of a person's name or likeness in some commercial venture. Thus it would be an invasion of privacy if you walked into a supermarket and found that a pickle manufacturer had, without your permission, put your face on a whole shelf of pickle jars. The best way for broadcasters to avoid privacy invasion suits based on unauthorized exploitation is to obtain written consent from subjects.

Well-known individuals, of course, can have more of a stake in these matters. In fact, over the last several years an offshoot of the commercial appropriation area known as the "right of publicity" has been articulated by the courts. In contrast with the traditional privacy area, which is based on the right to be left alone, the right of publicity is concerned with who gets the financial rewards when the notoriety surrounding a famous person is used for commercial purposes. In this regard, the right of publicity resembles a property right rather than a personal right and bears a little resemblance to copyright. In essence, the courts have ruled that famous people are protected against the unlawful appropriation of their fame. For example, Johnny Carson was successful in his suit against a manufacturer of portable toilets that were sold under the name "Here's Johnny!"

Protecting Sources

Since 1950 a conflict has developed between courts and reporters over the protection of news sources, notes, and news footage. Some background will be useful before we discuss the specifics.

There are two basic types of litigation. In a criminal trial the government seeks to punish someone for illegal behavior. Murder, rape, and robbery are examples of proceedings that would be covered by criminal law. Civil law involves a dispute between two individuals for harm that one has allegedly caused the other. Breach of contract, claims of overbilling, disputes between neighbors over property rights, defamation, and invasion of privacy are examples of civil suits. In a criminal or civil trial it is necessary for the court to have at its disposal any and all evidence that bears directly on the outcome of the trial in order to assure a fair decision.

Courts have the power to issue subpoenas, official orders summoning witnesses to appear and testify, in order to make sure all who have information come forth and present what they know. There are only a few exceptions to this principle, called privileges. No person is forced to testify against himself or herself. Husband–wife communication is also considered privileged. Other common areas of privilege are lawyer–client communication and doctor–patient conversations. For many years journalists have argued that their relationship with a news source qualifies as the same type of privilege. They argue that without a promise of confidentiality, many sources would be reluctant to come forward and the news-gathering process would be severely hindered. In fact, many journalists have been fined and sent to jail for failure to disclose the names of sources or for failing to turn over to the court notes, photos, and videotapes.

Before the 1970s the courts were reluctant to grant any privileges to journalists. Since then, however, journalists are in a better position thanks to several court decisions and the passage of state "shield laws," which offer limited protection for journalists. The landmark decision was handed down by the Supreme Court in 1972 in *Branzburg* v. *Hayes*. Originally regarded as a defeat for the principle of journalistic privilege, the decision actually spelled out guidelines that covered when a reporter might legally refuse to testify. To make a reporter reveal confidential sources and information, the government must pass a three-part test. The three-part test listed below is often used in civil proceedings but seldom used in criminal trials. The government must prove the following:

1. That the journalist has information that bears directly on the case.
2. That the evidence cannot be obtained from any other sources.
3. That the evidence is crucial in the determination of the case.

The government's success in passing this test varies with the legal context. Reporters are most likely to be required to testify before grand juries, particularly if the reporter witnessed criminal activity; they are least likely to be compelled to testify when the defense in a civil trial is trying to obtain information. Civil libel actions where the medium is the defendant create special problems. Some states don't permit the protection of a shield law if it would frustrate a plaintiff's effort to show actual malice.

Twenty-nine states have granted limited protection to journalists by enacting shield laws. These laws, of course, vary from state to state. In some states, protection is given to a journalist who refuses to reveal a source, but protection does not extend to notes, tape, and other media used in the news-gathering process. Moreover, some states have strict definitions as to who exactly is a journalist and is covered by the shield law. Several states require the journalist to prove that a source was actually promised confidentiality. Some states require that the information be published before the shield law is triggered. Other state laws list exceptions where the protection is not granted.

Cameras in the Courtroom

The controversy over cameras in the courtroom highlights an area where two basic rights come into conflict: the right of a defendant to a fair trial and the right of a free press to report the news.

The controversy began in 1932 during the trial of the man accused of kidnapping and murdering the infant son of national hero Charles Lindbergh. Newspaper, radio, and newsreel reporters helped turn the trial into a media circus and a special committee of the American Bar Association (ABA) was created after the trial to draw up media guidelines. This group recommended that a canon (labeled **Canon 35**) be added to the code of conduct of the ABA which would prohibit the broadcasting and taking of photographs of a trial. Many states enacted Canon 35 into law.

In 1962, the Supreme Court affirmed the ban on cameras and microphones in the courtroom but several justices noted that future technological advances in TV and radio might make broadcasting a trial less disruptive and suggested that it would one day be permissible. This prediction came true in 1981 when the Court ruled that televising a trial was not inherently prejudicial and left it up to the states to come up with systems to implement trial coverage.

Since that time, the trend has been toward more access. As of 1999, only three states—Mississippi, New York, and South Dakota—did not allow some form of coverage. In most states, the consent of the presiding judge is required and the judge controls the coverage. Currently, a cable network, Court TV, specializes in televising trials.

The merits of TV in the courtroom were subjected to fresh debate in the aftermath of the O.J. Simpson murder trial in 1994 and 1995. Despite some harsh criticisms, rules concerning cameras were not made more restrictive. On the other hand, despite a recommendation to the contrary by the Federal Judicial Conference, cameras are still not allowed in federal district courts; Supreme Court proceedings are not televised either.

REGULATING ADVERTISING

Advertising is a big business: about $62 billion was spent on broadcasting and cable advertising in 1998. Since advertising is such an influential industry, the government has enacted laws and regulations that deal with advertising messages.

Recent decisions by the Supreme Court have established that advertising does deserve some protection under the First Amendment. The Court, however, was unwilling to grant advertising the degree of protection that it gave to other forms of speech. Advertising that is accurate and truthful can be regulated by the state provided the state's regulation passes a three-part test: The regulation must serve a substantial government goal, advance the interests of the state and be narrowly drawn.

The above paragraph refers to ads that are accurate and truthful. But what about false and deceptive advertising? How is that controlled? The agency most visible in this area is the **Federal Trade Commission (FTC)**.

Congress set up the FTC in 1914 to regulate unfair business practices. In 1938 its power was broadened to include jurisdiction over deceptive advertising. Nonetheless, as far as advertising was concerned, the FTC remained an obscure institution until the consumer movement of the 1960s and 1970s when it became highly active in regulating questionable ads. (It even ordered some companies to run "corrective" ads to counteract any misunderstanding caused by their original ads.) After the move toward deregulation in the 1980s, the FTC assumed a much lower profile.

Like the FCC, the FTC is an independent regulatory agency with five commissioners appointed by the president for renewable seven-year terms. The FTC's Bureau of Consumer Protection handles advertising complaints. The FTC is charged with regulating false, misleading, and/or deceptive advertising and may investigate questionable cases on its own or respond to the complaints of competitors or the general public. The FTC may hold formal hearings concerning a complaint and issue a decision. Again, like the FCC, the FTC's decision can be appealed through the federal courts.

The FTC guards mainly against deceptive advertising, and over the years the commission has developed a set of guidelines that define "deception." Taken as a whole, the ad must have deceived a reasonable person. Any kind of falsehood constitutes deception. For example, a broadcast ad promising buyers a genuine diamond is deceptive if, in fact, what the consumer receives is a zirconium. Even a statement that is literally true might be judged deceptive. Wonder Bread ads claimed that the bread was fortified with vitamins and minerals that are necessary for healthy growth. Although literally true, the ad was ruled deceptive because it did not point out that every fortified bread contained the same vitamins and minerals.

The FTC, however, does recognize that there is room for reasonable exaggeration in advertising. Consequently, the commission permits "puffery" in subjective statements of opinion that the average consumer will probably not take seriously. Thus it would probably be OK for a restaurant to claim that it serves "the world's best coffee" or for a service station to advertise the "friendliest service in town." Puffery crosses over into deception when exaggerated claims turn into factual assertions of superiority.

The FTC has several enforcement means at its disposal. At the mildest level, the FTC can simply express its opinion about the questionable content of an ad, as it did in 1988 when it notified aspirin manufacturers that they should not promote aspirin as a preventive for heart attacks. Further, it can require that certain statements be carried in the ads to make the ads more accurate. For example, when some Listerine ads claimed the product killed germs that caused sore throats that came with a cold or fever, the FTC ordered the makers of Listerine to include a statement in their ads to the effect that Listerine was not a *cure* for sore throats associated with colds or fever. An appeals court upheld the right of the FTC to order advertisers to engage in such corrective campaigns even though the advertiser objected.

The FTC also can notify an advertiser that its ads are deceptive and ask that the advertiser sign a **consent decree.** By agreeing to a consent decree, the advertiser removes the advertising in question but does not admit that the ad was in fact deceptive. More than 90 percent of all FTC cases are settled by consent decrees. A stronger weapon is a **cease-and-desist order.** In this situation, the FTC issues a formal complaint against an ad and a formal hearing is scheduled. If after the hearing it is ruled that the ad was deceptive, a judge issues a cease-and-desist order and the company must stop airing the offending ad. Failure to do so results in a fine. In rare cases, when an ad might have injurious effects on the public, the FTC can seek an injunction to stop the offending ad quickly.

In practical terms, broadcasters and cable system operators should be encouraged to know that very few of the ads aired in any given year are likely to raise legal questions. In addition, since the advertising industry conducts most of its business in public, it is concerned with the harmful effects that might follow the publication or broadcast of any false or misleading ad. Consequently, the advertising profession has developed an elaborate system of self-regulation (see next chapter) that prevents most deceptive ads from being released. Networks also have departments that screen ads before they are accepted. Nonetheless, an occasional problem ad might crop up, which makes a knowledge of FTC rules and regulations helpful.

INTERNATIONAL OBLIGATIONS

American broadcasters also follow the rules of the **International Telecommunications Union (ITU).** The ITU is a United Nations organization that is responsible for coordinating the broadcasting efforts of its member countries. The ITU tries to minimize interference between stations in different countries, regulates radio spectrum allocations, assigns initial call letters to various countries (U.S. stations begin with W or K, Canadian stations with C, and Mexican stations with X), and works to improve telecommunications services in new and developing countries. The ITU is not a regulatory body like the FCC. It does not license stations; it has only the power that its member nations allow it to have. The ITU's main purposes are to encourage cooperation and efficiency and to serve as a negotiating arena where equitable policy regulation can be worked out.

The supreme authority of the ITU is given the somewhat ungraceful name of the Plenipotentiary Conference. Composed of representatives of all member nations, it meets every five to eight years. The most recent conference was held in 1998.

The World Administrative Radio Conferences (WARC) are another important part of the ITU. General WARCs, held at 20-year intervals, discuss and develop global communications policies. The last general WARC enlarged the shortwave broadcasting band and established policies covering satellite communications. The International Frequency Registration Board is a division of the ITU that maintains a master list of frequency use throughout the world. It allows individual countries to use certain frequencies without creating interference.

Over the years, the ITU has managed to concern itself largely with technical matters. Recently, however, politics have crept into ITU operations. As more third world nations joined the organization, the role of the ITU was broadened from merely dealing with technical matters to providing technical assistance to those countries that request it. In the last five years, the ITU has turned its attention to the Internet and has adopted new international modem standards as well as specifications for international videoconferences.

SUMMARY

- Broadcasting and cable regulation is based on two rationales: the scarcity theory and the pervasive presence theory. The regulation of the electronic media is influenced by the FCC, Congress, the courts, the White House, industry lobbyists, the public, state and local governments, and the operation of the marketplace.
- The Communications Act of 1934 and the Telecommunications Act of 1996 provide the groundwork for the regulation of the electronic media. The FCC implements these acts by assigning and renewing licenses. Although it does not license cable systems, the FCC does have some regulatory power over the industry. Section 315 of the Communications Act provides equal opportunities for political candidates on television stations.
- Copyright laws are important in broadcasting and cable. Music licensing is the method by which performers and composers are paid for the use of their work by broadcasters and cable operators. Cable systems

  also pay a fee for transmitting the signals of distant stations into their local markets. VCR owners can tape a program off the air for their personal use without violating copyright laws.
- Federal laws pertaining to obscenity apply to broadcasting and cable. In addition, the FCC has drafted special provisions that deal with indecent content on radio and TV.
- Cablecasters and broadcasters are bound by the regulations set down by the Equal Employment Opportunity Commission. Both the broadcasting and cable industries are also subject to antitrust laws.
- Several legal areas touch upon the practice of broadcast journalism: defamation, invasion of privacy, protecting sources, and using cameras and microphones in the courtroom.
- Advertising qualifies for protection as free speech under the First Amendment. The FTC is the main agency that regulates false and deceptive advertising.

KEY TERMS

scarcity theory   214
pervasive presence theory   214
Radio Act of 1927   215
Federal Radio Commission
   (FRC)   215

Communications Act of 1934   215
Federal Communications Commission (FCC)   215
Communications Satellite Act   215

Cable Communications Policy Act
   of 1984   217
Telecommunications Act of
   1996   217
Mass Media Bureau   217

SUGGESTIONS FOR FURTHER READING

Caristi, D. (1992). *Expanding free expression in the market-place*. New York: Quorum Books.

Carter, T. B., Franklin, M. A., & Wright, J. B. (1991). *The First Amendment and the Fourth Estate*. Westbury, NY: Foundation Press.

Carter, T. B., Franklin, M. A., & Wright, J. B. (1996). *The First Amendment and the Fifth Estate*. Westbury, NY: Foundation Press.

Corn-Revere, R. (1997). *Rationales and rationalizations: Regulating the electronic media*. Washington DC: Media Institute.

Creech, K. (1996). *Electronic media law and regulation*. Boston: Focal Press.

Dienes, C. T. (1997). *Newsgathering and the law*. Charlottesville, VA: Michie.

Holsinger, R. H., & Dilts, J. P. (1997). *Media law*. New York: McGraw-Hill.

Krasnow, E., Longley, L., & Terry, H. (1982). *The politics of broadcast regulation*. New York: St. Martin's Press.

Middleton, K., & Chamberlin, B. (1994). *The law of public communication*. New York: Longman.

Spitzer, M. (1986). *Seven dirty words and six other stories*. New Haven, CT: Yale University Press.

INTERNET EXERCISES

1. Visit our Web site at http://www.mhhe.com/beyond for study-guide exercises to help you learn and apply material in each chapter. You will find ideas for future research as well as useful Web links to provide you with an opportunity to journey through the new electronic media.

11 Self-Regulation and Ethics

Quick Facts

Date of first National Association of Broadcasters code for broadcasting: 1929

Date code abolished: 1983

Most influential citizens' group in TV history: Action for Children's Television

Approximate number of employees in CBS Department of Standards and Practices in the 1970s: 90

Number of employees in CBS Department of Standards and Practices in 1999: 13

The preceding chapter dealt with laws regarding broadcasting and cable. There are many situations, however, that are not strictly covered by law or FCC regulations. In these circumstances, broadcasters and cable professionals must rely on their own internal standards and/or organizational operating policies for guidance.

Consider the following example. You're the manager of a TV station in a medium-sized market. Your station has just acquired the rights to "The Jerry Springer Show," a talk show that has been criticized in the past for its emphasis on sensationalism, sleaze, and violent confrontations between the guests. The sales department has suggested that the show be scheduled at 4 P.M. so that it would generate a big audience that would flow into your local newscast. The sales manager notes that the show has big ratings in other markets and predicts that it will make a lot of money for the station.

The program director has some doubts, however. She has seen some previews of upcoming show segments. One is entitled "Dumped for Another Woman," which contains 130 bleeps of foul language and fistfights among the guests. Another program, called "My Daughter Is a Teen Prostitute," features a fistfight between a 19-year-old pregnant prostitute and her male prostitute uncle along with 120 bleeps. Yet a third, entitled "I'm Pregnant by My Brother," concerns a teenager who is pregnant by her half-brother but really is in love with her half-brother's older brother. At the end of the show another free-for-all breaks out.[1] The program director asks if it's proper to schedule this type of material at four o'clock in the afternoon, when many kids—just home from school—might be in the audience.

The sales director replies that the show displays a rating at the beginning warning people that it contains strong language and sexual themes. Parents who don't want kids to see this content can simply tell them not to watch. But, says the program director, what about all those kids alone in the house after school, before their parents get home; they have no one to supervise their watching. Doesn't the station have a responsibility to protect them from this material? Perhaps the station could show it late at night? The sales director points out that the show will make less money late at night and wouldn't

Programs such as "The Jerry Springer Show" can pose ethical problems for broadcasters.

help boost the ratings of the early newscast. What do you do?

In this situation the main consideration is not what is legal but what is the right thing to do. There is no law that says "The Jerry Springer Show" cannot be shown on TV at four o'clock in the afternoon. This and similar decisions boil down to a consideration of professional standards and personal ethics. In short, it's a matter of **self-regulation.** A consideration of self-regulation is important because the trend toward fewer formal regulations means that more and more decisions are being left to the discretion of broadcasters and program producers. Accordingly, this chapter focuses on (1) the major forces that influence self-regulation in broadcasting and cable and (2) ethics and its relationship to self-regulation.

---

[1] These are actual examples taken from programs in April 1998.

SELF-REGULATION IN BROADCASTING AND CABLE

This section examines (1) codes of responsibility and/or good practice, (2) departments devoted to maintaining proper standards, (3) the V-chip, (4) professional groups and organizations, and (5) citizens' groups.

Codes

Codes are written statements of principle that guide the general behavior of those working in a profession. Code statements can be prescriptive—"Thou shalt do this"—or proscriptive—"Thou shalt not do this." At one end of the spectrum they imply the minimum expectations of the profession (journalists should not plagiarize); at the other they embody the ideal way of acting (journalists should tell the truth). Professional codes are common in medicine, law, pharmacy, and journalism.

The NAB Code   Although many group-owned broadcasting stations adopted strict codes, probably the most famous of all in broadcasting was that developed by the National Association of Broadcasters (NAB). The NAB established the first radio code in 1929, just two years after the FRC was founded. In 1952, as TV was growing, the NAB adopted a code for it, too. By 1980 the two codes had been amended many times to keep up with the changing social climate. Adherence to the code was voluntary, and figures from 1980 show that about one-half of all radio stations and two-thirds of all TV stations were code subscribers. The NAB had a code authority with a staff of about 33 people who made sure that stations followed the codes. The only punishment the NAB could dish out to the violator, however, was revocation of the right to display the seal of good practice, a penalty that hardly inspired fear among station owners.

A glance at the codes themselves showed that they covered both programming and advertising. Included in the programming area were such diverse topics as news presentation, political broadcasting, religion, community responsibility, and programming aimed at children. The advertising section of the codes contained, among other items, guidelines about what products were acceptable, rules for the presentation of broadcast ads, and time standards suggesting limits on the time per hour that should be devoted to commercials.

The time standard provisions ultimately got the codes into trouble with the Department of Justice, which claimed in an antitrust suit that broadcasters were keeping the prices of ads high by artificially restricting the amount of commercial time available. The NAB, after a negative court decision, suspended the advertising portion of its code. Later, upon advice of lawyers, the NAB revoked the programming sections as well. By 1983 the codes ceased to exist.

Nonetheless, the codes still have some lingering impact. Although the courts said it was anticompetitive for groups of broadcasters to get together to produce common codes, it was still permissible for individual stations and group-owned stations to maintain their own codes. As a result, many stations still informally follow code provisions.

In 1990 the NAB's Executive Committee developed new voluntary programming principles. In order to avoid any of the legal complications that surrounded the original code statements, the NAB's legal department generated the principles and emphasized that there would be no enforcement of these provisions by the NAB or other groups. The new principles were entirely consistent with the philosophy of the original code but were restricted to four key areas: children's TV, indecency and obscenity, violence, and drug abuse. They urged special care in children's programming and that violence should not be portrayed excessively or in a gratuitous manner. Further, the guidelines noted that obscenity was never acceptable for broadcast and that all sexually oriented material should be presented with particular care. Finally, the principles recommended that glamorization of drug use should be avoided.

The government has recently pressured the broadcasting and cable industries to resurrect a more formal code of good behavior. In 1997, four senators introduced a bill that would have exempted the broadcasting and cable industries from antitrust laws to allow them to collaborate on programming guidelines in the hope that the industry would develop a new version of its code. The NAB opposed the bill as an example of government intrusion into free speech. More recently, a commission headed by Vice President Al Gore was considering a recommendation that the broadcasting industry adopt a new code of good conduct as part of a new public interest requirement on the industry as it moves toward the digital age. The NAB has expressed serious concern over such a provision. The final outcome of these new efforts was still unclear at this writing.

Issues: Competitive Pressures and Journalistic Standards

In early 1998, the ratings of CNN were falling. The number of Americans who were regular viewers had dropped by more than 30 percent since 1993. Increased competition from other all-news channels, such as MSNBC and Fox, had contributed to the decline. As part of an effort to increase ratings and raise the visibility level of CNN, the network, in cooperation with Time Warner, its parent company, launched a series called "NewsStand," a prime-time newsmagazine program. CNN had tried newsmagazines before but with little success. "Impact," the predecessor to "NewsStand," had never drawn more than a million viewers, far fewer than the audience the broadcast networks' magazine shows, such as "Dateline NBC" or "60 Minutes," normally attracted.

If CNN wanted to compete in this high-stakes marketplace, "NewsStand" would have to make a big initial impression. Fortunately for CNN, its reporters were working on a story that promised to be a blockbuster—the kind of story that would establish "NewsStand" as a major player in the world of prime-time TV journalism. The story, entitled "Valley of Death," alleged that, during the Vietnam war, the U.S. military, during a mission labeled Operation Tailwind, had used deadly nerve gas to kill defectors who were hiding in Laos.

The story aired on June 8, 1998, during the premiere edition of the program. It did bring immediate visibility to CNN, but not the kind of visibility the network had hoped for. Within hours of the broadcast, hundreds of comments denouncing the story as false came pouring into CNN. The Pentagon, retired General Colin Powell, and former Secretary of State Henry Kissinger labeled the report untrue, as did military personnel who were involved in the mission. CNN's own military adviser resigned in protest. As the criticism mounted, CNN took the unprecedented step of hiring Floyd Abrams, a lawyer with expertise on the workings of the media, to do a full investigation of the report. Abrams concluded that the broadcast was not fair and that the conclusions reached in the story were not justified by the evidence. Abrams recommended that CNN retract the story and apologize for it.

Media coverage dissected CNN's standards for checking the accuracy of its stories. Critics concluded that CNN did not follow its own standards in compiling the story. The checks and balances that generally keep inaccurate reports off the air did not work with regard to "Valley of Death."

On July 2, 1998, the story was retracted and Tom Johnson, CNN's president, formally apologized for airing it. The two producers who put together the story were fired, and an executive producer at CNN resigned.

How much of a role did the pressure to get ratings and the intense competitive atmosphere among all-news channels contribute to the breakdown of standards? This is a difficult question to answer, but most experts agree it played a part. Had CNN not been looking for a blockbuster story to give its premiere some clout and score a journalistic victory over its rivals, perhaps more scrutiny might have been given to the report.

In any case, CNN has now created a position called executive vice president for news standards. The person who fills this position is to make sure no inaccurate stories are broadcast.

Other Codes and Policies There are other noteworthy industrywide guidelines that deal with broadcast journalism and advertising.

The Radio and Television News Directors Association (RTNDA) has an 11-article Code of Broadcast News Ethics that covers items ranging from courtroom coverage to privacy invasions. The Society of Professional Journalists (SPJ) also has a code of ethics that covers all media including broadcasting. This code covers such topics as fair play, accuracy, objectivity, and press responsibility. The language of both codes is general and far-reaching. For example, from the SPJ code: "Seek truth and report it" and "Be accountable."

In the advertising area, the American Advertising Federation and the Association of Better Business Bureaus International have developed a nine-item code that deals with such topics as truth in advertising ("Advertising shall tell the truth . . ."), taste and decency ("Advertising shall be free of statements . . . which are offensive to good taste"), and responsibility ("Advertisers shall be willing to provide substantiation of claims made"). This code has been endorsed by the NAB and many other industry groups.

The absence of a general code of behavior for broadcasting and cable has given station managers and program directors a great deal of discretion in such matters as children's programming, artistic

Ethics: "60 Minutes" and the Suicide Doctor

On November 22, 1998, "60 Minutes" carried a segment that showed Dr. Jack Kevorkian, the "suicide doctor," administering a fatal injection to a terminally ill patient. Unlike previous programs about euthanasia, the moment of death was shown during the report.

The report launched a storm of controversy. "60 Minutes" was accused of running the report in order to hype its ratings (the segment was aired during an important ratings week). The *Boston Globe* said the report showed "60 Minutes" had entered "broadcasting's lower world." Still others charged that "60 Minutes" had been manipulated by a publicity-seeking self-promoter.

Some local stations refused to carry the report. The A. H. Belo Corporation, which owns six CBS affiliates, substituted a condensed local newscast into the program in place of the Kevorkian story. Most affiliates, however, decided to carry it.

"60 Minutes" defended itself by noting that, although the report was controversial, euthanasia was an important topic that deserved public attention and debate. Mike Wallace, the correspondent who did the segment, dismissed charges about pandering to the ratings by pointing out that "60 Minutes" had been a top-rated show for nearly 30 years and did not need to stoop to sensationalism to increase its audience. The executive director of the Freedom Forum also backed "60 Minutes," saying that the controversy over euthanasia was so significant that it needed to be aired even though it may have offended some people's sensibilities.

freedom, religious shows, programs devoted to important local issues, and acceptable topics. Management must be sensitive to the political, social, and economic sensibilities of the community; otherwise, a bad decision can cost a radio, TV, or cable organization credibility, trust, and, in the long run, dollars.

To help guard against bad decisions, many stations have developed their own policy guidelines covering sensitive issues. These station policies generally complement and expand the industrywide codes of conduct. Not surprisingly, the broadcast newsroom is the place where a written policy is most often found.

Written codes, however, are not without controversy. On the one hand, proponents of codes argue that they indicate to the general public that the media organization is sensitive to its ethical duties. Moreover, written codes of conduct ensure that every employee understands what the company views as proper or correct behavior; ethical decisions are not left to the whim of each individual. On the other hand, opponents argue that any company policy statement that covers the entire workings of the organization will have to be worded so vaguely that it will be of little use in specific day-to-day decision making. Further, opponents fear that a written code or policy statement might actually be used against a radio or TV station in court. For example, a private citizen who's suing a TV station for libel might argue that the station was negligent because it failed to follow its own written guidelines.

Many of the company codes that exist today tend to be proscriptive in nature and narrow in focus. Basically, they tend to spell out the minimum expectations for an individual employee. For example, many TV station policies forbid journalists from taking gifts from their news sources, or program directors from accepting gifts from program suppliers. Stations also have policies that bar employees from accepting free sports tickets and junkets or from holding outside employment that might conflict with their job at the station.

It's apparent that written guidelines can't do the whole job. In fact, most policy statements and codes fail to address the number-one ethical problem revealed by a survey conducted by *Electronic Media*: the conflict between making money and serving the public. Three out of four media executives agreed that the goals of making money and public service were sometimes in conflict. This is not surprising since most policy statements and guidelines are directed at the individual, whereas ethical problems are increasingly originating at the corporate level. For example, many stations and cable systems are owned by groups. How much of the profit made by a local operation should be reinvested back into the station and how much should go to shore up unprofitable operations in other communities or to finance new acquisitions? Should a TV station run sensational stories on its TV newscasts during sweep weeks to inflate its ratings? How much local news should be carried on a radio station if it means losing some money in the process? These are questions that codes seldom deal with.

Departments of Standards and Practices

The major television and cable networks maintain staffs to make sure that the networks' commercials and programs do not offend advertisers, affiliated stations and local cable systems, the audience, and the FCC. In prior years these departments, usually called standards and practices (S&P) or something similar, were large and influential. Their primary role seemed to be that of a moral guardian, shielding the audience from words and portrayals that main-stream society might find embarrassing or offensive. In the 1990s, as network audiences and profits de-clined, these departments were cut back. At CBS, for example, the standards and practices department was cut from 90 staffers to 13.

Moreover, the broadcast and cable networks ap-parently had become more flexible with their guide-lines as evidenced by the fact that only CBS and Comedy Central were willing to make their guide-lines public. The other networks were reluctant to re-lease theirs because they were too fluid to be pinned down in print.

The limits of acceptability, of course, have also changed dramatically over the years. Back in the 1960s, the network S&P departments decreed that Barbara Eden of "I Dream of Jeannie" couldn't reveal her navel on network TV and that Rob and Laura of "The Dick Van Dyke Show" couldn't be shown in bed together even though they were married. Liber-alization of standards began in the early 1970s with such shows as "All in the Family" and "Maude." In addition, cable, with its uncut and uncensored films, conditioned viewers to more permissive standards. By the 1980s, network S&P departments were grap-pling with programs about rape, homosexuality, racial prejudice, and abortion. The 1990s saw the net-works relax restrictions on language, provocative dress, and sexual themes. Words that would never be spoken by Rob and Laura now occur commonly in prime time. In addition, programs such as "NYPD Blue," "Ellen," "Nothing Sacred," and "Ally McBeal" pushed the envelope on subject matter.

A network's competitive position also influences its standards. The newer Fox Network, for example, in an attempt to catch viewers' attention, allowed shows such as "Married . . . with Children," "The

"Dawson's Creek," a series that deals with teenage sex and parental extra-marital affairs, was the most watched show among teens in 1999. The show also created an uproar among critics who thought it was sending an immoral message to young people.

Simpsons," "King of the Hill," and "When Animals Attack" to venture into areas that the older, more-established networks might have avoided.

Cable networks, of course, have a little more lee-way when it comes to controversial content but they also follow standards. Comedy Central, for example, runs the crude "South Park" late in the evening when fewer young children are in the audience, and MTV does the same with its explicit "Loveline" ad-vice program. MTV has also demanded cuts in music videos the network deemed too controversial in their original form. Premium cable channels, such as HBO and Showtime, have the greatest amount of latitude when it comes to presenting mature and sexual con-tent. The movie "Lolita" was carried by Showtime after the major Hollywood studios declined to dis-tribute it because of its controversial subject matter.

At the local level both broadcasting and cable op-erations pay close attention to questions of taste and appropriateness, but they do not have formalized departments that handle the task. Some group owners of stations have codes that they try to apply to all the stations they own, but most standards-and-practices decisions are made by managers or program executives. Further, not all decisions will be the same. The acceptability of certain TV or radio messages depends on several factors: (1) the size of the market, (2) the time period, (3) the station's audience, and (4) the type of content involved.

To elaborate, what's acceptable in New York City might not be appropriate for Minot, North Dakota. Standards vary widely from city to city and from region to region. The local radio, TV, or cable executive is usually the best judge of what his or her community will tolerate.

The time period also has a lot to do with acceptability. Stations tend to be more careful if there's a good chance that children will be in the audience. Programs and films with adult themes are typically scheduled late in the evening when few children are presumed to be listening. Cable movie channels generally schedule their racier films after 10:00 P.M.

The audience attracted by a station's programming is another important factor. Radio stations that feature a talk format with controversial topics usually spark few protests because their listeners know what to expect. Listener-sponsored Pacifica radio stations routinely program material that other stations would heartily avoid. Although they do get into occasional trouble (for example, the *Pacifica* case), the audience for Pacifica stations rarely complains.

Finally, the kind of program also makes a difference. Rough language and shocking pictures are sometimes OK for a news or public affairs program.

The V-chip

The **V-chip** represents an intriguing blend of legal regulation and self-regulation. Section 551 of the Telecommunications Act of 1996 requires TV set manufacturers to install a V-chip content-blocking device in every TV set that is 13 inches or larger. An FCC ruling stated that all new sets must be so-equipped by January 1, 2000.

The V-chip works in concert with a voluntary program rating system developed by the television industry that identifies programs with sexual, violent, or indecent content. After much discussion, the industry came up with a rating system that initially classified TV content according to its acceptability for various age levels:

"TV-Y"—programs suitable to "all children."

"TV-Y7"—programs "directed to older children," ages 7 and above.

"TV-G"—general audience.

"TV-PG"—parental guidance suggested.

"TV-14"—parents strongly cautioned for children under 14.

"TV-M"—mature audience only.

After complaints from public interest groups that this system was not informative enough, the ratings were later amended to include special advisories for specific content: "S" for sexual content; "L" for profanity and other strong language; "V" for excessive violence; and "D" for sexually suggestive dialogue. Thus, a program could be rated "TV-14—SLD." The ratings for each program are assigned by members of the television industry. The rating itself is electronically encoded in the program's transmission signal and appears on the screen at the beginning of the program.

When the V-chip becomes operational, parents can program the chip to block out content that they judge to be inappropriate for their children. For example, if parents are concerned about televised violence, they can use the V-chip to block any program that has a "V" in its rating. As of late 1998, all major TV networks had agreed to rate their programs, except NBC, which uses only the age ratings, and Black Entertainment Television, which does not use any ratings.

Broadcasters seem wary of the V-chip because they fear that a "TV-M" rating might discourage advertisers from buying time on a program. On the other hand, many in the creative community see the ratings system and the V-chip as an opportunity for them to create mature programs designed for adults. As for viewers, a recent survey reported in *Newsweek* found that 51 percent of parents don't pay attention to program ratings. Another national survey revealed that only 3 percent of parents knew that the "D" rating stood for suggestive dialogue. Finally, a 1998 study by the Kaiser Family Foundation discovered that more than 80 percent of the shows they sampled did not contain the appropriate content "D-V-S-L" label. In any case, the V-chip is a reality. Its effectiveness is still unclear.

Professional Groups

Professional groups are trade and industry organizations that offer their members advice about research, technical, legal, and management issues. The best known of these for broadcasters is the **National Association of Broadcasters (NAB).** The NAB has about 5,000 radio-station and 940 TV-station members, along with 1,500 individual members in the broadcasting industry. We have already examined the lobbying component of the NAB; its other services include designing public service campaigns, offering legal advice, conducting technology research, and maintaining an information library. In cable, the **National Cable Television Association (NCTA)** is the most influential group, with a range of services that parallels the NAB's. Other professional groups include the Radio Television News Directors Association, the National Association of Television Program Executives, the National Association of Farm Broadcasters, the Association of Maximum Service Telecasters, the National Association of Public Television Stations, and the National Association of Black-Owned Broadcasters, to name a few. A recent issue of *Broadcasting-Cablecasting Yearbook* listed about 175 national associations concerned with cable and broadcasting.

Professional groups contribute to self-regulation in both formal and informal ways. On the informal level, each group sponsors conventions and meetings where members exchange relevant business and professional information. These meetings offer ways for managers from one part of the country to learn how managers from other regions are handling similar problems. A station in Maine might find that a policy or set of guidelines used by a station in Ohio solves its problem. Organizational meetings let professionals get feedback from their peers. Professional organizations also set examples and demonstrate standards of meritorious behavior that members can emulate. The NAB, for example, reported that in 1997 radio and TV stations donated about $900 million in broadcast time for public service campaigns.

The most elaborate system of formal self-regulation by a professional group deals with national advertising. Basically, the process works like this. If a consumer or a competitor thinks an ad is deceptive, a complaint is filed with the **National Advertising Division (NAD)** of the Council of Better Business Bureaus. Most complaints are filed by competitors, but the NAD monitors national radio and TV and can initiate action itself. The NAD can either dismiss the complaint or contact the advertiser for additional information that might refute the complaint. If the NAD is not satisfied with the advertiser's response, it can ask the company to change or stop using the

ad. If the advertiser agrees (and most do), then that's the end of it. On the other hand, if the advertiser disagrees with the NAD, the case can be taken to the **National Advertising Review Board (NARB).**

The NARB functions much like a court of appeals. A review panel is appointed, the case is examined again, and the complaint is either upheld or dismissed. If the complaint is upheld, the advertiser is asked once again to change or discontinue the ad. If the advertiser still refuses, the case can be referred to the FTC or another government agency for possible legal action.

One of the problems with this system is that it takes a long time. In many cases, by the time the NAD has weighed the facts of the case, decided that the ad in question was truly deceptive, and notified the company to stop, the advertising campaign has run its course and the ad is already off the air. Nonetheless, although it doesn't have any legal or formal authority, the NAD/NARB system and the implied threat of legal action is taken seriously by most people in the industry.

Last, scholarly and academic organizations, such as the Broadcast Education Association and the Association for Education in Journalism and Mass Communication, contribute to self-regulation through their work with students. These and similar organizations urge colleges and universities to emphasize ethical and professional responsibilities in their curricula. Academic organizations also study and help clarify the norms and standards of the profession so that practitioners can have some guidance in making ethical decisions.

Citizens' Groups

In addition to shaping the legal and policy environment of broadcasting, citizens' groups (or pressure groups) exert a force for self-regulation by communicating directly with broadcasters. In recent years citizens' groups have been most vocal about three areas: (1) the portrayal of minorities, (2) the presentation of sex and violence, and (3) children's programming.

Portrayal of Minorities The concern over the portrayal of minorities began during the civil rights movement of the 1960s. African Americans correctly noted that few blacks appeared in network prime-time programming and that those few who did were usually shown in menial occupations. Their pressure

on the networks for more-balanced portrayals
ultimately led to more-important roles for blacks,
such as Bill Cosby's in "I Spy" and Diahann Carroll's
in "Julia."

The success of these efforts prompted Latinos to
campaign successfully for the removal of a commercial character known as the Frito Bandito, which
many found offensive. Ethnic stereotyping in a series
called "Chico and the Man" was also a target of Mex-
ican-American citizens' groups. Other groups, such
as Native Americans, Italian-Americans, the Gray
Panthers, Arab-Americans, and Asian-Americans,
have also pressured the networks to eliminate
stereotyped portrayals. The National Gay Task Force
has also lobbied the networks for a balanced portrayal of homosexuals.

A 1997 episode of "Seinfeld" in which a character
accidentally set fire to a Puerto Rican flag prompted
protests by the National Puerto Rican Coalition and
a subsequent apology from NBC. Most recently, a
1998 offering, "The Secret Diary of Desmond Pfeif-
fer," a controversial UPN series about a black butler
and advisor in the Lincoln White House, generated
criticism from African Americans about its portrayal
of slavery.

Presentation of Sex and Violence   The portrayal of sex
and violence is also a recurring topic of attention for
citizens' groups. The National Coalition on Television Violence focuses public attention on the problem by regularly publishing a list of the most violent
programs on broadcast TV and cable. The American
Medical Association (AMA) has joined with citizens'
groups in the campaign to reduce TV violence. In
1994, the AMA called upon the industry to develop a
new ratings system for film and video and for the
creation of a TV violence code. The Media Project at
the Center for Population Options has crusaded for
the responsible portrayal of family planning, sexual-
ity, and reproductive health. This group gives an annual award for outstanding programming in this
area. And the conservative American Family Association has campaigned against television programs
that the organization considers obscene.

Children's Programming   Programming for children
is another recurring concern of many groups, including the national Parent Teacher Association and the
National Education Association. Since the passage of
the **Children's Television Act of 1990** and the subsequent ruling by the FCC that stations devote three

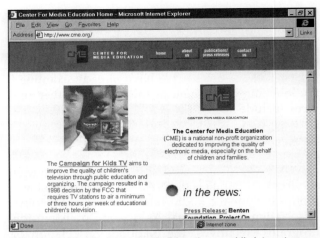

Home page of the Center for Media Education, a public interest group
interested in children's television.

hours a week to children's programs, the major focus
of children's television advocates has been the enforcement of these provisions. The Center for Media
Education, for example, maintains a Web site that
contains a description of the new legal regulations, a
listing of what programs the networks are presenting that meet the three-hour requirement, and information on how to read a TV station's public file to
see if the station is in compliance.

Effects   Citizens' groups pose special problems for
the self-regulatory attempts of the industry. They increase the sensitivity of programmers toward potentially offensive material, but at the same time they severely restrict the creative freedom of writers and
producers. Their cumulative effect thus may lead to a
kind of self-censorship. In addition, program producers are forced to walk a thin line between alternatives.
For example, gay citizens' groups are calling for increased portrayals of homosexuals in TV drama. If the
producers accede to the demands, they might risk offending a substantial part of their viewing audience.
Similarly, networks and production companies are
careful not to allow potentially harmful acts of violence to remain in a show, but even seemingly innocuous acts of aggression may still raise the ire of some citizens' groups. Satisfying everybody is not an easy task.

ETHICS

All of us deal regularly with ethical problems. For
example, suppose one of your teachers returns your
test with a grade of 95 on it. As you look through the

test, you realize your teacher made an addition mistake and your real score is 85. Do you tell your teacher? Or suppose the cashier at the bookstore gives you $25 in change when you were supposed to get only $15. Do you return the extra $10? Personal ethical principles are important in the self-regulation of broadcasting and cable, since many decision makers rely on them in situations that are not covered by codes or standards and practices. And since the many crucial ethical decisions of broadcasters and cablecasters are open to public inspection and criticism, ethical behavior is critical to those working in radio and TV. This section takes a brief look at the formal study of ethics and then examines how ethics might apply in the day-to-day world of TV and radio.

The Greek word *ethos* originally meant an abode or an accustomed dwelling place, a place where we would feel comfortable. In like manner, the study of ethics can be thought of as helping us make those decisions with which we are comfortable. In formal terms, ethics addresses the question, "Which human actions are morally permissible and which are not?" or, in more familiar terms, "What is the right thing to do?"

Ethics and law are related; both limit human activities. Laws, however, are enforced by sanctions and penalties, whereas ethics are enforced by our moral sense of the proper thing. In many cases the law and ethics overlap—the legally correct action is also the morally correct action. In other cases a decision that's perfectly legal may not be the best decision from an ethical standpoint.

Perhaps a brief and basic tour of the philosophical groundwork that underlies ethics might help.

Ethical Theories

Without getting too bogged down in the technical language of the philosophy of ethics, we first need to define two key concepts: teleological theories and deontological theories. A **teleological** (from the Greek, *teleos,* an end or a result) **theory** of ethics is one that measures the rightness or wrongness of an action in terms of its consequences. To say that it is unethical for a TV station to show a violent film in prime time when a lot of children are watching because some of them might imitate the film and hurt other people is a teleological judgment. A policy that forbids reporters from accepting gifts and consideration from the people they cover because it would hurt their journalistic credibility is another teleological judgment.

A **deontological** (from the Greek, *deon,* duty) **theory** does not concern itself with consequences; instead, it spells out those duties that are morally required of all of us. The source of these moral obligations can come from reason, society, the supernatural, or the human conscience. For example, a policy that forbids investigative TV journalists from assuming a false identity while researching a story because such actions constitute lying, an action forbidden by one of the Ten Commandments, is based on supernatural deontological grounds. Note that it doesn't matter if the consequences of the lying are beneficial to society. A lie is prohibited since it is counter to God's will as expressed in the commandments.

With that as a background, let's examine some specific ethical principles and see how they might relate to broadcasting and cable.

Utilitarianism   Probably the most popular and clearest ethical principle is a teleological theory, utilitarianism. **Utilitarianism** holds that a person should act in a way that produces the greatest possible ratio of good over evil. In other words, one should make the decision whose consequences will yield the greatest good for the greatest number (or the least harm for the fewest number). Under this principle the ethical person is one who adds to the goodness and reduces the evil of human life.

A broadcaster who chose to follow utilitarianism as an ethical standard would first have to calculate the probable consequences that would result from each possible course of action (this is not easy; sometimes it's impossible to predict all the consequences of a given decision). Second, the broadcaster would have to assign a positive or negative value to each probable consequence and then choose the alternative that maximizes benefit and minimizes harm.

To illustrate, suppose the sales manager asks the news director (let's assume that's you) at a given station to kill a story about health code violations at a local restaurant. The restaurant is one of the biggest advertisers on your station and has threatened to cancel if you run the story. From the utilitarian perspective you first define your possible actions: (1) run the story, (2) kill the story, and (3) run an edited version of the story without naming the restaurant involved. The consequences of killing the story are easy to predict. Your station continues to get money and stays in business, thus keeping everyone on your staff employed. It might also help the restaurant stay in business, since consumers who are health conscious might have stayed away had the story been aired. On the other hand, failing to run the story or running it minus the name of the offending restaurant might have significant negative effects. First, it might hurt the credibility of your news operation, particularly if other local media identify the restaurant. In the long run this might cause people to stop watching your newscast and hurt your revenues. Second, the morale in your news department might be negatively affected. Third, unwary consumers who eat at the restaurant might have their health jeopardized by the unsanitary conditions. Carrying the full story would help credibility, improve station morale, and warn unsuspecting members of the general public. In short, our cursory utilitarian analysis suggests that it would be better to carry the story.

Egoism   Another teleological theory is known as **egoism.** Its basic premise is simple: act in the way that is best for you. Any action is judged to be right or wrong in terms of its consequences for one's self. If decision A is more in your self-interest than decision B, then decision A is right.

Egoism was popularized by writer-philosopher Ayn Rand, who argued that a person should not sacrifice self to others. Rather, a person should have the highest regard and owe the greatest obligation to his or her own self. (Rand's book *The Fountainhead* is a forceful interpretation of this view. Incidentally, a movie of the same name, starring Gary Cooper, was based on this book, making it probably the only motion picture ever to be based on a formal ethical theory.)

Egoism sounds like an intellectual rationalization for doing whatever you please. But it goes deeper than that. Egoism doesn't preclude kindness or thoughtfulness toward others. In fact, it requires the individual to make a thoughtful and rational analysis of each choice to determine what exactly is best for the individual. Doing what is best for you frequently also entails doing what is best for others. In any case, egoism is an interesting example of an individualistic ethic that many have criticized as being paradoxical and inconsistent.

In our restaurant example, the news director goes through the same analysis as discussed earlier, but now he or she is not concerned about the consequences for the station, the restaurant, the public, or the news staff. The news director is interested only in what will be best for himself or herself. In this case the news director might well conclude that killing the story would harm his or her reputation as an aggressive, probing journalist and thus would run the story since, in the long run, the action would be beneficial to a news director's career.

Categorical Imperative   Probably the most famous deontological theory was developed by Immanuel Kant. Our proper duty, not the consequences of our actions, must govern our decisions. Kant argued that our proper course of action must be arrived at through reason and an examination of conscience. How do we recognize our proper duty? By subjecting it to the **categorical imperative:** Act only on those principles that you would want to become universal law. This philosophy is close to the famous golden rule in Western cultures. An ethical person should perform only those behaviors that he or she would like all to perform. What is right for one is right for all. In this context, "categorical" means without exception. What's right is right and that's the end of it.

Someone following the categorical imperative might handle the restaurant news story in this manner: Since holding back important information is not something that I would want everybody to do, the story must run. In this instance there is a categorical imperative against squelching the publication of important information. Therefore, it should not be done in this or other situations. Period.

The Golden Mean   Another deontological theory stems from the writings of Aristotle. A natural scientist, Aristotle grounded his theory of ethics in natural law. He noted that too much or too little of something was harmful. A plant would wither if given too little water but would drown if given too much. The proper course of action is somewhere between these two extremes. Moderation, temperance, equilibrium, and harmony are concepts that are important in his philosophy.

When faced with an ethical dilemma, a person using this theory begins by identifying the extremes and then searches to find some balance point or mean that lies between them—the **golden mean.** This may be easy or hard to do, depending on the situation. In the restaurant example one extreme would be to publish everything; the other, to publish nothing. Perhaps a compromise position between the two would be to air the story completely but also to provide time for the restaurant owner to reply to the charges. Perhaps the story might note that these are the first violations in the restaurant's history or include other tempering remarks.

Cultural Ethics   **Cultural ethics theory,** which is grounded in society as opposed to nature, holds that an individual is shaped by his or her culture. Our moral judgments are shaped by those we experienced when growing up and when entering other socializing environments such as school or work. Cultural ethics suggests that the individual accepts the discipline of society, adjusts to its needs and customs, and finds ethical security within it. There are no universals by which each culture is judged; each is self-legislative, determining its own rules of right and wrong. Moreover, many different subcultures within society may be relevant. An ethical problem encountered on the job might be assessed in the context of the workplace with all of its relevant norms.

In the broadcasting area, the practical application of this theory suggests that a station or cable system owner consult the norms of other media or of other businesses or of the general community before making an ethical decision. In the restaurant example the station involved might see how other stations are treating the story or have treated such stories in the past. Similarly, the way that other media, such as newspapers, handle the situation should be noted. Or the station might consult the managers of other stations throughout the area to get advice about the proper course to follow.

Situational Ethics   The theory of situational ethics also examines ethics in relative terms. Unlike cultural ethics, however, **situational ethics, or situationism,** argues that the traditions and norms of society provide inadequate guidance because each individual problem or situation is unique and calls for a creative solution. Decisions regarding how we ought to act must be grounded in the concrete details that make up each circumstance. Universal ethical principles like the categorical imperative might provide some guidance, but they are merely hints as to the correct course; they do not apply in every situation. A general principle that we endorse, such as "TV newscasters should always tell the truth," can be violated if the situation calls for it (such as broadcasting a false story to gain the release of hostages).

Of course, the way we see and analyze situations varies from person to person. No two individuals will define the same situation in exactly the same

terms. How we perceive things depends on our moral upbringing and our ethical values. Consequently, different answers are possible depending on how one assesses the situation.

In our restaurant example the entire situation must be examined before making a decision. Was the board of health on a vendetta against this particular restaurant? Has the restaurant recently changed management? How much money will actually be lost if the restaurant cancels its advertising? Could this revenue be replaced from another source? Have all the violations been corrected? These are some aspects of the situation that might be considered before a decision is made. From a situationist point of view there is no single "correct" answer to this problem.

"Doing" Ethics

A knowledge of ethical principles is useful for all those entering the radio and TV profession. First, it is important to have some predefined standard in place when a quick and difficult ethical call is required. Second, a personal code of ethics assures an individual of some measure of consistency from one decision to the next. Third, media professionals are often asked to explain or defend their decisions to the public. A knowledge of ethical principles and the techniques of moral reasoning can give those explanations more credibility and validity. Fourth, and most pragmatically, good ethics and good business generally go hand in hand, at least in the long run. Although short-term economic gains may result from making ethical compromises, one study done in the late 1970s showed that companies that ranked high in ethics also tended to rank high in growth and in earnings per share.

How can a person develop a set of ethical standards that will be relevant and useful in day-to-day situations? If you have read this far, you already have gotten a head start. The first step is to become familiar with enduring ethical principles, such as those just enumerated, or others that may be germane to your profession. For example, if the classical ethical theories do not seem helpful, you might want to consider the set of ethical principles proposed by Edmund Lambeth in *Committed Journalism*. Although designed for working journalists, his principles have relevance for everyone employed in broadcasting and cable. Lambeth suggests that an individual's decisions should adhere to the following principles:

Ethics: The Paradox of Egoism

Suppose that you are an advocate of the ethical position known as egoism. You believe that a person should always act in a way that promotes that person's own self-interest. Let's further suppose that you're a salesperson for a local radio station. You have been working for months to sell a large package of ads to a big company in your town. Your colleague comes to you one day to chat.

> COLLEAGUE: I have an ethical problem.
> YOU: Act in a manner that promotes your own self-interest.
> COLLEAGUE: I'm glad you said that. My brother-in-law knows the guy at that big company you've been trying to sell. My brother-in-law says that the guy trusts him and will buy advertising from anyone my brother-in-law recommends. I know how long you've been working on this one and I was going to get my brother-in-law to recommend you. But since you told me to act in my own self-interest, I'll get myself recommended, make the sale, and pocket a big commission. I knew you'd understand.
> YOU: Something is wrong here.

In this case recommending egoism to someone contradicts your own self-interest. It is not to your advantage to have everybody else pursue their own advantage. You are in the interesting position of having an ethical stance that you can practice yourself but cannot recommend to others.

1. Tell the truth.
2. Behave justly.
3. Respect independence and freedom.
4. Act humanely.
5. Behave responsibly.

Another model for journalists endorsed by many in the profession has seven principles or moral duties:

1. Don't cause harm.
2. Keep all promises.
3. Make up for previous wrongful acts.
4. Act in a just manner.
5. Improve your own virtue.
6. Be good to people who have been good to you.
7. Try to make the world better.

It matters little whether you subscribe to Aristotle's golden mean or principles suggested by Lambeth; the point is that you need to develop some underlying set of ethical principles.

Next you need to develop a model or plan of action that serves as a guide in making ethical choices. When a person is confronted with an ethical dilemma, the model serves as a blueprint for thinking. One possible model might be the following:

Stage one. Determine the situation. Compile all the facts and information that are relevant to the situation. Learn all you can about the circumstances that prompted the problems.

Stage two. Examine and clarify all the possible alternatives. Make sure you are aware of all your possible courses of action. (If you subscribe to a teleological theory of ethics, you may also have to assess the possible consequences of each action.)

Stage three. Determine what ethical theories or principles you will follow in the situation. Try over time to develop some consistency in the choice of theories or principles.

Stage four. Decide and act accordingly.

Ethics in the Real World

We have now seen some theories and models promulgated by philosophers who have the luxury of time to reflect on their various ramifications. In the real world of TV and radio, however, rarely do professionals have the time to reflect on their decisions. For example, in New York City a convict with a gun threatened to kill hostages if his demands weren't broadcast immediately by a local TV station. The police on the scene urged the station manager to grant this request. The station involved in this dilemma had about two minutes to decide what to do. That's probably not enough time to do a thorough utilitarian or Kantian analysis of the situation. (In real life the TV station agreed to the request and bloodshed was averted. Subsequently, however, the station was soundly criticized by local newspapers for giving a forum to a gunman.)

Moreover, many broadcasters and cablecasters enter their profession without a personal code of ethics.

Academic courses in media ethics became popular only in the early 1980s. Many current media executives were trained in selling, programming, or news but had to pick up informally along the way whatever ethical standards they have. In fact, many executives would probably be hard-pressed to articulate exactly where and how they developed their ethical standards.

Third, although some broadcast and cable organizations have codes of conduct or good practice, they are generally written in broad, general terms and may have little relevance to the individual. Companies rarely conduct education and training sessions in ethics. A new employee who expects the company to provide him or her with a ready-made set of ethics will probably be disappointed.

Finally, recent experience suggests that many ethical problems exist at the corporate level as well as at the individual level. The view that the only responsibility of business is to make a profit has come under attack by those who argue that since corporations have such a significant impact on the environment, their surrounding communities, and the individual consumer, they have an ethical obligation to serve the needs of the larger society. It is not surprising, then, that the number-one ethical problem that was cited in an *Electronic Media* survey done in 1987 was balancing corporate profits against public service. This suggests that employees of broadcasting and cable companies will be faced with ethical decisions throughout their careers. New employees will probably have to make choices about their own personal behaviors, while veterans who have risen to the managerial level will be making decisions regarding proper corporate policy. Personal codes of ethics must also accommodate the corporate situation.

In sum, a theoretical knowledge of ethical principles and analysis is helpful, but it must be tempered by an awareness of the nature of the day-to-day pressures in TV and radio.

Ethics: A Final Word

Many texts on media ethics present case studies that raise ethical problems for discussion. Students spend much time debating alternatives and find that there may be little agreement on the proper choice. Different ethical principles do indeed suggest different courses of action. Many students become frustrated by this and look upon ethics as simply a set of mental games that can be used to rationalize almost any decision. This frustration is understandable. It helps, however, to point out that ethical problems are not like algebra problems. There is no one answer that all will come up with. Ethical theories are not like a computer; they do not print out correct answers with mechanical precision. Abstract ethical rules cannot anticipate all possible situations. They necessarily leave room for personal judgment.

Ethical decision making is more an art than a science. The ethical principles and models presented here represent different perspectives from which ethical problems can be viewed. They encourage careful analysis and thoughtful, systematic reflection before making a choice. A system of ethics must be flexible, and it ought to do more than merely rationalize the personal preferences of the person making the choice. As Edmund Lambeth says in *Committed Journalism,* an ethical system "must have bite and give direction." In sum, this brief discussion of ethics is not intended to give everybody the answers. It was designed to present some enduring principles, to encourage a reasoned approach to ethical problems, and to foster a basic concern for ethical issues, recognizing all the while that many ethical decisions have to be made in an uncertain world amid unclear circumstances and with imperfect knowledge.

SUMMARY

- Personal ethics have become an increasingly important issue for broadcasters as the competitive atmosphere, fostered by deregulation, heightens. Station managers now must be accountable for regulating themselves. Codes, departments, professional groups and organizations, and citizens' groups all help promote responsibility.

- The acceptability of a message depends on the size of a market, the time period, the station's audience, and the type of content involved.

- Ethics and law share common threads. Both are restrictive measures. The difference lies in the fact that one is enforced by the state, whereas the other is enforced by personal judgment.

- There are numerous ethical theories that attempt to explain how a person determines right from wrong. Some major theories are utilitarianism, egoism, the categorical imperative, the golden mean, cultural ethics, and situational ethics.

KEY TERMS

Self-regulation   241
V-chip   246
National Association of
    Broadcasters (NAB)   247
National Cable Television
    Association (NCTA)   247
National Advertising Division
    (NAD)   247

National Advertising Review Board
    (NARB)   247
Children's Television Act of
    1990   248
teleological theory   249
deontological theory   249
utilitarianism   249

egoism   250
categorical imperative   250
golden mean   250
cultural ethics theory   251
situational ethics; situationism   251

SUGGESTIONS FOR FURTHER READING

Christians, C., Rotzoll, K., Fackler, M., & McKee, K.
    (1997). *Media ethics* (5th ed.). New York: Addison-Wes-
    ley.

Conover, C. (1967). *Personal ethics in an impersonal world.*
    Philadelphia: Westminster Press.

Ethical dilemmas. (1988, February 29). *Electronic media,*
    p. 1.

Fink, C. (1995). *Media ethics.* New York: McGraw-Hill.

Frankena, W. (1973). *Ethics,* Englewood Cliffs, NJ: Prentice
    Hall.

Goodwin, H. (1987). *Groping for ethics in journalism*
    (2nd ed.). Ames, IA: Iowa State University Press.

Gordon, D., Kihross, J., Merill, J. G., & Reuss, C. (1998).
    Controversies in media ethics. New York: Addison-
    Wesley.

Hausman, C. (1992). *Crisis of confidence.* New York:
    HarperCollins.

Klaidman, S., & Beauchamp, T. (1987). *The virtuous jour-
    nalist.* New York: Oxford University Press.

Lambeth, E. (1992). *Committed journalism.* Bloomington,
    IN: Indiana University Press.

Limburg, V. E. (1994). *Electronic media ethics.* Boston: Focal
    Press.

Merrill, J., & Odell, S. (1983). *Philosophy and journalism.*
    New York: Longman.

Meyer, P. (1987). *Ethical journalism.* New York: Longman.

Patterson, P. & Wilkins, L. (Eds.). 1997. *Media ethics: Issues
    and cases.* New York: McGraw-Hill.

INTERNET EXERCISES

1. Visit our Web site at http://www.mhhe.com/
    beyond for study-guide exercises to help you learn
    and apply material in each chapter. You will find
    ideas for future research as well as useful Web links
    to provide you with an opportunity to journey
    through the new electronic media.

Part Five   What It Does

Ratings and Audience Feedback 12

Quick Facts

 Year of first national radio audience survey: 1927

 Number of U.S. households with TV: 99 million

 Number of households in A.C. Nielsen's Peoplemeter sample: 5,000

 Number of households in Media Metrix's Internet ratings sample: 40,000

 Average length of a song hook used in radio call-out research: 8 seconds

Advertisers spend billions every year to purchase time on radio and television for their commercial messages. Not surprisingly, they like to know if their money is well-spent. For this to happen, they need information about how many and what kinds of people watch and listen. Enter the ratings.

This chapter discusses how to measure and evaluate what people are listening to or watching. The first part examines how ratings and ratings companies developed in the United States. The next sections will look at how data are collected, analyzed, and reported. The final section explores how additional feedback from the audience is gathered.

HISTORY OF AUDIENCE MEASUREMENT

Audience research first appeared in the 1920s when station owners became curious about the size of their listening audience. Early announcers requested listeners to drop a post card to the station reporting that they had heard a particular program and indicating whether the signal was clear. The need for more-detailed data became important when advertisers, particularly those who bought time on network radio, demanded accurate estimates of audience size. Consequently, the American Association of Advertising Agencies and the Association of National Advertisers formed the **Cooperative Analysis of Broadcasting (CAB)** in 1930.

The CAB collected data on network listening in 35 cities across the United States using the **telephone recall method.** Calls were placed at different times during the day to homes selected at random from phone directories, and respondents were asked to recall the programs that they had listened to.

One problem with the credibility of the CAB ratings was in fact this use of the recall method. Although asking a person to remember what he or she had heard in the last few hours is more accurate than asking the person about listening on a previous night, human memory is still open to failure.

The CAB operated until 1946, when it fell victim to another organization with a superior way of measuring the audience. The C. E. Hooper company introduced the **telephone coincidental method,** in which respondents were asked if they were listening to the radio at the time of the call, and, if the answer was yes, they were asked to name the program or the station to which they were listening. The coincidental method is an improvement over the recall method because it does not rely on the fallible memory of the respondent. The results of the Hooper surveys, called Hooperatings, were sold to advertisers, advertising agencies, and broadcasters.

In 1942, the A.C. Nielsen Company started a ratings service that used a different method, one that did not rely on the telephone, to collect data about radio listening. Nielsen connected a mechanical device, called the **audimeter,** to the radios of a randomly selected sample of people. The audimeter consisted of a sharp stylus that made a scratch on a roll of paper tape (later replaced by 16-millimeter film) in synchronization with the radio's tuning dial. After a period of time, listeners sent back the tape or film to Nielsen where the scratches were analyzed to reveal how long the set was on and to what station it was tuned.

Note that, whereas previous companies measured actual listening, Nielsen measured set use. The audimeter could determine only if the radio was turned on and to what station it was tuned. It could not determine who, if anyone, was listening. Nonetheless, advertisers preferred the Nielsen numbers, and in 1950 Nielsen bought out Hooperatings.

The audimeter moved to TV in the 1950s. A device was attached to every TV set in the home and families were instructed to open up the audimeter at the end of a week's viewing and send the film back to Nielsen for analysis. A Nielsen family received 50 cents per week for their cooperation. Data from the audimeters formed the basis for two Nielsen reports: the **Nielsen Television Index (NTI),** which reported the viewership of network programs, and the **Nielsen Station Index (NSI),** which did the same for local television markets.

Nielsen got a competitor in local TV ratings in 1949 when the American Research Bureau (later called Arbitron) began collecting ratings data. One of the problems with the Nielsen ratings was the lack of demographic data; the audimeter simply measured when the set was on and what channel it was tuned in to—it did not provide information about who, if anybody, was watching or listening. The Arbitron company solved this problem by using yet another data gathering technique—the **diary.** A sample of viewers was asked to record viewing in a specially prepared diary and to mail the finished diary back to Arbitron. In response, Nielsen introduced the diary as a supplement to its audimeters in 1955. Not to be outdone, Arbitron emulated Nielsen and introduced its own version of the audimeter in the 1960s.

A set-top box and a handheld keypad make up the Peoplemeter system.

Citing increased costs, Nielsen abandoned its radio ratings service in 1963 to concentrate on television. Shortly thereafter, Arbitron announced it would use its diary method to measure local market radio. From the mid-1960s to the 1980s, Nielsen alone provided network TV ratings and competed with Arbitron for local TV market ratings. Arbitron was the dominant company in radio ratings.

The mechanical measurement devices continued to be improved. Nielsen introduced the **storage instantaneous audimeter (SIA)** in several local markets during the 1960s and 1970s. This device sent information directly from the audimeter through phone lines to Nielsen's computers. The SIA made it possible to publish ratings the day after a program was broadcast.

Yet another mechanical device for measuring the audience was introduced in the late 1980s—the **Peoplemeter.** Developed by an English company, AGB Television Research, in an attempt to compete with Nielsen, the Peoplemeter was connected to the TV set and automatically recorded the channel and time. But it also had a new feature—a device that resembled a remote control with a numbered keypad. Each family member was assigned a unique code number. When he or she started watching TV, the family member was supposed to punch in his or her number on the keypad and then punch it again when

they stopped watching. This information was stored in the Peoplemeter and then transmitted via phone lines to central computers that had detailed demographic information about each family member obtained through a personal interview when the meter was installed. Thus, the Peoplemeter could determine exactly who was in the audience. Nielsen quickly introduced its own version of the Peoplemeter for use with its national NTI report. AGB was unable to secure enough clients for its new service and ceased operation in 1988.

Peoplemeters have several advantages over diaries. First, they aren't affected by memory. Many people forget to fill out their diaries. Second, the data are sent electronically to Nielsen, eliminating the problem of people who don't mail back their diaries. Moreover, unlike SIAs, which measure only set usage, the Peoplemeters report data about who is watching.

On the downside, Peoplemeters are relatively expensive to install and maintain. This means that changing homes in the sample is difficult. Second, children's viewing is hard to measure with the Peoplemeter. When the switch from SIAs to Peoplemeters took place, a 22 percent drop in children's viewing was reported. Children aged 2 to 11 are apparently inconsistent in logging in with the Peoplemeter and get bored with punching the buttons as

Peoplemeters have been around for many years in television but have yet to be used for measuring radio listening. For the last 35 years, Arbitron has been using the traditional method of pencil-and-paper diaries that their respondents carry around with them. This situation may change in the future, however, as Arbitron began testing a new personal portable meter (PPM) in early 1999.

The new PPM is about the same size as a pager. Respondents are asked to carry the device with them and push buttons that record when they listen. Inaudible codes carried in a radio's signal are recognized by the PPM and stored in its memory. Each night, respondents place the PPM in a special "docking station," which transmits the data to Arbitron's central computer for processing.

The first field test for the PPM will be done in Manchester in the United Kingdom. This area was chosen because it is served by a relatively few radio stations, making it easier to program the device. If the test is successful, the PPM might make it to the United States before 2003.

they watch TV. Finally, like the SIAs, Peoplemeters only measure at-home viewing. TV watching at work, in a bar, or in a college dormitory is not accounted for with the Peoplemeter.

Arbitron, Nielsen's chief rival in providing local market TV ratings, also introduced its own version of the Peoplemeter. The recession of the early 1990s, however, forced many local TV stations, which had previously subscribed to both Nielsen and Arbitron, to cancel one of their contracts in order to save money. The one they canceled was usually Arbitron, and in 1993 the company announced it was abandoning television ratings to concentrate on radio.

As of the late 1990s, the situation was as follows: Nielsen had no serious competitor in the television ratings business. In radio, Arbitron dominated local market radio ratings, although AccuRatings, started in 1992, provided some competition in about 50 markets.

The situation in TV, however, may change in the near future. Dissatisfied with Nielsen because of the high price of its reports and perceived shortcomings in the way it collects data, the broadcast TV networks and several advertising agencies funded the development of SMART (Systems for Measuring And Reporting Television) to compete with the national Nielsen ratings. The new SMART technology employs a Peoplemeter that is easier to use and easier to install. In addition, SMART promised that its regular reports and its custom analyses of data will be priced more cheaply than the Nielsen products. As of 1999, SMART was still searching for financing and its ultimate fate was still unclear.

THE RATINGS PROCESS
Measuring TV Viewing

Nielsen Media Research draws two different types of samples to measure TV viewing. The national sample used for the NTI is designed to be representative of the entire United States population. To draw this sample, Neilsen first selects at random more than 6,000 small geographic areas, usually blocks in urban areas or their equivalent in rural areas, and lists all households in these areas. Next, a sample of 5,000 households is drawn at random from the cluster of households in each area. Each household is then contacted, and, if it agrees to participate in the survey, a Nielsen representative installs a Peoplemeter and trains household members how to use it.

For the local market NSI reports, Nielsen first divides the country into more than 200 markets. Within each market, a sample is drawn from phone books and supplemented by random digit dialing in order to obtain unlisted numbers. Sample sizes vary by market but are usually in the range of 1,000 to 2,000 households. Nielsen measures local station TV viewing using two different techniques. In 44 of the largest markets, SIAs are attached to each television in the household and viewing data are gathered about "set tuning" behavior. This information is supplemented with demographic data collected by means of a diary that is sent to participating households. Each member of the household is supposed to record what program he or she is watching and send the diary back to Nielsen at the end of a week. Four times a year (February, May, July, and November), diary measurement is used to collect information from all 210 television markets in the United States. These measurement periods are called "sweeps," and the information from the diaries is used by local stations to determine advertising rates.

Processing the Data

Data from the Peoplemeter and the SIA samples are stored in the home devices until they are automatically retrieved by Nielsen's computers. In addition, program schedules and local system cable information are also checked to make sure the viewing data match up with the correct programs. All of this information is processed overnight and made available for customer access the next day. Diary information takes longer to process. The diaries are first mailed back to Nielsen where they are checked for legibility and consistency. The data are then entered into Nielsen computers and tabulated. It usually takes several weeks before these reports are available.

The Ratings Books

The NTI contains data on the estimated audience—divided into relevant demographic categories—for each network program broadcast during the measurement period. The report also features a day-by-day comparison of the audience for each of the major networks as well as an estimate of audience watching cable channels, independent broadcast stations, public TV, and premium channels.

The NSI is a little more complicated. Each local market ratings book contains a map that divides the market into three areas: (1) the metro area, where most of the population in the market lives; (2) the designated market area (DMA), where the stations in that market get most of their viewers; and (3) the NSI area, that portion of the market that surrounds the DMA and accounts for 95 percent of the total viewing audience in that market. NSI areas may overlap but DMAs do not.

The next section of the NSI contains special information, including the number of homes actually in the sample and demographic characteristics of the market. There are also notes about technical problems the stations may have had during the ratings period, such as being knocked off the air by a thunderstorm or power failure.

Audience estimates appear next. These numbers are broken down by time periods and by programs.

Thus, a station manager can see how a specific program is doing against its competition and how well it maintains the audience from the program that preceded it.

Nielsen also prepares several specialized reports: The Nielsen Homevideo Index provides measurement of cable viewing, pay cable, VCRs, satellite channels, and other video services; the Nielsen Syndication Service reports viewing levels of syndicated programs; and the Nielsen Sports Marketing Service tracks the viewing of particular sports teams. Nielsen also offers a special service that measures the Hispanic television audience.

Terms and Concepts in TV Ratings

There are three important terms in TV ratings. **Households using television (HUT)** represents the number or the percentage of households that have a TV set on during a specific time period.

The second term is **rating.** Specifically, a rating is the percentage or proportion of all households with a TV set watching a particular program at a particular time. A rating of 10 means that 10 percent of all the homes in the market were watching a specific program. Ratings consider all households in the market, not just those with TV sets in use.

The third term is *share of the audience* or **share.** The share is the total number of households watching a particular program at a specific time divided by the total number of households using TV. Thus, the share is based only on those households that actually have their TV sets turned on.

Some programs can have the same share but have different ratings. For example, let's pretend there are 1,000 households in our market. At 6 A.M., 100 of those 1,000 households have their TV sets on. Of those 100 households, 20 are watching "The Sunrise Home Shopping Show." The rating for this program would be 20 divided by 1,000, or 2 percent. The share would be 20 divided by 100, or 20 percent. Later that night, let's say at 9 P.M., 600 households are watching TV, and of those 600, 120 are watching "Frasier." The rating for "Frasier" would be 120 divided by 1,000, or 12 percent. The show's share of the audience would be 120 divided by 600, or 20 percent, exactly the same as that of "The Sunrise Home Shopping Show."

Here are the formulas for calculating ratings and shares:

$$\text{Ratings} = \frac{\text{Number of households watching a program}}{\text{Total number of households in market}}$$

$$\text{Share} = \frac{\text{Number of households watching a program}}{\text{Total number of HUT}}$$

For another calculation example, see the box "Calculating Ratings and Shares."

Measuring Radio Listening

The audience for programs on national radio networks is measured by **Radio's All-Dimension Audience Research (RADAR),** which conducts surveys of about 12,000 listeners using the telephone recall technique.

Arbitron is the leading company that provides ratings of local radio stations. Arbitron uses the diary method, and many of its procedures are similar to those used by Nielsen Media Research to measure TV viewing.

Arbitron draws its sample by randomly sampling phone numbers from a list compiled by a market research company. Numbers are also randomly generated to account for unlisted phones. The number of households drawn for the sample varies based on a statistical formula that takes into account the total number of households in the market. Sample sizes may range from 750 to 4,500 for local market surveys, with medium-sized markets having a sample size of about 1,000 diaries.

Those households that are selected by Arbitron are called and asked if they would like to participate in the survey. Arbitron mails a brightly colored package to each household that agrees. Inside the package are envelopes (for each member of the household over 11 years of age) that contain a diary, instructions, a letter of thanks, and about a dollar or so.

Diaries cover a one-week period beginning on a Wednesday. There is one page per day with a column for indicating when a person started listening to a station and when the person stopped. Another column asks the person to write down the frequency or call letters of the station while another records where the listening took place (in a car, at the office, at home, etc.).

Some simple demographic questions are included at the end of the diary. When the diary is completed, the respondent mails it back to Arbitron, where the next phase begins.

This home page contains useful information on how Arbitron conducts their radio surveys.

Processing the Data

Once received by Arbitron, the diaries are subject to several review procedures. The first review removes diaries that Arbitron considers unusable: those that come in late, those that are illegible, those missing demographic information, and so forth. Other reviews look for inconsistent information (e.g., reporting listening to a station that doesn't exist) and other minor errors (e.g., transposing the call letters of a station). The data are then entered into the computer for analysis.

The Radio Ratings Book

A local market radio ratings report is similar in format to its TV counterpart. The first page contains a map that divides the market into metro, DMA, and total survey areas, much like the NSI. This is followed by general market statistics—number of automobiles, housing values, retail sales data, and the like. Another section reports whether any radio stations conducted unusual promotions designed to artificially increase their audiences during the ratings period. The next section of the book presents demographic data about listeners categorized by dayparts. A station, for example, can easily find its rating among men 12 to 24 during the Monday to Friday 6 A.M. to 10 A.M. daypart. Other sections of the book summarize total time spent listening to the station, where the listening occurred, and the average audience size per station by quarter-hour estimates.

Events: Calculating Ratings and Shares

Let's use the following hypothetical data in our calculations. A ratings company samples 24,000 households (all having TVs) in a given market and determines the following for the 7:30 to 7:45 time period.

Station	Number of Sample Households Watching
WAAA	4,800
WBBB	2,400
WCCC	1,200
Other stations	1,200
	9,600 = HUT

Let's figure out WBBB's rating:

$$\text{WBBB's rating} = \frac{2,400}{24,000} = .10 \text{ or } 10\%$$

To calculate WBBB's share of the audience, we must first determine the total number of households using TV (HUT) during the 7:30 to 7:45 time period. To do this, we add $4,800 + 2,400 + 1,200 + 1,200 = 9,600$. WBBB's share, then, is

$$\text{Share} = \frac{2,400}{9,600} = .25 \text{ or } 25\%$$

Also note the following relationships:

(1) $\%\text{ HUT} = \dfrac{\text{rating}}{\text{share}}$

In our example

$$\%\text{ HUT} = \frac{.10}{.25} = .40 \text{ or } 40\%$$

This means that 40 percent of all the TV homes in the sample were watching TV from 7:30 to 7:45.

(2) $\text{Rating} = \text{share} \times \%\text{ HUT}$

In our example

$$\text{Rating} = .25 \times .40 = .10$$

This is simply another way to calculate the rating.

(3) $\text{Share} = \dfrac{\text{rating}}{\%\text{ HUT}}$

In our example

$$\text{Share} = \frac{.10}{.40} = .25 \text{ or } 25\%$$

This is another way to calculate the share.

Arbitron issues its *Radio Market Reports* for more than 200 local markets. Ratings reports are issued four times a year for larger markets. Smaller markets are measured less frequently.

Terms and Concepts in Radio Ratings

The basic unit of measurement is different for radio and television ratings. The basic unit for most television ratings is the household. For radio, the basic unit is the person. The formulas for ratings and shares for radio listening reflect this difference. Specifically, in radio

$$\text{Ratings} = \frac{\text{Number of persons listening to a station}}{\text{Total number of persons in market}},$$

and

$$\text{Share} = \frac{\text{Number of persons listening to a station}}{\text{Total number of persons using radio}}.$$

There are two other ratings terms that are more commonly associated with radio ratings. The cumulative audience (or **cume**) is an estimate of the total number of different listeners who listen to a given station at least once during the time part under consideration. In other words, cume is a measure of how many different people listen at least once during the week during the given day part.

Average quarter-hour persons estimates the average number of persons who are listening to a station within a 15-minute period. It is calculated by dividing the estimated number of listeners in a given time period by the number of quarter hours (four per hour) in that time period.

ACCURACY OF THE RATINGS

There are more than 99 million television households in the United States. The Nielsen Peoplemeter sample size is only 5,000, about 0.005 percent of the total. Is it possible for a sample this small to mirror accurately the viewing behaviors of the entire population? The answer to this question is yes, within limits. A sample doesn't have to be large to represent the whole population, as long as it is *representative* of the whole population. To illustrate, when you go to the doctor for a blood test, the doctor does not draw a couple of quarts of blood from your body. A blood test uses only a few milliliters. From this small sample, the doctor can estimate your red cell count, your cholesterol, your hematocrit and a number of other variables.

Imagine a huge container filled with thousands of coins—pennies, nickels, dimes, and quarters. Let's suppose that 50 percent of the coins are pennies but that this fact is unknown to you. The only way you could be absolutely *sure* what percentage of the coins were pennies would be to count every coin in the huge container, an arduous and time-consuming job. Suppose instead you took a random sample of 100 coins. If sampling were a perfect process, you would find that pennies accounted for 50 percent of your sample. Sometimes this happens, but more often you'll wind up with a little more or a little less than 50 percent pennies. It is also possible, but exceedingly unlikely, that you could draw a sample of 100 percent pennies or another of 0 percent pennies. The bigger the size of your sample, the more likely it is that your results will tend to cluster around the 50 percent mark.

Statisticians have studied the process of sampling and have calculated the accuracy ranges of samples of various sizes. One way of expressing accuracy is to use a concept known as the 95 percent **confidence interval**. This is an interval calculated from sample data that has a 95 percent chance of actually including the population value. For example, let's say the Nielsen Peoplemeter sample of 5,000 homes finds that 20 percent of households watched "Buffy the Vampire Slayer." Similar to our coin example, we probably wouldn't expect that exactly 20 percent of the 99 million TV households in the United States were also watching. By using statistical formulas, however, we can estimate the 95 percent confidence interval, which in this case, ranges from 18.9 percent to 21.1 percent. This means that we are 95 percent sure that, in the entire population of 99 million homes, somewhere between 18.9 percent and 21.1 percent are watching "Buffy."

To sum up this statistical discussion, Nielsen ratings are not exact estimates. They are subject to sampling error. However, when their margin of error is taken into account, Nielsen ratings (and other ratings based on a random sample) provide rather accurate estimations of audience viewing behavior.

Incidentally, there is an organization that strives to ensure reasonable accuracy in the realm of ratings: the **Media Ratings Council (MRC).** This council periodically audits Nielsen, Arbitron, and other ratings services to check on their methods and reports. The MRC is an independent body whose fees are paid by the ratings companies.

It should also be noted here that factors other than sampling error also have an impact on accuracy. Note that the above discussion was based on the assumption that the ratings were drawn from a random sample of the population. Although both Nielsen and Arbitron go to great lengths to gather data from a truly random sample, that goal is seldom attained: When contacted, many households in the original sample may refuse to cooperate; individuals in the Peoplemeter sample may get tired of pressing buttons and stop using it; people in the sample who agree to fill out a diary may get bored after a day or so and not return it; other diaries may be filled out illegibly; and Peoplemeters and SIAs are subject to mechanical errors. All of these factors contribute to a **nonresponse bias.** Nonresponse is a more serious concern for diary samples. In many markets, Arbitron may be able to use 50 percent or less of all the radio diaries it sends out.

Additionally, some people may not tell the truth. During a telephone coincidental survey, one of the authors heard the audio from the TV set in the background that was tuned to a wrestling match. When asked what program he was watching, the respondent replied, "the local newscast." Individuals with SIAs might tune their sets to PBS whenever they leave the house. Diary keepers might fill in many educational programs that they did not watch. These are examples of the **social desirability bias,** or providing answers that the respondent thinks will make him or her look more refined or more educated.

Both of these factors reinforce the fact that ratings are estimates of viewing and listening behavior. They are not exact. Nonetheless, they are the best available means for the industry to determine who is watching or listening to what or which programs.

USES FOR RATINGS

Local stations and networks use the ratings to see how they are doing in terms of their total audience. Typically, the bigger the audience, the more money stations and networks can charge for advertising. This is why "ER," which has a weekly audience of about 21 million households, can charge $565,000 for a 30-second commercial while "Working," with a weekly audience of 6 to 7 million homes, charges only $165,000.

In addition, ratings can be used to determine what types of people are watching. Advertisers are interested not only in audience size but also in audience type. A show like "Ally McBeal," for example, can charge higher rates, not because its total audience is particularly large, but because it attracts 18- to 49-year olds—an audience that many advertisers want to reach.

The sales staff at a station uses ratings to persuade potential advertisers that their stations attract the type of audience most likely to buy the advertiser's product. The salespeople at a radio station with a sports-talk format, for example, can show the owner of a cigar bar that an ad on their station would reach a predominantly male audience, a prime target for a cigar merchant.

The station's news department can use the ratings to see how much viewing occurs in neighboring communities. If the ratings show substantial viewing, the station might want to increase coverage of those areas to encourage continued viewing and better ratings.

These are just a few of the uses for ratings data. Keep in mind, however, that while the ratings are a handy tool, they are only one of several considerations that are used by broadcasters and cablecasters to make decisions. They are helpful, but as we have seen, they are not perfect.

MEASURING THE INTERNET AUDIENCE

Reliable data on the Internet audience is important because without such data advertisers are reluctant to spend money on net advertising. As in broadcasting and cable, advertisers want to know who is visiting a World Wide Web site, how often they visit, how long they spend at the site, and whether the cost is reasonable. Obtaining such data, however, is difficult. Despite their limits, the Arbitron and Nielsen audience data are generally accepted as industry standards. An industry standard for Internet audience measurement has yet to be developed.

Early attempts to measure Web page traffic were programs that measured "hits," or the number of times someone logged onto the page. A counter at the bottom of the page kept a running total of the number of visits. These numbers were notoriously unreliable since the programs measured hits in different ways depending on the server. Moreover, there were other programs that called Web sites over and over to inflate the number of hits. Advertisers preferred an independent organization that count the numbers.

From 1996 to 1997, several companies began to offer Internet measurement services. One of the first

Issues: Top-Rated Cable Programs

What are the highest rated shows on cable channels? Nielsen Media Research reported the following for the week of November 30, 1998. Perhaps you can see a pattern. (If you can't, check the box on page 182.)

Rank	Net	Program
1	ESPN	NFL Football
2	USA	World Wrestling Federation Wrestling (Tues.)
3	USA	World Wrestling Federation Wrestling (Wed.)
4	TNT	World Championship Wrestling Monday Nitro
5	Nickelodeon	Rugrats (Mon.)
6	ESPN	NFL Prime Time
7	Nickelodeon	Rugrats (Wed.)
8	USA	World Wrestling Federation Wrestling (Fri.)
9	Nickelodeon	Rugrats (Thurs.)
10	TBS	World Championship Wrestling Thunder

was Internet Profiles Corporation or I/PRO. I/PRO was a "site-centric" service that monitored the Web sites themselves and counted total hits, time spent reading each page, and limited demographic data about the visitors. In contrast, a competitor, Media Metrix (formerly PC Meter) used a "consumer-centric" approach. Media Metrix recruited a random sample of 30,000 users and mailed each participant software that ran in the background whenever the participant used the computer. Each month respondents sent back a disk that contained a record of usage of online services such as America Online, visits to Web sites, demographic information about the users, and a list of all software programs used by the respondent. Media Metrix used this data to construct a list of the top 25 most visited sites.

Another competitor, RelevantKnowledge, also used a consumer-centric approach. Using a panel of 11,000 users recruited through a random sample of phone numbers, RelevantKnowledge gathered data directly over the Internet using software that panel members downloaded from its Web site. Using the Internet allowed the company to provide overnight ratings on Web sites to its clients. Like Media Metrix, RelevantKnowledge also collected detailed information about its panelists.

Yet another company, NetRatings, used a panel of 10,000 recruited from the Web. NetRatings measured only net activity and collected detailed lifestyle profiles of all of its respondents. NetRatings also offered data about the number of people who were exposed to banner advertising. In late 1998, these four companies were joined by another formidable competitor, the A. C. Nielsen Company. Nielsen's service, NielsenNet, used a sample of about 10,000 recruited through random digit dialing. In addition to the usual data reports, Nielsen measures net usage on noncomputer devices, such as WebTV.

By early 1999, consolidation had reshaped the Internet measurement business. Media Metrix merged with RelevantKnowledge to create Media Metrix, Inc. The new firm offered monthly, weekly, and overnight reporting of results based on a sample of 40,000 people. About 250 companies, including Microsoft, IBM, and Netscape, were clients of the new company. In addition, NielsenNet announced plans to become a partner with NetRatings to create a measurement service with an initial sample of 6,000 respondents.

Two problems make it difficult to gather accurate Web data. First, much Web surfing is done at work. Server logs at sites such as CNN and ESPN show that most of their usage comes during the daytime.

Many businesses, however, have not allowed ratings companies to install tracking software on office computers because they fear the software might also be used to access confidential memos or sales data. Media Metrix is the only company that maintains a separate sample of about 1,000 business users, but most analysts think this is too small for reliable results. Other ratings companies try to compensate for this problem statistically. All research firms probably underreport office usage data, which severely hampers those sites aimed primarily at business users.

Second, since there are so many Web sites, it is necessary to draw huge samples to get reliable data on some of the lesser-used sites. It would be difficult, for example, to generate a reliable demographic portrait of the visitors to a certain site if only four or five people visited it during a month. Current sample sizes are adequate for only the most visited pages. Ad agencies would prefer a minimum sample size of about 12,000.

The next few years should determine which company or companies become the industry standard.

BEYOND RATINGS: OTHER AUDIENCE RESEARCH

Although audience ratings serve as the primary source of feedback for the electronic media industry, owners and managers often need additional information about who is listening and watching. This examines two broad categories of audience research that are used to supplement ratings data.

Music Research

Most radio stations play music. All stations want to play the right mix of music so that they will attract as large an audience as possible. They want to avoid playing new songs that their listeners dislike and to avoid playing popular songs so many times that listeners get tired of them (a phenomenon called **burnout**). Broadcasters use two methods to test music: call-outs and auditorium testing.

Call-outs **Call-out research** refers to a process whereby listeners are surveyed by telephone and asked to rate certain songs. About twenty **hooks**— 5- to 10-second cuts of the most memorable parts of the songs—are played, and the listener is asked to rate each song on several rating scales. One scale measures whether the listener likes the song, while another measures whether the song has reached the burnout stage. Programmers at the station can use the results of the survey to determine those songs that their audience wants to hear as well as those that have peaked in popularity.

The biggest disadvantage of the call-out method is that it can't be used to test new or unfamiliar music. Since it depends on familiar hooks, program directors and music directors must rely upon other techniques when evaluating new releases. One possible method is auditorium testing.

Auditorium Testing **Auditorium testing** consists of gathering a sample of 75–100 people in an auditorium or similar facility for about 60 to 90 minutes to evaluate musical selections—both new and familiar. Auditorium testing has two advantages over call-out research: It can test new songs, and it can test a much larger number of hooks. An auditorium test designed to rate familiar songs can test more than 300 hooks at a single session. Additionally, entire songs can be played so that the audience can rate music they have never heard before. Radio stations that are considering a format change use auditorium testing to examine reactions to the new format. Instead of a series of hooks, audience members hear longer portions of the proposed format, including music, promotional announcements, and DJ patter.

Market Research

Market research covers a variety of techniques used by broadcasting and cable programmers to gain more knowledge about their audiences and their audiences' reactions to programs and personalities.

Production Research Before spending huge sums of money to develop a new program or a TV commercial, networks, studios, and ad agencies may want to examine some early responses. **Concept testing** is used by production companies to gauge audience reactions to possible new program ideas. Audience members are given a one- or two-paragraph description of the concept behind a particular show and asked if they would watch it.

Commercials are sometimes tested with a **rough cut,** a simply produced version of the ad using minimal sets, little editing, amateur actors, and no special effects. These rough cuts are used to get a general sense about the direction and the approach of the

Videotaping a focus group session. The moderator is leading a discussion about a commercial that the group has just watched.

planned ad. Researchers realize that some low ratings of the rough cut are due to its unfinished nature.

New ads and programs may be tested using **continuous ratings.** Each seat in a special auditorium is equipped with a dial or a series of buttons that enable a viewer to rate continuously what he or she sees on a screen. One button may be marked "like a lot," while another might be marked "like a little," all the way down to a button marked "don't like at all." The responses are sent directly to a computer that keeps track of the average responses. Thus an advertiser might determine that the first 15 seconds of the commercial were well liked but the rest of the ad rated poorly.

A more realistic method for analyzing viewer reactions to a program is **cable testing.** A research company recruits a sample of 500 to 600 viewers from a typical market. The members of the sample are asked to watch the new program on a cable channel that is not assigned to a broadcast or a cable network. After the show, a survey is conducted among sample members to see what viewers liked or disliked about the program and to ascertain whether they would watch the program if it were regularly scheduled.

Focus groups provide more-detailed information about how people think and feel about an ad or a program. A **focus group** is a group of 6 to 12 people and a moderator who have a focused discussion about a topic. The members of the group are screened to ensure that they are appropriate for the research. For example, a radio station conducting a focus group to find out what listeners thought of its music programming would be careful to include only regular listeners in the group. Members are generally paid between $25 and $50 to participate.

The moderator usually has a prepared list of topics for the group to discuss. It is also the moderator's job to elicit responses from everybody in the group and to make sure the group stays on the topic.

Researchers recommend that more than one focus group be conducted for a particular topic. The results from a single group might be unique or idiosyncratic and lead to wrong decisions. The total number of groups used to investigate a topic depends upon how much the sponsoring organization can afford to pay, but the typical number of groups used is between four and six per topic.

Focus groups are best thought of as a diagnostic device. Their responses can reveal the reasons behind certain attitudes or behaviors. Since focus groups comprise small, nonrandom samples, it is dangerous to generalize their results to the total population.

Audience Segmentation Research Radio and television ratings books provide information on the different demographic segments of the audience. Programmers are able to determine whether particular programs do better among males or females and whether a show has a predominantly young or old audience. Demographic breakdowns, however, may not tell the whole story. The listening, viewing, and buying habits of a 20-year-old female living on a farm in Manhattan, Kansas, may be totally different from those of a 20-year-old female living in an apartment in Manhattan, New York City. Accordingly, many market researchers suggest classifying audience members along other dimensions.

Psychographic research segments the audience according to various personality traits. Audience members report their viewing and listening behavior and then rate their personalities on a number of different scales: independent–dependent; active–passive; leader–follower; relaxed–tense, romantic–practical, and so forth. The results can be used by program producers and advertisers. For example, if the audience for "20/20" scores high on the practical dimension, commercials that emphasize such themes as "saving money" or "seldom needs repair" might be emphasized.

Lifestyle surveys are similar to psychographic research but put more importance on values that may influence consumer behavior. There are many measurement scales used to segment audiences based on their lifestyles but the most well-known is VALS II—values and lifestyle segmentation—developed at the Stanford Research Institute. The test divides people into eight groups, including "Strugglers," "Strivers," "Achievers," and "Actualizers." Advertisers use the VALS II results to develop campaigns that are consistent with the values and orientations of their target audiences.

SUMMARY

- Audience estimates, expressed as ratings, are an important tool for broadcasters, cablecasters, Web site operators, and advertisers. Audience reports published by different ratings companies aid decision making in the industry.

- Early ratings companies, such as the Cooperative Analysis of Broadcasting and the C. E. Hooper Company used telephone surveys to measure radio listening. The A. C. Nielsen Company used a mechanical device attached to a radio or TV set to generate its estimates of the audience.

- Currently, the Arbitron Company uses diaries to measure radio listening, while the Nielsen Company uses a handheld device, called a Peoplemeter, along with set-top meters and diaries to measure TV viewing. Several companies use different techniques to measure Web site traffic.

- Ratings companies calculate ratings, share of the audience, households using TV, people using radio, and cumulative audience figures and publish their results online and in ratings books. The reports contain maps, demographic information, daypart results, and reports concerning specific programs. This information is used by networks, syndication companies, local stations, and advertisers.

- In addition to ratings research, radio stations use call-out research and auditorium testing to fine-tune their play lists.

- Broadcasters and cablecasters also use market research to pretest programs and commercials. Focus groups are conducted to investigate why certain programs and commercials are popular and others aren't.

- Finally, lifestyle research and psychographic research focus on personality traits and values in an effort to understand the audience further.

KEY TERMS

SUGGESTIONS FOR FURTHER READING

Beville, H. M. (1988). *Audience ratings* (2nd ed.). Hillsdale, NJ: Erlbaum Associates.

Chappell, M. N., & Hooper, C. E. (1944). *Radio audience measurement*. New York: Stephen Daye.

Fletcher, J. (1981). *Handbook of radio and TV broadcasting*. New York: Van Nostrand, Rinehold.

Lindlof, T. (1987). *Natural audiences: Qualitative research of media uses and effects*. Norwood, NJ: Ablex.

Marshall, C., & Rossman, G. (1989). *Designing qualitative research*. New York: Sage.

Nichols, J. E. (1990). *By the numbers: Using demographics and psychographics for business growth in the '90s*. Chicago: Basic Books.

Stewart, D. W., & Shamdasani, P. N. (1990). *Focus groups: Theory and practice*. Newbury Park, CA: Sage.

Webster, J. G., & Lichty, L. (1991). *Ratings analysis*. Hillsdale, NJ: Erlbaum Associates.

Wimmer, R., & Dominick, J. (1999). *Mass media research: An introduction* (6th ed.). Belmont, CA: Wadsworth.

INTERNET EXERCISES

1. Visit our Web site at http://www.mhhe.com/beyond for study-guide exercises to help you learn and apply material in each chapter. You will find ideas for future research as well as useful Web links to provide you with an opportunity to journey through the new electronic media.

Effects 13

Quick Facts

 Percentage of 1998 prime-time broadcast TV programs containing violence: 67

 Percentage of premium cable networks' (HBO, Showtime, etc.) 1998 prime-time programs containing violence: 87

 Percentage of Americans who get most of their information about political candidates from TV news: 57

 Average length of sound bite for political candidates on TV news: 9.7 seconds

 Most researched television program in history: "Sesame Street"

Do TV and radio have an impact on our lives? Ask yourself the following questions:

1. What rights does a person have when arrested?

2. While on a date, have you ever used a line or clever remark that you heard on TV?

3. When you're preparing for an important occasion, do you worry about dandruff, acne, perspiration, bad breath, ring around the collar, yellow teeth?

4. Did you ever consciously dress like a character you saw on TV?

5. How many cops are like the cops on "NYPD Blue"?

6. Do you vote differently because of televised ads for political candidates?

The answers to these questions will tell you how much of an impact TV and radio have had on your personal life.

Now consider the global scale. What impact have the broadcast media had on society? This question is a little more difficult to answer. Nonetheless, it's an important topic. Radio and TV have been, at various times, the alleged culprits behind a host of social ills. Television, it was claimed, made us more violent and antisocial, hurt our reading skills, decreased our SAT scores, fostered sexual stereotypes, and more. From a pragmatic standpoint society needs to know if, in fact, these allegations are valid, and if so, how to correct them. Consequently, this chapter briefly examines how we go about studying the impact of radio and TV, the changing views concerning media effects over the past 70 years or so, and the most current research about the effects of broadcasting in specific areas.

STUDYING THE EFFECTS OF THE ELECTRONIC MEDIA

There are many ways to examine the social consequences of the electronic media. Some scientists employ qualitative methods, in which they make direct observations and in-depth analyses of mass communication behaviors in natural settings. Other scholars use the critical or cultural studies technique that has been long popular in the humanities to provide a more interpretive look at the process of mass communication. Both the qualitative and critical/cultural studies approaches suggest new and different ways

of explaining and understanding the nature of the impact of electronic media. This chapter, however, focuses more on the traditional and pragmatic social science approach to mass media effects; it emphasizes those research questions that have implications for social policy.

In electronic media research, several techniques are used to gather data about audience effects. These techniques are wide-ranging, partly because historically the effects of mass communication have been studied by psychologists, social scientists, political scientists, and others. Not surprisingly, each discipline has relied on the technique most closely associated with it. Thus psychologists use the experimental method whereas sociologists use surveys. There are, however, many variations on experimental and survey research. In general, it's possible to say that there are three main social scientific methods:

1. Experimental methods, which can take place either in controlled "laboratory" conditions or in more natural "field" conditions.

2. Survey methods, which can either sample the subjects one time only or continue over time.

3. Content analysis, which is a systematic method for analyzing and classifying communication content.

Each of these three methods has its own built-in pros and cons. Knowing the advantages and disadvantages of these various techniques is important because they have an impact on the degree of confidence that we have in research results.

Laboratory experiments are done under tightly controlled conditions and allow researchers to focus on the effects of one or more factors that may have an impact on the audience. Usually at least two groups are involved; one group gets treated one way while the other is treated differently. The big advantage of lab experiments over other methods is that they allow researchers to make statements about cause and effect. In an experiment subjects are randomly assigned to experimental conditions and the researcher has control over most external factors that might bias the results, thus making the claim of cause and effect stronger. Their big disadvantage is that they are done under artificial conditions and behavior that occurs in the lab might not occur in real life.

Field experiments occur outside the lab. Sometimes a natural event occurs that creates the conditions necessary for an experiment, and sometimes

field experiments can be set up by the researcher. To illustrate, suppose one program is fed to one-half the homes on a special cable system while the remainder sees a different program. The effects of this single program could then be examined. The advantage of field experiments is naturalness; people are studied in their typical environments. The big disadvantage is the lack of control. Unlike the lab, field experiments are subject to the contaminating influences of outside events.

Surveys generally consist of a person's answers to a set of predetermined questions. Surveys are done through the mail, over the phone, or in person and usually involve some kind of questionnaire or other written document. The big advantage of survey research is its realistic approach. People in natural settings are asked questions about their typical behaviors. A big disadvantage with surveys is the fact that they can't establish cause and effect. After a survey a researcher can say only that factor *A* and factor *B* are related; that researcher cannot say that *A* causes *B* or that *B* causes *A*. A survey only establishes a relationship. Another disadvantage is that surveys rely on self-reports. It can only be assumed that respondents give valid and truthful responses.

Surveys can be done one time or they can be **longitudinal** (repeated over time). A **trend study** is one in which the same question or questions are asked of different people at different times. An example of a trend study would be a poll done six months before an election that asks which presidential candidate people intend to vote for and is then repeated with a different group of people a week before the election.

Panel studies are a special type of longitudinal survey in which the same people are studied at different points in time. The advantage in a panel study is that some evidence of cause and effect can be established, usually through sophisticated statistical analysis. The disadvantages include the fact that panel studies take a long time to do and they suffer from attrition—respondents die, move away, or get bored and are no longer part of the study group.

Content analysis studies segments of TV and radio content in order to describe the messages presented by these media. Such studies have been useful in defining media stereotypes and establishing a gauge of the amount of violence in TV programming. The biggest problem with content analysis is that it cannot be used alone as a basis for making statements about the effects of media content. For example, just because a content analysis establishes

that Saturday morning cartoons are saturated with violence, it doesn't necessarily follow that children who watch these shows will behave violently. That might be the case, but it would take an audience study to substantiate that claim—a content analysis by itself would be insufficient.

THEORIES OF MEDIA EFFECTS

These methods have been used to study the impact of mass media since early in this century. Throughout that time our view about the power of media effects has undergone significant changes as social science learns more about the various factors that affect media impact. As we shall see, there were periods in history when the media (including broadcasting) were thought of as quite powerful and other times when they were thought to have little effect. The current thinking seems to represent a compromise between these two extreme positions. The rest of this section briefly reviews the various theories concerning the effects of mass media that have evolved over the years.

Hypodermic Needle Theory

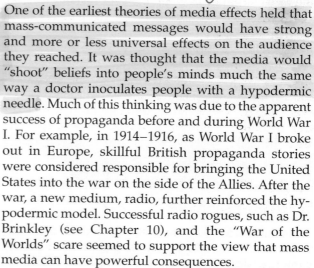

One of the earliest theories of media effects held that mass-communicated messages would have strong and more or less universal effects on the audience they reached. It was thought that the media would "shoot" beliefs into people's minds much the same way a doctor inoculates people with a hypodermic needle. Much of this thinking was due to the apparent success of propaganda before and during World War I. For example, in 1914–1916, as World War I broke out in Europe, skillful British propaganda stories were considered responsible for bringing the United States into the war on the side of the Allies. After the war, a new medium, radio, further reinforced the hypodermic model. Successful radio rogues, such as Dr. Brinkley (see Chapter 10), and the "War of the Worlds" scare seemed to support the view that mass media can have powerful consequences.

Reexaminations of the development of this model suggest that it was not so thoroughly accepted as once believed. In addition, some social scientists of this early period also argued that other factors should be considered when discussing the impact of the media. In any case, advances in experimental and survey research began to cast serious doubt on the hypodermic needle model. By the mid-1940s it was obvious that the model's assumptions about the way communication affects audiences were too simplistic. The pendulum was about to swing in the other direction.

Limited-Effects Theory

Persuasion, especially the political kind that goes on in election campaigns, was the main focus of this new line of research. Several studies indicated that the media did not have a direct effect on the audience, as was previously believed. The newly developed two-step flow theory suggested that media influence first passed through a group of people known as opinion leaders and then on to the rest of the audience. Further research posited that media influence was filtered through a net of intervening factors, such as a person's prior beliefs and knowledge and the influence of family, friends, and peer groups. The mass media were simply one of a great many determinants of how people think or behave.

This view brought some comfort to those who feared that the public might be brainwashed by skillful ideologues and clever propaganda techniques, since it suggested that they were unlikely to succeed. It also was appealing to mass media executives, who could use it to counter criticism that the media were the cause of various social ills.

The most complete statement of the limited-effects position (although he doesn't call it that) appears in a book by Joseph Klapper, *The Effects of Mass Communication*, published in 1960. Klapper reviewed the existing research and summed it up in a series of generalizations, the most widely quoted of which held that mass communication alone does not ordinarily cause audience effects but instead functions primarily to reinforce existing conditions.

Klapper's generalizations enjoyed popularity for nearly two decades; in fact, there are some who still subscribe to the limited-effects model even today. Nonetheless, keep in mind that the bulk of the studies reviewed by Klapper were done before TV became the dominant mass medium. In addition, although the most widely quoted of Klapper's conclusions concerned the reinforcement effect of the media, he also noted that there were occasions when the media could exert direct effects or when the mediating factors that generally produce reinforcement are absent or themselves help foster change. As TV became more prevalent and re-

searchers discovered more areas where media effects were direct, the limited-effects model gave way to a new formulation.

Specific-Effects Theory

The most recent theory of media effects represents a middle ground. Researchers realize that media are not all-powerful; they compete with or complement other sources of influence such as friends, family, and teachers. Nonetheless, there are circumstances under which specific types of media content might have a significant effect on certain members of the audience. Although this statement might not be entirely satisfying from a scientific standpoint, in the last few years communication researchers have made great progress in identifying how and when, and sometimes even why, mass media, especially broadcasting, affect individuals and groups. Accordingly, the answer to the question, "What are the effects of the mass media?" has become complex, as social scientists continue to define the circumstances, the topics, and the people for whom specific effects might occur.

The remainder of this chapter examines seven of the most investigated topics in recent broadcasting research: (1) the effect of violent TV programming on antisocial behavior, (2) perceptions of social reality, (3) sex-role stereotyping, (4) TV and politics, (5) TV and educational skills, (6) prosocial behavior, and (7) social impact of the Internet.

VIDEO VIOLENCE

It is appropriate that we first examine the media violence area. This subject is the most controversial, generates the most research, utilizes all of the four research techniques mentioned earlier, illustrates some of the problems in generalizing from research data, and is the one topic about which communication researchers know the most.

History

Concern about the impact of electronic media violence first surfaced during the 1930s when parents worried that gangster movies would corrupt the morals of young people. When television became popular during the 1950s, video violence became an issue. Congressional hearings examined the topic

Much video violence occurs in animated series aimed at children.

and concluded that watching TV was an important factor in shaping the attitudes and characters of its younger audience.

The urban violence and general unrest that characterized the mid-1960s sparked a new burst of interest in the topic. A presidential commission, the National Commission on the Causes and Prevention of Violence, reviewed the existing research evidence and concluded that violent behavior as depicted on TV had a negative effect on the audience.

A few years later the United States Surgeon General's Office sponsored a research effort involving 50 separate studies that examined this same area. After some debate and further congressional hearings, most researchers who participated in the project agreed that their findings indicated a causal link, albeit a weak one, between watching TV violence and antisocial attitudes and behaviors. In 1982, 10 years after the release of the original Surgeon General's Report, an update reinforced the original conclusion that TV violence was a cause of aggressive behavior.

Many studies appearing since the update have changed their focus to "effect size." This approach gets away from the simple question of whether TV violence has an effect on the audience and considers instead the more complicated question of how big an effect it has. Several researchers have disagreed over the significance of some of the relatively weak effects that have been discovered.

The most recent reincarnation of this issue occurred with the passage of the Telecommunications Act of 1996. In response to public and congressional pressure, the act contained a provision mandating that new TV sets be equipped with a V-chip that would allow parents to block out violent content (and other forms of objectionable behavior) from their TV sets. (The V-chip is discussed in more detail in Chapter 11).

So much for the history of this topic. Next, we review specific research evidence, pointing out its strengths and weaknesses, and conclude with an attempt to summarize the research consensus in this area.

Research Evidence

Experiments were one of the first methods used to investigate the impact of media violence. A series of studies done in the early 1960s documented that children could easily learn and imitate violent actions that they witnessed on screen.

A second set of experiments from the early 1960s

Figure 13–1

Simplified Diagram for Catharsis versus Stimulation Experiment

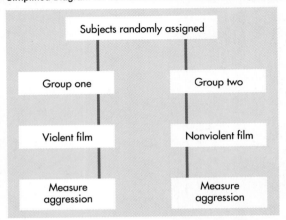

Figure 13–2

Survey Design Examining Effects of TV Violence

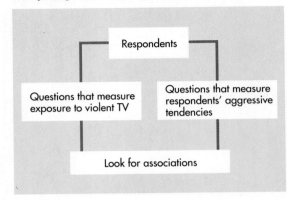

was designed to settle the debate touched off by two competing theories of media effects. On the one hand, the **catharsis theory** posited that watching scenes of media violence would actually reduce the aggressiveness of viewers since their hostile feelings would be purged while watching the media portrayals. Not surprisingly, this viewpoint was popular with many industry executives. On the other hand, the **stimulation theory** predicted that watching scenes of violence actually prompted audience members to behave more aggressively after viewing. The experimental design used to test these competing theories is presented in simplified form in Figure 13–1. The results of these and other experiments showed little support for catharsis. In fact, the bulk of the laboratory research argues for the stimulation effect. This is not to say that the catharsis hypothesis is categorically wrong. There may be some instances where it might occur. Most of the time, however, the likely end product is increased aggression.

These early experiments were criticized for their artificiality. They were done in the lab under controlled conditions and used violent segments that were not typical of what everybody saw on TV. Later experiments used more-realistic violent segments and more-relevant aggression measures. For example, several experiments used actual programs that contained about the average number of violent acts per hour in prime-time TV (about five or six). Additional experiments used more real-life measures of aggression. Several observed the actual interpersonal aggression of children in play groups or in classrooms. These and other more-natural measures

confirm that watching violence stimulates subsequent real-life aggression.

In sum, the results from laboratory experiments demonstrate that shortly after exposure to media violence, individuals, especially youngsters, are likely to show an increase in their own level of aggression. In fact, since the mid-1970s there has been a marked decrease in the number of lab experiments examining this topic partly because the results have been so consistent. More recent experiments have accepted the fact that exposure to violence facilitates subsequent aggression and have concentrated instead on factors that might increase or decrease the *amount* of aggression performed in response to media portrayals.

Laboratory studies are important because, as mentioned earlier, they help establish a plausible cause-and-effect pattern and control for the effects of extraneous factors. Still, the laboratory is not real life, and to be more sure of our conclusions we need to examine the results of research that is done outside the lab.

Surveys (also called correlational studies) are done in the real world. Although they offer little evidence of cause and effect, they do not have the artificiality of the lab associated with them. Most surveys on this topic incorporate the design of Figure 13–2. If the viewing of media violence is indeed associated with real-world aggression, then people who watch a lot of violent TV should also score high on scales that measure their own aggressive behavior or attitudes toward aggression. The results from a large number of surveys involving literally thousands of respondents across different regions, socioeconomic

Figure 13–3

Canadian Field Experiment Design

Community	Time one		Time two	
1	No TV	Measure aggression, media exposure, and related variables	One TV channel	Measure aggression, media exposure, and related variables
2	One TV channel		Two TV channels	
3	Four TV channels		Four TV channels	

statuses, and ethnic backgrounds have been remarkably consistent: There is a modest but consistent association between viewing violent TV programs and aggressive tendencies.

These results, however, are not without problems, like trying to establish cause and effect. Although viewing TV violence and aggression are related, TV viewing does not necessarily *cause* aggression. In fact, it's logically possible that aggressive individuals choose to watch more violent TV, which would mean that aggression could cause the viewing of violent TV. Finally, it's also possible that the relationship might be caused by some third factor. Maybe the real cause of aggression is a history of child abuse, and this in turn is associated with watching violent TV. Survey statistics would show a positive relationship between viewing violent TV and aggression, but the real cause might be something else.

Once again, to sum up, correlational studies provide another piece of the puzzle; they show that viewing TV violence and antisocial behavior are linked in the real world, but they don't tell us anything definitive about cause and effect. Remember, however, that lab studies can determine cause and effect and their results are consistent with the notion that TV viewing causes subsequent aggression. So far we have reason to be somewhat comfortable with that conclusion. But there is still other evidence to consider.

In the past 20 years or so, several field experiments were carried out to investigate the potential antisocial effects of TV violence. Recall that field experiments give us some basis for deciding cause and

effect but suffer from a lack of control of other, potentially contaminating factors.

The results from field experiments are somewhat inconsistent. At least two done in the early 1970s found no effect from viewing violent TV. One of these two, however, was plagued by procedural problems and its results should be accepted cautiously. On the other hand, at least five field experiments have yielded data consonant with the lab and survey findings. The main conclusion of these studies seems to be that individuals who watch a diet of violent programs tend to exhibit more antisocial or aggressive behavior. In some studies this effect was stronger than in others, but the direction was consistent.

Figure 13–3 shows the design used in one of these field experiments. In this case the experiment was based on natural circumstances. The researchers were able to identify a Canadian town that was surrounded by mountains and was unable to receive TV signals until 1974. This town was matched with two others, one that could receive only the Canadian Broadcasting Corporation (CBC) and another that could get the CBC plus the three U.S. networks. The towns were studied in 1973 and again two years later. Children in the town that had just gotten TV showed an increase in the rate of aggressive acts that was more than three times higher than those for children living in the other two towns.

On balance, the results from field experiments are not so striking as those using the lab and correlational methods. On the whole, though, they tend to support, although weakly in some cases, the notion that viewing violent TV fosters aggressive behavior.

Issues: Exposure to TV Violence and Psychological Trauma

The most recent large-scale survey to examine the impact of TV violence was published in the October 1998 issue of the *Journal of the American Academy of Child and Adolescent Psychiatry.* Led by researchers at Case Western Reserve University in Cleveland, the survey examined a large group of youngsters—more than 2,200—from both rural and urban neighborhoods.

The results were consistent with earlier findings. The more young children watched TV, the more likely they were to feel depressed, angry, anxious, and aggressive. Interestingly, girls who watched more than five or six hours of TV a day showed the highest level of these emotions, followed by heavy-viewing boys. Girls and boys who watched TV programs that contained a lot of violence were also more likely to report that they themselves behaved violently.

As with all survey research, these results do not prove that watching TV causes violence. It's entirely possible that children who are depressed or anxious to begin with simply watch more TV than others. Nonetheless, as the researchers point out, heavy viewing may be a clue that something in the child's life is not going well and needs attention.

There is one more piece to be added to the puzzle. Panel surveys, as noted earlier, are longitudinal research projects that examine the same individuals at different points in time. They are not plagued by the artificiality of the laboratory, and their design allows us to draw some conclusions about cause and effect. Since the early 1970s the results of several panel studies have become available for analysis.

The panel analysis begins with measurements of both real-life aggression and exposure to TV violence, taken at two different times. Next, the researchers determine if TV viewing as measured at time 1 is related to aggression at time 2. At the same time, the relationship between aggression at time 1 and TV viewing at time 2 is also assessed. If early TV viewing is more strongly related to later aggression than early aggression is to later TV violence viewing, then we have evidence that it's the TV viewing causing the violence and not vice versa. Figure 13–4 diagrams this approach.

Figure 13–4

Longitudinal Design to Study TV Violence

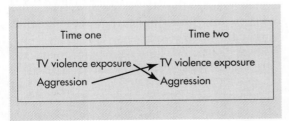

Several longitudinal studies done in the United States and Europe, including both panel and trend studies, have found, with some exceptions, similar results. The majority of the studies seem to suggest that the sequence of causation is that viewing TV violence causes viewers to become more aggressive. The degree of the relationship between the two factors is small and, in a few instances, difficult to detect, but it is consistent. In addition, the process seems to be reciprocal. Watching TV violence encourages aggression, which in turn encourages the watching of more violent TV, and so on.

Having reviewed evidence from four basic research methods, what can we conclude about the effects of violent TV on antisocial behavior? Laboratory experiments demonstrate that under certain conditions, TV can have powerful effects on aggressive behavior. Field experiments provide additional, although less consistent, evidence that TV can exert an impact in the real world. Surveys show a consistent but somewhat weak pattern of association between violence viewing and aggression. Longitudinal studies also show a persistent but weak relationship between the two and suggest a pattern whereby watching TV causes subsequent aggression. Unfortunately, few findings in areas such as this are unambiguous. Nonetheless, a judgment is in order. Keep in mind that some might disagree, but the consensus among social scientists seems to be the following:

1. Television violence is *a* cause of subsequent aggressive tendencies in viewers; it is not *the* cause since many factors besides TV determine whether people behave aggressively.

2. The precise impact of TV violence will be affected by many other factors, including age, sex, family interaction, and the way violence is presented on the screen.

3. In relative terms, the effect of TV violence on aggression tends to be small.

Does this close the case? Not quite. The third summary statement has been the focus of much current debate. The majority of researchers concede that there is some kind of causal link between viewing video violence and aggression, but several argue that the link is too weak to be meaningful. To be more specific, statisticians characterize the strength of any relationship in terms of the amount of variability in one measure that is accounted for by the other. For example, suppose a person was trying to guess your college grade point average just by looking at you. Chances are the person wouldn't do too well. Now let's show the person your SAT scores and let the person guess again. Chances are that the person will do a little better. Why? Because there is an association (a moderate one, at least) between GPA and SAT scores. In other words, they share some variation. The more shared variability there is between two measures, the better a person can predict. If two factors are strongly related, changes in one might account for 60 to 70 percent (or higher: 100 percent if perfectly related) of the change in the other. A person could make quite accurate predictions in this instance. If two factors are not associated at all, change in one would explain 0 percent of changes in the other. In this case a person's predictions would be no better than chance. Thus the strength of a relationship is measured by the variability explained. As far as TV violence and aggression are concerned, exposure to televised violence typically explains from about 2 to 9 percent of the variability in aggression. Knowing how much TV violence you watch helps a little, but not much, in predicting your aggression level. Put another way, between 91 and 98 percent of the variability in aggression is due to other causes. Given this situation, is the effect of TV on aggression really that meaningful? Does it have any practical or social importance?

This question is more political or philosophical than scientific, but research can offer some guidelines for comparison. The usual effect size found for TV violence's impact on antisocial behavior is only slightly less than that found for the effects of viewing "Sesame Street" and "The Electric Company" on cognitive skills of the audience. It's also only slightly less than the effect that a program of drug therapy has on psychotic patients. Indeed, several drugs in widespread use have therapeutic effects about as great as the effect size of TV violence and aggression. In sum, although the magnitude of the effect may not be great, it is not that much different from effects in other areas that we take to be socially and practically meaningful. Thus even though the effect may be small, this does not mean that it should be dismissed.

Finally, it should be noted that the bulk of the violence research was done when network TV was still the viewing norm. In today's viewing environment the audience can choose to watch cable offerings that show much more graphic violence than the networks ever could before. Further, even youngsters have access to violent movies on rented videocassettes; the *Friday the 13th* series and other slasher/stalker films, for example, contain much more realistically staged scenes of mayhem. One study in Great Britain has already suggested that youngsters who rent and view violent videocassettes also behave more aggressively in real life. The effects of these new distribution channels for violence have yet to be researched adequately. It appears that there will be much more written on the vexing topic of video violence.

A MEAN AND SCARY WORLD? PERCEPTIONS OF REALITY

The preceding section traced the impact of TV on the behavior of the audience. This section is more concerned with the impact of TV on how the audience thinks about and perceives reality.

The media, particularly TV, are the source of much of what we know about the world. The media, however, bring us more than simply information. They also, at least to some degree, shape the way we perceive the outside world. Or, put another way, the media affect the way we construct our social reality. For instance, what is it like to live in southern New Zealand? It seems probable that very few of you reading this book have had much of a chance to experience living in southern New Zealand or to talk to people who have. Consequently, a TV show on the life of the people who live there might have tremendous influence on your perceptions in this area. This isn't much of a problem as long as the media presentations accurately represent reality.

There are, however, many areas where the world presented on TV differs greatly from reality. For example, studies of TV entertainment content have shown that far more TV characters work in crime and law enforcement than do people in the real world. Criminals on TV commit violent crime far more often than do their real-life counterparts. Trials on TV are decided by juries more often than they are in reality. Leading characters in TV shows are almost always American; people from other countries are rarely shown. More people on soap operas have affairs and illegitimate children than do real people. More unscrupulous and treacherous people are shown on TV than exist in real life. Again, this wouldn't be much of a problem if people were able to separate the two worlds, TV and reality, without any confusion. For some, however, separating the two is not easy.

This is the focus of cultivation theory. **Cultivation theory** was popularized by George Gerbner and his colleagues at the University of Pennsylvania. In simplified form, the theory suggests that the more a person is exposed to TV, the more likely that the person's construction of social reality will be more like that shown on TV and less like reality.

The procedure first used to put the theory to the test requires a content analysis of TV to isolate those portrayals that are at odds with reality. A content analysis is a systematic and objective analysis of the messages portrayed on TV. The second step requires dividing audience members into heavy-viewing and light-viewing groups and then asking for their perceptions of various social events or situations. If cultivation theory is correct, then a lot of the heavy viewers should give answers more in line with the TV world, whereas a lot of the light viewers should give answers more in keeping with the real world. Figure 13–5 shows the basic model used for analysis.

Gerbner and his colleagues have done several surveys examining the cultivation effect. In one study adolescents were asked how many people were involved in some kind of violence each year, 3 or 10 percent (the TV answer); 83 percent of the heavy viewers gave the TV answer as compared with 62 percent of the light viewers. Another question asked how often a police officer usually draws a gun on an average day. The choices were less than once a day (the real-world answer) and more than five times a day (the answer more in line with the TV world). Three times as many heavy viewers (18 percent) as light viewers (6 percent) said more than five times a day.

Cultivation studies have received a fair amount of publicity in the popular press (*TV Guide* even carried

Figure 13–5

Design for Cultivation Analysis

TV viewing	Number giving TV answer	Number giving non–TV answer
High	A lot	A few
Low	A few	A lot

an article by Gerbner and his colleagues), and the theory has a certain commonsense appeal. Recent research, however, suggests that the process of cultivation is much more complex than originally thought.

In the first place, remember that most of the cultivation studies relied on the survey approach. Although the survey method can establish a relationship, it cannot be used to rule out other factors that might be causing the relationship. Consequently, more recent studies suggest that when other factors in the process (like age, sex, race, and education) are simultaneously controlled, the cultivation effect either is weakened or disappears.

In response to these findings, cultivation theory was revised to include two additional concepts—mainstreaming and resonance—that account for the fact that heavy TV viewing may have different outcomes for various social groups. **Mainstreaming** means that heavy viewers within social subgroups develop common perceptions that differ from those of light viewers in the same subgroup. For example, among light TV viewers, nonwhites are generally more distrusting than whites and are more likely to report that people will take advantage of you if they get the chance. Among heavy viewers, however, the gap between whites and nonwhites on this measure is significantly smaller. Heavy TV viewing has a homogenizing effect in this instance and brings both groups closer to the mainstream.

Resonance refers to a situation in which viewers get a "double-dose" from both TV and reality. For example, heavy TV viewers who live in a high-crime area have their belief in a scary world reinforced by both TV and their firsthand experience. They should show an exaggerated cultivation effect when compared with light viewers.

Also remember that surveys cannot establish cause and effect. Cultivation theory assumes that TV

Issues: How Cultivation Works

One of the more perplexing problems connected with cultivation research is explaining how the effect occurs. What mental processes account for television's having an influence on our perceptions of social reality?

A 1993 *Communication Research* article by L.J. Shrum and Thomas O'Guinn provides an initial answer. The results of an experiment conducted by the two support the following reasoning: Think of the memory part of your brain as a huge collection of filing cabinets. Each file drawer contains information about a specific process or thing. Thus one file drawer might be labeled "pizza" and another "morality" and another "courtroom trials." When you acquire information on any topic you stick a new file in the front of the file drawer and push the old files further to the back. When someone asks you for a judgment about something, you go to that particular file drawer and usually scan the files from front to back. If the front of the drawer contains a lot of files filled with information that you acquired from TV, you are more likely to respond with a judgment that more closely conforms to the TV world. Hence, if someone asks you what percentage of trials are decided by juries, chances are, if you're a heavy TV viewer, that when you consult that file drawer, the files in the front of the drawer will consist of material from TV: the O.J. Simpson trial, the Menendez trial, scenes from "Ally McBeal," and so on, almost all of which show jury trials. As a result, you will probably assume that a high proportion of trials in real life are decided by a jury rather than by a judge.

Conversely, if you don't watch a lot of TV, the files in the front of the drawer will contain different and diverse information. There will, of course, be some files filled with TV material but perhaps you've read some articles on law, perhaps your aunt or uncle is a lawyer who has told you stories about how often judges decide trials, perhaps you yourself were involved in a trial, and the like. Whatever the case, you may be more likely to give a lower estimate of jury trials.

The model suggested by Shrum and O'Guinn will obviously require further testing before we can accept its validity, but it does represent a significant step toward a deeper understanding of the cognitive roots of cultivation.

---

viewing is cultivating the subsequent perceptions of reality. It is possible, however, that people who are fearful of going out at night stay home and watch more TV, thus making the perception the cause of the viewing rather than the effect. Of course, the best way to sort out cause and effect would be an experiment, but since cultivation theory talks about the long-term cumulative effect of TV exposure, a definitive experiment would be difficult to design.

Other cultivation studies have tried to specify the conditions that are most likely to foster or inhibit cultivation. Although the results are not entirely consistent, it appears that cultivation depends on the following:

1. *The motivation for viewing.* Ritualistic, low-involvement viewing appears to be more potent than planned and motivated viewing.

2. *Amount of experience with the topic.* Studies have noted that cultivation seems to work best when audience members have only indirect or distant contact with the topic. This seems to contradict the resonance notion.

3. *Perceived realism of the content.* Cultivation appears to be enhanced when the viewer perceives the content of entertainment shows to be realistic.

More recent studies of cultivation theory have demonstrated that the research itself must be done carefully in order to avoid spurious findings. One study found that the amount of TV viewed that divides the high TV group from the low TV group must be chosen precisely or distortions will appear in the results. Other studies have found that the way the questions are worded and the precise topics to be evaluated will also have an impact. It should be obvious that a lot of research still needs to be done before we understand cultivation theory completely. It is also obvious that the area is an intriguing one and represents one of the few topics that have attracted research interest from sociologists, social psychologists, and mass communication researchers. The influence of TV on the way we construct social reality is likely to be an important research area for the foreseeable future.

SEX-ROLE STEREOTYPING

Somewhat related to cultivation analysis is the research area that examines the impact of stereotyping on viewers' attitudes. The women's movement of the 1960s and 1970s sparked interest in the way males and females were portrayed in TV programs. Early content analyses disclosed that men outnumbered women two to one in starring roles and that men appeared in a far greater variety of occupational roles. When they did appear, women were likely to be housewives, secretaries, or nurses. Female characters were also portrayed as passive, deferential, and generally weak, in contrast to male characters, who, on the whole, were active, dominant, and powerful. More recent content analyses have shown that females are now portrayed in a wider range of occupations but that little else has changed.

A number of studies about the effects of exposure to this material began to surface in the early 1970s. Many of these studies used the correlational approach, and, although they were not as rigorous as they could be, their findings generally supported what the cultivation hypothesis would predict: Youngsters who watched a lot of TV should have attitudes and perceptions about sex roles that are in line with the stereotypical portrayals on TV. In one study heavy TV viewers were far more likely than moderate TV watchers to choose a sex-stereotyped profession (for example, boys choosing to be doctors or police officers and girls choosing to be housewives or nurses). Another study noted that children who were heavy viewers scored higher on a standardized test that measured sex stereotyping.

Like cultivation analysis, the major problems with this sort of research are establishing causation and sorting out the impact of TV from other sources of sex-role information (schools, peers, parents, books, and so on). In an attempt to clarify the process, panel studies have examined the correlation between viewing and stereotyping. The results suggested that the causal connection evidently works in both directions: TV viewing led to more stereotypical attitudes and people with more stereotypical attitudes watched more TV, thus reinforcing the effects.

A second popular technique for examining the effects of TV on sex-role attitudes usually takes place in the laboratory and consists of showing subjects (usually youngsters) men and women in counterstereotypical roles (for example, a male nurse, a female mechanic) and then seeing if changes in perceptions occur. Results from these studies have found that exposure to this nontraditional content does seem to decrease sex-role stereotyping. In one typical experiment a group of girls saw commercials in which a woman was shown as a butcher, a welder, and a laborer. Another group saw commercials featuring women as telephone operators, models, and manicurists. After viewing, girls who saw the nontraditional roles expressed a greater preference for traditional male jobs than did the other group. Similar results have been found in at least a half dozen other experiments.

Taken as a whole these studies demonstrate that sex-role beliefs can be affected by the mass media. A qualification is in order here. It also appears that nontraditional portrayals can sometimes boomerang and reinforce the stereotypes they were meant to erase. In one study, first and fourth graders saw a tape about a visit to the office of "Dr. Mary" and "Nurse David." When asked immediately after viewing to describe what they had just seen, most of the male students referred to "Dr. David" and "Nurse Mary." Apparently some stereotypes are highly resistant to change.

BROADCASTING AND POLITICS

Even the most casual of political observers will concede that the broadcasting media, and TV in particular, have changed American politics. A new term, "telepolitics," has been coined to describe the way politics is now practiced. This section looks at the obvious and not-so-obvious influences of broadcasting on the political system.

Those who have studied the impact of media on politics generally divide the field into two categories. The first has to do with the influences on the ultimate political act—voting. Studies in this category examine how media help shape our election campaigns, our images of candidates and issues, our knowledge of politics, whether we vote, and for whom we cast a ballot. The second category includes studies of how media, TV especially, are changing the basic political structure and how we perceive it. We shall examine each category, but first let's look at the media, electioneering, and voting.

Media Influences on Voting Behavior

The past 50 years have seen rather striking changes in the way political scientists and mass communication researchers have viewed the importance of media in political campaigns. Early fears about the political impact of the media were shown to be unjustified by careful studies done in the 1940s and 1950s. Most people reported that factors other than

Music videos have been one place in which sexual stereotyping has been studied closely. Not surprisingly, all studies suggest that music videos constitute a place where females are portrayed in a distinct way. First, few female performers appear. Studies from several different years have found that males make up almost 80 percent of the artists who appear in music videos. Second, when women have appeared, either as performers or characters in concept videos, they tended to appear in seductive dress or various forms of undress. Third, several studies rated the portrayal of women in music videos according to a four-step sexism scale, ranging from level 1, "condescending," through level 4, "fully equal." As might be expected, level 1 accounts for most of video portrayals, ranging from 40 to 50 percent in various studies.

the media, such as their party affiliation and the opinions of respected others, were the most influential factors determining their vote choice. Since 1960, however, TV has assumed dominance as the most potent political medium and voters have tended to be less influenced by party ties and organizations. Accordingly, the potential for media impact may be on the increase.

One thing is certain. People get a lot of political information from the media during the course of a campaign. Candidates who get extensive coverage also show strong gains in public awareness. In 1992, Ross Perot went from a regional to a national political figure thanks primarily to TV coverage.

Moreover, the pattern of news coverage during an election campaign can help determine what political issues the public perceives as important, a phenomenon known as **agenda setting.** For example, if the media give extensive coverage to U.S. policy in Central America, audience members may think that this is an important issue and rate it high on their own personal agenda of political issues.

Voters, of course, get more than just issue-related information from the media. Another area of research is concerned with the role of TV and other media in forming voters' images of the candidates. In particular, political ads are designed to project a coherent and attractive image to voters. Studies have suggested that a candidate's image can be the dominant factor in many elections. As party identification weakens, voters tend to rely on a general image to help them make up their minds. This "image effect" seems strongest among uncommitted voters and is most noted during the early stages of a campaign.

When it comes down to the actual choices (1) whether to vote at all and (2) for whom to vote, the research is not so definitive as one might think. Voting behavior is a complex activity and many factors—interpersonal communication, personal

values, social class, age, ethnicity, party affiliation—along with media exposure come into play. To make it even more complicated, some people are unable to distinguish exactly what factors influence their choice. Existing research, however, does offer some conclusions. Not surprisingly, voters who learn a great deal about a particular candidate are likely to vote for that candidate. Certain kinds of media exposure are also related to voter turnout. Print media readership was found to be related to greater voter participation, whereas people who were heavy TV viewers were less likely to vote. Exposure to TV ads and other political TV programs was also related to turnout and voter choices, but this effect was most pronounced among those who had little interest in the campaign.

TV debates between or among presidential candidates have become a fixture of modern campaigns, and their results have been closely studied to determine what, if any, impact they have on voter preference. Numerous studies of the debates of the last six presidential elections generally agree that the debates reinforced preferences that were formed before the debates took place. Almost 6 out of 10 voters have made up their minds by the time the debates occur, and most viewers simply have their choice confirmed.

The two televised debates of the 1996 presidential campaign reinforced the above findings. Incumbent President Bill Clinton had a big lead over challenger Bob Dole going into the debates, and public opinion polls detected no change in his lead after the debates were over.

A final area that received recent research interest relates to the impact of **exit polls** on voter behavior. Exit polls can be used by the news media to predict election results before all the votes are in and all the polls are closed. Exit polls are not as influential in statewide elections because most news organizations

Negative ads during the 1998 midterm elections that focused on the Clinton-Lewinsky scandal apparently backfired for many political candidates.

refrain from making predictions until all the polls are closed in the state. Presidential elections are another matter. It has been speculated that an early prediction of a winner in a presidential race might deter people from going to the polls or cause them to change their vote choice. Research findings suggest that any impact of an early "call" depends on the perceived closeness of the race and how early the call is made. In general, however, the effects are likely to be limited and the influences of many outside factors are hard to sort out.

Media Impact on the Political System

Turning now to the second general area of research, the impact of the media on the political system as a whole, we find that there is less research available but the findings are no less important. One line of research suggests that political institutions and the media have become interdependent in a number of ways. Political reporters need information to do their jobs, and the government and politicians need media exposure. Thus public officials hold news conferences early enough to meet media deadlines, presidents have "photo opportunities," and correspondents accompany administration leaders on world trips. Further, many politicians have learned to stage media events that accommodate both sides: The politician gets exposure, and the TV reporter gets a 10-second "sound bite" for the evening news. This interdependence is also demonstrated by the change in political conventions. In prior years, conventions actually selected candidates. These days conventions are more like coronation ceremonies, closely orchestrated to maximize prime-time TV coverage.

The recent trend toward negative political advertising has also been a topic of concern. Definitive results about its impact have yet to be determined. On the one hand, many political consultants point to the success of several gubernatorial and senatorial

Events: Order in the Court?

Prospective jurors in Los Angeles County are allowed to watch TV while they wait to be assigned to a case.
Recently, however, the court decreed that "The Jerry Springer Show" was off limits to potential jurors. Why?
Bailiffs reported the program was causing fights to break out in the waiting room.

elections in the 1996 campaign that relied on negative advertising and were successful. On the other hand, several surveys and experiments have shown that negative advertising seems to make voters more cynical, less inclined to participate in political campaigns, and even less likely to vote. The level of negative advertising hit a new high in the 1998 midyear elections, and many observers suggested that it had a boomerang effect for several candidates.

To sum up the rather broad and complicated area of broadcasting and politics, research concerning the political impact of the media demonstrates the specific-effects viewpoint mentioned earlier. In some areas, such as building political knowledge, shaping political images, and setting agendas, the media effects are fairly direct and evident. In other areas, such as voter turnout and voter choice, the media work along with a host of other factors and their impact is not particularly strong.

TELEVISION AND LEARNING

It seems that every new medium has been indicted at one time or another for lowering the educational level of American youth. During the 1930s critics charged that radio was a negative influence on youngsters' school achievement and made it difficult for them to develop good study habits. In the mid-1950s, when TV took center stage, concern about its effects on children mounted quickly, but early studies failed to show convincing evidence that watching TV was related to poor school performance. These surveys did uncover some links between heavy viewing and poor academic performance, but the lack of conclusive evidence pushed the issue out of public focus. In the 1970s, however, the issue was rekindled, primarily as a response to an alarming dip in SAT scores. This section reviews the research on TV's effect on IQ, school achievement and reading.

The results of the research on the relationship between TV viewing and IQ are not surprising. Heavy viewers tend to have lower IQs than light viewers, and many critics have argued that watching TV actually lowers a person's intelligence. Further research

suggests that the association is not that simple. First, it appears that age is a factor. At least two studies noted that heavy viewing was actually linked to higher IQs in kids up to the age of 10 or 11 but that after 11 the relationship reverses. In sum, there appears to be a weak negative relationship between IQ and TV viewing, but age is a complicating factor. And, as is the case with surveys, the direction of causation is not clear.

When it comes to school achievement, the results are not conclusive but they also suggest a slight negative relationship. Youngsters who watch a lot of TV tend not to do so well at school as do their lighter-viewing counterparts. In one study of more than 600 sixth to ninth graders, high TV viewers tended to score lower on tests of vocabulary and language achievement than did light viewers, even when the effects of IQ were statistically controlled. Interestingly, TV viewing was not associated with math achievement scores. Surveys done among adults confirm that high TV viewers do less well on vocabulary tests, suggesting the negative relationship carries over from youth.

Another study indicated that the type of TV content viewed, along with the amount of viewing, was important in determining the precise relationship between TV and achievement. This survey found that children who watched a good deal of news and educational programs got better grades in school, whereas those who watched a lot of adventure shows got lower grades. A recent panel study among high school students, however, found no evidence of TV's effects on math and reading achievement after controlling for such confounding factors as parents' education level, IQ, race, and school attendance. In any case, virtually all of the studies showed the relationship, if one was found, to be relatively weak. In terms of the amount of variability explained, TV viewing generally accounted for about 1 to 4 percent of the variation in achievement scores, a link even weaker than that discussed between exposure to TV violence and aggression.

The relationship between TV and reading performance is hard to sum up. Although common sense might suggest that TV viewing has a negative influence on reading skills, the research has found no clear relationship. True, a few surveys have found a weak negative relationship between entertainment TV viewing and reading achievement scores, but at least one study has found the opposite.

A large-scale study published in 1990 sheds additional light in this area. This research used data gathered from a national sample of about 1,750 children over a four-year period. The children were first studied when they were 6 to 11 years old and then studied again four years later. Cross-sectional correlations done at one point in time were as expected: Negative relationships existed between the amount of TV viewing and IQ, reading skill, and arithmetic ability. When the relationships were examined longitudinally, however, the negative relationships disappeared. The best predictors of intelligence and aptitude were parents' educational level, race, size of family, and birth order.

On the more positive side, related research has shown that TV can teach youngsters specific skills that will help them develop reading competence. Research examining "Sesame Street" and "The Electric Company" showed that they helped children develop letter recognition and decoding skills, which promoted reading fluency.

Overall, the data offer some qualified support to the notion that TV viewing, at best, has a small adverse effect on IQ and school achievement. The results certainly support the conclusion that, excluding especially designed educational programs, TV offers no particular educational benefits to its young viewers; all the hours that youngsters invest in it carry no measurable scholastic rewards.

TELEVISION AND PROSOCIAL BEHAVIOR

It's tempting, of course, to blame all of society's ills on TV. To be fair, however, we should also point out that TV has had several positive or prosocial effects as well. Prosocial behavior covers a wider range of activity than does antisocial behavior. Usually a prosocial behavior is defined as one that is ultimately good for a person and for society. Some behaviors commonly defined as prosocial are learning cognitive skills associated with school achievement, cooperation, self-control, helping, sharing, resisting temptation, offering sympathy, and making reparation for bad behavior. Many of these prosocial acts are not so obvious or as unmistakable as common

antisocial acts; it's a lot easier to see somebody hitting somebody else than it is to see a person resisting temptation. In any case, this section takes a look at the more beneficial results of TV viewing.

First, as noted earlier, specially constructed programs can be effective in preparing young people for school. Without a doubt, the most successful program in this area is "Sesame Street." On the air for more than thirty years, "Sesame Street" is viewed by nearly six million preschoolers every week. Further, "Sesame Street" is the most researched TV series ever, and the available data highlight the success of the series. To summarize some of the major findings:

1. Children who viewed "Sesame Street" regularly, either in school or at home, scored higher on tests measuring school readiness.

2. The more children watched the program, the better their scores were.

3. Disadvantaged children who were frequent viewers showed gains almost as great as their advantaged counterparts.

4. Frequent viewers also seemed to develop more positive attitudes toward school in general.

5. Children who were encouraged to view the program showed more gains than those who were not encouraged.

The success of "Sesame Street" brought it high visibility and criticism. First, it was noted that "Sesame Street" seemed to enlarge the skills gap between advantaged and disadvantaged children. Although disadvantaged children frequently gained as much as advantaged children, fewer disadvantaged children were frequent "Sesame Street" watchers, leading to the net result that a larger proportion of advantaged kids gained by viewing. To cope with this criticism, educators looked for ways to encourage more viewing by the disadvantaged. The second criticism charged that the show's fast-paced style might cause problems when children entered the more slow-paced school environment. It was argued that heavy "Sesame Street" viewers might be bored and/or hyperactive as a consequence. This turned out to be a false alarm, and subsequent research has not linked these problems with frequent viewing.

The success of "Sesame Street" encouraged the production of "The Electric Company," a series whose goal was to teach reading skills to children in the early grades. Much like "Sesame Street," research designed to assess the effects of viewing this

Big Bird and his pals on "Sesame Street" are known the world over. Produced by The Children's Television Workshop, the show has been on the air for more than 30 years.

program found that viewers did better on tests of reading performance than did nonviewers. The program seemed to do best when viewed in school and supported by related curriculum materials.

Other programs that were constructed to get across prosocial messages about mental health or personal social adjustment have proven helpful. For example, viewers of "Mister Rogers' Neighborhood" were found to be more cooperative and more persistent than nonviewers. Another program, "Freestyle," was designed to alter sex-role stereotypes among 9- to 12-year-olds. An extensive research program disclosed that heavy viewers held less stereotypical attitudes than did light viewers. Two other shows, "Big Blue Marble" and "Villa Allegre," were also shown to have some success in improving attitudes toward minority groups.

All the series mentioned were designed for broad-

casting over the public TV system. Although public TV reaches a considerable audience, far more watch the commercial system. Is there any evidence about the prosocial effects of commercial TV? There is, and the main conclusions are not surprising. First of all, research sponsored by the TV networks found that children were able to perceive prosocial messages in commercial TV shows. One study showed that 90 percent of the audience for "Fat Albert and the Cosby Kids" were able to verbalize at least one prosocial message after watching specific episodes of the show. Do any of these messages have an impact on behavior? Studies examining the prosocial impact of TV, using both lab and survey techniques, have demonstrated that children who were exposed to specially chosen or constructed episodes of TV shows like "Lassie," "The Waltons," or "Superfriends" were more likely than nonviewers to score higher on a postviewing test of helpfulness. These effects, however, occurred in a tightly controlled environment and involved children performing tasks that were quite similar to what they saw in the program.

Surveys that link the viewing of prosocial TV with the performance of prosocial acts in real life are rare. One study done in the 1970s found a weak correlation between the two, an association that was even weaker than the correlation between viewing of TV violence and aggression. A recently published three-year longitudinal study of elementary school children in the Netherlands found no relation between viewing prosocial behaviors on TV and performing prosocial acts. One of the reasons for this lack of association might be that prosocial acts on TV are subtle and easier to overlook than violent actions. Also, it is not clear if exposure to prosocial material on TV nullifies antisocial portrayals or if each exerts an independent effect. Further, research has yet to establish if there are any critical periods during the development of children where the effects of prosocial—or antisocial—TV portrayals might have their maximum impact. Finally, no one has yet done an elaborate panel study examining prosocial behavior. Clearly much more work needs to be done before a complete understanding of this area is achieved.

In summary, TV seems to have several effects on behaviors that most would define as prosocial:

1. Television teaches certain cognitive skills that are necessary for school success.

2. Television shows can help reduce gender-related stereotypes.

3. Laboratory experiments suggest viewing commercial TV shows with definite prosocial messages can prompt subsequent prosocial behaviors, but this link has not yet been found to carry in any significant degree to real life.

Before closing this section we should point out that there are many more areas that might have been mentioned. For example, many communications researchers are now devoting increased attention to how individuals process messages in their brain—the study of the cognitive aspects of communication. Moreover, it should be clear by now that the research in many of these areas highlights the thinking embodied in the specific-effects theory discussed earlier in the chapter. Radio and TV usually operate along with a number of other factors to produce an effect, and trying to untangle the unique effects of the media can be quite frustrating. And although the study of media effects is still relatively new, the data are steadily accumulating. It also appears that the electronic media are not necessarily as powerful as many people have charged, although they can exert significant influence in specific instances. Finally, we have a lot more work to do, particularly since new media have transformed the media habits of the audience.

SOCIAL IMPACT OF THE INTERNET

The Internet is so new and changes so rapidly that it is difficult to make generalizations about its impact. There are, however, some preliminary findings that merit reporting.

First, surveys project that the number of Internet users is large and growing rapidly. A 1998 study by the Nielsen Company projected the total number of U.S. and Canadian users at about 58 million. Additionally, the demographics of Internet users are changing. When it first emerged, the Internet was used mainly by males and younger persons. In the past few years, however, more women and more older citizens have begun to use the net. Surveys done in 1998 found that almost 40 percent of net users were female and about 45 percent were over 40. Moreover, Internet usage was strongly related to education and income. Researchers found that about three out of four users had attended college and that about 45 percent had annual incomes of more than $50,000, compared with the 30 percent having this income status in the general population.

Time spent online seems to displace time spent watching television but doesn't seem to have much impact on other media use. Television viewing apparently suffers because a great deal of Internet usage is done in the prime-time evening hours, when people traditionally have watched TV. Internet users also spend more time reading newspapers and magazines than do nonusers and are also heavier radio listeners and movie-goers.

The Internet is also becoming another source of news for many Americans. A 1998 survey conducted by MSNBC found that about 20 million people regularly go online to obtain news about current events. Although this audience is still small compared with the number of people who regularly read newspapers or watch TV news, it appears to be growing. The online news audience is even larger during periods of national breaking news, such as during the White House sex scandal in 1998.

Research into the behavioral effects of Internet use is still in its embryonic stage. Much concern has arisen about the impact of exposure to the pornographic sites on the World Wide Web. One preliminary study suggested a relationship between viewing pornographic Web content and sexual abuse of females. This will obviously be an area that will attract much research interest in the future.

Social scientists are also examining a phenomenon called **Internet addiction**—a psychological dependence on the net that may cause people to ignore family, friends, and work as they spend most of their time surfing the net. Students are apparently one group at risk for this malady. One study found that high Internet use was related to lower grades; another found a correlation between college drop-out rates and high Internet use.

Finally, one study of the impact of the Internet on people's social lives turned up an unexpected result: A two-year panel study of 169 individuals found that Internet use appeared to cause a decline in psychological well-being. Despite the fact that most panel members were frequent visitors to chat rooms and made heavy use of e-mail, their feelings of loneliness increased as they reported a decline in the amount of interaction with family members and friends. The researchers concluded that the social interactions people have through e-mail and the Internet don't take the place of face-to-face relationships.

THE FUTURE: SOCIAL CONCERNS

New media technologies such as interactive, 500-channel cable and satellite TV systems, home computers and TV sets connected to the World Wide Web, interactive CDs, low-cost video phones and video conferences, and virtual reality raise new social concerns.

All this new hardware will increase the distance between the media-haves and the media-have-nots. New technologies slowly filter down to lower socioeconomic groups. The people who could most benefit from easy access to information are usually the last to get it because new technology is expensive. For example, computers that teach preschoolers how to read and how to count will be a tremendous education aid. They will be expensive, however, and perhaps only available to advantaged children. When these children enter school, the gap between their skills and those of disadvantaged children may be even greater than it is today.

The more money a family has to devote to entertainment and informational services, the more that will be available to them. At some point in the development of new technologies there will have to be a debate over the social issue of how to distribute equitably the informational wealth that these new technologies will bring.

With information comes political enfranchisement. The problem will not be whether a family has only 30 channels to watch or 500, but whether an individual has the ability to gather and control information. People who have little access to electronic databases will have less power than those who do.

Then there is the problem of information overload. Information overload hardly needs to be defined to college students who are studying 9 or 10 different subjects a year. The term generally refers to the feeling of confusion and helplessness that occurs when a person is confronted with too much stimulation in a limited time period. With 500 or more TV channels, video games, computers, and virtual reality systems, the consumer of the future will have more information available than he or she could ever use.

Last, there is the problem of escapism and isolation. The term "couch potato" came into vogue during the 1980s to describe a type of person who turned away from personal interaction and merely vegetated in front of the TV. How many people will become couch potatoes in the future when 500 channels of TV are routinely available? And, what about the virtual reality technology? Some people currently spend four or five hours in front of the TV set escaping into the virtual reality of sitcoms, game shows, and action/adventure programs. Others spend equally significant amounts of time trying to master the latest video games from Nintendo. How much more time will they spend in the far more beguiling and seductive world of virtual reality? Indeed, some critics of virtual reality have labeled it "electronic LSD" because many people find it addictive.

The new communication technologies will bring promise and peril. Just like the telegraph, telephone, radio, and TV that preceded them, they will bring fundamental changes to our lives. They will require difficult decisions from policymakers and from consumers alike. They will require us to learn more about them and what they can do. As Loy Singleton pointed out in his book, *Telecommunications in the Information Age,* the new technologies will best serve those who know how to use them.

SUMMARY

- The social effects of broadcasting and cable have been studied by using experiments, surveys, panel studies, and content analyses.

- Over the years various theories have enjoyed popularity as explanations for the effects of the media. The hypodermic needle theory considered the media a powerful persuasive force. This theory held that all people would have more or less the same reaction to a mass-communicated message. The limited-effects theory proposed just the opposite: Because of a variety of intervening variables, the media have little effect. Currently the specific-effects theory is in vogue. This theory argues that there are some circumstances under which the media have a direct effect on some people.

- The most researched topic in broadcasting is the effect of video violence on the audience. After more than 30 years of research, most scientists agree that there is little evidence to support the catharsis theory. Further, most agree that TV violence contributes, although in a small way, to the development of antisocial tendencies.

- There is less agreement among scientists about cultivation theory, which states that viewing large amounts of TV will distort a person's perception of reality. Evidence is mixed about this topic, and more research remains to be done. Television also seems to play a part in sex-role stereotyping.

- Broadcasting has had a major effect on politics. It provides political information, sets voters' agendas, establishes candidates' images, and has some limited influence on voters' attitudes.

- Television also seems to have a slightly negative relationship with education. Youngsters who watch a lot of TV do not do as well in school as those who do not watch as much.

- Preliminary research into the impact of the Internet is just beginning.

KEY TERMS

laboratory experiments   272
field experiments   272
surveys   273
longitudinal   273
trend study   273

panel studies   273
content analysis   273
catharsis theory   276
stimulation theory   276
cultivation theory   280

mainstreaming   280
resonance   280
agenda setting   283
exit poll   283
Internet addiction   288

SUGGESTIONS FOR FURTHER READING

Bryant, J., & Zillmann, D. (Eds.). (1986). *Perspectives on media effects.* Hillsdale, NJ: L. Erlbaum Associates.

——— (Eds.). (1991). *Responding to the screen.* Hillsdale, NJ: L. Erlbaum Associates.

——— (Eds.). (1994). *Media effects.* Hillsdale, NJ: L. Erlbaum Associates.

DeFleur, M., & Ball-Rokeach, S. (1989). *Theories of mass communication* (4th ed.). New York: Longman.

De Fleur, M., & Lowery, S. (1995). *Milestones in mass communication research* (3rd ed.). New York: Longman.

Graber D. (1997). *Mass media and American politics* (5th ed.). Washington, DC: Congressional Quarterly Press.

Huesmann, L., & Eron, L. (Eds.). (1986). *Television and the aggressive child.* Hillsdale, NJ: L. Erlbaum Associates.

Jeffres, L. (1986). *Mass media: Processes and effects.* Prospect Heights, IL: Waveland Press.

——— (1997). *Mass media effects.* Prospect Heights, IL: Waveland Press.

Kraus, S. (1988). *Televised presidential debates and public policy.* Hillsdale, NJ: L. Erlbaum Associates.

Larsen, O. (1994). *Voicing social concern.* Lanham, PA: University Press of America.

Liebert, R., & Sprafkin, J. (1988). *The early window* (3rd ed.). New York: Pergamon Press.

Milavsky, J., Kessler, R., Stipp, H., & Rubens, W. (1982). *Television and aggression: A panel study.* New York: Academic Press.

Pearl, D., Bouthilet, L., & Lazar, J. (1982). *Television and behavior: Ten years of scientific progress and implications for the eighties* (Vol. 2). Washington, DC: U.S. Government Printing Office.

Reeves, B. (1986). *Effects of mass communication.* Chicago: Science Research Associates.

Signorelli, N., & Morgan, M. (1990). *Cultivation analysis.* Newbury Park, CA: Sage.

Singletary, M., & Stone, G. (1988). *Communication theory and research applications.* Ames, IA: Iowa University Press.

William, T. (Ed.). (1986). *The impact of television.* New York: Academic Press.

Wimmer, R., & Dominick, J. (1999). *Mass media research* (6th ed.). Belmont, CA: Wadsworth.

INTERNET EXERCISES

1. Visit our Web site at http://www.mhhe.com/ beyond for study-guide exercises to help you learn and apply material in each chapter. You will find ideas for future research as well as useful Web links to provide you with an opportunity to journey through the new electronic media.

The International Scene 14

Quick Facts

 Number of languages broadcast by VOA: 53

 Annual license fee in Great Britain for owning radio and TV sets: @$160

 Number of continents: 7

 Number of continents with MTV: 6 (all except Antarctica)

 Number of local language versions of "Sesame Street": 19

Let's take a quick trip around the world and turn on some TV sets. First stop, Australia. You turn on the set and hey, that blonde girl looks familiar. Buffy and her friends Willow and Xander are on the track of vampires at Sunnydale High. Keep watching and you'll see some other recognizable U.S. TV stars— "Drew Carey" and "Everybody Loves Raymond" are also popular on Australian TV. Let's head north to Thailand. There on Thailand's Channel 3 Network are Scully and Mulder of "The X-Files," speaking the local language. Continuing northward, let's check out the television scene in Afghanistan. Thanks to Star TV, an Asian satellite network, the talk show fans in Afghanistan can now catch "The Oprah Winfrey Show" on a daily basis.

Let's head northwest into Russia where we can watch the latest episode of MGM's series, "La Femme Nikita" on NTV, a Russian network. Continuing into Europe, we find that the CBS-produced "Walker, Texas Ranger," is popular in Poland, while the U.S. soap, "The Bold and the Beautiful" is grabbing impressive afternoon ratings for Canale 5 in Italy. Another soap, "The Young and the Restless," does remarkably well in Greece. Crossing the English Channel, we can catch the latest episodes of "Friends" and "Frasier" on Channel 4 in Great Britain.

A hop across the Atlantic brings us to Argentina where "The Simpsons" is a top-rated show. Continuing north to Mexico, we find that the U.S. cartoon, "Alvin and the Chipmunks" is a popular afterschool show. Jumping north to Canada, we find a plethora of U.S. shows available, including "ER" and "Ally McBeal."

What can we learn from this quick trip? Obviously, that U.S. TV shows are popular all over the globe. But on a more general level, this information suggests that studying broadcasting as it exists solely in the United States might be too narrow a focus. Radio and TV signals and programs do not stop at national borders. Other countries have developed systems different from ours. It might be valuable to examine electronic media systems in a world context since such a perspective might give us a broader view of our own system. Furthermore, American production companies make a great deal of income from programs that are sold to foreign systems. Total revenue in 1998 was more than $2 billion.

As will be noted later, in Europe and many parts of the globe, commercial broadcasting has expanded and U.S.-made programs have become a staple on many systems. Although the initial surge of demand for U.S.

programming has subsided and a number of countries have enacted quotas that limit the amount of foreign-made programming on their systems, income from international sales of programs will continue to be an important consideration. In fact, many U.S. production companies now routinely test the ideas for new series to see if they have international appeal.

To begin, we need to define some terms. There are two basic ways to study world broadcasting. First, there's **comparative electronic media systems,** the analysis of media systems in two or more countries. Thus if we took the U.S. system and compared it with the electronic media operations of Canada and/or Great Britain, we would be practicing comparative analysis. Next, there's the study of **international electronic media,** the analysis of radio and video services that cross national boundaries. Programs can be deliberately aimed at other countries (as is the case with the Voice of America or the Voice of Russia) or they can simply spill over from one country to its neighbor (as happens between the United States and Canada). This chapter first looks at comparative analysis and concludes with an examination of international systems.

COMPARATIVE ELECTRONIC MEDIA SYSTEMS

Let's first turn our attention to electronic media systems as they exist in other countries, recognizing that certain international factors such as geography, global politics, and culture have an influence on national systems. The study of other systems allows us to see how other countries deal with basic problems such as freedom of expression, regulation, and access. The purpose of this section is not to prove that one system is necessarily better than any other but to give us a broader perspective from which to evaluate the U.S. system.

To accomplish this purpose, we shall first present a simplified model of the major differences between national systems and then look in detail at the operations of the electronic media in four specific countries.

Differences in Electronic Media Systems: A Model

In addition to the international factors mentioned above, the arrangement of a country's media depends on the nation's political philosophy, social history,

Figure 14–1

Typology of Broadcasting Systems

Ownership

Characteristics	Government agency	Government corporation	Private
Goals:	Mobilization	Education/Cultural enlightenment	Profit
Regulation:	Strong	Moderate	Weak
Financing:	Government	License fee/Tax Government subsidy/Advertising	Advertising
Programming:	Ideological/Cultural	Cultural Educational/Entertainment	Entertainment

and economic system. Trying to categorize the variations that exist among countries is a difficult task. One of the earliest attempts, made in 1956, identified four main classifications based on the country's press philosophy. Authoritarian systems used the media to promote governmental goals. Libertarian systems gave great freedom to the media and promoted a free marketplace of ideas. Social responsibility systems also argued for a free press, but in return for its freedom, the press had responsibilities and obligations to fulfill for society. Finally, the communist system regarded the media as a means to transmit social policy. Another formulation classified systems into three categories: (1) paternalistic (the government or whatever agency in charge of broadcasting knows what is best for the people and programs their systems accordingly), with the BBC in Great Britain serving as the prime example; (2) permissive (broadcasters are allowed by the government to do pretty much what they want), with the U.S. commercial system as the best example; and (3) authoritarian (the government controls the system and uses it to achieve its objectives), with the system in the former Soviet Union as the most vivid example. Other writers have sug-

gested additions or variations to these ideas.

Although the above notions are helpful, recent historical changes have meant that most countries now have diverse arrangements in which more than one of the above approaches is represented. The United States, for example, has a commercial system that fits the permissive approach and a public system (PBS) that is more inclined toward the paternalistic philosophy. For many years Finland had a strong state-run TV system modeled after the BBC. In 1994, however, the Finnish government licensed an advertising-supported network whose emphasis was more on entertainment than on cultural programming or public service. This new service promptly became the most viewed network in the country. Given this growth in diversity, a more complex taxonomy might be more useful. Figure 14–1 displays a classification system that shows how ownership affects four important characteristics: (1) goals, (2) regulation, (3) financing, and (4) programming. Keep in mind this model is a simplification and many variations exist. Nonetheless, let's look at the model in more detail.

There are three main ownership patterns. A broadcasting or cable system could be operated by a government agency, as in China, where it is controlled by the Ministry of Radio, Film and TV, and in Kenya, where it is controlled by the Ministry of Information and Broadcasting. The goal of this ownership type is, generally, mobilization of the population to achieve some goal. This goal might be nation building, as in Kenya, or it might be stability and social order, as in China. Strong regulation characterizes this type of setup. Censorship, either formally by the government or informally by the members of the press themselves, is common. Financing is typically achieved through a direct grant from the national budget, as in China, or by a direct grant supplemented by another type of revenue, such as advertising in Kenya. Programming on a system run by a state agency is primarily ideological in nature and promotes a national policy. There may be, however, some cultural programming as well. Entertainment is not a priority in this system.

A broadcasting/cable system could also be operated by a government-chartered corporation, such as the British Broadcasting Corporation (BBC) or the Canadian Broadcasting Corporation (CBC) or the U.S. PBS system. The goal of this form of operation tends to be enlightenment and information. Regulation is moderate, with most laws dealing with defamation and national security. Some content regulations, as in Canada, might also be present. Financing is achieved through a license fee, as with the BBC, or by a tax or a direct government subsidy supplemented by other revenue streams, such as advertising, as with the CBC. The programming on this type of system is a mix of cultural, educational, and entertainment.

The major goal of a privately owned system, such as that in the United States, is profit. Other goals, such as enriching the cultural heritage, serving the public interest, and informing the population, are also espoused, but the profit motive tends to be paramount. Regulation in the privately owned situation is generally weak. Financing is usually done through the sale of commercial time. Most of the programming is entertainment-oriented.

Keep in mind that most countries have one or more of these three systems in operation and each influences the others. In Great Britain, for example, the success of the commercially supported and entertainment-oriented ITV channel prompted the BBC to offer more mass-entertainment programming on its channels. Also remember what was said at the beginning of this section about systems' being influenced by social, economic, and political forces. The 1980s and 1990s saw the end of communism in Eastern Europe and the rise of the free marketplace economy. Consequently, many countries previously served by a state-run monopoly system now faced competition from privately owned stations and networks. Other countries, faced with economic problems, sold some of their state-run networks to private companies. Finally, since broadcasting signals don't stop at the border, people in countries where broadcasting was run by a state agency or by a government corporation saw examples of popular entertainment shows on systems not previously available to them from neighboring countries. As a result, pressure began to build on governments to move toward more mass-appeal programming.

ELECTRONIC MEDIA IN OTHER COUNTRIES

This section analyzes the systems in four countries along the dimensions of structure, economics, regulation, and content. These are not the only dimensions that could be analyzed, but they are among the most seminal. Moreover, it's not possible to analyze systems in every country. For our purposes, we have chosen only four. This should not suggest that these countries are more important than others; they simply offer better examples to bring out comparisons.

The four systems that will be analyzed are those of Great Britain, the People's Republic of China, Canada, and Kenya. The British system has been praised for its excellence and has served as a model for many other systems; it is also significant because it represents a good example of a pluralistic broadcasting system in a developed country. China provides an example of a government-controlled system of broadcasting. An examination of the Canadian system will illuminate the problems of maintaining cultural autonomy in the face of broadcast spillover from the United States. In addition, Canada, as an immediate neighbor of the United States, is a good candidate for study. Kenya demonstrates the special role of broadcasting in a developing nation. It also provides us with an opportunity to discuss the "new world information order."

The United Kingdom

Broadcasting in the United Kingdom and the United States developed at about the same time but underwent a markedly different evolution. Like many countries in Europe, Britain decided early that broadcasting should be a monopoly public service. Coupling this thought with the British tradition of strong independent public institutions, the government chartered the British Broadcasting Corporation (BBC) in 1927. The programming on this new service was essentially "highbrow," characterized by news, analysis, education shows, and classical music. Over the years, however, the BBC has diversified its radio programming by adding other, more-popular content. In the early 1970s there were four BBC radio networks in operation, one devoted entirely to rock music.

The BBC got into TV broadcasting in 1936 but, as in other countries, development was short-circuited by World War II. Television service resumed in 1946 and grew rapidly in popularity. The BBC enjoyed

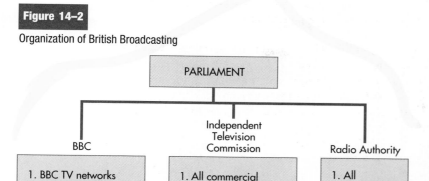

Figure 14–2

Organization of British Broadcasting

transition to digital television. The new digital format would allow the BBC and the commercial stations to increase the number of channels available to the audience. Sky Digital, a satellite-delivered service offering dozens of different channels, premiered in 1998. All in all, the 1990s were an eventful decade for British radio and television, and the digital era will undoubtedly bring about a more competitive television market in the United Kingdom.

monopoly status until 1954 when Parliament created a competitive, commercially sponsored TV system. Further competition came about in the early 1970s when local independent radio stations were authorized. In 1995 the BBC consisted of two national and several regional TV networks, four national radio networks, and several regional and local services. The rival commercial system had two national TV networks, approximately 50 local independent radio stations, and TV and radio news services.

VCR penetration was high, more than 70 percent. Cable TV was not growing as rapidly as in the United States, primarily because of a generally weak economy in Great Britain and because of an environmental protection act that makes it necessary for all cable to be buried rather than hung from poles. As a result, cable penetration was less than 5 percent in 1994. About 15 percent of the population was equipped to receive satellite television and this percentage was expected to grow to about 40 percent by the end of the century.

British broadcasting was deregulated and partially restructured in 1990. A new governing body was created for commercial TV, and more radio stations went on the air. A new commercial network, Channel 5, went on the air in 1997. British Sky Broadcasting used a direct-broadcast satellite system to compete with the BBC and the commercial stations. The charter of the BBC was renewed in 1996, and despite speculation that the BBC would start accepting commercials, the system was left unchanged. The BBC added a 24-hour news channel, and, in 1998, BBC Online made its debut on the Web. As the 1990s drew to a close, the BBC and commercial broadcasters were preparing for the

Structure   As portrayed in Figure 14–2, broadcasting in the United Kingdom is organized into a **duopoly.** There are two major broadcasting entities: the noncommercial BBC and the commercial sector. The BBC is a public corporation that is ultimately responsible to Parliament but whose day-to-day operations are generally free from interference. Operating under a royal charter, the BBC oversees the noncommercial national radio and TV system, the regional radio and TV services, and the BBC World Service. An American parallel to the BBC is difficult to find, since most government-chartered organizations tend to be politically involved from time to time. Perhaps the Red Cross, chartered by Congress but run by its own board of trustees, comes the closest.

The Independent Television Commission (ITC) and the Radio Authority regulate the commercial sector of British radio and television. The ITC oversees the operation of three TV networks: Channel 3—the oldest commercial network in Britain, Channel 4, and the newly established Channel 5. In addition, the ITC regulates all cable and satellite systems. The Radio Authority governs all independent radio stations.

Economic Support   Since the BBC is prohibited from making money by selling commercial time, it must turn to other sources for income. The system used by the BBC is a license fee, or receiver fee, that all set owners in the United Kingdom must pay to support broadcasting. This license fee system is fairly common in Western Europe but is unfamiliar to those in the United States, who are accustomed to "free" radio and TV supported by the sale of advertising. (A variation of the license fee system has been suggested from time to time as a means of supporting the

Tinky-Winky, Laa-Laa, Dipsy, and Po. The latest British group to invade America, the Teletubbies originated on the BBC.

public TV system in the United States, but so far this plan has not been adopted.) As of 1999 the license fee, set by Parliament and tied to the inflation index, was about $164 per year per household for a color TV set. (License fees support both radio and TV broadcasting but are imposed only on TV receivers.) The post office used to gather this fee, but in the early 1990s the BBC assumed responsibility for its collection. People who avoid paying it are subject to a heavy fine. About 60 percent of total license fee revenue goes to TV, about 25 percent to radio, with the remainder going for reserve and miscellaneous expenses.

The BBC also receives income from selling program guides, books, records, and other merchandise, such as Teletubbies toys. In 1997, the BBC added an additional revenue stream when it began UKTV, a service that takes past hit programs from the BBC and distributes them worldwide via satellite to consumers who pay a fee for the channel. After operating in the red for several years, the BBC had a positive cash balance in 1997, thanks in part to cost-cutting measures that included reducing its staff by 1,700 and to an increase in the annual license fee.

The commercial TV networks, on the other hand, receive no part of license fee revenue. Their income is derived from rental fees paid to them by local radio and TV franchises that use the ITC's transmitters and in turn make their money by selling advertising on their stations. The ITC has recently liberalized its rule concerning the placement of advertising. Advertisers may now sponsor programs and have more flexibility in where to place their ads within the show. Despite the more liberal rules, the ITC also has regulations governing the amount of time given over to commercials and the commercial copy itself. In 1998, advertising revenue on the independent networks amounted to about $4.2 billion, compared with the BBC's total license fee income of about $3 billion. (This difference is not unusual. In other countries having similar duopolies, advertising revenue generally exceeds license income.) When profits exceed a certain level, the government is empowered to levy a special tax on commercial broadcasters.

Law and Regulation   Government exercises a light hand with the BBC. Although technically the government has the final say, it has rarely exercised that power. The government, however, can exert significant pressure, as it did in the late 1980s and early 1990s when it prohibited the broadcasting of terrorist voices in connection with the violence in Northern Ireland. In addition, the Police and Criminal

Evidence Act of 1984 offered, in principle at least, some protection to journalistic materials—reporters' notes, photographs, news footage, and so on. In practice, however, requests from the police for such material have generally been approved by the courts.

The BBC's charter obliges it to cover activities of Parliament, forbids editorializing, and, as we have seen, prohibits commercials. In addition, the BBC has imposed regulations on itself. Its board of governors has enacted guidelines that state the BBC will treat controversial issues fairly, operate in good taste, and neither encourage nor incite crime. The Broadcasting Complaints Commission was set up in 1981 to consider charges of unfair treatment or invasion of privacy by both BBC and independent TV programs.

The ITC finds itself in an administrative as well as regulatory role. It operates within a framework set by legislation and is responsible for supervising programs in the public interest. The ITC selects the companies that will produce programs, supervises and controls program schedules, and regulates advertising. It issues lengthy program guidelines to the production companies, covering such things as matters of taste, portrayals of violence, charitable appeals, and accuracy in news broadcasts. Moreover, in accordance with the Broadcasting Act passed by Parliament in 1990, the ITC constructs and enforces a code that deals with advertising. One provision of the code, in contrast to the situation in the United States, prohibits advertising in programs intended for children. Moreover, no ads may be shown for any tobacco products.

Programming   Before 1993 the BBC produced almost all of its own programming. Critics complained that the BBC could save money by using independent producers as program suppliers. Consequently, new legislation required that the BBC purchase at lease 25 percent of its programs from independent suppliers. This cost-saving measure helped the BBC's financial situation. The programming on the commercial channels (Channels 3, 4, and 5) is all produced either by the company that holds the franchise or by independent producers. Channel 5 depends on outside production companies for all of its programs. Programming on the cable and satellite networks resembles the situation in the United States. There are dozens of services available, including the Discovery Channel, CNN, and ESPN, along with movies and sports channels.

The BBC has a somewhat stodgy reputation when it comes to programming (its nickname is "Auntie Beeb") whereas the commercial channels have a reputation for more mass-appeal programs. These images are not entirely accurate. The BBC, after all, produced the politically incorrect and rather offbeat "Absolutely Fabulous," which ran on Comedy Central in the United States, and the improvisational comedy "Whose Line Is It Anyway?" hosted by Drew Carey in its American version. The BBC also carries such mass-appeal shows as "Third Rock from the Sun" and "The Simpsons." At the same time, the BBC aired programs for more-select audiences, such as the period drama "Charles Dickens: Our Mutual Friend" and "The Antiques Roadshow." Channel 3, meanwhile, carried such mass-appeal shows as "Baywatch Nights" and "The Jerry Springer Show" but also the arts program "The South Bank Show." Channel 4's charter mandates that it serve those specialized tastes not generally catered to by Channel 3. Consequently, it features programming geared to selective audiences segments, such as the Generation X soap opera "So You Want to Be a Rock Star" and the landscape show "The Garden Doctors" along with some American sitcoms. The new Channel 5 is a more general-appeal service whose schedule is dominated by American imports, such as "Xena: Warrior Princess," and lifestyle shows.

Channel 3 gets the biggest share of the audience, about 40 percent, while BBC-1 and BBC-2 account for a combined total of about 33 percent. Channel 4 typically averages less than 10 percent of the viewing audience, and the new Channel 5 less than 5 percent. Much like the situation among the commercial networks in the United States, Channel 3's audience share has been dropping recently as viewers migrate to cable and satellite networks.

People's Republic of China

Broadcasting developed in China around 1940. Its development was hampered by World War II and internal fighting among China's various political factions. The first station, built with scavenged parts and utilizing a Russian transmitter, was immediately used by China's Communist party as a political tool. China's leader, Mao Zedong, decreed that the station should be used to keep in touch with areas of China that were controlled by the party and with guerrillas and armed forces in the other provinces.

After the Communists assumed power in 1949, radio became a major propaganda tool. From the beginning, the goal of Chinese broadcasting was to

Figure 14–3

Organization of Chinese Broadcasting

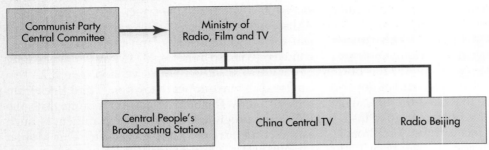

shape the development of Communist society. The government built new transmitting facilities and, to make up for the lack of receiving sets, installed loudspeakers for group listening in the rural sections of the country. In 1950, the Central People's Broadcasting Station (CPBS) opened in Beijing (in China, the word "broadcasting" refers to radio and not TV). China's international shortwave service, Radio Beijing, started about the same time. Local stations relayed the programming of the CPBS into the provinces. By 1960 more than 120 radio stations were providing the country with news, entertainment, public affairs, and educational and political broadcasts.

The 1960s and 1970s saw Chinese broadcasting influenced by the cultural revolution proclaimed by Mao Zedong. The programs during this period were propaganda-oriented, strident, and mostly political. Entertainment that was carried had to be in keeping with the goals of the revolution. After Mao's death in 1976, controls over the radio system were relaxed and service was eventually expanded to include six national radio channels. In the 1980s, China opened its doors to Western culture and the CPBS even began to play American rock music (called *yaogunyue*, translated literally as "shake-roll" music). At the same time, regulation of news was eased. All of that changed in 1989 with the demonstrations in Tiananmen Square. After a few days of tolerance the government cracked down on both the TV and radio media and instituted strict censorship.

Television started in China in 1958 with one station in Beijing. Lack of hardware and technology, however, hampered the development of TV. In addition, during the cultural revolution TV development was stopped entirely. Consequently, by 1970, there were only 30 stations in the entire country. Since 1976, however, TV has been China's fastest growing medium. In 1998 there were more than 2,100 TV, cable, and satellite stations. Roughly 90 percent of the urban population in China has access to a television set. About 70 million Chinese subscribe to cable. Some cities boast cable penetration rates higher than those in the United States. Cable TV reaches 96 percent of all Beijing households and 87 percent of those in Shanghai.

The Chinese government has become more liberal in its economic philosophy and has moved toward a free marketplace. As a result, commercials are far more prevalent on Chinese TV. Beijing TV even carries a home shopping network. In addition, several Western companies have agreed to coproduce television programs with Chinese firms. Western-style television from Hong Kong, newly incorporated into China, also attracts many Chinese viewers, as do satellite-delivered channels such as HBO and ESPN. In short, China is in the midst of a significant transformation. A country that was media poor is quickly becoming media rich. The impact of this transformation on China's political system and culture has yet to be determined.

Structure   Figure 14–3 illustrates the general structure of broadcasting in China. The Bureau of Radio, Film and Television controls Radio Beijing, the CPBS, and China Central Television (CCTV). Positions in this bureau generally go to Communist party members, which means that the party effectively controls the system. CCTV has eight networks that are relayed by satellite across the country. There are also provincial stations as well as stations that serve only the major cities. As mentioned above, cable systems are also located in major urban areas.

Events: Can You Tell Me How to Get to *Zhima Jie*?

"Sesame Street" has finally come to China. Although the learning-is-fun program has been airing for many years in countries across the globe, including Norway, Turkey, Argentina, and Germany, it was not available in China until mid-1998. Thanks to a more relaxed ideological atmosphere, "Sesame Street"—or *"Zhima Jie"* in Mandarin—will be broadcast by Shanghai Television to a potential audience of more than 100 million.

The program will retain its American format but will include mostly Chinese content. *"Zhima Jie"* is set in a Chinese neighborhood with a bicycle repair stand, noodle shop, public phone booth, and recycling center. Bert and Ernie have been replaced by Puffing Pig and Little Plum. The yellow-feathered Big Bird will not be present. The producers of "Sesame Street" have never allowed him to star in any of their foreign coproductions. Instead, the Chinese version will feature *Da Niao*, who will be introduced as Big Bird's Chinese cousin. Initial reaction to *Da Niao*, was mixed. Some of the children in the test audience thought his beak was too big. "He could snap a little kid's head off," said one Shanghai child. So far there has been no decision to include a Chinese Fortune Cookie Monster.

China is a huge country with a large landmass. In addition, its people speak a variety of languages and dialects. To accommodate this fact, China has developed both a national and a regional service. CPBS provides two national channels of programming, along with two channels beamed at Taiwan, along with special radio services in languages other than Standard Chinese, including Cantonese, Amoy, Hakka, Tibetan, and Mongolian. In addition, there are many provincial and local radio stations serving the various regions of the country. Local FM stations, targeted at a single village or farming community, are the fastest growing sector of Chinese radio.

China Central Television (CCTV) provides eight channels and 138 hours of programming every day. CCTV-1 is the primary service and broadcasts entertainment, news, and current events. CCTV-2 focuses on economic and social topics, while CCTV-3 airs operas and music. CCTV-4 is also known as CCTV International and provides varied programs targeted at overseas viewers. The other channels specialize in sports, movies, education, and the arts.

Financing Until the late 1980s, China's broadcasting system was supported entirely by government allocations from the national budget. The trend toward a free market economy, however, has changed all of that, and now commercials are a common sight on Chinese TV. Eager for foreign capital, the Chinese government has opened the airwaves to commercial advertisers. In 1997, commercials accounted for more than half of the revenue sources for the Chinese TV networks. Since China is the largest TV market in the world, advertisers are eager to get their messages aired. Furthermore, ad rates are a bargain. In the late 1990s, the most expensive price for a 30-second commercial on CCTV-1 was $134,000. Considering that CCTV-1 regularly reaches about 900 million viewers, this works out to about a 15-cent cost per thousand viewers. Commercials are grouped together and shown in three- to five-minute segments between programs.

Regulation Theoretically, at least, China exemplifies the Marxist-Leninist philosophy of total integration between the government and the media. This is illustrated by the fact that ultimate control over the CPBS and Chinese TV is exercised by the Central Committee of the Communist party. According to the philosophy expressed by Mao Zedong, the functions of the media are threefold: (1) to publicize party decisions, (2) to educate the people, and (3) to form a link between the party and the people.

Censorship is a given on Chinese TV and radio. The most common type of censorship is self-censorship, since journalists and media managers know from training and experience which stories and programs might upset the government. In addition, the party monitors the content of radio and TV stations and, if it wishes, can intervene.

This intervention was never more vivid than in the events that surrounded the incident in Beijing's Tiananmen Square in 1989. After a breakdown in the authority of the Communist party's politburo, students demonstrated for democracy in the square and TV cameras broadcast unprecedented pictures to the Chinese population. The hard-liners in the government cracked down, however, and 50,000 troops

The electronics revolution is worldwide as evidenced by this sign across from a Beijing, China, hotel.

fought their way into the square. News reports of the incident going out of China to the rest of the world were censored; the Voice of America was jammed. China Central TV was taken over by the military and members of the internal security force. Journalists who had sided with the students were ordered to do hours of grueling political study aimed at making them recant their prodemocracy views. In short, the government was back in control of the media.

Since 1989 the restrictions on the broadcast media have been relaxed a bit. China Central TV has been returned to civilian control. The official government philosophy, however, has not changed. An administrator from the Ministry of Television succinctly stated government policy in a 1994 press release: "No reactionary, pornographic, or violent programs or programs harmful to state security may be aired."

In actuality, the government has taken a relatively light approach concerning entertainment programs imported from the West. There are quotas that limit the amount of foreign programs during certain hours, but most imported programs are shown without incident. News coverage and programs dealing

with political ideology are scrutinized more closely. Chinese policy forbids the rebroadcasting of any news story other than those carried by official Chinese news agencies. An Asian satellite service was forced to remove the BBC news channel from its lineup before the Chinese would allow it to operate in their country. CCTV newscasts are closely monitored. There may be signs, however, that indicate perhaps a slight change in philosophy. The tradition of a free press that had existed in Hong Kong was allowed to continue even after control of that city reverted to China. Also, in 1998, CCTV carried live a press conference between President Bill Clinton and China's President Jiang Zemin in which the two discussed human rights and the 1989 Tiananmen Square violence, topics usually forbidden in the Chinese media.

The Chinese government has also been trying to regulate the flow of information over the Internet. The government has erected filters and "firewalls" to block sites deemed pornographic or subversive, including the *Los Angeles Times*, the *New York Times*, and the BBC. In addition, special security personnel monitor e-mail. Despite these efforts, many Chinese are able to access outside sources of information. In sum, the Chinese government is still somewhat concerned about the unsettling effect that unsupervised information might have on its citizens, but as more and more media choices become available, the government finds its task increasingly difficult.

Programming   Radio programming in China resembles the content of public radio in the United States. Programs consist of news, humor, storytelling, and music. AM radio is the mainstream service and has the biggest audience. FM radio tends to be localized and relies more on music. The two main CPBS channels provide about 40 hours a day of service, two-thirds of which is general entertainment. News, features, and advertising make up the rest of the schedule. Regional stations will also carry some CPBS programming but will originate about 12 hours per day of local programming, mainly music. Western music is played on many stations, and most Chinese are familiar with the latest trends in rock music, thanks to stations in Hong Kong.

The top-rated program on CCTV is their 7 P.M. newscast. The remainder of their schedule consists of variety programs, documentaries, cultural programs, and Chinese-made soap operas. A recent program schedule from CCTV-1 consisted of "Window of Science," "Cosmetology Training," and a drama entitled "Xue's Army." American-made programs show up every once in a while on CCTV. The 1997 National Basketball Association championship games were a big hit, and many cable networks carry The Nashville Network. Regional television networks, some based in Hong Kong and Shanghai, compete with CCTV. Their programs tend to be more entertainment-oriented than those of the government-run network.

Canada

Broadcasting in our northern neighbor has been shaped by its geography, cultural heritage, bilingualism, and the importance of its proximity to the United States. Almost 90 percent of the Canadian population lives within range of U.S. TV signals. Because of these factors, Canadian broadcasting has had to face some unique problems.

The origins of Canadian broadcasting generally paralleled those of the United States. Experimental licensing began in 1919, and three years later private commercial stations began broadcasting. As radio grew, so did concern about the ultimate future of broadcasting. On the one hand, the country's British heritage suggested a model such as the BBC. On the other hand, the proximity of the commercial system in the United States suggested another approach. In 1929, a government commission recommended the creation of a national company to provide a public broadcasting service throughout the country. This ultimately led to the creation of the Canadian Broadcasting Corporation (CBC) in 1936, whose main tasks were to provide a national radio service and to regulate Canadian broadcasting. This may sound reminiscent of the BBC, but there was a well-established system of private broadcasters in operation at the time who were allowed to continue operating—but under the regulation of the CBC. Thus, from its beginnings, Canadian broadcasting has represented a blend of the U.S. and British approaches.

Radio grew quickly, reaching 70 percent of the population by 1937. After World War II the CBC instituted FM broadcasting and started investigating the development of TV. Television became a reality in 1952, and, as in radio, both private and CBC stations were established. In 1958, after pressure from the private sector, a body separate from the CBC, known as the Board of Broadcast Governors, was established to regulate broadcasting. This in turn was followed by the Canadian Radio–Television Commission—now called the Canadian Radio–Television and Telecommunications Commission (CRTC)—which has the power over private stations and more limited authority over the CBC. Television networks, in both French and English, also started during the 1960s, as did cable TV. In fact, cable grew so rapidly in Canada, it is now one of the most "cabled" countries in the world, with about 80 percent of its homes wired. Much of this growth can be accounted for by the desire of Canadians to receive the full lineup of U.S. cable channels. The Canadians also pioneered satellite communication to cover the vast distances of their country. VCRs are also popular, with about 66 percent penetration.

The 1970s and 1980s were marked by some conflicts between the United States and Canada regarding the spillover of U.S. TV signals and lost advertising revenue. A trade agreement in 1988 finally solved most of these difficulties. Many U.S. series moved their production to Canada to save money. In the mid-1990s, the Canadian broadcasting and cable industries faced increased competition, fragmenting audiences, and dwindling advertising revenue.

In response, the CBC cut back on its expenses. In an effort to reduce programming costs, in 1997 the CBC announced it would no longer try to acquire high-priced American programming and would present all-Canadian programming in its place. In addition, more than 1,000 jobs were eliminated. Privately owned Canadian television and radio networks bounced back at the close of the decade as ad revenues jumped sharply from 1996 to 1998. Cable penetration passed the 80 percent mark in 1998 and two direct-to-home satellite networks began operation.

Structure   Broadcasting in Canada is officially described as a single system with two components. In practical terms, the Canadian system, like the British system, is a *duopoly*, a mix of the public and private, commercial and noncommercial. On the public side, as we have mentioned, the CBC is owned by the federal government and is the major broadcasting force in the country. It provides national radio and TV services through separate English and French networks. Unlike the BBC, however, the CBC relies on a number of privately owned stations that serve as affiliates and provide CBC programming to areas not served by CBC-owned stations. In addition, the CBC operates a special service for the sparsely populated north regions, an armed forces network, and Radio Canada International, its shortwave international broadcasting operation.

The private sector in Canadian broadcasting is made up of all commercial radio and TV stations that are not affiliated with the CBC. There are no privately owned radio networks in Canada, but there are private TV networks as well as several regional satellite and cable networks. Figure 14–4 provides a simplified representation of the Canadian system. Of course, as we have already mentioned, most Canadians can also pick up the major U.S. networks and many independent stations, or see American programs that are provided directly to Canadian stations.

Economic Support   The financial system that supports Canadian broadcasting also combines elements from the British and American systems. The CBC is currently supported by funds appropriated to it by Parliament and by revenue collected from the sale of advertising on many of its stations. (True to its British heritage, from 1923 to 1953 the CBC was also supported by a license fee on receivers.) In 1997, of CBC's total $1.1 billion budget, about 67 percent came from the government and about 33 percent from ad rev-

Figure 14–4

Organization of Canadian Broadcasting

Public Sector (CBC)
1. English TV network
2. French TV network
3. French Radio network
4. English Radio network
5. Radio Canada International

Private Sector
1. English TV networks
2. French TV networks
3. Independent radio stations

enue. The amount of money given to the CBC by the government is scheduled to decline until it reaches about $800 million annually, sometime in the next century. The revenues of private radio and TV broadcasters are generated primarily from advertising. In addition, as in the U.S. system, many cable channels are supported through direct subscriber payments.

Law and Regulation   Throughout the twentieth century, Canada has made extensive use of independent commissions and parliamentary committees in shaping its broadcasting policy. In contrast, the United States rarely relies on this technique, preferring to use Congress and the FCC. In many instances the recommendations of these Canadian commissions and committees have been enacted into law.

The current law governing Canadian broadcasting was enacted in 1976. This law established the Canadian Radio–Television Telecommunications Commission (CRTC), an independent authority charged with regulating and licensing all broadcasters and cable operators. In terms of structure and overall function, the CRTC is somewhat similar to the FCC in the United States. In 1991 Parliament revamped the Broadcasting Act and in 1993 proclaimed a new Telecommunications Act. These new laws were a recognition of the need to modernize and consolidate existing legislation in the changing world of broadcasting and telecommunications.

The one area in which Canadian regulation sharply differs from that of the United States has to do with regulation of programming. Canada does not have the equivalent of the First Amendment of the U.S. Constitution. The government, therefore, is free to take a more intrusive role into the everyday operation of radio and television stations. For example, the Broadcasting Act of 1991 emphasizes the nationalistic purposes and cultural goals of Canadian policy. It states that the broadcasting system should be owned and controlled by Canadians, should be predominantly Canadian in content and character, and should promote Canadian identity. Such language is necessary because 9 out of 10 Canadians live within 100 miles of the U.S. border and Canadians are worried that their national identity and cultural values will be overwhelmed by American broadcasting. Consequently, during the 1970s, quotas governing the minimum amount of Canadian content required to be broadcast were imposed on all domestic broadcasters. These rules are too complicated to explain in their entirety, but some specific examples will illustrate their scope and intent. For radio, 30 percent of all recorded music must be Canadian in origin (this means either the performer, composer, lyricist, or recording studio is Canadian). In addition, there are rules regarding diversity in radio formats. Canadian radio stations are allowed to play any kind of music but are not allowed to mix formats. For example, if a station has a country format, it has to play at least 70 percent country music. The other 30 percent can be anything the station wants, but no less than 70 percent must be country. There are also rules limiting how often a hit record can be played in a given time period. Many Canadian radio stations employ one full-time person just to deal with these federal regulations.

For TV, programs are scored according to a complicated point system, with points awarded to a program according to the nationality of the creative team (director, writer, performers, and so on). For CBC stations, Canadian programming must account for 60 percent of all content during the day. For private stations, 60 percent must be Canadian during the day and 50 percent at night. (Keep in mind that most Canadians also have access to U.S. stations, so that, even with these regulations, about 70 percent of all English-language TV available in Canada is from the United States.) In cable, there is a rule that obligates system operators to provide one Canadian channel for every American specialty outlet on their systems.

Canada is not alone in having legislation to protect its cultural heritage (Australia and several European countries have similar rules), but few countries seem to devote as much time and energy to defending national identity. Although much of the justification for quotas is based on an appeal for cultural autonomy, it should be noted that there are economic reasons as well. Broadcasting/cable in Canada is a multibillion-dollar industry, but it can ill afford to lose substantial advertising and production income to foreign countries.

The Canadian system has additional regulations that are not present in the U.S. system. From 6 A.M. to midnight, Canadian stations are limited to no more than 12 minutes of commercials per clock hour. This means that those 30-minute infomercials, common on U.S. TV at all hours of the day, can be seen in Canada only between midnight and 6 A.M. CBC policy calls for family-oriented fare in the 7-to-9 P.M. block, with adult programs scheduled no earlier than 10 P.M. (A few years ago, a somewhat similar policy in the United States was struck down by the courts.) Finally, in 1994, the CRTC adopted a new violence code that banned the depiction of gratuitous violence and began a national program classification system to work with the V-chip, a device that would block objectionable programming from television receivers. A variation of the Canadian V-chip system was recently adopted by the United States. (See Chapter 11.)

Programming   Since Canada is a multilingual nation, it must provide radio and TV programs in English, French, and other native languages. The CBC administers both an English-language all-news radio network and a French-language network that links most of the French-language stations in Montreal, Quebec, and Ottawa. In addition, the CBC provides a native-language service to residents in the far northern provinces. Network radio in Canada generally follows an eclectic approach, emphasizing music, news, and features. Private radio stations generally feature a format that emphasizes popular music and news. The CBC also operates an English and a French TV network. There are also several privately owned TV networks: CTV, an English net; TVA, broadcasting in French; Global Television and Chum, both English services; the Atlantic Satellite network, a regional satellite to cable service in Atlantic Canada; and Quatre Saisons, a private French-language service started in late 1986. Canada also has numerous cable systems, which reach about 30 million people, and two English and two French pay services.

Looked at in its entirety, Canadian TV tends to be entertainment-oriented, with about 75 percent of its programs in this category. News and public affairs account for about 14 percent, with sports programming (particularly hockey) making up the remainder. The private TV system tends to be a bit more entertainment-centered than the CBC. In a typical year, CBC programs average about 55 percent entertainment, 25 percent news and public affairs, and 20 percent sports.

Canadian-produced TV drama demonstrates high quality. Series such as "Wind at My Back" and "Black Harbour" have captured large segments of the viewing audience. The CBC "National News" is also popular, as is "Hockey Night in Canada." The programs on the commercial channels tend to be dominated by American series, such as "Ally McBeal" and "L.A. Doctors."

Kenya

The Republic of Kenya is located on the east coast of Africa. About the same size as the state of Texas, Kenya has about 20 million people who speak either Swahili or English. The literacy rate averages about 50 percent, higher in the urban areas, particularly around Nairobi, the capital, and lower in the rural areas. Kenya was a British possession until it achieved its independence in 1963. It is a republic, although in recent years Kenya has become a rigidly controlled, one-party nation, and government power over the press has increased.

Kenya belongs to that set of nations typically described as the third world. (A third world, or developing, country is one that is changing from an agrarian economy and colonial rule to an industrial economy and sovereignty.) The majority of countries in the world belong to the third world. As in many of these countries, the critical issue for Kenya is development. Indeed, the stress of political, economic, educational, and cultural development has strongly influenced its broadcasting system.

Radio began in Kenya in 1927 when the British East African Broadcasting Company relayed BBC broadcasts to British settlers in the area. In 1930 this company was renamed the Cable and Wireless Company and was given a monopoly on broadcasting for the East African Colony. In 1959, aided by a grant from the British government, this station was replaced by the Kenyan Broadcasting Corporation (KBC). Kenya received its independence in 1963, and the new government dissolved the KBC and turned it over to the Ministry of Information and Broadcasting, which renamed it the Voice of Kenya. Today the Voice of Kenya offers radio programs in Swahili and English as well as in about a dozen local languages.

Television began in 1963 with a station in Nairobi. A second station went on the air in 1970 in Mombasa. Television is still in its infancy; the Kenya Broadcasting Service (KBS) has only six TV cameras in the entire country. In 1998, it was estimated that about 35 percent of the population were regular viewers of TV, with most of these living in the urban areas. The state-run KBS enjoyed a monopoly in TV until 1990, when the Kenya Television Network (KTN), a commercially supported network, started broadcasting from Nairobi. In 1993, however, the government took control of the network, apparently because the network was giving too much airtime to political opponents of the government. Television companies from other countries have expressed interest in starting stations in Kenya, but, until recently, none had been successful. Finally, in 1998 after much political wrangling, the Nation Media Group, an African publishing company, was granted a license to start radio and TV broadcasts in the Nairobi area.

Structure   In Kenya, as in other third world countries, radio is the primary means of mass communication. Many citizens, particularly in the rural areas, cannot read, thus limiting the impact of newspapers. As we have mentioned, TV is generally confined to the urban areas of the country. Radio is inexpensive and portable; it can run on batteries and can be understood by all residents.

As currently organized, the Voice of Kenya, controlled by the Ministry of Information and Broadcasting, provides both English and Swahili programming. It also provides an educational service for schools and uses shortwave radio to reach people who live in distant villages. It has no international shortwave service. From its origin, the Voice of Kenya was charged with aiding in the task of national development. Its goal has been defined as "educating, informing, and entertaining Kenyans."

The TV system consists of one state-run network and one commercial network. Like radio's, the stated goal of the state-run TV network is to encourage national development. The commercial network puts more emphasis on entertainment.

Economic Support   The state-run Kenyan radio and TV services are supported by grants from the Kenyan government. Both the TV and radio networks are permitted to accept advertising, but the

The notion of a free flow of information is not universally accepted. Although recent advances in satellite television and the Internet have made it harder to censor the electronic media, many countries still try. Some examples:

- Cuba forbids its radio and TV stations from reporting news about U.S. sports.
- In Iran, satellite dishes are illegal, as are tapes that feature female vocalists.
- China blocks access to what it calls "subversive" Internet sites, including those of Penthouse, Amnesty International, and CNN. China also has 200 "Internet security guards" who patrol computer networks at state companies and ministries.
- The Taliban government in Afghanistan declared that TV was corrupting the country and ordered all TVs, VCRs, and satellite dishes destroyed.

revenue they collect is then turned over to the treasury. In theory, this money (and more) is returned to the stations when the government enacts its annual budget for broadcasting. A weak economy has caused problems for Kenyan broadcasting, and both TV and radio services have recently complained that they are underfunded. The commercial TV service, as its name implies, is supported entirely by revenue raised from selling advertising time.

Law and Regulation   Kenya does not score highly when it comes to press freedom. The government-run radio and TV services are tightly controlled, and censorship is common. Print media have slightly more freedom but are still closely monitored by the government. News programs are scrutinized by the Ministry of Information and Broadcasting for stories that might reflect badly on the state. Foreign journalists must be accredited by the ministry and to maintain their accreditation are expected to report what the government defines as the "truth." News from external sources is also supervised. The government TV channel, for example, carries CNN but blacks out any unfavorable mention of Kenya in CNN stories. Conversely, stories about the activities of the Kenyan president and the Kenyan Parliament are common features on the state-run channel.

Programming   Radio programs are geared for national development. Typical programs include literacy instruction, farming guidance, health education, and technological training. Television, centered in the urban areas, tends to be more news- and entertainment-oriented. Like many of its neighbors, Kenya has rules concerning the amount of foreign material that can be shown. Despite the entertain-

ment emphasis, the goal of national development is still present on the state-run channel. One program in Swahili, loosely translated as "What Has Happened," builds a sense of nationalism by focusing on the achievements of the country and its leaders. Another program, "Rural Development," as the name suggests, focuses on farming activities.

NEW WORLD INFORMATION ORDER

The Kenyan system provides a natural springboard for consideration of a controversy that's been called the New World Information Order. To simplify, the spokespersons for many developing nations argue that the United States and other Western countries dominate TV programming and the flow of news between developed and developing countries. This, in turn, leads to a form of cultural imperialism reminiscent of colonial times. To remedy this situation, developing nations want regulations concerning the amount and type of radio and television programming that crosses their borders. Those in the United States and other developed countries counter by arguing that there should be a free flow of information from one country to another and governments ought not have the power to censor information of which they don't approve.

This debate has cooled down in the 1990s, due in part to the trend toward privately owned media, the growth of free-market economies, and the emergence of satellite-delivered television and the Internet, two innovations that make it difficult to regulate content from out-of-country sources. As new governments replace the old and the gap between developed and developing countries narrows, it's possible this debate may subside.

INTERNATIONAL ELECTRONIC MEDIA SYSTEMS: A HISTORICAL PERSPECTIVE

Earliest attempts at wireless broadcasting were designed to see how far a signal would go. Chapter 1 notes that one of Marconi's striking achievements was the transmission of a signal from England to Newfoundland. Thus it was only natural for other inventors to try to send their signals even farther. One of the things they quickly realized was that the frequency of the radio signal was directly related to the distance the signal would travel (see Chapter 3). For example, using reasonable power, medium-wave signals (300–3,000 kilohertz) travel a few hundred miles during the day (farther at night). This makes them appropriate for domestic radio services but not suitable for international purposes. On the other hand, shortwave signals (3,000–30,000 kilohertz) travel much farther. Using sky waves, they are reflected by the ionosphere and with the right combination of power and atmospheric conditions they can travel thousands of miles. Thus it is not uncommon for a listener in North America to be able to pick up signals from Europe and Africa. Consequently, the earliest international efforts were generally confined to this part of the spectrum. (Of course, this increased distance has its price: Shortwave signals are subject to fading and interference.)

The first radio service designed to be heard by overseas listeners was started by Holland in 1927. The program was directed at Dutch citizens in Holland's colonial empire. The purpose of this service was to keep these people in touch with what was happening back in the homeland. Germany followed suit in 1929, and Great Britain began its Empire Service in 1932.

These "colonial service" stations, however, began to attract a secondary audience of listeners who were native citizens of the country receiving the signals. This paved the way for propaganda broadcasts from one nation to another for the purpose of political persuasion. In 1929, the Soviet Union All-Union Radio, with announcers speaking in both German and French, was broadcasting appeals to the working classes of Germany and France to unite under the banner of socialism. The late 1930s brought tension and war clouds to Europe. Nazi Germany's mobilization under Hitler included an active propaganda program over shortwave. By 1939 approximately 25 nations were involved in international political broadcasting, with Germany, Italy, France, the Soviet Union, and Great Britain the most active. Note that the United States was not a leader in early shortwave broadcasting. This period was the golden age of radio (see Chapter 1), and the commercial networks gave Americans all the news and entertainment they wanted. Further, the memory of World War I was still fresh, and a mood of isolationism—of not getting involved in Europe's problems—permeated the nation. Consequently, Americans paid scant attention to shortwave. World events, however, soon changed everything.

In December 1941 the United States was swept into war against Germany and Japan. Almost immediately the U.S. government instituted a program of shortwave broadcasts to blunt the impact of German propaganda. The new U.S. service, called the **Voice of America (VOA)**, made its debut February 24, 1942. VOA was quickly placed under the jurisdiction of the Office of War Information and spent the duration of the war encouraging America's allies and announcing to the rest of the world that the United States was determined to win the war.

World War II also saw a sharp increase in clandestine radio services. A **clandestine station** is an unauthorized station that broadcasts political programs, usually in the name of exile or opposition groups. The United States, Britain, and Germany all operated such stations. For example, Radio 1212 claimed to be a German station but was actually operated by the U.S. Army's Psychological Warfare Branch. The station broadcast to Germany news reports about air raids and battles that were kept secret by the Nazi high command. The real purpose of the station was to cause confusion and dissension in military ranks. On one occasion it misdirected a convoy of German trucks behind Allied lines where they were captured. Most of these wartime clandestine stations vanished when the war ended.

Yet another type of international broadcasting also began in this era—commercially supported shortwave stations. Radio Luxembourg started sending music, news, and ads to other European countries as early as 1933 and continued to broadcast until the war erupted. Radio Monte Carlo signed on in 1943 (it derived some money from ads but was primarily supported by Italy and Germany), and even the United States got involved in broadcasting commercially sponsored shortwave radio to Latin America and Europe. The war, of course, curtailed the U.S. effort, which would resurface a few years later.

Although the shooting war stopped in 1945, the propaganda war between East and West continued. The Soviet Union established international stations in Poland, Hungary, and Bulgaria that supported international communism. Not to be outdone, the VOA stepped up its propaganda efforts. In 1952 the VOA became part of the newly formed United States Information Agency (USIA). One of the stated goals of the VOA was "to multiply and intensify psychological deterrents to communism." The BBC's External Service also entered into the propaganda fray. Broadcasts in Russian began in 1946 and the BBC was urged by many politicians to stay tough on communism. Budget cuts and aging equipment, however, plagued the service for many years.

Other countries also became involved. International operations started in Japan and West Germany in the 1950s. China increased its shortwave programming from next to nothing in 1949 to about 700 hours weekly by 1960. Fidel Castro's Radio Havana, an AM station, signed on in 1961. The Soviet Union debuted a second international service in 1964, Radio Peace and Progress. For its part, the United States answered with several new systems. Armed Forces Radio Service (AFRS), which started in 1942 to serve military forces around the world, had about 300 stations by the late 1960s and established a large foreign audience. Radio in the American Sector (RIAS), broadcasting primarily to listeners in East Germany and East Berlin, began operation in 1946 and 10 years later was one of the larger systems operating in western Europe. Radio Free Europe (RFE) and Radio Liberty (RL), founded in the early 1950s, were given the task of encouraging dissent in Communist-controlled countries. Both stations were secretly financed by the Central Intelligence Agency until 1973, when Congress approved a new governing board.

International broadcasting grew even more during the 1960s and 1970s. More than 150 countries were operating stations during these decades. Much of this increase was due to former colonies' and developing nations' starting their own external services.

The end of the Cold War during the late 1980s and early 1990s caused a fundamental change in the structure and philosophy of international broadcasting. The democratization of many countries meant that the Voice of America and other U.S. services were no longer the only source of uncensored news. Both CNN and the BBC were available in many countries. Privately owned radio stations offering independent reports of the news cropped up in the former Soviet Union. In Africa, many FM stations were privatized and aired news unfiltered by the government. As a result, politically oriented programs decreased and were replaced by more public affairs, news, and entertainment programming. Nonetheless, the importance of the political dimensions of international radio was demonstrated by its role during the Gulf War and the attempted coup in Russia. In addition, the United States continues to operate Radio Martí and TV Martí, two broadcast services whose purpose is to provide Cubans an alternative source of news about national and international events.

Moreover, the Cold War ended just as a worldwide economic slowdown began. Consequently, many governments reexamined the goals and efficacy of their external services and took a close look at their budgets. The United States, for example, questioned whether Radio Liberty and Radio Free Europe were still necessary. After much discussion, the Clinton administration announced plans to merge the VOA, Radio Liberty, and Radio Free Europe under the United States Information Agency. The budgets of RL and RFE were cut, and, in an effort to save more money, their headquarters was moved from Munich to Prague. The German service, Deutsche Welle, also announced cuts in its budget, as did the BBC World Service, Radio Nederlands, Radio Moscow, and many others.

Private international broadcasting continued to be popular during the early to mid-1990s. The pioneer in this area was WRNO, New Orleans, a private station supported by the sale of commercials, whose signal reaches most of South America and parts of Europe. In 1994, WRNO became the first international station to broadcast a live concert on the shortwave band, when it aired a Pearl Jam performance from Atlanta. Many other private stations broadcast religious programming and are supported by donations.

VCR penetration has increased not only in the United States but also abroad. As of 1998, about 85 percent of TV-equipped households in Australia also had VCRs; Japan had about 75 percent penetration, as did France. Mexico had about 50 percent. Countries in which local programming is limited or heavily censored, such as in the Middle East, also have a surprisingly high percentage of VCR-owning households.

Perhaps the biggest trend, however, in international broadcasting is the increasing importance of television as an international medium. Although it has yet to attract the millions of listeners who listen to shortwave radio, there are unmistakable signs that international TV is coming into its own (see later in this section).

INTERNATIONAL RADIO BROADCASTERS

This section briefly examines the organizations of each of the top five international radio broadcasters as of 1999.

The Voice of America

In terms of program hours per week, the United States is the most prolific international shortwave broadcaster. The most powerful U.S. system is the Voice of America (VOA), now in its fifth decade of operation. As mentioned above, the United States also operates Radio Free Europe and Radio Liberty. These services have been at the center of several recent political controversies. During the administration of President Jimmy Carter, the mission of the VOA was to educate and inform the rest of the world about the United States; the VOA's propaganda role was de-emphasized. The Reagan administration reverted to the original mission of the VOA, and the service became a champion of American policies. The Reagan administration also spent more than $1 billion to modernize VOA's transmitters and studios.

The collapse of communism in Russia and Eastern Europe caused the United States to reexamine the role of the VOA and RFE/RL. Everyone agreed that the VOA must continue its operations, but the future of RFE/RL was in doubt.

In the late 1990s, in a move to save money, the VOA and RFE/RL were grouped together under the jurisdiction of the International Broadcasting Bureau, and the budget of RFE/RL was cut. In 1998, however, the mission of this service was expanded to include two new services, Radio Free Iraq and a Persian section of Radio Free Europe. For the short term, at least, it appears that RFE/RL will continue to broadcast.

The VOA broadcasts news, editorials, features, and music in 44 languages through a satellite-fed system of more than 100 transmitters and 32 domestic studios, most of them in Washington, D.C. Its major domestic transmitting facility occupies about 6,000 acres in Greenville, North Carolina, and other domestic transmitters are in California, Ohio, and Florida. The VOA also maintains relay stations in many foreign countries.

Reading the news at the VOA. The VOA reaches more than 120 million listeners every week.

The VOA estimates that about 120 million people worldwide are regular listeners, with about 60 million of these in Eastern Europe and Russia. In the last two years the VOA has provided more "how-to" programming for the emerging democracies in Eastern Europe. Recent programs have focused on explaining how the free-market system operates, how laws are made, and how the judicial branch of the government functions. Programming in the late 1990s included more emphasis on health and nutritional information aimed at developing countries.

Another VOA agency is Radio Martí, which went on the air in 1984 as a special service directed toward Cuba. It remained, however, outside the normal VOA chain of command, with its own presidential advisory board. In 1990 it broadcast about 122 hours per week. Radio Martí's transmitter is located in the Florida Keys, and since most Cubans have conventional rather than shortwave radio receivers, it operates at 1180 kilohertz in the standard AM band. In the early 1990s Radio Martí was joined by TV Martí.

The VOA is also moving to take advantage of developments in technology. VOA has recently gone on the Internet, allowing listeners to use their personal computers to receive VOA programs in 15 languages. To overcome some of the reception problems in the shortwave radio band, the service is also using satellites to beam its signal directly to more than a thousand local AM and FM stations, which rebroadcast the signal to their home countries.

The BBC

The BBC's World Service came into existence in 1948 when Parliament decided to merge the old Empire service with the European operations started during World War II. The BBC service is different from the VOA in that the British system is independent of government ownership. (It does, however, work closely with the British Foreign Office so that official government policies are represented accurately to the outside world.)

Programming on the BBC World Service is diverse and imaginative. Along with its highly respected news programs, there are many entertainment programs, including rock music, serious drama, sports, comedy, and features. The BBC has also introduced a series of international phone-in shows with guests ranging from politicians to Paul McCartney.

The BBC conducts a wide range of audience research. Data suggest that about 140 million adults regularly listen to the World Service in English and 44 other languages, including about 14 million in Russia. The BBC has 43 transmitters in England plus others in such places as West Berlin, Singapore, Ascension Island (in the mid-Atlantic), and Masirah Island (in the Persian Gulf). In addition, the BBC also leases time over VOA and Canadian transmitters in North America. As a result, few areas of the world are outside the BBC's range. Finally, the BBC also maintains an extensive monitoring service of international broadcasting. Both radio and TV programs from other countries are taped, translated, analyzed, and sometimes rebroadcast.

Radio China International (RCI)

The external service of the People's Republic of China got its start during the Cold War period of the late 1940s. It basically broadcast propaganda programs until the early 1970s when a thaw in U.S.–China relations caused a mellowing in its attitude toward the United States and an increase in nonpolitical content. In the 1990s, Radio China International (RCI) was suffering from outmoded and unreliable equipment. Nonetheless, the station has more than doubled its programming hours since 1960 and now transmits more than 1,400 hours weekly in about 40 foreign languages. Relay stations are located in Canada, Spain, France, French Guyana, Mali, and Switzerland. Reception in the United States is difficult and subject to interference.

During the June 1989 violence in Beijing, RCI broadcast a strong condemnation of the brutality used by the government in putting down demonstrations in Tiananmen Square. Shortly thereafter, however, the government cracked down on the station, which then began to broadcast the official government version of the events in the square.

About 80 percent of RCI's programs are devoted to cultural information about China, news, analysis, and commentary. The other 20 percent are mainly music. In addition, RCI produces a half-hour program called "The China Connection," which is distributed directly to local U.S. and Canadian stations that subscribe to it. Little is known about the audience research efforts of Radio China International, but surveys done by other international broadcasters suggest that it ranks behind the other major services in listenership. Its highest audience levels are in neighboring countries such as Thailand and India.

The Voice of Russia

During the days of the Soviet Union, this service was known as Radio Moscow and was one of the most influential international broadcasters. The demise of the Soviet Union and the resulting political turmoil have drastically reduced its importance. Renamed the Voice of Russia in 1993, the service broadcasts in 32 languages (for comparison, Radio Moscow broadcast in 82 languages) and provides a total of 67 hours of programming a day (about half of what Radio Moscow provided). Nonetheless, the Voice of Russia is still one of the five most popular international broadcasting services. Continuing budget cuts, however, make its long-term future somewhat uncertain. The Voice of Russia accepts no advertising and depends totally upon the government for support.

The Voice of Russia's programming is a mixture of news, entertainment, and financial programs. The English language service carries such programs as "Folk Box," which features Russian folk music, "Music at Your Request," and Joe Adamov's "Moscow Mailbag," which has been on the air more than three decades.

The large land mass of Russia enables the Voice of Russia to locate most of its transmitters on native soil and still be able to reach most of the world. Recently, in an effort to generate income, the service has been leasing its transmitters to other international broadcasters.

Like the VOA, the Voice of Russia can be heard on the Internet. Future plans call for the service to investigate moving away from the shortwave spectrum and using the AM and FM bands to carry its signal to various countries.

Deutsche Welle (German Wave)

The international radio voice of Germany first signed on in 1953, with broadcasts only in German. Operations quickly expanded, and, by the 1960s, programs were broadcast in 26 languages. The service continued to grow during the 1970s and 1980s, and by 1992 Deutsche Welle (DW), which incorporated the former East German international radio service when the two Germanys merged, was broadcasting more than 1,200 hours per week in 34 languages.

Deutsche Welle's (DW's) annual budget comes from the federal government and is funded at roughly the same level as the VOA or the BBC. It has two domestic transmitters and six others in Africa

and Asia. In 1992 it started leasing transmitters from the Voice of Russia to improve DW's coverage of Asia. Its programs focus on news, music, and German culture, with an occasional feature on the economic and social life within the country. DW has an extensive listenership, ranking just behind the VOA and the BBC. It draws particularly well in East Africa but has trouble getting its signals into Asia. Similar to other international broadcasters, DW is available on the Internet.

Unofficial International Services: Clandestines and Pirates

As mentioned previously, a clandestine station is an unauthorized station that beams propaganda at a country for political reasons. Because of their very nature, it's hard to get authoritative data on clandestines. One study published in the mid-1980s found that about 94 clandestines were then in operation, broadcasting to about 20 countries, with Iran and Cuba the most popular targets. For example, during 1980, when the Iran–Iraq war broke out, the Iraqis operated the clandestine Ahrav Voice of Al-Qadisyah, designed to reach dissident Arabs in Iran. The Iranians also sponsored a clandestine that broadcast to Iraq—The Voice of the Iraqi Islamic Revolution. Clandestine stations also cropped up during the 1991 Gulf War. After the Iraqi invasion, a station in Kuwait broadcast information to resistance fighters and the United States started clandestine stations that broadcast into Iraq. In 1998, clandestine stations were carrying antigovernment messages in Bangladesh and Sri Lanka.

In contrast, a pirate station, while also unauthorized, does not usually devote itself to political messages. Pirate stations generally program entertainment material. They typically operate outside a country (usually on a ship anchored beyond territorial limits) but can operate from within, depending on governmental leniency. Pirates became big news in 1958 when a number of them set up operations in the North Sea (between Britain and Scandinavia) and beamed rock music to the teenagers of Europe, whose musical tastes had been ignored by established national systems. The most famous of these early pirates was Radio Caroline (named after President John Kennedy's daughter). Supported by the sale of advertising, these stations had a literally stormy existence. North Sea gales would frequently threaten to sink them, and, in better weather, gov-

Events: Cannes or Click Here?

For the last 35 years, Cannes, the resort city on the French Riviera, has been the host of the annual MIP international television trade show where buyers and sellers meet and greet, wine and dine, and hammer out deals. For six days in the spring, Cannes resembles an international bazaar as program producers, hoping for big sales in the foreign syndication market, exhibit their wares for the global community.

Now, thanks to the Internet, these busy program executives may be spared that grueling week in the French sun, that expensive French wine, and that rich French food. Technology has made it possible to market, sell, and distribute TV programs to international buyers using the World Wide Web.

Here's how it works: A potential buyer visits a special Web page that lists all of the shows that are available. Under each show there is a list of all the languages in which the show is available. The buyer clicks on a language and sees a 5- to 10-minute full-motion video promotional clip from the program. If the buyer wants to purchase the program, he or she clicks on a button that displays a screen showing what territories and what language rights are still available. After selecting a desired territory, another screen appears listing the price. If all is in order, the buyer moves to another screen and completes a purchase order. Once finished, the buyer can then download the program to a DVD recorder. Total time for the transaction: about 30 minutes. Much more efficient than spending a week in a luxury French hotel. Right?

ernment ships would harass them. By 1967 the BBC and other national systems had started their own popular music programs, which weakened the pirates' appeal. Nonetheless, the pirate stations were credited with popularizing British rock music during the early 1960s.

Pirate broadcasting is not limited to radio. Television Nordzee operated for a time off the Dutch coast, beaming programs to Europe, and in 1988 a pirate station located on a fishing boat off the Florida Keys was broadcasting video to Cuba.

The United States has its share of pirates, but most U.S. pirate stations operate within the continental United States. Every once in a while, however, a problem may crop up as it did in 1987 when a ship in international waters broadcasting to New York City was shut down by the FCC. Pirate broadcasting might be less of a problem in the future as many would-be pirates find it easier and less hazardous to put their signals on the Internet.

INTERNATIONAL VIDEO

Most global video traffic consists of (1) TV signals, usually sent by satellite, designed to cross international borders, and (2) videotapes or films that are shipped from one country to another.

Satellite-distributed video, as has been mentioned, is one of the biggest growth areas in modern telecommunications, with both public and private broadcasters involved. On the public side, the Voice of America operates the Worldnet Television and Film Service, a global satellite system, which transmits live and taped U.S. programs to Europe and other parts of the world. In 1993, the BBC World Service joined British media company Pearson in a plan to broadcast a subscription-based channel first to Europe and then to other continents. Of all the public broadcasters, perhaps the German international service Deutsche Welle is the most ambitious. The organization has satellite-based television channels in German, and in Spanish and English. In addition, Deutsche Welle signals are also currently being beamed into the United States. Homes with the appropriate satellite dishes can pick up 14 hours of programming a day from the German broadcaster.

International news channels have also proliferated. CNN is seen in more than 170 million households and thousands of hotel rooms worldwide. The BBC operates a comparable service called BBC World. CNBC started international news and business reporting on its channel in 1996. MSNBC and Fox News are also distributed by satellite to other countries.

International TV is not simply confined to news. MTV is available on every continent except Antarctica and reaches 200 million homes. ESPN launched an international sports channel in 1988 and now beams its coverage into Asia, South America, Africa, Europe, and Australia. Similarly, the Cartoon Network and TNT have large global audiences. In

Europe, BSkyB, owned in part by Rupert Murdoch, delivers satellite programming to England and the mainland. Murdoch also operates an Asian satellite system that reaches about 180 million viewers. NBC also has a satellite channel that is seen in Asia and Europe. The WB network also reaches millions of homes worldwide.

Looking next at the tape and film area, the trade imbalance that characterizes much of the U.S. economy is completely reversed in TV. The United States imports only about 2 percent of its programming (mostly from Britain) while exporting a great deal. In 1998, for example, "Roseanne" was seen in England, Australia, New Zealand, Canada, and Finland. Viewers in Poland, Russia, and other European countries watched "Hollywood Squares." "Oprah" was seen in more than 130 countries, including Russia, where it was the number-one rated show in Moscow.

In the future, American-made programs might not be so prevalent because of laws that put a quota on imported programming and because many countries' own domestic TV systems can now produce professional and slick programs that rival those made in the United States. In fact, in many countries, most of the top-rated prime-time shows are locally produced. The U.S. shows tend to be shown in the daytime, in the early evening, or late at night.

SUMMARY

- A country's media system is dependent on political philosophy, social history, and economic structures. This is most evident when comparing the media systems of Great Britain, China, Canada, and Kenya since each of these countries differs greatly in these respects.

- The controversy surrounding the New World Information Order arises from the argument that Western nations such as the United States tend to dominate programming and the flow of news between developed and developing countries. With the emergence of media forms that are difficult to regulate, such as satellite-delivered TV and the Internet, and with changes in the government structure of many developing countries, the controversy seems to be lessening.

- International broadcasting started with the discovery that shortwave radio could travel long distances and could be used for propaganda. The United States did not get involved in international broadcasting until 1941, when it entered World War II. In the 1950s, the United States set up the Voice of America to counter propaganda broadcasts from the Soviet Union.

- Recent developments in the international broadcasting arena include the decrease of propaganda; cost-cutting measures going into effect at all major broadcasting organizations; a growing interest in private international broadcasting; and the growth of television as an international medium.

- The top five international broadcasters are the Voice of America, the BBC, Radio China International, the Voice of Russia, and Deutsche Welle, the German station. International services can also be heard over the Internet. The leaders in international TV are CNN, ESPN, MTV, TNT, and the BBC. American programs are still popular in other countries despite increasing competition from local productions.

KEY TERMS

comparative electronic media
   systems   292
international electronic media   292

duopoly   295
New World Information
   Order   305

Voice of America (VOA)   306
Clandestine station   306
pirate station   310

SUGGESTIONS FOR FURTHER READING

Bishop, R. (1989). *Qi Lai: The Chinese communication system*. Ames, IA: Iowa State University Press.

Boyd, D., Straubhaar, J., & Lent, J. (1989). *Videocassette recorders in the third world*. New York: Longman.

British Broadcasting Corporation. (1997). *Annual report and handbook*. London: British Broadcasting Corporation.

Canadian Radio Television Commission. (1997). *Annual report: 1996–1997*. Ontario, Canada: Canadian Radio Television Commission Information Service.

Chang, W. (1989). *Mass media in China*. Ames, IA: Iowa State University Press.

Fortner, R. S. (1993). *International communication.* Belmont, CA: Wadsworth.

Frederick, H. H. (1993). *Global communication and international relations.* Belmont, CA.: Wadsworth.

Gross, L. S. (1995). *The international world of electronic media.* New York: McGraw-Hill.

Howell, W. J. (1986). *World broadcasting in the age of the satellite.* Norwood, NJ: Ablex Publishing.

Laurien, A. (1988). *The Voice of America.* Norwood, NJ: Ablex Publishing.

MacDonald, B. (1993). *Broadcasting in the United Kingdom.* London: Mansell Publishing Co.

McPhail, T. (1987). *Electronic colonialism.* New York: Sage.

Merill, J. (1991). *Global journalism.* New York: Longman.

Mowlana, H. (1997). *Global information and world communication.* New York: Longman.

Passport to World Band Radio. (1990). London: International Broadcasting Services.

Rosen, P. (1988). *International handbook of broadcasting systems.* Westport, CT: Greenwood Press.

Soley, L., & Nichols, J. (1987). *Clandestine radio broadcasting.* New York: Praeger.

Wedell, G. (1986). *Making broadcasting useful: The African experience.* Manchester, United Kingdom: Manchester University Press.

World Radio–TV handbook. (1998). New York: Billboard Publications.

INTERNET EXERCISES

1. Visit our Web site at http://www.mhhe.com/beyond for study-guide exercises to help you learn and apply material in each chapter. You will find ideas for future research as well as useful Web links to provide you with an opportunity to journey through the new electronic media.

Glossary

account executive   Salesperson who visits local merchants to sell them broadcast advertising.

addressable converter   Device that allows pay-per-view cable subscribers to receive their programs.

adjacency   Commercial placement that immediately precedes or follows a specific television, cable, or radio show.

advanced television (ATV)   Improved resolution TV that is compatible with existing TV receivers.

affiliate   Local radio or TV station that has a contractual relationship with a network.

aftermarket   Alternative markets for TV series after they run on the major networks; syndication and overseas markets are examples.

alternator   Device that generates continuous radio waves; necessary for the broadcasting of voice and music.

American Society of Composers, Authors and Publishers (ASCAP)   Group that collects and distributes performance royalty payments to various artists.

amplifier   Device that boosts an electrical signal.

amplitude   Height of a wave above a neutral point.

amplitude modulation (AM)   Method of sending a signal by changing the amplitude of the carrier wave.

analog signal   Transduced signal that resembles an original sound or image; for example, a phonograph record contains analog signals.

area of dominant influence (ADI)   In ratings terminology, that region of a market where most of the viewing or listening of that market's TV and/or radio stations occurs.

ARPANET   Early version of the Internet.

average quarter-hour persons   In radio, average number of listeners per 15-minute period in a given daypart.

audience flow   Movement of audiences from one program to another.

audimeter   Nielsen rating device that indicates if a radio or TV set is in use and to what station the set is tuned. *See also* Storage instantaneous audimeter.

audio board *See* Mixing console.

audion   Device invented by Lee De Forest that amplified weak radio signals.

auditorium testing   Research technique that tests popularity of records by playing them in front of a large group of people who fill out questionnaires about what they heard.

barter   Type of payment for syndicated programming in which the syndicator withholds one or more minutes of time in the program and sells these time slots to national advertisers.

beam splitter   Optical device that dissects white light into its three primary colors: red, green, and blue.

bicycle network   A network that distributes programs physically by shipping tapes to various stations.

blacklist   List of alleged Communists and Communist sympathizers circulated in the 1950s; contained the names of some prominent broadcasters.

blanket rights   Music licensing arrangement in which an organization pays BMI or ASCAP a single fee that grants the organization the right to play all of BMI's or ASCAP's music.

blanking pulse   Signal carried inside the TV camera that shuts off the scanning beam to allow for persistence of vision.

block programming   In radio, programming to one target audience for a few hours and then changing the format to appeal to another group. Used by many community radio stations.

bumper   Segment that introduces a newscast after a commercial break.

burnout   Tendency of a song to become less popular after repeated playings.

Buying Power Index   A weighted measurement describing a specific geographic market's ability to buy goods, based on population, effective income, and retail sales.

Cable Communications Policy Act   A 1984 law that gave FCC limited power to regulate cable.

cable TV   Distributing television signals by wire.

call-out research   Radio research conducted by telephone to evaluate the popularity of recordings.

carrier wave   Basic continuous wave produced by a radio or TV station; modulated to carry information.

catharsis theory   Theory that suggests that watching media violence relieves the aggressive urges of those in the audience. There has been little scientific evidence for this position.

cathode ray tube (CRT)   Picture tube in a TV set.

C band   Satellite that operates in the 4–6-gigahertz frequency range.

channel   Frequency on which a station broadcasts.

channel capacity   In cable, the number of channels that can be carried on a given system.

charge-coupled device (CCD)   Solid-state camera that uses computer chips instead of tubes.

chromakey   Process by which one picture is blended with another in TV production.

clandestine radio services   Unauthorized broadcasts, usually political in nature, conducted by groups in opposition to the current government.

claw   In a motion picture projector, the device that grabs each frame of film by the sprocket holes and holds it in place in front of a light.

clearance   Process in which an affiliate makes time available for a network program. In syndication, refers to the number or percentage of TV markets in which a program is carried.

clone   Digital copy made from a digital master.

clutter   Commercials and other nonprogram material broadcast during program breaks.

coincidental telephone interview   Method of audience research in which a respondent is asked what radio or TV station he or she is listening to at the time of the call.

common carrier   Communication system available for public use such as the telephone or postal service.

community-service grants   Money given by the government to public TV stations to support programming of special interest in the station's broadcast area.

compensation   The amount of money networks pay to their affiliates for carrying the network fed program. Compensation rates are based on market size, ratings, and affiliate strength.

compulsory license   Fees paid by cable systems that use distant nonnetwork signals from other markets.

condenser microphone   Microphone that uses an electrical device to produce the equivalents of sound waves.

convergence   A trend whereby radio, television, and telephone communication are merged with the computer.

cooperative advertising   Arrangement in which national advertisers assist local retailers in paying for ads.

cooperative advertising (co-op)   A commercial where the cost is shared by the manufacturer of the product and the local retail outlet.

corporate video   Usually done in a business setting, video production intended for a specific audience and usually not for public use.

cost per thousand (CPM)   One measure of efficiency in the media. Defined as the cost to reach one thousand people.

cross-licensing agreement   Agreement made between or among companies that allows all parties to use patents controlled by only one of the parties.

cultivation theory   Theory suggesting that watching a great deal of stereotyped TV content will cause distorted perceptions of the real world.

cumulative audience   In ratings, the number of different households that watch or listen to a program in a specified time period. Also called the unduplicated audience.

dayparts   A way of dividing up the broadcast day to reflect standard time periods for setting advertising rates.

deflection magnet   Device that directs the scanning beam inside a TV camera.

demographics   Science of categorizing people based on easily observed traits. Age and sex, for example, are two common demographic categories.

dichroic mirror   Mirror that separates white light into red, green, and blue light. Used inside a color TV camera.

dielectric   Insulated middle portion of a coaxial cable.

digital audio broadcasting (DAB)   Broadcasting a radio signal using a binary code (0s and 1s).

digital audio tape (DAT)   High-quality audio tape that uses the same digital technology as a CD.

digital compact cassette (DDC)   Digital audio tape packaged in a cassette format.

digital signal   Transduced signal that consists of binary codes (0s and 1s) that represent the original signal.

direct-broadcast satellite (DBS)   Satellite transmission designed to be received directly by the home.

distance learning   Process in which educational material is distributed by video to students in different locations.

drop   In cable, that part of the system that carries the signal from the feeder cable into the house.

duopoly   (1) System of broadcasting in which two systems, one public and one private, exist at the same time, as in Canada. (2) Owning more than one AM or FM station in the same market.

dynamic microphone   Microphone that uses a diaphragm and electromagnets to change sound energy into electrical energy.

effective radiated power (ERP)   Amount of power a radio station is permitted to use.

electroencephalogram (EEG)   A physiological measure of brain waves used in broadcasting and cable research.

electroluminescence (EL)   Method of providing a flatscreen TV receiver.

electron gun   Device in a TV camera that produces a stream of electrons that scans the image to be televised.

electronic news gathering (ENG)   Providing information for TV news with the assistance of portable video and audio equipment. Also called electronic journalism (EJ).

encoder   Device that combines the red, green, and blue information in a color TV signal with the brightness component.

equalizer   Electronic device that adjusts the amplification of certain frequencies; allows for fine tuning an audio signal.

erase head   The part of a tape recorder that returns the metal filings to a neutral position, thus erasing any signal on the tape.

evening drive time   In radio, a peak listening period that extends from 3:00 to 7:00 P.M. when many people are commuting home from work or school.

exclusivity deal   In cable, an arrangement whereby one premium service has the exclusive rights to show the films of a particular motion picture company.

exit poll   Survey in which voters are asked about their voting decisions immediately after they leave the voting booth; used to predict the outcomes of elections before the polls close.

expanded sample frame   In ratings, a technique by which a sample is increased to include more minority groups.

fair use   In copyright law, a small portion of a copyrighted work that can be reproduced for legitimate purposes without the permission of the copyright holder.

fairness doctrine   Currently defunct policy of the Federal Communications Commission that required broadcast stations to present balanced coverage of topics of public concern.

false light   A type of invasion of privacy in which media coverage creates the wrong impression about a person.

feeder line   In cable, that part of the system that transfers the signals from trunk lines to house drops.

fiber optic   Cable used for transmitting a digital signal via thin strands of flexible glass.

fidelity   Degree of correspondence between a reproduced signal and the original.

field   Half of a complete TV picture; one field is scanned every sixtieth of a second.

financial interest and syndication rules (fin-syn)   FCC regulations limiting network participation in ownership and subsequent syndication of programs produced for the network.

focus group   Small group of people who discuss predetermined topics, such as a TV newscast.

footprint   Coverage area of a communications satellite.

format   The type of music or talk that a radio station chooses to program. Formats are usually targeted at a specific segment of the population. *See also* Demographics.

formative evaluation   In corporate video, testing the storyboard, script, and rough cut of the program to determine if these elements are designed as originally planned.

frame   Two fields or one complete TV picture; one frame is scanned every thirtieth of a second.

franchise agreement   A contract between a local government and a cable company that specifies the terms under which the cable company may operate.

frequency   Number of waves that pass a given point in a given time period, usually a second; measured in hertz (Hz).

frequency modulation (FM)   Method of sending a signal by changing the frequency of the carrier wave.

frequency response   Range of frequencies that a radio set is capable of receiving.

future file   Collection of stories to be used in upcoming newscasts.

galvanic skin response (GSR)   Measure of the electrical conductivity of the skin. Used in broadcast and cable research.

geosynchronous orbit   A satellite orbit that keeps that satellite over one spot above the earth.

globalization   Tendency for mass media firms to have interests in countries all over the world.

grazing   Method of TV viewing in which the audience member uses a remote-control device to scan all available channels during commercials or dull spots in a program.

gross impressions   The total number of advertising impressions made during a schedule of commercials. GIs are calculated by multiplying the average persons reached in a specific time period by the number of spots in that period of time.

gross rating points   The total number of rating points gained as a result of scheduling commercials. GRPs are determined by multiplying the specific rating by the number of spots in that time period.

headend   In cable, the facility that receives, processes, and converts video signals for transmission on the cable.

height above average terrain (HAAT)   Measurement of the height of a transmitter tower; used to classify FM stations.

helical-scan tape recording   Method of videotape recording in which the signal is recorded in diagonal strips.

high-definition television (HDTV)   Improved resolution TV system that uses approximately 1,100 scanning lines.

holography   Three-dimensional lensless photography.

homes passed   Number of homes that have the ability to receive cable TV; that is, homes passed by the cable.

hook   Short, easily identifiable segment of a recording.

households using television (HUT)   Number of households that are watching TV at a certain time period.

hue   Each individual color as seen on color TV.

hypodermic needle theory   Early media effects theory stating that mass communicated messages would have a strong and predictable effect on the audience.

independent   Station not affiliated with a network.

Interactive television   System in which TV viewers respond to programs using a special keypad.

international broadcasting   Broadcast services that cross national boundaries and are heard in many countries.

International Telecommunications Union (ITU)   Organization that coordinates the international broadcasting activities of its members.

internet   A global network of interconnected computers.

inventory   The amount of available advertising time a media outlet has to sell; unsold time.

ISP   Internet service provider; A company that connects subscribers to Internet.

keying   Process by which one video signal is electronically cut out of or into another.

kinescope   Early form of recording TV shows in which a film was made of a TV receiver.

ku band   Communications satellite that operates in the 12–14-gigahertz frequency range.

LAN   Local area network. A group of computers that are linked together.

laser optical media (LOM)   General term of CDs, videodiscs, and related devices that use a laser to read information.

license agreement   Arrangement between a syndicator and a TV station specifying the number of times a movie or TV show may be shown in a given time period.

limited-effects theory   Media effects theory suggesting that media have few direct and meaningful effects on the audience.

liquid crystal display (LCD)   Flat-screen display system being developed for use in TV receivers.

live assist   Form of radio production where local announcers and DJs are used in conjunction with syndicated programming.

local market agreement   Arrangement whereby a company that owns one radio station can manage assets of another station without violating FCC ownership rules.

local origination   Program produced by a local TV station or cable system.

lowband   That part of the cable occupied by channels 2 to 6 and FM radio.

low-power television (LPTV)   Television stations that operate with reduced coverage and have a coverage area only 12–15 miles in diameter.

luminance   Degree of brightness of a TV picture.

market   Specific geographic area served by radio and TV stations. The United States is divided into approximately 210 different markets.

midband   That part of the cable signal occupied by TV channels 7 to 13 and cable channels 14 to 22.

minidisc (MD)   A more compact version of the CD, about one-fourth the size of a standard CD.

minidoc   Multipart reports that generally air Monday to Friday on local TV stations. Each minidoc segment may only be three or four minutes long.

mixing console   Master control device in an audio studio that selects, controls, and mixes together various sound inputs.

modem   Device that connects computers to phone lines.

modulation   Encoding a signal by changing the characteristics of the carrier wave.

monopoly   The ability to exercise unrestrained power over a market; the existence of no real or effective competition.

morning drive time   In radio, 6:00 to 10:00 A.M. Monday through Friday when large numbers of people are listening in their cars.

multichannel, multipoint distribution system (MMDS)   System using microwave transmission to provide cable service into urban areas; also called wireless cable.

multichannel television sound (MTS)   Stereo sound and a second audio channel are multiplexed in the audio portion of the TV signal.

multimedia   System that combines TV set, computer, CD player, and telephone.

multiple-system operator (MSO)   Company that owns and operates more than one cable system.

multiplexing   Sending different signals with the same channel.

must-carry rule   Regulation which stated that cable systems had to carry the signals of all broadcast TV stations seen in the market served by cable.

National Association of Broadcasters (NAB)   Leading professional organization of the broadcasting industry.

National Cable Television Association (NCTA)   Leading professional organization of the cable industry.

national representative (rep)   Organization that sells time on a local station to national advertisers.

national spot sales   Advertising placed on selected stations across the country by national advertisers.

National Television System Committee (NTSC)   Group that recommended the current technical standards for color TV. Also refers to the North American standard for television broadcasting.

network compensation   Money paid by a network to one of its affiliates in return for the affiliate's carrying network shows and network commercials. *See also* Clearance.

network programming   Programs that are financed by and shown on TV networks.

news consultants   Research companies that advise stations about ways to improve the ratings of their news programs.

noise   Unwanted interference in a video or audio signal.

oligopoly   In economics, a situation in which there is limited or managed competition. In broadcasting, the condition of having limited number of competitors, which ensures that every outlet will find some audience.

open video system   An arrangement whereby a telephone company can offer television programs.

orbital slot   "Parking place" for a communications satellite in geosynchronous orbit.

oscillation   Vibration of a sound or radio wave.

overbuild   More that one cable system serving a community.

package   1. News story that includes pictures of the newsworthy event, the natural sound, and a reporter's voice-over. 2. Series of theatrical movies made available by a distribution company for sale to cable and broadcast TV stations.

panel method   Research technique in which the same people are studied at different points in time.

payola   Bribes given to DJs to influence them to play particular records on radio stations.

pay per transaction (PPT)   System of videocassette rental in which the motion picture production company receives a portion of the rental fee whenever one of its movies is rented.

pay per view (PPV)   System in which cable subscribers pay a one-time fee for special programs such as movies and sporting events. *See also* Addressable converter.

PEG channel   Cable station set aside for public, educational, or government use.

Peoplemeter   In ratings, handheld device that reports what TV show is being watched. Peoplemeters also gather demographic data about who is watching.

persistence of vision   Tendency of perceptual system to retain an image a split second after the image is removed from sight. Makes possible the illusion of motion in film and TV.

phi phenomenon   Tendency of perceptual system to "fill in blanks" between two light sources located close to one another. As one light blinks off and the other blinks on, the brain perceives the change as motion.

photon   Packet of light energy.

pilot   Sample episode of a proposed TV series.

pirate station   Unauthorized radio or TV station that generally broadcasts entertainment material.

playback head   In a tape recorder, the device that reproduces the signal stored on the tape.

playlist   List of records that a radio station plays. *See also* Format.

plugola   Gifts given to DJs for promoting a product on the air. Listeners are unaware that the DJ is being compensated for these mentions.

pods   A cluster of commercials, promotions, or other announcements.

preemption   Show that a network affiliate refuses to carry.

prime-time access rule (PTAR)   In general, a regulation that limits the TV networks to three hours of programming during the prime-time period. Exceptions are made for news, public affairs, children's shows, documentaries, and political broadcasts.

privatization   Trend in which former public or state-owned broadcasting systems are becoming privately owned.

promotional announcement (promo)   Short announcement to remind viewers or listeners about an upcoming program.

psychographic research   Research that uses personality traits to segment the audience.

psychographic variables   Psychological factors that explain audience behavior.

public service announcement (PSA)   Announcement for charitable or other worthwhile endeavor presented free of charge by broadcasters.

puffery   Allowable exaggeration in advertising claims.

pulse code modulation (PCM)   Method used in digital recording and reproduction in which a signal is sampled at various points and the resulting value is translated into binary numbers.

pure competition   In economics, a state where there is sufficient competition in the market place that prices of goods and services move toward actual cost. In broadcasting, having a sufficient number of voices in the marketplace to keep ratings and rates in a state of equilibrium.

Q score *See* TV Q.

Radio Act of 1927   Act that established the groundwork for modern broadcasting regulation.

rating   In TV, the percentage of households in a market that are viewing a station divided by the total number of households with TV in that market. In radio, the total number of people who are listening to a station divided by the total number of people in the market.

recording head   Device in a tape recorder that stores a new signal on the tape.

retracing   Scanning process that goes on inside a TV set.

right of first refusal   Network's contractual guarantee to prohibit a production company from producing a specific show for another client.

rotation   Mix or order of music played on a radio station.

rough cut   Preliminary rendition of an ad or a TV show produced so that viewers can get a general idea of the content.

sampling   1. Selecting a group of people who are representative of the population. 2. In digital signal processing, selecting a number of points along an analog signal and converting the signal into binary numbers.

satellite master-antenna television (SMATV)   System used in apartment buildings in which a master receiving dish and antenna on top of the building pick up TV signals, which are then transmitted by wire to dwelling units.

satellite news gathering (SNG)   Use of specially equipped mobile units to transmit live and taped remote reports back to a local station.

saturation   Strength of a color as seen on color TV.

scanner   Radio monitor that is tuned to police and fire frequencies.

scanning   Technique by which the beam of electrons inside a TV camera traces its way across an image.

scatter market   In broadcasting, commercial time that corresponds to the calendar year; the four quarters in the scatter market reflect the various seasons of the year.

sell-through   A tape designed to be sold directly to consumers as opposed to video rental stores.

sets in use   In ratings, the number of radio or TV sets that are in operation at a given time.

share   In radio, the number of people who are listening to a station divided by the total number of people who are listening to radio at a given time. In TV, the total number of households watching a given channel divided by the total number of households using TV.

sideband   Signals above and below the assigned frequency of a carrier wave at a TV or radio station.

signal-to-noise ratio   Amount of desired picture or sound information that remains after subtracting unwanted interference.

simulcast   Radio program aired in both AM and FM at the same time on two different stations. Also a TV show, usually a concert, carried by an FM station at the same time it is being televised.

single-system operator (SSO)   Company that owns and operates one cable system.

skip   Tendency of radio waves to reflect off the ionosphere and back to earth, then back to the ionosphere, and so on. Makes possible long-distance radio transmission.

SMATV   Satellite master antenna TV.

specific-effects theory   Theory that posits there are certain circumstances under which some types of media content will have a significant effect on some audience members.

spot sets   Segments in radio programming, such as commercials and promotions, which interrupt the normal programming content.

standing order   A commercial order that gives a certain time in the broadcast schedule to the same customer until the order is rescinded.

stand-up   Reporter standing in front of the camera providing an opening, bridge, or closing for a story. *See also* Package.

station   Organization that broadcasts TV or radio signals.

station identification   Station announcement broadcast at the top or bottom of the hour telling call letters and location or having station logo superimposed on the screen.

step deal   Contractual arrangement by which TV series are produced. Production proceeds in a series of defined steps, with the network having the option to cancel after each step.

stimulation theory   Theory suggesting that watching media violence will stimulate the viewer to perform aggressive acts in real life. Opposite of the catharsis theory.

storage instantaneous audimeter (SIA)   Computer assisted TV measurement device that makes possible overnight ratings.

storyboard   Drawings illustrating what a finished commercial or segment of a TV show will look like.

streaming   A technique that allows sound and moving pictures to be transmitted on the World Wide Web.

stripping   Scheduling the same show to run in the same time period from Monday through Friday.

subscription television (STV)   System that sends programs in scrambled form to TV sets equipped with decoders.

subsidiary communications authorization (SCA)   A service provided by FM stations using additional space in their channel to send signals to specially designed receivers.

summative evaluation   In corporate video, research that looks at the effectiveness of a completed program. *See also* Formative evaluation.

superband   That part of the cable signal that carries channels 23 to 69.

superstation   Local TV station that is distributed to many cable systems via satellite, giving the station national exposure.

survey   Research method that uses questionnaires or similar instruments to gather data from a sample of respondents.

sustaining program   Common in early radio, a program that had no commercial sponsors.

switcher   Device used to switch from one video signal to another. Can also be used to combine more than one video signal.

synchronization pulse   Signal that enables the output of two or more cameras and other video sources to be mixed together and also keeps the scanning process in the camera operating in time to coincide exactly with the retrace process in the TV receiver.

syndicated exclusivity (syndex)   FCC rule stating that local cable systems must black out programming imported from a distant station if it is being carried by a local station in the cable system's market.

syndication   The sale and distribution of programming directly to the station. First-run syndication involves products that have been specifically produced for airing in the syndication marketplace.

target audience   Specific group a radio or TV program is trying to attract.

target plate   Mirrorlike device inside a TV camera that holds the image while the image is scanned by the electron beam.

teaser   Clever line used to introduce a newscast.

Telecommunications Act of 1996   Federal law that allowed cable and telephone companies to compete, raised station ownership limits, and introduced the V-chip.

teleconference   Video link between individuals, frequently used for business conference.

teleports   Facilities that provide uplinks and downlinks with communication satellites.

teletext   Cable service that offers text and graphics displayed on the screen.

television receive-only earth station (TVRO)   Home satellite dish that receives TV programming.

tiering   Process of selling cable subscribers increasing levels of service.

timeshifting   Recording something on a VCR to watch at a more convenient time.

tip sheet   Radio industry publication reporting current musical preferences across the country.

total survey area (TSA)   In ratings, a geographic area where at least some viewing of TV stations in a given market occurs. *See also* Area of dominant influence.

tradeout   Swapping advertising time for a product or service.

transponder   The part of a communication satellite that receives a signal from an earth station and retransmits it somewhere else.

treatment   Short narrative used to sell an idea for a TV show or series to a production company.

trunk line   Main cable lines connecting the headend to the feeder cables.

turnkey automation   Radio station that is fully automated.

TV Q   Score that measures the popularity of TV celebrities.

TVRO   Satellite television receive-only earth station.

ultra-high frequency (UHF)   The portion of the electromagnetic spectrum that contains TV channels 14 to 69.

underwriting   Assisting a station in paying for a public radio or TV program in exchange for a mention on the air. Major corporations are the most frequent underwriters.

upfront sales   Network television time that is sold in the summer before the actual television season begins. Upfront sales are frequently for dayparts as opposed to actual programs.

uplink   Ground source that sends signals to a communication satellite.

URL   Universal resource locator; a unique address of an Internet site.

uses and gratifications   Research tradition that examines the reasons people use the media.

V chip   Device installed in TV sets that blocks out violent programming.

velocity microphone   Microphone that uses a thin metal ribbon and electromagnets to reproduce sound.

vertical blanking interval   Portion of the TV signal that occurs between fields; used to send teletext and closed-captioning.

vertical integration   Process by which a firm has interests in the production, distribution, and consumption of a product.

very high frequency (VHF)   The part of the electromagnetic spectrum that contains TV channels 2 to 13.

video news release (VNR)   In corporate video, a complete video package sent by a company to a news organization in an attempt to get broadcast time.

video on demand   Interactive service that allows customers to order the television programs and services they want when they want them.

videotex   Two-directional information service linking a data bank with computer terminals via cable or telephone lines.

video toaster   A personal computer that generates special video effects.

virtual reality   Computer system that creates three-dimensional images that users interact with by means of special goggles and gloves.

waveform   Visual representation of a wave as measured by electronic equipment.

wavelength   Distance between two corresponding points on an electromagnetic wave.

World Wide Web   Part of the Internet that contains sites featuring text and graphics.

zapping   Deleting the commercials when videotaping a program off the air for later viewing.

zipping   Fast-forwarding through the commercials when viewing a program recorded off the air.

Photo Credits

Index